An Exposition of the Four Gospels

VOLUME 1
Matthew/Mark

An Exposition of the Four Gospels

VOLUME 1

The Gospel of Matthew
The Gospel of Mark

Herschel H. Hobbs

BakerBooks
A Division of Baker Book House Co
Grand Rapids, Michigan 49516

Published by Baker Books
a division of Baker Book House Company
P.O. Box 6287, Grand Rapids, MI 49516-6287

Two-volume edition published 1996

Previously published in four volumes

Printed in the United States of America

ISBN 0-8010-5696-9

The Gospel of Matthew

CONTENTS

of the Jews. So this Gospel is fittingly called *The Gospel of the King*.

The basic English text used in this study is the Authorized or King James Version. Where other versions are followed it will be so indicated. However, this study endeavors to follow rather closely the Greek text (Nestles), but with a minimum of Greek words involved. At times the author makes his own translation where it seems of value in the exposition of a given passage.

It would be impossible for one to recall the source of all of the thoughts which comprise this study. But some of the basic volumes consulted may be mentioned.

William Barclay, *The Gospel of Matthew,* Volumes 1-2, Westminster, Philadelphia, 1956.

John A. Broadus, *Commentary on Matthew,* American Baptist Publication Society, Philadelphia, 1886.

A. B. Bruce, "Matthew," *The Expositor's Greek Testament,* Eerdmans, Grand Rapids, 1951.

W. A. Criswell, *Expository Notes on the Gospel of Matthew,* Zondervan, Grand Rapids, 1961.

William Hersey Davis, *Davis' Notes on Matthew,* Broadman, 1962.

Herschel H. Hobbs, *The Gospel of Matthew,* Baker, Grand Rapids, 1961; *Preaching Values from the Papyri,* Baker, Grand Rapids, 1964.

G. Campbell Morgan, *The Gospel According to Matthew,* Revell, New York, 1929.

E. H. Plumptre, *The Gospel According to Matthew,* Zondervan, Grand Rapids, 1957.

A. T. Robertson, *Word Pictures in the New Testament,* Volume 1, Sunday School Board of Southern Baptist Convention, Nashville, 1930.

J. W. Shepard, *The Christ of the Gospels,* Eerdmans, Grand Rapids, 1938.

As Matthew wrote to convince the Jews that Jesus was their King, this effort at exposition is made with the hope that it will lead many, both Jews and Gentiles, to receive Him as their King. It is in prayer to that end that this volume is sent forth.

Herschel H. Hobbs

First Baptist Church
Oklahoma City, Oklahoma

INTRODUCTION

This volume makes no claim to scholarship in the technical sense of that word. It is simply the effort of the author to interpret the life of Jesus Christ as it is recorded in *The Gospel of Matthew*. This effort at times leads us into the other Gospels and/or other writings in the New Testament. But the focal point is *Matthew*.

New Testament scholarship is not agreed as to the authorship of Matthew. An early writer named Eusebius quotes Papias as saying that Matthew wrote the *Logia* of Jesus in Hebrew (Aramaic). Did he also write the Gospel which bears his name? Whoever wrote it certainly made use of the Logia which was devoted to reporting the "sayings" or teachings of Jesus. There is no real reason why Matthew could not have written it. Indeed, if he did not write it, it is strange that it would bear his name, for he had been a publican or tax-gatherer for the Romans, a fact that would not make his a popular name among the Jews. It is this author's position that Matthew did write it. And so without going into a lengthy and technical discussion we shall proceed on that assumption.

The date of the writing of Matthew is linked to the dates of Mark and Luke. Since Matthew and Luke follow the framework of Mark it is generally agreed that Mark wrote his Gospel first, probably about A.D. 55. While at times, in keeping with their purposes, both Matthew and Luke depart from the chronology of Mark, it is significant that at no time do both of them do so in a given instance. Does Matthew precede Luke in date of writing? In all probability it does. Luke shows no evidence of having made any use of Matthew's Gospel. However, it is usually assumed that Luke did not write his Gospel prior to his sojourn in Palestine during Paul's imprisonment in Caesarea. He probably wrote it during this time or about A.D. 60. We cannot be dogmatic as to the date of Matthew, but it was written after Mark and probably before Luke. This would mean sometime between A.D. 55 and 60.

Matthew is generally regarded as having written for the primary benefit of the Jews. For this reason he makes great use of Old Testament prophecy, especially in the early part of the Gospel. He wrote to prove to the Jews that Jesus was the Christ or King of the Jews. So this Gospel is fittingly called *The Gospel of the King.*

The basic English text used in this study is the Authorized or King James Version. Where other versions are followed it will be so indicated. However, this study endeavors to follow rather closely the Greek text (Nestles), but with a minimum of Greek words involved. At times the author makes his own translation where it seems of value in the exposition of a given passage.

It would be impossible for one to recall the source of all of the thoughts which comprise this study. But some of the basic volumes consulted may be mentioned.

William Barclay, *The Gospel of Matthew,* Volumes 1-2, Westminster, Philadelphia, 1956.

John A. Broadus, *Commentary on Matthew,* American Baptist Publication Society, Philadelphia, 1886.

A. B. Bruce, "Matthew," *The Expositor's Greek Testament,* Eerdmans, Grand Rapids, 1951.

W. A. Criswell, *Expository Notes on the Gospel of Matthew,* Zondervan, Grand Rapids, 1961.

William Hersey Davis, *Davis' Notes on Matthew,* Broadman, 1962.

Herschel H. Hobbs, *The Gospel of Matthew,* Baker, Grand Rapids, 1961; *Preaching Values from the Papyri,* Baker, Grand Rapids, 1964.

G. Campbell Morgan, *The Gospel According to Matthew,* Revell, New York, 1929.

E. H. Plumptre, *The Gospel According to Matthew,* Zondervan, Grand Rapids, 1957.

A. T. Robertson, *Word Pictures in the New Testament,* Volume 1, Sunday School Board of Southern Baptist Convention, Nashville, 1930.

J. W. Shepard, *The Christ of the Gospels,* Eerdmans, Grand Rapids, 1938.

As Matthew wrote to convince the Jews that Jesus was their King, this effort at exposition is made with the hope that it will lead many, both Jews and Gentiles, to receive Him as their King. It is in prayer to that end that this volume is sent forth.

Herschel H. Hobbs

First Baptist Church
Oklahoma City, Oklahoma

The King
and the Kingdom

Matthew 1

The Birth of the King

Jesus Christ was not born to become a King. He was born the King destined to become the Saviour. All of this is contained in the first chapter of Matthew. Thus the evangelist speaks of (1) the genealogy; (2) the genesis; (3) the gospel.

The Genealogy (1:1-17)

How many modern readers have ever really studied this portion of Matthew's Gospel? To most of us this is simply a meaningless (?) list of *begats* somewhat like we find scattered throughout the Old Testament. For this reason the average reader begins with the account of Jesus' birth in 1:18. But to do so is to omit one of the most meaningful passages in the entire book. Surely Matthew must have had a purpose in including it. To him and his immediate readers it provides the key to the entire Gospel.

Matthew is writing to convince the Jews that Jesus Christ is both their King and their Saviour, their Messiah. And since the Jews placed great importance on genealogy, it would be unthinkable to them to accept Him as such without genealogical proof of a royal and spiritual lineage.

At the time of Jesus' birth Herod the Great sat on the throne of Judea, placed there and maintained by the power of Rome. But because he was not a full Jew his subjects never accepted him as their king. So out of spite he caused all genealogical records to be destroyed. Thereafter, he could claim as great a genealogy as any of the Jews.

Furthermore, before a Jew could aspire to the priesthood, he must prove his line back to Aaron. Even his wife must be able to trace her line back for at least five generations. So if Jesus were to be received as their High Priest or Saviour He must be able to furnish genealogical proof of a spiritual lineage.

It is in this dual light that we may understand the opening verse of the Gospel. "The book of the generation of Jesus Christ, the son of David, the son of Abraham." As "son of David" Jesus is of the royal line (cf. Rom. 1:3); as "son of Abraham" He is related to the spiritual promise of redemption (cf. Heb. 2:16).

However, this verse contains an even greater meaning. To David, God had promised an everlasting kingdom. It is obvious that this promise was not realized in Solomon or other of David's seed. Indeed, it was through this very seed that the kingdom declined and disappeared in the Babylonian captivity. So Matthew says that this promise is to be fulfilled through "Jesus Christ, the son of David. . . ."

Likewise, to Abraham and his seed God had promised the blessing of redemption of all nations. Again this promise was not realized through Isaac, Jacob, or any other of Abraham's immediate descendants. So once again Matthew says that the promise is to be fulfilled through the true seed of Abraham, "Jesus Christ . . . the son of Abraham" (cf. Gal. 3:16).

Following this opening verse, therefore, Matthew presents a triad of fourteen generations each (1:17): from Abraham to David; from David to the Bablyonian captivity; from the Babylonian captivity to Jesus Christ. But even this is not simply a listing of names. The first division begins with Abraham to whom God made His promise of redemption. It ends with David who led Israel to its zenith of worldly glory, but who did not lead them to fulfil the promise made to Abraham. The second division begins with Solomon in whom the spiritual decline began, and ends in the Babylonian captivity marking the destruction of David's earthly kingdom. The third division begins with the Babylonian captivity when Judah became a puppet nation, and ends with the birth of Jesus Christ. Here then we see promise, failure, and fulfilment. The promise of God's purpose; the failure of man in that purpose; the fulfilment of God's purpose through Jesus Christ.

Indeed, this genealogical arrangement is suggestive of a greater truth: God's purpose in the creation of man; man's failure through sin; God's dealing with sin through Jesus Christ. So whether we regard God's purpose as related to a nation or to individual men the message is the same.

Actually God's national purpose involved the saving of man as an individual. God made man in His own image, and endowed him with the capability of fellowship with God. Thus we see man's dignity and destiny. Only through divine intervention could man's dignity be restored and his true destiny achieved. And this is the gospel itself, a gospel which Matthew introduces with the genealogy of Him who is God's revelation in saving grace.

Which introduces us to a further element of Matthew's genealogy. Matthew was a Jew writing for Jews. It is significant, therefore, that he includes some non-Jewish elements in his genealogy. For instance, the Jewish man's morning prayer included thanksgiving that he was not a Gentile, a publican, or a woman. Matthew himself was a former publican. He includes two Gentiles (Rahab and Ruth) and four women (Tamar, Rahab, Ruth, and Bathsheba) in his genealogy. Furthermore, the Jews regarded adultery as a most grievous sin, punishable by stoning. Yet Matthew lists two adulterers (Judah and David) and at least two adulteresses (Tamar and Bathsheba). (Rahab is called "the harlot." The Hebrew word means "public woman." She could have been a woman engaged in public business, perhaps an innkeeper [cf. Josh. 2:1ff.].)

But be that as it may, the inclusion of these names is significant. Since they ran contrary to the thinking of his readers, the Evangelist must have included them with deliberate purpose. Was it not his way of saying that Jesus Christ was identified with all such, apart from sin? This was his method of declaring what Paul said when he wrote, "There is neither Jew nor Greek . . . bond nor free . . . male nor female: for ye are all one in Christ Jesus" (Gal. 3:28). Likewise, he sounds the note of Hebrews 4:15-16, "For we have not an high priest which cannot be touched with the feeling of our infirmities; but was in all points tempted like as we are, yet without sin. Let us therefore come boldly unto the throne of grace, that we may obtain mercy, and find grace to help in time of need."

Thus the barriers between Jew and Gentile, male and female, and saint and sinner are removed in Jesus Christ. Truly Jesus came not "to call the righteous, but sinners to repentance" (Matt. 9:13). All men and women are lost, and yet are equally precious in God's sight.

But even though Jesus is one with all men, He is separate from all men. As King, Jesus is identified with His people. Yet He is separate from them in majesty and glory. As Saviour He identifies Himself with them in their sin. But He himself is sinless that He might rescue them from the power of sin. This Matthew declares in 1:16. Note the change of the verb from "begat" to "was born." The former, which appears throughout this genealogical table, speaks of direct generation from father to son. But of Jesus Matthew says that He "was born" of Mary with no mention of a human father (cf. Luke 3:23). And this introduces us to the account of His birth.

The Genesis (1:18-20, 22-25)

"Now the birth of Jesus Christ was on this wise . . ." (1:18). The word "birth" is "genesis." It is the same word used for the first book in the Bible. God's natural creation is a "genesis." Likewise, His spiritual creation is called a "genesis." "In the beginning God created the heaven and the earth" (Gen. 1:1). "In the beginning was the Word... and the Word was made flesh, and dwelt among us... full of grace and truth" (John 1:1, 14).

Without question Matthew presents the birth of Jesus as a virgin birth. This is the significance of 1:16. Men may question the fact of the virgin birth, but to do so they must ignore or alter the Gospel records. For instance, Matthew Arnold, in the preface to his *Literature and Dogma,* may say, "I do not believe in the virgin birth of Christ because it involves a miracle, and miracles do not happen." But to do so is to speak contrary to Biblical evidence, and in a manner which is dogmatically unscientific and unscholarly. Or one may alter the text to suit his pre-judged position. The Sinaitic Syriac text of 1:16 reads, "But Joseph to whom the virgin Mary was betrothed, begat Jesus." The Ebionites denied the deity of Jesus. Apparently one of their scribes altered the text to harmonize with this position. But God causes even the wrath of man to praise Him. For the scribe failed to *doctor* the text of 1:18-25 which clearly teaches that Jesus was born of a virgin.

Despite this fact Moffat in his *New Translation of the New Testament* follows this late text, contrary to all early and more accurate Greek manuscripts, and renders 1:16, "... and Joseph (to whom the virgin Mary was betrothed) the father of Jesus, who is called 'Christ.'" Of interest is the fact that he also renders John 1:1c, "... the Logos was divine." And this despite the fact that the Greek reads, "... God [*Theos*] was the Logos" or "the Logos was God himself." Had John wanted to say "divine" he could have used *theios.* Scholarship? Or prejudice against the deity of Jesus? The record speaks for itself.

Along with the crucifixion and resurrection of Jesus, His virgin birth forms the triumvirate of salvation. Thus the gospel stands or falls upon those dynamic truths. What then may we say with regard to the virgin birth?

It is historically correct. The virgin birth is anticipated in Genesis (3:15). It is prophesied in Isaiah (7:14).[1] And it is affirmed by both *Matthew* and *Luke* whose historical accuracy has never been successfully contested. Apart from prejudice or ignorance of the facts, the virgin birth has never been denied or questioned.

Again, the virgin birth is scientifically trustworthy. Its most ar-

---

1 Note RSV, "young woman." This renders the Hebrew *almah,* a young unmarried woman, and so a virgin (cf. Matt. 1:22-23).

dent supporter is Luke "the beloved physician" (Col. 4:14). His medical training would have prejudiced him against such. But after careful examination of the evidence, this scientist-historian recorded the most beautiful and complete account on record that Jesus was "born of the Virgin Mary."

A miracle? Yes. But what is a miracle? It is an act of God which is contrary to the laws of nature *as we understand them,* but which is according to laws known only to God, and in keeping with His benevolent purpose. It is neither scientific nor scholarly for us to say what God can do. To reckon the virgin birth apart from God is one thing; to reckon it as a work of God is another. For as Luke himself records, "For with God nothing shall be impossible" (1:37).

Further, the virgin birth is morally necessary. For Jesus to be the Saviour He must be virgin-born. He must be free from sin both actual and inherited. It was in Adam's sin that the race died (I Cor. 15-22). It is through the seed of the woman that sin is to be conquered (Gen. 3:15). The significance of this statement is fully realized only in One who was born of a virgin.

Furthermore, the virgin birth is experientially affirmed. Logic alone cannot decide the matter. The final word belongs to the voice of experience. And through the centuries millions have found Jesus the answer to their deepest needs. He must, then, be more than a man. Those who deny the virgin birth will affirm His sinless life. And Bruce in his *Apologetics* (p. 410) says, "A sinless man is as much a miracle in the moral world as a Virgin Birth is a miracle in the physical world." J. W. Shepard summarizes the entire matter when he says, "The how of the incarnation is inscrutable, the why is incomprehensible, the fact is undeniable."[2]

However, it is of interest that Matthew employs no such argumentative devices to *prove* the virgin birth. In a manner marked by simplicity he assumes the fact, clearly stating that Jesus' mother "was found with child of the Holy Ghost [Spirit]" (1:18). But in so doing he provides us a glimpse of the family into which Jesus was born.

Without fanfare he introduces Mary, the mother of Jesus. There is no evidence whatever of the elaborate labyrinth into which she has been placed by certain historical theology or Mariolatry. He does not even tell us where she lived (cf. Luke 1:26-27). He simply says that she "was espoused to Joseph" and "before they came together, she was found with child of the Holy Ghost." Nevertheless, Joseph is called her "husband." To the modern mind these words

---

[2] *The Christ of the Gospels,* Eerdmans, Grand Rapids, 1947, p. 15.

sound strange and confusing. But to the ancient Jewish mind they were a normal statement of fact.

Among the ancient Jews marriage consisted of three phases: engagement; betrothal; and marriage. The engagement usually involved two children (Joseph may have been older than Mary by several years), and was usually arranged by either the parents or a professional matchmaker. When the engaged couple approached marriageable age the girl could refuse marriage, and, therefore, be released from the engagement. But once she consented, the betrothal was completed, and usually lasted for one year. During this time she lived with her parents. The couple was considered as husband and wife, although they did not enter into marriage relations. At this stage unfaithfulness was regarded as adultery. After one year the marriage was completed, and the bride went to live with her husband.

It was during the period of bethrothal that Mary was found with child. What a shock it must have been to Joseph! So far as he knew she had been unfaithful to him. The Scripture says that he was a "just man" or a righteous man. This means that he was not benign or merciful, but that he conscientiously lived by what is right. As a just Jew he adhered to the Law. And the Law said that for her act of *adultery* (as it seemed) she should be stoned to death (cf. Deut. 22:23). However, the Law also provided that for a lesser cause Joseph could put her away by giving her a bill of divorcement (cf. Deut. 24:1).

It is here that we see the love that Joseph had for Mary. Under the circumstances two courses of action were open to him. His sense of justice told him to "make her a public example" by which she would have died by stoning. But his sense of love prevailed. Therefore, "not willing to" do the former, he *wished* to put her away privately simply by giving her a bill of divorcement in the presence of witnesses.

Joseph could not have known it, but in his actions he became a foregleam of the gospel itself. According to his understanding Mary was guilty under the Law, and thereby was condemned to death. But in an act of grace he showed mercy. Thus his very gracious attitude was an acted parable of the grace of God extended to all men who are condemned under the Law but who may receive grace, mercy, and peace through Him whom God entrusted to the care of one who himself showed mercy.

And this man of grace and mercy was not long in receiving peace. Apparently Joseph pondered these things while lying on his bed at night, when the hobgoblins of doubt find us such easy prey. Doctor McNeile calls this tortured unrest "a short but tragic struggle between his legal conscience and his love." So when his love had won the battle, with his course of action settled Joseph fell asleep. And then he dreamed. According to the Jews this was a good omen. For to them a dream was a sign of God's favor. And this was indeed the case. For an angel of the Lord put his mind at ease. "Joseph, thou son of David, fear not to take unto thee Mary thy wife: for that which is conceived in her is of the Holy Ghost" (1:20). Literally, the angel said, "Stop being afraid." For that is exactly the state of Joseph's heart. And then God's messenger revealed to Joseph the mystery of the ages as he let him in on the purpose of it all (1:21).

No longer did Joseph hesitate. He stopped being afraid. Touched by the hand of God he learned what true grace really is. For no longer does he think of putting aside the Law as he merely sent Mary away to bear her fate alone. Instead he "took unto him his wife" (1:24). He identified himself with her condition. He bore her shame as his own. The neighbors would gossip. The stigma of fornication would fasten its stinging fangs in Mary's heart. But it would strike him also. The Talmud would record that Mary was conceived by a Roman soldier. Under the lash of public scorn Mary's tender flesh would quiver. But always between her and the lash stood Joseph. His strength became her strength. Surely God in omniscience chose her who was to be the mother of His Son. But with equal wisdom He placed His hand upon him who was to be His foster-father. Yes, Joseph shared Mary's shame. But he partakes of her glory also. And that glory is the glory of

The Gospel (1:21)

"And she shall bring forth a son, and thou shalt call his name JESUS: for he shall save his people from their sins" (1:21).

Surely Joseph must have smiled in his sleep. For not only was Mary true to him. God was moving in history to redeem his people. But is was a redemption far beyond even that which so just a man as Joseph could imagine.

"Thou shalt call his name JESUS . . ." The name "Jesus" is the Greek equivalent of the Hebrew word "Joshua," Jehoshuah or Yeshua, meaning "Jehovah is salvation." Now this was not a ready-made name for the Son of God. Actually it was a very common name among the Jews. Thus even in His name Jesus was identified with a lost humanity.

But God took an ordinary name and made it unique and apart from all names (cf. Phil. 2:9-10). Many men have been named

Winston. Many others have been called *Churchill.* But when you put them together they mean but one man, *Winston Churchill,* a man who by the sheer strength of his will rallied to victory a world which tottered on the brink of destruction. So *Jesus* might once have meant most any Jewish lad. But today it is a name above every name. For it denotes Him who was Jehovah in the flesh snatching a lost world from the depths of sin onto the heights of glory.

Conceived of the Holy Spirit, He is God. Born of the virgin Mary, He is man. He is the God-man in whose Person the personality of God and that of man could find interplay for salvation. Jesus is the focal point of all history. He is the One to whom prophecy pointed. And He is the One out of whom comes its fulfilment. He is ever *Emmanuel,* God with us (1:23; cf. Isa. 7:14). And Matthew cites this as the first of many prophecies which were fulfilled in Jesus.

"He shall save. . . ." Literally, "He Himself shall save. . . ." This is a most significant statement. For immediately thereafter Matthew refers to Isaiah 7:14. To understand his meaning we must consider the entire section of Isaiah 7-9. Ahaz, king of Judah, was confronted by an invasion by Syria and Israel. He sought deliverance through military alliances, soothsayers, and wizards. Isaiah urged him to trust in Jehovah. But Ahaz refused to ask him a sign from the Lord. So the prophet told him that nevertheless God would give him a sign. "Behold, a virgin shall conceive, and bear a son, and shall call his name Immanuel" (7:14). That this promise was not of immediate fulfilment is seen in Isaiah 8:1-4. Furthermore, Isaiah clearly sees this as a future work of Jehovah as is revealed in 9:6-7. (Note the promise concerning David's throne in verse 7.) Matthew sees the birth of Jesus as the fulfilment of this promise.

Evidently Matthew had a dual purpose in citing this prophecy. It positionizes Jesus in the line of God's redemptive purpose. But it also declares the kind of Saviour that He will be. The period in which Jesus was born was characterized by many false "messiahs." The world, both Jew and Gentile, was looking for a *saviour.* But it still followed the ways of Ahaz. The monuments and inscriptions of the time abound in the title "Saviour" ascribed to the Roman Caesars and others. And even though the Jews looked for a Saviour from Jehovah, they thought in terms of a military Messiah who would destroy their oppressors and set up David's throne in Jerusalem by which they would rule the world.

Even after two thousand years the world still looks for salvation from among its own kind. But it is a salvation which takes little account of God or the sin-problem. The frustration found on every hand is eloquent testimony to such futile hopes. So the message of Matthew 1:21 is as applicable to our day as it was in the time of Ahaz or the first century. Through the din of confusion and desolation of the twentieth century still comes the still small voice of God's Word. "He himself [and no other] shall save..." (cf. Acts 4:10-12).

This salvation is to be "from their sins." The word "sin" means to miss the mark. Man has missed the mark of God's will. And Jesus alone can save or deliver us from such. Note that the word "from" is *apo,* away from. So He shall save "away from sins." It may be *away from* sins not yet committed as well as *out of* (*ek*) sins already committed. Matthew does not in this verse specify the *how* of this salvation. It must be ascertained within the context of the entire Gospel.

"He shall save *his people* from their sins" (1:21, author's italics). To whom do the words "his people" refer? The popular concept was that it included only the Jews. And if this verse be treated in isolation this might well be the case. However, even this Jewish Gospel relates Messiah's blessings to other than the Jews (cf. 15:21ff.). Not every citizen of national Israel is to be regarded as "his people" (cf. Matt. 3:9). Even in the Old Testament this concept holds. The true seed of Abraham was not a national entity but a spiritual remnant. And this concept is attested by the apostle Paul (cf. Rom. 9:6-13; 11:1-4). John says, "God so loved the world [inhabited earth]..." (3:16).

So "his people" are, literally, "the people of him" or "the people belonging to him." This new relationship is not genetical or political, but spiritual (cf. Matt. 12:46-50; Rom. 11:17-36; I Peter 2:9-10). The salvation which God offers in Jesus Christ is not universal but particular. It is particular in that it is available for all who will receive Him as their Saviour.

Thus this most Jewish of all the Gospels extends the hand of hope to Jew and Gentile, male and female, saint and sinner alike. The Rahabs and Ruths, the Judahs and Davids, the Tamars and Bathshebas, yes, the Josephs and Marys may rejoice in hope. For in "Jesus Christ, the son of David, the son of Abraham" God has moved in history to provide redemption to all who come to Him in repentance and faith. This is the message of Matthew 1. It is the *good news* of the gospel.

Matthew 2

The Response to the King

The overall purpose of Matthew to present Jesus as the fulfilment of prophecy is clearly seen in the second chapter of his Gospel. For it is built around four such Old Testament passages. He was born in Bethlehem (Mic. 5:2). He was called out of Egypt (Hos. 11:1). His birth was accompanied by great sorrow (Jer. 31:15). He shall be called a Nazarene (Isa. 53:2-4).

However, throughout the Gospel there also runs the purpose to present Jesus as King and Saviour. And even within this purpose there are also intermediate purposes wherein by first one emphasis and then another, the Evangelist presents different facets of the picture of Jesus and His relationship to His contemporaries. These also contain timeless truths which make this Gospel of value to all men in all ages of history.

Therefore, in the second chapter we see various responses to Jesus as King and Saviour. And these may be noted as (1) the response of inanimate nature; (2) the response of the Gentiles; (3) the response of the Jews; (4) the response of the world; (5) the response of God.

The Response of Inanimate Nature (2:2)

"For we have seen his star in the east . . ." (2:2). Who can think of the birth of Jesus without thinking of a star? Even if you never read the Bible at all, you could not live through a Christmas season without knowing that somehow a big bright star was connected with this event. And while this star may mean different things to different people, it certainly suggests to us the response which inanimate nature gave to its King and Saviour at His birth.

Many efforts have been made to explain the "Star of Bethlehem" by natural means. According to astronomical records Halley's comet was seen streaking across the sky about 11 B.C. But this was too early for Jesus' birth. He was born "in the days of Herod the king" who died in 4 B.C. It is generally agreed that Jesus was born about two or three years prior to Herod's death, or between 7 and 5 B.C.

Of greater interest is the suggestion of the astronomer Kepler. He notes that there was a conjunction of Jupiter and Saturn in

7 B.C., to which was added Mars in 6 B.C. This comes within the probable time of Jesus' birth. But this does not concur with the language of Matthew. The Greek word for a group of stars is *astron*. Matthew uses *aster,* a single star. Someone has suggested that the Magi had poor eyesight, so that the phenomenon looked like one star. But this thought within itself is preposterous. And especially so since C. Pritchard's calculations, verified at Greenwich, show that those "planets could never have appeared as one star, for they never approached each other within double the apparent diameter of the moon."

Furthermore, the account in Matthew allows for no such speculation. The star which the Magi saw while they were in the "east" appeared to them a second time in Palestine. It "went before them [from Jerusalem to Bethlehem], till it came and stood over where the young child was" (2:9). Had it been a normal star it would have been as far from them in Palestine as in the "east."

But the most striking testimony is that it was "his star," the star of Him "that is born King of the Jews" (2:2). We are justified by the record, therefore, to say that this star was created and designed for this one specific purpose. Quite obviously it involves a miracle, an extraordinary event. But the entire context is that of extraordinary events. If we accept any of them as true, as we do, where shall we cease to believe the record? Astronomers tell us that the universe consists of at least twelve quadrillion (twelve followed by fifteen zeros) solar systems, each containing billions of stars. If God could create so many stars, why could He not create one more in keeping with His laws and for His benevolent, saving purpose? As God said, "Let there be light: and there was light" (Gen. 1:3), so He said, "Let His star come into being," and it was so.

Thus we see inanimate nature responding to God's sovereign will as it heralds the birth of His Son as King and Saviour. And this is but the first of many such evidences. The response of men to Jesus was varied. But nature with one accord bowed to His will.

John suggests this thought when he says, "He came unto his own [things], and his own [people] received him not. But as many as received him, to them gave he power to become the sons of God, even to them that believe on his name" (1:11-12). Yes, He came unto His own material universe, and it *welcomed* Him. Water, wind, vegetation, rocks, and physical disease responded to His word. Seasons, seed-time and harvest, all respond to His will. "The heavens declare the glory of God; and the firmament showeth his handywork" (Ps. 19:1). In the realm of inanimate nature Christ is King. His law is absolute.

And even though the evil one works through nature to accomplish his malevolent purpose (storms, earthquakes, etc.), even so the material universe "groaneth and travaileth in pain together until now," waiting for its redemption through Him who is its King and who will be its Saviour (cf. Rom. 8:19-23).

The Response of the Gentiles (2:1, 9-12)

The "wise men" (Magi) have been the object of much legendary thought. One of the early traditions said that there were twelve. But today the traditional number of three is almost universal. However, the New Testament does not say how many there were. The number *three* is derived from the number of gifts that they brought. One legend holds that they were kings. They are even given the names of Caspar, Melchior, and Balthasar. Still another tradition says that they came from Asia, Africa, and Europe; and that they represent Shem, Ham, and Japheth. In a cathedral in Cologne one will even be shown what is supposed to be their skulls.

But the New Testament justifies none of these. It simply says that they were "wise men from the east," probably some area east of Palestine.

Now who were these Magi? The word *magos* probably was of Babylonian origin. Other than in Matthew 2 it appears in the New Testament only in Acts 13:6, 8 where it is rendered "sorcerer." However, this is not the significance of Matthew 2.

The ancient historian, Herodotus, speaks of a Median tribe called the Magi. The Medes were a part of the Medo-Persian empire. Following an unsuccessful revolt against the Persians the Magi became a tribe of priests, much like the Levites of Israel. Subsequently they became skilled in philosophy, medicine, and natural science, especially astrology. It is this last field of study which brings them into our story.

Among the ancients (and some moderns) it was thought that the stars control our destiny. Thus a man was said to be born under a certain star. Since the stars were unvarying in their courses, they suggested the order of the universe. If a star unknown to them suddenly appeared in the heavens, they regarded it as heralding some great event as though God were breaking into His ordered universe to announce such. Thus we may well understand the excitement "in the east" when "his star" appeared.

However, the note of primary interest to us at this point is that the Magi were non-Jews, and, therefore, were Gentiles. So at the birth of Jesus we see Gentiles traveling many miles that they might worship the Christ child. And in a Jewish Gospel this fact is of significance. Is it not Matthew's way of saying that He who was rejected by the Jews evoked such a response from the Gentile world?

Now why, when the Magi saw this star, did they journey to Jerusalem? Two answers may be given. In the first place they came from a land in which many Jews dwelled. At the time when the "remnant" of Jews returned to Palestine at the end of the Babylonian captivity, many voluntarily remained in Babylonia where they were engaged in business and other relationships. Among other things they had their religion and scriptures. They held on to their Messianic hope. It is entirely possible that the Magi had learned of this hope from them.

In the second place, at this very period in history the world had a strong feeling of expectation that something unusual was about to occur, and this expectation was related to Palestine. Even the Roman writers reflect this feeling. Referring back to this time Suetonius in his *Life of Vespasian* says, "There had spread all over the Orient an old established belief, that it was fated at that time for men coming from Judea to rule the world." The same thought is found in the *Histories* of Tacitus. Josephus mentions it in his *Wars of the Jews.* At about the time of Jesus' birth the Roman poet, Virgil, wrote of the golden age that was to come. It is understandable then that in this period the term "Saviour" was applied to many rulers, including Augustus, the very Roman Caesar who was reigning when Jesus was born. The hope which was so precious to the Jews had had a remarkable effect upon the Gentile world as well.

So it was that when these Magi discovered a new star in the heavens, it suggested to them that a momentous event was at hand. They interpreted it to mean that God was about to intervene in history. The expectation so prevalent among the Gentiles was about to be realized. The hope of the Jews was nearing substantiation. And since these two traditions centered in Judea, the Magi set their faces westward. It was natural that they would go to Jerusalem, the capital of Judea. Where else but in the king's palace would they inquire about the birth of a King? And having been directed to Bethlehem, they continued their journey.

Apparently they had not seen the star since leaving their homeland. So naturally they rejoiced when upon leaving Jerusalem the star appeared again. It "went before them, till it came and stood over where the young child was" (2:9). What happened to the star no one knows. Evidently when it had accomplished its purpose it disappeared, never to shine again. A beautiful legend says that it fell into a well in Bethlehem, where on occasion it may still be seen by those who believe. But it is only a legend.

Note that the Magi found Jesus in a house (2:11), not in a manger. It was at least six weeks (some say two years) after Jesus' birth before the Magi arrived. In all probability their arrival came after Jesus had been presented in the temple (cf. Luke 2:22ff.), which occurred when He was six weeks old. By this time Mary and Joseph were living in a house.

And when the Magi saw Jesus they "fell down, and worshipped him..." (2:11). So here we see Gentiles worshipping Him who was "born King of the Jews." He was their King also. They were only a few Gentiles out of so many. Only a few sheep out of the fold other than the Jews (cf. John 10:16). Merely a trickle, but they foretold that flood from the nations who would come saying, "Sir, we would see Jesus" (John 12:21). How ingeniously Matthew weaves into his Jewish Gospel the universal Saviourhood of Jesus! First Rahab and Ruth, and now the Magi. But it is the gospel nevertheless.

The Magi did not come empty-handed. It is fitting that those coming to the King shall bring Him gifts. Empty-handed worship is hardly worship at all. "...and when they had opened their treasures, they presented unto him gifts; gold, and frankincense, and myrrh" (2:11).

And none of these gifts is without significance. Gold is the gift for a king. Frankincense is symbolic of prayer. Myrrh, used to embalm the bodies of the dead, is a symbol of suffering. So in their gifts the Magi recognized Jesus as their King, their God, and their Saviour. Would that all men, both Jew and Gentile, might do so!

The Response of the Jews (2:4-6)

Since Herod was only a half-Jew he would know little and care less about the Jewish scriptures. So when the Magi inquired about the new-born babe, he called in the chief priests and scribes to ask where Christ should be born. In reply they quoted Micah 5:2 to him. "And thou Bethlehem, in the land of Juda, art not the least among the princes of Juda: for out of thee shall come a Governor, that shall rule my people Israel" (2:6). Note that they gave Herod a ready answer (2:5). They knew the answer, but did nothing about it. Why?

Certainly they knew the reason for Herod's inquiry. The entire city seemed to know (2:3). One would suppose that they would have joined the Magi in their pilgrimage to Bethlehem. Instead they adopted an attitude of complacency. And we may well inquire as to such a response to the exciting news.

In the first place, they were mortally afraid of Herod. At the outset of his reign he had slain the Sanhedrin. And even though a generation had elapsed since then, they knew that they were no safer than the merest whim or caprice of the wicked despot. So as soon as they had done his bidding they hurried out of his presence into the comparative safety of their temple, a temple which even Herod had built for them. It is always a sad spectacle when religion is under the domination of the State!

In the second place, the scribes were so absorbed in the letter of their religion that they had lost its spirit. Evidently the answer to Herod's question came from the scribes. For the chief priests or Sadducees did not even regard the prophetic writing as Scripture. They accepted only the five books of Moses as such. But the scribes were Pharisees who accepted all of the Old Testament as inspired Scripture. The scribes were those Pharisees who were experts in the Scriptures and Law.

However, although they knew the contents of the Scriptures, they did not discern their true meaning. Jesus said to them, "Ye search the scriptures; for in them ye think that ye have eternal life: and they are they which testify of me. And ye will not come to me, that ye might have life" (John 5:39-40). They were too concerned with searching the written Word of God to be concerned with Him who is the living Word.

In the third place, the chief priests had little concern for the Messiah. They were so absorbed in the *status quo* that they resisted any idea of change. Under the Romans they enjoyed a semblance of power and no small economic gain. The attitude of the Sadducees is clearly expressed by Caiaphas. After Jesus became a threat to the *status quo,* he said, "If we let him thus alone, all men will believe on him: and the Romans shall come and take away our *place* and our nation" (John 11:48, author's italics). But they were entirely unconcerned with a baby born to peasant parents.

So the response of the Jews to the birth of Jesus was one of total indifference. A remnant here and there received Him. But as a whole they rejected Him. So absorbed were the chief priests and scribes in their rituals, legal discussions, and quest for wealth and power, that they ignored Him who "was born King of the Jews." A sad spectacle, to be sure, but one that has been repeated times without number. For these Jews are not alone. They but suggest all of those who become engrossed in their own affairs, even sacred things, to the utter disregard of Him who came that men might have life, and have it more abundantly.

The Response of the World (2:2-3, 7-8, 16-18)

When Herod heard of Him that was "born King of the Jews... he was troubled, and all Jerusalem with him" (2:2-3). The words "born King of the Jews" struck terror in Herod's heart. And well they might do so. For Herod was king of the Jews not by birth but by *appointment* of the pagan Romans. And Jerusalem also might well be troubled. For she knew to what cruel excesses Herod could go when his suspicious nature was aroused.

To understand this portion of the Gospel we must rehearse the sordid record of him who has been called Herod the Great. A. T. Robertson calls him "Herod the Great Pervert."

Herod was half Jew and half Idumaen. His father was Antipater the Idumaean who by a series of exploits gained favor with the Romans. Thus he was appointed procurator of Judea. Through his influence his son, Herod, in 47 B.C. was appointed governor of Galilee, where he so performed as also to gain the favor of Rome. This, plus much intrigue, led him to receive from Augustus Caesar the appointment as king over Palestine, an appointment which later was renewed by Marc Anthony. Thus from 40 B.C. until his death in 4 B.C. Herod reigned as king in Jerusalem.

His reign was one of many mighty achievements. He won many military victories. He was a great builder, ranging all the way from single structures to entire cities which he dedicated to his Roman masters. He was a strange combination of genius and madness, compassion and cruelty. On one occasion during a famine he emptied his treasury to buy food for his people. But his record of murder far exceeded his deeds of mercy.

Herod was insanely jealous of his position and power. He tolerated no rivals. Immediately after his accession to the throne he put to death the entire Sanhedrin, the ruling body of the Jews in religious and civil affairs. During the course of his bloody reign he executed many members of his own family: his popular high-priest brother-in-law, Aristobulus; his two favorite sons, Aristobulus and Alexander; his favorite wife, their mother, Mariamne; Antipater, another son; the brother and mother of Mariamne; and her uncle, his faithful adviser. Any sort of suspicion, whether well-grounded or not, was sufficient cause for such bloody deeds. Augustus Caesar said that it was better to be Herod's sow (*hus*) than his son (*huios*), for the former had a better chance to live.

So hated and feared was Herod by his people that he knew they would rejoice at his death. Therefore, just before his death he ordered that when he died, the heads of prominent families should be executed, in order that there would be mourning throughout the land. Fortunately, this order was not carried out.

Even so such a record enables us to understand Matthew 2. Much has been made of the fact that no non-Biblical source mentions the slaying of the babes of Bethlehem. In all there were probably about twenty. But in the light of Herod's bloody record such an event would hardly be considered newsworthy. It was news only as it related to the redemptive purpose of God, a purpose which receives scant notice from any worldly choniclers.

We have called Herod's response to Jesus "the response of the world." For Herod and all that he stands for is suggestive of all worldly aims and ambitions which set themselves against Jesus. Such powers are always troubled when they are confronted with the Christ of God. On one occasion Jesus said, "Now is the judgment of this world..." (John 12:31). The word "judgment" is "crisis." The world is always in a "crisis" when it comes face to face with Jesus.

Why was Herod troubled? Because he occupied a throne which rightly belonged to Jesus. He saw Him as a threat to his position. Whenever any man or system enthrones himself/itself in opposition to Jesus, it is confronted with a crisis and is troubled. Suppose that Herod had joined the Magi in true worship of Jesus as he laid his crown at His feet. What would have happened? Jesus would have returned it to him enhanced in glory and strength. But he did not do so.

Instead he feigned a desire to worship the Christchild that he might destroy Him. And in so doing he destroyed himself. The world still bows in mock worship before the Lord, and then goes on its wicked way. Jesus is none the less glorious. But empires fade and fall as they are broken on Him who is the Chief Cornerstone of God's purpose in history. Jesus survived Herod and his evil designs. The empire which crucified Him is but a broken memory. And Jesus will survive all worldly systems which oppose Him now!

The Response of God (2:12-15, 19-23)

Despite the evil of men God works in all things for good to those who love Him, and who fit into His will and purpose. The rage of Herod caused the flight into Egypt, a flight which may well have been financed by the gifts from the Magi (2:11, 13). Because no help could be expected from the indifferent and fearful Jewish leaders, God provided for His Son a haven of safety among pagan people. Thus He could say, "Out of Egypt have I called my son" (2:15). The prophet spoke more than he knew when he wrote of Israel (Hos. 11:1).

God worked in the brief accession of Archelaus, Herod's son, and a true son of his father, to cause Mary and Joseph to by-pass Judea and return to Nazareth. Thus Matthew can say, "... that it might be fulfilled which was spoken by the prophets [note the plural; cf. 2:5, 15, 17 where the singular is used], He shall be called a Nazarene" (2:23). No one prophecy can be cited for this. In all probability the root of the word "Nazarene" ("Nazareth" does not appear in the Old Testament) is the same as that for "shoot" or "branch" (cf. Isa. 53:2-4).

Thus Matthew closes this phase of his Gospel with the thought that though Jesus appeared as One of little honor in men's eyes, He was the true life out of the seemingly dead root in dry ground (cf. Isa. 53:2). The *root* of God's promises through Abraham and David seemed dead indeed. But by God's grace and power it sprouted, and though men despised so little a thing it became the Tree of Life to all who come to Him.

Yes, there was a star, "his star," the response of inanimate nature to the benevolent will of God. Those who responded to follow this star found Him who is the Desire of all nations. Those who ignored it continued to walk in the darkness of sin.

How glorious for those who follow the star. How tragic for those who do not. But God's star of hope still shines for those who will look up and follow on to know the Lord.

George Bernard Shaw in his *St. Joan* has the word for us. In the coronation scene in Rheims Cathedral Joan tells of hearing the voice calling her to deliver France. But Charles, the weak king, interrupts her. "O, your voices, your voices! Why don't the voices come to me? I am King, not you." Joan replies, "They do come to you; but you do not hear them. When the angelus rings you cross yourself and have done with it; but if you prayed from your heart, and listened to the trilling of the bells in the air after they stop ringing, you would hear the voices as well as I do."

Hearing voices or seeing the star—the meaning is the same. "And when they saw the star, they rejoiced with exceeding great joy" (2:10)!

Matthew 3

The Presentation of the King

In Matthew's Gospel there is a gap of perhaps twenty-seven years between Jesus' return from Egypt to Nazareth and His sudden appearance in the Jordan valley as a grown man. The "silent years" were not vital to the author's purpose. A Jewish rabbi entered his public ministry when he reached the age of thirty years. So when Jesus reached that age (Luke 3:23) He emerged from the privacy of Nazareth onto the stage of His public ministry. It is at this point that Matthew resumes his gospel record. Thus the third chapter may well be called "The Presentation of the King." It revolves about (1) the messenger; (2) the message; (3) the Messiah.

The Messenger (3:1, 3-4)

The messenger is John the Baptist or the Baptizer. We are not prepared by Matthew's preceding record for this person. Alexander Maclaren says, "John leapt, as it were, into the arena full-grown and full-armed."

We know from Luke's account that he was a second cousin of Jesus. He was the son of Zacharias and Elizabeth, Mary's cousin. Tradition says that his parents died when he was a child, and that he was brought up in the desert. At any rate Matthew simply introduces him as a desert wind from out of nowhere.

There is dramatic effect in his sudden appearance. Malachi 4:5 says, "Behold, I will send you Elijah the prophet before the coming of the great and dreadful day of the Lord." As Elijah "leapt . . . into the arena full-grown and full-armed" (I Kings 17:1), so John the Baptist suddenly appeared in the wilderness of Judea. He was even dressed like Elijah (II Kings 1:8, "raiment of camel's hair, and a leathern girdle about his loins," 3:4). Doctor Plummer holds that "John consciously took Elijah as a model." Whether or not this is true, the likeness is there nevertheless.

"In those days came [cometh] John the Baptist preaching in the wilderness of Judea . . ." (3:1). The word "cometh" is a historical present tense. So with imagination we see him striding through the wild country of Judea, a barren land bordering on the Dead Sea and the Jordan River. And he came "preaching." This word means to speak as a herald of the king, with the authority of the king, a message which is to be heeded and obeyed.

That Matthew presents John the Baptist as the herald or forerunner of the King is seen in verse 3. "For this is he that was spoken of by the prophet Esaias, saying, The voice of one crying in the wilderness, Prepare ye the way of the Lord, make his paths straight" (cf. Isa. 40:3; Luke 1:76; John 1:23). This prophecy related primarily to the return of Israel from Babylonian captivity, accompanied by their God. But Matthew sees its fuller meaning in the coming of the Lord as King, leading His people out of the exile of sin. And John the Baptist goes before Him to prepare the way.

In ancient times there were few highways. So when the king visited a city workmen were sent before him either to build a road or else to repair one that had fallen into ruin. Low places were filled in; high places were leveled; the road was made straight and smooth (cf. Isa. 40:4). The road into the hearts of the Jews had fallen into disrepair, and must be made usable by the King. A new highway must be constructed into the hearts of the Gentiles. And the Baptist was sent to prepare the way for the King.

Note the nature of this man. He was fearless and domineering before the people, the religious leaders, and kings (cf. Mark 6:16ff.). But before his King he was only a "voice." He was a true ambassador who spoke not his own message but that of his King. He proclaimed with authority, but it was an authority outside and above himself. He declared the truth with no fear of the consequences for himself. Nor did he wait for a congregation. He began preaching to the few people who lived in this wilderness, and the power of his message spread. So that the multitudes left their cities and villages to hear him. Even the Pharisees and Sadducees deigned to come to listen to this strange, unrefined son of the desert. For his words rang with compelling authority. A. T. Robertson with barbed wit notes that "some preachers start with crowds and drive them away." But not so with John. He started with a message, and the crowds came to hear him. What a lesson for those of us who propose to be heralds of the King!

The Message (3:2, 5-12)

It had been four hundred years since the voice of a prophet had been heard in Israel. And the hearts of the people were hungry for such. This hunger is reflected throughout the Jewish non-Biblical writings of the period between the Testaments. For instance, Antiochus Epiphanes, the Syrian ruler, desecrated the temple in Jerusalem, even sacrificing a sow on its altar. A successful revolt under the Maccabees ensued. When the temple was cleansed and re-dedicated, the question arose as to what to do with the stones of the altar. Finally, it was agreed to put them away with the hope that a prophet would come and tell them what disposal to make of them.

So we can readily understand why the people came to hear John the Baptist. For here, after four hundred years, was a man who had the ring of God in his voice. His message electrified the nation. As we examine this message we discover a challenge, a condemnation, and a consolation.

The challenge: "Repent ye: for the kingdom of heaven is at hand" (3:2). These were startling words to the Jewish minds and hearts. The prophets had pointed to such a kingdom which was to come. And now John, the last of the prophets, says that it is at hand. The kingdom of heaven draws near.

Actually the verb rendered "is at hand" is a perfect tense expressing a past fact, present reality, and a continuing effect. The word "kingdom" (*basileia*) means sovereignty, royal rule or power. Both "kingdom of heaven" and "kingdom of God" are used interchangeably in the various Gospels. They speak of the "reign [sovereignty] of God." Thus we may understand the words "is at hand." God is not about to establish His sovereignty. It is timeless, past, present, and future. But in an especial way He is about to declare His sovereign rule, not merely in the natural universe but in the hearts of men.

How near this "kingdom" is John does not say. Paul uses this same word to speak of one who was at the point of death (Phil. 2:30). So in effect John says that the "kingdom" is at the point of being declared. Already the signs of its immanency appear. The King even then approaches Jordan. Wherever the King is there is the "kingdom." So "the kingdom of heaven is at hand."

But perhaps an even more startling word to the Jews was the word "repent." For it declares the basis upon which one may become a part of this kingdom. One rabbi said that if all Israel would repent for one day the Messiah would come. But, even so, their concept was that when He came all Israel would be in His kingdom. However, John does not say, "Repent ye, that the kingdom may come." Instead he says, "Repent ye: for the kingdom of heaven is at hand." It is a matter of how one is related to it. And note that the verb "repent" is a plural form. It is a call for all to repent, Sadducees and Pharisees (vv. 7-8), publicans and sinners, Jew and Gentile.

Now John would have excited little interest had he called on the Gentiles to repent. For this was a common doctrine among the Jews. The Pharisees would probably have said, "Amen," had he called on publicans and sinners to repent. But to engulf the whole Jewish nation in the challenge was an unheard of thing. However, John does not tone down his message even in the face of the proud religious teachers and rulers of the nation. Instead he singles them out for particular emphasis. To them he said, "Think not [stop thinking] to say within yourselves, We have Abraham to our father: for I say unto you, that God is able of these stones to raise up children unto Abraham" (v. 9). They did not say it, but they were thinking it. And in flashing words John erases their false presumption. For the kingdom of which he speaks is not based upon natural generation but upon regeneration (cf. John 3:1ff.). And its subjects are to show outward evidence of the inward change (v. 8).

Which brings us to consider the meaning of the word "repent." John A. Broadus calls this the worst translation in the New Testament. The word "repent" is of Latin derivation (*repoenitet*) and means "to be sorry again." The Greek has a word to express this idea (*metamelomai*, cf. Matt. 27:3). But the word used in Matthew 3:2 is *metanoeō*. It means to change one's mental attitude and conduct (cf. v. 8). This involves a decided turning around so as to alter the entire direction of one's life. From going away from God you come to God. Once you hated God, now you love Him. You once loved sin, now you hate it. From rebellion against God you turn to serve Him. Such is more than a mere mechanical reformation. It involves an entire change of your nature.

So this last of the prophets continues the message of those who went before him. "Turn ye [cf. Joel 2:12; Isa. 55:7; Ezek. 33:11, 15]; for the kingdom of heaven is at hand."

Multitudes heeded the message of the Baptist. From Jerusalem, Judea, and from both sides of the Jordan they came. The crowds just kept on coming, as is seen in the imperfect form of the verb "went out" (*exeporeueto*, continuous action in past time). "And were baptized of him in Jordan, confessing their sins" (3:6). The words "were baptized" also render an imperfect tense of the verb *baptizō*. Not that individuals kept on being baptized. But as each one confessed his sins he was baptized. There was a regular procession of such.

The word *baptizō* means to dip, immerse, or submerge in water. One classical use of this word is used to describe the sinking of a ship. It was sometimes used in the Greek papyri of one being overwhelmed or submerged in trouble (cf. Matt. 20:22).

The Jews had a form of baptism called "ablutions" which symbolized ceremonial cleansing (*baptismos,* the act of baptism, cf. "washings" in Heb. 9:10). They practiced proselyte baptism for Gentiles who embraced the Jewish faith. So John had a ready form for those who expressed their willingness to embrace his message and its import.

But, even so, the baptism of John is not to be confused with the rite of Judaism. For in Acts 19:3 John's baptism is called a *baptisma.* In contrast with *baptismos* (see above) *baptisma* connotes not the act but the meaning of the act (cf. I Peter 3:21). So John's baptism was not a rite of ceremonial cleansing. It symbolized the subject's repentance, as shown by the confession of his sins, and his willingness to become a part of the kingdom which was at hand. Happily, in response to his challenge, many submitted to John's *baptisma.* But some did not.

Therefore, John's message was also one of condemnation. To the Pharisees and Sadducees he cried, "O generation of vipers, who hath warned you to flee from the wrath to come?" (3:7). This was a common figure in the wilderness. Sudden fires would spring up in the dry vegetation, and borne by the hot desert winds would sweep across the land. Snakes and vermin would flee before the flames in quest of safety. What stinging words these were to the religious and social elite. Like a whip lash they crackled in their ears and laid bare their hearts. They were not present out of heart-hunger, but for critical inspection. John calls them a brood of snakes fleeing before God's "wrath."

There are two words in the New Testament for "wrath," *orgē.* and *thumos.* The former is used here. It means God's abiding opposition to sin. Thayer distinguishes between these two words. *Orgē* is indignation which has arisen gradually and become more settled (cf. Rom. 1:18). *Thumos* is passion as angry heat, suddenly boiling up and soon subsiding (cf. Rev. 14:10; but note *orgē* in Rev. 16:19). But John says that these Jewish leaders are fleeing from God's settled and abiding anger against sin.

There is tremendous meaning in John's choice of the word *orgē.* We may think of God's wrath in a given instance as a *thumos* which suddenly boils up and then subsides. Like a flash fire which for a brief time consumes everything that it touches. But it is soon burned out. And those who fled from it may once again dwell in comparative safety—until it boils up again. But God's *orgē* is not some temporary punishment. It is His abiding punishment. It is His abiding opposition to sin. You flee from it in one place only to find that it is everywhere, and burning continuously. So with no place to flee, you are permanently abiding in it. Thus John might as well have asked not "who" but "where" will you flee from this wrath? In such a fire there is only one place of safety. Not before the flames, but where they have already been. At Calvary God's *orgē* did its worst to Jesus, our Substitute. The only place of safety for your soul is not in fleeing *from* God's wrath, but in fleeing *to* Calvary.

Nor should any Israelite presume upon his privileged position as a child of Abraham. The Jews said that Abraham had an excess of merit with God, enough to guarantee each of his descendents a place in the kingdom of God. This is much the same idea which holds that certain *saints* can make available to any one praying to them their excess merits (?) with God. But John relieves us of any such supposition. God can raise up stones as children of Abraham. Thus he gets down to the bedrock of the matter. One's relationship to God is an individual matter.

This is evidenced in his change of metaphors (3:10). God does not save men *en masse* any more than a farmer saves orchards *en masse*. Trees which bear no fruit are cut down and cast into the fire. Such a time had come to Israel as is seen in verse 10. Note "And *now*..." (author's italics). Jesus will usher in a new order of things, a new way of regarding one's relation to God. The time of Judgment is at hand.

However, John's message is not one of condemnation bereft of hope. For the one coming after him will baptize in the Holy Spirit and fire. The idea of the Spirit was precious to the heart of the faithful Jew. He longed for the promise made through Isaiah. "... I will pour my spirit upon thy seed, and my blessing upon thine offspring" (44:3).

The Hebrew word for "spirit" is *ruach* (Greek, *pneuma*), meaning breath or wind. And it had many happy associations in the Hebrew mind. At creation the Spirit of God worked (Gen. 1:2). God *breathed* life into man. Elijah heard the mighty *wind*. And the Spirit came upon men to give God's revelation of truth. So to be baptized in the Holy Spirit meant re-creation, life, power, and the understanding of God's truth.

What does John mean by the baptism of "fire"? Some see it as a purifying element. Which of course is true in certain cases. But is that the connotation here? We must interpret it in its immediate context.

Note that in this passage *fire* appears three times, one implied

(v. 7) and two specific (vv. 10, 12). In each of these the idea is that of judgment. Wind (Spirit) and fire are two of the basic elements of power. How one relates himself to them determines whether they destroy or serve. This contrast is implied in this passage.

These two ideas are clearly stated in verse 12, immediately after he speaks of the baptism of Spirit and fire. Realistically John draws a contemporary picture which may be seen in Palestine to this day. "Whose fan is in his hand, and he will throughly purge his floor, and gather his wheat into the garner; but he will burn up the chaff with unquenchable fire." Here we see the work of *wind* and *fire*.

Animals tread out the grain leaving it mixed with the chaff. With the winnowing fan or shovel both grain and chaff are tossed into the air. The *wind* blows the chaff away leaving the heavier grain to drop on the floor. Henceforth the grain is stored in the garner, and the remaining chaff is used for fuel.

So the Wind of God will separate the grain from the chaff. Only that which is rightly related to the King will be stored in God's garner, the Kingdom. The chaff will be burned in unquenchable fire. Note that the King will thoroughly cleanse (*diakathariei*) his threshing floor. Not one grain will be lost. Not one bit of chaff will escape the fire. Salvation and judgment. These are to be the works of the King. This is the message of the gospel (cf. Rom. 1:16-18, note "righteousness of God" and "wrath of God"). And John the Baptist preached both as he heralded the coming of the King. No man can claim to be the King's herald who does less.

The Messiah (3:13-17)

"Then cometh Jesus from Galilee to Jordan unto John, to be baptized of him" (3:13). Once again we have the historical present (cf. 3:1). In this word Matthew follows every step of Jesus from Nazareth to Jordan. The fame of John's preaching had reached the little town in Galilee. The hour had come for the presentation of the King.

"Then cometh Jesus...." The time is probably A.D. 26. The place is the Jordan River near Bethany. "Then" refers to Jesus' hour. But it involves more. It speaks of the exact moment when Jesus appeared before John. John had finished his message (3:12-13). The herald had fulfilled his mission. There but remains that he should present the King. No blast of trumpets is heard, unless it be the preaching of John. Quietly, simply the King stood face to face with His ambassador.

What a meeting this was! The grizzly son of the desert and the quiet carpenter of Nazareth. But no coming together of two men has affected the world as did this. Had there been a previous meeting of these two? Their mothers had met as they carried their babies in their wombs. Even then John leaped in recognition of the King. The probability is that never before had they stood face to face, unless it had been as children probably at some feast in Jerusalem.

But somehow John knew that before him stood the King. Perhaps as while he was in his mother's womb so now John responded to the innate deity and purity that were in Jesus. Although he had been given a sign as to the identity of the King (cf. John 1:33), instinctively he knew Him at first glance.

When John protested that he should be baptized of Jesus rather than to baptize Him, Jesus replied, "Suffer it to be so now: for thus it becometh us to fulfil all righteousness" (3:15). So both John and Jesus went down into the water, and John buried the King in the waters of baptism.

Heaven itself bent low for the occasion. For as Jesus, the Son, came up out of the water, God the Spirit, as a dove descended and lighted upon Him. God the Father spoke in approval of the Son. Thus we see the triune God joining in the presentation of the King. Did anyone save John and Jesus see the "dove" or hear the "voice"? From the record it would appear not (but cf. 4:3). But henceforth the herald must decrease that the King might increase (cf. John 3:30).

Invariably the question is asked as to why Jesus was baptized and as to the significance of His baptism. The answer to this question calls for an analysis of the event.

"To be baptized" (v. 13) is an infinitive of purpose. So Jesus sought baptism with a definite purpose in view. Certainly it did not involve repentance. For Jesus had no sin innate or actual, for which to repent (cf. Matt. 3:14). His sinlessness is at the very heart of the gospel. Nor did Jesus submit to baptism merely to set an example for others. His purpose in baptism is found in His words "to fulfil all righteousness" (v. 15).

While the word "righteousness" (*dikaiosunē*) sometimes refers to that which God requires in man, it more often refers to God's activity whereby He enables man to achieve the state of righteousness which He requires (cf. Rom. 1:17). And this righteousness is embodied in Jesus Christ (cf. Rom. 10:3-4). And in His baptism Jesus fulfilled this righteousness in three ways.

In the first place, He identified Himself with the ministry of John the Baptist. He authenticated John's ministry and message. But He did more. He linked Himself to John's ministry. John heralded the coming of the King. Jesus is the King. John preached a message of salvation and condemnation. It is in the person and work of Jesus that men will be either saved or condemned. So the ministry of John did not end in a blind alley. It naturally moved from the herald to the King, from the message to its fulfilment. And the transition came when John baptized Jesus in Jordan.

In the second place, Jesus in His baptism identified Himself with sinful men whom He came to save. Those who submitted to John's baptism did so on the basis of repentance from and confession of their sins, and upon the basis of their willingness to participate in the kingdom which was at hand. And when Jesus submitted to John's baptism He was saying, "I am one with you [apart from sin]. As you have dedicated yourselves to become a part of the Kingdom of heaven, I dedicate myself to do that which will make possible your entrance into it."

The apostle Paul defines the meaning of the cross when he says, "For he hath made him to be sin for us, who knew no sin; that we might be made the righteousness of God in him" (II Cor. 5:21). In similar fashion we may speak of Jesus' baptism. He who needed no repentance became one with those who did, in order that the righteousness of God might be fulfilled in them through Him.

In the third place, Jesus' baptism symbolizes that which He would do for the salvation of lost men. Thus in His burial in and resurrection from the watery grave we see His death, burial, and resurrection through faith in which men shall be saved. This is the substance of the gospel. Not water baptism as such (*baptismos*). But its meaning (*baptisma*).

So Jesus' baptism was not merely an event. It was the prophecy of a greater event, namely, that which He did to fulfil or fill full the righteousness of God in Christ Jesus (cf. Rom. 10:6ff.).

It is in this light that we may understand that which followed Jesus' baptism. When Jesus came up out of the water the heavens parted, and the Spirit of God "like a dove" descended and lighted upon Him (v. 16). Luke says that the Holy Spirit descended "in bodily shape like a dove..." (3:22). Thus we see the anointing of the King by the Holy Spirit. He was not *anointed King*. He was

King anointed. Anointed for what? He was anointed for sacrifice.

This is the significance of the *dove.* The dove is symbolic of gentleness, innocence, and meekness. The Levitical law prescribed one dove, along with a lamb, or two doves only for the poor, as a sacrificial offering (Lev. 12:6; 14:22; cf. Luke. 2:24). This would be the primary thought suggested to Matthew's Hebrew readers. So as one who was gentle, innocent, and meek Jesus would be the sacrifice for sin. As a lamb (cf. John 1:29) and dove for those who could afford it, or two doves for the poor, so Jesus will be the comprehensive sacrifice for sin for all who will receive Him. He will be offered "through the eternal Spirit" (Heb. 9:14). As the dove He is weak in His sacrifice. As the Spirit He is powerful in His salvation.

Yes, at the very inception of His public ministry the King is anointed for sacrifice. This is quite contrary to the popular Jewish concept of the Messiah. And in this fact lies the significance of the voice from heaven (v. 17). "This is my beloved Son, in whom I am well pleased" (cf. Matt. 17:5). A. T. Robertson calls "I am well pleased" (*eudokēsa*) a timeless aorist tense, expressing the Father's good pleasure in the Son at all times.

But why were these words spoken at this very moment? The King has just been anointed, not for military exploits as the Jews expected, but for sacrifice. It is not easy for men to accept disappointment concerning their dreams, no matter how erroneous they may be. The pressure would be upon Jesus constantly to deny the Father's will and to accede to popular demand. But in every such hour He would hear the Father's voice of approval for the way of the cross. And He who delighted always to do His Father's will would be strengthened thereby.

As Jesus heard these words His mind would hearken back to Psalm 2. Here the Father speaks of His begotten Son to whom He will give the heathen for an inheritance. He shall be His "king upon my holy hill of Zion." Though the heathen (and Jews) shall rage and kings shall plot, the Son is promised victory. His victory shall be not by military conquest but by spiritual sacrifice. He will go through the cross to the throne. The One whom the Father now approves He will one day raise and crown.

As at His baptism the triune God manifests Himself, so in the cross and resurrection He will be present. The King will be "declared [horizoned].... the Son of God with power, according to the spirit [Spirit] of holiness, by the resurrection from the dead" (Rom. 1:4). In Jordan's waters the King is presented for sacrifice.

In heaven's brightest firmament He will one day be presented in majesty and glory.

Yes, the kingdom of heaven is at hand. And the King goes forth to claim His kingdom.

Matthew 4:1-11

The Nature of the Kingdom

The King has come to establish His kingdom. What kind of kingdom will it be, and by what method will it be brought into being? These were vital questions then as they are now. For upon their answer hangs the very nature of this kingdom, its ideals, aims, and efforts. That God had an ideal kingdom in mind is everywhere evident in Scripture. But this did not mean that it was impossible for that ideal to be delayed or even destroyed. God created man in His own image. That was His ideal. But the image was marred or destroyed by sin. Would the same fate await His kingdom?

When God created the material universe He did so by methods of His own choosing with no possibility that they be altered. But in the realm of personal relationships God does not force His will upon other persons, even the person of His Son. It must be espoused through conscious, personal choice. And choice involves the possibility of another will being followed.

It is in this light that we must understand the temptation experiences of Jesus. For even the Son of God was given the right of choice. And the choices which He made in His initial temptation experience, after His baptism, determined the very nature of the kingdom of God, or even if there should be such a kingdom at all.

In this regard three things call for our attention. Thus we shall examine (1) the tempter; (2) the fact of temptation; (3) the temptations of Jesus.

The Tempter (4:1)

At this point Matthew introduces a new principal character into his story. He calls him "the devil." And he presents him as a personality. This is in harmony with the entire teachings of Scripture. Many deny that such a person exists, insisting instead that evil, like germs, is in the air. Which is exactly what he wants us to do. If we regard him merely as some impersonal, evil influence, or even make of him a caricature, we fall victim to one of his chief weapons. Thus he disarms us so as to leave us helpless before him.

One man insisted that there is no devil because he had never met him. You do not meet the devil if you are going his way. But once you change directions he will become a very present reality.

However, simply to deny the existence of the devil does not destroy him. It is more reasonable to accept the personality of the devil than to attempt to explain the existence of evil in some other way. To deny the personality of the devil is to run counter to the burden of Biblical teaching.

It is not within our purpose to delve into the mystery of the origin of the devil. In all likelihood he was a fallen angel who rebelled against the sovereign rule of God. Our point of emphasis is that he is in the world working against both God and man. He challenges God's sovereignty in the universe. He is called the prince of devils (Matt. 9:34; 12:24), implying that he has under his command a host of devils or demons who do his bidding. And the Bible presents him as one of great power, second only to that of God Himself.

The Bible ascribes many names to the devil each of which speaks of his nature and work. He is called Adversary (I Peter 5:8), Apollyon (Rev. 9:11, destroyer), Beelzebub (Matt. 12:24, probably out of contempt for the pagan god, Baal), Belial (II Cor. 6:15, worthless), Deceiver (Rev. 12:9), Dragon (Rev. 12:3), Enemy (Matt. 13:39), Evil One (Matt. 13:19), Father of lies (John 8:44), Murderer (John 8:44), Sinner (I John 3:8), and Tempter (Matt. 4:5). In seventy-four out of eighty-three times that he is mentioned he is called either Satan or Devil.

Matthew introduces him as "the devil," the definite article with a masculine noun implying personality. (But note that Jesus calls him Satan, 4:10). Thirty-eight times in the New Testament he is called "devil" (*diabolos*). The word "devil" means slanderer. He slanders God to man (Gen. 3:4) and man to God (Job 1:9-11). Thus he is called by Jesus "a liar, and the father of it" (John 8:44).

But a most interesting fact about the devil is that when he appears to man he never appears as the devil or in his true personality. In Eden he appeared to Eve as a serpent, perhaps a beautiful, graceful, flying serpent. Paul says that he transforms himself into an angel of light (II Cor. 11:14). And for this reason he is all the more deadly an adversary. If he appeared to men in his true self they would flee from him. But because he does not, men are ensnared by him.

An equally impressive truth is that the devil always appears before God in his true light (cf. Job 1:6ff.; Matt. 4:10). God knows him for who he is. And while God permits him to go so far in his nefarious work, He has determined limits beyond which he cannot go (cf. Job 1:12; 2:6). Of course, in personal relations this is with respect to those who trust in God. In the end those who completely align themselves with Satan, together with him and his angels and powers, will be cast into the lake of eternal fire (Matt. 25:41; Rev. 20:10, 14-15). Jesus Christ was manifested to destroy the works of the devil (I John 3:8).

So Satan is at war with God. He has contested God's sovereignty in the universe. And while the battle rages even in the natural elements (cf. Rom. 8:19ff.; I Cor. 15:24-28), the main arena of conflict is in the personality of man. And in this arena Satan's principal weapon is *temptation.*

The Fact of Temptation (4:1-3a)

It is unnecessary that we present evidence to establish this fact. It is the experience of every man. However, it is vitally necessary that we understand the nature of temptation.

The Greek word for "tempt" is *peirazō.* Together with its Hebrew equivalent it means to test or to try in order to prove. It may mean to test in order to prove one good or evil. In each usage the context must decide. For instance, in Genesis 22:1 we read of God's purpose to "tempt Abraham." He was not testing him to induce evil. His purpose was to prove Abraham's faith. Likewise in the case of Job. God *permitted* Satan to test Job to prove him faithful. James says that God tempts or tests no man with a view to producing evil (1:13).

On the other hand, Satan's testing is always for the purpose of seducing his victim. He tested Job in an effort to prove him faithless. Satan never tests a man to prove him genuine but in an effort to find a flaw in him. And we would do well to remember that He is ever the deceiver and an enemy of souls.

How does the devil tempt man? Contrary to much popular thinking he never assails us in our baser nature. He attacks us in our higher selves. Every power which God bestowed in us is good when used as God intends. But Satan seeks to pervert these powers to his own evil purposes. W. Hersey Davis once defined sin as "an illegitimate expression of a legitimate desire."

Let us gauge this definition in the light of divine revelation. In general terms we may say that temptation is with respect to physical appetites, aesthetic senses, and spiritual desire. This is evident in the initial record of temptation. "And when the woman saw that the tree was good for food [physical appetite], and that it was pleasant to the eyes [aesthetic sense], and a tree to be desired to make one wise [spiritual desire, Gen. 3:5], she took of the fruit thereof, and did eat . . ." (Gen. 3:6).

Now none of these is evil within itself. To say that Satan always attacks us in our baser nature is to fall victim to his wiles. Rather he seeks to seize upon legitimate desires and guide them toward an illegitimate expression. So the truth is that Satan attacks us in the nobler aspects of our natures. But he does so that he might debase them to his own nefarious ends.

The most picturesque portrayal of temptation is found in James 1:14-15. Stating that no man is tempted (to do evil) of God, he says, "But every man is tempted [tested], when he is driven away of his own lust and enticed. Then when lust hath conceived, it bringeth forth sin: and sin, when it is finished, bringeth forth death."

Notice that James uses the word "lust" twice. This word means "desire." It may be good or evil desire, according to the context. For instance, Jesus said, "With desire I have desired to eat this passover with you before I suffer" (Luke 22:15). Here our Lord uses both the noun and verb in the good sense. Likewise, Paul speaks of "a desire to depart and to be with the Lord" (Phil. 1:23). But in Romans 7:7 Paul uses this same word in the evil sense.

Now applying this dual meaning of the word to James 1:14-15, we discern the nature of temptation. In verse 14 the word "lust" (desire) speaks of the natural, God-given desires which reside in man: physical appetites, love of the aesthetic, and spiritual ideals. But in verse 15 it connotes these same desires after they have been perverted by Satan. So a literal translation of these verses may read thusly. "But every man is tempted, when he is drawn away by his own legitimate desire, and is baited [as a fish]. Then when perverted desire has conceived, it gives birth to sin: and sin, when it is full grown, brings the abortion of death."

This is a terrible picture of how Satan lures and entraps us. A fish takes the bait through a legitimate desire for food. In the same fashion Satan baits us. But once he has us on his hook, this legitimate desire becomes a perverted or misused one. Then the evil desire conceives with our wills thus giving birth to sin. However, it is an abortive birth. The child of this unholy conception is not the beautiful living thing which Satan promised. Instead it is death itself. "For the wages of sin is death . . ." (Rom. 6:23).

Now when we relate the fact of temptation to Jesus several questions arise. Was He tempted in His divine or human nature?

Were His temptations real? Was it possible for Him to yield to them? How did He overcome them?

It is evident from the record that Jesus was tempted in His human nature. James says, "... for God cannot be tempted ..." (1:13). In each of Jesus' temptations He was tested with respect to His human body and/or the purpose for which as man He came into the world. Thus our High Priest identified Himself with us in our times of testing (cf. Heb. 4:15-16).

And for this reason His temptations had to be real. He was tempted in the same areas that Eve was tempted: physical appetite (Matt. 4:3); aesthetic sense (4:5f.); spiritual desire (4:8f.). Luke says that He was tested in "all the temptation" (4:13). Literally, "all temptation," or every *kind* of temptation. This does not mean every specific temptation but all areas in which it is possible for one to be tempted.

But the question which gives us the most difficulty is *could Jesus have yielded to these temptations?* Our first impulse is to say, "No." But is this the right answer? Of course, as God He could neither be tempted nor yield to temptation. But He was tempted not in His divine but human nature. We must never forget that He was God as though He was not man. But we must likewise remember that He was Man as though He were not God. It is just as great an error to deny His human nature as to deny His divine nature. Both are mysteries beyond our comprehension. But they are facts nevertheless.

Therefore, we are bound to say that in His human nature He could have yielded to temptation. Or else His temptations were not real. And, if not, then He pretended to be tempted when He was not. Which would make Him guilty of hypocrisy, the sin which He condemned more unmercifully than any other (cf. Matt. 23). We do Jesus a greater injustice by saying that He could not have yielded than to say that He could.

Indeed, we do Him no injustice at all when we admit the possibility that He could have fallen before Satan's wiles. For who knows the power of temptation the more? Those who surrender at the first skirmish, or one who endures its hottest fires but still overcomes? The answer is obvious. And because Jesus endured "all the temptation" without yielding to it, He is able to help us to overcome also. Yes, Jesus had the possibility to yield. But even more wonderful—He had the power *not* to yield. And in that truth is His glory and our hope. For He "was in all points tempted like as we are, *yet without sin*" (Heb. 4:15, author's italics).

Which brings us to the final question. How did Jesus overcome these temptations? Let it be admitted that He had no innate sin in His nature. There were no antecedent sins in His past which made Him susceptible to present sin. But somehow, in a manner beyond our understanding, His temptations were real and had to be overcome. How did He do it?

For one thing He did not call upon the divine power within Himself. Indeed, it was at this very point that Satan tempted Him. He fought and won the battle by relying upon the power which was available to Him in His human nature.

For forty days Jesus had prayed and fasted as He communed with His heavenly Father. He was aware of God's presence with Him and within Him. He was conscious of God's will and purpose for His life. He knew the consequences if He forsook them. He recognized Satan for who he was. He knew his nefarious purpose. He met each temptation forthwith. Not for one second did He allow Satan to sink his hook in Him. He refused to be baited. And every temptation He turned back with the Sword of the Spirit, which is the Word of God. In keeping with the exhortation of James 4:7 He submitted Himself unto God, resisted the devil, and he fled from Him.

Other than Jesus' innately sinless nature there is no weapon which He used against Satan that is not available to us. And since He has broken the power of sin, all who rely completely on Him may know victory in every time of testing. In His life Jesus demonstrated that sin is not a necessary ingredient in true manhood. In His death and resurrection He provided a way of escape for all who will believe on Him. In the hour of trial we can be more than conquerors through Him that loved us (Rom. 8:37).

The Temptations of Jesus (4:3-11)

We have noted something of the "how" of Jesus' temptations. But this still leaves unanswered the "why." Why was it necessary that Jesus be tempted? We may assume that it was necessary. For Matthew tells us that He was "led of the Spirit into the wilderness to be tempted of the devil" (4:1). Mark says that immediately after His baptism the Spirit "driveth him into the wilderness" (1:12). "To be tempted" is an infinitive of purpose (cf. 3:13, "to be baptized"). So once again we see God's purpose being fulfilled. It is of interest to note, therefore, that the temptations of Jesus were brought about as a part of God's plan. The initiative was with God, not Satan. But once again we must note the difference of purpose. Satan tempted Jesus to prove Him faithless. God permitted Him to be tested to prove Him faithful.

In all the world there probably is not a more likely place for these temptations to take place than in the wild country just west of Jericho. Even to this day as one drives through or flies over it this area appears to be forsaken by man and God. Scarcely would one find a human being dwelling in it or travelling through it, except by the nearby Jerusalem-Jericho road. But even this was so infested by robbers as to be called the "Ascent of Blood." During His forty days in this wilderness Jesus' only companions were "the wild beasts" (Mark 1:13).

We cannot be certain as to where exactly the temptation took place. Tradition locates it on Quarantania, a mountain which rises fifteen hundred feet above the Jordan Valley. And it could well be the place, for it is about six or eight miles from the traditional place of Jesus' baptism.

At any rate after forty days of fasting our Lord was confronted by the devil. Was it a face to face meeting? There is no valid reason to think differently. To be sure temptations can be psychological. But if we permit the Scriptures to speak for themselves, we must conclude that the devil appeared to Jesus in bodily form.

It is perfectly natural that at this point in His ministry Jesus should be tempted. Great hours of spiritual victory are always followed by spiritual depression. The mountains give way to the low places. It is true of us; it was true of Jesus.

However, more than mere psychological reaction is involved in this experience of Jesus. He has just been presented as the King. The anointing of the Spirit and the voice of heavenly approval are still fresh in His memory. The King so anointed and approved sets forth to secure His kingdom. What kind of kingdom shall it be? What shall be its purpose? How will it be established? These questions most likely were in Jesus' mind as He prayed and fasted for forty days. And then the devil came to Him. Three times he tempted Jesus. And each temptation had to do with the nature of His kingdom.

The first temptation. "If thou be the Son of God, command that these stones be made bread" (4:3).

Note that the devil assumes that Jesus is the Son of God. In the Greek "if thou be the Son of God" is a condition of the first class which assumes a thing to be true. Jesus had just heard the voice of the Father so declaring Him. John heard it. And so did Satan. Therefore, he does not begin by planting doubt in Jesus' mind. Instead, he says, "You are the Son of God. Why not use the power that is yours? You are hungry. Why not turn these stones into bread and eat? You made them stones. You can also make them bread."

So many subtle suggestions are involved in the devil's words. In effect he says, "So you are the Son of God. You have divine power. How do you know that it works? Why not try it to see?" Or, "You have come to establish your kingdom. But you are famished. Suppose that you starve in this wilderness. Where will your kingdom be then? But you have the power to remedy that. Why not do so?"

Thus, while admitting that Jesus is the Son of God, the devil endeavors to plant distrust in His heart as to the love and power of God. At the same time He seeks to get Jesus to work a miracle for His own selfish gratification. Even here he suggests that in establishing His kingdom Jesus avoid the way of suffering.

But there is more in this temptation. Satan said, ". . . command that these stones be made bread." "Comand" is an imperative form. Thus Satan *commands* Jesus to command. He seeks to take charge at the beginning. On whose will shall the kingdom be established? Satan's or God's? This fundamental principle must be settled at the outset.

Furthermore, is the kingdom to be based upon the King's selfish indulgence or upon His service? The pattern of the ancient world was the former. Is Jesus to follow the ways of the world or the way of God?

The late queen of Holland as a little girl stood looking out the window at the people passing by. Turning to her nurse she asked, "Do all of these people belong to me?" The nurse replied, "No, my child, you belong to all these people." Which attitude should Jesus take?

Again, was the kingdom to be founded upon material things or upon a spiritual experience? Would Jesus seek man's allegiance by offering him "bread"? Would the King minister only to man's animal nature? Or would He provide for His soul? All of these things were involved in the first temptation.

In reply Jesus wielded the Sword of the Spirit as He said, "It is written, Man shall not live by bread alone, but by every word that proceedeth out of the mouth of God" (4:4; cf. Deut. 8:3).

Man must have bread. But bread alone cannot suffice for his needs. Better to be without bread than to be without God.

Jesus was ever conscious of man's physical needs. However, He realized that man's greatest problem is not poverty or hunger but sin. Indeed, sin is the principal cause of the material problems of men. The earth produces abundantly and enough for all. But sin causes some to hoard and others to be in want. For many the sin problem is aggravated by the very abundance of things which they possess. "For what is a man profited, if he shall gain the whole world, and lose his own soul?" (Matt. 16:26).

The kingdoms of this world are largely founded upon "bread." The group which promises the most in material prosperity more than likely will be elevated to power. Catering to the selfish interests of the citizenry is standard political procedure, even though the so-called gratuities are paid for out of the recipients' own pockets. But history reveals that such governments are short-lived.

Nero sought to hold his power over the Roman populace with circuses and bread. But when boats arriving from Egypt were found to contain sand for the arenas rather than wheat for bread, the populace revolted. It was the beginning of the end for Nero, who died a suicide.

The height of Jesus' popularity with the multitudes came with the feeding of the five thousand. But when He refused to be a "bread" Messiah the crowds left Him. He paid a price in numbers. But He gained in that He continued to build His kingdom out of those who sought Him not for loaves and fishes, but because they found in Him the living bread of God which "giveth life unto the world" (John 6:33).

The second temptation. "If thou be the Son of God, cast thyself down: for it is written, He shall give his angels charge concerning thee: and in their hands they shall bear thee up, lest at any time thou dash thy foot against a stone" (4:6; cf. Ps. 91:11-12).

From the wilderness the devil transported Jesus to the highest "wing" of the temple in Jerusalem. This was probably that section on the southeast side of the temple which was four hundred and fifty feet above the Kidron Valley. Even today when one looks down from this dizzy height it is an awesome spectacle. Hegesippus says that it was from this place that James, the half-brother of Jesus, was flung to his death in the valley below.

This temptation was threefold in nature. It was directed toward the natural human weakness which produces dizziness when one looks down from high places. It was designed to cause Jesus to put to the test the promise of God. It was related to the nature of the kingdom which Jesus came to establish. The first of these is quite obvious. But the other two call for closer examination.

As we examine the second element of this temptation several things are worthy of note. The devil again assumes the deity of

Jesus: "If thou be the Son of God. . . ." Furthermore, he issues a second command: "Cast thyself down . . . ." He seeks to impose his assumed sovereignty even over the Son of God. There is nothing sacred to him. And then he appeals to Scripture (cf. Ps. 91:11-12). Satan can quote Scripture also.

But note how he misapplies and misquotes it. The promise made in the psalm was never intended to be so used. It calls on us to trust God, not dare Him. And in quoting this passage the devil omitted one very important phrase, "to keep thee in all thy ways." The way proposed by the tempter was not the way prescribed for the Son of God.

This is one of Satan's favorite tricks. He does not use but mis-uses (abuses) the Word of God. Just because a sermon or a book contains much Scripture does not necessarily mean that it declares truth. The Scripture is true in its context. But by removing it from its true setting one may misuse it so as to declare error. The hearer or reader should be like the men of Berea who "searched the Scriptures daily, whether those things [preached by Paul] were so" (Acts 17:11).

Furthermore, Satan entraps us by mis-quoting Scripture. How many times have you heard someone say, "Resist the devil, and he will flee from you" (James 4:7b). This is not true. For the Bible does not say this. It says, *"Submit yourselves therefore unto God.* Resist the devil, and he will flee from you" (author's italics). And that makes all the difference in the world.

What is Satan's purpose in so tempting Jesus? He reminds Him that He is God's Son. God has promised to protect Him. Why not put God to the test to see if He will keep His promise? Had Jesus done so it would not have been an act of faith but of doubt.

But the third aspect of this temptation is even more relevant to the situation. In effect the devil was suggesting how Jesus should esablish His kingdom. Perform the spectacular! Dazzle the people! Fling yourself out into space, and float down as though upheld by an unseen hand! Then the people will accept you as the Messiah.

But Jesus did none of these things. Instead, seeing the subtle designs of Satan, He quoted again from God's Word. "Thou shalt not tempt [put to the test] the Lord thy God" (4:7; cf. Deut. 6:16).

Jesus trusted in God, but He never pushed God into a corner. He never created situations in which God would have to deliver Him by miraculous means. Instead He deliberately avoided such until His "hour" came. Nor did He work miracles merely to display His power before doubting men. He refused to give "signs" of His deity upon demand.

"Why? Because He knew that the kingdom of God was not to be founded upon *razzle dazzle.* Men were to come to Him not for entertainment but in faith unto salvation. The former is of the world; the latter is of God.

You can draw a crowd by dealing in the spectacular. But this does not necessarily mean that you are building the kingdom of God. Too often men ask bread, and we give them stones. Risky performances designed to display one's faith may not be faith at all. It may be pushing God into a corner, daring or testing Him to see if He will keep His word. Those inclined to do so would do well to ponder long Jesus' answer to Satan on the pinnacle of the temple.[3]

The third temptation. "All these things will I give thee, if thou wilt fall down and worship me" (Matt. 4:9).

Jesus and the devil are back on "an exceeding high mountain." From Quarantania Jesus could see the international highways leading to all the nations of the ancient world (Europe, Asia, Africa). "In a moment of time" (Luke 4:5) the devil showed Jesus "all the kingdoms of the world [*cosmos*], and the glory of them" (Matt. 4:8). This was most likely a psychological picture. But note that Matthew does not say "world" (cf. Matt. 24:14, *oikoumenē,* the inhabited earth) but *cosmos,* the orderly arrangement of the universe. So that which Jesus saw was more than the *earth.* It was the sovereignty of the *cosmos* itself.

Satan claims sovereignty in both the earth and the universe. And he offers to resign his claim for one act of worship by the Son of God. Note that here Satan does not command Jesus. Instead, he suggests a condition which is not fulfilled but which may be fulfilled (Greek, condition of the second class). (This within itself suggests the possibility that Jesus could yield to his temptation.)

Suppose that Jesus had bowed before the devil. The sovereignty which he proposed to give is not his to bestow. He is a usurper of power. Furthermore, had Jesus succumbed to his wiles He would have received no kingdom. Rather the very moral structure of the universe would have collapsed. *Even the sovereignty of God would have been destroyed!*

---

[3] Note Mark 16:8. The oldest and most accurate manuscripts of *Mark* end with 16:8. Most likely the remainder of this chapter is not genuine Scripture.

So once again we see the nature of the kingdom of God. How is it to be established? In effect the devil suggests that Jesus take a short-cut to the throne. Avoid the cross! Later in this study we shall see how ardently the devil worked to keep Jesus off the cross. For he knew that thereby he would be dethroned and Jesus enthroned. Even to the followers of Christ the devil says, "Compromise with sin. Avoid the preaching of the cross. Take the quick, easy way, and all men will follow you."

But Jesus did not take the tempting bait which Satan offered. Once again He drew the sword of the Spirit. "Get thee hence, Satan [Begone, Satan!], for it is written, Thou shalt worship the Lord thy God, and him only shalt thou serve" (Matt. 4:10).

Thus Jesus rejected the way of Satan to follow the way of God. An analysis of these three temptations shows that they all turn upon a contrast of the kingdoms of the world, their ideals, ways, and purposes; and the ideals, ways, and purposes of God in His Kingdom. Jesus knew that His kingdom was not of this world (John 18:36). Nor could it be etablished through worldly ways. He must go to the throne through the cross and empty tomb. It is the long, the hard way. But it is the right way. It is God's way. So He turned from the way of the world to follow the way of God. Those who propose to follow Him will do well to tread the path over which He chose to go.

"Then the devil leaveth him, and, behold, angels came and ministered unto him." But note that the angels came only after He had vanquished the foe. However, the devil will return again and again. But unperturbed the Saviour will walk the road of God. For that road alone leads to that day when "the sovereignty of the cosmos became the [undisputed] sovereignty of our Lord and of his Christ, and he shall reign unto the ages of the ages" (Rev. 11:15, author's translation).

The Proclamation of the King

Matthew 5

The Citizens of the Kingdom

Matthew does not find it in his purpose to record the early Judean ministry of Jesus and other related events (cf. John 2:13—4:54). Instead he plunges immediately into His Galilean campaign which occupied so much of His public ministry. He does not take Jesus to Judea until shortly before His crucifixion. This is most significant in a Gospel addressed to the Jews. John records several visits of Jesus to Jerusalem prior to the final one. And Luke includes a Judean ministry not found in the other Gospels. It would seem, therefore, that Matthew is emphasizing the rejection of Jesus by the Jews. According to his Gospel the first time that Jesus presented Himself to Jerusalem He was crucified. This is not a conflict in the records. It is merely Matthew following his purpose as the other Evangelists did theirs. Indeed, we cannot fully understand Matthew's account without taking into consideration the rising opposition to Jesus recorded in Luke and John.

At any rate Matthew brings Jesus to Galilee directly after the temptation experience. The immediate occasion was the arrest of John the Baptist (4:12), an account which he reports fully in Chapter 14. Realizing that this would be His own fate eventually but that His "hour" had not come, Jesus left the hostile atmosphere of Judea for the more tolerable one in Galilee. Galilee was a populous region which had come under Greek influence, and so was more willing to receive new ideas. Thus we can understand why Jesus spent the greater part of His public ministry here.

Shortly after His return to Galilee Jesus removed from Nazareth (cf. Luke 4:16-31) to Capernaum, a city on the northern shores of the sea of Galilee, where He established His headquarters for His Galilean campaign (4:13). From this center He began to preach the gospel of the kingdom, His message being the same as that of John the Baptist (4:17). During this time He called His first disciples (4:18-22). In three brief verses Matthew describes the expanding ministry of Jesus (4:23-25). And then he records the Sermon on the Mount (chaps. 5-7).

If we follow Matthew alone this would appear to come early in our Lord's ministry. But in his *A Harmony of the Gospels* A. T.

Robertson places it near the middle of His public ministry. Luke says that this Sermon came immediately after Jesus had chosen the twelve apostles (6:12-16; cf. Matt. 10:1-14; Mark 3:13-19). We cannot be certain as to the place where this sermon was delivered. Matthew simply says that it was on a mountain (cf. Luke 6:17-19). The Horns of Hattin more nearly fit the description than any other place.

To whom was this sermon delivered? Some hold that it is simply a compilation of Jesus' teachings which were spoken on various occasions. But to this writer the arguments for such a position are far from convincing. We prefer to regard it as one sermon delivered at a specific time and for a definite purpose. Matthew says that it was delivered to Jesus' disciples (5:1-2). Luke includes the multitudes along with the disciples (6:17-19). In all probability it was delivered primarily to Jesus' disciples, with the multitudes listening also. It was not delivered for the benefit of unbelievers. It is not a plan of salvation. Oswald Dykes calls it "The Manifesto of the King," delivered to His subjects. It may well be called "The Constitution of the Kingdom of God." It describes the citizens of the kingdom (chap. 5); the values in the kingdom (chap. 6); and the relationships within the kingdom (chap. 7). In this chapter we are concerned with the first, "The Citizens of the Kingdom." As we do so let us note (1) the quality of the citizens; (2) the function of the citizens; (3) the motive of the citizens.

The Quality of the Citizens (5:3-12)

This quality Jesus describes as "blessedness" or "happiness." The Greek word rendered "blessed" (*makarios*) is a very interesting word which is difficult to translate into English. Certainly "happy" does not render its full meaning. For the basis of "happy" is "happening." It describes a condition which depends upon that which happens to one. So it is related to outward circumstances.

We can best understand *makarios* when we examine its usage. William Barclay points out that *hē makaria* (feminine form) was used by the ancients to describe Cyprus as *The Happy Isle*. Cyprus was so beautiful and fertile that it was said that one needed to go nowhere else. For there one could find everything necessary for a full, complete life. So in describing the kingdom citizen as *makarios,* Jesus says that he contains within himself all that is necessary for the abundant life. His life is full and complete regardless of outward circumstances. Thus *makarios* is expressive of

Jesus' words, "...my peace I give unto you: not as the world giveth, give I unto you" (John 14:27).

Therefore, Jesus gives us eight "Beatitudes" to express the quality that abides in the life of His people. Notice that in each case the word "are" is in italics, showing that it does not appear in the Greek text. So *makarios* is an absolute; it is an unchangeable condition. Furthermore, note that these beatitudes are related in a progression of ideas. They do not describe eight different types of people, but an abiding and progressive condition in one person in eight different types of experiences. The former four deal with the Christian's relation to God; the latter four have to do with his relation to men.

"Blessed the poor in spirit: for theirs is the kingdom of heaven" (v. 3). The word "poor" is *ptōchos*. Another word, *penēs,* means a working man who provides for his own needs, but with nothing left over. But *ptōchos* means absolute or abject poverty. It is used of the beggar Lazarus (Luke 16:20), who was absolutely destitute and dependent upon others for the bare necessities of life.

But Jesus speaks of one who is "poor in spirit." There is no virtue in either poverty or wealth as such in the material sense. One who is poor in spirit is one who recognizes his absolute poverty in spiritual things. He lacks the self-sufficiency of the Pharisee (Luke 18:11-12). He knows that within himself there is nothing to justify him before God. Like the publican he can only cry out for mercy (Luke 18:13). He desires to be something more than he is, and realizes that it can come only from one outside himself. He needs *grace,* not justice. "Poor in spirit" describes the condition known in theology as *conviction* of sin. Jesus says that only such a person can become a citizen of the kingdom of heaven.

"Blessed they that mourn: for they shall be comforted" (v. 4). The word "mourn" means to mourn for the dead. It is the strongest word for mourning in the Greek language. In the Septuagint it is used of Jacob's mourning when he thought that Joseph was dead (Gen. 37:34). So Jesus says that he who is "poor in spirit" mourns for his sins. Realizing his own sinfulness and unworthiness he is plunged into deep mourning, not only for what his sins have done to him but to God also. Thus he knows "godly sorrow" which "worketh repentance" (II Cor. 7:10). So conviction is followed by *repentance.*

Such a person, Jesus says, shall know the comfort of the Holy Spirit. For the words "shall be comforted" (*paraklēthēsontai*) are akin to "Comforter" (John 14:16, *paraklētos*) The Holy Spirit brings conviction for sin which, in the seeking heart, results in repentance.

"Blessed the meek: for they shall inherit the earth" (v. 5). Unfortunately the English word "meek" suggests "weak." But the Greek word which it translates is a virile word. Among other things it means one who, recognizing his shortcomings, is free from pride and filled with humility. Thus he is teachable. He is willing to enroll as a disciple under a teacher (cf. Matt. 11:28-30). He commits himself to one who can supply his lack. Thus he believes in or commits himself to the Teacher. This is his expression of *faith* (*pisteuō,* believe, commit, have faith). As one who has committed himself fully to the King, he inherits the land (*gēn*) or the Kingdom. He has been "born again" (John 3:3).

"Blessed they which do hunger and thirst after righteousness: for they shall be filled" (v. 6). Hunger and thirst are the most demanding of appetites. For the kingdom citizen these appetites will be directed toward righteousness. The self-righteous man knows no such desire. But the one who has received the righteousness of God in Christ Jesus keeps on hungering and thirsting for God's righteousness. It possesses his very soul. He is never satisfied with his present state, but craves more and more of the God-kind-of-righteousness. He keeps on growing in grace and in the knowledge of his Lord and Saviour Jesus Christ (II Peter 3:18). This is the equivalent of *sanctification.*

Dedicated or set apart (sanctified) to the service of the King, the kingdom citizen will continue to grow and develop in that dedication. Thus he will "be filled." The Greek word so rendered was used of feeding and fattening cattle. So the kingdom citizen who hungers and thirsts after righteousness will be thoroughly satisfied, and will attain the purpose for which he receives sustenance.

Thus in four short verses Jesus runs the gamut of one's Christian experience: grace, conviction, repentance, faith or commitment, and sanctification. It is that which is involved with being "in Christ" (cf. II Cor. 5:17). But this relationship is to express itself in the kingdom citizen's relationship to men. Therefore, Jesus continues.

"Blessed the merciful: for they shall obtain mercy" (v. 7). The kingdom citizen has become such not through God's justice but through His mercy. Therefore, he should show mercy to others. To fail to do so is evidence that he has not received mercy from God (cf. Matt. 18:23ff.).

The Greek word rendered "mercy" is *eleēmōn,* meaning active pity. Its Hebrew equivalent (*chesedh*) means to get inside one's skin so as to become completely identified with another. Thus you see through his eyes, think with his mind, and experience his own innermost feelings. It is akin to the thought contained in the Greek word *sunpaschein* (to sympathize), to suffer together with. So to be merciful is to identify yourself so completely with another that his condition becomes yours, and then to act accordingly. Thus we see the element of *Christian service.*

This is exactly what God in Christ did for us. We are to do the same for others in their need. And in showing such mercy one receives it from others in return. Doctor Bruce calls this "a self-acting law of the moral world."

"Blessed the pure in heart: for they shall see God." The word "pure" means "unmixed, unadulterated, without alloy." It is pure gold without alloy. Applied to the heart, as here, it means a heart with unmixed motives, a heart that is loyal under all circumstances. Thus the kingdom citizen should serve God with a pure heart, a heart that can be trusted. He is wholly devoted to his King. No evil comes between his soul and his Saviour. This is suggestive of the privilege of *communion* and *prayer.*

Such a person shall see God. This figure is drawn from the Oriental court where the king lived in seclusion. The only intercourse with him was through a trusted official. This minister could approach the king at all times. So one whose heart is pure shall see God. He can come into His presence because the King knows that his will is that of his Lord. This is made possible only through Christ (cf. Heb. 4:15-16).

"Blessed the peacemakers: for they shall be called the children of God" (v. 9). Christ the King is a peacemaker between God and man (Col. 1:20-22) and between man and man (Eph. 2:12-18). The kingdom citizen must be the same. The message of peace is the message of the gospel. Here then is the *missionary motive.* Men shall find peace within themselves and among themselves only as they become kingdom citizens.

Peacemakers shall be called the children of God. This is more than relationship. It involves character. Furthermore it speaks of the outward expression of inward being. Such will be called by others "children of God."

All of the above qualities call for the separated life. And a life separated from the world can expect to receive the hatred of the world (cf. John 15:18-19). Therefore, "blessed they which are persecuted for righteousness' sake: for theirs is the kingdom of heaven . . ." (vv. 10-11). Jesus never promised His followers an easy time in this world. Citizens of the kingdom of heaven can expect opposition from the kingdom of evil. But they are to be sure that the persecution, reviling, and false speaking are unmerited. When they suffer it is to be as Christians (cf. I Peter 2:11ff.; 3:14ff.) not as evil doers. The King does not ask His subjects to endure anything that He has not endured. And they are to *rejoice* in their trials, knowing that "if so be that we suffer with him, that we may be also glorified together" (Rom. 8:17).

So the King sums up the whole of the kingdom citizen's experience: grace, conviction, repentance, faith, sanctification, Christian service, communion, missions and joy. All of this He gathers up in the word *makarios*. Because (note "for" in each verse) he is a citizen of the King he shall find within himself ("Christ in you," cf. Col. 1:27) all that is necessary for a blessed life, uncaused or unmoved by any outward circumstance. It is wholly the work of the King.

The Function of the Citizens (5:13-16)

From this marvelous picture of the quality of kingdom citizens Jesus proceeds to give it a practical application. The Christian is not merely to be sufficient within his own being as such. He is to bring that quality of being to bear upon life about him. Thus Jesus describes him as "salt" and "light."

"Ye are the salt of the earth . . ." (v. 13). In so speaking Jesus paid His followers one of the highest of compliments, as indeed it is today. To say that a man is "the salt of the earth" is to speak of him in the highest of terms.

In the ancient world salt was a precious commodity. The Greeks called it divine. Roman soldiers were often paid in salt, hence the word "salary" (Latin, *sale*). From earliest times salt was considered an offering to the gods. All Hebrew meat offerings were to be salted. (Lev. 2:13). As one drives along the Mediterranean coast of Lebanon today one sees salt bins along the shore. So scarce is salt that they catch the sea water in the bins. The sun evaporates the water, leaving the salt. Thus we can understand the fact that the ancient Romans regarded salt as a symbol of purity. They said that salt came from the purest of all things, the sun and the sea. This symbol of purity adds great force to Jesus' words. But primarily His words meant two things to His hearers.

To them salt was a preservative. In a hot climate without refrigeration meat spoiled quickly. To preserve it it was *salted down.* In this manner it was saved from corruption and decay.

The kingdom citizen is to be a preserving element in society. In order to do its work salt must come into contact with that which it preserves, but it never becomes an identical part of it. The Christian cannot live in a world apart from his environment. But he should never become a part of it. He is to be in the world but not of it. Salt is a silent but effective preservative. Likewise, the Christian does not call attention to himself. But there should be that antiseptic quality about him which creates a pure and wholesome condition in whatever circle he may move.

Furthermore, salt adds flavor to food. So the kingdom citizen is to give to life a zestful flavor. His entire life should be such as to reflect the very joy of living. Too many Christians feel that they must show their piety by a *pious* attitude. A woman was asked if she would become a Christian. She replied, "No, I am sad enough as it is." She had observed Christians who were insipid rather than salt. Jesus came to give life more abundant. The Greek word for "abundant" means "overflowing all the edges around," like a cup filled to overflowing. The kingdom citizen will bless others by the overflow out of his life.

Jesus warns that salt may lose its "savor." It becomes tasteless and useless. This figure causes difficulty for interpreters. It is contended that salt never loses its flavor. But John A. Broadus cites an instance where piles of salt near the Dead Sea were found to be tasteless. William Barclay also cites a Palestinian custom of putting salt under ovens to enable them to hold their heat. In time the heat produced a chemical change in the salt so that it was incapable of retaining the heat. Thus it was thrown out to be trampled over. It may be that Jesus used a common proverb which grew out of these or other facts unknown to us.

But whether or not salt can lose its flavor, Christians can lose theirs. Thus insofar as their mission as salt is concerned, they lose their usefulness. It may be because of some sin, attitude, or mere idleness. Thus their lives become insipid. There is here the case of lost opportunity. Talents unused are talents lost. Therefore, instead of being a preservative or of giving meaning to life, life simply passes them by. They receive only scorn as the world tramples them under its feet as it rushes on to corruption, despair, and loss.

Furthermore, Jesus said, "Ye are the light of the world" (v. 14a). Thus the King says that His citizens are to be like Himself. "I am the light of the world" (John 8:12); "ye are the light of the world." Of course, there is a difference. He is light within His very nature (John 1:4). The Christian receives light from Him. The world is to see Jesus in us.

A light is meant to be seen. And if we are light the fact of it cannot be hid (v. 14b). As men do not light a lamp and hide it, so the Christian's light is not to be secret. Someone had said that there is no such thing as secret discipleship. If you are lighted you will shine. And if you do not shine you have never been lighted.

As with salt so with light, the emphasis is on a quiet but effective witness for Christ. A light does not call attention to itself. It points the way through the darkness. It warns the traveller of danger. Furthermore, light does not rid a room of darkness by physical force. It shines, and the darkness flees. Someone has said that it is better to light one little candle than merely to curse the darkness.

Therefore, Jesus says, "Let your light so shine..." (v. 16). In Greek "shine" is an imperative tense. He commands light to shine. Shining, therefore, is not a matter of choice but of obligation. Again, the word "so" is the first word in the sentence, so it is emphatic. Jesus says, "So shine...." "So" refers back to the two illustrations. So shine as a city set on a hill, and as a lamp on a lampstand. We are to shine before men, not in some hermit's cave or in an ivory tower.

We are to let men see our *good* works. In the Greek there are two words for "good." One (*agathos*) refers to the quality of goodness. But the word used here is *kalos* (*ta kala erga*) which in addition to goodness carries the idea of attractiveness or beauty. Some Christians are *good,* but they are repulsive to others in their goodness. Jesus says that the kingdom citizen is so to live as to attract men, not to himself, but to God. The hypocrite can shine with outward goodness in order to receive the plaudits of men. The Christian is to shine in such beauty that men shall recognize that he is shining with a light greater than himself. Thus they will glorify the Father which is in heaven.

So even though the Christian is *makarios,* sufficient within himself, he is to recognize that his sufficiency is not of himself but of God. Therefore, as he has received, so he is to give in order that that which he possesses may become the possession of all men. He exists for no other purpose.

The Motive of the Citizens (5:17-48)

In the kingdom of God what is to be the citizen's relation to the Law or the old dispensation? This is the burden of this section of the Sermon. Actually it deals with the motive of kingdom citizens with regard to the Law.

Literally Jesus says, "Stop thinking that I am come to destroy the law, or the prophets: I am come not to destroy, but to fulfil" or to fill full. The law and the prophets refer primarily to the Old Testament. But to Jesus' listeners this phrase would include all of the scribal laws laid down as interpretation of the Scriptures. The Pharisees lived by the letter of the Law, not its spirit, and made God's revelation a burden to be borne, not a power to elevate the soul.

It is likely that the disciples were thinking, "Well, at last we shall be rid of all that. We shall be free." Jesus read their minds, and so said, "Stop thinking such thoughts. I am not come to set aside the law, but to fill it full of meaning." Indeed, He is the fulfilment of the Law. And not one *iota* or one *yod* (the smallest letters in the Greek and Hebrew alphabets respectively) shall pass away until all is fulfilled (v. 18).

In the meantime, the righteousness, or keeping of the law, of the kingdom citizen is to exceed that of the scribes and Pharisees (v. 20). The latter meticulously kept the letter of the law. The former is to capture its spirit. The former kept the law with a view to credit before God and man. The latter is to keep it out of love for both God and man with no thought of personal reward.

To illustrate this principle the King selects six pertinent points in the Law. And in each instead of lowering the standard prescribed in the *letter* He lifts it to the higher standard of the *spirit*. Thus more is expected of one under *grace* than of one under *law*. Note that the repeated phrase "But I say unto you" is the word of the King.

The first example has to do with the law against murder (Exod. 20:13; Matt. 5:21-26). If you take another's life you must give yours in return. So said the law. But the letter stopped there.

However, Jesus goes beyond physical violence to spiritual attitude. Two angry men may be brought before the local court (*krisis*) to settle their difference. To call one "Raca," empty-headed or stupid, one may be brought before the supreme court (*sunedrion,* Sanhedrin). But to call one a "fool" (*mōre,* scoundrel, contempt for heart and character) is to be in danger of "hell fire" or "the Gehenna of fire." "Gehenna of fire" refers to the Vale of Hinnom, south and east of Jerusalem, where fire consummed the garbage of Jerusalem. Jesus used this figure to refer to the place of eternal punishment.

The point is that the Christian should have such a high regard for human personality that, not only will he not commit murder, but will not even be guilty of anger or contempt toward another. He cannot even worship at God's altar if his brother has ought against him, probably for one of the above-mentioned offenses (vv. 23-24). A difference with your fellowman is a difference between you and God. For this reason it is far better for the Christian to negotiate a difference, even to his own material loss, than to fight for one's rights. These are strong words, but they are the words of the King!

The second example deals with the law against adultery (Exod. 20:14; Matt. 5:27-30). The law forbade the overt act. Jesus forbids the inner attitude which produces the act. A. T. Robertson says, "Jesus locates adultery in the eye and heart before the outward act." To look on a woman to lust after her is to commit adultery in the will. The only thing which prevents the overt act is lack of opportunity or fear as to the consequences. How these words strike home today when so much emphasis is placed on the display of sex!

In effect Jesus is saying that the Christian should place such a high value on personality, his own and that of another, that he will not entertain even evil desires. In Oriental hyperbole He says that it is better to lose an eye or a hand, the physical organs involved in the lustful look or touch, than to be guilty of so great a sin (vv. 29-30). "Hell" is "Gehenna" (cf. v. 22). This punishment is reserved for the lost man. Which implies that the kingdom citizen will not be guilty of such sin.

The third example is related to the second. It concerns the law concerning divorce. Both of these evils strike at the very heart of the home. In Deuteronomy 24:1 Moses provided that for rather unreasonable causes a man might put away his wife. Only he must give her a bill of divorcement. In Matthew 19:8 Jesus says that Moses did so because of the hardness of the Israelites' hearts. His regulation was an improvement over the current practice in his day.

But Jesus says that such should be done only for fornication. Such an act broke the oneness of the marriage (cf. Matt. 19:1-9). Some scholars hold that this is not genuine Scripture, since both Mark and Luke omit this one cause. But there are insufficient grounds on which to do so. An analysis of the very nature of marriage makes this a reasonable statement in keeping with the divine nature of the marriage relationship. (For a further treatment of this matter refer to Matthew 19:1-9 in this volume.) In a time of easy divorce this is a most pertinent passage which present-day kingdom citizens would be wise to heed.

The fourth example is drawn from the custom of taking oaths in court or in business transactions. This may be in relation to Exodus 20:7 which prohibits the taking of the name of Jehovah in vain (cf. Lev. 19:12). While this involves profanity, it more directly relates to the practice of using the name of Jehovah in oaths. The Jews swore by all kinds of things to show their sincerity in their dealings with one another (cf. Matt. 5:34-36). To swear by some things was considered more binding than by others.

But Jesus says that the kingdom citizen should be so honest and trustworthy that such things are unnecessary. His word should be his bond. When he says, "Yea," he should mean "yea." When he says, "Nay," he should mean "nay." There is no place in the Christian's profession for talking out of both sides of his mouth or for split-tongued dealing.

The fifth example touches upon the law of retaliation (Exod. 21:24; Matt. 5:38-42). The kingdom citizen should not exact vengeance against wrong. In verses 39-40 Jesus is speaking in hyperbole. We are to resist evil as such (cf. Matt. 23), but are not to retaliate for evil done to us. Jesus Himself protested when struck on His cheek (John 18:22-23), but He did not strike back. These paradoxical statements startle us, but they should make us examine our attitudes and motives. Paul says that Christian love does not keep books on the evil done against it (cf. I Cor. 13:8d). This is the sense here.

Verse 41 draws upon a custom of the day whereby an official or soldier might press a citizen into service to run an errand or to carry a load (cf. Matt. 27:32). The Jews resented such at the hands of foreign oppressors. Jesus says that the kingdom citizen will do more than he is asked and without grumbling. He will return good for evil.

The final example has to do with personal relationships (Matt. 5:43-47). Leviticus 19:18 says, ". . . thou shalt love thy neighbor as thyself. . . ." But the Rabbis corrupted this by adding, ". . . and hate thine enemy," words which are not found in the Scripture. Jesus repudiates this. The kingdom citizen is to love his enemies. (He is to return blessing for cursing; good deeds for hate);[4] and prayer for persecution (v. 44).

[4]This passage is not found in some ancient manuscripts, but it seems to fit the context here.

God bestows His blessings upon all men without discrimination (v. 45), not only upon His friends but upon His enemies as well. Even upon the kingdom citizen God has bestowed His saving love and grace while he was yet numbered among the ungodly (Rom. 5:6). If he is to be a child of his Father, or be like Him, he must do the same.

There is no virtue in loving those who love us. Even the lowest of sinners does that (v. 46). If you greet only those who greet you, the same is true. In other words the kingdom citizen is to go out of his way to show forth Christian winsomeness which will be an outward witness of his inward relationship to the King. These words (vv. 44-47) are but an enlargement upon 5:13-16.

The King closes this section of His sermon with a most startling exhortation. "Be ye therefore perfect, even as your Father in heaven is perfect" (5:48). The word "perfect" renders the word *teleios.* It is the goal or aim of the life of the kingdom citizen. A kindred word, *telos,* connotes the means whereby we shall achieve the *teleios.* The *teleios* is the absolute standard of our Heavenly Father. The *telos* is the contents of Matthew 5.

Quite obviously, therefore, this Sermon is intended only for the kingdom citizens. It is not a social manifesto for the world. The perfection which is in the Father is the goal of His children. It is not something which we shall realize within ourselves. It is the God-kind-of-righteousness which is in Christ Jesus. He is our righteousness before God.

But having received this righteousness, we are to strive to be like our Heavenly Father. This involves sanctification wherein we are dedicated to God and develop in that dedication. In His perfection God is complete in His character and in His work. In this life the kingdom citizen shall not achieve such completeness. But he is to keep on keeping on as he grows in grace, knowledge, and service.

Only thusly may he show forth those qualities which demonstrate that He is a child of God, a citizen of the kingdom of God.

Matthew 6

The Values in the Kingdom

The kingdom man is a citizen of two worlds, the earthly and the heavenly with each striving for the mastery. As such he is the battleground between God and man and between God and mammon. In the final analysis it is a struggle between God and Satan. And the kingdom citizen is the arena of conflict. When Satan loses man's soul to God, he seeks to destroy the joy and effectiveness of his Christian life.

In this struggle the issue revolves about the matter of values. The world has its set of values, and the kingdom of God has its set of values. Which values will be uppermost in the life of the kingdom citizen? That is the burden of Jesus' message as recorded in Matthew 6.

Note that in no sense does Jesus condemn the various actions as such which He describes in the chapter. He warns against the peril of doing them for the wrong purpose. Here again we see Satan attacking in the realm of righteousness to pervert it into sinful practice. He strikes at legitimate desires in order to give them an illegitimate expression. It is possible to do the right thing in the wrong way. Thus the *good* becomes the enemy of the *best.*

As we examine Matthew 6 let us do so under three headings: (1) the kingdom citizen and righteousness; (2) the kingdom citizen and loyalty; (3) the kingdom citizen and purpose.

The Kingdom Citizen and Righteousness (6:1-23)

Jesus begins with a warning which might well cover the entire chapter. "Take heed" (*prosechete,* v. 1) renders an imperative form which means to apply the mind. Followed by the negative particle (*mē*), as here, it means to beware. So it is a warning against danger. G. Campbell Morgan calls it the "flaming sword" which Jesus sets forth to guard holy ground. And the holy ground is "righteousness" (*dikaiosunē*).

This is the reading of the earliest and best manuscripts. Jesus is not warning against doing deeds of righteousness. The entire Sermon teaches to the contrary. Nor does He discourage righteous deeds "before men" (cf. 5:16). He warns against the subtle temptation to do them "to be seen of men." "To be seen" (*theathēnai*) is an infinitive of purpose. You can see the English word "theatrical" in this Greek word. So our righteous deeds are not to be theatrical performances put on merely for men to see. Otherwise we have no reward with our heavenly Father.

Now it is as natural as breathing for the Christian to do righteous deeds. It is a part of his nature. But they are not that which make him a Christian. They are the fruit and not the root of the matter. And their true purpose is not for self-glory but for God's glory (cf. 5:16). But knowing the nature of the Christian, Satan seeks to destroy this purpose by making them deeds of selfishness rather than deeds of righteousness. If he succeeds he robs God of His glory and the Christian of his true reward.

To the Jew the principal deeds of righteousness were alms, prayer, and fasting. So Jesus illustrates His warning by showing the wrong value placed upon them by some.

Of all the righteous deeds of the Jew alms was the greatest. Indeed in many cases "righteousness" and "alms" were synonymous terms. So our Lord begins with the giving of alms. "Therefore [the warning in v. 1] when thou doest alms, do not sound a trumpet before thee, as the hypocrites do in the synagogues and in the streets, that they may have glory of men" (v. 2).

"Sound a trumpet" causes some difficulty to interpreters. For no actual incident of such is found in Jewish writings. It may have been the custom of blowing on some instruments to call beggars to oneself. Such instances have been observed among Hindu priests in India. But the thought is that of any act designed to call attention to one's beneficence. Jesus calls it *sounding a trumpet.* The Greeks said, "Playing their own flutes." We say, "Blowing your own horn."

Jesus calls such people "hypocrites." This is the harshest name that He ever applied to men (Matt. 23). And He is the only person in the New Testament to use it. Actually it means "play actor," and follows naturally the words "to be seen" in verse 1. Such a giver is not sincere. He is only playing a role that he might receive the applause of men. He has no concern to bring glory to God, but to himself.

Of such a person Jesus says, "Verily I say unto you [a very solemn statement], they have their reward." "Reward" (*misthon*) is the same word used in verse 1. But there is a difference between the two uses. This is seen in the verb "have." In verse 1 it is *echete,* simply "have." It is a present tense expressing continuous action. "They keep on having." This means permanency as well as repetition. So the one who performs righteousness for God's glory not only has his reward as a permanent possession, God keeps on rewarding him. Who can estimate the complete reward in heaven for one righteous act done for God's glory!

But in verse 2 "have" renders a compound verb *apechousin*. It is the same word as in verse 1 with the preposition *apo*, which gives it an intensive meaning. We would say, "They really have their reward." This verb also is a present tense. But in this case it means "They keep on having their reward" in the sense that there is no other reward and never will be. And what is "their reward?" "That they may have glory of men." Nothing more. What they sought they received.

This meaning is enhanced by the usage of this verb (*apechō*) in the papyri. It was a commercial term meaning "paid in full." When a man receipted an account, he wrote *apechō*, "I have all that is coming to me. I have been paid in full. The account is closed."

This is the meaning as Jesus used it. If you give alms to "have glory of men," you have it. You have been paid in full. The account is closed. You have no glory with God.

From the wrong motive in giving Jesus turns to the right one. And this is to be the motive of the kingdom citizen.

"But when thou doest alms, let not thy left hand know what thy right hand doeth" (v. 3). In the Greek "thou" (*sou*) is the first word in the sentence, and so is emphatic. Jesus contrasts the kingdom citizen with the hypocrites. Instead of an open display for self-glory, the giving of alms is to be "in secret" (v. 4) for God's glory.

Some people see in this an admonition against any kind of open giving. For this reason they refuse to sign a pledge card or to use church envelopes. Some wit remarked that if he gave as little as some people he would not want his left hand to know what his right hand was giving either. But I have known some conscientious and generous givers who would slip their gifts to the church treasurer on the side. Or else "drop it in the plate." However, Jesus is not teaching about church finances but about alms giving. In Matthew 5:16 He commands us to shine before men.

The Jews themselves placed emphasis on "secret" giving in their teachings. One such reads, "He who gives alms in secret is greater than Moses." In keeping with this one Rabbi dropped money behind him so as not to see who picked it up. William Barclay reminds us of a room in the temple called The Chamber of the Silent. People who wished to atone for some sin placed money there to be taken by the poor without the donor knowing their identity. But unhappily among the Jews, as among the Christians, there were those who were ensnared by Satan into giving only for self-aggrandizement. It is these who fell under the condemnation of the Lord, even as they do among most men.

Therefore, the point of this passage is that of giving with the right motive. It should be for God's glory, not self-glory. There should be no thought of reward from men. This Jesus emphasizes when He said, "... thy Father which seeth in secret himself shall reward thee..." (v. 4). "Openly" is not in the best manuscripts, so not a word of Jesus. Our Lord does not say whether the reward will be secret or open. It may be either or both. This is purely incidental to what Jesus is saying.

What He emphasizes is the fact that "the Father of you... shall reward you." One manuscript adds *autos,* Himself, "shall reward you." While this word does not appear in the best manuscripts, that is certainly the thought which Jesus expressed. It is God's reward as opposed to men's reward. Alms given for man's praise receives man's reward. Those given for God's glory receive God's reward.

The second deed of righteousness so important to the Jew was prayer. Wherever he was at 9:00 A.M., noon, and 3:00 P.M., he was supposed to pray. For one who wished to "make a public show" (*phanōsin*) of piety it would be a simple matter for him to be at some prominent street corner. Or else he welcomed the opportunity to pray aloud in the synagogue. Jesus called such people "hypocrites." They too made a theatrical production of prayer. And like the first "hypocrite" (v. 2), they too "have their reward." They pray to be seen of men. Men see them. God does not hear them. They receive their receipt. Paid in full. The account is closed. That is all.

Again Jesus contrasts the attitude of the kingdom citizen with that of the hypocrites. For literally He said, "You but when you pray..." (v. 6). The kingdom citizen is to enter his "closet" and shut the door. A "closet" could be any secret place, even the secrecy of the heart. This is not a prohibition against public prayer. For Jesus Himself prayed publicly on many occasions. The point is that we are to shut out the world, or any thought of worldly acclaim, and to commune with God. The reward in this experience is the same as in the case of almsgiving (vv. 4, 6).

Nor is the Christian to indulge in empty repetition as do the pagans (v. 7). Pagan worshippers repeat prayer phrases. They fill prayer wheels with written prayers and turn the wheels, thinking that with each revolution each prayer goes up to their gods. In Japan I have seen prayer papers decorating a tree like a Christmas tree. Jesus condemns such. For we pray not to some pagan deity, but to our heavenly Father who knows our needs better than we do (v. 8). Christian prayer can be uttered in a pagan manner. Prayer is not some battering ram by which we gain entrance to God's treasury. It is a receptacle by which we receive that which He already longs to give to us.

The third deed of righteousness treated by Jesus is fasting. He does not condemn fasting as such, but fasting in the wrong spirit and for the wrong purpose. Indeed, He assumes the practice of fasting.

But when the "hypocrites" fast they are merely playing a part (v. 16). They assume a "sad countenance" which they do not feel. They "disfigure their faces," probably with ashes and other "make-up" to hide their real attitude. They fast not in their hearts, but make a show of such before men. And they too have their reward. "Paid in full."

Again Jesus draws the contrast between the hypocrites and the kingdom citizen (vv. 17-18). In brief Jesus says that when the Christian fasts, he is not to give an outward appearance of such. In modern terminology He says that he should groom his hair, wash his face, and give a good appearance before men. His fasting is to be "unto the Father" and in his heart and spirit. He, too, will be rewarded by the Father.

So Jesus gives a threefold teaching as to kingdom values. In each instance He uses the word "when" (*hotan,* vv. 2, 5-6, 16). This word never refers to *time* but *condition.* These righteous deeds are not to be perfunctory acts done on a schedule. They are to be performed when our inner condition calls for them. We are to give alms out of the goodness of our hearts. We are to pray from a sense of spiritual hunger. We are to fast when our souls are burdened. The outward expression is to be the result of an inward condition.

It is in this light that we may understand verses 19-23. Here Jesus is not thinking about material "treasures." He is applying the lesson concerning rewards. It is a question of kingdom values as opposed to worldly values. Worldly values are corruptible and temporary. The plaudits of the throng soon fade. When a man criticized another, someone remarked, "But I thought that he had done you many favours." The man replied, "Yes, but he has not done anything lately." So are the rewards of the world.

But the rewards of the heavenly Father are abiding and secure.

Which do you prefer? Your concept of values will be shown by the place in which you seek to accumulate your treasures. "For where your treasure is, there will your heart be also" (v. 21). It is just as true to say, "For where your heart is, there will your treasure be also."

Jesus closes this lesson with vivid imagery (vv. 22-23). While some see difficulty in the details, the meaning is clear. A "single" eye is one with clear vision. An "evil" eye is one with an astigmatism which produces a blurred vision. It is one which is trying to focus on both worldly and heavenly values. The result is that one sees neither clearly.

A. T. Robertson gives this a humorous turn. He envisions a cross-eyed or cock-eyed person with one eye focused on the treasures of earth and the other proudly rolled up toward heaven. Such is a life filled with darkness. If the Christian's life is to be filled with light, he must first of all focus his spiritual eyes on those values which are legal tender in heaven.

The Kingdom Citizen and Loyalty (6:24-32)

The first section of this chapter naturally flows into the second. For one's concept of righteousness will determine the center of his loyalty. So Jesus continues to contrast worldly and heavenly values.

"No man can serve two masters" (v. 24). This is a self-evident fact. But it is even more evident in the Greek text. "No one is able to be a slave *(douleuein)* to two masters." The master of a slave owned him absolutely. He required undivided loyalty and service.

The word used here for "serve" means "to be a slave." It is used twenty-five times in the New Testament. The noun form *(doulos)* is used one hundred and twenty-five times. At times these words refer to the institution of slavery. At others they are used in the spiritual sense. For instance, Jesus said, "Whosoever committeth sin is the servant [slave] of sin" (John 8:34). Paul called himself "a servant [slave] of Jesus Christ" (Rom. 1:1). With two exceptions (8:9; 26:51) Matthew always uses this word *(doulos)* as related in parables of Jesus which draw a spiritual lesson from the institution of slavery. The only two uses of the verb in Matthew are found in 6:24. So we may conclude that in this verse Jesus is using a current social situation to express a spiritual truth.

The two masters involved are God and mammon. "Mammon" is a Chaldean word for the money-god or devil. In this sense mammon is used of the entire system of materialism, the system of the world of which Satan is called the "prince" (John 12:31). In the names "God and mammon" Jesus gathers up all that he has said thus far in this chapter, and gives it a very practical application. So it is a question of who will be your God? To whom will you give your loyalty? To the heavenly Father or to the system of worldly values?

Now it is worthy of note that both God and mammon call for absolute loyalty. Neither will consider a compromise. Alas, some seem to think so, but such thinking is false. Jesus said literally, "Ye are unable to God to be a slave and to mammon." Every one's effort to do so is a betrayal of both. Therefore, a man must make a choice. This is expressed in the words "hate" and "love." For they were used commonly in this fashion (cf. Mal. 1:3; Rom. 9:13). Jesus reinforces this thought with a Hebrew parallelism. "He will hold to the one, and despise the other."

So Jesus says that the kingdom citizen must give undivided loyalty to his King. He cannot roll one eye toward heaven, and focus the other on the things of earth. To center values in himself is to serve mammon. To evaluate life in terms of heaven is to serve God. And, of course, this involves the element of Christian faith. Jesus is not telling lost people how to be saved. He is telling kingdom citizens how they must live. They are to live a life of faith, faith in eternal rather than temporal values.

This He illustrates in verses 25-32. "Therefore" – because "ye cannot serve God and mammon" – "I say unto you, Take no thought for your life, what ye shall eat, or what ye shall drink; nor yet for your body, what ye shall put on. Is not the life more than meat, and the body than raiment?" (v. 25).

Jesus is not teaching irresponsible living. Certainly a man needs food, drink, and clothing. But the word "thought" means "anxiety" even as it did in old English at the time when the King James Version was translated. Actually the Greek word basically means "to divide the mind." "Mind" in this sense involves the whole of one's self. So Jesus is repeating what He said about the eyes. As the kingdom citizen is to have a "single" eye, so he is to have a single mind or self. He is not to be divided in loyalty between God and mammon. between heavenly and worldly values, between glorifying God and simply looking out for one's self. He is not to be a split personality. But he is to find the full realization of his personality in undivided loyalty to God.

Actually the word "life" (*psuchē*) in this context means the principle of animal life. It is that life which is common to both man and beast. It is the life which indwells the body. The body needs food and clothing. But Jesus warns against one living simply for or at the animal level. He is also *spirit*. In fact, man is not a body *(sōma)* and has a spirit *(pneuma)*. He is a spirit and has a body. The body will perish. The spirit is immortal. It is a confused sense of values indeed which makes his body the center of his loyalty, with no concern for his spirit.

Then our Lord cites fowls and flowers to prove His point (vv. 26, 28-29). Birds are not idle, but neither are they anxious. Flowers grow, but they grow from within. The Christian is to work to provide the necessities of life. But they are not to be the *end* of life, only a means to provide and preserve a life dedicated to the service of God.

Who by being divided in mind or loyalty can add one cubit to his "stature" (v. 27). "Stature" is used in the papyri for both height and length of life. Either makes sense here. However, in view of the context ("life") the latter seems more appropriate. Anxiety certainly does not lengthen one's life. Indeed, it more likely will shorten it.

Inordinate anxiety is a pagan quality (v. 32a). The attitude of the kingdom citizen should be one of faith (v. 31), a faith which is grounded in the goodness of God (v. 32b).

The Kingdom Citizen and Purpose (6:33-34)

What then shall be the driving purpose in the life of the kingdom citizen? Jesus answers this question when He says, "Seek ye first the kingdom of God, and his righteousness; and all these things shall be added unto you" (v. 33). So reads the King James Version. But the Greek text is more explicit. In the best manuscripts "of God" is absent. The word rendered "his" may be either "his" or "its," depending upon whether it refers to "God" or "kingdom." So in the absence of "of God" in the best manuscripts, the meaning is "its."

Thus Jesus commands the kingdom citizen to "seek [imperative] the kingdom and the righteousness of it." This can hardly be used as a text for a sermon to lost men. Often a lost man says when asked if he is a Christian, "Well, I live by the Sermon on the Mount." This Sermon was not given to tell lost men how to be saved. Indeed, if it is difficult for a saved man to live by its teachings, it is impossible for a lost man to do so. This Sermon was delivered to kingdom citizens who were already in the kingdom. It is laying down the principles by which they are to live.

Therefore, Jesus' command is not for kingdom citizens to get into the kingdom. He is saying that their primary concern should be to seek to bring in the kingdom and its righteousness. To be sure by their very practice of kingdom righteousness they will lead others to desire to be a part of the kingdom.

This exhortation encompasses the entire sermon up to this point. Indeed, it is the balance between that which precedes (chap. 5-6) and that which follows (chap. 7). By exemplifying the qualities of kingdom citizens (5:3-12) they will be both salt and light in a corrupt and darkened world (5:13-16). Living by the spirit rather than the letter of the Law (5:17-48), they will show forth the true nature of the kingdom. By having a true sense of values as opposed to the values of "play actors," they will personify the righteousness of the kingdom in its superiority to the self-righteousness of the world (6:1-22). To do this they must give absolute loyalty to God (6:24-32). Such will produce the completely balanced personality of a kingdom citizen, which is the best advertisement of what God can do with a life that is wholly surrendered to Him.

"All these things" encompasses the true values set forth in Chapter 6. The kingdom citizen who by his life demonstrates the qualities inherent in kingdom righteousness will be recognized by men. But this recognition will be all the more glorious in that men will look beyond the citizen to see the King. And with the issue of kingdom values settled, the citizen will learn to trust the King for the necessities inherent in his "life" *(psuchē)*.

And then Jesus closes this portion of His Sermon by exhorting His disciples not to be divided in their selves over the future (v. 34). The future may loom before us with foreboding clouds. But through faith in the King we can face them when they come. "Sufficient unto the day is the evil thereof." It is difficult enough to live in the present without being distracted over the future.

With design we have delayed our treatment of "The Model Prayer" (vv. 9-13) until this point. For we believe that we can best understand it as we view it in retrospect. In this chapter Jesus is dealing with the very heart of the outward expression of the Christian religion. And as religion is primary in man's relation to God, so prayer is the primary expression of that relationship.

In "The Model Prayer" Jesus is not praying but teaching. He is teaching His disciples how they are to pray. It would be more fitting to call this "The Disciples' Prayer" than "The Lord's Prayer." For it is a prayer which only a disciple can pray. Until one can say "Our Father" in the Christian sense of these words, he cannot pray the remainder of the prayer.

Someone has described this prayer as the words of a child to his Father, a worshipper to his God, a citizen to his King, a servant to His Master, a beggar to his Benefactor, a sinner to His Saviour, and a follower to his Guide. But, even so, this is not a mere ritual to be repeated (v. 7). It is a guide in prayer as one endeavors to live the life of a kingdom citizen. In this light after verse 9 this prayer becomes an outline of Chapter 6 in reverse.

"Thy kingdom come. Thy will be done, in earth as it is in heaven" (cf. vv. 33-34). The first concern of the kingdom citizen should be to "seek . . . the kingdom and its righteousness."

"Give us this day our daily bread" (cf. vv. 24-32). Therefore, the kingdom citizen is to trust in God for the necessities of his life (*psuchē*).

"And forgive us our debts, as we forgive our debtors" (cf. vv. 19-23). Thus in our relationship to both God and man we shall have treasures in heaven.

"And lead us not into temptation, but deliver us from evil" (cf. vv. 1-18). God leads us into testings even as we determine the values of the true righteousness. If we follow Him fully, He will deliver us from Satan and his wiles as he endeavors to get us to pervert even our righteous deeds into sinful practices.

We are so weak, and the demands are so great. Only through prayer may we hope to live up to the standard of values inherent in kingdom citizenship. But in the full answer to the elements of "The Model Prayer" we can be more than conquerors through Him who loves us, and who knows our needs even before we ask. What we cannot do within ourselves, God can do through us.

Matthew 7

The Relationship within the Kingdom

The kingdom citizens are to be a separated people. However, this does not mean that they shall live in isolation. Paul cautioned the Corinthian Christians not to mingle with evil doers, whether they be professing Christians or not (cf. I Cor. 5:9ff.). But he points out that this does not mean that they are to withdraw from the world altogether. "For then must ye needs go out of the world" (v. 10). The Christian is to be "salt" and "light." He is to be in the world but not a part of it.

So the kingdom citizen's life involves relationships, both within and without the kingdom. And the message of Matthew 7 is designed to give guidance in these relationships. A study of this chapter reveals three: (1) the kingdom citizen's relationship to other citizens; (2) the kingdom citizen's relationship to pseudo-citizens; (3) the kingdom citizen's relationship to kingdom principles.

The Kingdom Citizen's Relationship to Other Citizens (7:1-14)

The very nature of kingdom righteousness carries within itself the possibility of being perverted into the spiritual sin of wrong attitudes. The citizen who excels in righteousness will be tempted to pass judgment on those who do not. This was evident within the little band of disciples itself (cf. Matt. 20:20-28; note especially v. 24).

So Jesus says, "Judge not, that ye be not judged. For with what judgment ye judge, ye shall be judged: and with what measure ye mete, it shall be measured to you again" (Matt. 7:1-2). In condemning James and John the ten revealed that they possessed the same ambitions (cf. Matt. 20:25-28). "Judge not" means literally, "stop judging." So they were already guilty of such.

The word "judge" (*krinō*) means to decide between two things and to reach a decision. It may be used of legal matters, values, or persons. The thought is that of weighing evidence and reaching a decision or passing sentence. A *krisis* may be the court of judgment (Matt. 5:21-22) or it may be the sentence passed on the basis of the act of judging. And a *krima* (judgment, v. 2) is the punishment inflicted or the carrying out of the sentence. The word *krisis* does not appear in this passage, but it is implied in the word "judge."

So Jesus warns against the tendency of a kingdom citizen to sit in judgment, to pass and to carry out the sentence with respect to another kingdom citizen (cf. "brother" in v. 3). This, of course, deals not with legal judgment, but with judgment involving moral and spiritual values and personal relationships. Now this does not mean that the Christian is not to exercise discrimination. This chapter explicitly says that he is to do so (vv. 6, 9-11, 13, 15ff.). The thing prohibited is censorious, sharp, unjust criticism.

Now why is the kingdom citizen not to sit in such judgment? In the first place, he is incapable of being a judge. He does not, yea, cannot, know all the facts in the case. No true judge will hand down a judgment until he has heard all of the available evidence. In American jurisprudence a man is considered innocent until proved guilty. It is not the accused's responsibility to prove himself innocent. It is the court's responsibility to prove him guilty beyond all reasonable doubt. If this be true in legal processes, how much more so should it apply in Christian relationships.

If this principle be observed, then it becomes impossible for us to render such final judgment. Therefore, it remains for God alone to judge in such fashion. It is so easy to call another person a *hypocrite* (cf. 6:2 for this word). But it is worthy of note that in the New Testament only Jesus applies this word to a person. Who else can know if one is *play acting?* Who else comprehends all of the circumstances, or can discern the motives of the heart?

In the second place, the word "judgment" (*krima*) implies pre-judgment. In the papyri this word is never used of a trial which ended in acquittal. Therefore, while "to judge" suggests the weighing of evidence, "judgment" implies that one is judged in order to prove one guilty, not innocent. Of course, this applies only to the "judgment" of men. For God is a righteous Judge.

Jesus is not talking about the processes of law necessary to a well-ordered society. He is talking about exercising private judgment, and especially between Christians. No man should take the law into his own hands. Neither personal nor mob vengeance is right. And if this be true in society generally, it most certainly applies in Christian relationships.

Captious criticism in its very nature is designed to condemn. "Let's get the trial over so we can hang him" is an attitude found all too often among those who should exercise Christian love.

In the third place, Jesus says that when we pass judgment on others, we are in reality judging ourselves. Our own "judgment" judges us (v. 2). And the sentence which we carry out against others will be carried out against us.

The judgments of men are so fallible. When Abraham Lincoln delivered his Gettysburg Address it was pronounced a failure. But history declares it to be one of the truly great utterances of man. Those who with improper evidence condemned this address were really condemning their ability to judge. If I should judge Handel's *Messiah* as not being good music and composition, it would merely show that I was incapable of appreciating good music.

Now Jesus illustrated this matter of judgment with an obviously comic stituation (vv. 3-5). A "mote" (*karphos*) is a speck, as dust, or a small chip of wood or straw. A "beam" (*dokos*) is a large beam of wood. So Jesus envisions a play-actor (hypocrite) having a large beam of wood in his own eye and trying to remove a small chip of wood or a particle of dust from another's eye. The scene is intended to be ridiculous. But it is no more ridiculous than for one Christian to set himself up as the *watch dog* over another Christian's actions. The words "behold" and "consider" are most picturesque. One Christian looks with horror on the faults of another, but does not set his mind on his own shortcomings. Because of this he is unable to get close enough to his brother to enable him to rid him of his sins.

A critical Christian is not a loving Christian. This is especially true when his own sins (beam) are greater than those of his brother (mote). And this is implied in the comparison. By inference Jesus says that the spiritual sin of carping criticism is even worse than the sins of the flesh. He does not excuse either. But whereas fleshly sin destroys the body spiritual sin destroys the spirit. In other words, while God abhors all sin, He looks with most disfavor on sins of the spirit—pride, prejudice, and judgment of others.

Note that Jesus called the self-righteous brother a "hypocrite." He never used this word for those who were guilty of the scarlet sins of society, or for one guilty of sins of attitude but who did not appear to be self-righteous. He applied it to those, like the Pharisees, who set themselves up as judges of others, while they themselves were outwardly clean but inwardly filthy (cf. Matt. 23).

What is the proper attitude for the Christian toward his brethren? First of all, he is to see that his own life is clean. Then in lovingkindness he is to render aid to those who are less so.

This is seen in a comparison of the words "behold" (v. 3) and "shalt see clearly" (v. 5). "Behold" (*blepō*) means to look at a thing. "To see clearly" (*diablepō*) means to see through a thing. The carping critic merely sees another's faults. The Christian attitude is to see through them in order to understand the person and his condition. Such discernment will bring sympathetic understanding, thus creating a bond of love between the two Christians. Then the stronger will be able to help the weaker, not only to overcome his faults but to avoid others.

But what about the exercise of moral judgment with respect to non-Christians? Jesus says that this is to be rendered with moral discrimination. For He admonishes, "Give not that which is holy unto the dogs, neither cast ye your pearls before swine, lest they trample them under their feet, and turn again and rend you" (v. 6).

Numerous interpretations have been given to this. Some hold that we are not to witness to those who resent it. But the New Testament draws no distinctions at this point. One suggests the meaning to be that Christians should not discuss holy things in the presence of those who can neither understand nor appreciate them. But is this the meaning in this context of rendering judgment? It seems that a more appropriate explanation is possible.

"Dogs" and "swine" were both unclean to the Jews. Therefore, in the Christian context they suggest non-Christians. Obviously Jesus employs a Hebrew parallelism (the same thought expressed in two different ways). But suppose that we think of "dogs" and "swine" separately. Both are unclean. Now imagine a dispute between them. This suggests a controversy between two who are not Christian brothers. The Christian is asked to settle or judge their dispute. Obviously he should do so on Christian principles, principles which neither disputant is capable of comprehending or appreciating. To do so is to give holy things to dogs and pearls to swine. The result is that both refuse your counsel and turn on you in the process. The Christian should not become involved in useless controversies. He would better spend his time and effort in trying to make kingdom citizens out of aliens.

How is the kingdom citizen to achieve the standard which Jesus proposes that he exercise in the matter of judgment? Not in his own power to be sure. Jesus says that it can be done only through prayerful effort. "Ask, and it shall be given you; seek, and ye shall find; knock, and it shall be opened unto you" (v. 7). This is a promise concerning prayer generally. But the specific promise here is as to moral and spiritual discrimination. We are to *ask* for it, *seek* it, and *knock* on the door of God's grace until we find it. Notice the progression of ideas. We are to *ask* God for it. He may give it forthright. But if in His own wisdom He proposes another way, we are to *seek* it as by His grace God develops it within us. Furthermore, we are not to stop short of achieving it (knock). These three words are *present imperatives.* Jesus commands us *to keep on asking, to keep on seeking, and to keep on knocking.*

Such persistent effort is promised success (v. 8). This does not mean that we can ask for anything that we want, and get it. This specific promise is made respecting the quality of moral discrimination which God wants us to have. If that for which we pray is, in God's wisdom, harmful or unnecessary then God refuses. Our heavenly Father knows better than an earthly father how to give good things to His children (vv. 9-10). But note that God gives "good things" to His children, not necessarily that which they think is good (v. 11). Certainly moral and spiritual discrimination is a *good thing.* God will give it to us if we ask, seek, and knock.

And then Jesus sums this whole thing up in what we call the Golden Rule (v. 12). "Therefore [7:1-11] all things whatsoever ye would that men should do to you, do ye even so to them. . . ." These are eighteen words which can change your life as a Christian from what you are into what Christ wants you to be. Only thus will you be able not to judge but to discriminate.

Now these words are not a substitute for regeneration. A man cannot be saved by "living by the Golden Rule." Nor is this "Rule" meant to be applied by people of the world. To do so would make this best of all *rules* into a vicious thing. For criminals to live by this rule would produce a crime wave of unprecedented proportions. Suppose that all bank robbers should suddenly decide to live by the Golden Rule. What would a bank robber wish "that men should do" to him? Rob a bank and give him the money! Apply this to any crime of violence or to those of a subtler nature, and the result is the same.

No, the Golden Rule was not given to the world. It was given to kingdom citizens to guide them in the matter of their relationships. It is "golden" only as it is applied within the framework of Christian moral and spiritual principles.

Some insist that this is not a unique teaching of Jesus. To prove their case they cite similar (?) teachings of other great teachers. But you cannot find this rule anywhere else other than in the teachings of Jesus. Hillel, the Hebrew, said, "Do not do to thy neighbour what is hateful to thyself." Socrates, the Greek, said, "What stirs your anger when done to you by others, that do not do to others." Confucius, the Chinese said, "What you do not want done to yourself, do not do to others." Identical with Jesus' Golden Rule? Even similar? At first glance, perhaps. But under close examination they are farther apart than the poles.

Wherein lies the radical difference between them? Theirs are *negative* and *passive*. Jesus' is *positive* and *active*. Theirs is silver. Christ's is golden. Hillel, Socrates, and Confucius say, "Avoid doing to other people what you do not want done to you." Jesus says, "Think of what you would like for a person to do for you. Then go and do it for him." A man can live by the former, and let people starve to death so long as he does not strike them dead. But for one to live by the latter he must seek to feed a starving man so that he may live.

Oh, there is difference enough! The tragedy is that too many Christians do not even live up to the Silver Rule, to say nothing of the Golden Rule. And for that reason our souls are shriveled, our witness is blunted, and the fellowship of churches is destroyed. We become a stumbling block to the world rather than a stepping stone toward God. It is no wonder that Jesus placed such great emphasis upon the matter of the relationship between kingdom citizens and other such citizens. Truly, the kingdom of God would come, and God's will would be done in earth as it is in heaven, if every Christian would show the same compassion and understanding to other Christians as he wants them to show to him. Because thereby we would truly be "salt" to a rotting world and "light" to a stumbling humanity to guide it to God.

To show such an attitude will not be easy. But it is not impossible. This is the meaning of verses 13-14. The "strait gate" is the narrow gate. The way to destruction is a wide gate opening into a broad way. And it is always crowded with people living meaningless lives whose end is destruction. But the Christian way is a narrow way. It is confining, but it leads to life.

"Life" in this sense does not mean *salvation*. For these words were spoken to those who already were in the kingdom of God. This "life" is the abundance of living which should be the experience of every Christian. It is the full realization of that state of living which the king desires for His subjects. Such will be the fruit of all that He has set forth thus far in the sermon.

It is of interest to note that in a similar statement recorded by Luke (13:24), Jesus says, "Strive to enter in at the strait gate...." The word "strive" (*agōnizomai*) is used in the papyri for fighting in warfare. The figure here is of soldiers storming the gates of a city. So the citizens of the King are to storm the narrow gates of the city of abundant Christian living. This is further evidence that Jesus is not speaking of *redemption* but of *sanctification*. We are redeemed not by *striving* but by grace. Once we are kingdom citizens we are dedicated or sanctified to the King. Then by His grace we are to "strive," by His grace, to enter into the full realization of the dedicated life. As we wage this warfare all the forces of Satan "strive" to defeat us in our purpose. But "we are more than conquerors through Him that loved us" and gave Himself for us (Rom. 8:37).

The Kingdom Citizen's Relationship to Pseudo-citizens (7:15-23)

We have seen that, while the kingdom citizen is not to sit in judgment with respect to his fellow-citizens, he is to exercise moral and spiritual discrimination. And this is especially true as he distinguishes between true citizens and pseudo-citizens, or those claiming citizenship in the kingdom of God but do so falsely. In other words, the Christian is not to be gullible so as to be taken in by everything which moves under the guise of Christianity. This was a much-needed admonition then as it is now.

"Beware of false prophets" (v. 15). The word "beware" (*prosechete*) is the same as "take heed" in 6:1. It is a warning against enemies in both cases. "False prophets" renders one word, *pseudoprophētōn*. They were false teachers of error. There were many such in the Old Testament. Later Jesus will predict "false Messiahs and false prophets" (Matt. 24:24). One has but to read of the Judaizers and Gnostics as reflected in the epistles to see how necessary this warning of Jesus was. It is a timely and timeless warning, as may be evidenced even today.

Now who is a false prophet? He is not everyone who just happens to disagree with you. Nor is he one who expresses Christian truth in words and forms different from yours. There is the sound of orthodoxy in familiar words, and of heterodoxy in unfamiliar words. However, the test is not in the wrappings but in the substance.

There was no man more prepared to stand for the defense of the gospel than Paul (cf. Gal. 1:6-10). But hear his words in Philippians 1:15-18: "Some indeed preach Christ even of envy and strife; and some also of good will . . . what then? notwithstanding, every way, whether in pretence, or in truth, Christ is preached; and I therein do rejoice, yea, and will rejoice."

Wherein lay the difference? The latter were those who with mixed motives toward Paul preached Christ. The former were those (Judaizers) who preached a false gospel under the guise of being Christian teachers. These were "false prophets" whom Paul opposed with all his heart. The others were those who differed with Paul personally but who were true to Christ. Like John Wesley Paul is saying, "If thy heart be as my heart, give me thy hand." Paul did not agree with them in every detail, nor did they with him; but each preached Christ in his own way. Each was true to Christ. These are not those against whom Jesus warns us.

A false prophet was one who pretended to follow Christ, but whose purpose was to oppose Him. They were really "wolves" disguised in "sheep's clothing." They had the appearance of Christians, but lacked the experience which makes one a follower of Christ.

The greatest danger to the cause of Christ on earth is not the enemy from without, but that which is within. This is true of a nation; it is true of the kingdom of God on earth. Paul warned of such. In Act 20:29-30 he spoke of grievous wolves which would enter the fold, not sparing the flock. In this context it appears that he is speaking of persecution from without of which there was much. But then he warned, "Also of your own selves shall men arise, speaking perverse things, to draw away disciples after them." These were the false prophets who assumed the guise of Christian teachers.

Persecution from without has never really harmed the Christian cause. Instead, it has purified and solidified it. Its greatest damage has come from within. Already in the first century there were false teachings at work which ultimately perverted the very stream of Christianity, and which persist to this very day. Denials of the deity of Christ, perversion of the teaching as to His person and work, the nature of salvation and of the church are but a few of the false doctrines of those who were as "ravening wolves" destroying the flock and leading many astray after them.

The kingdom citizen is to beware of such. He is not to indulge in carping criticism of every other citizen who does not speak eternal truth in his own vocabularly. But he is to beware of pseudo-citizens who as false prophets seek to destroy from within. Obviously this calls for moral and spiritual discrimination. What, then, is to be the guage of such discrimination?

Jesus said, "Ye shall know them by their fruits" (vv. 16, 20). "Know" is the verb "to know" with the prefix *epi* (*epiginōskō*, to recognize or have full knowledge). So we may recognize false prophets by their fruits, not by their words. You can judge a character by its fruits. A system of thought submits to the same test. To make this test you must wait until the time of harvest. It may be early or late. But it is the final test from which there is no appeal.

And then our Lord drives home His point. "Do men gather grapes of thorns, or figs of thistles?" (v. 16). The answer is self-evident. Someone said, "You may tie grapes on thorns and figs on thistles. But they will not grow there." This reaffirms Jesus' lesson about false prophets. A wolf may wear wool, but he cannot grow it. It is contrary to his nature.

Apparently Jesus had made His point. You can see His listeners shaking their heads in a negative answer. So Jesus continues, "Even so every good tree bringeth forth [keeps on making] good fruit. A good tree cannot bring forth evil fruit, neither can a corrupt tree bring forth good fruit" (vv. 17-18). Thus Jesus pounds home His lesson. G. Campbell Morgan calls attention to this. By affirmation (v. 16a), question (v. 17b), renewed affirmation (v. 17a), negation (v.17b), and renewed negation (v. 18) He echoes and re-echoes this truth. You judge a prophet by his fruit or his life.

Jesus does not delineate the meaning of "evil fruit." But it is anything that produces evil. It may be simply the absence of the good. Or it may contribute to pernicious evil. A false prophet may wear a prophet's clothes and speak a prophet's words. But if they are not genuine their fruits will reveal them to be false.

Actually, Jesus is summarizing the whole of His sermon at this point. He has dealt with the qualities, attitudes, and purposes of the kingdom citizen. Anyone who does not possess these is not a kingdom citizen; he is a pseudo-citizen, a false prophet. So what are the fruits of a false prophet or a pseudo-citizen?

If he does not possess the qualities of a kingdom citizen (5:3-12) he is a pseudo-citizen. Unless he is "salt" and "light," he is a pseudo-citizen (g:13-16). If his religion be mechanical or of the letter rather than of the spirit (5:17-48), he is a pseudo-citizen. And if he is a carping critic rather than a person of Christian love and discrimination (7:1-14), he is a pseudo-citizen. One does not become a kingdom citizen simply by practicing the elements of this sermon. He endeavors to practice them because he is a kingdom citizen. "By their fruits ye shall know them" (7:20).

How these words challenge us! This sermon is not some merely ethical pronouncement. It blazes with the reality of life and of death. We are prone to say with the Jews of old, "This is an hard saying; who can hear it?" (John 6:60). But they are the words of the King! We must hear them. And we must practice them. The kingdom citizen himself finds them difficult. The pseudo-citizen finds them impossible. And so the world passes them off as idealism with no semblance of practicality. But any time that a kingdom citizen practices any one of them, however imperfectly, he knows that they are in truth "the way, the truth, and the life." We may do a sorry job at living these principles, but to each of His citizens the King says, "Be ye therefore perfect, even as your Father which is in heaven is perfect" (5:48). The goal is still there. Let us strive upward to reach that goal!

It is perfectly natural, therefore, that the king would issue the warning found in 7:21-23. For the kingdom is not words but deeds. It is even more than deeds. It is a spirit, a relationship to the King. Even the most discriminating kingdom citizen may not be able to detect the false prophets. But the King knows. And in the final harvest of the age (v. 22) He will declare their judgment. If their fruit be evil, like a corrupt tree they will be cut down and be cast into the fire (v. 19). But the kingdom citizen, like a good tree, will go on bearing good fruit unto the King forever and forever. We may not be "perfect" now, but the all-wise Husbandman prunes, fertilizes, and cares for us that when He shall appear we shall be like Him.

The Kingdom Citizen's Relationship to Kingdom Principles (7:24-27)

How may you know that you are a kingdom citizen? This question Jesus answers in the closing verses of this sermon. Notice that He pictures two builders. One He likens to a man who "heareth these sayings of mine, and doeth them" (v. 24). He is a wise man. The other "heareth these sayings of mine, and doeth them not" (v. 26). He is a foolish man.

Furthermore, Jesus says nothing about a difference in building materials. We may infer that each used the same insofar as their outward appearance is concerned. The difference is not in the material but in the foundation. The one is built upon "the rock"; the other built upon "the sand." And this is most significant.

"Rock" is *petra,* a ledge rock which serves as the foundation of a house or a cliff (cf. Matt. 16:18b). We shall treat this matter fully when we come to the cited passage. Suffice to say that this "rock" is Christ Himself. So the kingdom citizen is one who has founded or trusted his life on the "rock."

This becomes all the more significant when we go back to the beginning of the sermon. Who is he who has built on the *rock*? This Jesus declares at the outset (5:3-6). He is the one who is "poor in spirit" or who has been convicted of his sins; one who *mourns* or who has repented of his sins; one who is "meek" or who has submitted himself in faith to Christ as His Saviour; one who hungers and thirsts after more and more of the God-kind-of-righteousness. Such a person, having received a right relation to God, will seek a right relation to man (5:7-12).

And then the movement shifts from what a kingdom citizen is to what he does. But without this fact of *being*, the *doing* is false from beginning to end. The man who does not found his house on the rock may go through the same motions as the one who did found his house on the rock. But there is a vast difference. Because he builds for himself, not for the King. He hears "these sayings of mine," and thinks that he is doing them. But his *doing* is outward and mechanical, selfish and sinful. Therefore, he hears but does not do.

Until you have a right relationship to the King, you cannot serve or obey Him. Go through this entire sermon after 5:12 and hear once again what Jesus is saying. He is not merely speaking words. He is declaring a relationship. Without that relationship one's deeds are evil fruit, no matter how outwardly righteous they may appear to be.

And the testing time reveals whether they are good or evil. Note that in verses 25-27 each house underwent the same testing. Word for word these verses read in the English (the Greek has different words for "beat upon" but the meaning is the same), until you come to the statements of result. There the words change. "And it fell not: for it was founded upon [the] rock" (v. 25). "And it fell [note the absence of "not"]: and great was the fall of it" (v. 27). The difference was in the foundation. The one was founded upon Christ. The other was founded upon nothing. You cannot be rightly related to kingdom principles until you are rightly related to the King.

Matthew closes this account by noting the effect of the sermon, not on the disciples alone, but on the "people" (*hoi ochloi*, the crowd or multitude). They were accustomed to hearing the rote repetitions of the scribes as they quoted first one authority and then another. But Jesus spoke as one "having authority." Literally, "as having authority." The word "authority" renders *exousia*, meaning "out of being." It is an authority which comes from the very nature of one's being (cf. Matt. 28:18, "power" is this word). Here we see the kingly authority of Jesus expressing itself in His teachings.

The crowds were "astonished" (literally, "kept on being amazed") at the teachings of Jesus. Alas, the "crowds" are still amazed at the Sermon on the Mount. Some have committed it to memory. How many have committed it to life? What is even more important, have you committed yourself to the King?

The Business of the King

Matthew 8

The Authority of the King (I)

The Sermon is ended. The people recognized the King's authority in the realm of His teaching. His principles were noble enough. But was this all that Jesus had to offer? It is one thing to declare high-sounding words, but could He match them with astounding deeds? The answer to this question is found in Chapters 8 and 9.

A comparison of Matthew's chronology with that of Mark shows a difference. Mark's gospel is the earliest of the four. And Matthew and Luke usually follow his framework. But Matthew does so in keeping with his purpose. He is not concerned with giving a chronological account of the life of Jesus. His primary concern is to present Jesus as the King. And he groups his material to accomplish that purpose. His Jewish readers would understand that as a legitimate literary device.

It is in this light that we may understand the contents of Matthew 8-9. The author is showing that not only does Jesus have *authority* in the realm of teaching, but that His *authority* resides in other phases of life also. What He has the authority to say He has the power to perform.

So in Matthew 8 the evangelist is declaring the authority of Jesus. It naturally divides itself into (1) the authority of the King over disease; (2) the authority of the King over nature; (3) the authority of the King over demons; (4) the authority of the King challenged. It is well at this point to note that in each case Matthew records the response to each of Jesus' demonstrations of authority.

The Authority of the King over Disease (8:1-22)

The first demonstration of authority was in regard to leprosy. The crowds followed Jesus down from the mountain (v. 1). Suddenly a leper was seen running toward Him. You may be certain that the crowds parted to let him through. For leprosy was the most loathesome of diseases.

There were two different types of leprosy. One type began with little nodules which gradually covered the entire body. They became ulcerated and gave off a foul discharge. The eyebrows came out, and the eyes developed a staring condition. As the vocal chords became ulcerated the voice became raspy or coarse. This type of leprosy usually ended in mental decay, a coma, and death in about nine years. The other kind of leprosy began with loss of sensation at the nerve ends. Muscles wasted away, and as the tendons contracted the hands became as claws. Then came the ulcers. Progressively fingers, toes, hands, and sometimes the feet dropped off. Thus a man died by degrees over a period of from twenty to thirty years.

When a man contracted leprosy, he was ostracized from society. He was not allowed to enter into any city or walled village. To the populace he was regarded as dead. Thus lepers usually lived in caves or in abandoned tombs. A leper was not allowed within six feet of a clean person. If the wind was blowing from him toward another person, he must keep at a distance of one hundred feet. And wherever he went he was required to keep his hand or a cloth over his mouth as he cried, "Unclean, unclean." No one dared to touch him lest he contract the disease also.

This leper came and worshipped Jesus. The word "worshipped" renders a word (*proskuneō*) which was used of the worship of deity. It usually meant to prostrate oneself before one, and to kiss his feet, his garment, or the ground before him. So the leper recognized Jesus as the Messianic King or Divine Helper. Therefore, when he addressed Jesus as "Lord" he meant more than mere respect. He saw in Jesus one who was of the supernatural realm.

Note his appeal. "Lord, if thou wilt, thou canst make me clean" (v. 2). He recognized that Jesus had the power to help him. But was He willing to do so? He had faith in Jesus' power. He was uncertain as to His will. This is expressed in the form of his question. It is a condition of the third class, undetermined, but with the prospect of being determined (cf. 4:9b). Jesus had spoken of love and compassion. Here was the supreme test of "Salt." Would Jesus be equal to His words?

The leper's uncertainty reflects the common attitude of the Jews toward his kind. It was unheard of for anyone to show them kindness, unless it was by one's own family or friends. One Rabbi boasted that he had thrown rocks at a leper to keep him away from him. Would this Rabbi be any different? "Thou canst, if thou wilt."

Leprosy was a type for sin. How many lost sinners, due to our attitude toward them, ask the same thing of us? "Thou canst, if thou wilt." You have the message of life for us by which we may be cleansed from sin. But do you will to give it to us? It is so easy to ignore them, even to throw *rocks* of scorn at them. That is the way of the world. It should never be the way of kingdom citizens. For it was not the way of the King.

The crowd must have gasped when Jesus reached out and touched the leper (v. 3). Jewish law forbade such. And even if it had not, a man would scarcely have done so. But Jesus did. He was not afraid of contamination. Here then is divine love in action, even as shortly before He had been divine love and wisdom speaking matchless truths. His love bridged the chasm which society had erected, as He reached out the hand of help to the helpless.

And then the glorious words, "I will; be thou clean." Literally, "I am willing." The leper said, "You can, if you are willing." Jesus said, "I do, because I am willing." Enabling power and willing love performed a miracle. "Be thou clean." This is an imperative form. So we see divine authority in action.

Yes, it was a miracle. For "immediately his leprosy was cleansed." Not a gradual cure, but immediately. This is the first specific miracle of Jesus recorded by Matthew, although he gave a general account of such miraculous healings in 4:23-24. And it is significant that the disease was leprosy, the most terrible of diseases among the Jews. But Jesus' authority prevailed even over it.

It is fitting at this time to examine the miraculous element in the ministry of Jesus. How shall we explain it? Some disregard it altogether as merely an element of a non-scientific and superstitious age. But this is to find refuge in agnosticism simply by ignoring the problem. What does this do to the character of Jesus? How do you explain the miracles recorded by Luke the physician? Indeed, how do you explain the miracle of salvation? Others see in certain of Jesus' miracles a type of psycosomatic medicine or psychiatric treatment. This would reduce Jesus to little more than a super-psychiatrist. This can hardly explain His place in history. Nor does it even apply to many of Jesus' miracles such as the one at hand.

Perhaps a definition of miracle would help us. A miracle is an act of God contrary to the laws of nature as we understand them, but not contrary to natural law as God understands it, and performed in keeping with God's benevolent will and purpose. Once you admit God the problem is simplified. And when you reckon with His benevolent will and purpose, miracles are to be expected. For the miracles recorded in the Bible do not upset the laws of nature. They restore them to their intended purpose. Therefore, when we see the King performing miracles, we see Him asserting

His authority to restore natural law which has been perverted by Satan. The Gospel of John calls these mighty works "signs" (*sēmeion*), signs of Jesus' deity (2:1ff., note v. 11). Jesus never performed a miracle on demand as a selfish display of His power. Nor did He do so for His own needs. He did so to restore the normal processes of nature, which within itself testified to His authority and person.

Note Jesus' own response to His miraculous healing of the leper (v. 4). "See thou tell no man." The King did not wish to precipitate undue excitement on the part of the people or hostility on the part of the rulers or the religious leaders. His hour had not yet come.

But, even so, He recognized the rules of an orderly society. God through Moses had commanded that a healed leper should go to the priest, show "testimony" (Matt. 8:41, evidence) of his cure, and perform certain sacrifices (Lev. 14). Afterward the leper was pronounced clean and permitted to return to society. So Jesus said, "But go thy way, show thyself to the priest, and offer the gift that Moses commanded, for a testimony unto them" (8:4).

The King exercised His authority to restore the processes of nature. He did not ignore the laws of God and thus upset the processes of society. He came to do the will of Him who sent Him. Authority under authority, accomplishing the purposes of God!

This thought seems to introduce the second demonstration of the King's authority over disease (Matt. 8:5-13). Jesus had just returned to Capernaum which served as His headquarters during His Galilean ministry. He was met by a centurion who besought Him to heal his servant who was a bed-ridden paralytic ("palsy," Greek, *paralutikos*). Matthew calls the servant a *pais* (boy), but Luke calls him a *doulos* (slave) (7:2). He was a youthful slave.

Now several things are of interest concerning this centurion. He was a Roman officer commanding one hundred soldiers. As such these officers were the backbone of the Roman army. Apparently they were men of high caliber. For the New Testament always presents them in a good light. Luke notes of this particular centurion that the elders of the Jews appealed to Jesus on his behalf, "saying, That he was worthy for whom he should do this: for he loveth our nation, and he hath built us a synagogue" (7:4-5). Apparently he was a man of wealth. Even today tourists may view the ruins of a synagogue which was probably built on the site of the synagogue built by this centurion.

The character of this man is further seen in his attitude toward his slave. Slaves were usually regarded as nothing more than property. A paralytic slave might well have been destroyed, since the owner had the right of life and death over him. But this centurion evidently loved the boy. Therefore, he swallowed his Roman pride and appealed to Jesus on his behalf.

In response to his appeal Jesus said, "I will come and heal him" (Matt. 8:7). The word "heal" commands our attention. Jesus used the word (*therapeuō*) which means basically to serve, to treat medically, then to cure or to restore to health. The word for miraculous healing is *iaomai*. Of interest in this regard is the fact that Luke the physician says in Luke 9:11 that Jesus healed (*iato*) those in need of treatment (*therapeias*). Also in Acts 28:8 Luke uses *iaomai* of the miraculous healings of Paul. But in 28:9 he speaks of those who were healed (*therapeuō*). William Ramsay sees this latter as the medical practice of Luke. But these words were not always distinguished, since at times both are used of Jesus' healing ministry.

However, it appears that in the case of the centurion's servant the distinction is preserved. Jesus said, "I will come and heal [*therapeuō*] him." Or it could mean "treat" him. At any rate the centurion replied that Jesus could heal (*iaomai*) him from a distance and simply by saying the word (v. 8). And verse 13 uses this latter word of the healing that was done. This is suggestive of the faith of the centurion.

But the point of this event seems to turn on the word "authority." Jesus asserted His authority over Jewish regulations which forbade a Jew to enter the home of a Gentile. And the centurion responds to this implied authority when he says that he is unworthy for Jesus to enter his house. Furthermore, such is unnecessary, since Jesus can heal from afar and by a word.

And then we see the key to the story in the centurion's words "For I am a man under [*hupo*] authority, having soldiers under [*hupo*] me . . ." (v. 9). He was under the authority of his superiors yet soldiers under his authority did his bidding. Whether or not the centurion meant to say this, his words are suggestive of the authority of Jesus. He was under the authority of His Father's will, yet within Himself there was authority over the power of disease. So once again authority under authority performed a miracle.

Jesus marvelled at this man's faith (v. 10). He had faith to believe that Jesus could heal miraculously simply by a word spoken at a distance. Furthermore, in his finite authority he recognized the authority which was resident in Jesus. The question which was in the minds of the Jews was answered in the words of a pagan Gentile. Thus Jesus said, "I have not found so great faith, no, not in Israel" (v. 10). He sees this as a foregleam of the great Gentile host who will enter the kingdom of heaven, while those who thought that they were "children of the kingdom" by virtue of their natural birth will be "cast out into outer darkness" (vv. 11-12).

Jesus spoke the healing word, and the servant was miraculously healed that selfsame hour (v. 13). The faith of the centurion was rewarded as the authority of the King over disease was asserted.

The third demonstration of the King's authority over disease occurred in Peter's house (vv. 14-15). This healing was done in private, showing that the basis of Jesus' healing ministry was not for public acclaim but out of a heart of love and mercy.

Peter's mother-in-law was sick of a fever. It was probably malaria, which was common in the marshy areas about the sea of Galilee. She was bedridden with this disease. In this case Jesus touched her, and the fever "left her." "Left" is an aorist tense, expressing an immediate action. So this was a miraculous healing. This is further seen in the fact that she arose, and ministered unto them. Not only did her fever *leave* her, but her strength *returned* to her immediately!

Word had gotten around that Jesus was back in Capernaum. So at eventide the people came with their demon-possessed and sick (v. 16). Mark notes that this happened on the Sabbath day (1:21ff.). Since the Jews were not allowed to bear burdens on the Sabbath, they waited until the Sabbath ended at "even" to bring their sick to Jesus. And He cast out the demons and healed the sick. Here "healed" is *therapeuō*. So we see the word used here of miraculous healing as is evident from the verse.

Matthew closes this record of the King's authority over disease by noting that it is a fulfilment of prophecy. "Himself took our infirmities, and bore our sicknesses" (v. 17, cf. Isa. 53:4). So the King not only has authority in words but in deeds of mercy as well.

The Authority of the King over Nature (8:18-27)

Having shown the King's authority over physical disease, Matthew now proceeds to recount His authority in the realm of nature. At the close of a busy day Jesus departed from Capernaum to cross to the eastern side of the Sea of Galilee. Note His reason for leaving. "Now when Jesus saw great multitudes about him, he gave commandment to depart unto the other side" (v. 18). At first glance this seems to be a strange reaction to the crowds on the part of Jesus. He must have had a reason. The miracles of the day had caused great excitement. The volatile Jews were ever ready to acclaim some popular leader their Messiah in the military sense of the word. So probably feeling that His presence might touch off such a demonstration, Jesus departed from Capernaum. His hour had not yet come, and He did not wish to cause a scene which might well bring the Roman authorities down upon Him.

Furthermore, Jesus did not welcome followers on such a basis. He wanted men to come after Him out of a true faith and understanding of discipleship, not out of a momentary emotional enthusiasm which would soon subside or out of a wrong conception of what it meant to follow Him. That there was danger of such is evidenced by two extreme reactions which occurred just before He departed.

"A certain scribe came, and said unto him, Master [*didaskalos*, teacher], I will follow thee whithersoever thou goest" (v. 19). He proposed to become a disciple without counting the cost. But Jesus gently rebuffs what A. T. Robertson calls "a 'bumptious' brother full of self-confidence and self-complacency" by reminding him of the cost of such an impulsive decision (v. 20).

Note that here for the first time in Matthew Jesus uses the title "Son of man" (cf. Dan. 7:13). This was Jesus' favorite self-designation. It is not found in the Gospels on any lips but Jesus', except in John 12:34 where His questioners quoted His words. It appears in Acts 7:56 where Stephen so refers to Him. John uses it twice in Revelation (1:13; 14:14). Jesus avoided the terms "Christ" and "Son of David" in direct reference to Himself, although He accepted the titles when used by others. These words carried a highly nationalistic meaning to the Jews. And so to avoid this mistaken meaning of these terms Jesus preferred the title "Son of man." It, too, was Messianic in nature, but without the nationalistic connotation. Furthermore, this title stressed His identification with man as the Representative Man.

At this point "another of his disciples" (not one of the Twelve) said, "Lord, suffer me first to go and bury my father" (v. 21). The father was not dead. But according to custom a son was supposed to stay with his father until his death. Then after his death he was free to live his own life. He was willing to follow Jesus, but only after he had fulfilled his filial duty. Whereas the "scribe" was overly enthusiastic, this "disciple" was overly cautious.

But Jesus replied, "Follow me; and let the dead [spiritually] bury their dead [physically]" (v.22). If a man is to follow Jesus, that has the prior claim.

So in two brief interviews Jesus gently rebuked the one and then the other. A man must count the cost if he would follow Jesus. But once he decides to follow Him, he must give to Him loyalty over all other claims placed upon him.

So having disposed of these two matters Jesus and His disciples embarked to cross the lake. After a hard day Jesus slept the sleep of exhaustion in the rear of the boat (Mark 4:38). The sea of Galilee is six hundred and eighty feet below sea level. It is subject to sudden winds sweeping down from Mount Hermon through the canyons which empty into the sea. Suddenly this usually quiet lake became a boiling cauldron as it was seized upon by one of these squalls. Mark (4:37) and Luke (8:23) call it a whirlwind (*lailaps*) beating in sudden gusts. But Matthew uses the picturesque term *seismos megas* (v. 24). It was as though "a great earthquake" (great tempest) had seized the sea. The water rocked and rolled as giant waves covered the ship. The disciples were terrified as they thought they would surely be destroyed.

But through it all Jesus "kept on sleeping" (imperfect). It was not the sleep of indifference but one of perfect faith. Thus we see the contrast of fear versus faith. The disciples were fearful not only for themselves but for Jesus. What would happen to His mission if He were drowned at sea? But Jesus slept the sleep of faith, knowing that His destiny was to be otherwise.

When it seemed that all was lost the disciples awakened Jesus with the cry, "Lord, save us: we perish" (v. 25). In the Greek this is most dramatic. "Lord, save us at once [aorist], we are being utterly destroyed!" (present passive).

In contrast to the futility of the disciples note the fortitude of the Saviour. He is the very essence of confidence as He says, "Why are ye fearful, O ye of little faith?" (v. 26). In effect, why should they be fearful when they are with Him? And He rightly describes them. "O ye of little faith" renders one word *(oligopistoi)* meaning one whose faith is small and weak.

When Jesus is in our boat we have nothing to fear. For God's purpose rides with the King. We may seem overwhelmed with difficulty. But with the Lord on our side, we are more than conquerors. For this is the victory which overcomes the world, even our faith in Him.

And then the King asserted His authority. "He . . . rebuked the wind and the sea. . . ." The word "rebuked" is an aorist form of the verb "to reprimand strongly." One time (aorist) He strongly reprimanded the elements of nature. "...and there was a great calm." "Was" is also an aorist tense. So *immediately* the raging wind and sea became calm. This is evidence of the miraculous. For had this been due to natural causes, the wind would have subsided gradually, and the sea would have become placid in the same manner. Note the contrast: "a great tempest" and "a great calm." The difference was the authority of the King.

And then we see the result (v. 27). It is a contrast between astonishment and achievement. The disciples wondered at the person of Jesus. "Even the wind and the sea obey him." Apparently the disciples had not been overly impressed with the healing miracles. But His authority over nature inspired their wonder and awe. The word for "marvelled" is an ingressive aorist tense, and the word "obey" is a present tense. Literally, "The men began to marvel...and the winds and the sea keep on obeying him."

It would seem, therefore, that the disciples began to see Jesus in a new light. He was not only a master of words (chaps. 5-7) and a healer of diseases (8:2-15), but His authority extended even to the mighty forces of nature. He is King in the intellectual, physical, and natural realms. But there is more to come. For He is King in the spiritual realm also.

The Authority of the King over Demons (8:28-32)

Presently Jesus and His little company were on dry land. It was the country of the Gadarenes. The King James Version reads "Gergesenes" (v. 28). But the best texts read "Gadarenes." Mark (5:1) and Luke (8:26) read "the country of the Gerasenes." We cannot be certain as to the location. Even today one may visit the ruins of the city of Khersa (Gerasa). But this is some miles from the sea. However, it is in the district of the city of Gadara. So all three Evangelists are correct in their description of the area.

At any rate when Jesus arrived in the area He was confronted by two demon-possessed men (v. 28). Mark and Luke mention only one. But they evidently centered on the leading one, or the one possessed of a legion of demons (Mark 5:9). There is no necessary conflict here.

Thus we are introduced to a phenomenon which has been the center of much discussion and dispute. Is there such a thing as demons? Or is this merely the belief of an ignorant and superstitious age? Again, does the New Testament use demon possession to describe conditions which are today given more sophisticated medical terms? To be sure the symptoms often described are those which today denote certain mental and bodily illnesses. The case at hand suggests maniacs who were criminally insane. But the fact remains that the New Testament does speak of demons as a reality. Did Jesus accommodate His terminology to a mere superstition? If so, was He intellectually dishonest? To admit this is entirely contrary to His character.

Among the ancients there was a wide-spread belief in demons. And while this belief often bordered on the superstitious, there is no real reason why this should be identified with the New Testament teaching about demon-possession. John A. Broadus points out that demoniacal possessions are not mentioned in the Old Testament, the Apocrypha, nor the Jewish Mishna. But they are mentioned repeatedly in Josephus. Edersheim shows that the New Testament phenomenon is quite different from the popular Jewish idea of demons. But in view of the absence of such in the above-mentioned writings, save Josephus whose writings were somewhat contemporary with the New Testament, this makes the New Testament treatment of such all the more significant.

The four Evangelists repeatedly speak of demons as real, a position with which Jesus agrees. At times we even find Jesus carrying on conversations with them. They show a supernatural knowledge (Matt. 8:29), even declaring Jesus to be the Son of God. To be sure, Jesus forbade them so to declare Him (cf. Mark 1:34; Luke 4:41). This was probably due to two things. He did not wish to precipitate a premature witness before His followers were prepared to receive it. Nor did He wish to throw Himself open to His enemies' accusation that He was in league with them, an accusation which they made in due time (cf. Matt. 12:24). It is quite evident that both the Gospel writers and Jesus accepted demons as real beings. And with their testimony we agree.

This poses another question. Why should this phenomenon coincide with our Lord's presence on the earth? We agree with Doctor Broadus (*Matthew,* in loco) when he says, "The Eternal Word was then manifesting himself in the flesh; and thus the great struggle which is always going on was brought out into visible appearance, so as to exhibit in a visible and striking way the absolute powerlessness of the evil spirits to contend against God."

Therefore, when Jesus arrived in the country of the Gadarenes He found these two demon-possessed men (v. 28). They lived among the tombs. Because of their maniacal tendencies men had sought without success to bind them with fetters and chains (cf. Mark 5:4). The residents gave this graveyard a wide berth in fear of them. It is evident that Jesus had no fear of them. He knew their nature.

And they recognized their master. For they cried, "What have we to do with thee, Jesus, thou Son of God? art thou come hither to torment us before the time?" (v. 29). While they knew Jesus for who He was, they were also aware that they had nothing in common with Him. Furthermore, they knew their final destiny (cf. Matt. 25:41; Rev. 20:10). They surmised that the Messiah was come to administer punishment before that great and terrible day of the Lord.

Now we come to another passage which causes difficulty to some. Jesus was now in an area largely populated by Gentiles. Nearby a herd of swine was feeding. Some hold that demons do not like to be disembodied (cf. Matt. 12:43ff.). So the demons, knowing that they were about to be cast out of the men, asked to be allowed to enter into these swine (v. 31). Jesus permitted them to do so. And the swine suddenly "ran violently down a steep place into the sea, and perished in the waters" (v. 32). This indicates that demon-possession was no normal physical malady. The swine did not gradually become insane. The word "went" is an aorist tense, suggesting sudden action. The same is true of the word "ran." This was an instantaneous effect brought on by the hogs themselves being suddenly possessed by demons.

Now the problem which some see is that Jesus in this miracle permitted the swine to be destroyed. However, this seems to be straining at a gnat and swallowing a camel. Who can reckon property or animal values as over against human values? Is not this within itself an acted parable in which Jesus shows the destructive power of evil in the human soul? A real event, to be sure, but with a great spiritual lesson.

But Matthew is not quibbling over minor details. His purpose is to show the authority of the King over demons. He came to destroy the works of the devil and to save men from his power. That He is capable of doing so is clearly demonstrated in this encounter.

The Authority of the King Challenged (8:33-34)

What a strange anti-climax to so great a demonstration of kingly authority! For the swine herders ran to their masters to report the event (v. 33). They "told every thing." This included what had happened to the men who had been freed from the demons, as well as that which had occurred to the swine. The word "told" *(apēggeilan)* is akin to the word "showed" *(apēggellon)* in Acts 26:20 with reference to preaching the gospel. These swine herders had a *gospel* to preach to their masters.

But what was their response to it? "The whole city came out to meet Jesus: and when they saw him, they besought him that he would depart from their coasts" (v. 34).

Why did they ask Jesus to leave? Was it because of the loss of the swine? Perhaps. This is the usual interpretation. But it appears that there was more behind this than mere material values. Both Mark and Luke say that when the people saw what Jesus had done, "They were afraid" (Mark 5:15). This is the reaction of the entire city, not just that of the owners of the swine. Was not the real reason, therefore, that they were frightened in the face of such a display of supernatural power? These people were Gentiles who lived in fear of their gods. So such a demonstration struck fear in their hearts. They did not know a God of love and mercy.

How many people fail to respond favorably to God's overtures of grace, not simply because of fear of economic loss, but because of awe and dread in the presence of divine power and that which it demands of them!

At any rate Jesus did not consider them beyond redemption. For He told the healed men to return to their homes, and to declare that which Jesus had done for them (Mark 5:19). There is no record that He ever returned to this area. But He left a witness behind.

Nevertheless in the outcome of this event as recorded in Matthew we see the climactic effect of the entire chapter. The authority of Jesus was unquestioned by disease, nature, and demons. Only the will of man challenged it, Truly, "He came unto his own [things], and his own [people] received him not" (John 1:11).

God's power is absolute over *things,* even demons. But He has made man a free personality with the right of choice. He will not violate the personality of man; nor will He coerce His will. But He stands ever ready in the power of His very being (authority, *exousia*) to save all who will respond to His overtures of grace.

Matthew 9

The Authority of the King (II)

From the country of the Gadarenes Jesus returned to "his own city." We know from Mark that this was Capernaum. Already Jesus was closely identified with His adopted residence. The Nazarene had become a Capernaumite.

Thus we are introduced to Matthew 9 in which the Evangelist continues to show the authority of the King. This truth is set forth in five incidents as (1) the authority of the King over sin; (2) the authority of the King over social custom; (3) the authority of the King in religion; (4) the authority of the King over despair; (5) the varied reactions to the authority of the King.

The Authority of the King over Sin (9:2-8)

It was not long before word of Jesus' return became known. The crowds gathered about the house where Jesus was staying, probably that of Peter. Presently there came four men bringing a bed-ridden paralytic ("palsy," *paralutikon*) to Jesus. This suggests the faith of the friends rather than that of the patient. But they could have been bringing him at his own request. Mark gives a more detailed account of this incident (2:3ff.), which clearly shows the determination of these friends to bring the man before Jesus. What a lesson in faith and faithful works for us!

But once they had brought the man to Jesus, things took an unexpected turn. Obviously the man was in need of healing. But Jesus said nothing about his physical condition. Instead, He said, 'Son, be of good cheer; thy sins be forgiven thee." "Forgiven" means to send away. It is a present passive form with the aorist effect of immediacy. The passive voice means that the sins were sent away by another, Jesus. But the point to note is that Jesus dealt with the man's spirit before He healed his body.

Three reasons suggest themselves as to why Jesus did this. In the first place, He pointed out the prior need of the spirit over the body. In the second place, He recognized the common belief that all sickness was the result of sin. He did not Himself accept this theory (cf. John 9:1ff.). But He used it to teach a great spiritual truth. Now the man was a sinner, as are all men. Some specific sin may have caused his illness, but not necessarily so. To be sure all sickness is the result of sin in the sense of evil at work in the world. But Jesus rightly chose to deal with this man's specific sin problem before He dealt with the health problem. Physical healing was often used as a means to induce spiritual faith, then as it is now. But the ultimate purpose of healing should be to bring faith in the Saviour. In many instances, even today, we must deal with the sin problem before we can cope with the physical need.

But among the Jews the belief was strong that a man could not be cured of physical illness until he was forgiven his sin. Rabbi Chija ben Abba said, "No sick person is cured from sickness, until all his sins are forgiven him." So Jesus began at the place of their understanding.

In the third place, Jesus used this belief to demonstrate His power to forgive sins as well as to heal bodies. Thus the evidence of His authority would be undeniable.

That Jesus rightly diagnosed the situation is seen in the fact that "certain of the scribes said within themselves, This man blasphemeth" (v. 3). This is the first mention of the Pharisees (scribes were Pharisees) appearing in opposition to Jesus. Hereafter they will be much in evidence throughout the remainder of Jesus' ministry. In fact, in this one chapter they accuse Jesus of blasphemy (v. 3), immorality (v. 11), lack of piety (v. 14), and of being in league with Satan (v. 34).

Their first accusation was not oral but mental and spiritual. The scribes' minds thought out of evil hearts (v. 4). They regarded Jesus' act of forgiving sin as blasphemy. Note the scorn in their attitude. They did not even dignify Jesus with a name. Instead they thought, "This one blasphemes." He was assuming to Himself an authority which belongs only to God (cf. Mark 2:7). In their own minds they could say nothing worse about a man.

But God causes even the wrath of man to praise Him. Because in Jesus' response to their evil thoughts, by their own words He showed that He was God Himself (vv. 4-7). Is it "easier to say, Thy sins be forgiven thee; or to say, Arise, and walk?" The former act the scribes might deny, even argue it away in theological debate. But the latter would be irrefutable evidence before their eyes and the eyes of even the common, unlettered masses.

So Jesus continued, "But that ye may know that the Son of man hath power on earth to forgive sins, (then saith he to the sick of the palsy,) Arise, take up thy bed, and go unto thine house" (v. 6). The bed was a pallet. Two words call for examination: "know" and "power." "Know" is a form of *oida*. Another word for "know" was *ginōskō*, meaning to know by experience, such as seeing, hearing, or participation. *Oida* expresses the knowledge which results from seeing through an experience to form a conviction of the heart. It may well be called "soul knowledge." So Jesus proposes to give them an outward knowledge, which, if they properly see through it, will result in soul knowledge.

However, in this context the more interesting word is "power." This is the same word which in Matthew 7:29 is rendered "authority" (exousia). It speaks of the authority which is resident in Jesus' very being. So the issue here is the King's *authority* over sin.

The scribes gained experiential knowledge (*ginōskō*), but they failed to perceive unto soul knowledge (*oida*). The evidence was complete. One minute they saw a helpless paralytic lying on his pallet. The next they saw a strong man carrying his pallet home. A miracle, both physical and spiritual, before their very eyes. Their eyes saw it, but their hearts denied it. Convinced against their wills, they were of the same opinion still. They still accused Jesus of blasphemy. But the multitudes marvelled and praised God as the One who gave "such authority [*exousia*] unto men."

The same evidence, then as now, produces such different effects in men. It is not the evidence but men's hearts which make the difference.

The Authority of the King over Social Custom (9:9-13)

This event deals with Jesus' calling of Matthew and the teachings which came out of it. We have noted Matthew's custom to ignore chronological order when it suits his purpose to do so. And this is certainly a case in point. For A. T. Robertson's *A Harmony of the Gospels* locates this event prior to the Sermon on the Mount. And this is important as we shall see presently.

As Jesus passed by the custom house He saw Matthew busy at his task (v. 9). For he was a tax-gatherer, a publican (cf. 10:3). There was no more despised group among the Jews. Under the Roman system the privilege of collecting taxes in a given area was farmed out to the highest bidder. He, in turn, must regain the cost plus his profit in the transaction. So all kinds of oppressive measures were used in collecting taxes. The "publicans" were the Jews who collected the taxes. They were regarded as traitors to their people, and were universally hated. Therefore, they were put in the same class with the lowest of sinners, so that "publicans and sinners" became a term of utter contempt.

Matthew was such a Jew. Mark (2:14) and Luke (5:27) refer to him by his Hebrew name, Levi. Since he was stationed at

Capernaum, he was probably an agent of Herod Antipas who ruled in this area under the Romans. He was "sitting at the seat of customs" or toll. Either he collected toll from ships crossing the sea of Galilee or from caravans on the route which ran from Damascus to Egypt. Apparently he had had previous contact with Jesus. For when Jesus said, "Follow me" ("keep on following me," present tense); "he *arose,* and *followed* him" (author's italics, both aorists). He did not hesitate, but immediately left his despised job to enter into a glorious career.

We may well ask why Jesus called such a man to be one of His inner circle of disciples. Certainly it was not in order to win popular acclaim. Of course, Jesus came to save all men. But evidently Matthew was already a disciple of Jesus. This call involved more. May we not say that Matthew possessed a gift which would make him especially fitted to serve Jesus in a given capacity?

As a customs collector Matthew was accustomed to keeping records. It is even possible that he could use shorthand, for such did exist at that time. If this be a reasonable surmise, then you can almost see him sitting within hearing of Jesus to take down verbatim what He said. It is Matthew who gives us the more complete record of the Sermon on the Mount. He includes more of Jesus' teachings than the other Evangelists. It is usually agreed, from Papias, that he was the author of a document called *Logia* (sayings or teachings). This was written before the Gospels, and contained many of the elements of the life of Jesus not found in Mark. It consists largely of discourses. So this adds weight to the suggestion as to Jesus' purpose in calling Matthew. Matthew probably penned the first account (*Logia*) dealing with the ministry of Jesus.

But even this does not explain why Matthew places the account of his call at this point in his Gospel. We must understand this in the light of his purpose. He is dealing with the authority of the King. And this event plus that which follows shows Jesus' authority with relation to social custom. Despite the fact that Matthew was a social outcast, Jesus called him into the most blessed fellowship in the world. He became one of the *intimates* of the King.

And this example of the King's authority is compounded in the scene at the banquet which Matthew gave in honor of his new way of life and of the One whom he now served. It is to be expected that along with Jesus and His disciples Matthew would invite his friends, "many publicans and sinners" (v. 10).

So once again the King was not bound by the narrow social customs of the prejudiced Jews.

The Pharisees resented this, and made it an occasion of further criticism. Their question in verse 11 involved what they considered to be an immoral act on the part of Jesus. He actually dared to have social fellowship "with publicans and sinners!" Apparently the Pharisees came right into the banquet hall. For when Jesus overheard their question, He took up the conversation. He did not seek to justify His actions to them. So fixed were they in their prejudice that it would have been a useless effort. But He did use it as the occasion to show the utter stupidity and sinfulness of their attitude.

"They that be whole [in good health] need not a physician, but they that are sick" (v. 12). Where else would you expect to find a doctor but with the sick? The Pharisees were pseudo-physicians who were afraid of germs. You do not cure patients by condemning them, but by loving and caring for them. We should be surprised to find Jesus anywhere other than among the "publicans and sinners." How this example of the King, the Physician of souls, condemns those of us who seek to follow Him!

And then Jesus condemns them out of their own Scriptures of which they were masters (v. 13). He quotes from Hosea 6:6. "I will have mercy, and not sacrifice." "Go ye and learn what that meaneth," says Jesus. Oh, they knew the words, but they had never learned their meaning. They were long on "sacrifice" but terribly short on "mercy."

The conclusion of the whole matter? "For I am not come to call the righteous, but sinners to repentance." The word "not" is first in this sentence, and so emphatic. Jesus states in a negative fashion His positive purpose. In so doing He does not imply that the Pharisees are righteous. But with biting sarcasm He condemns their attitude of self-righteousness. They criticized Jesus for eating with "sinners." Why should He eat with the Pharisees? On occasion He did. But that is not the point here. By their own attitude these Pharisees claimed to be "righteous." Jesus did not come to call such. However, He did come to call both publicans and Pharisees but only on the basis that they were sinners in need of a Saviour.

So with authority the King brushed aside man-made customs which stood in the way of His redemptive purpose. He never broke the laws of God. But customs which were vicious in their very nature fell before His authoritative mission.

The Authority of the King in Religion (9:14-17)

It was not unusual for groups to stand about and watch those eating at a feast. Apparently, in addition to the Pharisees, a group of the disciples of John the Baptist was present. So when the Pharisees stepped back to lick their wounds, John's disciples stepped forward to add their criticism to the occasion. They approached Jesus Himself with the question, "Why do we and the Pharisees fast oft, but thy disciples fast not?" (v. 14).

It is sad to see the Forerunner's disciples critical of Jesus. But John was in prison, and here was Jesus at a banquet apparently unmindful of their teacher's fate. John the Baptist probably would not have attended such a banquet under any circumstances. Furthermore, it may have been one of the Jewish fast days. And here were Jesus and His disciples at a banquet.Whether this was the point at issue or the general matter of fasting, it reflects Jesus' attitude toward fasting for fasting's sake. Jesus did fast on occasion, but it was in keeping with His inner need, not the days on a calendar.

So the problem involved not merely a banquet scene. It reflects the contrast between religion as taught by the Jews and that as revealed through Jesus. Fasting was one of the most important religious duties under Judaism. Thus in His reply Jesus, in effect, declared His authority in setting forth the relationship which Christianity should bear to Judaism. And in doing so He spoke three parables.

The first parable had to do directly with the Jewish practice of fasting. "Can the children of the bridechamber mourn, as long as the bridegroom is with them?" (v. 15). Fasting suggested sadness in contrast to the present banquet atmosphere. Jesus likens His disciples' present position to those who are attending the banquet of a bridegroom. His example would be perfectly clear to His audience.

In Jewish life for a week after the wedding the bridgegroom and bride entertained their closest friends known as "children of the bridechamber." It was a time of feasting and rejoicing. So Jesus likens the present relationship between Him and His disciples to such a happy occasion. Mourning would be out of place. So now they rejoice. "But the time will come when the bridegroom shall be taken from them, and then shall they fast." Here Jesus refers to His death. Truly they shall fast and mourn. But even then they shall rejoice after that the Bridegroom is seen to be alive forevermore. So in the larger context Jesus is saying that those who follow Him shall know joy unspeakable. Even their Christian fasting will be tempered by the knowledge that they serve a living Lord. Life in the new revelation through Jesus will be free from the frustrations which were so evident in Judaism.

The second and third parables deal specifically with the relationship which Christianity bears to Judaism. The figures employed by Jesus were those of patching old clothes and of putting wine into wineskins (vv. 16-17). These were common illustrations taken from the life of the people, as were all of Jesus' parables.

"No man putteth a piece of new cloth unto an old garment, for that which is put in to fill it up taketh from the garment, and the rent is made worse." "New cloth" was undressed or unshrunken cloth. When it became wet it shrank. And in the process it would tear the old cloth. So the *schism* would be larger than the original hole. Jesus did not come to patch up Judaism, but to weave a new spiritual cloth altogether.

"Neither do men put new wine into old bottles [wineskins]." One can still see in eastern lands liquids carried in containers made from the skins of goats. "New wine" was still fermenting. If it were put in an old, brittle skin, the gases produced by fermentation would burst the skins, and lose the wine. New wine is put into new skins which are elastic. They will stretch to suit the need. And thus the wine is preserved.

This is an obvious comparison between Christian truth and that which was taught by Judaism. New ideas call for new means of expression. Of interest is the fact that Jesus used two different words for "new." The former is *neos* meaning the new as contrasted with the old. The latter is *kainos* which expresses the idea of newness but also that the *old* is obsolete. So the new truth is to be expressed in new and adequate terms. The immediate context involves the fasting or mourning of Judaism and the joy of the Christian revelation. The old faded garment can only detract from the beautiful new cloth. Nor is the old able to bear the truth involved in the new. The symbolism and system associated with the old dispensation is obsolete, and therefore cannot contain the meaning of the new dispensation. The symbols of *law* cannot contain the message of *grace*. "Grace" is not something to be sewed on to the system of law. The two are self-contradictory. Neither can *grace* be poured into *law*. Grace negates law, and law negates grace. So in such an attempt, both are lost.

Thus the King in His authority declares that the two shall not be combined. But despite this fact through the years men have tried to do so. And the result is tragic. To endeavor to preserve Old

Testament systems of worship and priesthood in Christian dress is but an effort to patch the old with the new. To equate the meaning of Christian ordinances with the rite and ceremony of Judaism is to pour the new wine into old skins. The meaning of the new is lost in the old.

Christianity finds its roots in the spiritual message of the Old Testament. But it is not to be identified with it. Christian truth is God's revelation in Christ who fills full the law. The law finds its full meaning in Christ, not Christ in the law.

The Authority of the King over Despair (9:18-31)

This section contains the account of three miracles performed by Jesus. The cases involved have one thing in common. They involve the element of despair. The daughter was dead (vv. 18-19, 23-26). The woman with an issue of blood had tried every possible cure to no avail (vv. 20-22). There is nothing more hopeless than blindness (vv. 27-31). Yet in each instance Jesus changed despair into joy. The King has authority to overcome despair and to produce hope and gladness.

The banquet was interrupted by a ruler of the synagogue who sought Jesus' help when all else had failed. His daughter was dead. The aorist tense says, "My daughter just now died" (v. 18). But the ruler had faith to believe that Jesus could restore her to life.

It is remarkable to see such faith in one in his position. As the ruler of the synagogue he was the very essence of Judaism. He was in charge of the synagogue, its building, services, and personnel with respect to worship. Since this man was responsible for inviting those who taught and conducted worship, he doubtless on occasion had chosen Jesus for this ministry (cf. Mark. 1:21-22). The people had commented about Jesus' "authority" as a teacher. Furthermore, the ruler had seen Jesus cast an unclean spirit out of a man in his very synagogue (Mark 1:23ff.). Again the people had noted that "with authority commandeth he even the unclean spirits, and they do obey him." So there was a basis for this ruler's faith in Jesus' *authority* to raise the dead.

When Jesus arrived at the ruler's home He found a typical scene as the people mourned for the dead (v. 23). But Jesus put the mourners out of the house, saying, "The maid is not dead, but sleepeth" (v. 24). And they laughed him to scorn, for they knew that she was dead. Some hold that "sleepeth" means that she was in a coma. But this word (*katheudō*) is used for *sleep* in the sense of death (cf. I Thess. 5:10).

The authority of Jesus in the presence of death is seen in the simple words, "He took her by the hand, and the maid arose" (v. 25). And while no mention is made of joy replacing despair, it is implied in the words, "And the fame hereof went abroad into all the land" (v. 26).

Despair comes to all, the small and the great. But despair which in faith drives us to Jesus is dispelled into joy. It was true with the ruler of the synagogue. It can be true of us. For He has authority, not only over evil spirits, but over death itself.

While Jesus was on His way to the ruler's home, a woman in despair came to Him (vv. 20-22). She had had an issue of blood for twelve years. Literally, "And, behold, a woman having a hemorrhage twelve years." Because of this she was considered unclean, preventing her from being with other people and from participating in worship (cf. Lev. 15:25-27). By Jewish law she should not even have been in the crowd. But her deed was one of desperation. She had tried everything to find a cure, but to no avail. The Talmud sets forth at least eleven different cures for her condition, some medical and others pure superstition. She probably had tried them all. Furthermore, she had consulted physicians. Mark says that she "had suffered many things of many physicians, and had spent all that she had, and was nothing bettered, but rather grew worse" (5:26). With a physician's touch Luke says, "... neither could be healed of any" (8:43). She had an incurable disease.

So in her desperation she dared the wrath of the crowd in order to come to Jesus. This woman had faith in Jesus, even if it was a superstitious faith. She felt that if she could but touch the fringe of His garment, the tassels which hung from the edge of the outer garment (cf. Num. 15:38), she would be healed. Jesus honored even her superstitious faith. For He said, "Daughter [note the tenderness], be of good comfort; thy faith hath made thee whole [aorist tense, immediacy] ... from that very hour" (v. 22). Despair gave way to *comfort* through the authority of the King!

The third situation of despair involved two blind men (9:27-31). Blindess was and is a common disease in Palestine. So these men would have remained comparatively inconspicuous had they not come into contact with Jesus. They would have been but a part of that flotsam and jetsam which ever floats aimlessly on the sea of misery. But because they dared to come to Jesus, they stand as a prime example of His authority over despair.

Note that they followed Him in the street "crying and saying, Son of David, have mercy on us" (v. 27). Literally, they "kept on crying and kept on saying [present tense], have mercy [at once, aorist imperative] on us." This speaks of the intensity and urgency of their appeal. So far as they knew this might be their one chance to be healed, and they made the most of it.

For the first time in *Matthew* we see Jesus in direct address called "Son of David" (cf. 1:1). Jesus never used this title in direct reference to Himself. It was a term which in the Jewish mind carried a highly nationalistic meaning. It spoke of the belief that the Messiah would be a political and military one. And since this was contrary to Jesus' mission, He avoided this title to discourage the fanaticism of the Jews with regard to Him. On occasion He commented on His relation to David when others used the term. But He never used it with reference to Himself.

This may explain why Jesus did not respond to the cry of these blind men until He was in the privacy of a home (v. 28). Perhaps He also wished to test their sincerity. At any rate when they came to Him in the house (Peter's house?), He asked, "Believe ye that I am able *to do this?*" In response to their affirmative answer, Jesus *touched* their eyes, saying, "According to your faith *be* it unto you. And their eyes were *opened* . . ." (vv. 29-30). The author's italics indicate aorist forms which speak of *one point* action or immediacy. So this was not a gradual cure but a miracle. They believed in a miracle, and they received one.

And notice that this was in response to their faith. Man's faith plus the King's authority! It is ever thus.

Jesus strictly charged that they should not tell this. Note His care to prevent a precipitated revolution. But so great was their joy that they spread the glad news abroad. How strange it is that even though Jesus charged them with silence, they published it abroad. Yet we who are charged to publish glad tidings are so derelict in doing so.

Nevertheless the case for the King's authority was thoroughly established. He was not only a speaker of the word but a doer of it also. Evidence enough to convince all whose minds and hearts were open to receive the truth. But what was the result?

The Varied Reactions to the Authority of the King (9:32-38)

To compound the evidence, as though to drive a final nail in the board, Matthew records the healing of "a dumb man possessed with the devil" (v. 32). And then came the verdict.

The multitudes "marvelled, saying, It was never so seen in Israel" (v. 33). In the Greek this is a very strong declaration.

"Never" renders a word (*oudepote*) which means "not ever" or "never absolutely." "Seen" is an aorist tense. So literally they said, "It was absolutely never seen at any time in Israel."

The "multitudes" were the vast crowd of ordinary people, so much in need, who had received no help from the Pharisees, their religious leaders. Instead they were the objects of their scorn. But here was One who not only had the authority, but the compassion as well, to meet their needs. Such a people with a sense of need will always marvel at Jesus. And the greater the need the greater the marvel.

"But the Pharisees said, He casteth out devils through the prince of devils" (v. 34). They could not deny the authority which was resident in Jesus. They could only malign its source. "In league with the devil," they said (cf. 12:22ff.). They were set in their ways. Through a deep-seated pride they would admit no need. Blinded by prejudice they could not, would not see. In the face of infinite authority they continued in their sins. And their descendants are legion. If we reject the authority of Jesus there is nothing that even He can do for us!

But their cynicism did not defeat the cause of Jesus. For He continued to teach, preach, and heal (v. 35). The needy multitudes ever moved Him to compassion. They were tired (fainted) of the burdens placed upon them by the Pharisees, but were given by them no power to bear them. The word "fainted" renders a word (*skullō*) meaning to be plundered or vexed (papyri). So like bewildered sheep which were plundered by their false shepherds, they were tired and had lain down. This last thought is expressed by the word "scattered" (*rhiptō*) It is used of men cast down and lying prostrate on the ground suffering from mortal wounds. The wolves dressed in shepherd's clothing had ravaged the flock.

In such a multitude Jesus saw an abundant harvest waiting to be gathered. But there were so few laborers (v. 37). So Matthew concludes this section with an earnest plea from Jesus (v. 38). "Pray ye therefore the Lord of the harvest, that he will send forth laborers into his harvest." The words "pray" and "send forth" are aorist forms, suggesting urgency. Note that it is "his harvest." So one who responds to this call is in the service of the King.

How seldom do we "pray" for more servants of the King! And how hesitant are many who hear the call! "Send forth" means "to thrust forth." Thus Jesus suggests that God has to push or force a man into obedience when he resists the call of the King. How much more wonderful when we recognize the King's authority to call and to perform through us. It is even more glorious when the *called* share the King's compassion, so that to answer the call is not simply a duty to be performed but a privilege to be seized and enjoyed.

Matthew 10

The Heralds of the King

The King sends forth His heralds to proclaim the gospel of the Kingdom. The field truly is white unto harvest. So the Lord of the harvest thrusts forth His laborers into the harvest field. And while their particular mission has an immediate nature, it will not be finished until the second coming of Christ at the end of the age. This broader view must be kept before us if we are to comprehend the contents of Matthew 10.

This chapter naturally divides itself into five sections. So let us examine it as follows: (1) the call of the heralds; (2) the mission from their call to the crucifixion; (3) the mission from Pentecost to the destruction of Jerusalem; (4) the mission from the fall of Jerusalem to the end of the age; (5) the dual response to the mission.

The Call of the Heralds (10:1-4)

In keeping with his purpose to present the life of Christ in a topical arrangement, Matthew delays the listing of the Twelve until the time when Jesus sends them forth on a definite mission. That they had already been chosen is seen in the Evangelist's use of the definite article (Greek, "the twelve disciples of him"). Already they are regarded as a group set apart from the larger body of disciples. Furthermore, the "twelve disciples" (10:1) are now designated as "twelve apostles" (10:2). "Disciples" are learners. "Apostles" are those who are sent forth. The King has taught them; now He sends them forth to practice that which they have learned. There will be other lessons, as there will be other missions. But the time of their own public ministry has arrived.

Furthermore, the King imparts to them the "power" designed to authenticate their mission (10:1). This word "power" is the word for "authority" (*exousia*) which we have noted often in this section of the Gospel. The "authority" which Jesus possesses within Himself He bestows on His heralds. For they are to go in His name.

Worthy of note is the fact that in 10:2 we find Matthew's only use of the word "apostle." In Hebrew thought an apostle was not merely a *messenger*. He carried with him the *delegated authority* of the one who sent him. The Talmud says, "The Apostle of any one is even as the man himself by whom he is deputed." Therefore, we can understand the authority which was later attributed to the Apostles. Likewise, the order of Matthew's words takes on a natural sequence. To the "twelve *disciples* he gave . . . power [authority] . . . Now the names of the twelve *apostles* . . ." (author's italics). So in effect the mission of the apostles was the mission of Jesus. To receive them was to receive Him; to reject them was to reject Him (cf. 10:12-15, 40).

In the New Testament there are four listings of the twelve apostles (Matt. 10:2-4; Mark 3:16-19; Luke 6:14-16; Acts 1:13). A comparative study of these lists reveals many interesting things. For instance, in each list Peter is always first and Judas Iscariot is always last, except in Acts 1:13 where his name does not appear. He is always described as the betrayer of Jesus. The position of Peter's name does not necessarily imply a position above the others. Certainly Jesus was the leader of the Twelve at this time. And there is ample evidence in the New Testament, including Peter's own testimony (I Peter 5:1)), that the early Christians did not regard him as being over the others.

A closer look at the Twelve reveals three groupings of four with Peter, Philip, and James the son of Alphaeus heading each group respectively. Whether this is significant or not, it is just as reasonable to assume their leadership by groups as to regard Peter as the leader of the Twelve. His name heading the list may best be explained by the fact that, being more forward than the others, he was usually their spokesman.

There are three groups of brothers among the Twelve: Peter and Andrew; James and John; James the Son of Alphaeus and Judas the brother of James. James and John were related to Jesus through their mothers. And James was destined to become the first Christian martyr (Acts 12:2).

A study of the various names by lists shows an apparent discrepancy, since one list carries one name for a person and another gives a different name. This is due to the fact the men had more than one name. We know that Simon was also called Cephas and Peter, the last two being the Aramaic and Greek respectively of the same name. Matthew was also called Levi; Thomas was called Didymus. Didymus is simply the Greek translation of Thomas, meaning "a twin." Simon the Cannanean (true reading of 10:4) is also called "the Zealot" (Luke 6:15). "Zealot" is the Greek equivalent of "Canaanean." This referred to a fanatical revolutionary group dedicated to the overthrow of Roman rule in

Palestine. It was their activity which finally brought on the Jewish War (A.D. 66-70), resulting in the destruction of their nation.

But it is of even greater interest to note the type of men whom Jesus chose for this intimate group. At the time when Matthew wrote his Gospel they were well known among his readers. Hence the scarcity of details about them. But certain items of interest may be pointed out. Peter, Andrew, James, and John, after John the Baptist, were the first four people to receive Jesus as their Messiah. They were four fishermen who were partners in the business. Philip (not the "evangelist," cf. Acts 8:5) was an early convert who in turn brought Bartholomew (Nathanael, John 1:43ff) to Jesus. Thomas was a heroic doubter (cf. John 11:16; 20:25). But note that he only demanded the proof which the rest of the Twelve already had. Matthew was a despised publican, and Simon the Zealot was a former revolutionary. Judas, the only one of the Twelve who came from Judea, was a devil from the beginning. (We shall deal more fully with him later in this volume.)

The outstanding thing about these men is that they were not outstanding. They were just plain men, each perhaps possessing some particular quality which Jesus wished to develop for use in His Kingdom. We may well imagine that Jesus had studied His growing band of disciples carefully, singling out first one and then another. Finally, after a night of prayer (Luke 6:12ff.), He chose these twelve. To the casual observer they may appear to be a rather motley group. But they were just ordinary men chosen to do an extraordinary task in the service of God. And their first assignment was a preaching mission throughout Galilee.

The Mission from Their Call to the Crucifixion (10:5-15)

The divisions of the Scripture here and throughout this chapter are not arbitarily made. They contain instructions given by Jesus relative to the program of preaching the gospel of the Kingdom. But as you examine them it becomes clear that there are definite breaks in the thought. Even between verses at the points of divisions one enters into a new atmosphere. Furthermore, certain instructions do not seem to be universal in character, while others are. We shall point these out as they appear. It is quite evident that verses 5-15 are applicable only to the period ending with the crucifixion and resurrection of Jesus.

Having chosen the "twelve," Jesus sent them forth (v. 5). "Sent forth" renders the verb which is akin to the word for "apostles." He sent them forth with His "authority" to cast out demons and to heal the sick. These miracles would lend evidence that the authority of God was in their preaching. Furthermore, Jesus "commanded" them. This word was often used of the issuing of an imperial command. So the King issues His imperial command to His soldiers as they march forth to do battle against the evil that is in men's hearts. In so doing He defines the area of combat (vv. 5-6), the weapon to be employed (vv. 7-8), and the equipment necessary for the campaign (vv. 9-15).

The area of combat is confined to "the lost sheep of the house of Israel." Therefore, they are not to go into the way leading to the Gentiles. Nor are they to enter Samaria which was populated with half-Jews. They are not to go east across the sea of Galilee (Gentile country), neither north into Syria (Gentile country), nor south into the land of the Samaritans. Their present responsibility is an evangelistic tour of Galilee. It is quite evident that this command did not extend beyond the resurrection. For Matthew 28:19 is a command to disciple all nations.

Why did Jesus confine the present effort to the Jews? Certainly it was not due to a narrow nationalism on the part of Jesus. His own witness was borne to both Samaritans and Gentiles. His purpose is first to present the gospel of the Kingdom to the Jews, His own people after the flesh. They shall be given the first opportunity to respond to His Kingship. And Jesus did not propose to encourage undue prejudice on their part by including the Gentiles and Samaritans as such in this particular effort. While not agreeing with their own prejudiced opinion, Jesus took it into consideration as He made a wise and practical approach to the matter.

In fact, it is logical that the mission should begin with the Jews. In background and training they would be the most natural soil in which to sow the seed of the new order. If they received their Messiah the new age would dawn, and would become a bright new day for the entire world. In His term "lost sheep of the house of Israel" Jesus implies that they have lost their way. Doctor Bruce notes that the King spoke this more in pity than in blame. They were as sheep having no shepherd. They were *lost* because they had been *led astray* by false shepherds. So He proposes to offer Himself as the Good Shepherd to lead them back to the will and way of God.

The weapon which the apostles were to use was the proclamation of the gospel of the Kingdom (v. 7). They are commanded to "preach" or, literally, to "go on preaching." The word "preach" renders the word meaning "to herald" or "to proclaim." It was used of announcing the results at athletic games. But more to the point here, a *herald* was an officer of the government who went about declaring the proclamations of the king. As a representative of the king he was to be heeded and obeyed.

So the King sends forth His heralds, His authoritative apostles, to proclaim to the Jews, "The kingdom of heaven is at hand." This is not the full gospel which will later be preached to all nations. Such a message must wait on the cross and resurrection. But this message is that the King has come to set up His Kingdom. This was the same message heralded by John the Baptist and by Jesus Himself. It was authoritative then, but even more so in the mission at hand. For in truth the King is beginning the campaign that shall not end until God says, "It is enough," in the glorious and final appearance of our Lord at the end of the age.

He has sounded forth the trumpet
  That shall never sound retreat;
He is sifting out the hearts of men
  Before His judgment seat;
O be swift, my soul, to answer Him!
  Be jubilant, my feet!
Our God is marching on.
—Julia Ward Howe

But what about equipment for this campaign? This Jesus deals with in verses 8b-15. There is the element of urgency in His words. Literally, Jesus said, "Do not acquire for yourselves either gold, or silver, or brass in your girdles" (v. 9). Note the descending value of the coins. They are not to wait to get such things. Nor are they to pack a *travelling* or *bread bag.* This is the meaning of the word "scrip" (v. 10). They are not to be loaded down with extra clothing, not even an extra walking staff. Mark 6:8 says that they should take one staff. Apparently Jesus means that they are not to take an extra one, the same provision as with clothing. In essence, they are to start out right now, just as they are. The King's business requires haste.

However, there is another element suggested in these instructions. For Jesus introduced them with the statement "Freely ye have received, freely give." James Moffatt translates this, "Give without being paid, as you have got without paying." J. W. Shepard renders it, "You have received without cost, give without pay."

This charge plus the admonition not to take a "scrip" or "wallet" suggests that they are not to be beggars for the necessities of life. Deissmann cites an inscription which shows that a "scrip" could be a beggar's collecting bag. This inscription at Kefr Hanar in Syria reads, "While Christianity was still young the beggar priest was making his rounds in the land of Syria on behalf of the national goddess." It refers to the custom of pagan priests begging for their deity. So "scrip" could mean a begging bag, very much like the Hindu priests use begging bowls today to acquire from the people their daily rations. The apostles do not serve a pauper King, and, therefore, should not themselves be beggars. "For the workman is worthy of his meat" (v. 10).

Of course, they must have food and lodging along the way. This passage is not intended to forbid a *paid ministry*. Instead it specifically teaches one. The point is that they are not to be encumbered with efforts to earn for themselves (v. 9) the necessities of life to the neglect of their spiritual ministry. They are to render it with no thought of remuneration. But remuneration is to be provided by those whom they serve. They are to be neither *providers* nor *beggars* (vv. 9-10). But they are to be provided for by benefactors.

This is the import of verses 11-13a. Wherever they go the apostles are to seek out those homes where, because of a kindred interest in the Kingdom, they will be provided with life's necessities. They are not to procure such from unbelievers. Certainly this would forbid a tax-supported ministry. The servants of the King are to abide in homes that are "worthy." That is, a home which would welcome both the messengers and the message. Finding such a home the apostles are to "salute it" (v. 12), or express good wishes upon it. They are to give it the traditional oriental benediction of "Peace be unto you" (v. 13).

However, an *unworthy* home or city, one which refuses both the messenger and the message—when they depart they are to "shake off the dust of your feet" (v. 14) against it. This was a strong oriental expression of condemnation. When a Jew passed from a Gentile land into his own *holy land,* he shook the pagan dust from his sandals. Those who refused the message of the King were so to be regarded. Years later we see Paul and Barnabas doing this very thing in Antioch in Pisidia (Acts 13:51). But they did this in response to Jewish opposition. With the Jewish and pagan seekers (Acts 13:42-44) they had great patience. It was here at Antioch in Pisidia that the apostles definitely turned to the Gentiles (13:45-46).

This seems to be the import of Jesus' instructions to the Twelve. Those who receive them and their message are to be blessed with their presence and ministry. Those Jews who refused it are to be left to their decision. And for such it will be more intolerable in the Judgment than for Sodom and Gomorrah, cities which the Jews regarded as having no place in the world to come.

The Mission from Pentecost to the Destruction of Jerusalem (10:16-23)

Suddenly the entire picture changes. From homes and cities which refuse to hear them, the apostles find themselves as sheep among wolves (v. 16). And that which follows might well serve as an outline of the Book of Acts. It is quite apparent, therefore, that Jesus is looking beyond the crucifixion and resurrection to the experiences of His followers when the lines of battle will be more tightly drawn. The things described in this section certainly did not happen during the lifetime of Jesus. Therefore, they must refer to a time after His ascension. When we approach them from this point of view, the picture comes into clear focus.

The word "behold" prepares us for a shock (v. 16). Already we can see the wolves rending the flock. This was no accident, nor did it come as a surprise to Jesus. "I send you forth as sheep in the midst of wolves." In the Greek the pronoun "I" is written out rather than simply being present in the verb form itself. Furthermore, it comes first in the statement. Hence it is doubly emphatic. In effect Jesus says, "I, even I, send you forth...." Here again we have the verb from which comes the word "apostle." So with the authority of the Shepherd the sheep are to go among the wolves.

Such an ordeal will require both wisdom and courage. Jesus expressed it in proverbial fashion. "Wise as serpents, and harmless as doves." The serpent was symbolic of intellectual keenness and shrewdness (Gen. 3:1). The dove suggests simplicity (Hos. 7:11). So the apostles are to be characterized by an intellectual keenness which is expressed in simplicity or singleness of heart. A. T. Robertson comments that "either without the other is bad." Alone, the one produces evil and the other results in gullibility. But together they produce the spirit which enabled the early Christians successfully to storm the citadels of sin. The same quality will produce the same results in any age.

So Jesus warns against such men as are characterized by "wolves." "For they will deliver you up to the councils, and they will scourge you in their synagogues" (v. 16). This refers to purely Jewish persecution. The word "deliver up" means to hand over to a court for judgment. It is the word used for the Jewish rulers delivering Jesus up to Pontius Pilate (Matt. 27:2), and Pilate delivering Him to the soldiers for crucifixion (Matt. 27:26).

In this context, however, the reference is to persecution carried on by the Jews as such. The word "councils" refers to both local courts (Acts 12:1ff.) and to the Sanhedrin (cf. Acts 4:1ff.). The reference to scourging in the synagogues suggests the disciplinary session of Jewish religious bodies (cf. Acts 5:40).

But in verse 18 Jesus promises persecution carried on by both the Jews and the pagan Romans. And the description is exact. For repeatedly the Christians were judged by the civil authorities on accusations brought by the Jewish religious leaders (cf. Acts 16:5ff.; 18:12ff.; 21:27-28).

So in verses 17-18 the persecution of the Christians following Pentecost is vividly described. When "the Way" was a movement confined to Palestine the persecution was Jewish. But as it spread throughout the Roman empire, there was a persecution involving both Jews and Gentiles, sometimes acting independently and sometimes jointly. W. Hersey Davis notes that only in the period from Pentecost to the destruction of Jerusalem were the Christians persecuted by both Jews and Gentiles. Furthermore, he points out that since the fall of the Jewish state in A.D. 70 there is no record of a Christian being scourged in a Jewish synagogue.

But such persecution is to become "a testimony against them [Jews] and the Gentiles" (v. 18b). A literal translation reads "unto a witness to them and to the Gentiles." Their persecution gave the apostles opportunities which would have come in no other way to preach the gospel before the Sanhedrin (Acts 4:5ff.; 5:27ff.) and before the Roman governors and King Agrippa (Acts 24:10ff.; 26:1ff.). We may well conclude that because of Paul's bonds Nero heard a sermon or two. And the Holy Spirit spoke through these heralds of the King as they stood before the tribunals of men (vv. 19-20).

Furthermore, this period will be characterized by divisions within families (v. 21). As the gospel spreads it will penetrate the family circle. The bitterness of such strife is reflected in this verse. Brother against brother, father against child, and children against parents. Those reaching forth for the new order will be set against those holding on to the old order. And history records that many Christians went to their death upon accusations brought by members of their own families!

In all of this the apostles shall not escape (v. 22). For Jesus' sake they will be hated by all men who are opposed to Him. This truth is reflected in Acts 17:6. "These that have turned the world upside down are come hither also." Persecuted by religion, by the state, and by the family. Yet they are to remain faithful. And those who endure "to the end shall be saved." "Saved" here does not refer to salvation of the soul. The apostles already enjoyed this state. This word is used in many ways: to be healed, to be rescued from danger, to be saved from sin, or to be saved from failure. Certainly this is a promise of protection, of patient endurance, and of a successful venture in witnessing for the Lord. Even if they die in the process they will be received into eternal habitations. This is a promise for our age as for every other age.

During this period the apostles are not to tarry in useless controversy (v. 23). They are to flee from one persecution to another, not as cowards but as men with a mission. If men will not hear them in one place, they are to flee to another. Because there are so many who have not heard. The time of this period of ministry is limited. "Ye shall not have gone over the cities of Israel [to say nothing of the Gentiles], till the Son of man be come" (v. 23).

This statement by Jesus is the cause of great difficulty. Some (e.g. Moffatt) hold this to refer to the immediate tour of Galilee. Before they finish their mission Jesus will come after them. Others refer this variously to the Transfiguration, Pentecost, or the Second Coming of Christ. Those holding to this last position conclude that Jesus was mistaken as to the divine timetable. But did Jesus refer to any of these?

Any great intervention in history on the part of God was considered as a "coming." In the light of Jesus' reference to the "cities of Israel" does this not refer to the destruction of Jerusalem? Certainly this event is intermingled with Jesus' discussion of "the end of the age" as recorded in Matthew 24. The fall of Jerusalem marked the end of the Jewish state. Thereafter there would be no "cities of Israel" in the strictest sense. So Jesus is simply placing the terminal event for this period of His instruction. This is all the more reason for haste in their mission to Israel. History itself records that thereafter the emphasis in Christian missions was toward the Gentile world.

The Mission from the Fall of Jerusalem to the End of the Age (10:24-31)

The emphasis in this section is on the Christian's identity with Christ (vv. 24-25). "A disciple is not over the teacher, nor a slave over his owner" (v. 24, author's translation). So the Christian should not expect to fare better than his Lord. It should be sufficient for a pupil to be as his teacher, and a slave as his owner

(v. 25). And if Jesus' enemies accuse Him of being the very devil himself, His followers can expect the same treatment. So not only is the Christian through the ages to be identified with the suffering of Christ, Christ likewise will be one with him in his suffering. When men malign you they are maligning Christ. When they persecute you they persecute Him also (cf. Acts 9:4).

So completely identified is Christ with His people that it is impossible for one to malign or mistreat the one without doing the same to the other. What an indictment are these words of Jesus against each one of us!

Nevertheless, the gospel must be preached (vv. 26-27). It must not be kept hidden, but must be *heralded* from the housetop. The heralds of the King must go marching through the ages with no fear as to what men may do to them. Instead they must be fearful of failing in the mission which God has entrusted to them (v. 28). In the meantime, they may rest in the assurance that He who watches over the sparrows will watch over them (vv. 29, 31). Even the hairs of your head are numbered (v. 30). And the enemies of Christ cannot pluck out even one but that God takes note of it. What a comfort these words are to the Christian who endures suffering for Christ's and the gospel's sake!

The Dual Response to the Mission (10:32-42)

Jesus anticipates a dual response to the message of His heralds. Some will "confess" Him and others will "deny" Him (vv. 32-33). This has ever been the case. The words "confess" in verse 32 are future tenses which cover all future time. It is as true today as it was in the first century.

To "confess" is to declare a thing to be true and to commit one's self to it. A Christian confession, therefore, is an open declaration as to the truth of the gospel in Christ, and an open commitment to Him. Our Lord leaves no room for *secret discipleship*. In the original language the reading is "confess in me" and "confess in him." This is more than a verbal statement. It involves faithful commitment "in Christ," to walk "in the sphere of" (*en*) Christ. "In me" and "in him" suggest the intimate union between Christ and the believer. In effect Jesus says that the person who says before men, in word and in deed, "He is mine," of him Christ will say before the Father, "He is mine."

By the same token those who "deny" Christ before men, He will also "deny" before the heavenly Father (v. 34). There is no "in me" or "in him" here. It is outside of Christ that the denials take place. The first "deny" is an aorist tense followed by the accusative case. This means complete denial and separation from Christ. The second "deny" is a future form involving all future time. One good reading of the word rendered "deny" is "to disown." So if you "disown" Christ before men, He will disown" you before His Father. In the Greek "I . . . also" in both of these verses is one word (*kago*). It sets Jesus' reaction in contrast to the reaction of man. The message of these verses involves the finished work of redemption through the crucifixion and resurrection. So Christ has done all that even God can do to redeem man. The final issue waits on man's decision. Confession and denial on the part of Christ means only His recognition of a fixed and final state in the heart of man.

And then Jesus startles His listeners with a dramatic statement. "Think not that I am come to send peace on earth: I came not to send peace, but a sword" (v. 34). "Think not" is an aorist subjunctive preceded by a negative particle. Literally it means "Stop thinking." It is so easy to think that an acceptance of Christ is followed by peace. In one sense this is certainly true. But in our relationships with others it may result in conflict, not peace. The King demands absolute loyalty. And this may well lead to conflict. The gospel unites us to Christ, but it may divide us from men. It may even produce division within family relationships (vv. 35-36).

The words "send" in verse 34 are aorist forms (sudden action) of a verb meaning to cast or to throw. So just as His apostles were thinking of peace, Jesus hurls a sword into their midst. When a man is confronted with the gospel he is faced with a decision. It may involve loyalty to Christ as opposed to loyalty to the most intimate of earth's relationships, the family. In such a case a true Christian must choose Christ before even parent or child. The word "loveth" involves choice not simply emotional response. You can love your family in the sense of emotion and still "love" Christ in the sense of your will. But even this involves conflict.

Even one's physical life must be secondary in one's relationship to Christ (v. 38). To take a cross meant to die on a cross. Jesus' listeners were familiar with the scene where a condemned person bore his own cross to the place of crucifixion. So if one is to be worthy of Christ he must be willing to die for Him. These are strong demands, but they are the demands of the King who accepts no lukewarm discipleship.

And then Jesus climaxes this truth with a paradoxical statement. "He that findeth his life shall lose it: and he that loseth his life for my sake shall find it" (v. 39). "Findeth and "loseth" are aorist participles denoting final, definite point action. They refer to the definite point action. They refer to the definite and final fixing of one's attitude. The word for life (*psuchē*) in each instance can mean either the animal principle of life or the spiritual principle of life. Actually there is a contrast of the two meanings here. If one places his emphasis on the natural, physical life, he will lose the spiritual life; and *visa versa*. So here we have a paradox. We lose by finding and find by losing. The Christian life is a paradox. Jesus found the true meaning of His life by losing His physical life. And so do we.

In closing this discourse Jesus turns from the messengers to those who receive them and thus share in their ministry (vv. 40-42). It is beautiful and fitting that the King should close on this note. For not all to whom the heralds are sent will refuse them or persecute them. Some will receive them kindly and will accept their message.

Eight times in verses 40-41 Jesus uses the word "receive." Six times He uses one word (*dechomai*) which means to receive kindly in the sense of hospitality or a welcome. Twice He uses the word (*lambanō*) meaning to receive into one's hand. Here it speaks of receiving a reward. The sense of these two words is that those who welcome the heralds will receive to themselves a reward for their kind hospitality. The element of reward suggests the end of the age. So from sending out His first apostles, the King now thinks of the rewards for service which He will distribute at His second coming. There are present rewards, to be sure; but they are as nothing when compared to the final reward when all of the fruits of our labors are in.

However, there are even greater truths involved in these verses. In verse 40 we see the intimate identity between the heralds and the King. In Jewish thought to welcome one's messenger was the same as receiving the one who sent him. So in giving hospitality to the heralds the host is giving hospitality to the King and His message. Furthermore, in this kindly act the host welcomes the Father Himself into his home (v. 40b). What a blessing which comes to the home or life which extends hospitality to the servants of the Lord!

A great preacher told me that through the years he had made it a point to entertain great preachers in his home. His primary purpose was to bring his children into contact with these dedicated personalities. But an even greater blessing accrued to his home. For in entertaining them he was host to the Lord, even

God Himself. He entertained, not angels, but God unawares.

But Jesus goes on to say that one who offers hospitality to a prophet or a righteous man for the sake of such also receives the reward due to them (v. 41). He does it with no thought of remuneration. But the reward is forthcoming nevertheless. Not everyone can be a prophet. But he can receive the reward of a prophet. For in his simple act of hospitality he shares in the prophet's ministry. If you cannot play first violin, you can at least play second fiddle. And He who reckons reward in the judgment will bestow His gratuities not on the basis of performance but on the basis of faithfulness in one's own sphere.

Who can reckon the value of a simple deed done in the name of or for the sake of a disciple of Jesus? Even a cup of cold water so bestowed becomes an act of infinite magnitude in the sight of God. The world gives its reward to its own. And heaven gives its reward to its own. The world headlines the deeds of those who are of the world. It may pass by with scant notice those who serve the King. But even the humblest deed done in His name is emblazoned in box-car letters across the headlines of heaven.

And that will be reward enough for the heralds of the King.

Matthew 11

The Authentication of the King

The ministry of the King has now progressed to the point that definite reactions to Him may be seen. Already these have been noted in a general way. But in Matthew 11 the Evangelist records an incident which reveals four very definite attitudes with reference to His person and work. And in each instance the matter issues in an authentication of the King and His mission. This we shall see as we note (1) the perplexity of John the Baptist; (2) the unreasonableness of the age; (3) the impenitence of certain Galilean cities; (4) the response of the "babes."

The Perplexity of John the Baptist (11:2-15)

As Jesus continues His busy ministry John the Baptist languishes in Herod's prison at Machaerus (cf. Matt. 14:1-12). He had been placed there because he had denounced the unholy marriage of Herod Antipas to his sister-in-law Herodias. Apparently he was allowed to see his disciples on occasion. And they brought to him reports on the works of "the Christ" (v. 2). This is the only time in his narrative portions where Matthew uses this official title of Jesus.

So hearing these reports John sent two of his disciples to Jesus with a question. "Art thou he that should come, or do we look for another?" (v. 3). "He that should come" renders two words *ho erchomenos* meaning "the Coming One." It was a term used in the Minor Prophets to refer to "the Christ." And the word "another" (*heteros*) means "another of a different kind." So the question reads literally, "Are you the Coming One, or do we look for another Christ of a different kind?"

What was the reason for this question? Some expositors hold that John had his disciples to ask it for their own benefit. Perhaps they had asked this very question of their teacher. So he had sent them to Jesus in order to get the answer.

Others see this inquiry as evidence of doubt on John's part. This rugged man of the outdoors is imprisoned in a dungeon. He had identified Jesus as the Messiah. But Jesus seems so indifferent to John's plight. Could John have been wrong about Jesus? So finally this doubt had so eaten at John's vitals that he sent his disciples to Jesus for an answer.

That there is a question in the Baptist's mind is quite evident. But are we justified to say that he harbored doubt in his mind? Certainly he had been positive in his identification of Jesus. And the John which we know was made of too rugged a material to wilt under adversity. At least this was Jesus' own estimate of him (cf. 11:7ff.). An examination of this passage reveals that John's problem was more one of perplexity than of doubt.

To understand fully the intent of John's question we must analyze his message in the light of the prophetic picture of the Messiah as found in the Old Testament. There we see two very clear and diverse portraits of the Messiah. In the Major Prophets He is seen both as a Suffering Servant and a reigning King. But in the Minor Prophets the Messiah is one of judgment, destroying evil and punishing the wicked.

We cannot say that John the Baptist was unaware of the Suffering Servant passages. For in John 1:29 he says of Jesus, "Behold the Lamb of God, which taketh away the sin of the world." He is definitely seen as the sin bearer. But an examination of John's preaching as recorded in Matthew shows that he was also cognizant of the Messianic picture found in the Minor Prophets. His "axe is laid unto the root of the trees" (3:10), and His "fan is in his hand, and he will throughly purge his floor ..." (3:12). So John's message was definitely one of judgment against evil (3:7-12).

Now John hears of the works of the Christ. He is going about Galilee teaching, preaching, healing, and raising the dead. When He encounters opposition He debates rather than destroys. And all the while John lies in a dungeon. Where is the judgment against evil? Surely the time is ripe for such. But he hears nothing which would indicate that it is forthcoming. Perhaps there is impatience along with the Baptist's perplexity.

And John is not alone in this condition. After almost two thousand years we see evil forces continue to stride with bloody boots throughout the earth. Doubting minds and impenitent hearts still reject the will and work of the Lord. We wonder why with a stroke of His might He does not chop down the unfruitful trees and cast the chaff into furnaces of fire. In effect, we are asking, "Art thou he that should come, or do we look for another?"

So when John asked this question it was one of impatience and perplexity. Actually he seems to be wondering if there is to be one or two Messiahs. That Jesus fell into the pattern of the picture given by the Major Prophets was quite evident. But is He also to fulfil the role depicted in the Minor Prophets, or do we look for another Messiah of a different kind for the ministry of judgment? We must not judge John from our vantage point but his. His question was not one of doubt but of perplexity. He was sincere in asking it. He was in search for an answer to a real problem, the solution of which was important to him and to us.

However, while we must not judge John from our vantage point, from it we can analyze his question for our own benefit. Sometimes we are so close to a problem that our very position makes a solution difficult. W. A. Criswell suggests that we can look at two stars in the sky. From our position they seem to be very near one another. When in reality they are millions of miles apart. So John saw the two pictures of the Messiah. From his point of understanding he expected them to be fulfilled simultaneously. When actually in God's plan they were two distinct ministries of the Christ, but separated by many years of history. Already over nineteen hundred years have intervened. How much longer it will be we do not know. But from our vantage point we know that in His first coming the Christ fulfilled the role of the Suffering Servant. At His second coming He will fulfil the role of the Judge.

Even in His first appearance there was the mingling of the two elements in His ministry. For alongside His teachings of truth and love, He also taught God's judgment with respect to sin. His very call to repentance implies a judgment. You may reject God's offer of salvation in Christ, and to all outward appearances not experience the wrath of God against sin. But judgment is promised and sure, if not in this life then in the world to come. In His first coming Christ is our Saviour; in His second coming He will be the Judge of all who refuse to believe in Him as Saviour and Lord.

It is well to note, however, that John did not allow his perplexity to fester into doubt. Through his disciples he brought it to Jesus. And as mist disappears before the morning sun, so did he receive the answer designed to dispel his problem.

Note carefully Jesus' method of dealing with John's problem. He did not debate issues or bemean him who wrestled with an honest question. He simply referred to His works. "Go and show John again those things which ye do hear and see" (v. 4). He pointed out those things which were evident to his natural senses. What do you hear? What do you see? These are the evidences which Jesus submits to each of us. The Chinese have a proverb that one picture is worth a thousand words. So Jesus gave to John a picture, not an argument.

And this is the most convincing argument of all. Jesus healed a blind man in Jerusalem. Later the Jews asked him to give an opinion about Jesus. "He answered and said, Whether he be a sinner or no, I know not: one thing I know, that, whereas I was blind, now I see" (John 9:25). The man was no theologian. But he had had an experience. And that experience was his gospel to unbelieving hearts. John did not dis-believe. But Jesus gave to him the answer to his perplexed mind and heart.

We are not to suppose however, that Jesus' answer was without prophetic significance. "The blind receive their sight, and the lame walk, the lepers are cleansed, and the deaf hear, the dead are raised up, and the poor have the gospel preached unto them" (v. 5). John the Baptist was the last and greatest of the prophets. We may be certain that his mind was filled with the prophetic message concerning the Christ. So in effect, Jesus reminded him of the prophecies of Isaiah, whose preaching centered in the Suffering Servant. Perhaps John's mind harked back to Isaiah 29:18-19. "And in that day shall the deaf hear the words of the book, and the eyes of the blind shall see out of obscurity, and out of darkness. The meek also shall increase their joy in the Lord, and the poor among men shall rejoice in the Holy One of Israel." Most assuredly he recognized Isaiah 61:1 in the words "and the poor have the gospel preached unto them" (cf. Luke 4:18-21).

So in effect Jesus is telling John to re-examine the Scriptures. Did not he himself say that Jesus is "the Lamb of God, which taketh away the sin of the world?" These people were bound in the prison house of sin—their bodies, minds, and spirits. Judgment can wait. In the meantime Jesus must break the power of sin. He must first reveal God as One of mercy and love. Man must be given the opportunity of fleeing from the wrath of God. The work which Jesus is doing is the work of the Suffering Servant who "hath borne our griefs and carried our sorrows" (Isa. 53:4).

Jesus concluded His answer with the words, "And blessed [happy] is he, whosoever may find no occasion of stumbling in me" (v. 6, author's translation). The word "blessed" is the same word used in the Beatitudes. So Jesus says that the one who finds no occasion of stumbling in Him by God's grace shall be sufficient within himself. There is a mild rebuke of John in this. But it was the tender exhortation of Him who understands and who never turns a deaf ear to a cry of need. We may well imagine that when John received the report of his disciples, there was fulfilled in him the prophecy of Isaiah 29:24. "They also that erred in spirit shall come to understanding, and they that murmured shall learn doctrine."

Perhaps as John's disciples departed there was a murmur of

disapproval in the crowd concerning John. So Jesus turned from His mild rebuke to an enthusiastic eulogy of His imprisoned herald (11:7-15). Evidently these people had seen and heard John in the Jordan valley. So Jesus actually rebuked them with a series of questions. Did they see in John a frail reed bending to every shift in the blowing wind (v. 7)? Instead he was a mighty oak standing against the evil wind currents of his day. Did they see in John a soft-living "yes man" to a sensuous king (v. 8)? His present plight was the result of his rebuke of some. He was a prisoner in Herod's dungeon, not a courtier in his court.

They had gone to hear John because they thought him to be a prophet of God (v. 9). But Jesus says that he is more than a prophet. The prophets had looked down the centuries, and had seen Messiah's day. But John himelf was the fulfilment of prophecy. For had not Malachi, the last of the Old Testament prophets, said, "Behold, I send my messenger before thy face, which shall prepare thy way before thee"? (v. 10; cf. Mal. 3:1). And had not Malachi concluded this verse with the very words, "Behold, he shall come, saith the Lord of hosts?" And Jesus is "the coming one" (cf. v. 3).

And then Jesus spoke in superlatives. "Verily I say unto you. ..." This was His way of introducing a very solemn utterance. "Among them that are born of women there hath not risen a greater than John the Baptist ..." (v. 11). What a tribute for any man to pay to another! But, most of all, what a tribute for the Lord Himself, who knows all men, to pay to one. We could wish that John's disciples had heard and carried back to him these words from his Lord. They would have been as balm to his soul. In all probability they would have been his last thoughts as the sword of the executioner descended to bring to an end such a life. It would have been as though before his arrival on the other side of Jordan John had heard the words "Well done, thou good and faithful servant: thou hast been faithful over a few things, I make thee ruler over many things: enter thou into the joy of thy Lord" (Matt. 25:21).

But then Jesus said a very strange thing. "... notwithstanding he that is least in the kingdom of heaven is greater than he" (v. 11). There is none born of women who is greater than John. Yet the least in the kingdom of heaven is greater than John! What did Jesus mean? Certainly He did not mean that John was not a part of the commonwealth of God. Rather He is saying that John is greater in character than all others. His function surpassed that of all others. There is to be but one forerunner of the Christ, and he was he. But the least in the kingdom of heaven is greater than John in privilege. A. T. Robertson says that he is the end of one age, "until John" (v. 13), and the beginning of the new era. All who come after John stand on his shoulders.

However, there seems to be another thought involved in Jesus' words. John had sent his disciples to Jesus with a question of perplexity. He could not understand the role which Jesus was now filling. But the "least in the kingdom of heaven" can now see the significance of that role. In the light of the cross and the resurrection, things which John did not live to see, the Christian knows the judgment of God upon sin in both its penalty and power. Furthermore, he is privileged to know that He who came once for redemption will come again for judgment. John saw the axe laid at the root of the tree. He saw the fan in Messiah's hand. But he did not see Him use them. But we know the end from the beginning. And we can wait. This is the patience of the saints.

Our Lord closes this particular trend of thought with a most difficult statement. "And from the days of John the Baptist until now the kingdom of heaven suffereth violence, and the violent take it by force'" (v. 12). The difficulty hinges upon the verb form "suffereth violence." It could be either a middle or a passive form. It appears in the New Testament only here and in Luke 16:16 where it reads, ". . . and every man presseth into it."

Some expositors would make these two statements one, with Matthew and Luke using them in different thought contexts. Thus they make Jesus to say in Matthew that only those enter into the kingdom who do so out of a sense of desperate need. They are anxious to enter and to pay whatever price is necessary to do so. This would seem to be Luke's meaning, and which would give his usage of the verb the middle force. But is this the sense in Matthew?

A. T. Robertson, following Zahn, suggests that Matthew uses the middle voice, meaning that the kingdom "forces its way" like a rushing mighty wind. Hort, seeing the middle voice, holds that Jesus means that since John the Baptist violent and impetuous throngs gather about Jesus. However, none of these seems to fit the context.

May we not see Matthew's form of the verb to be a passive voice? If so, it would mean that men seek to force the kingdom into a particular mold by violent means or meaning. The law and the prophets proclaimed the coming kingdom. It definitely had two facets, suffering and judgment. But by the time of John the Baptist the former aspect was largely lost in an emphasis upon the latter—

so that Israel looked for a Messiah who would be a mighty conqueror wreaking judgment upon the enemies of Israel. He would establish an earthly kingdom, and with Him Israel would rule the world. Even John the Baptist, seems to have had this idea predominantly in mind. So that when Jesus actually came no man really understood the true nature of the Messianic role or kingdom. Therefore, from the days of John the Baptist they had sought to force Jesus into a role which corresponded to their own ideas. Even John's latest question centered about this conflicting view. Because Jesus refused such a role the Jews rejected Him as their Messiah.

This statement of Jesus should not be interpreted as a criticism of John. Instead it was His effort to show His listeners the true role which He must fill and the true nature of the kingdom which He would establish. The facts are that the prophet Malachi (4:5) had said that Elijah the prophet would precede "the great and dreadful day of the Lord." But at what distance would he precede the Coming One? Jesus certifies that John the Baptist is the "Elijah" to whom Malachi referred (Matt. 11:4). But in the light of Jesus' reply to John's question, He also declares that the Coming One is to be both the Suffering Servant and the Judge respectively. He does not state the time element involved, although it is implied in the remainder of this chapter (cf. vv. 19-24).

In the meantime Jesus cites the work that He is doing as proof that He is truly the Christ. "He that hath ears to hear, let him hear" (v. 15).

The Unreasonableness of the Age (11:16-19)

In a brief section Jesus draws a conclusion based upon the foregoing incident. Whereas John was concerned about the two distinct pictures of the Christ, that generation seemed to care for neither. He likens it to "children sitting in the markets, and calling unto their fellows" (v. 16). This was a picture drawn from life. The "market" (*agora,* cf. Acts 17:17) was usually a street where people gathered to talk and trade. Such a place usually was a bedlam of noise both animal and human. And mingled with the din were the voices of children at play. Any visitor to the Near East today is familiar with such a scene. It is likely that Jesus as a boy had joined with other children to play in the market place in Nazareth while their elders visited and bargained. Such a scene may have been transpiring about Jesus as He spoke.

But the figure of "children" implies the impetuous and changing nature of Jesus' contemporaries. In the Greek text the word "fellows" is simply "others." But it is the same word used in Matthew 11:3, meaning others of a different kind. The "children" wanted to play. But the "others" did not. So the children said, "We have piped unto you, and ye have not danced; we have mourned unto you, and ye have not lamented" (v. 17). These two figures suggest a wedding and a funeral, a joyful and a sad occasion. In effect, they said, "We asked you to play wedding, but you did not want to play. We asked you to play funeral but you refused." It was not a question of which game to play. The "others" did not want to play at all. They were totally indifferent to the whole affair.

Jesus applies this figure to the reaction which His generation gave to both John the Baptist and to Him. "For John came neither eating nor drinking, and they say, He hath a devil. The Son of man came eating and drinking, and they say, Behold a man gluttonous and a winebibber, a friend of publicans and sinners."

John was not a social being, so they called him insane. Jesus was a social being, so they called Him immoral. Two such diverse approaches, yet they rejected both. The trouble was not with the two men. They just did not want to play. They were so absorbed in the spirit of the age that they were indifferent to the whole matter. This within itself shows that verse 12 does not mean that the multitudes were trying to force themselves into the kingdom of heaven.

However, there is a deeper meaning in Jesus' words. Actually they contrast the two pictures of the Messiah as found in the Old Testament prophets. While John was not the Messiah, there were some who thought that he might be (cf. John 1:19-20). We must interpret this Johannine passage in the light of the Synoptic gospels. Here we find a picture which definitely falls into the pattern of the Messianic role of judgment. And while John enjoyed a brief popularity, it soon waned so that now he is totally rejected by his generation. He is in prison, while life goes on its usual way. We may explain John's loss of popularity by his own choice to recede into the background in favor of Jesus (cf. John 3:28-30). The work of the forerunner was finished when the Christ appeared. However, we must not attribute such a motive to his generation. They lost interest in him when they learned that he was not the Messiah. After a brief response to John's call to repentance on the basis of a coming judgment, the people soon lapsed back into their accustomed ways. They did not want to play funeral.

On the other hand, Jesus came in the role of the Suffering Servant. He was concerned about people and their needs. He taught their minds, healed their bodies, rid them of demons, and raised the dead. Yet that generation's response to Him was more of a surface enthusiasm than that of a spiritual commitment. His enemies criticized Him for being a social being, especially with the needy and sinful. The masses saw His miracles as a hope for their worldly political ambitions. While they soon neglected John, the prophet of judgment, they also rejected Jesus when He made it clear that He would not fit into their role of a military Messiah (cf. John 6). They wanted no part in a Suffering Servant Christ. So while they did not want to play *funeral* with John, neither did they want to play *wedding* with Jesus. An unreasonable attitude, to be sure, but one which was born of their indifference and pre-occupation with other things.

However, this attitude is not confined to the first century. It is characteristic of every age. Men are indifferent to the gospel of judgment. They take lightly the gospel of redemption. Why? Because they simply have no interest in either game, funerals or weddings.

During World War II the story was told of a meeting between Roosevelt, Churchill, and Stalin. When Stalin rejected proposal after proposal, he was asked to give a reason for his attitude. He replied with a story. One Arab refused to lend another Arab his rope, saying that he needed it to tie his camel. When the other Arab reminded him that he did not own a camel, he said, "I know. But when you do not want to lend your rope, one excuse is as good as another."

Finally, Jesus said, "But wisdom is justified of her children" (v. 19). So reads the King James Version. This is probably the correct reading in Luke 7:35, although some strong manuscripts there use "works" rather than "children." However, the best manuscripts of Matthew read "works." So Matthew reads, "But wisdom is justified by its works." Apparently this refers back to 11:5 where Jesus cites His works as proof of His Messiahship.

God's wisdom had planned the conduct of both John and Jesus. And His wisdom is justified by the results accomplished. God had a purpose for each, and each performed accordingly. "Ye shall know them by their fruits" (Matt. 7:16).

However, the theme running throughout this passage centers in the two pictures of the Messiah. So the ultimate meaning of Jesus' words must be found in that context. In God's wisdom the Christ is to be both Suffering Servant and Judge. And Jesus is saying that time will justify both facets of His work. A. T. Robertson notes that "is justified" is a timeless aorist tense. So whether in the first century, in the twentieth, or in the entire scope of history God's wisdom is justified or set right in the overall ministry of His Christ.

In effect, Jesus is saying that time will tell. Men may reject either one or both views of the Christ. The Johns may be perplexed, and generations may be indifferent. But the play is not over. We must not judge the play by one scene or even one act. For when history has run its course the Christ will appear in all of His glory, the Saviour now, but then the Judge. In the meantime we must trust in the wisdom of God. The fruits justify the claims of the Christ.

The Impenitence of Certain Galilean Cities (11:20-24)

At this juncture Jesus began "to upbraid the cities wherein most of his mighty works were done, because they repented not" (v. 20). This is not a sudden outburst of wrath on the part of Jesus. It is wrath, to be sure, and shows that the Suffering Servant can also impart judgment. But it is a wrath mingled with sorrow. For the word which Jesus used (*ouai*) may denote either pain or displeasure. It is translated as both "woe" and "alas."

But if we see this only as an expression of pain or displeasure, both of which are present, we miss the intent of the passage. Actually Jesus is continuing His answer to the question brought to Him by John's disciples. Although they have departed, Jesus uses this opportunity to teach those who remained. He is still setting forth evidence that He is the Messiah. For, in effect, He is saying that He is not only the Suffering Servant, but He is the Judge also. As the former, Jesus performed "mighty works" or miracles in Chorazin, Bethsaida and Capernaum. But they "repented not." So now He is the Judge who foretells their judgment both in history and at the end of the age (vv. 21, 23).

We have no record of Jesus' ministry in Chorazin. But He doubtless did many mighty works in cities and villages of Galilee and elsewhere of which we have no record (cf. John 20:30; 21:25). We do know about Bethsaida (cf. Mark 8:22ff.) and Capernaum (cf. Mark 1-2). The point is that they did not repent after seeing the "works" of the Suffering Servant. Thus they will know the punishment of the Judge. They have already been judged in history. There is absolutely no trace of Chorazin today. The site of Bethsaida is disputed. And Capernaum, a once mighty city, is nothing but a small village which is an attraction to tourists. The word "hell" in Matthew 11:23 is "Hades," the realm of the dead. A city which once enjoyed dreams of grandeur truly has been brought down to the abode of the dead.

But that is not all. There still awaits the final judgment when the Christ will sit on His throne of judgment. At that time it will be more tolerable for Tyre and Sidon than for Chorazin and Bethsaida (v. 22). The fate of Capernaum will be worse than that of Sodom, one of the most wicked cities in the ancient world (v. 24). Its very name has become the name of one of the worst of sins, "sodomy."

However, here we must think in terms of the inhabitants of these cities, not so much acreage and stone. Cities and nations are judged within the context of history. Their inhabitants may, and do, suffer judgments in time. But their final judgment will come at the end of the age. And at that time citizens of these cities who rejected Christ will receive a greater judgment than will the citizens of these Old Testament cities who never knew Him. Why will this be so? Because they sinned against the greater privilege. They were indifferent to their opportunity.

It is a great privilege to be confronted with Christ. But it is also a great responsibility. And the woes pronounced by Jesus upon these cities apply to any city, nation, or individual who sins against the privilege of being confronted with Christ, His gospel, and His claims.

So the lesson contained in these verses (20-24) is that we may be indifferent to Christ. We may sin against our privilege. But that does not alter His person. He is still the Christ. He is both Suffering Servant and Judge. If we reject Him as the former, nevertheless, we must face Him as the latter. For the day will come when "at the name of Jesus every knee should bow . . . and every tongue should confess that Jesus Christ is Lord, to the glory of God the Father" (Phil. 2:10-11). Some will have done so willingly and joyfully. But even those who refuse Him, by the power of His might will be forced to acknowledge that Jesus who lived among men was the Christ and is the Lord of all. Those in heaven will praise Him as Lord. Those in hell will be forced to admit that He is Lord.

So Jesus said to His listeners, "The final judgment will be an eternal testimony that I am the Christ of God, both Suffering Servant and Judge." Happy are those who acknowledge Him as such now!

The Response of the "Babes" (11:25-30)

Jesus concludes this teaching session with a prayer (vv. 25-26), a declaration (v. 27), and an invitation (vv. 28-30). Some expositors prefer to regard this section as being entirely removed from that which precedes. But to do so is to miss its meaning. For the thought flows naturally from the former into the latter as great music rises to a grand crescendo.

It is so natural that "at that time" Jesus should burst forth in prayer. John is perplexed, the generation is unreasonable, and the cities are indifferent. Any other person would have been tempted to complain and to give up. But not so with Jesus. Instead He prays, He worships. What a lesson for everyone who meets with the same attitudes as they try to serve Him!

What did Jesus pray? He did not complain to God or denounce men. He praised God "because thou hast hid these things from the wise and prudent, and hast revealed them unto babes" (v. 25). It seemed good in God's sight to do so (v. 26). Literally, "It was wellpleasing in thy sight." Weymouth translates it, "For such has been thy gracious will." And Jesus praises the Father that His will has been done.

Two groups of people Jesus mentions in this prayer: the wise and prudent and the babes. The "wise" are those who possess natural ability and intellect, and who place their entire emphasis upon knowledge. The "prudent" are those who place things side by side, and through reason draw a conclusion on the basis of the evidence. In this context they had placed the two pictures of the Christ alongside one another, had reasoned from the evidence, and had drawn a conclusion based upon their knowledge.

But they had limited evidence. They did not see the end from the beginning. They drew their conclusion only from what they saw, not from the infinite wisdom of God. And, even so, they looked at the evidence through prejudiced eyes. The Christ must behave according to their own pattern, or else He was not the Christ. It is no wonder that they came out with the wrong answer.

Is not this the trouble with much scientific and theological thinking today? It is one thing to be a scientist. It is another thing to be a Biblical theologian. It is one thing to be a philosopher. But when the scientist endeavors to subject God to a purely scientific examination, difficulty ensues. And when a philosopher seeks to apply his speculative processes to theology, the result is the same. There are some things which do not submit themselves to the laboratories of science, for instance, love. The deepest elements of truth cannot be *placed side by side,* in order to draw a conclusion. Not within the realm of man's limited knowledge, at least. We simply must recognize that our evidence is incomplete, and that, at best, we are prejudiced beings. Until we possess all of the knowledge which is known to God, and can weigh its evidence in absolute sincerity, we are in no position to be dogmatic about the things of the Spirit.

On the other hand "babes" suggest those who are willing to be taught. They do not have all of the answers to life. The Greek root of this word means "not speaking," suggesting immaturity and a willingness to receive. Such a person realizes that he does not know everything, and so is willing to receive. Now Jesus says that these have received that which the wise and prudent have missed.

For what, then, did Jesus thank the Father? Not that the wise and prudent had failed to discern His true nature. But that spiritual truth is not limited to them. It is possible for them to know Him, but it is not by knowledge alone. The thing for which Jesus is thankful is that this great understanding of Him is not by knowledge but by revelation. Thus it is open to all who will receive it. And regardless of one's wisdom and prudence, he must come to Jesus as a *babe,* submitting himself to Him and opening his heart and mind to receive Him who is Truth. Many of the *wise* and *prudent* are also *babes.* And they are thrice blessed. Not simply because they are wise or prudent, but because they are babes. Revelation, not reason, is the means whereby fully we may comprehend the Christ.

It is on this basis that Jesus makes His declaration (v. 27). "All things are delivered unto me of my Father: and no man knoweth the Son, but the Father, neither knoweth any man the Father, save the Son, and he to whomsoever the Son will reveal him."

What are we to understand by "all things"? G. Campbell Morgan relates this to "these things" in verse 25. However, this does not seem to agree with the language. "These things" *(tauta)* refers to something specific. We have related it to the two pictures of the Christ. But "all things" *(panta)* is an inclusive word. It is sometimes used of the universe in its several parts. With the definite article *(ta panta)* it refers to the universe as a whole. So here, without the article, it would appear to include every single particle of knowledge and/or element which comprises the universe. Or we may regard it as involving the totality of the mystery of God as revealed in Christ. This passage (11:25-30) has a definitely Johannine note in it. So we can comprehend what Jesus is saying by reading John 1:1-18 (cf. Col. 1:15ff.; 2:9).

The thought suggested in this verse (v. 27) is the utter impossibility of comprehending Christ through wisdom and prudence alone. Such comprehension must come by divine revelation. The words "knoweth" are words for *full knowledge.* No man in his wisdom and prudence "fully knows" the Son. Only the Father possesses such knowledge. Neither does any man by wisdom and prudence "fully know" the Father. Only the Son does that. The only way that we can *fully know* God is through the revelation of the Son. "He that hath seen me hath seen the Father," said Jesus (John 14:9). Conversely no man can *fully know* the Son except through the revelation of the Father.

We can know some things about God and Christ through wisdom and prudence, provided that we bring them to God as "babes" willing to receive God's revelation. But we cannot know "all things" by the ingenuity of our intellects. However, the more of truth that we learn about the natural universe the greater Christ appears to us.

The achievements of the nuclear age have not destroyed faith in Christ. They have confirmed it. In the light of the atomic structure of the universe John 1:3 takes on added meaning. "The universe in its several parts came into being through him, and apart from him not one thing [one atom] came into being which has come into being" (author's translation). Furthermore, the marvels of the space age enhance the glory of Christ beyond our comprehension. As you think of the far reaches of outer space, think what this means to Colossians 1:16. "Because in the sphere of him the universe as a whole was created, the things seen [planets?] and the things not seen [atoms?]... the universe as a whole through him and unto him stands created" (author's translation). Thus Christ is the Creator of the universe from atoms to solar systems. It was created in the sphere of Him *(en);* He was the immediate Agent in creation *(dia);* He is the Goal of creation *(eis).*

Or even more to the point, read Colossians 1:17. "... and in the sphere of him the universe as a whole holds together" (author's translation). Paul is saying that Christ is the center of the universe. Science has long since shown that the sun is only the center of one solar system. One astronomer says that according to our best telescopes there now appear to be twelve quadrillion solar systems each with its own sun. A quadrillion is 1 followed by 15 zeroes! This certainly gives added credibility to Paul's astounding statement.

In our own galaxy there are about 100 billion stars stretching over a distance of 500 quadrillion miles. Already there have been observed over a billion other galaxies with a total of 100 sextillion (1 followed by 23 zeroes) stars now visible. Who can tell what even more powerful telescopes may reveal? We can only exclaim, "How great is Christ!"

But, even so, our wisdom and prudence have not touched the hem of the garment of Christ's magnitude. A full knowledge of

Him can come only through God's revelation. And that revelation centers in God's saving love.

Christ wants to reveal to us the Father. And he wants to be revealed to us by the Father. It is no wonder, then, that He breaks forth in the greatest of all invitations. "Come unto me, all ye that labor [in agonizing toil] and are heavy laden, and I will give you rest [I will refresh you or will rest you up]" (v. 28).

To whom is this invitation directed? To John and all the Johns who wrestle with honest perplexity. To every unreasonable age. To impenitent cities and men. To the "babes" who search for knowledge. Whatever your problem or need, Jesus says, "Come unto me ... and I will rest you up." Oh, what a glorious invitation to the multitudes, all ye that endure wearisome toil and bear heavy burdens!

And then Jesus tells us how to come. "Take my yoke upon you, and learn of me..." (v. 29). The words "take my yoke" were a Rabbinical figure to enroll under a teacher. To take Jesus' yoke is to become His disciple. This figure corresponds to being "born again." The second you are born again you become a child of God. Thereafter follows a life of growth and service. To enroll in Jesus' school is to commit yourself to Him as your Teacher. The second you submit to Him you become His pupil or disciple. Thus begins a life of growth in grace, knowledge, and service for Him. And those who come to Him will find that His yoke is easy (kindly), and the burden which He places upon us is light (v. 30). The load may be ever so heavy, but He is a meek and humble Teacher who understands our weaknesses and needs. And in His strength, "the toil of the road will seem nothing, when we come to the end of the way."

Thus Matthew closes the account of the authentication of the King. Men may be perplexed over His Messiahship, but He is authenticated by the works that He is doing. An unreasonable age may be indifferent to His claims, but His work through the ages will justify God's wisdom as seen in Him and the role which He fills. Cities and men may obstinately continue in unrepentance in the face of His mighty works, but His claims will be authenticated in the final judgment at the end of the age. But the "babes," ah, the "babes" will discover what the wise and prudent fail to see. For it will be revealed to them of the Father by the Holy Spirit. And all who come to Him in faith will know Him in an ever expanding knowledge and experience by His grace.

And He still calls us out of perplexity, indifference, and unrepentance. Will you hear? Will you heed? Only thus will you "find rest unto your souls" (v. 29).

Matthew 12

The Opposition to the King

From the early days of Jesus' ministry it was evident that a growing conflict would develop between Him and the religious leaders of the Jews. It was inevitable that the opposition on the part of the latter toward Jesus would reach a climax. And Matthew records it in this chapter.

To understand Matthew 12 we must recognize that among the Jews in His day the three most sacred things were the temple, the ceremonial law, and the institution of the Sabbath. But of the three the Sabbath was held in a unique regard. Other religions had their temples and sacrifices. But only the Jews had their Sabbath. So in a peculiar way it was the distinguishing feature of their religion as over against all others. It is understandable, therefore, that they would be most sensitive at this point.

At intervals throughout His ministry up to this time Jesus had shown His disregard for the Jews' misconception of these matters (cf. Matt. 9:11; John 2:13ff.). In response there had been criticisms and grumblings on the part of the Jewish leaders. But the issues came to a head with respect to the Sabbath day. John records a controversy over the practice of Jesus healing on the Sabbath in Jerusalem (chap. 5). According to Robertson's *A Harmony of the Gospels* the event in Matthew 12 followed shortly thereafter. And the fact that he first mentions the Sabbath in this chapter is significant. He uses it as the occasion to recount the growing opposition of the Pharisees toward Jesus. If we follow the chronology of Mark and Luke (which is likely correct), we find that the remainder of Chapter 12 actually came later in the Galilean ministry. But in keeping with his purpose the Evangelist relates them together as comprising the climax of this opposition.

It is important, therefore, that we shall follow carefully the events in Matthew 12. The chapter may be divided into (1) the conflict over the Sabbath; (2) the conflict over Jesus' power; (3) the demand for a sign; (4) a pathetic postlude.

The Conflict over the Sabbath (12:1-21)

Jesus and the Twelve, returning from Jerusalem to Galilee, were passing through a grain field (v. 1). Paths were left in the fields over which people might walk. The time was probably between Passover and Pentecost when the grain was ripening. And it was on a Sabbath day. The disciples were hungry, so they began to pluck the heads of grain, rub away the chaff, and eat the grain. According to Deuteronomy 23:35 this was permissible so long as they did not use a sickle to cut the grain.

Apparently this little company was accompanied by some Pharisees, who were ever on the alert for some basis upon which to criticize Jesus. So they said to Him, "Behold, thy disciples do that which is not lawful to do upon the Sabbath day" (v. 2). What they were doing was legal. Their charge of illegality was with reference to the day on which they did it. So it was not a question of morality but of Sabbath observance. And their charge was directed not against the disciples but against Jesus for permitting them to do so.

Now the question at issue is not Sabbath observance as such. One should find no grounds in this passage for ignoring Scriptural teachings to this effect. The point at issue had to do with the interpretation of the fourth commandment (cf. Exod. 20:8-12). This commandment simply forbade work on the Sabbath. But the Jewish interpreters had proceeded to define work. They laid down thirty-nine basic actions, and then subdivided these into literally hundreds of prohibitions. The end result in many cases was downright silliness.

For instance, a man could not carry a burden on the Sabbath. And a burden was defined as anything which weighed as much as two dried figs. Learned (?) debates were held as to what one could or could not do on the Sabbath. One favorite topic had to do with a man and his donkey. He arrived home just at sunset on Friday or the beginning of the Sabbath. Should he unload his donkey? To do so involved work for him. Not to do so meant work for the donkey. Should one eat an egg laid on the Sabbath? For the laying involved work for the hen. One should not draw a stick along the ground, for that was plowing. A woman should not look in a mirror on the Sabbath. She might see a grey hair and be tempted to pluck it out. That was regarded as work.

More to the point of our study, the Jews interpreted the law to forbid reaping, threshing, winnowing of grain, and the preparation of food on the Sabbath. Thus in their sight the disciples were guilty of Sabbath-breaking on all four counts. To the Jews plucking a few heads of grain was *reaping;* rubbing out the grain in their hands was *threshing;* blowing the chaff from the grain was *winnowing;* and the overall was a *preparation of food!* It is against such a background that we must view Jesus' reply to His critics.

Thoroughly did our Lord refute their position. The Pharisees regarded their Scriptures as law, prophets, and writings (historical books, Psalms, Proverbs, etc.). So in answering them Jesus swept aside their meticulous rules to get back to authoritative sources. First, He cited the *writings.* David and his men had eaten the sacred shewbread in order to appease hunger (vv. 3-4; I Sam. 21:1ff.). Second, He cited the *law* (v. 5). Numbers 28:9-10 commanded the priests to work on the Sabbath as they made sacrificial offerings. Third, He cited the *prophets* (v. 7). Hosea 6:6 says that God desires mercy and not sacrifice. And in each of these runs the theme that human need takes precedence over a mere letter interpretation of the law. Jesus did not in any sense discredit the law. Rather He interpreted it in the light of the basic Biblical teaching of the infinite worth and dignity of human personality before God.

Furthermore, in addition to these three citations Jesus set forth two principles. He is greater than the temple (v. 6). He is the Lord of the Sabbath (v. 8). So, in effect, Jesus struck at the Jews' mistaken attitude toward ceremonial law, (vv. 3-5, 7), the temple (v. 6), and the Sabbath (v. 8). But because the Pharisees had raised the Sabbath question He climaxed His answer by stating His true relationship to the Sabbath. In the Pharisees' eyes this would be an even greater claim than that with regard to the temple.

In claiming to be "Lord" (owner) of the Sabbath Jesus actually makes claim to deity itself. For the Sabbath had been given by Jehovah. It belonged to Him, therefore He was its Lord or Owner. Jesus makes the same claim for Himself. Since He gave the Sabbath in the first place, He can do with it as He wills. But note that in no sense did He devaluate it. Instead He rescued it from the death of the rote rules of men to breathe into it once again the life of the spirit. Mark 2:27 says, "The sabbath was made for man, and not man for the sabbath." The Pharisees had the opposite conception. What God intended for a blessing they had made a burden. So Jesus simply placed the Sabbath within the purpose of God.

It is well that we should re-emphasize the fact that these teachings of Jesus are not grounds for making the Lord's day into a holiday. An examination of the verses under consideration reveals that Jesus dealt with three specific things: deeds of necessity, worship, and mercy. A study of His own life reveals that He practiced what He preached. If we follow in His steps and obey His teachings the Sabbath will truly be a blessing and not a blight or burden.

The sequel to the event in the grain field took place in a synagogue on the same day (vv. 9-13). Present was a man with a withered hand. The Pharisees had no comeback for Jesus' reply with respect to the disciples' actions in the grain field. But apparently they expected Him to heal the man. So in the synagogue they confronted Him with a question. In effect they said, "So much for labor on the Sabbath. Is it lawful to heal on the sabbath days?" Since the Lord had answered them previously from the Scriptures, they were at a disadvantage to contradict Him. So they sought some other ground upon which "they might accuse him."

The question of healing on the Sabbath was also a much debated one among the Jews. Many rabbis held that healing was work, and, therefore, forbidden on the Sabbath. But in their discussions various positions evolved. It was generally agreed that where life was in danger treatment was permissible. But the question was as to what disease might be considered as endangering life. Obviously the man with the withered hand did not fall in this class. One position said that you could treat a person to keep him from getting worse but not to make him better. The Talmud said, "One who has a sore throat must not gargle with oil; but he may swallow oil (for food), and if that cures him, all right." It is evident that the Pharisees' question was both touchy and tricky.

In His reply Jesus argued from the lesser to the greater. He asked His critics which one of them, if he had a sheep to fall in a ditch on the Sabbath day, would not pull it out? There was even a division among the Jews at this point. Some rabbis held that you could make the sheep comfortable and feed it, but you could not take it out. But the general opinion was that you could take it out of the ditch.

Therefore, on that assumption Jesus added, "How much then is a man better than a sheep?" The answer was obvious. So Jesus concluded, "Wherefore it is lawful to do well on the sabbath day [s]." The outcome of such a conclusion is that if it is lawful to do good on the Sabbath, it would be sinful to do otherwise. Thus the Lord completely turned the tables on His critics. Had they answered in disagreement they themselves would have appeared in a bad light. Therefore they remained silent as Jesus healed the man before their very eyes.

When a man cannot answer with logic or some other authority, he has but one recourse short of agreement—violence. The Pharisees had no intention of agreeing with Jesus. So they left the synagogue, "and held a council against him, how they might destroy him" (v. 14). By "destroy" they meant "kill." Mark notes that they conferred with their hated enemies the Herodians, the champions of the house of Herod (3:6). What strange bedfellows! Yet they temporarily resolved their differences in their common hatred for Jesus. Already the Jewish rulers in Jerusalem had sought how they might kill Him (cf. John 5:18). And now the same plot spreads to Galilee. But it was the same crowd and the same plot. Like their fellow-conspirators in Jerusalem, the Pharisees and Herodians doubtless sought to justify their actions on the basis that Jesus broke their Sabbath regulations and claimed to be Lord of the Sabbath or God Himself. But their true reason was jealousy and fear that He would destroy their own position.

The irony of the entire matter is that these men, who had such great qualms of conscience about rubbing out a few grains of barley or healing a man on the Sabbath, would on that day plot the murder of One who did the will of God always. Consistency, thou art indeed a jewel!

Knowing their evil designs Jesus left the synagogue and went elsewhere. He was not afraid. But He will die, not according to the plots of men, but according to the purpose of God (vv. 15-21). As He went the multitudes followed Him, not the Pharisees. And He healed their diseases—on the Sabbath still. The carping critics may challenge His methods, but they will not stop His work. And it is ever thus!

The Conflict over Jesus' Power (12:22-37)

This event begins what is called the "Busy Day" in Jesus' ministry. It involves the material through Chapter 13, and, following Mark's chronology, the events found in Matthew 8:18, 23-34. But Matthew following his topical arrangement limits the present section to the former material.

Sometime after the Sabbath controversy Jesus healed a demon-possessed person who was dumb and blind (v. 22). The multitudes "were amazed" or "stood out of themselves." So much so that they asked, "Is not this the son of David?" (v. 23). This was definitely a Messianic title (cf. Matt. 21:9). In the Greek text this form of question invites a negative answer. But this merely shows the people's caution in the presence of the hostile Pharisees. The people definitely meant this to be a Messianic appellation. It is interesting to note the spiritual perception of ordinary people unless they are misled by some hostile, so-called theological authority. However, it should be noted that their concept of the Messiah was far-removed from its true meaning. Jesus Himself avoided this title since to His contemporaries it carried a nationalistic connotation.

But even this title the Pharisees denied to Jesus. For when they heard the people's question they replied, probably by whispering among themselves, "This [one] doth not cast out devils, but by Beelzebub the prince of devils" (v. 24). Note the Pharisees' contempt for Jesus. They did not call Him by name. They simply said, "This one" or "This fellow" (*houtos*). They could not deny the fact of the miracle, for it was witnessed by the crowd which followed Jesus. Their only recourse, other than to agree that Jesus was the son of David, was to claim that He worked by the power of Satan.

The title Beelzebub or Beelzebul was an adaptation of the words Baal-Zebub, the fly god of Ekron (II Kings 1:2-3, 6, 16). Baal was the pagan god of the Canaanites. The name means "lord." This was the god whose worship was brought into Israel by Jezebel. The combination of this name with *flies* was probably due to the fact that when this god of nature was in the ascendency, as seen in the growing season, Palestine was overrun by flies. Hence Baal-zebub, the fly god. In later years to show their contempt for this pagan god, the Jews attributed this name to Satan. So the Pharisees called him "the prince of demons" (*daimonia*). They likewise showed their contempt for Jesus and His work by saying that He worked miracles by the power of Satan.

It has been noted that they probably made this accusation in whispers or in an undertone so that Jesus would not hear them. Nevertheless Jesus "knew" their secret thoughts, and proceeded to answer them openly (v. 25). In a series of irrefutable examples Jesus showed the absolute unreasonableness of their charges.

First, if the charge of the Pharisees be true, then Satan is defeating himself. "Every kingdom divided against itself is brought to desolation; and every city or house divided against itself shall not stand" (v. 25). Jesus recognizes two distinct kingdoms, the kingdom of righteousness and the kingdom of evil. These are at war against one another. Now if Jesus casts out demons by Satan's power, Satan is fighting against his own kingdom. In verse 26 the definite article appears with "Satan" in both uses. Literally, "If the Satan the Satan is casting out, against himself he is divided." It is not Satan casting out another Satan, but Satan casting out himself. "How shall then his kingdom stand?" If this be the case then the Pharisees should be happy over this fratricidal war. Why then are they so unhappy?

Second, if Jesus' casting out demons was a work of Satan, by whom did the Pharisees' "children" claim to cast out demons? These "children" were the students of the Pharisees. At this time it was a common practice for the Jews to profess to cast out demons. Josephus tells of the curious, superstitious methods employed by these exorcists, such as using a remarkable root, with incantations which they claimed were handed down by Solomon. In Acts 19:13 we read of certain Jewish exorcists who thought that there must be a magical charm in the name of Jesus in which Paul worked miracles, and which they sought to use with tragic results for themselves.

Now Jesus does not authenticate the claims of these "children" of the Pharisees. He took their own false claims and by them threw them into a dilemma. For if their charges be true their own students shall be their judges. Either they themselves are in league with Beelzebub, or else their charges against Jesus are false. In either case they condemn themselves.

Third, if the Pharisees deny that they are in league with Beelzebub, then they must admit that Jesus is working by some other power. And the only other power available is that of the Spirit of God (v. 28). In order to get out of the dilemma into which Jesus has placed them, they are forced to admit that He works by the Spirit of God. If this be true, "then the kingdom of God is come unto you" (v. 28). The word "come" means to come beforehand or unexpectedly. In the aorist tense, as here, it suggests a sudden appearance. So "the kingdom of God is burst upon you."

Quite obviously this miracle was by a superhuman power. If not Satan's then it must be of God. And if it be of God, then it is God's kingdom triumphing over Satan's kingdom. If it be the victory of God's kingdom, then Jesus must be the King. Why then were the Pharisees opposing the kingdom of God and its King? If they were not acting in such a devilish manner one could almost feel sorry for them. They were really taking a logical thrashing.

Fourth, Jesus' very act proved that He was superior to Satan. "Or else how can one enter into a strong man's house, and spoil his goods, except he first bind the strong man? and then he will spoil his house" (v. 29). This parable is fraught with meaning. The "strong man" is Satan, suggesting his power. His "house" is the region which is subject to him, either the world generally or else the spirits of individual men. "Goods" (instruments) are the demons through whom he operates. The *binding* is the limit which has been placed upon his tyranny by Jesus' act of healing the demoniac. And "spoil his house" refers to the final victory which the King will achieve over the king of evil powers. The word "spoil" means to plunder thoroughly. Every soul which Jesus snatches from Satan's clutches is a spoil of the war which must end in total victory for the King.

We may well imagine that Jesus looked about at the multitude as He spoke the words in verse 30. They must choose sides. "He that is not with me is against me; and he that gathereth not with me scattereth abroad." Jesus throws down the gauntlet not only to the Pharisees but to the people as well. He recognizes the hopeless cleavage between Himself and the Pharisees. They have accused Him of being in league with Satan. With unanswerable logic He has proved otherwise. It is they who are in league with Satan. The struggle between the King and Satan is raging. In such a conflict there can be no neutrality. Either the people are with Him or else they are against Him. Which shall it be—Christ or Satan, Christ or Pharisees? The harvest is being garnered. Either they are helping to gather it in, or else, with the Pharisees, they are scattering it to the four winds. The choice is theirs as to the side on which they shall be.

And the challenge still stands. One cannot be indifferent to the claims of Christ. The struggle between good and evil offers no neutral grounds. To claim neutrality is to oppose the King. For His conflict with Satan involves the issue of life or death. If we are not aligned with the Lord we are defeating the very purpose of His redemptive mission. So our indolence becomes opposition. Broadus comments that "if we are not yielding Christ our whole heart, we are really yielding him nothing."[5]

At this point Jesus spoke some of the darkest words which ever fell from His lips. And as we consider them we should remember that they are not the words of some sadist. They were uttered by Him who is infinite in love and mercy. But they are the words of the King, and therefore carry divine authority.

"All manner of sin and blasphemy shall be forgiven unto men: but the blasphemy against the Spirit ["Ghost" in KJV; "Holy" not in best manuscripts, but genuine in verse 32] shall not be forgiven unto men" (v. 31). Thus Jesus spoke of what is called the unpardonable sin. "Blasphemy" means "slander" or "defamation." It comes from the verb *blasphēmeō* which means to speak slander-

[5] *Commentary on Matthew,* American Baptist Publication Society, Philadelphia, 1886, p. 27.

ously or insultingly so as to defame one's character or reputation. Note that Jesus said that "all sin and blasphemy shall be forgiven" except the blasphemy of the Spirit. Of course this forgiveness is based upon repentance and faith. But for the blasphemy of the Spirit there is no promise of forgiveness.

Naturally the question arises as to the nature of this sin which is unpardonable. There are many popular but false assumptions concerning it. A man in a fit of anger blasphemes, and thinks that he has committed this sin. Some hold it to be profaning the name of God. Others regard murder as unpardonable. Again, rejecting Christ until death is so regarded. Even some Christians occasionally feel that they are guilty of this sin. Let it be said that a Christian cannot commit the unpardonable sin. For he is already saved by grace through faith in Christ, and has been sealed by the Holy Spirit (cf. Eph. 1:13-14). Nor do the conditions found in the context fit any other of these sins.

Jesus specifically said that "a word against the Son of man... shall be forgiven" (v. 32). It is the speaking against the Holy Spirit which is unpardonable "neither in this world [age], neither in the world to come." Here Jesus used the word "Holy" in connection with "Spirit" as though to contrast Him with the *evil* spirit as seen in Satan.

In order to understand this word of Jesus let us reconstruct the scene which brought it forth. The Lord had just performed a deed which unmistakably involved a supernatural spiritual power. The people saw it, and asked, "Is this the son of David?" They inferred that the miracle was one by the power, or Spirit, of God. But the Pharisees, seeing the same evidence said that it was wrought by the power, or spirit, of Beelzebub (Satan). The deed itself was a good one, and only God is good (cf. Mark 10:18). Yet the Pharisees attributed this good deed to Satan who is altogether evil. Therefore, if they were correct then this deed itself was an evil one. So in any case they called good evil and evil good.

Now in this light let us examine the nature of this sin. First, it was not a sin of impulse. The Pharisees did not impulsively utter these words of blasphemy. They came as the result of a long process of opposition to Jesus and His work. Second, it was a sin of knowledge. They did not speak these words in ignorance. The people had the same knowledge, and attributed the miracle to the power of God. The Pharisees attributed it to Satan. Third, it was a sin of deliberate choice. They had accompanied Jesus and had observed His work. Repeatedly they had spoken against Him. But now they are faced with a choice. Before their very eyes a miracle has been performed. They cannot deny the fact. They can only decide as to its source. They have but two choices, the Holy Spirit of God or else the evil spirit of Satan. Therefore, despite the evidence that a good work had been performed upon this demoniac, they chose to attribute it to the evil spirit and not to the Holy Spirit. So crusted were their hearts in their opposition to Jesus that they had lost the power to discern between good and evil. Or else discerning it, they with full knowledge chose the evil and rejected the good. In the words attributed to Satan by John Milton in *Paradise Lost* (Book IV, line 108) they said,

> So farewell hope, and, with hope, farewell fear,
> Farewell remorse; all good to me is lost.
> Evil, be thou my good."

Why is blasphemy against the Son of man pardonable, but blasphemy against the Holy Spirit unpardonable? Many years ago B. H. Carroll stated it in this fashion. If you blaspheme against God the Son, the Spirit remains. But if you blaspheme the Spirit, nothing remains. You are left without God and without hope, both in this world and in the world to come. It is true that the Holy Spirit is God revealing the Son in His saving ministry, convicting of sin, drawing the sinner to the Saviour, and effecting regeneration. Therefore, if one rejects this ministry of the Spirit, there can be no forgiveness or salvation.

But there is even a further word to be said. It is clear in Matthew 12:28 that the Spirit of God represents Deity in general. Therefore, to reject the Spirit is to reject Deity. It is to shut one's life to God altogether, and to throw one's life open to Satan and his evil designs. *Rejecting* the Spirit is not to be confused with *resisting* the Spirit. One may resist the Holy Spirit for a time as did Saul of Tarsus. Saul honestly did not believe that Jesus was the Son of God. But when on the Damascus road he was confronted with the living Christ, he ceased to resist the Spirit to become His most powerful instrument in evangelism. But one should not presume upon the mercy of God. For so long as one resists the Spirit he is outside of God's grace. Every refusal of His convicting work leaves him more resolutely determined against the Lord. Who can tell when, like the Pharisees, this may evolve into a full and final rejection of the Holy Spirit?

Is it possible to blaspheme the Holy Spirit today? Some hold that it is not, since they claim that this sin was confined to the age of miracles or the apostolic age. But is not the new birth and the subsequent development in grace the greatest of all of Jesus' miracles? In that light we would hold that this sin is possible today. If one sees this mighty work of God being done, yet refuses it for himself, is he not in effect saying that it is not a good work but an evil one? If so, is it not the work of Satan and not of the Spirit of God? And even if one acknowledges it as the good work of God yet deliberately chooses *evil* as his *good,* is he not repeating the sin of the Pharisees? Who can tell when this moment of final and fatal decision will come for him?

Let it be said that if you think that you have committed the unpardonable sin, you have not done so. Your very consciousness of sin is evidence that the Holy Spirit is still convicting you of sin. It is far more likely that the person who repeatedly claims that he has no sin from which to be forgiven has committed this sin (cf. I John 1:10). Of course, the person who continues to resist the Holy Spirit until death is guilty of *an* unpardonable sin, for there is no pardon for the unregenerate in the life beyond (cf. John 3.18). But this is not *the* unpardonable sin of which Jesus spoke. He was speaking of a sin committed in life and for which there is no forgiveness *"in this age"* (author's italics) as well as in that which is to come. It is the sin of deliberate choice and in the light of full knowledge whereby one fully and finally rejects God from his life and chooses the will and way of Satan.

John A. Broadus summarizes it in these words. "The conditions, then, under which this unpardonable sin of blasphemy against the Spirit of God is committed, are (1) that there shall be a work manifestly supernatural, unmistakably the work of God and not of man, and (2) that one shall, in determined and malignant opposition, insultingly ascribe to Satan this which he knows to be the work of God."[6]

It is the author's conviction that such is possible today. For to see the work of regeneration and all that it entails in others, to recognize it as the work of God, and yet to insult the Holy Spirit by refusing it fully and deliberately as though it were a work of Satan, is "in determined and malignant opposition, insultingly [to] ascribe to Satan this which he knows to be the work of God." How shall one be certain that he will never commit this sin? By fully, willingly, and immediately surrendering himself to God in Christ through the power of the Holy Spirit. For

---

[6] *Ibid,* p. 272.

There is a time, we know not when,
  A point we know not where,
That marks the destiny of men,
  For glory or despair.

There is a line, by us unseen,
  That crosses every path;
The hidden boundary between
  God's patience and His wrath.
—Joseph A. Alexander

A word needs to be said about the closing verses of this section (vv. 33-37). The nature of a man's character will be revealed by the fruits of his life (vv. 33-35). And this is especially true of one's words. The unpardonable sin was one of words, but words which revealed a malignant character. An "idle word" is an ineffective, useless word. This does not refer to light, pleasant conversation. For such may be most effective and useful in one's daily concourse. The power of speech is one of the most distinctive things about a man as over against an animal. It has power for either good or evil. The warning of Jesus is that every word which we speak is remembered of God. And we shall face each one of them in the judgment as revealing our true natures. Of course speech will not be the only basis of judgment. Words will be but one evidence of the character which we bring to the judgment seat. Men are saved or lost by the relationship which they have with Jesus Christ. If our words, like those of the Pharisees, reveal that we have rejected Christ, they will be one evidence of our condemnation. Conversely if they reveal that we are His, they will be one evidence of that fact. In this sense shall we be "justified" or "condemned" by our words.

But one other thought is involved in this teaching. There is the basis of rewards for the Christian. Idle, useless, ineffective words will be as works that are burned up (cf. I Cor. 3:15). But useful, effective words will enhance the glory that shall be ours. How carefully we should guard and weigh our words!

The Demand for a Sign (12:38-45)

The Scribes and Pharisees sought to counterattack against the onslaught of the King. "Master [teacher], we would see a sign from thee" (v. 38). They chose to ignore the sign which had been given, and which they had attributed to the power of Satan. Which is but one evidence of the malignancy in their souls. Bruce calls this demand, "impudent, hypocritical, insulting." Nevertheless they asked for a "sign" as proof of His deity and His right to speak as He had just done. In Matthew 16:1 they will repeat this request in conjunction with the Sadducees. There they will ask for a "sign *from heaven*" (author's italics). This addition was probably due to the Sadducees who did not believe in the supernatural (cf. Matt. 16:1-4).

Jesus refused the request, saying that the only sign which they would receive would be "the sign of Jonas" (v. 40). This sign was Jesus' resurrection from the dead. As Jonah was in the belly of the great fish for "three days and three nights" so would the Son of man be in the heart of the earth or tomb.[7] But even this sign they will refuse (cf. Matt. 28:11ff.). Therefore, the men of Nineveh will condemn Jesus' contemporary generation (cf. v. 39) in the judgment. For they believed and repented at the preaching of Jonah. "And, behold, a greater than Jonas is here" (v. 41), but they do not believe Him. Furthermore, that generation will be condemned also by "the queen of the south" (cf. Sheba). For she came a great distance to hear the wisdom of Solomon. "And, behold, a greater than Solomon is here," but they do not hear Him.

The word "condemn" (*katakrinō*) is used in the papyri as a legal term meaning to find guilty and pronounce sentence. The punishment resulting from the sentence is expressed by *katakrima.*[8] So the actions of the Ninevites and the queen of Sheba will serve as evidence to convict that faithless generation.

From this general reply to the Pharisees Jesus became more specific as He relates a parable in which He condemns the emptiness of the teachings of the Pharisees. He is still thinking of that generation which is the product of the religious emptiness so characteristic of the Pharisees as a group.

An unclean spirit comes out of a man. The coming out may be voluntary or forced. But in this case the latter seems to be true. So disembodied the spirit wanders through "dry places, seeking rest, and finding none" (v. 43). This figure reflects the popular view that demons inhabited desert places until they found an opportunity to inhabit the bodies and souls of men, and to afflict them with the fever and burning thirst of madness. But when the evil spirit found no rest, or a place of contentment, he said, "I will return into my house from whence I came out" (v. 44). Notice that he considered the person *his* dwelling place. Satan is ever the intruder, but in his deceit claims man for his own. When the

---

[7] Some are disturbed by this time element. For a discussion of it see Matthew 28:1.

[8] See Hobbs, *Preaching Values from the Papyri,* Baker, Grand Rapids, 1964, pp. 69ff.

spirit returned he found the man's life "empty, swept, and garnished" (v. 44). The emphasis is upon the word "empty." It was ever so clean and seemingly beautiful, but it was *empty*.

An examination of these words is most revealing. The words "swept" and "garnished" are both perfect passive participles. The former (*sesarōmenon*) means to be swept or cleansed with a broom. The latter (*kekosmēmenon*) comes from the verb *kosmeō* which means to arrange, set in order, to adorn or decorate. It is the word from which comes the English word "cosmetics." But the word "empty" (*scholazonta*) is a present participle of *scholazō,* meaning to be unemployed, to be at leisure, or to be empty.

Now note the first two words. The passive voice means that someone else did these things to the man's life. And the perfect tense suggests a finished work or a thorough job. But the last word, in the present tense, says that his life kept on being unemployed, at leisure, or empty. Whoever swept and garnished his life failed to put anything in it to take the place of the evil spirit which had departed. So if we give this phrase a free interpretative translation it reads, "Someone did a thorough job of sweeping the house clean with a broom, arranging the furniture in order, even decorating and adorning it, but leaving it unoccupied, unused, and empty." What a text for a sermon on the tragedy of a religion which has an outward form but no inner vitality!

The sad ending of the parable is that this evil spirit found "seven other spirits more wicked than himself" (v. 45), and the eight took up their abode in the man's life. So he was worse off than at the beginning when he was possessed of only one evil spirit.

This parable was a pointed condemnation of the Pharisees and their religious system. Indeed, it is a recital of Israel's history and a prophecy as to her end. Notice that Jesus concludes the parable with the words "Even so shall it be also unto this wicked generation," which in verse 39 He has described as "evil and adulterous." Adultery in this sense is used in the Bible for idolatry. And it is in this thought that we find the key to the parable.

The man possessed of an evil spirit suggests Israel's sin of idolatry which beset her from the Exodus until the Babylonian captivity. During the Exile she was to all intents and purposes cured of such. The evil spirit moved out. It was in the period immediately following the return from the Exile that the Pharisees came into being as a religious sect. At the beginning they rendered a valuable service among the Jews. Through their zeal for Jehovah and the law it seemed that idolatry was banished from among the Jewish people forever. They did a thorough job of sweeping the house clean of all pagan debris. Through their emphasis upon the Law and their meticulous teaching of it they arranged every religious truth in order; they divided and subdivided every truth *ad infinitum*. They even adorned, decorated, or cosmetized the whole with their rite and ceremony and an outward show of hypocrisy. But in the process they left the house of Israel empty.

What is the result? A far more insidious idolatry and evil replaced the demon who was expelled: the worship of the material, pride, prejudice, arrogance, hate, self-righteousness, and spiritual blindness. Jesus sees the end in the frightful war with Rome which will end in the destruction of Jerusalem and the nation. One has but to read Josephus' account of the atrocities, crimes, fanaticism, and suffering which accompanied this event to comprehend the meaning of Jesus' words, "The last state of that man is worse than the first."

So our Lord charges the Pharisees with the very condition which will soon come to fruition in such a bloody ordeal. The crowning act of their emptiness will be their rejection of the greatest of all "signs" as to the identity of the King whom they have so recently charged with being in league with Satan. And the greater tragedy is that they took their generation down with them! This should be warning enough for all who propose to teach for God.

A Pathetic Postlude (12:46-50)

Even while Jesus was delivering His solemn discourse against the Pharisees, His mother and brethren had been standing outside the house, desiring to speak to Him (v. 46). They were unable to get inside because of the crowd (cf. Luke 8:19). Who were these "brethren"? Matthew names them in 13:55. Some, wishing to perpetuate the virginity of Mary, insist that they were either cousins or else children of Joseph by a former marriage. But beyond this *wish* there are no grounds for believing other than that they were children of Joseph and Mary, born after the virgin birth of Jesus. That they entered into normal marriage relations after Jesus' birth is strongly implied in Matthew 1:25. Furthermore, Luke 2:7 calls Jesus her "firstborn son" (*prōtotokon*; not genuine in Matt. 1:25, but implied). Had he wished to call Him her "only begotten" son he could have used *monogenē* (cf. John 3:16).

Why had they come? Some identify them with the "friends" in Mark 3:21 who thought that Jesus was "beside himself." And this is a possible identification, although it is difficult to harmonize this with Mark 3:31 where they are specifically mentioned. They may have been standing outside throughout the incidents recorded in Matthew 12:22-44. It is also possible that they are separate from the "friends," but had heard the reports which were going about. Since Jesus' brethren did not yet believe on Him (cf. John 7:5), His zealous work could have been an embarrassment to them. Did Mary share this feeling, or was she drawn into it for the sake of family harmony? Perhaps Mary herself had proposed this action in order to get her son away from the stress and strain of the multitudes and the rising enmity of His foes. Or is all of this mere conjecture? From the record itself their only purpose could have been a desire to visit with Him.

At any rate when Jesus heard of their presence (Matt. 12:47) He asked, "Who is my mother? and who are my brethren?" (v. 48). And then turning to His disciples He said, "Behold my mother and my brethren! For whosoever shall do the will of my Father which is in heaven, the same is my brother, and sister, and mother" (vv. 49-50). At an earlier time Jesus had inferred to His mother that she must not presume on her relationship to Him (cf. John 2:4). Now He extends this to include all of His earthly family. From His birth until the beginning of His public ministry Jesus lived in the normal relationship of a son and half-brother. But from that time on He deprived Himself of family ties to give Himself fully to His mission. Thereafter, the tie with Jesus was one of faith in Him. This bond constitutes a far more intimate fellowship than that of family itself. If we would "do the will of my Father" we must experience the same.

So even the members of Jesus' earthly family group are no longer to see Him as *son* and *brother*. He is to be *Saviour* and *Lord*. When James, Jesus' half-brother, wrote his epistle, he did not lay claim to any human relationship to Jesus. He referred to himself as "a servant of God and of the Lord Jesus Christ" (1:1).

When Jesus took from Mary and her children the privilege of human family ties, He gave to them, and to us, a relationship far greater and richer—that of Saviour and Lord. For all who receive Him become "sons of God" (John 1:12), "heirs of God, and joint-heirs with Christ" (Rom. 8:17).

Matthew 13

The Teaching of the King

The King had been teaching in the house where the object of His words were the hostile Pharisees. They had clearly shown that they were not open to receive His truth. In fact this attitude was evident in that generation generally. So Jesus began a new departure and a new method in teaching. Since men generally had refused to hear Him, He began to concentrate more and more on the Twelve. And He used a method of teaching, the parable, which was designed to set forth truth clearly, but only to those who could discern it.

Therefore, the Lord took the Twelve and went from the house to the seaside (v. 1). But the crowds followed. They so pressed upon Him that He finally sat in a boat where all might see and hear (v. 2). But even though the multitudes heard His words, the teaching was primarily for the Twelve.

It is of interest to note that the parables in Matthew 13 all deal with the kingdom of heaven. In keeping with the spirit of the age the disciples thought of an earthly kingdom brought into being by a mighty fiat of the Messiah. It was so necessary that they should understand its true nature and manner of growth. Already Jesus was looking toward the end of His earthly ministry. It is something over a year, possibly fifteen months, before that time. So we shall see the King concentrating more and more upon teaching the Twelve. And He will employ the parabolic method in an increasing fashion.

As we consider the teaching contained in Matthew 13 we note (1) the method and purpose of teaching; (2) the sowing of the kingdom; (3) the social relation of the kingdom; (4) the growth of the kingdom; (5) the value of the kingdom; (6) the teachers in the kingdom.

The Method and Purpose of Teaching (13:10-17)

We shall begin where the disciples did. Even while Jesus delivered His first parable they were wondering as to His reason for doing so. When the first parable was finished they came to Him (they were probably in the boat also) and asked, "Why speakest thou unto them in parables?" (v. 10). Heretofore He had used parables. But on the whole His teaching had been more forthright as He plainly declared the nature of the Kingdom and called men to repentance. Why use the parabolic method indeed?

What is a parable? The word "parable" (*parabolē*) means "a casting alongside." In the Old Testament it translated *mashal,* a proverb. In a sense a proverb may be a condensed parable, even as a parable may be an expanded proverb (cf. John 16:25, 29 where "proverb" suggests "parable"). But in the New Testament the parable takes on the nature of a story of varying length. It was one of the favorite methods of teaching by Jesus, and He used it with consummate skill.

Now we must not confuse a parable with a fable, a favored method of teaching with certain Greeks (cf. Aesop and Phaedrus). A fable did not necessarily adhere to the realm of possibility. But parables are true to life. While the parables told by Jesus may not have happened, they could have. In fact, the very point of a parable was to take some situation which was found in everyday life and *cast it alongside* a spiritual truth in order to enable the hearers to comprehend the latter. It takes on something of the nature of an illustration in modern discourse. The best illustration is one which relates incidents, either real or imaginary, which depict life incidents common to the hearers. This Jesus did with superlative skill as He drew lessons from the ordinary everyday happenings of His contemporaries.

A parable has been called "an earthly story with a heavenly meaning." Someone said that a parable is the handle by which we pick up a spiritual truth, and take it home with us. That this is true may be seen in the abundance of Jesus' teachings which are best remembered because of their relation to one of His parables. It is always necessary to relate the related incident to the spiritual truth which it is designed to convey.

This is the essence of Jesus' answer to the disciples' question. "Because it is given [has been given] unto you to know the mysteries of the kingdom of heaven, but to them [the Pharisees and the multitude] it is not given [has not been given]" (v. 11). The word "mystery" (*mustērion*) was a common one in the religious thought of that day. The mystery-religions of the east had spread over the Roman empire as the result of the religious vacuum which existed. Among other things they claimed to have certain *mysteries* or secrets known only to the initiates of those religions but unknown to outsiders. So the word "mystery" came to be used in the Christian sense of those elements of divine truth which from the beginning had been hidden in the mind of God, but which were now in Christ and the gospel revealed to those who were capable of comprehending them (cf. Eph. 3:4-5). Jesus was now revealing some of these secrets concerning the kingdom of heaven.

It is in the above light that we can understand the words "has been given" in verse 11. This sudden adoption of the parabolic method of teaching was not a deliberate attempt on Jesus' part to hide His teaching from the Pharisees and the multitude. Such would be a contradiction of all that we know about Him. He did not come to hide the light of truth but to reveal it. However, the words "has been given" suggest some prior action of God which is now being carried into effect. It "has been given" to certain ones to understand truth who have the capacity to do so. Also this ability "has not been given" to those who shut their minds and hearts against the truth. "Mysteries" were known only to those who were initiates of the mystery-religions. The "mysteries of the kingdom of heaven" were/are comprehensible only to those who were in the kingdom or who had/have yielded themselves to the King. And while the parables were delivered primarily for the Twelve, they would also be understood, in measure, by others who had given themselves to the King. Of course, as we shall see even the disciples had to ask for explanations, but the light of truth would gradually filter through to those who possessed the capacity to receive it.

Jesus uttered this thought when He said, "For whosoever hath, to him shall be given, and he shall have more abundance: but whosoever hath not, from him shall be taken away even that he hath" (v. 12). To those who have even the smallest capacity the truth shall be given. And they shall receive a growing comprehension in "more abundance." But to those who have not this capacity, the parables themselves would serve to emphasize their incapacity, leaving them in greater spiritual dullness.

The things of God cannot be comprehended by men with fleshly minds. For they must be spiritually discerned. To some even the gospel is a stumblingblock and foolishness. But to those who believe in Christ, it is the power and wisdom of God. The same applies to every truth of God. If men do not understand it, they have no one to blame but themselves. A man can dwell in darkness while the world is filled with sunshine. If he would have the light he must open the blinds. And what is true of a man's home is true of his soul.

So Jesus said that He spoke in parables because those outside the kingdom saw, but they really did not see; they heard, but they really did not hear; nor did they understand (v. 13). In them Isaiah's prophecy was filled up like a cup to overflowing (vv. 14.-15). "For this people's heart is waxed gross" or is calloused. This expresses a passive form. They themselves had made their hearts so. "They heard heavily with their ears" (literal meaning). Note "their eyes they have closed." They closed their own eyes lest they should see. They heard heavily so as not to hear. They made their hearts calloused in order not to understand. It was their doing, not God's. They did not wish to be converted or healed. So Jesus could only recognize their own self-made predicament, and act accordingly. Therefore, He spoke in parables.

But then He pronounced a beatitude upon the eyes and ears of the disciples (v. 16). For they were about to see and hear things that God's servants of old had desired to see and hear, but did not (v. 17). The mysteries of the kingdom of heaven were now to be revealed. And the disciples were privileged to see and hear. Because they were able to do so, we too are blessed beyond measure as we search for the *secrets* of the mysteries of the kingdom of heaven.

The Sowing of the Kingdom (13:3-9, 18-23)

The parable of the sower relates the fact of the sowing of the seed ("word," v. 19) of the kingdom in different types of soil, with the subsequent results. In each case the seed was the same. The difference was in the soil. So this might well be called "the parable of the soils."

"Behold, a sower went forth to sow" (v. 3). It was a common sight in Galilee to see a farmer sowing grain. But in order to catch the picture fully we must understand the method used. And since the emphasis is placed upon the soil rather than upon the seed, it is well to begin at that point. Jesus envisioned four types of soil in the field. In Palestine the fields were laid out in long narrow strips. In between the strips were footpaths made hard by the pounding of the feet of passersby. Within the field itself the soil would be of varying kinds. Palestine is underlaid by limestone rock. And in places it would be covered only by a thin layer of soil. Other soil, rich and deep within itself, would contain the small roots of thorn bushes which had been cut away and burned. Still other soil would be rich and deep, and without the thorn roots.

Two methods of sowing seed were used. One was to put a sack of grain on a donkey's back, cut holes in the sack, and walk the donkey over the field scattering the grain as it ran from the holes in the sack. Another method, and probably the one in view here, was for the farmer himself to walk over the field scattering the grain in the *broadcast* method, a custom still followed in many parts of the world. As he scattered the grain it would fall upon the various kinds of soil.

From the original text it is entirely possible that some farmer actually was sowing grain nearby. For Jesus mentioned "the sower" (definite article), not just "a sower" (KJV) or any sower. So, in effect, Jesus seized upon an actual event to teach a great spiritual truth. "Look at that sower there sowing seed!" And as He spoke the scene probably unfolded before their very eyes (vv. 4-8).

As the farmer scattered the seed some of it fell on the hard footpaths, where it had no chance to take root. Others fell on the thin soil above the limestone rock. Still others landed in the soil encumbered with the thorny roots. While some fell in the rich loamy soil which was free from such.

Even as they watched this picture unfold, birds which usually gathered at such a scene hastily flew down and ate the seed along the footpaths. And Jesus stimulated His hearers' imaginations to show what would happen to the rest. The seed which fell on the thin soil would not be covered deeply. And warmed by the sun reflecting from the limestone rock it quickly sprang up. But the same rock kept it from taking deep rootage. Furthermore, as the warm season set in the greater heat from the rock caused it soon to wither and die. The case of the seed among the thorns was somewhat different. The plants lived. But the thorns also grew. They took nourishment from the soil needed by the wheat. They crowded the wheat, literally, "choked them off," so that it was sickly and yellow. If it bore anything at all, it was a scanty harvest. But the seed which fell on the good soil flourished; it bore fruit, "some an hundredfold, some sixtyfold, some thirtyfold" (v. 8).

Note that even here the soil had different capacities, but each yielded a good harvest according to its ability. We must not press the exact amounts too far. However, Genesis 26:12 suggests the possibility of the hundredfold yield. The point in Jesus' figures is that this soil did bear an abundant harvest in varying amounts.

We are fortunate to have Jesus' own interpretation of this parable (cf. also 13:36ff.). But before we examine it, it will be well to consider some of the principles involved in the interpretation of Jesus' parables. As a rule they were designed to teach one great truth, with details being incidental to that truth. In certain cases He did apply the details. But where He does not, it is well that we exercise caution in doing so. From Jesus' own example it is evident that the details must be considered in order to get the lesson of the parable. But these should never be pressed beyond that point. Any interpretation of a detail which is foreign to the central truth should be avoided. Or else we shall distort the picture which is portrayed. It is clear that our Lord followed these principles. He interpreted the details, but He never lost sight of the one great truth which they were designed to teach.

"Hear ye therefore the parable of the sower" (v. 18). The word "ye" (*humeis*) is written out. It is, therefore, emphatic. It shows that this interpretation was spoken only to the Twelve. The Pharisees and multitudes had made their hearts calloused, they listened with heavy ears, they had closed their eyes to the truth. Had they heard the interpretation they would not have comprehended it. But apparently the disciples had an expression of wonder on their faces. While they did not understand the parable, they had given themselves (except Judas) to the King. They were, therefore, capable of receiving this inner truth.

From His own words it is clear that Jesus' emphasis soon passed from the *sower* and the *seed* to the *soil*. He called it "the parable of the sower" because it was a sower who inspired the lesson. The sower in question could be Jesus Himself as He deposited the seed in the soil of men's hearts. But in the nature of the case he more likely corresponds to anyone who proclaims "the word [preaching, cf. I Cor. 1:18, *logos* is rendered "preaching"; the word used here] of the kingdom" (v. 19). Throughout the age, which culminates in the return of the Lord, the gospel is to be proclaimed or *broadcast*. And in the process it will fall upon varying soils with corresponding results. That is the one great truth contained in this parable.

Note that in verse 19 Jesus' emphasis passes from the *sower* and the *seed* to the *soil*. And the "soil" is interpreted to mean *people*. "Anyone hearing the word of the kingdom..." (literal translation). Anyone, regardless of his identity, hears the word. But then Jesus goes on to identify four various types of hearers. In His own ministry He encountered all four of them. Every person who *broadcasts* the gospel will do the same thing. So this interpretation is both timely and timeless.

However, it should be noted that not all expositors are agreed at this point. For instance, G. Campbell Morgan[9] holds that in verses 19-23 the words "he which received seed" should read "*he*

---

9 *The Gospel According to Matthew,* Revell, New York, 1929, *in loco.*

that was sown" by the wayside, upon rocky places, among thorns, or upon good ground. Thus he holds that the meaning is not that of the same seed sown into the hearts of different men, but that it is the casting of a man into a certain age or generation.[10] To support this he cites the good seed in the parable of the tares as meaning "the children of the kingdom" (v. 38). But this is to interpret one of Jesus' parables by another, a procedure which is not justified. In the parable of the tares there are two kinds of seed, good and bad (vv. 24-25). But in the parable of the sower there is but one kind of seed. Furthermore, it is "the word of the kingdom," not "the children of the kingdom." In the one it is the "word" sown; in the latter it is the "children" sown. And there is no justification in reading the latter back into the former.

Now Morgan agrees that in the parable itself the emphasis is upon the soil. But he insists that in Jesus' interpretation He shifts the emphasis from the soil to the seed. He bases this position upon his translation of the words "This is he which received seed by the wayside" (v. 19), which he renders, "This is he that was sown by the wayside."

But a literal rendering reads, "This is the alongside the path being sown." So Morgan is correct in his translation of the passive form of the participle "being sown." But is he, or the Authorized Version, correct in the translation "he"? The question is as to what or to whom "this" (*houtos*) refers. Does it refer to a man? Being masculine in gender, it could. But it could also refer to "word" (*logos*) which is also masculine. If we considered this verse alone, this would be the more likely case. But this same word "this" (*houtos*) also occurs in verses 20, 22-23. So in order to be consistent we must examine it as a whole.

In verses 20, 22-23 where Jesus said, "He that received the seed," He used the definite article *ho* ("the one") rather than *houtos* ("this"). And so these examples read literally, "The upon the stony places ["among the thorns," v. 22; "upon the good ground," v. 23] being sown." But in each of these instances Jesus followed these words with "This [*houtos*] is the one hearing the word." The "word of the kingdom," not a man, is the seed that was sown. Furthermore, in these verses *houtos* is followed by the words "is the one hearing the word." Literally, "is *the* word hearing" (author's italics). Note the first "the" in this sentence. It is a definite article belonging to "hearing," or "the one hearing."

---

[10] Cf. Plumptre, *The Gospel According to Matthew,* Zondervan, 1957, *in loco.*

So in all three verses we have two definite articles followed by a participle. In the former cases the article is related to "being sown," with the place of sowing being designated by the various soils. Thus this article would refer to the seed being sown in the soil. But in the latter usages the article is combined with the "ones hearing." And this would refer to a man, corresponding to "anyone hearing" in verse 19, or to the one in whom the seed was sown. So in this case "the one hearing" would be the soil. Note that in verse 19 nothing is said about "the one hearing." The hard path did not receive the seed. It merely lay on the ground to be taken away by the birds. But in the other verses the seed was heard; it was received into the soil. Thereafter, the point of the parable is what happened as the result of the seed, "the word of the kingdom," being in various types of soil.

But this still leaves us with the word *houtos* ("this"). To what do these four uses of the word refer? We have noted that in verse 19 where this word first appears, the words "the ones hearing" do not occur. In this case the seed was not received. It was merely thrown on the hard ground. Now in the absence of any other words, Morgan and others translate this as meaning "he that was sown." However, if we take this *houtos* in company with the others in verses 20, 22-23 the case is not so simple. For in these usages the word *houtos* joins the statements about "the . . . being sown" and "is the word hearing." Does *houtos* refer to the former or to the latter? If it refers to the latter then "the . . . being sown" is synonymous with "the one hearing." In this case Morgan is right. Jesus' emphasis in interpretation was upon the seed or the the man sown in a given age or generation. But if *houtos* refers to "the . . . being sown," then Jesus' emphasis was upon the soil into which the seed is sown. We should keep in mind that to adopt Morgan's position we must distort Jesus' own words in verse 19, where He clearly said that the seed is "the word of the kingdom." But we do not have to stop with that.

Going back to *houtos* in verse 19 we note that it introduces the words "the one being sown alongside the way." This suggests Jesus' words in the parable itself (v. 4). In verse 4 He says literally, "And in the sowing with respect to him, some fell alongside the way" (*para tēn hodon*). Now in verse 19 He speaks of "the alongside the way being sown" *(ho para tēn hodon spareis).* This is preceded by *houtos estin,* "this is." What is? The experience related in the former part of verse 19. Is this not, therefore, Jesus' way of saying that that interpretation corresponds to the part of the parable about seed which fell on hard ground? And since "seed" in verse 19 is defined as "the word of the kingdom," it cannot possibly refer to "the ones hearing" in verses 20, 22-23. So we must look for another meaning for *houtos* in these verses. May we not then say that in these verses, as in verse 19, *houtos* is used by Jesus to relate these given interpretations to the corresponding examples in the parable? Whereas in verse 19 He gives the interpretation, in which no one received or heard the word, and then relates it to the parable; in the other cases He states the condition in the parable, and then gives the interpretation in which the men received or heard that which was sown, with varying results according to the condition of the soil.

In this case the seed is "the word of the kingdom." The soils are the different men who hear with varying results. Thus Jesus was consistent in both the parable and in His interpretation. He did not perform mental gymnastics by leading His hearers to concentrate on the soil, and then suddenly tell them about the seed. He was consistent in both counts. The *seed* is "the word of the kingdom." The *soils* are the varying attitudes of the hearts of men. And the results in both cases are the same.

After this long but necessary detour into critical analysis, we are now ready to see Jesus' interpretation of the parable itself. It is well to keep in mind that Jesus was not speaking of any given age in history. What He said is applicable to any period or person in any age. If it be insisted that this is a "kingdom of heaven" parable it should also be stated that these parables are dealing with "the mysteries of the kingdom of heaven." These principles were true even when they were hidden in the heart of God. However, their revelation at this time makes them even more pertinent in the gospel age. But so much for this. What does the parable mean?

Jesus said that "the word of the kingdom" is to be sown. It is to be scattered abroad. And in the process it will fall upon many different kinds of hearts which He likened to various types of soil. The response given to this "word" will reveal the charactertistics of the heart. And as we study these it is quite evident that Jesus was dealing not only with those who heard Him directly, but with all who shall hear His messengers through the ages.

First, there are the hearers whose hearts have been hardened by the traffic of the age (v. 19). This is obviously the type which Jesus had set forth in verses 14-15. They have made calloused their hearts, they hear with heavy ears, and they have closed their eyes; lest they should hear, understand, and be converted and healed. Jesus said that they hear with their ears, they know the meaning of the words, but do not understand with spiritual comprehension. Not only do they not receive the seed but they repel it. The result is that Satan snatches it away, and they are left as though they had not heard. This is an apt picture of the Pharisees, Judas Iscariot, and multitudes of others who set their hearts against "the word of the kingdom."

Second, there are those who correspond to the thin layer of soil covering the limestone (vv. 20-21). They hear the *word,* and immediately with joy receive it. They suggest superficial hearers who are joyful in committing themselves to the kingdom without recognizing what is involved. They are like the man who said, "Master, I will follow thee whithersoever thou goest" (Matt. 8:19). In reply Jesus warned him to count the cost before making such a commitment.

Such a person has no root in himself. The *word* sprouts in enthusiasm, but never penetrates into his heart or spirit. And when individual trials or persecutions come, he soon withers and dies. He is caused to stumble in the way. This does not teach "falling from grace." Rather it suggests that vast body of *surface* believers, like the crowd which turned from Jesus when He made demands upon their claim to follow Him (cf. John 6:66). They are in favor of a King and a Kingdom. But it must be according to their wills, not the will of God.

Third, there are those whose lives illustrate the thorn infested soil (v. 22). Such receive the *word,* and it takes root and grows. These are genuine believers. But they are those who fall short of a full commitment to Christ. They have the strength of purpose, but they lack a unity of spirit. Their lives are filled with the thorns of "the care of this world, and the deceitfulness of riches." The care of this world" reads literally, "The divided mind of the age." They endeavor to serve both God and mammon (cf. Matt. 6:24). Like the man in the Sermon on the Mount they have eyes with a double focus. They have one eye set on heaven and the other set on the world (cf. Matt. 6:22-23). They are deceived by the promises made by Mammon. Thus the *word* is choked. The plant lives, but it is puny and bears little or no fruit. Alas, their tribe is myriad!

Fourth, there are those hearers whose lives are like the good soil (v. 23). Unhindered by the "thorns" they flourish and bear an abundant harvest, each according to his several ability. They "understand" the word of the kingdom. This is more than intellectual comprehension. It suggests that the spirit of the hearer responds to the life which is in the *seed,* and the result is a rich harvest in the kingdom.

So the meaning of this parable is quite simple when we let Jesus say what He says. The "word of the kingdom" is to be sown *broadcast* in the world. In every case the seed is the same. The difference is in the soil. Someone may suggest that the sower should be careful where he sows the seed. So to insist would destroy the lesson of the parable. The gospel is not for a selected few. It is to be proclaimed to all men. But every man is responsible for what he does with it. Jesus never told His servants to be successful, but to be faithful. We are to sow the seed, and leave the results with Him.

The Social Relation of the Kingdom (13:24-30, 36-43)

Immediately following His interpretation of the parable of the sower, Jesus related another. It would appear that He now once again addressed the entire multitude. Matthew calls this another parable of the same kind *(allēn)* in that it deals with the kingdom of heaven, and that the topic is still that of a sower. But it is different since in this one the seed is not "the word of the kingdom" but "children of the kingdom." It teaches not the reaction of the soils to the seed, but that the children of the kingdom will bear a social relationship to others. Matthew notes that Jesus "put forth" another parable. The words "put forth" mean "placed alongside." So alongside the first parable Jesus places another.

As in the case of the former, the latter is true to life. A man sowed good seed in his field (vv. 24-30). But at night while he and his servants were sleeping, his enemy came and sowed tares among the wheat. Literally, "he sowed upon" or "resowed" the field. The word rendered "tares" is one (*zizania*) which means "darnel" or bastard wheat. The plant resembles wheat, but the grains are black. It is impossible to tell the plants apart until the grain forms. Darnel is not only unfit for food; it is positively noxious (Plumptre). Such an act of resowing an enemy's field was a common practice in that day.

When the grains formed this evil deed was discovered. The servants asked if they should pull up the darnel. But the owner negated the idea, since to do so would damage or pull up the wheat. He said to let them grow together until the harvest. At that time they could be separated. The darnel would be burned, but the wheat would be gathered into the owner's barn. Implied in this is the patience of the owner. He will not risk damaging the wheat, possibly having the servants to mistake wheat for darnel. He knows that in the end he can defeat his enemy's purpose, and destroy the darnel in the bargain.

It was not until Jesus had dismissed the crowd, and He and the Twelve were in the house (probably Peter's), that they asked Him to explain the meaning of this parable. They asked Him to explain only the two parables. Apparently they understood the others. But since these two were outwardly similar, yet different, they asked for an explanation of the latter as He had given of the former.

An analysis reveals that while both parables deal with the act of sowing and reaping, they are designed to teach different things. In the former the sower is not identified. He could be, and probably is, either Jesus Himself or anyone else who sows the word of the kingdom. But in the latter the sower of the good seed is identified as "the Son of man" (v. 37). Furthermore, the field is not the hearts of men but "the world" (*cosmos,* v. 38). This is an important point to remember. The good seed are "the children of the kingdom." The darnel is identified as "the children of the wicked one" or the devil. In the former the wicked one snatched away the seed from the hard places. Here he resows the field with his own children. Finally, Jesus identifies the harvest as the end of the age, and the reapers as the angels (v. 39). There is a similar meaning in the parable of the net (vv. 47-50).

Now what may we understand as the meaning of this parable? Keep in mind that "the field is the world." The word *cosmos* basically denotes the broad expanse of God's creation. But it was also used in the restricted sense to refer to the world. And that is probably Jesus' meaning here. But note again that the field is the world. It is not the kingdom of heaven or the church. It has no reference to either the church general or the church local. The children of the wicked one are not in the kingdom of heaven. Nor are they in the church in the strictest sense. Of course, some may be in the membership of some local church. But that is not the point of the parable. "The field is the world." So this parable is no ground for permitting flagrant, unregenerated sinners to remain in the church. Jesus will deal with this matter in Matthew 18.

Nor are the children of the wicked one to be identified with heretics, as some early interpreters insisted. They are not in the church but in the world. It will save us from many false interpretations if we will nail down the fact that the Interpreter Himself said, "The field is the world."

What then did Jesus teach? He taught that as He is sowing the children of the kingdom in the world, the devil in an endeavor to defeat God's purpose is resowing the world with his children. The former are those who have received the King, and who have submitted to His will and way. Conversely, the latter are those who have rejected the King, choosing rather to follow Satan's will and way. And the two are in the world together. Each is known by his fruits.

Jesus did not promise to isolate His people from society. They are to be in the world but not a part of it (cf. John 17:11-16). Paul exhorted the Corinthian Christians "not to keep company with fornicators." But he adds that they are not to isolate themselves from them altogether "for then must ye needs go out of the world" (I Cor. 5:9-10). They are not to participate in their sins, nor are they to associate with them socially. But they must be prepared to live in the world with them.

Furthermore, since the wheat and the darnel grew in the same field they must expect to share the same experiences—rain, drought, heat, and cold. By the same token the children of the kingdom must expect to share the same outward experiences as shall be common to the children of the evil one. Life is filled with varied experiences, good fortune and bad, sickness and health, trials and triumphs. The wheat cannot expect to enjoy the good without also enduring the bad. Our Lord does not seal us off from the stern realities of life. Being a Christian does not constitute an automatic insurance policy against such. But the Christian will experience the keeping power of God through such (cf. II Cor. 12:7-9). He must expect to endure the same hardships which befall the non-Christian. And in it all he must never act like darnel. He is always to bear wheat, for such is his very nature.

Since Jesus did not identify the "servants" we must assume that they are the servants of the Son of man. We might even say that they are the preachers, pastors, or any other who aspires to work for the Lord. And every one of such knows the temptation at times to call the wrath of God down upon the children of the wicked one. Not upon sinners as such who wait upon their ministry of the word of the kingdom. But upon those perpetrators of evil which seek to destroy everything which is sacred and holy, even to destroying the children of the kingdom or their efforts to bear fruit. During World War II how often did one hear "Why does not God destroy Hitler?" Or today, "Why does not God destroy the atheistic Communists?"

But here again we learn that the Householder is more patient than His servants. He does not work by some divine thunderbolt.

He chooses to work through His servants. And who of us can tell the *wheat* from the *darnel?* Or, if we could, who can uproot the *darnel* without injuring or destroying the *wheat?* "No," He says, "Be patient. When the harvest time comes all things will be made right. Then the fruit of each will be made manifest." The Son of man shall send forth His reapers, the angels (cf. Rev. 14:17-20), who will "gather out of His kingdom all things that offend [cause to stumble], and them that do iniquity." (v. 41). Here "kingdom" may well be rendered "sovereignty" or the rule of God in the universe (cf. I Cor. 15:24-28). This is not to be regarded as "the kingdom of heaven." All things are under God's sovereignty or rule, even the children of the wicked one. But all things are not a part of the kingdom of heaven.

Following this reaping the darnel will be burned in "the furnace" (Gehenna), and the wheat will be gathered into My barns (heaven). I can wait. And so can you? And while the servants continue to cry, "How long, Lord, how long?" He continues to wait until the harvest of the world is ripe. And then comes the reaping and the separation. The Householder knows best. And we can leave the separation to Him at the time and place of His own choosing. In the meantime the children of the kingdom must go on bearing fruit unto His glory.

The Growth of the Kingdom (13:31-33)

In two brief parables the King sets forth the nature of the growth of the Kingdom. The Jews, including the disciples, thought of the kingdom in terms of a great and glorious beginning by earthly standards. Jesus' purpose is to show that it will have a small, rather insignificant beginning, but will grow to vast proportions. And this growth will be gradual and without outward pomp and splendor. Jesus gave no interpretation to these parables. Apparently their meaning was clear to the disciples, although they pose certain problems for modern expositors.

The parable of the mustard seed is relatively simple. Beginning with the smallest of seeds known to the disciples (Jesus was not speaking with botannical exactness but in popular language), it produces a plant which is larger than other herbs which Jesus called a tree. The Palestinian mustard is different from ours. So much so that birds roost in its branches (vv. 31-32). Strangely enough some expositors see the birds as symbols of evil (cf. Matt. 13:4, 19), suggesting that evil will through the centuries indwell the church. However, this is not a parable of the church as such, but of the kingdom [sovereignty of heaven]. Nor should we borrow from one parable to interpret another. The simple truth is that the seed of the kingdom, small in its beginnings, will ultimately grow beyond all human expectations.

The parable of the leaven is more complicated. "The kingdom of heaven is like unto leaven which a woman took, and hid in three measures of meal, till the whole was leavened" (v. 33). Here Jesus drew upon one of the commonest of events to declare a great truth. In Palestine a housewife usually baked enough bread at one time to last for several days. The three measures of meal (flour) would be something more than a bushel. (Some see the "three" as meaning the Trinity, but without justification. Jesus was simply stating a common fact of life.) And in preparing the dough for baking the housewife would deposit in it a small piece of leavened dough kept from the previous baking. This, in turn, would silently leaven the whole lump.

To what did Jesus refer by the leaven? Many able expositors see this as the quiet working of evil as it permeates the Christian movement in this age. They hold that "leaven" as used in the Bible always refers to evil. And so that must be Jesus' meaning here. But several things may be said to the contrary.

First, leaven does not always refer to evil. In Leviticus 23:17 the law required that bread baked with leaven should be used as wave loaves offered to the Lord. Should we offer to the Lord that which is mixed with evil? Second, we should not force into the meaning of one passage the symbolic meaning of another. For instance, the figure of a lion is used to refer to both Satan (I Peter 5:8) and Jesus (Rev. 5:5). Third, we must not force Jesus' imagery into a preconceived mold. Clearly He did use leaven as a symbol of evil with respect to the teachings of the Pharisees and Sadducees (cf. Matt. 16:6ff.). But to insist that leaven has this meaning in the parable under consideration leads to greater difficulties. For instance, in the one parable of the tares He used "seed" to symbolize both good and evil ("darnel" was "seed"). In the parable of the net (vv. 47-48) He used the symbol of a fish in the same way. It is far simpler to let Jesus say what He says in a given parable than to deal in what A. T. Robertson calls "exegetical jugglery." We should endeavor to discern the *point* of each parable, and avoid pressing of the meaning of details where Jesus Himself did not do so.

In this light, therefore, we conclude that Jesus is simply saying that the kingdom of heaven is placed in the world as a piece of leaven is placed in the dough. From a very small beginning it will permeate the whole. If it be insisted that in its process of working leaven is destructive, then it may be noted that in the gradual growth of the kingdom it too will destroy those things which hinder its progress. But it will continue to spread until it has leavened the entire lump. This last thought points to that time when the sovereignties of this world shall become the sovereignty of "our Lord, and of His Christ" (cf. Rev. 11:15).

So in the parables of the mustard seed and the leaven Jesus employed a Hebrew parallelism to declare the same truth in two ways. Note that in each case the growth is silent and gradual; it is from within, but it is effective. Unlike the expectations of the age the kingdom will not begin nor will it proceed with a great outward show of pomp and splendor. But it will effectively progress in God's own way until it achieves His purpose. But the end will indeed be glorious.

The Value of the Kingdom (13:44-46)

Again in brief but vivid parables Jesus set forth the superlative value of the Kingdom. But of value to whom?

The kingdom of heaven is like a treasure hid in a field (v. 44). A man finds it, hides it, and for joy sells all that he has to purchase it.

This too was a common scene taken from life. Through the years many such treasures had been buried in the ground. It may have been done by some owner for safe keeping. Or by a band of robbers who expected to return and claim it. But either through death or some other cause, the treasure was not claimed. A man might own the field without knowing that it was there. But another discovered it. And since the owner of the land would benefit by such a treasure, the man acted as is seen in the parable. The question of morality enters into the picture. Did the man act dishonestly? Apparently so. But this does not mean that Jesus approved his act, any more than He approved of slavery when He referred to it. He is merely relating an incident true to life in order to declare a spiritual truth.

But before looking at the truth let us note the parable of the pearl of great price (vv. 45-46). Here again the figure was a familiar one. A pearl buyer seeking "goodly" or beautiful pearls. He found one of superlative value. So to possess it he sold all that he had and bought it. Here again Jesus employed a Hebrew parallelism in order to teach one great truth.

Obviously both parables teach the same thing. But what is it? Some hold it to mean that the Kingdom is of such value that a man should be willing to part with everything in order to possess it. But what can a man pay for such a treasure or pearl of superlative value? "What shall a man give in exchange for his soul?" (Matt. 16:26). Therefore, it seems that we must look elsewhere for the meaning.

The more natural meaning would be to see the purchaser in each case as Jesus Himself. The Kingdom is of such great value to Him that He *spent* all that He had in order to purchase or possess it (cf. Acts 20:28). It requires no extended treatment of this thought to see that it embodies every facet of the gospel. We do not purchase the Kingdom. But we enter into the Kingdom through faith in Him who paid the supreme price that it might become His own personal possession.

The Teachers in the Kingdom (13:51-58)

Having concluded these teachings about the kingdom of heaven Jesus asked His disciples, "Have ye understood all these things? They say unto him, Yea, Lord" (v. 51). They probably had not understood fully. But they had gained an insight into these great truths. Henceforth they too will become teachers (scribes) of these same truths.

In order to do so they must be able to bring forth from their own treasures of knowledge things "new and old" or *fresh* and *ancient.* (v. 52). They must be able properly to relate these new truths to the old. When properly understood the true picture of the King and His Kingdom is found in the Old Testament. But they must be so "instructed" as to be able to relate this new revelation to the old. From this time forth the King will focus His efforts on enabling them to do so. They will prove at times to be poor pupils, but they have a great and patient Teacher (cf. Luke 24:44ff.).

Much of the conflict in Christian thought through the centuries has stemmed from failure rightly to relate the *new* with the *old.* We would do well to ponder long these closing words of the King, as we sit at His feet to learn the true treasures of truth which He brought and which He is.

Following these words Jesus paid a final visit to Nazareth (vv. 54-58). It is a sad picture to see that once again they rejected Him (cf. Luke 4:16-31). Familiarity had bred contempt. "A prophet is not without honour, save in his own country, and in his own house." Other people heard Him gladly. His own refused to heed His marvelous teachings. But they were the greater losers. For "he did not many mighty works there because of their unbelief."

The greatest of Teachers, and yet they remained in spiritual darkness! May we not learn from this a lesson? We must not become so familiar with the teachings of Jesus that we shall lose the eternal truths which they convey.

The Withdrawals of the King

Matthew 14

The King's Answer to Despotism

With His final rejection by Nazareth (Matt. 13:54-58) Jesus brought His Galilean ministry to an end. It is now just one year before His crucifixion. During this intervening period Jesus will concentrate more and more on preparing His disciples for that event.

So at this time the King began a series of four withdrawals from Galilee which involved approximately six months from the feast of the Passover to the feast of Tabernacles (A.D. 29). Five reasons prompted these withdrawals. First, there was the natural desire for rest. Second, Jesus wished to be alone with the Twelve for their special training. Third, He wished to discourage the growing fanaticism of the multitudes lest they precipitate a nationalistic rebellion against Rome. Fourth, Jesus recognized the increasing opposition of the Pharisees. Fifth, He wanted to get out of the territory of Herod Antipas who was showing signs of hostility toward Him. It was this last reason which Matthew gives as Jesus' immediate reason for leaving Galilee.

We have noted Matthew's purpose of developing the life of Jesus from the topical standpoint. Therefore, it appears that in Chapters 14-16 he is setting forth Jesus' answers to the forces which ultimately will nail Him to the cross, namely, despotism (Chapter 14), tradition (Chapter 15), and false teachings (Chapter 16).

Chapter 14 opens with a perfect picture of despotism. And the subsequent events in this chapter bear a direct relationship to it. The chapter naturally divides itself into (1) the hostility of Herod; (2) the compassion of Christ; (3) the menace of the multitude; (4) the demonstration of deity.

The Hostility of Herod (14:1-11)

Herod Antipas was a despot after the order of the ancient world. And while he ruled under the authority of Rome, still he wielded its delegated authority after the fashion of an oriental potentate. It was such a kingdom which the Jews envisioned for the Messiah, only they, with him, would be the rulers, not the subjects. And it is in this light that we may best understand Matthew 14.

Matthew introduces this chapter by pointing out that the fame of Jesus had spread even to the royal palace of Herod. But instead of inspiring hope in him, these reports engendered despair instead. And then Matthew breaks into this account with a parenthetical statement as to its cause.

As a young man Herod Antipas had married the daughter of Aretas, the king of Arabia. But while in Rome he seduced Herodias, his niece and the wife of his brother, Philip, a private citizen. Thereafter, without difficulty, he persuaded Herodias to divorce her husband. He also divorced his own wife, and the two were married. Herodias was only too glad to exchange being the wife of a private citizen for becoming the wife of royalty.

No sooner had this iniquitous marriage taken place than did John the Baptist denounce it. Notice that Matthew does not refer to Herodias as Herod's wife, but as "his brother Philip's wife" (v. 3). It was not a true marriage in God's sight. The Mosaic law specifically forbade that a man should marry his brother's wife while the brother still lived (Lev. 18:16). "For John said unto him, It is not lawful for thee to have her" (v. 4). "Said" is an imperfect tense of the verb. It expresses repeated action in past time. Literally, "John kept on saying...." It took great courage for this desert preacher so to challenge his ruler. But he kept on saying it, probably to his preaching audiences, and finally to Herod himself.

Mark tells us that Herod held John in great respect as a righteous and holy man. He knew that John was telling the truth. But Mark also says that "Herodias had a quarrel against John" (Mark 6:19). Literally, "Herodias had it in for John." So it was probably at her insistence that Herod had John arrested and imprisoned in his fortress-castle at Machaerus, a stronghold on the southeastern edge of the Dead Sea. Furthermore, Mark tells of Herodias' efforts to kill John, but he was protected by Herod. It appears from Matthew 14:5 that when Herod could no longer resist her demands, he fell back on the claim that he did not kill John out of fear for the multitude who regarded John as a prophet. But Herodias hated, plotted, and waited. And finally her opportunity came.

It was at a banquet in honor of Herod's birthday (14:6ff.). Using her daughter, Salome, as her tool, she evoked from Herod a drunken promise to give the young lady whatever she wished. Incited by her mother she asked for the head of John the Baptist on a platter. And though it grieved Herod, he consented. When Salome received this bloody viand, she presented it to her gloating mother. Thus the great herald of the King fell victim to hate, alcohol, and sin of the vilest sort.

If the Old Testament had its Ahab and Jezebel, the New Testament has its Herod and Herodias. With the possible exception of Jezebel, Herodias is the most nefarious woman mentioned in the Bible. And both Jezebel and Herodias had a weak Ahab and Herod respectively to stand in their evil shadows.

It is against this background that we may understand Herod's reaction when he heard of the mighty works of Jesus. "This is John the Baptist; he is risen from the dead; and therefore mighty works do shew forth themselves in him" (Matt. 14:2). The best manuscripts of this passage read literally, "And through this one the powers keep on working in him." The "powers" refer to the vast and vague powers of the invisible world. So this was a form of superstitious dread in Herod's imagination. John himself did no miraculous works. But who could say what a dead John *redivivus,* or brought again from the dead, might do? So the king was in a terrible state. A. B. Bruce says that he had "the Baptist on the brain." And on his soul, no doubt.

The disciples of John the Baptist, ignoring the danger which their deed entailed, claimed their teacher's headless body, and gave him a decent burial. And then they brought the sad news to Jesus (v. 12). "When Jesus heard of it, he departed thence by ship into a desert place apart" (v. 13).

What Herod had done he would try again. He had sought to murder truth, but it had risen again. But this would not stay the hand of this despot. He had refused the truth which challenged his conscience. One would think that this new and greater revelation of truth would have brought him to his knees in repentance. But such is not the course of despotism. Once it has shown its brute power it will show it again. For to turn back is to lose its power. So Jesus wisely put Himself beyond its reach. He departed to an area outside of Herod's domain.

But in His departure Jesus gave His answer to despotism. He did not argue with it. Nor did He oppose it. He simply left it to its fate. Given time it will destroy itself as indeed it did. For Herod was destined to die in exile in Gaul. But in the meantime Jesus ignored Him. He departed from him. But not until Herod in his crazed evil had rejected Jesus.

Why did Jesus withdraw from Galilee? Surely it was not out of fear. Later in His ministry some friendly Pharisees warned Him to get out of Herod's territory (Perea), "For Herod will kill thee" (Luke 13:31). To which Jesus replied, "Go ye, and tell that fox,

Behold, I cast out devils and I do cures today and tomorrow, and the third day I will be perfected. Nevertheless I must walk today, and tomorrow, and the day following: for it cannot be that a prophet perish out of Jerusalem" (vv. 32-33). So Jesus departed from Galilee simply in order not to tempt the despotic Herod. Jesus will die, but it will be according to God's will, not Herod's.

However, a deeper and more underlying principle is involved in the withdrawals of the King. It involves the contrast between the true King and Kingdom and the false. So His action was in reality a rejection of the tetrarch and all that his position implied. If Herod rejected Jesus, Jesus also rejected him. God never fully and finally rejects a man until the man has first done the same with respect to God. But when a man makes it clear that he wants no part in God's purpose, God passes him by as He continues His saving purpose for those who will receive it.

Herod maintained an interest in Jesus, but it was only one of casual curiosity. And the gospel record shows that Herod never saw Jesus until He was sent to him by Pilate (Luke 23:7ff.). Even then the tetrarch regarded Jesus only as a passing amusement. But when Jesus refused to respond to his wishes, Herod "set him at nought, and mocked him" (v. 11). He held Him in contempt. And Jesus responded in kind. So Herod never heard a word from Jesus' lips, nor did he see one deed performed by His merciful hands.

It is no wonder then that Jesus neglected him and his kind. Despots may strut and oppress in their cruel and temporary power. They may hinder the work of God, but they do not destroy it. For as Jesus said, "My kingdom is not of this world: if my kingdom were of this world, then would my servants fight, that I should not be delivered to the Jews: but now is my kindom not from hence" (John 18:36). The kingdom of God has no part in despotism other than to judge it. So Jesus departed from Galilee.

The Compassion of Christ (14:13-21)

The events which transpired beyond the lake were a further answer of the King to despotism. For they demonstrate the contrast between His attitude toward men and kingship and that held by the despotic rulers of His day.

The first of these contrasts is seen in the miraculous feeding of the multitude. Despotism looks upon men as tools for its service and as objects of its exploitation. Jesus saw them as opportunities for service and objects of His saving love. This contrast of attitudes is sharply drawn in Matthew 20:25-26. "Ye know that the princes of the Gentiles [pagans] exercise dominion [lord it over] over them, and they that are great [in a wordly sense] exercise authority [tyranny] upon them. But it shall not be so among you: but whosoever will be great among you, let him be your minister; and whosoever will be chief among you, let him be your servant [*doulos,* slave]."

Herod showed his despotic rule by beheading one of his subjects who dared to oppose him. Jesus will demonstrate His greatness by extending compassion to those who need His ministry. He did not ask if they loved Him or were loyal to Him. He served them because they were in need. So in the feeding of the multitude the King, in effect, says that one's greatness is not to be seen in how many people serve him, but in how many people he serves.

When Jesus arrived beyond the lake He found that the crowds had preceded Him (Matt. 14:13). And in spite of the fact that He had left Galilee to escape the crowds, He did not upbraid them. Instead He "was moved with compassion toward them, and he healed their sick" (v. 14). This was a time consuming work. So "when it was evening [probably the first of two Jewish evenings, about 3:00 p.m.], his disciples came to him, saying, This is a desert [deserted, few villages] place, and the time is now past; send the multitudes away, that they may go into the villages and buy themselves victuals" (v. 15).

Within itself this verse involves a further contrast between the attitude of Jesus and that of His disciples. That the disciples shared their Lord's compassion for the people is quite evident. They were hungry and something should be done about it. But it never occurred to them that the Lord had a plan by which to meet that hunger. Instead they came to Jesus with their own plan. And it was the plan which might well have been followed by some Herod. So in their attitude they showed a mixture of Christian concern and worldly action. Their compassion they received from Jesus, but their program they might well have derived from their worldly ruler. Let the people be fed, but let them feed themselves!

An examination of verse 15 reveals two mistakes commonly found among the Lord's people. In the first place, the Twelve expressed their own will rather than seeking Jesus' will. The words "send . . . away" translate an aorist imperative form of the verb. It is a command for immediate action. "Send the multitudes away immediately." So they sought to instruct Jesus rather than to seek His instructions.

How often do we make carefully designed plans which express

the human will, and then ask that the Lord shall bless them. It is little wonder that such plans more often than not end in failure or else yield meagre results. A far better procedure would be to spend time in prayer seeking the revelation of God's will. God is under no obligation to bless *our* plans and programs. But the very power of the universe is dedicated to the accomplishment of God's purposes. Jesus never ran ahead of His Father, nor should we.

In the second place, the disciples proposed that the multitudes find help from sources other than Jesus. "Send them away"—away from us, away from Thee.

Christian people share a general concern for the fainting hungry multitudes. We want them to be saved and fed. But if not by our words then by our attitudes we say, "Let them find sustenance elsewhere." "Into the villages" suggests the attitude so prevalent today to rely upon those sources in society—political, civic, cultural, and economic—which endeavor to meet the pressing needs of men. To be sure each of these has its place in a complex society. But they cannot take the place of the spiritual ministry which the Lord has deposited in His churches. They may meet the surface needs of men. They treat the symptoms but they do not cure the disease. We do not make better men by improving society. We improve society by making better men. And men are made *better,* not by outward reformation, but by inward regeneration. And the latter ministry is given to the churches which are charged with the responsibility of preaching the gospel of spiritual salvation.

"Buy themselves victuals" further suggests that each man be left to his own resources, with no regard to the spiritual power which is resident in Jesus. In the Greek text "themselves" is written out, rather than simply being included in the verb form. So it is emphatic. Let them help *themselves,* but they should expect no help otherwise. No question is raised as to the availability of sufficient food for so great a throng. Or whether or not they even possessed the money with which to purchase it. But just "send the multitude away"—anywhere, but do not expect us to lend a hand.

When such an attitude prevails it should come as no surprise if the multitudes forsake the churches. Even an animal will go where he is fed. But if it comes to the feeding trough, only to find it empty, it will seek provender elsewhere. And the human species is no different.

Now what was Jesus' reply to such an attitude? "They need not depart; give ye them to eat" (v. 16). Literally, "Give to them you to eat." "Give" is also an aorist imperative. So it is Jesus' command in reply to the disciples' command. They said, "Send the multitude away." Jesus replied, "Give ye them to eat." They said, "Villages." Jesus said, "Ye." They said, "Themselves." Jesus said, "Ye." And this is ever His reply.

No matter how hard we may endeavor to be rid of our responsibility our Lord ever holds us to it. We may refuse it, but we cannot escape it. We may send men away, but we are the losers—along with them.

What was the problem of the disciples? They failed to recognize the resources which were at their disposal through the power of Jesus. They thought of outward mechanics with no regard for spiritual dynamics. To the Lord's command they replied, "We have here but five loaves, and two fishes" (v. 17). Five barley cakes and two dried fish, the food of the poor. John adds a further detail. "There is a lad here, which hath five barley loaves and two small fishes: *but what are they among so many?*" (6:9, author's italics). Perhaps this was the boy's lunch which his mother had prepared for him that morning. T. L. Holcomb once remarked that the greatest miracle that day was not that Jesus multiplied them into a feast, but that this growing boy still had his lunch uneaten by the middle of the afternoon!

Even so, Jesus said, "Bring them [the loaves and fishes] hither unto me" (Matt. 14:18). He then had the people to sit down in orderly groups, "by hundreds, and by fifties" (Mark 6:40). Note the organization that none would go unfed. Jesus does not despise organization so long as it becomes a means and not an end unto itself.

And then followed the miraculous feeding of the multitude (Matt. 14:19-21). "Five thousand men, beside women and children." How many? Perhaps fifteen or twenty thousand in all! Note the procedure. Jesus gave thanks, broke off pieces of the food, and gave it to His disciples, who in turn gave it to the people. He did not suddenly transform the meagre fare into an abundance of provisions. Mark says literally, "He broke in pieces [aorist tense, sudden action] the bread, and kept on giving [imperfect tense] to the disciples in order that they might set before them; and the two fishes he divided [aorist tense] to all" (6:41). In the aorist tenses you can almost hear the quick snapping of the brittle cakes and dried fish. And in the imperfect tense we see Jesus repeatedly giving the portions to the disciples to distribute among the crowd. Like the widow's meal barrel it seemed that the food would give out with each feeding. But also like it there was always enough through the power of the Lord.

Of further interest is the fact that Jesus supplied the food, but He gave it to His disciples to distribute to the people. This is a highly suggestive thought. There is no limit to the power of the Lord. But always between Him and the people stand His disciples. The Lord works through His people. Through divine wisdom He involves us in His ministry to the multitudes. He provides the food, but His command still is "Give ye them to eat."

The success of the effort is attested in the words, "And they did all eat, and were filled: and they took up of the fragments that remained twelve baskets full" (Matt. 14:20). The words "were filled" render a word which well may be translated "were gorged" (cf. Rev. 19:21). So the magnitude of the miracle is seen not only in the number of the people but also in the full stomachs and in the leftovers!

Numerous efforts have been made to explain away this miracle. One suggestion is that the disciples found food stored in a cave, probably Roman military supplies! Another even more ingenious one is that Jesus and the disciples shared their lunches with a few people. Then this generous act inspired others to do the same, setting off a chain reaction of sharing! But neither of these is supported by even a figment of Scriptural authority. It takes more faith to believe these explanations (?) than to accept the Biblical account. A. T. Robertson never said a wiser thing than "Let the Bible say what it says!"

Once you accept the deity of Jesus the remainder of the problem is easy. If He by known natural laws could multiply a handful of grain into a harvest, why could He not also by laws known only to Himself multiply the substance in completed form?

Back of this event is an additional message for the followers of Jesus in all ages. Apart from Jesus no one is sufficient. But in Him all things are possible (cf. Phil. 4:14). Note the order of this miracle. (1) The disciples had but little. (2) They brought it to Jesus. (3) Jesus blessed and multiplied it. (4) He gave the several portions to His disciples. (5) The disciples gave the food to the people. (6) The people ate and were filled. (7) The residue exceeded even that with which they began. (8) The more one gives away in the Lord's name the more he has.

Did the news of this miracle reach the ears of Herod? In all probability it did. If so, was its message lost to his sin-crazed mind? Evidently so. Nevertheless, Jesus had given a dramatic answer to Herod's despotism. Herod said, "The kingdom is mine." Jesus said, "The Kingdom is mine." Herod said, "The people belong to me." Jesus said, "I belong to the people." The former asked, "What can the people do for me?" The latter asked, "What can I do for the people?" The despot said, "Because a man displeased me he must die." The Saviour said, "Because all men disobey me I must die." The tetrarch said, "John is risen from the dead, and evil powers work in him." The Lord said, "I am risen, and all authority is given unto me." Herod lost his kingdom through greed, and ended his days in lonely exile and disgrace. Jesus gained His kingdom through suffering, and is set down at the right hand of God where He is forevermore King of kings and Lord of lords.

The Menace of the Multitudes (14:22-23)

Matthew gives but two verses to what was the great crisis point in Jesus' public ministry. But in this brief account he records Jesus' answer to both the disciples and the multitude as to the false and the true nature of the King and the Kingdom of God.

That the feeding of the multitude was an event of greatest importance in Jesus' ministry is attested by the fact that it is the only incident in His life, prior to Passion Week, which is related by all four gospel writers. What was its significance? It marks the acme in Jesus' popularity with the multitudes. Thereafter, with rare exceptions, it will recede until finally the people will forsake Him and He will be nailed to the cross. Why?

In order to answer this question we must combine the accounts of Matthew and John. (John wrote his Gospel after the other three, and often fills in details lacking in the others.) And when the two records are put together the picture is quite clear.

First, let us look at John 6:14-15. "Then those men [the five thousand], when they had seen the miracle that Jesus did, said, This is of a truth that prophet that should come into the world. When Jesus therefore perceived that they would come and take him by force, to make him a king, he departed again into a mountain himself alone."

The multitude went wild with excitement. The miracle of the loaves and fishes set off a demonstration the likes of which had not been seen in Jesus' ministry. The best manuscripts of John read "miracles" (plural). The Greek word is *sēmeia,* signs, the word which John always employs for Jesus' miracles. They were "signs" of His deity. Now "signs" in verse 14 could refer to the miracles mentioned in John 6:2 (cf. Matt. 14:14). But it also could be regarded as referring to all of Jesus' miracles performed in Galilee up to this time. The enthusiasm of the people had increased gradually as they had seen Jesus heal the sick and raise the dead. But the miraculous feeding was the fuse which set off this demonstration.

To these Galileans this *sign* was conclusive proof that Jesus was the Messiah. With one accord they "said" (aorist tense), "This is of a truth that prophet that should come into the world." "That prophet" refers to Deuteronomy 18:15 (cf. John 1:21) Moses said, "The Lord thy God will raise up unto thee a Prophet from the midst of thee, of thy brethren, like unto me; unto him ye shall hearken." This verse the Jews related to the Messiah. Furthermore, note that "that shall come" translates "the coming one" (*ho erchomenos,* cf. Matt. 11:3) which was also a Messianic title found in the Minor Prophets. We have seen that this title was connected in the Jewish mind with their political ambitions with reference to the Messiah. So with a double emphasis the multitude declared that Jesus "of a truth" was the Messiah. And to them "Messiah" had a political and military connotation.

But why should the loaves and fishes set off such a demonstration? Note that Moses had said that the "Prophet" would be "from the midst of thee [Galilee?], of thy brethren [Jew], like unto me [Moses]." Through Moses God had fed the Israelites in the wilderness. And the Jews believed that the Messiah would do the same thing, only on a greater scale (cf. John 6:31). So the loaves and fishes were the "sign" which proved to them that Jesus was the Messiah.

They were ready to proclaim Him as such, and then march against Rome. With Him as their leader they would be invincible. He could feed them, so they would need no supply corps. If they were wounded He could heal them, so there would be no necessity for a medical corps. Neither would there be need for recruitment. Each time one of them was killed, Jesus could raise him from the dead.

So it is no wonder that by force they sought to make Him their king. This was Satan's temptation all over again to forsake God's role as a spiritual Messiah to become a nationalistic one. Had the people succeeded it would have destroyed all that Jesus had done and must do. Therefore, once again the King refused to follow the will of Satan. And in refusing Satan Jesus once more turned His back upon despotism to follow the will of His Father.

Unfortunately the followers of Jesus have not always been as wise as their Leader. For through the ages they have sought to establish the Kingdom of God by force of arms, political alignment, economic and social enterprise, and/or other programs which would substitute outward bigness and power for inward spiritual strength. These are the programs of the "people." But *vox populi* is not always *vox dei*. It may be *vox diaboli*. The voice of the people is not necessarily the voice of God. It may be the voice of the devil. There are no shortcuts to glory. The ways of the world are not the ways of God.

It is at this point that Matthew takes up the story. "And straightway Jesus constrained [forced] his disciples to get into a ship, and to go before him unto the other side, while he sent the multitude away" (14:22).

Note the sequence. (1) Jesus sent the disciples away. (2) He dismissed the multitude. Why this order? Did He first send the disciples away to get them out of this revolutionary atmosphere? Or was it necessary to send them away before He could quiet the people? It is not out of reason to say that they had been at the bottom of the whole thing. For they too entertained the false concept of Jesus' role.

If so, then Jesus' action was a rebuke to them as well as to the multitude. It is one thing for Him to have to contend with Herod and the fanatical multitude. But the situation was compounded by the failure of His inner circle of disciples to understand His role and Kingdom. Nevertheless Jesus made it quite clear to all three groups that His Kingdom was not of this world. He refused to be a *bread* Messiah. The needs of men ran far deeper than that. And though His choice meant a cross rather than a worldly sceptre, even now He set His face to go to Jerusalem. He would attain a throne to be sure, but the path leading to it must first lead Him to the cross.

We are not surprised, therefore, to read that "he went up into a mountain to pray" (v. 23). Certainly it was a time to pray. One year before the crucifixion, and still no one understood the nature of His Kingship and Kingdom. In such a situation most mere men would have given up in discouragement. But Jesus was no *mere man*. Nevertheless, He needed to pray. To pray for strength within Himself. To pray for the multitudes who wandered as sheep without a shepherd. To pray for the Twelve that they may come to a true knowledge as to His nature and purpose.

But for the moment "he was there alone" (v. 23). It was more than mere physical loneliness. It was a sense of spiritual loneliness. He was alone in a world that did not understand Him, which had failed to comprehend His mission, and which will soon forsake Him. Yes, He was alone. But was He? For in prayer He found fellowship with His Father in whose presence no man is ever truly alone.

The Demonstration of Deity (14:24-33)

We may well imagine that the Twelve were in a bad mood as they rowed their way back across the sea of Galilee. Whether or not they had instigated the attempted revolution, they were not averse to it. And now it had failed. To the best ability of their understanding Jesus had missed a grand opportunity. And their own dreams of grandeur had been dashed to the ground.

But presently they had other troubles to engulf them. For the sea became a boiling cauldron of unrest. The wind was contrary, and their little boat was tossed by the waves. The troubled sea was a likely counterpart to their troubled spirits.

It was in such a condition, early in the dark hours of the morning, that the disciples saw Jesus coming to them walking on the waves. Thinking that they were seeing an apparition or ghost (Greek, *phantasma,* phantom), they were "terrified" (v. 26). But Jesus calmed their fears, saying, "Be of good cheer; it is I; be not afraid" or "stop being afraid." And then followed the episode of Peter walking on the water (vv. 28-32).

Matthew alone tells this story. We can well understand why Mark omits it. According to early tradition Peter was probably the source of Mark's information for his gospel. If so, Peter probably avoided telling of this incident. There is no known reason why Luke and John omit it except that it was already recorded by Matthew. But a more interesting question is as to why Matthew recorded it. He did not include material without a purpose. And assuredly the Holy Spirit had a definite reason for leading him to include it in his account.

May we not relate it to the events of the previous day? The disciples had had their faith in Jesus shaken. If He was not the Messiah (after their own fashion), then who was He? It was to reassure them that Jesus came to them on the water. Some insist that Peter's request to walk on the water was a presumptuous one. But Jesus said, "Come." And He never invites us to do presumptuous things. He had a purpose in inviting Peter to do so. As long as Peter kept his eyes on Jesus he walked on the waves. But when he looked at the tossing sea, he became afraid and began to sink. Realizing his own weakness he cried for Jesus to save him. And He did so. Then Jesus said, "O thou of little faith, wherefore didst thou doubt?" Literally, "Wherefore were you pulled two ways?"

Doubtless this question referred to Peter's experience. But back of it was a greater doubt, a doubt which was shared by the rest of the Twelve. Yesterday they saw Jesus feed the multitude. "Of a truth" He is the Messiah. But they had been caught up in the turbulent sea of an attempted revolution built about their false concept of the Messiah. So long as they kept their eyes on Jesus they were safe. But when they permitted their gaze to be fixed on the tossing waves of an erroneous public opinion they began to sink. Their faith faltered.

But now they see Jesus walking on the sea. Peter's experience parallels their own. And Jesus saves him only to ask, "Wherefore didst thou doubt?" Why were you pulled two ways? Not only with respect to the Saviour and the sea, but concerning the Messiah and the multitude? They were drawn to Jesus by a faith that was fixed in Him and His mission. Though they fully did not understand Him or it, yet they had dedicated their lives to Him. But they were also drawn by the popular, mistaken view concerning His person and work. So in their perplexity they are crying to Him even in the confusion of their hearts. And Jesus responds to their cry.

Presently Jesus is in the ship with them, and the sea is calm. And they "worshipped him, saying, Of a truth [*alēthōs*, the same word used by the multitude in John 6:14] thou art the Son of God" (Matt. 14:33). The disciples needed that assurance. The events of yesterday had disturbed them. But now they are reassured. They still do not comprehend fully the nature of the King and Kingdom. But they know Him. And they are convinced that He is God's Son. And they will follow on to know the Lord.

What a beautiful ending to a tragic story. Within a few hours the crowds will forsake Jesus when He makes it clear to them that He definitely will not fit into their Messianic pattern (John 6:66). Even the Twelve will look after the departing crowds with uncertainty (v. 67). But as in Peter's experience they had been reassured, so in his words they will say, "Lord, to whom shall we go? thou hast the words of eternal life. And we believe and are sure that thou art the Christ the Son of the living God" (vv. 68-69).

So this little worshipping congregation (Matt. 14:33) remains true. Here, then, is the King and His Kingdom—the faithful disciples and all like them who follow Him in faith. Not a despot and his cringing subjects, but a Saviour and His friends. Yea, the Son of God and all those who through Him may become the sons of God.

Even though Jesus' answer to despotism had been lost on Herod and the multitude, it had found a lodging place in the hearts of His disciples. It is not yet clear to them, as, indeed, it will never be to Judas Iscariot. But Jesus has made a beginning. The first lesson is over. But there are others yet to come. And gradually the light will dawn, the sun of understanding will rise unto a perfect day. The Twelve are not the best of pupils, as even we are not. But they have the best of teachers. And He is their hope—and ours.

Matthew 15

The King's Answer to Tradition

Following the feeding of the five thousand Jesus returned to Galilee, probably to Capernaum. This event occurred just prior to the feast of the Passover (cf. John 6:4). Due probably to the rising enmity of the Jewish leaders, Jesus did not attend this feast. It was sometime after the feast that a deputation of Pharisees from Jerusalem appeared in Capernaum (Matt. 15:1). They would hardly have left Jerusalem prior to or during the feast. Evidently the scorching attack of Jesus upon the Pharisees had been reported in Jerusalem (cf. Matt. 12:22ff.). At any rate this special group came up from Jerusalem to confront Jesus again. And in the issue at hand we see the vast chasm which existed between current Judaism and the teachings of Jesus. And as in Chapter 14 the King gave His answer to despotism, so in Chapter 15 He gives His answer to tradition. In so doing the King further sets forth His Kingdom as distinct, founded upon divine principles rather than upon human traditions.

The events in this chapter may be noted as (1) the conflict between tradition and the Law; (2) the conflict between tradition and spiritual religion; (3) the conflict between tradition and evangelism.

The Conflict between Tradition and the Law (15:2-9)

"Why do thy disciples transgress the tradition of the elders? for they wash not their hands when they eat bread" (v. 2). With this question the Pharisees confronted Jesus with what to them was a serious theological problem. The question had nothing to do with hygiene but with ceremonial religion. Nor was it a matter of the Mosaic law, but of the "tradition of the elders." A tradition was something that was passed along (*paradosin*) from one group or generation to another. The word might be used in a good or in a bad sense, depending upon the context. For instance, Paul used it in the good sense to refer to certain teachings which he had handed over to the churches (cf. I Cor. 11:2, "ordinances"; II Thess. 2:15; 3:6). But he also used it to refer to those teachings which had been handed down from preceding generations (cf. Gal. 1:14; Col. 2:8). It was in this latter sense that the Pharisees used it in

Matthew 15:2 where it definitely carries the bad meaning. The word "tradition" is used today by Roman Catholics to refer to that body of teachings which they hold in addition to the Scriptures themselves.

In a sense the traditions of the elders stemmed from certain Scriptural teachings. In the Mosaic code, particularly Leviticus, certain types of flesh were regarded as unclean (cf. Lev. 11). Lepers were unclean (cf. Lev. 13). This was quite obviously done with reasons of health in mind. Certain other laws dealt with uncleanness as making one unfit for worship or other spiritual service. Specific rites were prescribed for removing this uncleanness.

But in this as in many other matters of the Law the Jews went to extremes in their interpretation and application of these laws in their oral law or tradition. For instance, all Gentiles were regarded as outside the mercy of God. A Jew who brushed against a Gentile in the marketplace was defiled. Anything, even the soil, which a Gentile touched was considered unclean. The Jews kept pots of water available in their homes for cleansing purposes both of themselves and their vessels (cf. John 2:6-8) which might have been touched by a Gentile.

The matter of washing the hands before meals (some even did so at intervals during meals) was related to the above reasons. But it also involved sheer superstition as well. Demons were thought to dwell on the hands whence they might get on the food and into the body. So the issue at hand involved both superstition and racial pride and prejudice. It is important to remember these items as we proceed with Jesus' answers.

However, there was even a broader issue involved, the conflict between the Law and tradition. The rabbis taught that it was more important to obey the traditions of the elders than to keep the Law. The Talmud, traditional Jewish law, says, "The words of the Scribes are more lovely than the words of the law; for the words of the law are weighty and light, but the words of the Scribes are all weighty." Again, "My son, attend to the words of the scribes, more than to the words of the law." This sounds a distinctly modern note when we recall the Roman Catholic position that their traditions carry more authority than the teachings of the Scriptures.

The tradition about handwashing was of particular importance. Some rabbis taught that to neglect it was as bad as to be guilty of adultery or other gross crimes. The story is told of Rabbi Akiba being in prison. When his water ration was reduced, he used it to wash his hands before eating rather than to drink it. His reason was that he would rather die of thirst than to transgress the institutions of his ancestors.

But it should be remembered that this and other rituals of cleansing had nothing to do with hygiene or bodily cleanliness. They were related to ceremonial cleanness, and were related to religious righteousness. They struck at the very heart of true religion. And in regard to the Jews' relations to other people they were positively vicious. It requires no application to see how the same attitude toward tradition affects our own relationship to both God and man.

In His reply Jesus turned the tables on the Pharisees (vv. 3-6). "Why do ye also transgress the commandment of God by [because of] your tradition?" He did not deny that His disciples had disregarded their tradition. But He did not consider it a sin. Rather He regarded it as inconsequential. For this was merely a commandment of men. But He accused the Pharisees of a far greater sin. They were guilty of breaking God's law because of their tradition. The word rendered "transgress" basically means "to turn aside" or "to deviate from the way." It is used in the papyri in the sense of breaking one's word or of disobeying the terms of a legal contract. So Jesus accused them of deviating from the Law of God. They had agreed to keep it, but had broken their word. They had entered into a covenant relationship with God, but had disobeyed the conditions of the covenant. This last sense is especially meaningful. For their covenant with God involved their being a priest-nation to the Gentiles (cf. Exod. 19:56). But their attitude toward them made it impossible for them to turn the nations to God. And all because of their tradition!

As a specific example of this Jesus did not cite one of the ceremonial laws which were of a temporary nature, and which were to be fulfilled in Him. He cited one of the Ten Commandments which are basic in God's moral law. He cited the fifth commandment which had to do with the most sacred of human relationships. "Honour thy father and mother: and, He that curseth father or mother, let him die the death" (v. 4; cf. Exod. 20:12; 21:17). The latter was the penalty for violating the former.

Now that was God's Law. But what was their tradition? "But *ye* say" (v. 5, author's italics). "Ye" is written out, and so is emphatic. It is what the Pharisees said in contrast with what God said. It is always tragic when what we say contradicts what God has said. Then Jesus referred to one of the traditions of the elders. Despite God's commandment they taught that if one's parents needed financial assistance, he could simply say of his possessions,

"It is a gift," and was thereby relieved from any responsibility for his parents. Mark 7:11 calls this gift "Corban." It was a gift dedicated to God's service. But according to custom one did not have to name a date when such a dedication was to take place. It might be at the end of one's life, thus giving him the use of his wealth until he died. Or such a dedication might even end when the one died to whom he spoke the magic word "Corban." Not only did he escape the responsibility by the tradition, but he was forbidden by the elders to do otherwise even if he changed his mind (cf. Mark 7:12).

It was a vicious tradition indeed. Furthermore, it "made the commandment of God of none effect." The word which is rendered "made of none effect" means without authority or null and void. It emptied the very meaning of God's commandment. So with this one illustration Jesus pulled the mask of mock piety from their faces to reveal them as the hypocrites which they were (vv. 7-8). In this light how utterly ridiculous was their charge against the disciples. How empty was their lip-worship which was void of any heart-worship (v. 9).

But the greater tragedy is that this was the sum total of their religion. We can well understand why Jesus said that if our righteousness does not exceed theirs we cannot enter into the kingdom of heaven (cf. Matt. 5:20). Tradition, no matter how venerable it may be, cannot suffice for the Word of God. It is no wonder then that the King repudiated such as He came to bring life indeed to all who will receive it. There was no room for coexistence between the two. And even though His repudiation of their system ultimately nailed Him to the cross, Jesus did so nevertheless. For the issue was more than mere semantics. It involved the matter of eternal life or eternal death, then as it does now.

The Conflict between Tradition and Spiritual Religion (15:10-20)

That which follows may seem rather commonplace to the modern reader. But to His immediate hearers it was one of the most revolutionary things that Jesus ever spoke. For it cut across the whole system of Judiasm. Thus the King threw down the gauntlet to those who posed as the teachers of religion in His day. This issue was that of formal traditionalism as over against spiritual religion.

Note that He spoke it to the multitude even though the Pharisees also heard (v. 10). He wanted the multitudes to hear the challenge that He made. The fact that the King recognized the serious import of His statement is seen in His words "Hear, and understand." He wanted them to hear it. And, what is more, to understand it with spiritual comprehension. Because what He was about to say not only cut to the heart of this false form of religion; it also set forth the very heart of true religion.

"Not that which goeth into the mouth defileth a man; but that which cometh out of the mouth, this defileth a man" (v. 11). In these words Jesus did not quote from any rabbi. Nor was He citing any precept of the Mosaic code. In a very real sense He was setting aside the Old Testament laws about the clean and the unclean. He is the King stating a new principle altogether. This does not mean that the Mosaic code as to the clean and the unclean was not a teaching of God. For it was. As previously noted, some of these laws were hygienic in nature. Therefore, we must not press unduly the implications in Jesus' words with respect to certain forbidden foods. They were unfit for human consumption. For instance, pork harbors two worms, trichina and tape worm, which may be passed on to human beings. Under certain conditions of cooking these may be destroyed. But in ancient times such food was better avoided. As we shall see presently even Acts 10:9-15 primarily was designed to teach a spiritual truth. It was that which was uppermost in our Lord's mind.

Many of the ceremonial laws of clean and unclean were in a sense God's *primer* designed to teach morality. So in reality Jesus did not abrogate the law. But as in the Sermon on the Mount He raised it to a higher meaning. From ceremonial or outward morality He raised it to the level of the spiritual. Thus He taught a higher concept of purity, a purity which is guaged not by that which enters the mouth but by that which comes from the mouth.

However, there is an even profounder lesson in Jesus' words. The tradition of the elders had extended the laws of the clean and unclean to make them a cleavage between Jew and Gentile. What God had given to the Israelites to distinguish them from their pagan neighbors, the Jews had made a source of pride for themselves and of prejudice toward others. And it was this attitude which had defiled them and made them unclean, or unfit for God's service as a priest-nation. That this thought was involved in Jesus' words is seen in Peter's housetop vision at Joppa (cf. Acts 10:9-15). "What God hath cleansed, that call not common." "Common" (*koinos*) is from the same verb used in Matthew 15:11 for "defileth." In Acts the idea of animals (10:12-15) was incidental to a greater truth. God was about to send Peter to witness in the house of Cornelius, a Gentile, who to Peter was "common" or "defiled." So the real lesson of Peter's vision was that the chasm between Jew and Gentile must be removed in order that God's servants might lead them to the Lord. In a veiled form this was the import of Jesus' words in Matthew 15:11, a lesson which He presently will demonstrate to the Twelve (vv. 21ff.). But for the moment He set it forth as a spiritual principle in contrast to the tradition of the elders.

At a later time, apparently to the disciples privately, Jesus enlarged upon His words. The Twelve had seen the venom of hatred in the Pharisees' eyes following Jesus' revolutionary words. Evidently they themselves did not understand their Lord's teaching. They too were inoculated with the traditional approach to religion. And so there was a mild rebuke in their words, "Knowest thou that the Pharisees were offended [caused to stumble], after they heard this saying?" (v. 12). Evidently the Pharisees had accused Jesus of false teaching in His new idea. And since they were the accepted teachers of the Law, the Twelve thought that their own interpretation should be heeded. But Jesus did not back up on His declaration. Instead He warned the Twelve against the Pharisees. "Every plant, which my heavenly Father hath not planted, shall be rooted up" (v. 13). This was not primarily a reference to the Pharisees as persons. It was directed at the system of religion which they represented. The traditions of the elders were not of God. It did not matter what the Pharisees thought of Jesus or of His teachings. Their entire system of religion was to be destroyed.

So "let them alone" (v. 14). That was what Jesus was doing, and He commands (*aphete,* imperative) the Twelve to do the same. They were but blind guides leading the blind. And those who followed them would with them fall into a ditch. This was a proverbial saying. One day in Jerusalem our party saw one blind man leading another. It was doubtless a common sight in Jesus' day.

They were timely words. But they are also timeless in their meaning. In the physical sense it is a tragedy. But tragic beyond compare is to see the spiritually blind following spiritually blind leaders. Jesus is the Light of the world. And those who forsake Him and His teachings to follow empty tradition will always wind up in the ditch of emptiness and nothingness.

This was too much for the Twelve, even as it is for multitudes today. So Peter, speaking for the group, asked Jesus to "declare unto us this [the] parable" (v. 15). By "parable" he referred not to the blind leaders but to Jesus' revolutionary statement in verse

11. Note that Peter called this a parable. In the strictest sense it was not a parable. It was a principle. But Peter endeavored to tone down its meaning by calling it a parable. Jesus did not correct his mistaken terminology, but proceeded to enlarge upon the truth which He had declared.

In reply Jesus asked, "Are ye also yet without understanding?" (v. 16). "Yet" may better be rendered "even yet." In spite of Jesus' teachings they still did not understand. "Ye" is written out, and so emphatic. It contrasts them with the Pharisees. They were like the Pharisees for they lived in a Pharisaic environment. Their outlook on religion was Pharisaic. But not for this reason alone should we be patient with them. For we also are too largely slaves to the external in religious morality and purity. If after almost two thousand years we are so largely without understanding, how can we condemn them?

And then Jesus tried again. "Do not ye yet understand" (perceive)? This verb is akin to "mind" *(nous)*. So Jesus expects us to use our minds. And then He used a very homely illustration (v. 17). That which we eat passes through the body and is cast out of it. The things which really defile a man or make him common *(koinoi)* or unclean are the things which come out of a man's heart through his mouth (v. 18). The "heart," of course, is not the physical organ or the emotions. It refers to the whole of man's inner being. And then Jesus lists some of these things: "evil thoughts [cf. racial pride and prejudice], murders, adulteries, fornications, thefts, false witness, blasphemies" (v. 19). For a commentary on these words we should read Matthew 5:21-48. And for a modern parallel we should compare the stringent food and drug laws with the loose standards of morality and the crime which abound. We are so careful about what goes into our mouths, and are so careless as to that which comes out of them! So we have not yet perceived the meaning of Jesus' words.

And then Jesus summed up the whole of this teaching by referring back to the Pharisees' accusation with respect to eating "with unwashen hands" (v. 20). The whole import, then, has to do with the tradition-bound teachings of the Pharisees and the spiritual teachings of Jesus. But while the King left the blind guides to lead the blind, unfortunately the matter did not end there. For through the centuries, even until now, tradition continues to stifle the spirit of religion set forth by our Lord. And it has caused multitudes of the spiritually blind to fall into the ditch of spiritual ignorance, even worse, of being eternally lost, instead of walking with certainty on the highway of the King.

The Conflict between Tradition and Evangelism (15:21-39)

Following this latest clash with the Pharisees, Jesus took the Twelve and departed on His second withdrawal from Galilee (v. 21). And on this journey He made His only departure from the land that was outside the traditional land of Israel. He went to the region of Tyre and Sidon, a distance of about thirty miles from Capernaum. It is just south of modern Beirut, Lebanon.

Why did the King choose to go here at this particular time? Of course, there were the basic reasons. It was outside the domain of Herod Antipas. The Pharisees would be less likely to follow Him into this *unclean* or Gentile area. He would escape the crowds in Galilee and the oppressive heat of the valley into the comparative quiet and the cool breezes of the sea coast. But such a region would also give Him opportunity to teach the Twelve. And it is this last reason which probably led Jesus to this particular area, for it afforded a lesson which the disciples needed to learn at this time. With deliberate design it seems that Jesus chose this area in which He might teach in a real life situation that which He had set forth in words. So He moved from the classroom into life itself. He is still answering the question as to tradition. And in this particular instance He shows how the tradition of the elders stifled the priest-nation's mission of *evangelism* to the other nations of the world.

When this little band arrived in the region of Tyre and Sidon "behold, a woman of Canaan came out of the same coasts" (v. 22). The word "behold" suggests Matthew's purpose in recording this event. He especially calls attention to this "Canaanitish woman" (literal meaning) with this word which may be translated "look!" In Mark's account she is called a "Greek [*Hellēnis*], Syrophenician by birth" (7:26). Writing for the Romans he simply identified her as a Greek or Gentile since she was non-Jewish. But Matthew is careful to point out that she was a "Canaanitish woman." And this is significant. As such she was a Semite but not an Israelite. She was a descendant of the people who occupied Canaan before the Israelites came into Palestine. So she was of the very people from whom God had sought to keep Israel separated through the laws of clean and unclean. And this is the very point of the entire incident. For by that which followed Jesus put into practice the very principle which He had enunciated in Matthew 15:11. It is the same principle which God taught to Peter in Acts 10:9-15. No man by virtue of his race is to be regarded as "unclean" or as being outside the sphere of the possible working of God's grace. The tradition of the elders had put a barrier between the Jews and other people. By His example as well as by His teaching Jesus demonstrated that they are capable of faith, and through faith to receive God's grace. Thus He removed this barrier to evangelism.

This woman cried to Jesus, "Have mercy on me, O Lord, thou son of David; my daughter is grievously vexed with a devil" (v. 22). Was the word "Lord" used by her as a term of worship or merely as a title of respect ("sir")? In all probability it was the former. The title "son of David" shows that she recognized Jesus as the Messiah. Like the widow of Zarephath she may have been a worshipper of the true God. Possibly she had heard about Jesus from those of her area who had heard Jesus in Galilee (cf. Mark 3:8; Luke 6:17) and had seen Him cure many of their diseases. Maybe she had hoped that some day she might present her own problem to Him. So when word reached her that He was in that region she came to Him. Matthew says that she "kept on crying" (imperfect tense) to Jesus. Literally she said that her daughter was "badly demonized."

And then Matthew reports the strange reaction of Jesus to her plea. "But he answered her not a word" (v. 23). In the Greek "not" *(ouk)* precedes the verb. So it is emphatic. He did not answer her one word. Why this silence on Jesus' part? In the light of that which precedes in this chapter, we certainly cannot say that Jesus shared the belief that as a Canaanitish woman she had no right to ask or expect that He would grant her plea. Some hold that Jesus' purpose was to permit her to keep crying in order to strengthen her faith. However, this seems to be out of character for the Lord. Nor can we agree with those who see this as the power of continued prayer to overcome divine reluctance, inspire divine sympathy, and cause Jesus "to pass beyond the ordinary limits of His appointed work" (Plumptre). This would make Jesus act in direct contradiction to what He had been saying about the tradition of the elders.

It is in the light of this teaching alone that we can understand the actions of Jesus throughout this incident. What better way could He show the vicious nature of the traditions of the elders than by assuming them Himself, and thus showing how they applied in a specific case. It is so easy to lay down a tradition in general terms. It is something else when we see it in operation as it ignores a particular case of personal need. So Jesus played this role of tradition to the hilt, as in an acted parable He unmasked it before His disciples for the vicious thing that it is. And in this woman we may see a picture of the entire non-Jewish world crying to the priest-nation for help, but they answered them not a word.

The Twelve, still enslaved to this tradition, came to Jesus and "kept on beseeching" (imperfect tense) him to send her away (v. 23). Note the two imperfect tenses. She "kept on crying," to Jesus and the Twelve "kept on beseeching" Him to send her away. She was making a spectacle of herself and them, and they were embarrassed. Literally they say, "Send her away at once [aorist imperative]; for she keeps on crying [present tense] after us." They were as anxious to get rid of her as she was to get help from Jesus. We may assume from the Lord's answer that they were asking Him to grant her request. But it was not out of sympathy for the woman or her daughter. They wanted Jesus to grant her request in order that she would go away, and they would not be troubled further by her. They were the tradition of the elders personified.

Jesus' reply in verse 24 was directed to the disciples, but probably was heard by the woman. "I am not [was not] sent but unto the lost sheep of the house of Israel." Some hold this to mean that Jesus was not yet ready to expand His ministry beyond the Jewish nation. They cite His instructions to the Twelve in Matthew 10:6. "But go rather to the lost sheep of the house of Israel." However, this is to interpret Jesus' words out of context. In Matthew 10:6 He was instructing the immature disciples as to their present ministry. But in Matthew 15:24 He is stating a condition concerning His own mission. If this be interpreted as limiting His present ministry then it contradicts another event in it. For Jesus did heal at the request of a Roman centurion (Matt. 8:13). There is no documentary evidence that he was a Jewish proselyte as some claim. His building of a synagogue was interpreted by the Jews only as being an expression of His love for the Jewish nation (Luke 7:4-5). And Jesus Himself saw in this Roman proof that others than Jews would believe in Him (Matt. 8:10-11). We can more aptly find Jesus' own concept of His mission in John 10:16, "And other sheep I have, which are not of this fold."

If this be taken as true, then what did Jesus mean by His words in Matthew 15:24? May we not say that He was still demonstrating the vicious nature of the traditions of the elders? That is exactly what they would have said. Even when the Messiah came He would come only to "the lost sheep of the house of Israel." Certainly the hated and despised Canaanites would have no place in His ministry. And we can hope that since the disciples did not answer Him, that they were beginning to learn Jesus' object lesson.

Then we see one of the most pathetic scenes in the life of Jesus. "Then came she and worshipped him, saying, Lord, help me"

(v. 25). Whether she actually worshipped Jesus or merely prostrated herself before Him as some hold, the effect is the same. This poor woman simply cast herself at Jesus' feet begging for her child. She made no claim of being worthy of His mercy. She made no mention of her race. She was just a poor woman in desperate need. One would think that this would have broken Jesus' heart, as no doubt it did. However, He was not doing this for her good or to test her faith. Her faith had clearly spanned any chasm which might have existed. Jesus was teaching His disciples a lesson. And evidently their hearts were not yet broken. The greater the woman's desperate plea, the more it condemned the tradition of the elders. So the Lord drove home still another lesson.

Jesus replied to the woman, "It is not meet [*kalon,* good or fitting] to take the children's bread, and to cast it to dogs" (v. 26). The Jews called themselves God's children, but called the Gentiles "dogs." So Jesus drove another barb into their attitude, an attitude which continued to cling even to the Twelve. Actually Jesus toned down the term. For He used the word *kunarion,* little house or lap dogs, not the wild vicious dogs which roamed the streets and fields. But His reference definitely was to the attitude of the Jews toward all other people. How Jesus' words strike at our own evil attitude toward other people whom we regard as *unclean!*

But this poor woman was equal to the occasion. For with a ready wit she replied, "Truth [yea], Lord: yet the [little] dogs eat the crumbs which fall from the master's table" (v. 27). She did not ask to sit at the Lord's (*kurios,* master, Lord) table. Accepting the Jews' label as a "dog" she only asked to sit under the table, and catch an occasional crumb or small morsel which might fall to the floor. She did not ask that the "children" (Jews) be deprived of their food. But taking her place as a little dog, she claimed Him as her Master and asked only for the crumbs of His mercy.

That was too much! The negative lesson was over. "O woman, great is thy faith" (v. 28). The word "thy" *(sou)* is written out, and so is emphatic. It was her faith in contrast to the lack of faith in Israel (cf. Matt. 8:10). Even the Twelve could see this. Despite the attitude of the Jews as seen in the tradition of the elders, this despised Canaanitish woman had demonstrated that even she could exercise faith in the Christ.

And then Jesus taught the greatest lesson of all. "Be it unto thee even as thou wilt" (v. 28). The King granted her request; He looked with favor upon her prayers. "And her daughter was made whole from that very hour" (v. 28). So the blessings of the Kingdom were extended even to Canaanitish "dogs" who came to the

King in faith. Doubtless the disciples never forgot that lesson. And neither should we.

Matthew 15 closes with a scene located in the Decapolis, a Gentile or Greek area. This was Jesus' third withdrawal from Galilee. Mark says that following the incident of the Canaanitish woman Jesus went through Sidon (7:31). This is the only time in Jesus' public ministry where He probably saw the Mediterranean sea. We may well imagine that He looked unto "the isles of Chittim" (Jer. 2:10) whence would come many to believe on Him.

But the significant point is that Jesus went from the area of the Canaanites into a Greek area. In the light of Matthew's purpose we may wonder why he does not mention that Jesus went into the Decapolis. However, he was familiar with Mark's account, and the location of this incident was probably well known to his readers.

At any rate Jesus did go into this predominantly Greek area. For the Decapolis was a region comprising ten cities (hence the name *Deca polis)* occupied by Greeks or Gentiles. Matthew notes that Jesus healed many in this area (vv. 30-31). But the significant thing to remember is that as the result of this "they glorified the God of Israel." Why the "God of Israel?" This suggests that these were Greek people, pagan people, who "glorified" not their gods but "the God of Israel." And this would seem to be the point in Matthew's account. In defiance of the tradition of the elders Jesus was ministering to these Gentile, pagan people! He extended His mercy not only to Canaanites but to Greeks as well.

This healing ministry was followed by the feeding of the four thousand (vv. 32ff.). Some insist that this is a repetition of the account of the feeding of the five thousand. But there is no legitimate reason to do so. Certainly Jesus Himself mentioned both events (cf. Matt. 16:9-10). If we examine the incident of the four thousand in the light of Matthew's purpose the reason for it is quite clear. He is still recording Jesus' demonstrated reply to the accusation of the Pharisees concerning the tradition of the elders. Jesus healed the Jews. He healed the Gentiles. He fed the Jews. He fed the Gentiles. His ministry to the one is His ministry to the other. So He completely refutes the tradition of the elders. He extends His mercy to the *clean* and to the *unclean.* In God's sight neither is unclean because of race, but because of sin. And Jesus came to minister not to races as such but to sinners as such.

If by this time we have not learned the lesson of the King, further emphasis will serve no purpose. The attitude which is characterized by the tradition of the elders was in direct contrast to God's law, to a spiritual concept of religion, and to the evangelistic program which is to encompass all races, all men. And it continues to be so. If the Twelve needed this lesson, so do we. Jesus' mission is not founded upon the traditions of men but upon the commandments of God, not upon outward ritual but upon inward purity, and not upon the isolation of racial pride and prejudice but upon God's redeeming love for all men. Only by a recognition of these truths and the practice of them can we be found in the will of Him who said, "Not that which goeth into the mouth defileth a man; but that which cometh out of the mouth, this defileth a man." "What God hath cleansed, that call not thou common" (Acts 10:15)!

Matthew 16

The King's Answer to False Teachings

After the feeding of the four thousand Jesus and the Twelve made a brief visit to Magdala on the western shores of the sea of Galilee. He was back in the region of Herod, but for only a brief time. It was summertime, and the weather in the area was unbearably hot. So continuing His purpose to concentrate on the private teaching of the Twelve, they will soon depart for the mountains. This withdrawal will comprise several weeks and possibly months. However, Matthew's account of it involves less than two chapters. But they contain some of the most vital material in the life of our Lord. The issues at hand were rushing to a violent climax which pointed toward Jerusalem and the cross.

In Matthew 16 the Evangelist records the King's final answer to those forces which will accomplish His death. The issue at hand is that of false teachings as these are epitomized in the Pharisees and Sadducees. This chapter naturally divides itself into (1) the coalition of opposition; (2) the challenge of Truth; (3) the confession of Peter; (4) the cross of Christ.

The Coalition of Opposition (16:1-4)

While still in Magdala Jesus was confronted by the Pharisees and Sadducees. We have seen the Pharisees opposing Jesus from the beginning. But previous to this time Matthew mentions no open opposition to Jesus on the part of the Sadducees. Now these two diverse groups have combined against Him. G. Campbell Morgan calls this "the coalition of criticism." It is this coalition which will result finally in Jesus being nailed to the cross.

In all probability the Pharisees alone would never have killed Jesus. They might have argued Him to death, but on their own they would hardly have resorted to violence. However, the Sadducees were a different matter. They had little time for debate. Being realists they tended more toward action. These two elements, however, made a vicious combination, the fanaticism of the Pharisees and the deadly resoluteness of the Sadducees. It was under the leadership of Caiaphas, a Sadducee, that this coalition finally gave the word that Jesus must die (cf. John 11:47ff.).

What a strange coalition this was! We are so prone to use the term "Pharisees and Sadducees" that we yoke them together. But no two groups of Jews could be found which were farther apart.

The Pharisees were traditionalists. Conservative in theology they accepted all of the Hebrew Scriptures as the Word of God. Furthermore, they added to them the teachings and traditions of their oral law which to them were more important than the Law itself. They believed in spirits, angels, miracles, the work of the Holy Spirit, though not as we understand Him, and the resurrection from the dead. They cared little for politics as such, rather holding tenaciously to the Messianic hope. But their hope was for a political-military Messiah who would overthrow their foreign oppressors and set up His own kingdom of which they would be a vital part.

The Sadducees, on the other hand, were the rationalists of their day. They accepted only the five books of Moses as Scripture. They did not believe in spirits, angels, miracles, or the resurrection of the dead. To them belief in the supernatural was mere superstition. Their religion was more of an ethical code involving moral principles which man must achieve with no help from unseen powers. In fact, they were more concerned with politics than with religion. Far less numerous than the Pharisees, yet they were the wealthy, ruling class among the Jews. They entertained no Messianic hope, and were interested only in maintaining the *status quo*. To do less would have endangered their privileged position. It was only because they saw in Jesus a threat to this position that they came out against Him.

It is quite natural that the Pharisees and Sadducees were avowed opponents of each other. The former regarded the latter as corrupt, wealthy plutocrats who consorted with the enemies of Israel. And the latter looked on the former as fanatical back-numbers who were out of step with the times. Nevertheless, we see them joining hands against Jesus. They lost their mutual distaste in their common hatred for Him who dared to violate their traditions on the one hand, and to threaten their position on the other. And so they combined against what they regarded as their common enemy.

Matthew 16:1 says that they "tempted" Jesus. This word basically means to test or to try something. It may be to prove one genuine or to prove one false. The context gives the word its shading. And as used here it means to test in order to prove one false, and so to *tempt*. They demanded a sign which would prove Jesus' claims regarding Himself. But the last thing which they wanted was for Him to grant their wish.

Note that they asked for a sign "from heaven." They did not ask for a sign *from earth.* And this is significant. The Sadducees felt safe in asking it. For they did not believe in the supernatural. And Jesus' failure to produce one would dispose of Him in short order. But the Pharisees did believe in the supernatural. The point of their demand was that they distinguished between signs *on earth* and signs *from heaven.* Jesus had given them an abundance of earthly signs which they did not accept. They believed that even demons could work such (cf. Matt. 12:24). But a sign from heaven was quite another matter. What they meant by a sign from heaven we do not know. But evidently they wanted some visible demonstration which would be a final demonstration of God's presence and power—perhaps for the sun to stand still, the moon to turn to blood, fire to fall from heaven, or some other miraculous phenomenon. But their very attitude was such that they did not expect such to happen. Therefore, they too could dispose of Jesus as a fake or as one in league with demons.

But Jesus did not fall into the trap set by either. The same brilliance of mind that He displayed on Tuesday of Passion Week He demonstrated here. Instead of complying with their demand, Jesus used it as an occasion to point out their spiritual blindness. They were adept at reading the signs in the sky (16:2-3). They knew that a red sky in the evening was a sign of fair weather, and that a red and lowering sky in the morning meant stormy weather. William Barclay reminds us of a similar saying in current use today.

> A red sky at night is the shepherd's delight;
> A red sky in the morning is the shepherd's warning.

However, these worldly wise men were incapable of discerning "the signs of the times." The whole world was full of God, but they could not see Him. Events of eternal spiritual import were transpiring before their very eyes. But having eyes they saw not.

However, are we any better? A generation which performs marvels in the material, scientific sphere is all too often unaware of the workings of God. We trace the path of the stars, but are unable to see the course of God in history. And we, like they, are left to blunder on in spiritual darkness.

What was Jesus' final word in response to their demand? They were "an evil and adulterous generation" (16:4). The word "adulterous" had no reference to moral evil. Jesus used it in the sense of the Old Testament. Idolatry was regarded as spiritual adultery. These Pharisees and Sadducees had forsaken a vital experience with the living God to bow before their gods of dry traditionalism and harsh rationalism. And, therefore, no sign would be given to them except the sign of Jonas, or of Jesus' resurrection (cf. 12:39ff.). Jesus never performed a miracle on demand. Instead He pointed them to a greater miracle, one which they refused to believe when it was given.

"And he left them, and departed." To them Jesus gave the same answer as that which He gave to Herod. He left them to their own choice. They had demonstrated beyond doubt that they would have none of Him. The choice was theirs, not His. He merely recognized the condition which they had created. He was like a surgeon who operates on a man only to find him filled with a malignancy. He did not cause it. But he must act accordingly. He merely sews him up, and waits for the inevitable. So Jesus recognized their hopeless condition. "He left them, and departed."

In reality Jesus' departure from them was the answer of truth to error. He did not argue with them uselessly. There is no point in debating needlessly with a mind that is wholly committed to false teachings. For a man "convinced against his will is of the same opinion still." Jesus had revealed the light and they had refused it. So instead of wrangling with their erroneous views, He departed to proclaim the truth. This is the only effective answer which truth can give to error. "He left them, and departed."

How terrible are these words. And yet they express the attitude even of God in the face of one who irrevocably rejects Him. Jesus will not violate human personality by forcing Himself upon man. He offers Himself, but He will not coerce man. When Jesus departed from them, the Gospel record reveals that the Sadducees never saw Him again until the events of Passion Week. Like Jerusalem, their house was left desolate. He that hath ears to hear, let him hear!

The Challenge of Truth (16:5-12)

With this final word to the constituted religious leaders of the Jews, Jesus and the Twelve departed from Galilee on their fourth withdrawal. Apparently they left hastily, for the disciples carried no provisions (16:5). As they traveled along the way, beyond the sea of Galilee, Jesus taught them. "Take heed and beware of the leaven of the Pharisees and of the Sadducees" (16:6). The reference to leaven suggested to them the thought of bread (v. 7). They too were bound to the material. So Jesus censured them for their failure to understand (vv. 8-11). They had so soon forgotten the two miraculous feedings that they should worry about Jesus' ability to provide for their physical needs! "Then understood they how that he bade them not beware of the leaven of bread, but of the doctrine [the teaching] of the Pharisees and of the Sadducees" (v. 12).

Actually Jesus said two distinct things to them. "Take heed" to their teaching. The word is the word to see a thing and to retain the image which they saw (*horaō*). Literally Jesus said, "Look at it, be acquainted with it, or stare at it." They were to understand it, not only its words but its meaning. And then they were to "beware" of it, or to hold themselves away from it or against it. In the double use of the present imperative Jesus commands His disciples to *keep on looking* at their teaching and to *keep on bewaring* of it.

And what was their teaching? Traditionalism and rationalism respectively. These elements were and are the arch enemies of the truth as revealed in Jesus.

The Pharisees accepted the Scriptures as the revealed and inspired Word of God. But they so added to them with their traditions as to stifle the spirit in their insistence upon the letter. In such a fashion they sought to make the Scriptures say more than they said. Thus they became a burden rather than a blessing. Religion became merely the rote observance of laws and regulations. This legalism served to defeat a spiritual relationship with God as it placed its emphasis upon outward ritual and ceremonial purity.

The Sadducees, on the other hand, accepted only that portion of the Scriptures which coincided with their own preconceived ideas. If the Word of God approved of their system, well and good. But if not, then their ideas must prevail. Since they did not believe in the supernatural, then the Biblical accounts of the supernatural simply could not be true. The natural result was their belief that the Kingdom of God could not be brought in by supernatural power. Therefore, it must be produced by human means. Such a religion naturally degenerated into a crusade of social and political action. It had no place for inward change in the nature of man. Material prosperity and political power were to the Sadducees synonymous with *utopia*.

We have but to look about us to see the timeless nature of Jesus' warning. Men who either add to or subtract from the Word of God comprise those who would reduce the Christian religion either to a form of ritual and outward conduct, or else to a form of social and political action which takes little or no account of man's basic problem—his sinful nature. But neither can suffice for the needs of men. Jesus rebelled against both in His day, and there is no reason to believe that He regards either any differently today. He says to us as He did to the Twelve, "Keep on taking heed and keep on bewaring of the leaven of the Pharisees and of the Sadducees." Be aware of them; know their methods and aims; but avoid them as you would a plague. For to do otherwise is to miss the true meaning of Truth, of the King, and of His Kingdom.

The Confession of Peter (16:13-20)

Ultimately the path of this little band led them "into the coasts [region] of Caesarea Philippi" (16:13). And here we come to the very watershed of the gospel. All that went before and all that comes after this event flow from it. Jesus is now only six months away from the cross. Does anyone understand Him and His mission? If not, can they be brought to comprehend? For upon that understanding rests the very outcome of all that He has come to do. Therefore, with determined purpose Jesus picks this place for the supreme question. "Who am I? And what is the purpose and method of my mission?" It would appear that Jesus selected this place with deliberate design. For it brought Him into an environment suggestive of everything which opposed Him.

Caesarea Philippi was located about twenty-five miles northeast of the sea of Galilee. It was the northern extremity of Jewish territory at the headwaters of the Jordan river. The region was in the domain of Herod Philip, the brother of Herod Antipas. The city itself was built upon a rocky cliff which was several hundred feet high. The cliff rested on a large strata of rock (cf. Greek, *petra,* Matt. 16:18).

But the significance of this location for Jesus' purpose was its religious and political associations. George Adam Smith identifies it as the site of Dan which long had been associated with Hebrew worship and later with Baal worship. But in later years it had been identified with the worship of the Greek god Pan, the god of nature, who was said to have been born in a cave which was nearby. The association with this god is seen in the fact that until Roman times the town was called Panias. Herod the Great built here a temple to Caesar Augustus. Thus it was also identified with the political-religious cult of emperor worship. This element is also seen in the fact that at a later date Herod Agrippa called the town Neroneas in honor of the emperor Nero. At the time when Jesus was there it was called Caesarea Philippi. Herod

Philip had enriched and beautified the temple built by his father, and called the town Caesarea or Caesar's town. He added his own name Philippi to distinguish it from Caesarea, the city on the Mediterranean coast.

So the region had many mingled associations. It was a reminder of the Hebrew religion. But it also had a very definite pagan flavor as seen in the worship of the Greek god Pan. Furthermore, its association with Roman emperor worship carried the dual idea of the political state combined with the decadent religion. All of these elements were in direct opposition to everything which was related to Jesus, His person, purpose, and Kingdom. And it was in such an atmosphere that Jesus put His disciples to the test as to their own concept of Him and His mission.

"Whom do men say that I the Son of man am?" (16:13). Possibly the disciples were in a holiday mood. The place was filled with the monuments of ancient kings and conquerors as well as the relics of past and present religions. The Twelve may have been absorbed in viewing them as they sought to identify first one and then another.

The question of their Master brought them back to the present reality. One can almost feel the sudden silence which seized upon them. Then one by one they began to answer. "Some say that thou art John the Baptist; some, Elias; and others, Jeremias, or one of the prophets" (v. 14). Jesus was different things to different people. Some shared with Herod Antipas the idea that He was a continuation of the Baptist. Or He was Elijah, the prophet who would precede the Messiah. Or He is like Jeremiah the weeping prophet. Or some other prophet. Any one of these would have been a compliment to most men. But note that in kindness they did not mention some of the names given to Jesus by His enemies.

Jesus did not ask this question to seek information. He was perfectly aware of what other men were calling Him. What He wanted was to prepare the Twelve for the question of all questions. What was their conception of Him? Had He succeeded in imparting to them any understanding as to His identity and mission? They had observed Him for possibly three years. But had they discerned Him? That there was something unusual about Jesus was evident in their replies to His first question. But that was not enough. If the Twelve shared only these popular ideas about Him, then He had failed. But the time had arrived when He needed to know. And so, perhaps with bated breath, Jesus put to them the supreme question.

"But whom say ye that I am?" (v. 15). Literally, "But ye

[plural] whom me ye say to be?" The emphasis is upon "ye." It matters little what others say. If this little group has grasped the right answer there is hope. So "Ye, whom say ye that I am?"

If there was silence at the first question, that which followed this one was the silence of a tomb. Who would answer? Each seemed to wait for some other. Finally, the silence was broken. Simon Peter, speaking for all, said, "Thou art the Christ, the Son of the living God" (v. 16). Again the word "you" (*su*) is written in the text, and so it is emphatic. "You," in contrast to all others, "are the Christ, the Son of the God the living."

Peter's use of the word "you" sets Jesus apart from all others. Not only Pan and Caesar. But Elijah, Jeremiah, John the Baptist, and the entire roll of the prophets. These latter served definite purposes in the economy of God. But they were but servants in the house of God. No such designation could be applied to Jesus. He is the Son in the house. The former knew God from afar. But Jesus knows Him in the intimacy of the Godhead. Said Jesus of Himself, "He that hath seen me hath seen the Father" (John 14:9).

Doubtless at this time Peter could not have given a theological or philosophical dissertation on the relation of Jesus to the Father. But he knew enough for a beginning. There were yet many things which the Twelve needed to learn. But somehow the light had broken through the clouds of a wrong concept of Jesus and of the Messiah, so that they understood that somehow He was the Messiah, God's Anointed, and His Son. The light will grow brighter with the passing of time and the further unveiling of God's purpose in Christ until each of them can grasp the meaning of Paul's words, "For God, who commanded the light to shine out of darkness, hath shined in our hearts, to give the light of the knowledge of the glory of God in the face of Jesus Christ" (II Cor. 4:6).

But the light of hope also shined in the heart of Jesus. Wonderful and musical were the words of Simon. For Jesus saw the light of understanding beginning to break forth in the minds and hearts of this inner circle of His disciples. Though other men may be confused, and some even closed of mind and heart, these understood. And out of such would the King build His Kingdom.

And so Jesus spoke another beatitude. "Blessed art thou, Simon Barjona [son of John]: for flesh and blood hath not revealed it unto thee, but my Father which is in heaven" (v. 17). And because Peter spoke for the others, this beatitude was bestowed on all of them (Judas excepted) and others who come to this same realization. No matter what the confusion of thoughts and opinions about Jesus might be among those who only knew Him casually. This conviction about the King would make His followers sufficient within themselves as they faced the storm of hate which one day soon will break upon them. Anchored to this rock of faith they will be able to ride out the storm.

And note the source of this conviction. It came not through the rationalism of the Sadducees, neither by the outward rituals of the Pharisees. Nor did it come through the worldly pomp and splendor of despotism. It was a revelation from God through His Holy Spirit. Which comprises a lesson for us. We do not arrive at a proper concept of Jesus through the reason of the mind. He does not become real and personal by means of ritual. Nor do we find Him in the grandeur and glory of the world. We discover Him through the whispering of the Spirit of God in our hearts. The Christian religion is not discovered by man; it is revealed of God. And in this sense it is distinct from every other religion. Of course, the Hebrew faith came by revelation. And New Testament Christianity is the flower of which it is the root.

Only by divine revelation could the disciples come to such a concept of Jesus. By every worldly standard it was in contradiction to rational evidence. Amid the splendors of paganism, as evidenced by the beautiful white marble temple of Herod, this declaration was an absurdity. A lowly peasant carpenter "the Christ, the Son of the living God!" Yet through the ministry of these untutored yet believing men, and those who would come after them, in less than three hundred years Tiberius Caesar's successor would proclaim the religion built upon this *carpenter* as the official religion of the Roman Empire. And regardless of the subsequent effects of this proclamation, it speaks nevertheless of the spiritual power which was resident in Him who was revealed as "the Christ, the Son of the living God."

And then Jesus continued. "And I say unto thee, Thou art Peter . . ." (v. 18). "And I" is one word in the Greek (*kagō*), and so it is emphatic. Who is this speaking? "The Christ, the Son of the living God." And what does He say? "Thou art Peter. . . ." The word "Peter" *(petros)* means a rock or a little stone. When Jesus first met Simon He predicted that he would one day become a *petros* (cf. John 1:42). And now He says that he has become one. And what was the evidence that he had fulfilled Jesus' prophecy about him? His confession concerning Christ. So unstable and uncertain was Simon Barjona. But now he is a man of strength. The "rock" will soften here and there. But heated in the fires of the crucifixion and tempered in the cooling waters of the resurrection, he will one day stand before the enemies of Christ and declare, "...by the name of Jesus Christ of Nazareth, whom ye crucified, whom God raised from the dead, even by him doth this man stand here before you whole" (Acts 4:10). Nowhere do we find Jesus' power to transform men better illustrated than in the person of Simon who is called Peter. He has not yet arrived completely, but he is on the way.

With this Jesus spoke words of the greatest import. "And upon this rock I will build my church; and the gates of hell shall not prevail against it" (v. 18). Now that this little band has declared its conviction as to the Person of Jesus, how shall this faith be shared with others? It will be through the church. And thus Jesus begins to unfold the "mystery" which has through the ages been hidden in the heart of God how that He will declare His work of redemption "through the church" (Eph. 3:10). It will be accomplished through Christ. It will be declared through the church.

This is the first time that the word "church" appears in the New Testament where it appears one hundred and fifteen times. It renders a Greek word *(ekklesia)* meaning "assembly" or "the called out ones." Jesus Himself used this word only twice (cf. Matt. 18:18-20), but His usages are significant as we shall see presently.

So Jesus proposes to build His church. Upon what or whom does He plan to build it? "Thou art Peter, and upon this rock I will build my church." Roman Catholics cite this passage as proof that they are the only true church, and that Christ built it upon Peter as the first pope. They hold that since Jesus used the singular ("thou," *su ei Petros*) that He spoke to Peter as an individual, and that he is the "rock." Thus they speak of the primacy of Peter.

But is this the correct meaning? Since Peter spoke *for* the Twelve may we not assume that Jesus spoke *to* the Twelve through Peter? To be sure in the first clause He singled out Peter by name. But are we necessarily to assume that He spoke to Peter alone in the second clause?

An examination of the New Testament fails to reveal any primary position being accorded to Peter. To be sure his name always appears first in the lists of the apostles (cf. Matt. 10:2f.; Mark 3:16f.; Luke 6:14f.; Acts 1:13f.). But this is no sign that he was their leader. The constant struggle for position among the Twelve indicates that they did not hold Peter as being any different from them. Certainly Peter occupied no such place during Jesus' lifetime for He was the leader of the Twelve. And beginning at Pentecost their leader was Jesus' other Self, the Holy Spirit. The lists of apostles were made up after Jesus' death. That Peter did assume a certain amount of leadership following the Ascension is clear. But it well could be due to his natural impetuosity. However, even this does not imply primacy and authority. The church in Jerusalem was under the leadership of James. And it looked with askance upon Peter's evangelistic activity in Caesarea, accepting it only by a vindication through the Holy Spirit and a report from their committee sent to investigate the matter. Peter occupied no primary place at the Jerusalem Conference (Acts 15). Paul did not recognize any peculiar place or authority as being accorded to Peter (cf. Gal. 2:7-11). Peter himself claimed no special place of leadership among the early Christians. He regarded himself as a "fellow elder" with others (I Peter 5:1).

What then is the meaning of Jesus' words in Matthew 16:18? When we examine the words *petros* (Peter) and *petra* (rock) we note immediately that they are not related. For the former is a masculine gender, and the latter is a feminine gender. The word *petra* means a ledge rock such as the ledge rock upon which the city of Caesarea Philippi rested. It was a foundation rock. A *petros* was a little stone such as might be broken off of a *petra.* It partook of the nature of the *petra,* but it was not a *petra.*

Now to what does *petra* refer? Some hold that it refers to Peter, not as a person, but as a type of all who make the confession which he made. Others relate it to the faith as revealed in the confession. But either of these leaves much to be desired. The overall teachings of the New Testament regard Jesus Himself as the foundation of the church (cf. I Cor. 3:10-11). It is held by some that Jesus spoke in Aramaic, and that in that language the distinction between *petros* and *petra* does not hold. Even so in the Old Testament, when used in the symbolic sense, "rock" always refers to deity. Paul clearly says, "...for they drank of that spiritual Rock that followed them: and that Rock was Christ" (I Cor. 10:4; cf. Exod. 17:6).

It would appear, therefore, that *petra* refers to Christ Himself. He is the rock upon which the church will be built. And it will be built out of those *petroi* (stones) which partake of the nature of the *petra* through their confessions of faith in Jesus as "the Christ, the Son of the living God." This may well have been in the mind of Peter when he wrote, "Ye also, as lively stones [*lithoi*], are built up an spiritual house..." (I Peter 2:5). Peter is but one among many building stones made alive through Christ, and with which He is building His church.

A second question confronts us in this verse. What did Jesus mean by the "church"? Some hold that the word "church" in the New Testament sense always refers to the local church. While others see in it the twofold sense of both the local church and the church general as being composed of all of the redeemed through all the ages. Still others use it in the sense of a given denomination. Suffice it to say in this last regard that the New Testament never so uses the word. The early Christians knew nothing about *denominations* as we know them. But what of the other two uses? Out of the one hundred and fifteen times that the word *ekklesia* appears in the New Testament at least ninety-two times it refers to the local church. But there are other uses where it clearly refers to the church in the general sense. Jesus Himself seems to use the word in both the general and in the local sense (cf. Matt. 16:18; 18:17).

Perhaps we can best understand the meaning of Jesus' words by considering the word "church" in its fuller usage in the New Testament. We have seen that the word itself means "assembly" of free cities (cf. Acts 19:39). When a matter needed to be settled the citizens were called out *(ek,* out of; *kaleō,* call; so *ekklesia,* the called out ones) of their homes and shops to assemble as a group of citizens for debate and voting on the matter. As such they functioned as a purely democratic body acting within the framework of the laws of the Empire.

But *ekklesia* also had a Hebrew connotation. In the Septuagint it translates the Hebrew word *qahal,* referring to the nation of Israel assembled before God or a general assembly under theocratic rule (cf. Deut. 31:30; I Chron. 29:1, congregation; Judg. 21:8, assembly). The word *ekklesia* is so used twice in the New Testament (cf. Acts 7:38; Heb. 2:12). Thus the word had both a local, democratic meaning and a general, theocratic meaning. And both must be kept in mind if we are to comprehend Jesus' words.

We have become so involved in the meaning of both "rock" and "church" that we have largely lost sight of what Jesus actually said. For the emphasis in the Greek text is on neither of these words. It is on the word "my." "My" is written before the word "church" instead of after it. And so it occupies the emphatic position. Thus in effect, Jesus is saying, "The Greeks have their assembly; the Hebrews have their assembly. And upon this rock [Christ] I will build *my* assembly." So the assembly of Christ will be distinct from the Greek and Hebrew assemblies. And yet it will partake of their basic natures. It will be a purely local and democratic assembly operating under the Lordship of Jesus Christ or the laws of the Kingdom of God. And it will be a general assembly of all the redeemed of God through the ages and under His theocratic rule.

It might be argued that the church in this latter sense will become a reality only when all of the redeemed of all the ages are assembled before God in heaven. However, this is to put undue stress upon both time and space where neither is justified in terms of their relation to God who is Spirit. The fact is that Jesus spoke within the thought context of His listeners, and we must leave it there. Nor are we justified in pressing the general sense of "church" into present day ecumenical molds. For this also was not in Jesus' mind. We shall do well to let Jesus say what He said, nothing more, nothing less.

However, we are not through with verse 18. For still another question calls for an answer. What is the meaning of "the gates of hell shall not prevail against it?" It is true that the powers of hell shall not be able to overcome or successfully resist the church. But this is not taught in this verse. For the English word "hell" renders the Greek word *hades,* meaning the abode of the dead. It is the Greek equivalent of the Hebrew word *sheol,* the place of departed spirits. Therefore, the meaning has to do with death. The word "prevail" means to have strength against. So the gates of *hades* shall not have strength against the church. "Gates" are used to keep people out or else to shut them in. People are not storming the "gates of *hades*" in order to get in. Those inside are storming the gates endeavoring to get out. And Jesus says that the gates of hades shall not have strength to hold them in the realm of the dead. It is, therefore, His promise that the church, or those who make up His church, shall not be held in the clutches of death. It is a promise of the final resurrection from the dead as well as of the abiding and living nature of His church. The church of the Lord Jesus Christ will endure through the ages serving Him, and beyond the ages in eternal fellowship with Him. This is the glorious prospect of all those who in truth confess Him to be "the Christ, the Son of the living God."

But how shall the church serve Christ in this age? This question Jesus answers in verse 19. "And I will give unto thee the keys of the kingdom of heaven: and whatsoever thou shalt bind on earth shall be bound in heaven: and whatsoever thou shalt loose on earth shall be loosed in heaven."

Here again we find a conflict of opinions as to Jesus' meaning.

Those who hold that Peter was the first pope insist that the "keys" are his insignia of office. Thus they involve the right to retain or forgive sin, a power which he in turn passed on to his successors in office. It is further noted that "thee" (*soi*), as in verse 18, is singular, referring to Peter alone. However, we should remember that as Peter spoke for the Twelve, so Jesus speaks to the Twelve. And if one cares to press the point of the singular pronoun, it may be pointed out that in Matthew 18:18 where Jesus makes the identical statement the verbs are plural. Therefore, we may assume that as in Matthew 16:19 Jesus spoke through Peter to the Twelve, in Matthew 18:18 He speaks directly to the Twelve. And He does so in the context of reference to the local church (cf. 18:17), not to any individual or even to the Twelve alone.

What then did Jesus mean by the "keys"? The keys in a house were entrusted to a slave who was the "steward" of the owner. Furthermore, the phrase "binding... loosing" was a Rabbinical term relating to the scribe as a teacher. In Rabbinical language "to bind" was "to forbid," "to loose" was "to permit." Keys are for locking or opening doors. So the "keys of the kingdom of heaven" would refer to either shutting its doors to prevent entrance or else opening its doors to permit it. What is it which constitutes the right to enter into the kingdom of heaven? It is one's confession of the King as "the Christ, the Son of the living God." In essence, therefore, this involves the gospel, the life, death, and resurrection of Jesus from the dead. These elements of the gospel are not yet clearly defined in the minds of the apostles. But Jesus is looking beyond the events to their proclamation through the ages. So He is here committing to His church the gospel which it is to preach throughout the world until the end of the age. The church can either bind or loose it.

And this thought introduces again the meaning of binding and loosing in terms of the Christian gospel. In the Greek text of "shall be bound.... shall be loosed" the verbs are what is called the *periphrastic future perfect passive.* This form expresses an action which took place in the past but whose effect is still existing in the present, and will continue to be in effect in the future. Literally, "shall have been bound... shall have been loosed." In effect, the binding and loosing were in heaven, are still there, and will continue to be there. And the passive voice speaks of this binding and loosing as being done by one other than man on earth, or by God Himself.

So what did Jesus actually say? He said that heaven has already decreed that if we bind the gospel on earth, it is bound and stands bound in heaven. If we loose the gospel on earth, it is loosed and stands loosed in heaven. Heaven or God has decreed that men shall be saved by hearing and believing the gospel. If we bind it on earth by failing to proclaim it, heaven has no other way by which men shall be saved. But if we loose it on earth men will hear, and those who believe it shall be saved.

So Jesus has committed the "keys" to us as His stewards of the gospel. It is a glorious privilege, but it is also a tremendous responsibility. We have within our hands the power to transform the world. If the world is not won to Christ it will not be Christ or the gospel which has failed. It will be His church which has played truant to the faith which our Lord has placed in us. God forbid!

But, strange to say, after all of this Jesus forbids the Twelve to tell any man that He is the Christ (v. 20). This, of course, was not a permanent ban on the gospel. Rather Jesus knows that they are not yet ready to use the "keys." They know that He is the Christ. But they do not yet comprehend the full and true meaning of the term. Had they gone forth that moment to tell men that He was the Christ, they would have proclaimed a political, military Messiah. Nor were the people ready to receive the message with comprehension. They, too, had the wrong concept of His Messiahship. So to proclaim Him as the Christ at that point would have produced revolution instead of regeneration. The disciples had learned the first lesson well. But there is so much more to understand.

The Cross of Christ (16:21-28)

And Jesus proceeds immediately to the next lesson. "From that time forth began Jesus to shew unto his disciples, how that he must go unto Jerusalem, and suffer many things of the elders and chief priests and scribes, and be killed, and be raised again the third day" (v. 21).

Was this a new note in the teaching of Jesus? Did it suddenly occur to Him that this was to be His fate? He has rejected a political kingdom or despotism, the traditions and rituals of the Pharisees, and the social and political ambitions of the Sadducees. Now does He finally realize that they will wreak their vengeance upon Him? To say these things would be contrary to the record and to His own Person as the King.

The truth of the matter is that Jesus had spoken of these things in a veiled fashion from the beginning. He portrayed them in His baptism. John records them as a "sign" which Jesus gave to the

Jewish authorities on the occasion of His first visit to Jerusalem in His public ministry (2:18-22). And this sign He had repeated to both the Pharisees and Sadducees (cf. Matt. 12:39-40; 16:4). So this was no new note in Jesus' message.

However, it is here that He begins to speak plainly about it to His disciples. Only six months remain before His death. And they must be prepared for it. For this is the very heart of the "keys" which He has entrusted to them. And they must be ready to use them intelligently when the moment comes. The fact that Jesus "began" to teach these things implies that He continued to do so.

Notice that Jesus did not say that these things *will* take place, as though they were future events over which He had no control. The word is not "will" but "must." He *must* go to Jerusalem. He *must* suffer. He *must* be killed. He *must* be raised again the third day. The word rendered "must" is one meaning "it is necessary" (*dei*). So that of which Jesus spoke was in the plan and purpose of God. These things are divine imperatives, and not merely a human martyrdom.

However, note that His words did not end in a note of tragedy but of triumph. For He "must . . . be raised again the third day." This is not the word of one who submitted to the inevitable. It speaks of His faith in the glorious purpose of God whereby He will provide redemption for a lost human race. Too often we stop short of these final words. Jesus on a cross, yes. But that is only half of the gospel. Stopping there in our preaching we merely relate history's greatest tragedy. But continuing to the end of the story we proclaim God's greatest triumph. The early Christians never stopped at the cross in their faith or message. The glorious truth is not simply that Jesus died on a cross. For many men had so died. The ringing note of the gospel is that He arose from the dead. He is not merely a dead Jesus on a cross, but a living Presence through the ages. The gates of *hades* did not have strength against Him. And that is our message, even our hope.

Apparently Peter's mind stopped on the words "and be killed," so that he failed to hear "and be raised again the third day." For he replied, "Be it far from thee, Lord: this shall not be unto thee" (v. 22). A. T. Robertson translates "be it far from thee" as "God have mercy on thee" (*hileōs*). And we note in passing that God had no mercy on His Son in order that He might extend His bountiful mercy unto all who will believe in Him. But Peter recoiled from such a thought. In reply he used the strongest sort of double negative. Literally, "Not never shall be this to thee" (*ou mē estai soi touto*). It was as though Peter had perfect assurance that he and his companions could prevent it. Certainly they could not stay the forces working against Jesus. But most of all they could not defeat the purpose of God working in Jesus.

Jesus was quick to react. Matthew says that He "turned." He uses the aorist tense describing quick, immediate action. But Mark notes clearly that He turned from Peter and toward the others, as though He did so in revulsion to Peter's words (8:33). "Get thee behind me, Satan: thou art an offence [stumbling-block] unto me: for thou savourest [mindest] not the things that be of God, but those that be of men" (v. 23). Peter, who had so recently been a stepping-stone to Jesus, is now a stumbling-block on the road of God's purpose. He who had spoken the revelation of God now speaks the words of Satan. It is the oft-repeated temptation of the wilderness all over again. How sad that not only Peter, but we also, are so often stumbling-stones in Jesus' path of redemption as we misrepresent Him in both word and deed!

Jesus said that Peter spoke not the mind of God but the mind of men. For such is the favorite tool of Satan. Peter spoke the spirit of his age and of ours. The demand for a crossless Christ continues. The cross is to many still a stumbling-block and to others foolishness. But it is ever in the plan and purpose of God. When we rob Jesus of the cross and the subsequent resurrection, we take from Him His greatest glory. We make of Him merely an ethical teacher *par excellence* and nothing more. The gospel is emptied of its message, and men continue to wander hopelessly in the morass of sin. It is no wonder, then, that Jesus turned in revulsion from Peter. And He continues to do so to those who mind not the things that be of God but of men.

If Peter rebelled against a cross for Jesus, he was in for another shock. For Jesus continued, "If any man will come after me, let him deny himself, and take up his cross, and follow me" (v. 24). For a cross awaits all who propose to follow Jesus. We try to tone down these terrible words by referring to our own comparatively easy burdens as our crosses. But there was no mistaking the meaning of Jesus' words on the part of the Twelve. It was customary to require a condemned person to bear his own cross to the place of crucifixion. So in effect Jesus said that if anyone proposes to follow Him, he must be willing to die for Him. The words "deny" and "take up" are aorist imperatives of immediate action. They command an immediate renunciation of self and a taking up of the cross. There is no way of toning down these words without destroying their meaning.

Jesus never promised that we should have an easy time in following Him. If the world hated Him, it hates us. Both He and His people are a judgment upon the world. And the world has but one answer, the cross. In fact, the cross is God's only answer to the world. But it is His answer of love.

In paradoxical fashion Jesus summarizes the whole matter. "For whosoever will save his life shall lose it: and whosoever will lose his life for my sake shall find it" (v. 25). Losing by saving; saving by losing. This is the very paradox of life.

In the English version it appears that Jesus used a series of future tenses. But the original text reads otherwise. Literally, "For whosoever may will his life to save, he shall lose it: and whosoever may lose his life for my sake, he shall find it." As Jesus said, "If any one will to come after me" (v. 24) knowing that a cross awaits him, so He said that one "may will" to play it safe. But in so doing he will lose his life. Conversely, in the decision to follow Jesus one "may lose" his life. But in so doing he will find life.

The word "life" (*psuchē*) may be rendered either "life" or "soul." Obviously this is a play on the word which in verse 26 is translated "soul." In verse 25 the emphasis is upon "life," but "soul" is involved also. The athlete who saves his physical life from training and discipline will lose his spiritual life as expressed in the joy of victory. The student who saves his mental life from the arduous toil of study, will lose the spiritual life of a sense of accomplishment. But by the same token the one who loses his life in pursuit of a worthy goal will find life in the achievement of it.

This principle operated in the life of Jesus. Had He saved His life from following God's purpose, He would have lost it in a meaningless existence. In like fashion if we will to save our lives from the cross which awaits us in following Him, we shall lose life in the bargain. Only by losing self in Him may we find our true selves through Him.

"For what is a man profited, if he shall gain the whole world, and lose his own soul? or what shall a man give in exchange for his soul" (v. 26). "Soul" or "life," the meaning is the same. For in a very real sense the totality of "soul" involves "life" also.

The world offered its rewards to Jesus, but He refused them for the greater goal. It makes the same offer to us. If we would follow the King we must make the choice of the King. If you sell your soul for the "whole world," or all that the world has to offer, and yet lose your soul in the transaction, you have made a bad bargain. But once having done so and wishing to call off the deal, what will you pay to buy back your soul? The world has no legal tender in the Kingdom of God. You must give yourself to the King if you would be in His Kingdom.

This is no idle speculation. "For the Son of man shall come in the glory of his Father with his angels; and then he shall reward every man according to his works" (v. 27). Now God's Anointed offers Himself as the Saviour. Then He will sit on the throne of judgment.

From the many New Testament pictures of the Judgment we know that the fate of every man as to heaven or hell will already have been decided by his acceptance or rejection of Jesus. But at the Judgment He "shall reward *every man* according to his works" (author's italics). There will be degrees of reward for the saved and degrees of punishment for the lost (cf. Luke 12:47-48; I Cor. 3:12-15). And this truth enhances the meaning of Matthew 16:24-26.

Jesus closes this lesson with the words, "There be some standing here, which shall not taste death, till they see the Son of man coming in his kingdom" (v. 28). Does Jesus refer to the crucifixion and resurrection, Pentecost, the destruction of Jerusalem, or to His second coming? Some, holding to the last event, conclude that Jesus was mistaken. But we are not compelled to take such a position. In verse 28 the Lord is using apocalyptic language, in which any great intervention of God in history was regarded as a "coming." So certainly Jesus was speaking of some event or events which happened within the lifetime of "some" who heard Him. All but Judas lived through the events up through Pentecost when the proclamation of the Kingdom was loosed upon the world. Some of them, at least John, lived through the destruction of Jerusalem which marked the end of the Jewish economy, when Christianity came to be regarded fully not as an extension of Judaism but as the final and complete revelation of God in redemptive history. All of these events, or any one of them, considering the crucifixion and resurrection as one, fulfil the meaning of Jesus' words.

The point of emphasis is that the Kingdom will endure. The redemptive work of Christ will suffice. The forces which were then arrayed against Jesus will perish. But even "the gates of *hades* will not have strength against" either Him, His church, or His Kingdom.

"Even so, come, Lord Jesus" (Rev. 22:20).

Matthew 17

The King and His Glory

The period of the King's withdrawals from Galilee is rapidly moving toward a grand climax. Like some grand symphony Jesus' unveiling of Himself has passed from one stirring movement to another. And now there comes the tremendous crescendo. The movement in Matthew 16 was one of mingled lights and shadows, triumph and tragedy, heavenly revelation and satanic temptation. For there we see the King through the eyes of men, some viewing Him in idle curiosity and others through divine revelation. However, even the latter soon became the eyes of demonic insinuation.

But in Matthew 17 we view the King not as man sees Him but as God sees Him. Thus we see the Son of man transfigured in all of His glory.

This event came one week after the scene at Caesarea Philippi. We can only surmise what transpired during this time. But finally Jesus took Peter, James, and John and went up into "an high mountain." Some would identify this mountain with Mount Tabor in Galilee. But this is hardly likely. For the scene suggests a place of seclusion. The top of Mount Tabor was the site of an armed fortress and a castle. A more likely location is Mount Hermon. It is a "high mountain" having an elevation of above nine thousand feet. On a clear day it may be seen from the Dead Sea over one hundred miles away. Furthermore, it is in the region of Caesarea Philippi. So in all probability it was somewhere in the lofty slopes of this towering peak that heaven bent low to reveal the Son of man in a glory never before seen on this earth.

Therefore, as we view this heaven-saturated scene we are in the "holy mount" indeed (II Peter 1:18). And Matthew 17 naturally divides itself into three sections: (1) the purpose of the transfiguration; (2) principles of the transfiguration; (3) postlude of the transfiguration.

The Purpose of the Transfiguration (17:1)

The transfiguration was no isolated event in the life of Jesus. It is definitely related to the events recorded in Matthew 16:13-28. In his account of these incidents Luke says that "after these sayings" Jesus went into the mountain with His three disciples (cf.

Luke 9:18-27; Matt. 16:13-28). So we may assume that the latter was an outgrowth of the former. The transfiguration was an act of God who does nothing without a purpose. What then was the purpose of the transfiguration? Was it for the benefit of Jesus, the disciples, or both?

If this event was for Jesus' benefit, it appears to have been only indirectly so. Some hold that it was for the purpose of encouraging Jesus to continue to walk the way of the cross. But the record shows that He clearly refused Peter's suggestion that He should do otherwise. There is an element of truth in the thought that it was to strengthen Jesus in His resolve to do so. But even this does not fully explain the reason for His transfiguration.

Now it is quite evident that our Lord was disturbed by the turn of events at Caesarea Philippi. We may even admit that in His humanity He was discouraged by them. But this had nothing to do with His prospect of the cross. So in whatever way we may seek to identify Jesus with the purpose of the transfiguration, it must be upon some other basis.

The primary purpose of the transfiguration related itself to the disciples. This would explain why Jesus took three of them with Him into the mountain. These were critical days of intensive instruction for them. Only six months remained before wolves would ravage the fold and the Shepherd be taken from the sheep. And they had just recently demonstrated that they were not prepared for so great a trial.

To understand the transfiguration we must go back to the scene at Caesarea Philippi. Peter and the other disciples reached a new height of understanding with respect to Jesus when he confessed, "Thou art the Christ, the Son of the living God." But shortly thereafter they plumbed the abysmal depths of misunderstanding when Peter rebuked Jesus concerning the cross. And an examination of the language reveals that this was not an isolated incident. Matthew 16:21 says, "From that time forth began Jesus to shew unto his disciples, how that he must... be killed." Matthew 16:22 says, "Then Peter took him, and began to rebuke him...." In both verses "began" is an aorist tense denoting a point in time when these things began. Also "to shew" and "to rebuke" are present infinitives expressing repeated action. So it appears that Jesus *began* and *continued to show* the necessity of the cross. And Peter *began* and *continued to rebuke* Jesus regarding it. It may well be that this dialogue continued throughout the following week, with the other disciples siding with Peter either vocally or by their silence. G. Campbell Morgan sees this interim as one of estrangement between Jesus and the Twelve.

The Twelve regarded Jesus as the Christ to be sure. But they were children of their age. So their concept of the Messiah was still far from that which was necessary if they were to proclaim Him as the Saviour of the world. Furthermore, their very familiarity with Him was such that they even dared to argue with Him as to the role which He must fill.

It was in this state of affairs that Jesus called Peter, James, and John to accompany Him into the mountain. Luke says that He "went up into a mountain to pray" (9:28). And for what did He pray? In the light of Matthew 16:23-28 we can hardly say that He prayed for courage to face the cross. But in view of subsequent events may we not surmise that Jesus prayed for the Father to give to the disciples just such a revelation as came through the transfiguration? They must somehow be led to see Him as He truly is, to understand His role, and to view Him not as one to be commanded but as the only One to command. What the disciples had failed to comprehend by line upon line and precept upon precept, what they did not grasp fully even by revelation, they must be taught by a divine demonstration which could neither be misunderstood nor forgotten. "And as he prayed" (Luke 9:29) the Father answered His prayer immediately. For He "was transfigured before them" (Matt. 17:2).

We must not be too hard in judging the disciples in their failure to understand Jesus otherwise. It is so easy to sit in judgment after the event. But would we have done any better? For the mystery of the incarnation still defies human understanding. To multitudes it is incredible. And to the majority of us who believe it to be a fact of history, it has failed to become the commanding principle of our lives. Even those who accept the Christ of the cross largely demand a crossless discipleship. But still the Saviour patiently calls and waits for us to crucify self in a full commitment to Him. And as we hesitate a lost world wanders in indecision and unbelief. Still the soul of Jesus is restless as He yearns for the souls of men.

> The soul of Jesus is restless today;
> Christ is tramping through the spirit-world,
> Compassion in His heart for the fainting millions;
> He trudges through China, through Poland,
> Through Russia, Austria, Germany, Armenia;
> Patiently He pleads with the Church,
>   Tenderly He woos her.

The wounds of His body are bleeding afresh
  for the sorrows of His shepherdless people.
We besiege Him with selfish petitions,
We weary Him with our petty ambitions,
From the needy we bury Him in piles of carven stone,
We obscure Him in the smoke of stuffy incense,
We drown His voice with the snarls and
  shrieks of our disgruntled bickerings,
We build temples to Him with hands that
  are bloody,
We deny Him in the needs and sorrows of the
  exploited—"least of His brethren."
The soul of Jesus is restless today,
But eternally undismayed.

—Cyprus R. Mitchell[11]

The Principles of the Transfiguration (17:2-9)

We come now to one of the sublimest events in the life of Jesus. Every facet of it is filled with infinite meaning. And the persons involved in it are of timeless significance: Jesus, the heavenly visitors, the heavenly Voice, and the disciples.

In answer to Jesus' prayer He "was transfigured before them: and his face did shine as the sun, and his raiment was white as the light" (Matt. 17:2). The word "transfigured" renders a Greek word (*metamorphō*) from which comes our word *metamorphosis.* It means a change of form. A. T. Robertson in his *Word Pictures in the New Testament* (*in loco*) says, "It really presents the essence of a thing as separate from the *schēma* (fashion), the outward accident." So in His transfiguration Jesus appeared in His true essence as the God-man. He was in this moment no less man or no less God. But this metamorphosis showed His fusion flashing forth—perfect deity and perfect humanity.

This was not a light shining upon Jesus from without. It was His deity shining forth from within. The wick of His essential deity, which from His birth had been turned down low, was suddenly turned up to burn in the brightness of His true glory. "His face did shine as the sun." The sun does not give off reflected light. It is the source of natural light which shines forth out of its very nature. Likewise out of His very nature as deity did the face of Jesus shine. When Moses came down out of the mountain from communing with God, his face shone with the reflected glory of God which had come upon him from without. However, it was a glory soon to fade. But the face of Jesus shined with His own glory

---

11 *Christ and the Fine Arts,* Cynthia Pearl Maus, Harper, New York, 1938, p. 717.

emanating from within. And the glow of His person coming through His raiment caused it to be "white as the light."

However, the emphasis in Matthew's words is not that Jesus was transfigured, but that He "was transfigured *before them*" or before the disciples (author's italics). Who can deny that on other occasions, when Jesus alone in the night had communed with His Father with no human eyes to see it, His deity had illuminated His body in perfect accord with God? But whether or not this be true, this particular incident was for the benefit of His disciples. And whether or not they fully comprehended its meaning, it was a scene which they would never forget.

Suddenly there appeared with Jesus two heavenly visitors, Moses and Elijah. And their presence is most significant for the occasion. There are many reasons why this is true. For they had many things in common. Both had wrought significantly for God. It was through Moses that God had given the Law and had entered into a covenant relation with Israel. It was through Elijah that God had sought to call Israel back to the Law and to the terms of the covenant. Both men had left the world under unusual circumstances. Moses had died, and presumably was buried by the hand of God. Elijah had been translated without seeing death, being taken to heaven in a whirlwind. Yet both stand together on the mount with their separate identities in the after life and recognizable to the disciples. Both of these things are significant in our understanding of life after death.

But the overall significance of these two men is that they are suggestive of the old order which finds its fulfilment in Christ. The Jews commonly referred to their Scriptures as "the law and the prophets." In their thinking Moses was symbolic of the Law, and Elijah was symbolic of the prophets. Furthermore, in this capacity they are representative of that host of Old Testament "saints" who died in faith that God would redeem those who called upon Him. So in this gathering on Mount Hermon we see law (Moses), prophecy (Elijah), and grace (Jesus). The law and the prophets were talking with Him who is the embodiment of God's grace. And of what were they speaking?

Luke says that they "spake of his decease which he should accomplish at Jerusalem" (9:31). Actually the word "decease" should be rendered "exodus." It is the exact word used for the book of Exodus which takes its name from the exodus of Israel out of Egypt. So it embodies more than Jesus' decease or death. It involves that plus His resurrection and ascension, or the manner of His exodus out of this world and back to the glory of heaven.

We are not to suppose that Moses and Elijah were urging Jesus to walk the way of the cross. For such was unnecessary. But their very presence served to emphasize the necessity of it. For they and all others like them were in heaven "on credit," looking toward the time when the Christ of God would die for their sins and be raised for their justification. Without this heaven would be depopulated and hell would be inhabited by all those who had died in faith, looking for the time when Shiloh would come and establish their peace with God.

It is at this point that we can pause to see the full significance of the transfiguration. The law and the prophets are fulfilled in Him who is the gift of God's grace. Apart from Him the law is condemnation and the prophets are empty indeed. But in Him the righteousness demanded by the law finds fulfilment, and the promises held forth in the prophets become realities. And all because of who and what Jesus is in His person.

Even before God had created man, in the council chambers of eternity the Son had said to the Father, "Sacrifice and offering thou wouldst not, but a body thou hast prepared me . . . lo, I come . . . to do thy will, O God" (Heb. 10:5,7). Perfect in His deity the Son took on the form of a man. For thirty-three years He has endured the trials and conflicts of man, yet without sin. Not one time has He deviated from the will of the Father. Despite the repeated efforts of Satan and Satan-inspired men, He has turned His back upon the spirit of the world and of the age to walk perfectly in the path of divine purpose. And now He stands upon the mountain not only perfect in deity but perfect in humanity. Had there been one flaw in His character He would have been killed by the surging of divine voltage in His body. But because He was perfect God and perfect Man, "his face did shine as the sun, and his raiment was white as light." And soon He will hear once again the spoken approval of His Father. Morgan suggests that had He so chosen, He might have returned immediately to heaven. But it would have been a heaven bereft of those who had trusted or would ever trust in Him. And while He would have had the glory which was His before the universe came into being, even He would have been deprived of that glory which was to be His as Saviour (cf. Phil. 2:9-11).

So Moses, Elijah, and Jesus talked of His *exodus*. Thenceforth we see in Jesus an eagerness, almost an impatience, for the cross. For it is only thus that God may highly exalt Him and give to Him "a name which is above every name: that at the name of Jesus every knee should bow . . . and that every tongue should confess that Jesus Christ is Lord, to the glory of God the Father" (Phil. 2:9-11). What name possibly could be above and beyond every other name? *Jesus,* Jehovah is salvation! "Thou shalt call his name JESUS: for he shall save his people from their sins" (Matt. 1:21).

And how shall He do this? Through His perfect life as He satisfies the demands of God's holiness and righteousness. Through His perfect sacrifice for sin as God is in Christ reconciling the world unto Himself. Through His resurrection as He triumphs over sin and death. Perfect in His humanity. Perfect in His deity. Now He stands in physical night upon Mount Hermon. Then He will stand amid spiritual night upon Mount Calvary. And as He was glorious in the glow of Hermon, so He will be glorified through the throe of Calvary.

But even into this heavenly scene there intrudes the discordant notes of men. The disciples had been asleep while Jesus was praying (cf. Luke 9:32), but had been awakened by this glorious scene. They were terrified by it. And if they had heard the conversation about Jesus' exodus, it apparently had failed to register in their minds. So in such a state Peter spoke to Jesus. Luke notes that he spoke, "not knowing what he said" (9:33). He was still in a daze, or else did not comprehend the entire import of the event.

At any rate Peter said, "Lord, it is good for us [including the disciples] to be here..." ((Matt. 17:4). In effect he said, "Lord, this is what we mean. This glory is what we desire for you and for us. You speak of a cross, but that is not glory but shame and suffering."

Again we must not judge the disciples too harshly. For even though they still did not grasp the full significance of the role of Jesus, they loved Him nevertheless. And Jesus loved them in spite of their failure. They had caught the vision of glory, but they preferred to forget the cross. And, alas, they speak for us. For we also are willing to share in Christ's glory, but are perfectly willing to forget the suffering. Paul reminds us that the two cannot be separated. Through our faith in Christ we are "heirs of God, and joint-heirs with Christ" (Rom. 8:17). And we are willing to stop at that point. But Paul continues. "If so be that we suffer with him, that we may be also glorified together" (8:17). This might well be a commentary on Jesus' words, "If any man will come after me" (Matt. 16:24). Man ever dreams of a crown. But Jesus still speaks of a cross. It is through the cross to the crown.

There is no other way. Jesus walked it. And if we would follow Him, so must we.

Peter continued to speak. "If thou wilt, let us make here three tabernacles; one for thee, and one for Moses, and one for Elias." It was about the time for the feast of Tabernacles. So Peter proposes that they celebrate it in the mountain. Truly Peter spoke, not knowing what he said. He understood the words, but he was unaware of their implication.

For even as he was speaking "a bright cloud overshadowed them" (17:5). Travellers still note how quickly clouds form on Mount Hermon. But this was no ordinary cloud. It is suggestive of the Shekinah glory or the visible presence of God out of the cloud. "This is my beloved Son, in whom I am well pleased; hear ye him."

There are two things embodied in this statement. In the first place, there is the approval of Jesus by the Father. As at His baptism He was well-pleasing to the Father, so here after three years He is still approved of God. But note that there is one difference. Whereas at His baptism these words were spoken to Jesus, here they are directed to the disciples. They were caught in the cross-current of prevailing opinions about Jesus. And while they accepted Him as "the Christ, the Son of the living God" still they had questioned Jesus' own words as to His mission. So to them the Father says, "No matter what others may say or think about my beloved Son, He is still well-pleasing to me." How the disciples needed that word! But do we not need it even more?

In the second place, God's voice was one of rebuke to Peter and the others. "Hear ye him." They are to believe Him when He speaks of the cross. They are to listen when He speaks of the nature of His kingdom. They are to hear Jesus, not Moses, Elijah, the Pharisees and Sadducees, nor any other of the myriad of voices of a confused age. And this is a timeless rebuke. For in every age, even ours, men seek a voice which will lead them out of their "bondage, sorrow, and night." But apart from Jesus there is no sure word of prophecy. Only as we listen to Him and obey His words shall we be able to find and do God's will which alone is the answer to the problems which perplex us.

But one cannot escape the fact that there is more involved in God's rebuke. "Hear ye him" in contrast to Moses and Elijah, the law and the prophets. For they are fulfilled in Him. The old order merges into the new. Jesus and Jesus alone is the embodiment of God's complete revelation. Law and prophecy give way to grace. The old covenant is replaced by the new. Jesus says nothing which contradicts either the law or the prophets. But apart from Him they have no abiding meaning. They are as mighty rivers which are swallowed up in a desert of frustration. But in the mighty Son of God they merge to form the river which truly makes glad the city of God.

Underlying this rebuke is the sinful suggestion of Peter as stated in Matthew 17:4. Many have speculated as to the nature of this sin. Some see it as the sin of selfishness. For Peter it were better to remain in the glory of the mountain rather than to return to the need of the valley. Possibly so. But in the light of God's rebuke we are inclined to look elsewhere for the answer. Actually in Peter's suggestion he placed Jesus on a level with Moses and Elijah. "One for thee, and one for Moses, and one for Elijah."

This is a sin which is quite popular in our day. In some circles it is fashionable to regard Jesus as just one of many in the line of God's revelation of Himself to man—Moses, Elijah, Isaiah, Jeremiah, Buddha, Mohammed, and many other great teachers. But those who would regard Jesus other than God make Him only a man. To them He is the greatest prophet, but still only a prophet; the greatest teacher, but still only a teacher; the greatest man who ever lived, but still only a man. This is contrary to the teachings of Scripture and to the experience of life. Jesus is unique, apart, and above all others. To equate Him with man, even the greatest of men, is to miss the mark of His true person and work. The purpose of the transfiguration was to lead His disciples, then and now, to see Him as He is—truly God and truly Man.

The closing verse of Matthew's account of the transfiguration is pregnant with eternal truth. "And when they had lifted up their eyes, they saw no man, save Jesus only" (17:8). Jesus only! Moses and Elijah had vanished from the scene. And with them the binding nature of the systems which they symbolize. They had made their contribution to the economy of God's eternal purpose. But their work found its fulfilment in *Jesus only*. Thenceforth He will proceed to Jerusalem to seal the new covenant in His blood, a covenant in which law will give place to grace. Those who speak forth for God will have a new message and mission. And a lost world will look up with new hope.

On the way down from the mountain Jesus charged the disciples that they should "tell the vision to no man, until the Son of man be risen again from the dead" (Matt. 17:9). They had seen the vision, but they did not yet fully comprehend its meaning. But they would never forget it. James will be the first of the Twelve to seal his witness in a martyr's blood. But Peter will one day write of the vision in the "holy mount" (II Peter 1:17-18). And because of it he can say, "We have also a sure word of prophecy [cf. Elijah]; whereunto ye do well that ye take heed, as unto a light that shineth in a dark place [cf. Mt. Hermon], until the day dawn, and the day star arise in your hearts." And John late in the first century will write, "And the Word was made flesh, and dwelt among us, (and we beheld his glory, the glory as of the only begotten of the Father,) full of grace and truth... and of his fulness have all we received, and grace for grace. For the law was given by Moses, but grace and truth came by Jesus Christ" (John 1:14, 16-17).

The Postlude of the Transfiguration (17:10-27)

From the glory of the mountain Jesus returned to the suffering of the valley. For there He healed the demon-possessed boy (17:14-21). Luke and John record an intervening ministry before Passion Week. But Matthew, in keeping with his purpose, takes Jesus through Galilee and Perea to Jerusalem and the cross.

But before this final journey Matthew records two incidents of significance. "And while they abode in Galilee, Jesus said unto them, The Son of man shall be betrayed into the hands of men: and they shall kill him, and the third day he shall be raised again. *And they were exceeding sorry*" (17:22-23, author's italics). Jesus continued the teaching which he had begun at Caesarea Philippi. But there is a difference in the response of the disciples. Now there is no protest, only sorrow. They have accepted the truth of Jesus' role as the Suffering Servant. The transfiguration had done its work. And the disciples are on their way to understanding and preparation for the time when the Shepherd will be taken from the sheep.

The closing verses relate the incident of Jesus' miracle whereby money was procured to pay the temple tax for Himself and Peter. Even though He is the Lord of the temple He accepts the obligation placed upon Him by those in charge of the temple. He still identifies Himself with man. Until His redemptive work is accomplished He rejects His privilege for His obligation. And in so doing He reveals His greatest glory—that of the Saviour of men.

The Counsel of the King

Matthew 18

The King and Kingdom Greatness

The Twelve were in a bad way. Their own plans and schemes had gone awry. They dreamed of thrones. But Jesus spoke of crosses. And His words had punctured their dreams. Nevertheless they continued to think in terms of their opportunity to achieve greatness. Mark notes that on their journey back to Capernaum the disciples disputed as to which of them was the greatest (9:34). It is strange to see that following the transfiguration Peter, James, and John should enter into such. But the remainder of the disciples as yet knew nothing about it (cf. Matt. 17:9). However, Jesus' seeming favoritism in taking the three into the mountain probably had aroused the jealousy of the nine. Hence their dispute.

At any rate when they arrived back in Capernaum Jesus accosted them as to their "reasoning in the way" (Mark 9:33; Luke 9:46). The Twelve hesitated to answer Jesus. But finally they opened up and asked Him to settle their problem for them. And their question introduces us to the subject of kingdom greatness.

Therefore, as we examine Matthew 18 we find Jesus answering their question. And His answer involves (1) the standard of kingdom greatness; (2) the expression of kingdom greatness; (3) the degree of kingdom greatness.

The Standard of Kingdom Greatness (18:1-14)

"Who is the greatest in the kingdom of heaven?" (Matt. 18:1). So reads the King James Version. But the oldest and best manuscripts of Matthew add one significant word, "then." "Who then is greatest in the kingdom of heaven?" The word "then" suggests a contrast between the standard of greatness as held by the disciples and that which is implied in Jesus' concept of the kingdom. All of this harks back to the words of our Lord in Matthew 16:21-27. The spirit of the age regarded greatness in terms of pomp and splendor, of power and servants. But the King had spoken of death and suffering, of self-denial and service. Now in this new light "who then is greatest in the kingdom of heaven?"

In reply to their question Jesus "called a little child . . . and set him in the midst of them" (v. 2). The incident may have occurred in Peter's home, and this could well have been one of his children. How like Jesus it was to use simple things to teach spiritual truth. And what a contrast this child presented. The disciples in adult selfishness disputing as to positions of greatness. The child probably busy at play and totally oblivious to their problem. The Twelve thinking of sitting alongside Jesus on thrones of glory. The child standing alongside Jesus (cf. Luke 9:47) in untarnished simplicity. In effect Jesus said in this acted parable, "You want to know about heavenly greatness? Here it is in the person of a little child."

Now what is there so great about a little child? What are some of the characteristics of such? Comparative innocence, simplicity, forgiveness, faith, and almost infinite possibilities of development. And all of these are suggestive of that which Jesus proceeds to reveal.

For having called attention to the child Jesus said, "Verily I say unto you. Except ye be converted, and become as little children, ye shall not enter into the kingdom of heaven" (v. 3). This was a most solemn statement by our Lord as seen in His use of the word "verily." And why this solemnity? Because before you can be great in the kingdom you must first be in it. Literally Jesus said, "Except ye turn, and become as little children, ye shall not enter into the kingdom of heaven."

Some encounter difficulty at this point. Jesus was speaking to the disciples. Does He mean that they are not now in the kingdom of heaven? This can hardly be the meaning, since there is abundant Scriptural evidence otherwise. To be sure the disciples in their worldly standard of greatness are traveling in the opposite direction from kingdom greatness. In that sense they most certainly must turn and enter into the childlike attitude. But this is only incidental to Jesus' meaning.

Actually He is speaking in general principles. The disciples did not ask, "Which of us shall be greatest in the kingdom of heaven?" But *who* shall be greatest? What is the gauge of kingdom greatness? So in reply to this general inquiry Jesus speaks in kind. Before anyone can hope to achieve kingdom greatness he must be a kingdom citizen.

When we examine this verse two words stand out—"turn" and "become." So one must *turn* and *become* as little children. Now these words are suggestive of two definite experiences which theologians describe as *regeneration* and *sanctification*. To be regenerated is to be born again. Even an adult must be born again as a little child. And to be sanctified is to be dedicated or set apart to the service of God. The moment one is born again he is sanctified. He is set apart for God's service. Thereafter he must grow and develop in this dedication. Both of these words are in the aorist tense, suggesting a definite, instantaneous action. The former is in the passive voice, meaning that something is done to one by another. Thus one's conversion is an act of God. The latter word is in the middle voice, meaning that something is done within one's self. But even this is an act of God's grace as one submits himself to God (cf. Phil. 2:12-13). And whereas the word "turn" suggests one definite experience, the word "become" speaks of a continuing or continuous one. You may enter into the kingdom of heaven by *turning* and *becoming* as little children. But to achieve greatness you must continue in the becoming experience.

And this is the significance of the phrase "as little children." What is the principal characteristic of a child? It is imperfection with the possibility of growth and development. So Jesus does not set forth perfection as the requirement for one to enter the kingdom of heaven. Instead He implies imperfection. You must be born again as a child of God to be sure. But in that state you must recognize your imperfection. You have not *arrived* simply because you have become a Christian. You have only *begun.* If you would become great in the kingdom you must remain teachable.

This thought is involved in Matthew 18:4. "Whosoever therefore shall humble himself as this little child, the same is greatest in the kingdom of heaven." Now the child does not humble himself. He is humble by nature. He is open to instruction and growth. The Christian must have the same quality if he is to achieve kingdom greatness. Even though Jesus does not require perfection, it is the goal toward which we are to strive (cf. Matt. 5:48). And to the degree that we achieve that perfection or Godlikeness to that degree we achieve kingdom greatness.

Beginning with Matthew 18:5 Jesus applies the figure which He has drawn. "And whoso shall receive one such little child in my name receiveth me." Is He speaking here of an actual child or of those who are little children in Christ who are striving to develop and grow into kingdom greatness? Either figure makes sense. However, it is probably the latter to which Jesus is referring. He has made His point, and now He applies it. The "little child" is qualified by the word "such" which seems to refer to the person who humbles himself as a little child. A. B. Bruce comments at this point. "The real child present in the room passes into an *ideal* child, representing all that the spirit of ambition in its struggle for place and power is apt to trample under foot."[12] That this could refer to a child young in age is quite evident. But the emphasis seems to be upon the childlike spirit to which Jesus has been referring. But in either case the words of Jesus carry tremendous significance.

In verse 5 the words for "receive" mean more than mere reception. They involve a warmth of love and care which expresses itself in helpfulness for the little child or one of childlike spirit who is endeavoring to grow into his potentiality. And Jesus identifies Himself with such little ones. Thus He exalts the position of the spiritual teacher to almost infinite importance. The task of such a teacher may at times be a discouraging one, as indeed it was for Jesus, but the possibilities are tremendously great. And as one sees Jesus Himself in the process, his task takes on an aura of glory beyond any earthly reward.

However, the opposite is also true. For to be a cause of stumbling for such an one is of the gravest consequences (v. 6). Here also the meaning of "these little ones which believe in me" is ambiguous. But the meaning is applicable to either a little child or a childlike believer, preferably the latter. As such struggles to achieve his potential greatness in Christ we should beware that we do not despise him in putting a stumbling stone in his path. Rather than to be guilty of such it would be better if we should die. "It would be better for him that a millstone were hanged about his neck, and that he were drowned in the depth of the sea" (v. 6). The "millstone" in question is not the small stone turned by hand, but the large stone turned by an ass. Furthermore, "the depth of the sea" means far out in the open sea. Jesus is using strong language. Rather than for a man to place a stumbling stone before one of these little ones, it would be far better if the largest of millstones were hanged about his neck and he were cast into the deepest part of the sea to rise no more.

Now the world is filled with stumbling stones ("offences," v. 7). They may be positive and vicious sins. They may be the allurements of the world which lead the Christian out of the path of God's will. Or they may be the un-Christlike attitude of supposedly stronger Christians who look with contempt upon these weak, struggling little ones. At any rate these causes of stumbling will

12 *The Expositor's Greek Testament,* Vol. 1, Eerdmans, Grand Rapids, 1951, p. 237.

come to everyone who strives to live for Christ. The Christian does not live in a moral vacuum. He is to be in the world but not of it. Nevertheless, despite the prevalence of such stumbling stones, Jesus pronounces woe upon those who allow themselves to be the cause of such stumbling. It is a terrible thing to cause another to sin or to be complacent with regard to those things which entice the weak to sin. The Christian cannot afford to be indifferent to such.

And then Jesus turns from the one who causes the stumbling to those little ones who are in danger of being caused to stumble (vv. 8-9). For in both verses He uses the third person singular of the verb which means to cause to stumble (*skandalizei*). If your hand or foot causes you to stumble cut it off. Or if your eye does so pluck it out. In oriental fashion Jesus says that it would be better to go through life maimed or with one eye than to fail to achieve the greatness of the kingdom of heaven. In our wordly view these may seem to be extreme statements. But when viewed with eternal import they are reasonable indeed.

Note the consequences of failure to achieve kingdom greatness. In verse 8 Jesus speaks of one being cast "into everlasting fire." In verse 9 He uses "the Gehenna of fire." Does Jesus here refer to the punishment of the soul in hell? These terms are often used by Jesus in this manner. But are we so to understand Him here? It all depends upon how we interpret the ones to whom Jesus is speaking.

There are three possible objects of these words. Some hold that Jesus is speaking to those who cause these little ones to stumble. Bruce comments, "Since the offender is the greater loser in the end, it is worth his while to take precautions against being an offender."[13] But this hardly seems to fit the context. In verse 6 the offenders are referred to as those who cause the little ones to stumble. But in verses 8-9 the thought is that parts of a person's own body cause him to stumble. So it would seem that Jesus is speaking not of the offender but of the victim.

Again, it may be that the warning is given in general terms as in verse 3. If so, then the meaning is that one's bodily members cause him to stumble as he seeks to enter into the kingdom of heaven. In this case the meaning in verses 8-9 would refer to eternal punishment in hell for those who fail to enter the kingdom of heaven by not being converted and not becoming as a little child.

However, we must remember that the basic thought in this

---

[13] *Ibid,* p. 238.

chapter is not that of getting into the kingdom of heaven. It pertains to the question "Who then is greatest in the kingdom of heaven" (v. 1). It would appear, therefore, that the most likely reference in verses 8-9 would be to "these little ones which believe in me." (v. 6). Not all stumbling stones come from others. They may also come from the weaknesses in one's own self. So it appears that Jesus is warning immature, struggling Christians not to fall victim to the latter. It would be better to go through life maimed, and achieve kingdom greatness, than to be physically whole and fall short of this spiritual goal.

In this light, therefore, to what does "everlasting fire" and "hell fire" (Gehenna of fire) refer? Jesus is speaking to those who have already believed in Him and are, therefore, in the kingdom of heaven. In the light of the abundant teachings of the New Testament to the contrary, we can hardly see these references as meaning that these little ones shall lose their redemption and go to hell. What then is the thought in Jesus' mind?

We have seen that "the Gehenna of fire" refers to the Vale of Hinnom outside the city of Jerusalem (cf. Matt. 5:22). It was here that the worthless garbage of the city was consumed by unceasing fires. Jesus often referred to this as a figure of hell. But we are not necessarily bound to that figure in every instance. The context must decide in each case. If our surmise be correct here, then it could hardly refer to hell in this context. A more likely meaning could be that of wasted lives. These little ones are in the kingdom of heaven. But this does not necessarily imply the greatness under consideration. A child may be born into life yet fail to develop into a strong, useful person. He possesses physical life but misses the deeper meaning of life itself. Likewise, one may be born again, yet fail to develop into the kind of Christian which God intends that he shall become. He possesses spiritual life as such in the sense of regeneration, but he misses the full goal of that life. He fails to achieve kingdom greatness. His life is sanctified to God, but he does not develop in that sanctification. He has laid the foundation in Jesus Christ, but that which he builds upon this foundation is worthless. It is but garbage fit only to be cast into the Vale of Hinnom.

It was this thought which Paul had in mind in I Corinthians 3:11-15. "If any man's work shall be burned, he shall suffer loss: but he himself shall be saved; yet so as by fire" or through fire. Alas, how many are in the kingdom but who fail to achieve kingdom greatness!

And now, having warned the "little ones," Jesus returns to His general audience (vv. 10, 12-14). No Christian is to "despise" or "think down on one of these little ones." As we see these little ones endeavoring to develop in kingdom greatness, we are not with superior air to look down upon them. For "in heaven their angels do always behold the face of my Father which is in heaven." This does not mean that each believer has his own guardian angel. Angels are God's "ministering spirits, sent forth to minister to them who shall be heirs of salvation" (Heb. 1:14). John A. Broadus comments on this verse. "However humble in the estimation of worldly men, believers have angels as their attendants, sent forth to serve God for their benefit, and these angels of theirs enjoy in heaven, the highest dignity and consideration, like persons admitted to the very presence of a monarch, and allowed, not once, but continually, to behold his face. The seclusion in which Oriental monarchs live made this image very expressive."[14] Surely such who are so honored in heaven should not be despised on earth.

Matthew 18:11 (KJV) reads, "For the Son of man is come to save that which was lost." This statement suddenly breaks into the context. It makes Jesus inject a word about the "lost" into His teaching about "these little ones." (Note that the word "lost" does not appear in the parable of the sheep, vv. 12-14.) However, this verse obviously is not a part of Matthew's Gospel. It does not appear in the earliest Greek manuscripts and many other early writings. It was evidently borrowed by some copyist from Luke 19:10 where it is genuine. So to delete it here loses nothing from Scripture. By doing so it does remove a break in Jesus' train of thought.

For in the following parable our Lord continues His thought as to the value of one of these little ones. He is as a wandering, not a lost, sheep which has strayed from the flock. The shepherd does not despise it. Rather he searches until he finds it, and brings it back into the flock. "Even so it is not the will of your Father which is in heaven, that one of these little ones should perish."

What a lesson in Christian mutual care and nurture! (cf. Heb. 12:12-16). The sheep does not wilfully stray away. It does so inadvertently as it becomes encompassed by other interests. The same is true of these little ones. But the heavenly Shepherd does not despise them. Instead He claims those who are His own, that He may strengthen and guide them toward the kingdom greatness which He proposes for them. If we would be great in the kingdom of heaven we must follow in the steps of our King.

---

[14] *Ibid.*, p. 385.

The Expression of Kingdom Greatness (18:15-20)

This section is actually a continuation of the thoughts involved in verses 12-14. Jesus has just illustrated how the heavenly Father seeks out a wandering child. Now He applies this truth to the attitude which the strong Christian should have toward such. If he is to express kingdom greatness himself, he must not despise the wandering little one but must seek to find him and assist him in achieving kingdom greatness. In so doing Jesus gives to us the procedure whereby we should deal with an erring brother. The entire example presupposes the relationship within a local church fellowship.

Jesus supposes the case of a Christian who has fallen into sin. "Moreover if thy brother shall trespass..." or sin (v. 15). The King James Version adds "against thee." This would imply a personal difference between two Christians. For the word "brother" is used in the Christian sense. However, the words "against thee" are absent from the best manuscripts. These would appear to have been added by a copyist, probably in the light of the question raised in verse 21. The example which follows could well involve a personal difference. But the lesson is even more forceful if these words be omitted. Furthermore, without them the thought naturally flows from the parable of the seeking shepherd and the wandering sheep to that of a seeking Christian and a sinning one.

"If thy brother may sin" (literal translation). Here is one of these little ones who has gone astray. He has not necessarily sinned against one particular brother. But he has sinned, and his sin reflects against the entire church. No Christian sins in isolation. As a part of the body of Christ any malfunction on the part of an erring brother affects the entire body (cf. I Cor. 12:26). And the body must be concerned about every member.

What is to be the attitude of the stronger member toward the weaker? Certainly the former cannot ignore the latter. But what is he to do? Jesus says, "Go and tell his fault between thee and him alone." That this is wise counsel is seen in the fact that the normal procedure is just the opposite. The usual practice when we see a Christian brother living in sin is to tell everyone but the one who is at fault. In so doing we help him not at all, and we do harm to the entire Christian fellowship. Sometimes the widespread gossiping reports have no basis of fact. And this is compounded tragedy indeed. In fact, the gossiping may even be the greater sin. But even if the report be well grounded to talk about it to others is the action of one who is least in the kingdom, not the greatest.

Jesus says that when you see a brother sin you should go to him privately and face him with the matter, not in censorious criticism but in a sympathetic spirit. This is not the easiest procedure, but it is the Christian one. Christian people are responsible for one another. The author of Hebrews gives wise counsel when he says, "Wherefore lift up the hands which hang down, and the feeble knees; and make straight [even] paths for your feet, lest that which is lame be turned out of the way; but let it rather be healed... looking diligently lest any man fail of the grace of God; lest any root of bitterness springing up trouble you, and thereby many be defiled" (12:12-13, 15).

If such care be between you and the erring brother *alone,* there is more likelihood that he will be brought to see the error of his way. Public rebuke could serve to arouse his anger and pride, and make it more difficult to win him away from his erring path. But if it be a personal affair conducted in the right manner he will be more likely to respond in kind. If so, Jesus says, "Thou hast gained thy brother." You have rescued him from a life of sin, and have gained him back to the fellowship of the church and to a fruitful life for Christ. Jesus never crushed a bruised reed or quenched a smoking flax. Instead, He endeavored to bind up the bruise and to nurse it back to health. He sought to blow the breath of God upon the faltering flame and enable it to burn brightly once more. And if we would follow in His footsteps we must do the same.

But suppose that the erring brother does not heed your counsel. What then? Our Lord says that you should take one or two other brethren with you to plead with him (v. 16). Such a procedure involves five things. It becomes more than merely a personal matter between you and the sinning brother. It avoids one Christian being vindictive against another. It shows the broader concern of the church. It provides witnesses to the effort to win him away from sin. And it provides ample evidence for the church in case the effort fails. This method of dealing with such matters is in keeping with the words of Deuteronomy 19:15. "One man shall not rise up against a man for any iniquity, or for any sin, in any sin that he sinneth: at the mouth of two witnesses, or at the mouth of three witnesses, shall the matter be established" (cf. John 8:17; II Cor. 13:1). Thus all parties concerned are protected from undue haste in a matter of such serious import. And it provides that it shall be done decently and in a proper order.

In the event that the sinful brother refuses to hear this group, there remains but one final recourse. "Speak [*eipon*] to the church" (v. 17). Some interpreters see a difficulty in this mention of the local church. Holding that the church as such did not yet exist, they regard it as a later addition and not a genuine teaching of Jesus. Still others insist that Jesus is speaking prophetically, with the thought that the church did not come into being until the day of Pentecost. However, neither of these positions is necessarily valid. For certainly the necessary conditions for a *church* are present here: a group of baptized believers banded together under the Lordship of Christ to carry on His work. A. B. Bruce sees the Twelve as the "nucleus" of the church. There is no genuine reason to regard this teaching as other than one of Jesus.

Note the progression in dealing with a sinful member. First, there is the private, personal phase. If it succeeds the matter should end there with no publicity. Second, there is the effort within a small, unofficial group. Third, failing in both of these efforts, there is the public airing of the matter. It may not be the most pleasant thing in the world, but the fellowship of the church must be guarded from sinful pollution. If our forefathers sinned in being overly zealous in this regard, we sin in neglecting the matter altogether.

But having exhausted every means of reclaiming such a person, if he refuses to heed the will of the church, Jesus says, "Let him be unto thee as an heathen man and a publican" (v. 17). Again some question whether or not this is a genuine saying of Jesus because of the harshness of the sentence handed down. But this is to disregard the judgment side of His nature. There is none so tender, loving, patient, and kind as Jesus. But all of these attributes are to be regarded in the light of His righteousness and holiness. He gave His life to purchase His church. It is His purpose to present it to Himself as a holy Bride.

Furthermore, there is significance in the words "heathen" and "publican." Even though this sinful person is called a "brother," does not this imply that one who is a member of the local church, but who repeatedly refuses to break with his sin, is not really a Christian "brother" after all? If not, then he has no place in the Christian fellowship. But even if he be regarded as a real believer, Jesus counsels harsh methods in a final effort to reclaim him.

Such an example of church discipline is found in I Corinthians 5:1-5. Here the purpose of this discipline is "to deliver such an one unto Satan for the destruction of the flesh, that the spirit may be saved in the day of the Lord Jesus" (v. 5).[15] Indeed, this passage gives to us the pattern to be followed in carrying out Jesus' instructions. I Corinthians 5:4 says, "In the name [authority] of our Lord Jesus Christ, when ye are gathered together [passive voice, suggesting that someone calls the church together] ... with the power of our Lord Jesus Christ." The church so gathered together acts within the authority and by the power of the Lord Jesus Christ.

This same thought is present in Jesus' own words. Matthew 18:18 says, "Whatsoever ye shall bind on earth shall be [shall have been] bound in heaven: and whatsoever ye shall loose on earth shall be [shall have been] loosed in heaven." Note the plural form of the verbs ["ye shall bind ... loose"]. The same words which Jesus spoke to the church through Peter (Matt. 16:19) He now speaks directly to the church as a body. If in administering church discipline we act in the loving spirit of Jesus, we also act in His authority. Heaven has already decreed that this shall be the case. In other words heaven approves in advance the action of the church assembled when it acts under the Lordship of Jesus Christ.

This thought is further enhanced in verses 19-20. "That if two of you shall agree on earth as touching any thing that they shall ask, it shall be done for them of my Father which is in heaven. For where two or three are gathered together in my name, there am I in the midst of them." Popularly these verses are regarded as promises regarding prayer. In one sense this is true. But more directly they refer to God's approval upon the actions of a Christ-directed church. Jesus is emphasizing what He has said in verse 18. Such action is to be taken in prayer apart from any vindictive spirit. The church should recognize its inability to act without divine guidance. And when such is sought in symphonious fashion it will be given. The verb "agree" is *sumphoneō*. It was used primarily of musical instruments that make the same sound, then of harmony, *symphony*, where the sounds agree even though they are not identical. So even though in a church business meeting there may be different *sounds*, when they achieve a symphony the heavenly Father will hear and answer. Verse 20 is our Lord's promise to be present in such a gathering if it be "in my name." He is there in spiritual presence with His authority and power (cf. I Cor. 5:4) This promise applies in any church business meeting. And no local church should propose to transact the Lord's

---

[15] II Corinthians 2:4-8 suggests that the erring brother repented and was to be restored to the church's fellowship. Note the remedial purpose.

business under any other condition. If any church (or any individual Christian) would express kingdom greatness it cannot do so otherwise.

The Degree of Kingdom Greatness (18:21-35)

Jesus' teaching about the expression of kingdom greatness in the corporate body of the church naturally leads to its expression in individual Christian relationships. And in such a progression of thought Matthew points up the degree of kingdom greatness as seen in the matter of personal forgiveness.

We are not surprised to hear Simon Peter's voice injected into the scene. It is very well to speak of dealing with a brother who may sin in a general sort of way. But what shall be my attitude toward one who sins against *me*? This is the import of Peter's question. "Lord, how oft shall my [Christian] brother sin against me, and I forgive him? till seven times?" (v. 21). He may have had someone in mind, even one of the Twelve. Peter thought that he was being unusually generous. For the rabbis taught threefold forgiveness. The Babylonian Talmud reads, "When a man sins against another, they forgive him once, they forgive him a second time, they forgive him a third time, but the fourth time they do not forgive him." So Peter was willing to go beyond the second mile. Is any one of us so generous?

But if Peter thought that he spoke generously, we can certainly say that he raised a very practical question. A brother sins against us, and we conjure up enough Christian grace to forgive him. How pious we feel! But no sooner do we forgive him than he does us another wrong. And with unusual generosity we forgive him again. And then comes another wrong. How long shall we continue to forgive? Is not there a point beyond which we are no longer expected to forgive? Until *seven times?*

But notice Jesus' reply. "I say not unto thee, Until seven times: but, Until seventy times seven" (*hebdomēnkontakis hepta,* v. 22). Just how many times did Jesus mean? Did He mean seventy plus seven or seventy times seven? Some expositors, on the basis of Genesis 4:24, see this to mean seventy-seven times. A. T. Robertson notes that in the *Testament of the Twelve Patriarchs,* Benjamin VII. 4, it is used in the sense of seventy times seven. He also points out that had Jesus used *heptakis* He definitely would have meant four hundred and ninety times. Most scholars see the meaning to be four hundred and ninety times.

But even this does not really state Jesus' meaning. Peter thought in terms of legalism or mathematics. He would count the times up through seven and end it there. One can hardly imagine the same person sinning against you seventy-seven times, to say nothing of four hundred and ninety times. Jesus is not thinking in terms of either legalism or mathematics. In the Greek text He said, "Not I say to you until seven times." The negative is emphatic. He vigorously brushes aside all thought of legalism and mathematics to lift the matter into the realm of the *evangelic* (Bruce). He means limitless forgiveness. In other words the Christian who would achieve kingdom greatness must not count grievances. He must live in the spirit or atmosphere of forgiveness. McNeile says succinctly, "The unlimited revenge of primitive man has given place to the unlimited forgiveness of Christians."

The apostle Paul caught this spirit when he said that Christian love (*agape*) "thinketh no evil" (I Cor. 13:5). "Thinketh" renders a bookkeeping term. Literally, "Christian love . . . does not keep books on the evil done against it." This suggests a ledger containing debits and credits. If someone does you a wrong you put it down as a debit against the wrong doer. And it can only be offset by the credit of some good deed done to you. Such was the thought behind Peter's question. But Christian love does not so conduct itself. Jesus says that if you have this love, if you act in terms of kingdom greatness you will be limitless in your attitude of forgiveness.

Of course, a complete renewal of unbroken fellowship rests upon the repentance of the one who does the wrong (cf. Luke 17:4). But, even so, one who aspires to greatness by kingdom standards must cultivate a forgiving heart. Your willingness to forgive will be an effective call to the sinful brother's repentance.

Jesus drives home this lesson in forgiveness with one of the most picturesque of His parables (vv. 23-35). Notice that He began with the words "Therefore [cf. vv. 21-22] is the kingdom of heaven likened unto a certain king, which would take account of his servants" (*doulōn,* slaves). So this parable is to be understood in terms of kingdom relationships, not that of those outside of the kingdom. Jesus is still answering the question as to greatness in the kingdom of heaven (v. 1), not the manner by which one enters into the kingdom. The thought of *remaining* in the kingdom is foreign to this entire chapter.

The parable deals with a slave or officer in the kingdom who owes his king the equivalent of $12,000,000. Unable to pay the debt he pleads for mercy. In turn the king forgives the entire debt. But instead of being grateful for his king's gracious act, the servant in turn demands that another servant pay him a debt of

$17.00. Jesus says that he "took him by the throat." He began to choke him (imperfect tense) and kept on choking him. This was a standard Roman practice in dealing with debtors. Livy tells how their necks were twisted. And Cicero says, "Lead him to the judgment seat with twisted neck." Thus Jesus implies that a kingdom man is acting like a pagan. The Greek text says that the debtor "kept on beseeching" and the unmerciful one "kept on not willing" to grant his plea (imperfect tenses).

The debtor pleaded for time in which to pay. Instead he was cast into prison "till he should pay the debt." How could he pay it if he were in prison? Other servants reported the matter to their lord. The word "told" is a very strong word. They gave a complete and clear account of their fellow-servant's unmerciful action. The result was that he himself was delivered to the tormentors "till he should pay all that was due unto him" (v. 34).

The picture is quite evident. We accept the boundless forgiveness of our heavenly Father. But we are so unwilling to grant even the smallest forgiveness to our fellow-Christians. At times it appears that we are more forgiving toward outsiders than we are toward those with whom we should enjoy the closest of all relationships. And such an attitude yields the direst consequences.

Jesus concludes, "So likewise shall my heavenly Father do also unto you, if ye from your hearts forgive not every one his brother...." "Their trespasses" is not found in the best manuscripts although the thought is present.

What are we to understand by these words? Some see in them evidence of purgatorial punishment. However, the fact that the slave could never pay back that vast debt negates this possible meaning. So we must see rather a punitive judgment. But what is this judgment? It must be remembered that in interpreting a parable we must not press every little item. Rather we must seek to determine the overall lesson the parable is intended to teach.

This parable could be interpreted to mean that if a Christian acts like a pagan he shall be treated like a pagan. This does not mean to lose one's redemption. For the servant was still related to his lord. Or it could mean that in one's unforgiving spirit he demonstrates that he is not a Christian at all. In his first epistle John points out that our love for our Christian brethren is an evidence that we are children of God. "He that loveth not knoweth not God; for God is love.... Beloved, if God so loved us, we ought also to love one another.... If a man say, I love God, and hateth his brother, he is a liar: for he that loveth not his brother whom he hath seen, how can he love God whom he hath not seen? And this commandment have we from him, That he who loveth God love his brother also" (I John 4:8, 11, 20-21).

But a more probable meaning is found if we relate the parable and Jesus' conclusion to the chapter as a whole. The basic question in Matthew 18 is that of "Who then is greatest in the kingdom of heaven?" The parable implies a kingdom relationship. Jesus' final conclusion is directed toward the Twelve. And as noted previously, apart from Judas, they must be regarded as being in the kingdom. So the point is not how to get into the kingdom or to remain therein. It is as to how one may achieve kingdom greatness. And this quality is likened unto a little child. Its expression is seen in one's attitude toward one of these little ones. A kingdom-citizen cannot be said to possess kingdom greatness if in a superior attitude he despises a weaker but struggling brother. And this truth is clearly depicted in Jesus' parable.

So what may we conclude from these things? A servant of the King belongs to Him by right of redemption. He is in the kingdom relationship. And nothing can change that fact, not even prison and suffering. However, one may be in the kingdom and yet fail to achieve kingdom greatness.

One is in the kingdom by right of his redemption from *sin*. But one's day to day growth in kingdom greatness involves, along with other things, his repeated forgiveness of *sins*. "If we say that we have no sin, we deceive ourselves, and the truth is not in us. If we confess our sins, he is faithful and just to forgive us our sins, and to cleanse us from all unrighteousness" (I John 1:8-9). The actions of the servant suggest that he was not conscious of the contrast between his action and that of his king. Being unaware of his sinful practice he could hardly confess his sin. Hence no forgiveness of it. But he still remained in the kingdom even in prison.

Of course, if one presses the literal meaning of the words "till he should pay all that was due unto him," this position runs into difficulty. However, we must not lose the overall message by dwelling only on this one facet of the parable. We must view the whole in the light of the question "Who then is greatest in the kingdom of heaven?" If so, Jesus is saying that one without an unforgiving spirit is not the greatest but the least in the kingdom of heaven. Oh, the tragedy of shrivelled souls because of unforgiving spirits!

It is at this point that we may comprehend "delivered him to the tormentors." A. B. Bruce properly notes that "the word, chosen to suit the king's mood, represents a subjective feeling rather than an objective fact." The unforgiving spirit is not only in this prison of selfishness but is tormented by the demons which inhabit such a prison. It is little wonder that there are so many unhappy Christians. Forgiven of God but unforgiving toward others.

Until you, by the grace of God, overcome such a beggarly spirit you will never achieve the kingdom greatness which the King desires and proposes for all of His subjects. Lord, help us to forgive our debtors even as Thou hast forgiven our debts!

Matthew 19

The King and Personal Problems

The King now departs from Galilee on His final journey to Jerusalem. Luke and John relate an intervening ministry of Jesus in Judea and Perea. But, in keeping with his purpose, once Matthew has completed his account of the Galilean ministry and that of the withdrawals he takes Jesus directly to Jerusalem for the final week and that which followed. On this journey Jesus followed the normal route taken by Jews. He went down the eastern side of the Jordan through Perea (19:1). As He traveled He was followed by great crowds. Therefore, He continued His ministry of teaching and healing (19:2). It was while in Perea that the Pharisees once again accosted Jesus with a question. Thus Matthew introduces us to the King's teaching concerning personal problems.

Of course, all of Jesus' teachings in one way or another dealt with personal problems. But in Matthew 19 we are faced with two very definite ones and the resultant teachings growing out of them. We may divide this chapter into (1) the problem of marriage and divorce; (2) the reaction of the disciples; (3) the problem of wealth; (4) the question of the disciples.

The Problem of Marriage and Divorce (19:3-9)

That the Pharisees confronted Jesus with an ever-pressing problem is quite evident. But they did not seek information. After all, what could this peasant carpenter teach them about a matter to which the scholars had given so much attention? Their purpose was to test Him in order that they might discredit Him before the people who followed Him.

"Is it lawful for a man to put away his wife for every cause?" (v. 3). This was a lively question then as it is now. The case at issue here does not involve a merely legal separation but the matter of remarriage. This was the problem among the Jews even as it is the problem today.

To comprehend the pertinency of this question we must note that there were two schools of thought concerning it. The school of Hillel advocated the liberal view of divorce for every cause. The school of Shammai held that the only ground for divorce (and remarriage) was adultery. These extreme positions grew out of their interpretation of Deuteronomy 24:1-2. Moses said, "When a man hath taken a wife, and married her, and it come to pass that she find no favour in his eyes, because he hath found some uncleanness [unseemly thing] in her: then let him write her a bill of divorcement, and give it in her hand, and send her out of his house. And when she is departed out of his house, she may go and be another man's wife."

Now the two schools of thought grew out of two phrases in this law. Hillel put his emphasis on "some unseemly thing," saying that this meant anything which displeased the husband. He said that he might divorce her even if she burned his food. Rabbi Akiba noted "she find no favour in his eyes" to mean even if he found someone more beautiful. On the other hand Shammai interpreted "some unseemly thing" (uncleanness) to refer to adultery. The Hebrew phrase means a "matter of nakedness." It would seem, therefore, to involve some indecent, shameful act. Quite naturally the position of Shammai was very unpopular among the Jews as it is in our time. The teaching of Hillel was and is quite convenient. And it is in this light that we can understand the purpose of the Pharisees' question. They did not ask Jesus to explain Deuteronomy 24:1. They asked Him if the school of Hillel was correct—"for every cause." It is obvious that they expected Jesus to take the stricter view of Shammai, which would have made Him unpopular with the people.

It is so tragic to see so grave a matter settled on the basis of convenience and personal choice. Society would not for one moment condone surgery "for every cause" or capital punishment "for every cause." But in the matter of the home and marriage, the basic foundation stones of a well-ordered society and matters which are far more precious to a man and a woman than physical life itself, the trend is toward "for every cause."

But Jesus was not drawn into the snare of the Pharisees. He made no mention whatever of either Hillel or Shammai. Nor did He stop with Moses. He went back to the divine concept of marriage in the beginning.

"Have ye not read, that he which made them at the beginning made them male and female, and said, For this cause shall a man leave father and mother, and shall cleave to his wife: and they twain shall be one flesh? Wherefore they are no more twain, but one flesh. What therefore God hath joined together, let not man put asunder" (19:4-6; cf. Gen. 1:27; 2:24).

In dealing with divorce Jesus did not begin with the point of crisis. He went back to God's own design for marriage as an abiding state. Later when asked by the Pharisees as to Moses' law He said, "...from the beginning it was not so" (v. 8). "Was" renders a word meaning a permanent condition. God did not ordain marriage to be broken. Nor does He alter His purpose to suit the changing mores of given generations. Since marriage is a foundation stone in society God set a permanent and abiding state of marriage. Divorce was not a part of that plan.

As we analyze Jesus' words as to the nature of marriage three aspects emerge: physical, social, and spiritual. Note that Jesus moves from the least to the greatest.

First, marriage is physical. "...at the beginning made them male and female...and they twain shall be one flesh?" (vv. 4-5). Within itself neither male nor female is complete. Marriage suggests completeness. In such a state each complements the other as the two become *one flesh*. "Wherefore they are no more twain, but one flesh" (v. 6). This is the physical aspect of marriage.

Second, marriage is social. "For this cause shall a man leave father and mother, and shall cleave to his wife" (v. 5). Thus Jesus spoke of monogamy, one husband for one wife, and one wife for one husband. They break the family ties up to that point, and bring into being their own home and family, one that is dearer and more intimate than any tie previously known. This, of course, involves the satisfaction of the legal requirements of society in marriage. These elements comprise the social aspects of marriage.

Third, marriage is spiritual. "What therefore God hath joined together, let not man put asunder" (v. 6). Marriage is based upon man's ability to love, a gift which comes from God. The spiritual aspect of marriage then is an indissoluble union bound in the ties of sacred love.

Note that Jesus did not say "who" but "what" God has joined together. He is speaking of the marriage relation which God has made. "Joined together" literally means "yoked together" which was a common verb for marriage. A. T. Robertson notes that it is a timeless aorist indicative form, meaning that it is true always. Therefore, Jesus said, "Let no man sever" or "disunite" it (literal translation).

Now when we reverse the order of these aspects what do we find? Marriage is spiritual. It is based upon true love. It is social. One man and one woman satisfying the demands of society by legally and publicly being married. Marriage is physical. This man and woman in love and legally married consummate their marriage in the physical union thus becoming one flesh. Such a marriage is of God. It is that which He ordained in the beginning, a condition which He intends to be a permanent relationship. In such a relationship one man and one woman assume certain obligations. There is the obligation of love. There is the obligation of establishing and mantaining a basic unit of a well-ordered society, a godly home and family. There is what Paul calls the obligation of a conjugal physical relationship (cf. I Cor. 7:2-5).

All of these things are involved in the divine purpose of marriage. So in reply to the Pharisees' question Jesus simply points them back to God's ideal, not man's desires.

Failing to trap Jesus with one question, the Pharisees asked another. "Why did Moses then command to give a writing of divorcement, and to put her away?" (v. 7). Note that the Pharisees added to Moses' law. He did not "command... to put her away." He only commanded that if a man did put away his wife he should give her a bill of divorcement. This was actually an improvement upon the current practice prior to Moses' command. A man merely sent his wife away. So Moses' act was not permission to divorce one's wife; it was designed to protect the rights of the wife who was put away.

But again the Pharisees were not in search of information. They sought to trap Jesus into contradicting the Mosaic law. This would have appeared to be a grievous sin in the eyes of the people. However, Jesus again avoided their trap. He said that Moses gave this law "because of the hardness of your hearts... but from the beginning it was not so." He still holds them to the original intent of the institution of marriage.

And then Jesus gives His own interpretation of the divine intent in marriage with respect to the matter of divorce. "And I say unto you, Whosoever shall put away his wife, *except it be for fornication,* and shall marry another, committeth adultery: and whoso marrieth her which is put away doth commit adultery" (v. 9, author's italics). Note that Jesus' words are more exacting than those of Moses.

In His statement did Jesus grant any ground for divorce and remarriage? Scholars are divided as to their question. Some deny that Jesus did so teach. They base their position on the claim that the words "except it be for fornication" are not genuine words of Jesus, but are a later addition by some scribe to tone down Jesus' words. They point to the fact that in a similar statement recorded in Luke 16:18 he omits this statement as found in Matthew 5:32. And that Mark in reporting the incident under consideration does not include the exception as recorded in Matthew (cf. Mark 10:11-12).

However, in both instances the argument against Matthew's accounts is one from silence which is the weakest of all arguments. Because Jesus did not say "except it be for fornication" in Luke 16:18 is no ground for contending that He did not say it in Matthew 5:32 and 19:9. The teachings are on entirely different occasions. The reasoning about the argument from silence also holds as between Matthew and Mark. Certainly there is good manuscript authority for the genuineness of Matthew's usages. They appear in some of the best manuscripts. The *exception phrase* is in keeping with even the most conservative school of Jewish thought (Shammai) as to the meaning of Deuteronomy 24:1. McNeile argues against the genuineness of these "saving clauses" because Matthew would not represent Jesus as siding with the school of Shammai. A. T. Robertson comments tersely, "Why not, if on this point Shammai agreed with Jesus?" In fact it is reasonable that Jesus would use this exception, if He agreed with it, since the original question involved "for every cause."

But there is yet another thought which clears up the apparent discrepancy between Matthew and Mark. In Matthew 19:9 this statement is clearly directed to the Pharisees. But in Mark 10:11-12 the statement is directed to the disciples "in the house" (Mark 10:10) at a later time. They asked Jesus to explain His teachings concerning marriage and divorce. Since they had heard Him state the *exception,* which was accepted generally among the Jews, there was no point in repeating it to them.

Now in this light what may we understand Jesus to mean by "except it be for fornication?" Jesus has pointed out the ideal state of marriage with no provision for divorce. A marriage should be made with this concept as the goal, one man for one woman until death separates them. But granted that this is true, our Lord recognized one act of infidelity as breaking the marriage union. To comprehend this let us go back to the threefold nature of marriage as spiritual, social, and physical.

A true marriage must be based upon holy love involving the blessing and sanction of God. It involves a legal contract demanded by society. And it must be consummated in willing physical union of the sexes. Furthermore, it must be in that order: spiritual, social, physical. Now in essence Jesus says that a marriage can be broken only in the reverse of that order: physical, social, spiritual. If the legal tie only be broken, and the spiritual and physical remain, the marriage still holds. According to Jesus' words if both the love and legal ties of marriage be broken, and the physical tie remains, there is still a marriage in God's sight.

In Matthew 19:5-6 Jesus said, in effect, that, assuming a relationship of love, and following the legal or social marriage, with the physical union God declares the two parties "joined together." "They twain shall be one flesh." One can be one flesh with only one person. Paul warns against becoming one with a harlot (cf. I Cor. 6:16). If one becomes one flesh with another, the original oneness is broken. The innocent party may choose either to forgive, as taught in the book of Hosea, or else to regard the marriage as broken. By dissolving the legal contract the innocent party is free as though the guilty party were dead. The former is free to marry again, but the latter is not.

In a personal letter written in 1930 G. Campbell Morgan, the prince of expositors, says of Matthew 5:32, "So far as I am concerned, however, I am perfectly clear in my conviction that in the case of divorce on the ground of fornication the innocent party is absolutely free to marry again. I should have no hesitation in conducting the marriage service for such an one. I should refuse to marry the guilty party." [16]

The writer finds himself in agreement with this statement. Many will not do so. But he would point out that this, which he considers to be a genuine teaching of Jesus, lifts the matter immeasurably above the teachings of Moses, Hillel, and the promiscuous practices of modern society. It gets back to the basic and divine intent of marriage. It declares the sanctity of marriage. It stands as a flaming sword to defend it against everything that debases, defiles, or destroys marriage and the home. It challenges every prospective groom and bride to weigh carefully the issues involved. It issues a summons to every husband and wife to stand together on the threshhold of your home and your love to guard them against those things which would destroy the most precious of all human relationships.

Perhaps some may read these words who find yourselves divorced and remarried without this one Scriptural grounds for doing so. What can you do? To dissolve the marriage could cause only additional harm and woe to others—to society and, perhaps, to children. Jesus gave no specific word at this point. But the principles laid down by Him do point the way. Together confess your sins to Him, ask and receive His forgiveness and forgive one another. Then lay your marriage and home upon His altar,

---

16 *This Was His Faith*, Revell, Westwood, N. J., 1952, pp. 294f.

determined to make both all that God intends that they shall be. And as you do so, He will be in your midst to help and to bless.

The Reaction of the Disciples (19:10-15)

Quite naturally this teaching of Jesus upset the disciples as indeed it does many today. It is quite evident that their sympathies lay with the school of Hillel. But so stringent were the words of Jesus that the disciples came to Him privately (cf. Mark 10:10) for further instructions.

Said they, "If so be the case of the man with the wife, it is not expedient to marry" (v. 10, author's translation). If this be the only reason for dissolving a marriage, then it is better not to marry at all. In effect, this was not so much a complaint as it was a recognition of the high standard which Jesus had set for marriage. So if one is going to be true to God, he had better live in celibacy.

But notice Jesus' reply. "Not all have the capacity with respect to this saying" (v. 11, author's translation). To what "saying" does Jesus refer? Certainly not His own saying about marriage. For if so He is about to contradict all that He has said (cf. v. 12). The "saying" is that of the disciples: "it is not expedient to marry." The word rendered "receive" means to have room or space in one's nature for something, hence "capacity." In other words not all men have the capacity to live the celibate life. The only ones who have this capacity are those "to whom it is given" (v. 11). And then Jesus says that some are born "eunuchs" or incapable of the marriage relationship, others are made such by men (it was a widespread practice in that day, especially where a male slave was to serve the women in his master's household), and others voluntarily forego marriage in order the better to serve the Lord with undivided interests (v. 12; cf. I Cor. 7:32-34). Jesus concludes this statement by saying, "The one having the power to have this capacity, let him have this capacity" (v. 12, author's translation).

In so stating Jesus does not place any particular virtue on celibacy. He is not advocating monastic orders. He is simply stating a fact in answer to a question. The one having the capacity for celibacy should not look with disdain upon the married person, or *vice versa*. Jesus says that each person must decide his role in the kingdom of God for himself. But the entire passage places heaven's blessing upon marriage as the norm which God intends for men and women.

The teaching of Jesus was interrupted by the pleasant incident of parents bringing their "little children" (Luke says "babes"

18:15) that He might place His hands upon them and pray (v. 13). What a tender sight! And yet it has its darker undertones. For the disciples rebuked the parents for doing so. Why did they do this? It may have been for the very human reason that their coming interrupted Jesus, and they wanted to hear more on the subject under discussion. It may have been due to solicitous concern for Jesus' own welfare. He was too busy to be bothered with little children. But they misjudged Jesus. For He was ever attentive to the needs of the little ones. Mark says that He was moved with indignation or anger at the act of the Twelve. At any rate the incident brought forth one of the most beautiful and beloved sayings of Jesus. "Suffer [permit] little children, and forbid them not, to come unto me: for of such is the kingdom of heaven" (v. 14). How poverty stricken we should be without these words! And we are indebted to the dullness of the disciples for them. But this is another instance where God overrules the mistakes of men to turn them into a blessing—if we trust in Him.

So the scene closes with a picture beautiful beyond description. "And he laid his hands on them, and departed thence" (v. 15). Mark is even warmer in his account. "And he took them up in his arms, put his hands upon them, and blessed them" (10:16). He loved them, pressed them to His bosom, placed His hands upon them, and pronounced His blessing upon them. The parents would never forget it, nor would the children. We may well suppose that in later years many of these children became His disciples.

We should never despise the little ones. They need to be won to Christ as do all others. And most children are capable of exercising faith in Him much younger than we usually suppose. Their potential for Christ is so great. Therefore, it is not only what they are but what they may become which is of such great importance. The university president had caught something of the spirit of Jesus. When asked why he always tipped his hat when speaking to little boys, he replied, "I never know but that I am speaking to a future president of the nation."

The Problem of Wealth (19:16-26)

Jesus had left the house and was again journeying toward Jerusalem. He probably was still in Perea. Suddenly there came one running and kneeled before Him (cf. Mark 10:17). He was a young man of great possessions. Luke says that he was a ruler, probably the ruler of a synagogue (18:18). He came to Jesus with a problem. "Teacher, what good may I do in order that I may have life eternal" or life of the ages (v. 16, author's translation)?

In the Authorized Version the young man addresses Jesus as "Good Master." But in the best manuscripts of this passage the word "good" is absent. However, it is genuine in the Gospels of Mark and Luke. Likewise, whereas they address Jesus as "Good Master" they do not use the word "good" with reference to that which the young man asks. Instead they read, "What shall I do . . . ?" Nevertheless the word "good" appears in all three accounts. In the former it refers to Jesus; in the latter it refers to that which is to be done. The Gospel writers often relate the same incident but in different words. In any event the net meaning is the same.

The same difference is carried throughout the various accounts. In Mark and Luke Jesus replies, "Why callest thou me good?" But the best manuscripts of Matthew read, "Why askest thou me concerning the good?" In all other matters the accounts follow substantially the same wording. However, in the overall the messages are similar. But let us follow the account in Matthew.

We see a young man with high ideals. He desires eternal life or that life which is age-abiding. The emphasis here is not so much on length but upon the quality of life. Too often we think of eternal life as beginning after death. But eternal life both as to endurance and as to quality may be a present possession. And that is what this young man desires.

But note his concept as to how he may have this life. "What good may I do in order that I may have eternal life?" What may he do? He thought of it as resulting from his own good works. In his mind were those ethical and moral deeds which were in keeping with the spirit of the age in which he lived. It was for this reason that Jesus challenged his question. "Why askest thou me concerning the good? one there is who is good" (v. 17). Mark and Luke identify this "one" as God. Jesus means that *goodness* must not be measured by the moral and ethical standards which have grown up about the customs of a given people or in a given age. There is but one true standard of goodness, and that is from God who is perfect goodness. So to think of goodness one must not be content with the mores of society, but must seek after goodness as designed of God.

Therefore, Jesus says, "If thou wilt enter into life, keep the commandments" (v. 17). Does this mean that one can have eternal life by keeping the Ten Commandments? That is what Jesus says. But we must remember that Jesus is probing this young man's heart. The fact is that because of man's sinful nature it is impossible for him perfectly to keep these commandments. It is for this reason that God offers salvation by grace. And that is what Jesus is endeavoring to get this man to see.

You may ask why it is that if God knew that man could not keep the commandments He should wait so long to reveal His plan to save men by grace? Why the centuries of stumbling and failing? The answer is that God knew that man could not, or would not, keep the commandments. But man did not know it. And so man was left free to endeavor only to fail. It was only then that man would be willing to cast himself upon the free mercy of God. It was this very thing that was involved in Jesus' dealing with the rich young ruler.

In response to Jesus' challenge to keep the commandments, he asked, "Which?" (v. 18). Actually the word "which" refers to *kind.* What kind of commandments shall he keep? Does this distinguish between the Mosaic code and rabbinical rules? Possibly so. At any rate Jesus refers him to the Mosaic code or the Ten Commandments. In so doing He cites the five having to do with murder, adultery, theft, false witness, and honoring father and mother. He omits the one about covetousness (Mark mentions "defraud" which probably refers to this one). But Matthew adds the words "Thou shalt love thy neighbour as thyself" (v. 19). In essence this involves the tenth commandment, even as it was regarded as a summary of the last six (cf. Matt. 22:39). So in effect Jesus referred the young man to the last six commandments. These are the commandments which have to do with man's relation to other men. Note that Jesus did not quote the first four commandments which refer to man's relation to God. So Jesus actually said, "Live in a right relationship with other men."

In all honesty the young man replied, "All these things have I kept" or guarded. "From my youth up" is not in the best manuscripts. He had carefully guarded against breaking any of these commandments. And it is quite possibly so insofar as overt acts were concerned. He had not murdered. Neither had he committed adultery. Nor had he stolen or borne false witness against his neighbor. As a dutiful son he had honored his parents. He had been a model citizen and neighbor. So far as rote rules of conduct were concerned he had made a good score.

Yet he asked, "What lack I yet?" None of these things had brought satisfaction. His soul is still empty. Some see this as self-complacency or pride. However, there is no reason to question his honest admission that he still senses his lack of eternal life. He was like multitudes who keep the letter of the law but fail to achieve its spirit. He thought in terms of quantitative goodness rather than of qualitative God-likeness. The truth is that while he thought that he had kept these six commandments, he had not. For with his great wealth and position he apparently had done nothing to relieve the poverty and misery which abounded about him. He had done no harm, but neither had he done any good. His was a negative sort of goodness. He was good, but he was good for nothing.

And that is why Jesus shocked him with His demand. "If thou wilt be perfect [complete], go and sell that thou hast, and give to the poor, and thou shalt have treasure in heaven: and come and follow me" (v. 21). Did Jesus mean that he should become a pauper? Not at all. The New Testament does not despise riches as such. It says much about the stewardship of wealth, but it does not condemn it if it be acquired and used righteously.

Why then did Jesus make such a demand?

It was noted above that Jesus did not mention the first four commandments, or those which deal with man's relation to God. Did He ignore them in dealing with this man? Did He teach a merely social religion? To the contrary He was leading the young ruler to see that true religion is more than social. It is that to be sure, but it is more than that. And while it may seem strange to say so, in Jesus' counsel to sell his goods and give the money to the poor He was saying that true religion first of all involves a right relation to God. So in effect in verse 21 Jesus was quoting the first four commandments to the young man or at least that which they involve.

The rich young ruler thought that he had kept the commandments. Yet in his attitude toward his wealth he was certainly guilty of breaking the first one "Thou shalt have no other gods before me" (Exod. 20:3). And James says that if we break one commandment we are guilty of all (2:10). The young man unconsciously had made his wealth his god. And this idolatry negated his every effort toward self-righteousness. It is no wonder that he felt an emptiness in his soul. So Jesus told him to get rid of that which stood between him and God. Instead of being mastered by his wealth he should prove to be its master.

And our Lord says this to every man. Not every case necessarily involves wealth. It may be any number of things: pride, self-will, beauty, popularity, intellect, prejudice, or some coddled sin. But whatever it is that stands between you and a full allegiance to God, Jesus says that you must get rid of it. All of the social righteousness which you may perform cannot substitute for a right relationship to God. For when you have done all, you will still ask, "What lack I yet?"

But when the young man heard that saying, he went away sorrowful, but he went away. He almost had eternal life in his grasp, but he failed to take hold of it because his hands and heart were engaged in holding on to his god. The incident which began with such high hopes ended in the bitterness of despair. And, alas, his kind are myriad!

But he was not the only sorrowful person in the group. We may be sure that Jesus watched him sadly as he went away. For "Jesus looking upon him loved him" (Mark 10:21 RV). He loved him for who and what he was, for what he might become within himself, and for what he could mean to the kingdom of God. And He looks with sorrow upon every person who chooses to follow the gods of this world rather than to find eternal life in allegiance to God.

As Jesus watched the young man going from Him He said to His disciples, "Verily I say unto you, That a rich man shall hardly [with difficulty] enter into the kingdom of heaven" (v. 23). He did not say that he could not do so, but that it was difficult for him to do so. Not because he is wealthy but because his wealth proves a stumbling stone in his way. It is so tempting for one to place his trust in things. An abundance of wealth tends to invite a sense of self-sufficiency. This may be true in worldly relationships. But wealth is not legal tender in the kingdom of heaven. A wealthy man must be saved in the same manner as anyone else—by acknowledging his inability and unworthiness, and in faith receiving the grace of God through Jesus Christ. But the fact that one is rich in material things makes it exceedingly difficult so to humble himself. It was especially true in Jesus' day when wealth was regarded as God's approval of a person. This same insidious thought still lurks within modern man to ensnare multitudes. The *up-and-outs* need Christ as much as do the *down-and-outs*. But in the nature of things the former finds it more difficult than the latter to recognize this need.

Indeed, Jesus said, "It is easier for a camel to go through the eye of a needle, than for a rich man to enter into the kingdom of God" (v. 24). This is a strong statement indeed. And from earliest times efforts have been made to tone it down. One such effort was to see a textual error in the word for "camel" (*kamēlos*). It was held that the true reading should be *kamilos,* a cable or large rope. But there is no reason to hold to this idea. The word *kamilos* does not appear in any classical writing or in the papyri. It is found in no reputable manuscript of Matthew. Indeed the best Greek scholars hold that this word was invented in an effort to explain this passage. The best manuscripts of Matthew all read "camel." Another effort was to claim that the word "needle" referred to a small door in the Jaffa gate in Jerusalem, through which a camel might enter only by being stripped of its burden and crawling through on its knees. This is a most suggestive figure. But there is no evidence that there was any such door either in a Jerusalem gate or in any other Palestinian town at that time.

No, the point of Jesus' figure was to state an impossibility. His thought is that no man, rich or poor, by his own efforts can enter into the kingdom of heaven. It is understandable, then, that the disciples should ask, "Who then can be saved?" (v. 25). To them wealth was an evidence of God's good pleasure upon a man. And now Jesus dispels that view by stating that it may become a handicap in receiving God's approval. But Jesus answers their question by saying that while it may be impossible for a man to save himself, nothing is impossible to God (v. 26). Man must enter the kingdom of heaven by the grace and power of God. A man is not saved by position, power, or possessions. He is saved by becoming as a little child, bare of self-reliance and submissive to the will and purpose of God. The old saying is eternally true that the ground is level at the foot of the cross.

The Question of the Disciples (19:27-30)

Jesus had told the rich young ruler to forsake his goods and follow Him. In that light Peter, speaking for the Twelve, asks, "Behold, we have forsaken all, and followed thee; what shall we have therefore?" (v. 27). In the Greek text "we" is written out, and so is emphatic. It sets the Twelve in contrast to the young ruler. Jesus had promised him eternal life if he would forsake his wealth and follow Him. The disciples proudly claim to have fulfilled that condition. And they want to know what reward they shall receive.

The very fact that they would ask this question indicates that they misunderstood Jesus' words. To be sure they had left business, home, and family to follow Jesus. But their action had been prompted partially by a selfish purpose. They expect to receive more than they have renounced. However, Jesus does not rebuke them for this. He patiently endeavors to lead them to an understanding of His Kingdom and the nature of its rewards.

What did Jesus mean in Matthew 19:28? The word "regeneration" (*palingenesia*) is found in the New Testament only here and in Titus 3:5. In the latter case it refers to the cleansing of the new birth. But in Matthew 19:28 the sense seems to be that of a new birth for the entire cosmos at the second coming of Christ (cf. Rom. 8:20-22). This word was used by the Stoics in the sense of the renewal of nature. Plutarch uses it of the appearance of souls in new bodies. We must not pin Jesus down to a literalist meaning. He is speaking in apocalyptic language. We can only say that He points to a restoration of all things to the condition which God intends (cf. Acts 3:21). It speaks of the glorious return of the Lord when He shall sit upon "the throne of his glory."

Clearly Jesus says that the twelve apostles also "shall sit upon twelve thrones, judging the twelve tribes of Israel" (v. 28). This could hardly mean that only Israel will be judged or that a given apostle will judge a given tribe. The figure is drawn from the custom of an oriental monarch sitting upon his throne in public to hear complaints and petitions and to render judgments. Alongside him sat his counsellors to assist in this work, Other references of a similar nature are found in the New Testament (cf. Luke 22:30; Rev. 4:4). In I Corinthians 6:2 Paul says that the "saints shall judge the world." We cannot be dogmatic as to what Jesus meant. But in God's own secret wisdom the disciples who have left all to follow Jesus will be exalted.

In verse 29 Jesus extends His promise of reward to include all others who have forsaken houses, brethren, sisters, father, mother, children, or lands (Luke 18:29 includes "wife") for His sake. The King James Version says that they shall receive an "hundredfold." The best manuscripts read "manifold." In either event does this mean that in heaven such shall have many wives, etc.? The answer obviously is in the negative. This within itself warns against a literal interpretation of these words of Jesus. The exact meaning is hidden behind the veil of God's mysterious wisdom. The whole of it may be summed up in the words "and shall inherit eternal life." But note that while they "receive" rewards they "inherit" everlasting life. This would imply that while there may be differences in rewards they all inherit eternal life. Beyond that we can leave the details with God.

However, Jesus warns that there will be surprises at the judgment. "But many that are first shall be last; and the last shall be first" (v. 30). Shall we interpret this with reference to time? Did the apostles think that those who first began to follow Jesus should receive greater rewards than the others (cf. Matt. 20:1-16)? At any rate Jesus is saying that rewards will not be distributed according to man's standards or timetable but according to the sovereign will and judgment of God (cf. Matt. 20:1-16). Certainly some who think that they are great by men's standards will find that they do not rate so high by heaven's standards. Conversely some who by worldly standards do not fall among thhe *great* will be considered so at the final judgment.

Some years ago Toyohiko Kagawa was described as the world's greatest living Christian. When asked about this he replied that he did not know who deserved that title by God's standard. It might be some lowly Christian woman who lived in the slums of some great city, unheralded and unsung by her fellowmen.

This is apparently the meaning of Jesus' words. But certainly there will be surprises in that great final day. How disappointing it will be for some of the "first"! How glorious it will be for some of the "last"! We can leave the decision with Him who makes no mistakes.

Matthew 20

The King and Kingdom Reward

Matthew 20 is a continuation of the subject treated in Matthew 19:16-30. In Matthew 19 Jesus is dealing with a problem. In Matthew 20:1-16 He is explaining His answer. The closing part of this chapter shows how little the Twelve understand the entire matter. Nevertheless the burden of this chapter deals specifically with the subject of reward in the kingdom of heaven. A preview of its contents divides it into (1) the principle of kingdom reward; (2) the request for kingdom privilege; (3) the road to kingdom greatness.

The Principle of Kingdom Reward (20:1-16)

Jesus illustrates this principle with a parable. "The kingdom of heaven is like unto a man that is an householder . . ." (v. 1). The picture was a common one. Early in the morning, probably at six o'clock or at the beginning of the Jewish day, he went to the marketplace. There he found day laborers waiting to be hired. He bargained to pay them a *denarius* or about seventeen cents. This was a day's pay for a laborer or a soldier. And so they went to work in the vineyard. Later at the third hour (9:00 A.M.) he went back to the marketplace to hire others. But notice that he bargained for no set wage, promising to pay them "whatsoever is right," not *lawful* but *right*. They had no legal contract, nor did they ask about wages. Instead they were glad to work, and trusted the householder to do that which was right. The same thing happened at the sixth (noon) and the ninth hours (3:00 P.M.) Finally at 5:00 P.M. He returned to find other laborers. In reply to his question as to why they were not working they said, "Because no man hath hired us" (v. 7). So the householder sent them into the vineyard to work for one hour, until 6:00 P.M., promising them that they would receive what was right.

Now the stage is set. The workers have gone into the vineyard at intervals. But only the first group has been promised a definite wage. The others are glad to have work whatever the pay, and trust their employer to do the right thing by them. But Jesus was no idle storyteller. He was teaching a lesson. But what is He saying?

Recall that this parable follows immediately after His words "But many that are first shall be last; and the last shall be first." However, even this summarizes His teaching with regard to Peter's question about rewards. And it grew out of the incident about the rich young ruler. The question of Peter implies that, unlike the young ruler, the Twelve have left all to follow Jesus. Therefore, their reward should be great or the greatest. And in point of time their sacrificial following preceded all others.

In this light the parable takes on meaning. The householder is Jesus Himself, and the vineyard is His kingdom. "Early in the morning" suggests the beginning of His public ministry. The first laborers to be hired, therefore, relate to the Twelve themselves. The other laborers correspond to those who will be called into the vineyard from time to time leading up to the second coming of Christ. The Householder will continue to call laborers into His vineyard right up to the very end.

But how are we to understand the wages or the *denarius?* This was all that a laborer could expect for a full day's work. Anything beyond that was governed by the goodness of the Householder. But He definitely promised to pay the *denarius.* May we not say that the *denarius* corresponds to eternal life? This was the subject under consideration in the incident of the rich young ruler (19:16-17). And while Jesus said that those who followed Him would *receive* a reward, He said that they "shall *inherit* everlasting life" (19:29, author's italics). The reward was due to the goodness of the King; eternal life was due to His *integrity.* In the beginning, while the Twelve may have envisioned kingdom greatness, the King promised them eternal life. And like the first group of laborers the Twelve had entered the Lord's vineyard with that understanding.

So much for the Twelve. What about those who should come after them? Actually we know that they too were/are promised eternal life. But to have so stated would have spoiled the point of the parable. Though they come into the Kingdom from time to time after the Twelve, they do not quibble as to wages. They trust the Householder to do what is right. The whole point of the story is that the Twelve were thinking that due to their priority in time, length, and degree of labor they should receive some special reward not given to the others.

Now we come to the pay-off. At the close of the day the householder instructed his steward to pay the laborers their wages. This was in keeping with the Mosaic law (cf. Deut. 24:15). With design he instructed that those who came to work at the eleventh hour should be paid first (v. 8; cf. 19:30). Each one of them received a *denarius,* the same amount promised to those who went to work at 6:00 A.M.

Finally the steward came to those who entered the vineyard first (v. 10). We may well imagine their eager anticipation as they saw how generous the householder had been with the eleventh hour group. You can almost hear their minds calculating the amount that they would receive. A *denarius* for one hour's work! For twelve hours surely they would receive twelve *denarii.* But to their dismay they also received each a *denarius.*

And then the grumbling began (v. 11). For that is exactly what the word "murmured" means. Furthermore, it is an imperfect tense. They began to grumble and kept on grumbling. And as they progressively received their wages the noise increased. Listen to them. "These last have wrought but one hour, and thou hast made them equal unto us, which have borne the burden and heat of the day" (v. 12). They had endured the toil and scorching wind of a long day. The others had worked only one hour, and that in the cool of the day. And yet each received the same wage. The first group felt that they were justified in their complaint.

But notice the householder's answer (vv. 13-15). He addressed them or their spokesman as "Friend." Plumptre points out that this word is used by Jesus with a note of censure (cf. Matt. 22:12; 26:50). In Matthew 11:16 He uses it of the companions of little children, but contrary children. So we may understand it as a respectful address but with a note of censure. "I do thee no wrong: didst thou not agree with me for a penny (*denarius*)?" He paid them exactly what he promised. There had been no mention of a bonus. So he continued. "Take that thine is, and go thy way: I will [to] give unto this last, even as unto thee." The word "take" means "take up" (*aron*). Either they had left the *denarius* on the table or else contemptuously had thrown it to the ground. So take it up and be gone! Had they been paid first and had gone their way there would have been no grumbling. They would have been satisfied. But that is the very point of the story. The householder paid what they bargained for. Beyond that he could do as he willed with the others. And note his final word to them. "Is thine eye evil because I am good?" The evil eye was the divided eye or the one out of focus (cf. Matt. 6:23). Their eyes had a double focus – on the *denarius* and on an expected bonus.

Now what is the lesson which Jesus is teaching? He concludes the parable by applying the words of Matthew 19:30. "So the last shall be first, and the first last" (v. 16). (The words "for many be called, but few chosen" are not in the best manuscripts.) Notice that Jesus reverses the order of the words: "last" and "first." This is the lesson of the parable.

The Twelve had entered the Lord's vineyard on the promise of eternal life. They received it. Likewise do all those who come after them. But Jesus implies that the Twelve, because of their prior commitment, are thinking that they should receive a *bonus* in addition. However, Jesus says that the last person who believes on Him prior to His second coming will receive the same basic gift as the first (Andrew and John) who believed on Him. He gave to the first what He promised. And He gives to all what He wills. For eternal life is His to bestow as He wills according to His grace. He does not bestow it indiscriminately, but upon all who enter into His vineyard. No one should expect more, for all are unprofitable servants.

So the basic teaching of this parable is that God through Christ bestows His gifts as He wills, according to His sovereignty and by His grace. In the light of Matthew 19:28-29 there will be rewards in addition to eternal life. The Twelve will sit on thrones. The others will receive "manifold." But the King's rewards will be bestowed not on the basis of request but upon the basis of divine will. Nor will they be bestowed in degree on the basis of priority in time but on the basis of individual attitude and of the *goodness* (grace) of the Householder.

The lesson of this parable was both timely and timeless. The attitude held by the Twelve is unfortunately one that continues to plague the cause of Christ. And the censure of such on the part of the King is unchangeable. He does not discourage the idea of kingdom rewards as such. His teachings abound in God's promise to reward those who diligently serve Him. The trouble is not with the reward but with one's attitude toward it. No man should serve the Lord out of a sense of expectancy alone. He should do so for the joy of serving and of doing the will of God. Certainly he should not make requests or demands either of the Lord or of his fellow-servants. Eternal life is the present possession of all who believe in Him. We should leave the matter of rewards to His sovereign will and boundless grace.

The Request for Kingdom Privilege (20:17-24)

In between verses 16 and 17 Jesus and His company seem to have crossed the Jordan river and are nearing Jericho (cf. Mark 10:46). Jesus is definitely "going up to Jerusalem" (Matt. 20:17). A strange sense of awe has swept over the group (Mark 10:32). As though eager to achieve His destiny Jesus is walking ahead of the group. But at a given point He draws the Twelve aside for private instruction. He makes one further effort to get them to understand His mission. In verse 18 He repeats what He has said previously about His coming suffering at the hands of the Jewish leaders. He will be betrayed and condemned to death. But then Jesus adds a new note of the foreboding event. "And shall deliver [hand over for execution] him to the Gentiles [Romans] to mock [Mark adds "spit upon him"], and to scourge, and to crucify him" (v. 19). For the first time Jesus uses the word "crucify." Heretofore He has said that He would be killed, but now He specifies the manner in which He will die. The cross has been referred to in a general way, but now He definitely applies this terrible word to Himself. "Crucify" could mean but one thing to the disciples. Their Lord was to be executed as a common criminal. One would think that this would most certainly shock the Twelve into an awareness of the coming event. But Luke notes that they failed to understand (18:34). Along with this the promise of the resurrection also fell upon deaf ears. So completely obsessed were they with the thought of a political Messiah that it was almost impossible for them to see any other concept of Jesus.

But again we must not sit in judgment upon them. For if they failed to comprehend before the event, we have become so familiar with it after the event that these words continue to fall upon calloused ears and hearts. For we also think in terms of personal ambitions and power in kingdom enterprises. And that which stabbed the Saviour's heart then wounds Him still.

Even so we are hardly prepared for that which happened hard upon Jesus' words about His approaching death. Heretofore the Twelve have disputed among themselves as to kingdom greatness. When accosted by Jesus about this they have even asked Him to explain as to its nature. But now there comes a bold and brazen request for personal privilege and power. And even its source adds emphasis to the shock. For it comes from those whom we have come to regard as possessing unusual spiritual understanding – John and James.

Mark says that the two brothers approached Jesus directly (10:35). But Matthew notes that the request came from both them and their mother (20:20). He also records that they came "worshipping" or as one kneeling before the King. In response to Jesus' request as to what they wanted, the mother replied, "Grant that these my two sons may sit, the one on thy right hand, and the other on the left, in thy kingdom" (v. 21). And this in spite of the lesson which Jesus had taught in the parable! Apparently their minds were still fastened upon His words about the apostles sitting on thrones with Him. The "right hand" and "left" represent the two chief thrones with Jesus, or the places of first and second power next to Him. The mother asked these positions for her sons who shared in her ambitious request.

Why would she be so bold as to make such a request? It is generally conceded that she was Salome (cf. Matt. 27:56; Mark 15:40), and the sister of Mary, the mother of Jesus. If so, then she was Jesus' aunt, and John and James were His first cousins. It would seem, therefore, that she was presuming upon a family relationship. Furthermore, her two sons were members of the inner circle of disciples along with Peter (cf. Matt. 17:1). It may be that she felt that Jesus had discredited Peter (cf. Matt. 16:23). John is repeatedly referred to as "the disciple whom Jesus loved" (John 13:23; 19:26; 20:2). If we may assume that John 13:23 states a general pattern, then John enjoyed a favored place by Jesus when they reclined at meals. In this light, therefore, she would naturally assume that since someone must occupy these important positions they should naturally go to her sons. Apparently there was nothing wrong with her logic.

But there was much wrong with her understanding and that of her sons. They still failed to comprehend the nature of the Christ and His kingdom. And this was shared by all of the others. For even after the resurrection they still thought in terms of a worldly political kingdom (cf. Acts 1:6).

However, we must continue to warn ourselves against judging them too harshly. For if they failed to understand when they lived so close to the events under consideration, what about those of us who enjoy the vantage point of two thousand years after the events? The atmosphere of selfish ambition in the kingdom and its affairs continues to cling to us like a poisonous vapor. So what Jesus says in reply to this request should be taken personally by each one of us.

"Ye know not what ye ask" (v. 22). Note the plural form of these verbs. The reply was to both mother and sons. And the verbs themselves are of significance. "Know" (*oidate*) is a verb which speaks of the perception of experiential knowledge until it becomes a conviction of the soul. They knew the words which they spoke, but they had not seen through them to their meaning. Furthermore, "ask" (*aiteisthe*) is an indirect middle voice meaning "ask for yourselves." Jesus says that theirs was a selfish request. Nor did they comprehend that which they were asking for themselves. They were asking for a throne, little knowing that if they were to reign with Jesus they must also suffer with Him (cf. Rom. 8:17; II Tim. 2:12; Rev. 3:21). And that was the farthest thing from their minds.

But Jesus faces them with this very fact. "Are ye able to drink of the cup that I shall drink of, and to be baptized with the baptism that I am baptized with?" (v. 22). The word about baptism does not appear in the best manuscripts of Matthew. But it is genuine in Mark 10:38. And so for completeness we may consider it here. What did Jesus mean by these figures of speech? Obviously He was speaking of great suffering. The "cup" was commonly used among the Jews for either great joy or great sorrow (cf. Ps. 23:5; Jer. 25:15). In this context it would refer to the latter. Later we find Jesus using this very figure to refer to that which was involved in His death on the cross (Matt. 26:39; John 18:11). This seems to refer not so much to physical death itself, but to the fact that Jesus became *sin* in the process. We shall deal with this more in detail at that point. The reference to "baptism" involves Jesus being overwhelmed or submerged in the sorrow and suffering which the cross epitomizes. This word is so used in the papyri of one being overwhelmed by calamities.

So Jesus challenges them with the suffering which must precede the throne. And they accepted His challenge, so they thought, as they said, "We are able." Let us not think of this as arrogance but of ignorance. How could they possibly enter fully into the experience which awaited Jesus? In later years as John reflected upon his answer it must have put him to shame. But give them credit for being sincere insofar as their understanding permitted. Perhaps they thought of some military conflict by which Jesus would establish His kingdom. And this would appeal to these "sons of thunder" (Mark 3:17). Peter himself avowed the same loyalty as Jesus stood in the shadow of the cross (cf. Luke 22:33).

But none of them could grasp the full meaning of Jesus' words. It is far easier to stand bravely in physical combat than to endure spiritual trials triumphantly. Many a person who has stood without flinching before the mouth of a blazing cannon has proved to be a moral and spiritual coward. To follow Christ to the uttermost calls for more than physical courage, although that cannot be despised. It involves a resoluteness of soul to do our duty when all others about us are failing. It was such a courage which sustained Jesus in His hours of greatest trial. And we cannot say, "We are able," unless we are capable of doing the same.

Though He knew that the two brothers fell far short of understanding the import of their words He did not rebuke them. Instead He said that they would be called upon to prove their claims (v. 23). And to the extent that man is able to do so they did. James was the first of the Twelve to pay with his life for his faith in Jesus (cf. Acts 12:2). John would live to a ripe old age, but he would suffer persecution and exile (cf. Rev. 1:9). Although it is only tradition there is a legend that he was the last of the apostles to be martyred. According to this he finally was forced to drink poison, and then plunged in boiling oil. Whether this be true or not, it probably stems from this saying of Jesus.

But, even so, Jesus says that the places of privilege requested by John and James are not His to bestow (Matt. 20:23). The rewards of the kingdom are "for whom it is prepared of my Father." The word "prepared" is the perfect indicative passive form of the verb (*hetoimazō*) which means to make ready or prepare. So this matter has already been prepared by the Father, and it stands prepared. Matthew 25:34 says that this was done "from the foundation of the world." Thus it is not a matter to be decided on the spur of the moment, on the basis of the accident of natural birth, nor to be bestowed for the asking. And if we follow through on Matthew 25:34 we learn that it is bestowed on the basis of service rendered in the name of Jesus with no thought of reward (cf. 25:34-40).

It is always pleasing to see someone rewarded for a service well rendered. However, it is a sad picture to see a person who is constantly self-seeking, and renders a service with no motive other than the plaudits of men. The saddest picture of all is to see service rendered under the guise of religion whose only purpose is to be seen and rewarded by men. In the Sermon on the Mount Jesus says that such will receive what they seek. They may be rewarded of men but that is all. They are paid-in-full. There is no reward from God for such. But happy is he who serves the Lord out of the very joy of serving. Because he shall not lose his reward. For when the Lord returns He "will make manifest the counsels of the hearts: and then shall every man have praise of God" (I Cor. 4:5).

What was the reaction of the other ten apostles to this request? Matthew notes that "they were moved with indignation against the two brethren" (v. 24). This expresses strong resentment. They were not outraged concerning the bad taste that such a request had been made at so serious a time. Their indignation was due to the fact that the two brothers had beaten them to it, and that they had sought to gain an unfair advantage through personal and family relationships. There is no darker picture within this sacred fellowship than to see these men who were so close to Jesus struggling for power and privilege within the kingdom of heaven. But it may well be said that he among us who is without the same sin, let him cast the first stone at the Twelve.

The Road to Kingdom Greatness (20:25-34)

Sadly but patiently Jesus called the Twelve to Him. They seem to be so unteachable. But the Lord does not give up. He does not rebuke them for desiring kingdom greatness. Instead He seeks to guide them to a proper understanding of what that greatness really is.

"Ye know that the princes of the Gentiles [pagan rulers] exercise dominion [lord it over] over them, and they that are great [the grandees] exercise authority [play the tyrant] upon them" (v. 25). This is a description of pagan greatness. That is the standard that the Twelve are following. But Jesus says, "It shall not be so among you" (v. 26). The negative is emphatic. Literally, "Not so shall it be among you." Thus Jesus sets the kingdom standard of greatness over against that of the pagan world. "But whosoever will be [may will to be] great among you, let him be your minister [*diakonos*]; and whosoever will be [may will to be] chief [first] among you, let him be your servant [*doulos*]" (vv. 26-27).

Notice the words *diakonos* and *doulos*. A *doulos* was a bond-servant or slave. Paul was fond of calling himself a *doulos* of Jesus Christ. A *diakonos* was also a slave. It is our word for "deacon," although it basically means a slave who did menial service. The derivation of this word is uncertain. It is comprised of two words, *dia,* through, and *konis,* dust. A. T. Robertson says that it may mean one who raises a dust in his haste to serve.

This was a complete reversal of popular opinion as to greatness then and now. The pagan or worldly standard of greatness is gauged by the number who serve you. But the kingdom measure of greatness is the number whom you serve. It was the standard followed by Jesus Himself (v. 28). Even He came not to be served but to serve. When He washed the disciples' feet He embodied this very principle (cf. John 13:4ff.). They came into the upper room arguing as to which was the greatest (cf. Luke 22:24). Each probably was seeking the chief place at the table for the Passover meal. Jesus repeated the teaching as to diverse standards of the pagans and of the kingdom. And then He rinsed their feet. This was a service performed by a slave of the host. And since Jesus had no such slave, He performed the service Himself. Truly He came to serve and not to be served.

But Jesus added one significant phrase. "And to give his life a ransom for many" (v. 28). This is the only occasion where this word "ransom" (*lutron*) is used in the New Testament (cf. Mark 10:45). Previously Jesus has spoken of His death. But here for the first time He speaks of it in terms of a *ransom* for many. A ransom was the price paid for the freedom or deliverance of a slave or a captive. So Jesus says that His death will be the price which He will pay for the release of those who are slaves or captives of sin. Thus He speaks of the substitutionary atonement. Because the word "for" *(anti)* means "in the place of." Jesus will die in the place of those who are to be ransomed.

The word "ransom" causes some difficulty among theologians. To whom is the ransom paid? Certainly we cannot say that it was paid to Satan. For that would make him superior to God. Many theories have evolved from this question. Suffice it to say that the ransom was paid in Christ, and He paid it to Himself.

The apostle Paul gets to the heart of the matter in Romans 3:23-26. "For all have sinned, and come short of the glory of God" (v. 23). But they have been "justified freely by his grace," or free-for-nothing, "through the redemption [*apolutrōseōs,* thorough redemption, a form of the root word for *lutron*] that is in Christ Jesus" (v. 24). Man sinned. And because God is just He could not ignore the sin. Since the wages of sin is death, someone must die for man's sin in order to satisfy the holy nature of God. In his sinful state man abides in death. But because God is love He could not leave men hopelessly in such a state. Therefore, in Christ and His death on the cross God paid the price for man's sin. Thus He became "just and the justifier of him which believeth in Jesus" (v. 26). It is this last phrase, "which believeth in Jesus," that gives meaning to our Lord's words in Matthew 20:28, "a ransom for many." Not all, but many. He provided salvation or a ransom for all who will believe in Him as Saviour. This does not teach universal salvation. Jesus provided salvation for all men. But it becomes effective only for those who receive it through faith in Him. It is for those "which believeth in Jesus."

However, there is one other significant thought in Jesus' words "to give his life a ransom for many." The Twelve are thinking of thrones. Our Lord says that even He will ascend His throne through the cross and the empty tomb. If the Twelve aspire to thrones they must travel the same road. They must die to self and find the true meaning of life in their King. Truly they must in their finite way drink of His cup and experience His baptism. Kingdom greatness for us is not by the asking but by the deserving. This is the way which has been prepared of the heavenly Father. And there is no other way either in the first or in the twentieth century. He that hath ears to hear, let him hear!

Matthew closes Chapter 20 with a touching and significant incident (vv. 29-34). As Jesus and His company (a great multitude) were leaving Jericho on the way to Jerusalem, two blind men sat on the roadside begging. This is a common sight now as it was then. Hearing that Jesus was in the group they began to cry, "Have mercy on us, O Lord, thou son of David." Probably they had heard of His miraculous power. The crowd, indifferent to their need, sought to silence them. But that served only to increase their cries. Jesus stopped near them to ask, "What will ye that I shall do unto you?" They make no mention of alms. Such worldly things have receded in their desires. "They say unto him, Lord, that our eyes may be opened." Jesus had compassion on them, touched their eyes, and they received their sight. And then they followed Him. What a relief to Jesus that these men asked for sight rather than for preferential privilege in His kingdom.

There is almost a symbolic significance in this event. "Lord, that our eyes may be opened." The Twelve might well have prayed this prayer. For having two good eyes they saw not. And we too should breathe this petition. For even though we behold the things of earth we can scarcely perceive the things of heaven. Grant, Lord, that our eyes may be opened!

The Triumph of the King

Matthew 21

The Presentation of the King

From Jericho Jesus and His company travelled the fifteen miles up the Roman road to Bethany. He had definitely set His face to go to Jerusalem for the final showdown with the Jewish rulers and nation. If we follow Matthew alone this would be His first visit to the Holy City during His public ministry. However, we know from Luke and John that He had made several trips to Jerusalem or its environs. But Matthew in accord with his purpose in writing his Gospel records this one visit. For three and one-half years the King had delivered His message relative to the kingdom. During this time there had been a rising enmity toward Jesus on the part of the Jewish leaders. Now the King will challenge them and the nation in their capital city itself. He will officially present Himself as their King to be either received or rejected.

For this occasion the King chose the Passover (cf. John 12:1). And it was fitting that He should do so. For it was the most important of all the Jewish feasts. Since it commemorated Israel's deliverance from Egyptian bondage, there was always a sense of expectancy among the Jews that another great deliverance would come at such a feast. John 11:56 implies an unusual state of excitement at this particular Passover. The people were aware of the hastening climax which must inevitably come between Jesus and the Jewish rulers. In fact the latter had given orders that anyone having knowledge of Jesus' whereabouts should report it, in order that they might seize Him (John 11:57). So the people sensed that something was about to happen. There was widespread speculation as to whether or not Jesus would come to the feast (John 11:56).

A further reason why this feast was fitting for the presentation of the King was that at this time Jerusalem was always crowded with Jews. Every adult male Jew living within twenty miles of Jerusalem was required to attend the Passover. But every Jew, no matter where he lived, hoped to attend this feast at least once in his lifetime. Thirty years after this particular Passover the Roman governor took a census of the lambs slain at such a feast. The number was about two hundred and fifty thousand. And since one lamb was required for ten people this would mean that two and one-half million people would be involved. This gives some idea as to the number of Jews who were faced with a decision concerning Jesus. And this decision involved Jews both in Palestine and from among the Dispersion.

As we examine the presentation of the King Matthew 21 may be divided as follows: (1) the royal entry; (2) the assertion of kingly authority; (3) the challenge to kingly authority; (4) the exercise of kingly authority.

The Royal Entry (21:1-11)

The entrance of Jesus into Jerusalem on what we call Palm Sunday has traditionally been called His "Triumphal Entry." But it carries none of the meaning contained in those words. To the contrary it was the very opposite. In that day a triumphal entry was the occasion when some King or general returned from a victorious war, usually riding upon a white horse as a symbol of victory, and bringing with him his trophies of victory. If we would see Jesus' "Triumphal Entry" we must read Ephesians 4:8 where Paul describes His victorious return to heaven.

When Jesus rode into Jerusalem He came as one "meek, and sitting upon an ass," which suggests a King of peace. He came not after the *victory* but before the *battle*. He was the King-Messiah presenting Himself to His capital city and to His people. So His entrance was not a "triumphal entry" but "the royal entry" of one who came as the Prince of peace.

Everything about the royal entry shows careful and deliberate planning on the part of the King. According to John 12:1 He arrived in Bethany probably on Friday afternoon. It was six days before the Passover, so He chose the opportune time at the beginning of this week which to the Jewish mind symbolized deliverance. We are not told where Jesus stayed from Friday afternoon until Sunday morning, but His abode was probably at the home of Martha, Mary, and Lazarus (cf. John 12:9-11). Evidently it was during this time that Jesus made all the necessary arrangements for His royal entry.

It is at this point that Matthew picks up the story. Early on Sunday morning Jesus and His disciples were in Bethphage, a village on the eastern slopes of the Mount of Olives near Bethany (v. 1). From here the Lord sent two of His disciples "into the village over against you" (probably Bethany) to secure an ass. He told them that they would find "an ass tied, and a colt with her" (v. 2). The fact that the ass was tied suggests previous preparation (cf. Mark 11:4). Furthermore, if the owner said anything to them (cf. Mark 11:5), they were to say, "The Lord hath need of them; and straightway he will send them." This was evidently a prearranged signal between Jesus and the owner.

The incident is highly suggestive of secrecy. For apparently the Twelve themselves knew nothing about it beforehand. It seems that Jesus Himself had made arrangements to borrow these animals, probably from one of His followers, without even letting him know the purpose for which they were to be used. It was only that "the Lord hath need of them."

Why this secrecy? Because the King was moving according to a divine timetable. His hour was approaching, but it had not yet arrived. In the economy of God certain things were necessary before that hour. Messianic prophecy must be fulfilled (cf. v. 4-5; Zech. 9:9). The King of peace must make His royal entry into Jerusalem. The nation must see Him as the King-Messiah. The chief priests and Pharisees had given orders for His arrest. For Jesus to have revealed His plans even to the Twelve would have told Judas in advance where He would be. He must not enter Jerusalem as a criminal in bondage. He must do so as a King. We shall see throughout the following chapters that at every step Jesus is the King ordering the events according to God's will. And while the wills of men will most surely be involved, involving their guilt, we see the sovereign God ordering all things toward His divine will and redemptive purpose. If Jerusalem rejected Him, as they did, He will be rejected as her King.

When the disciples returned they made a saddle of some of their garments, and placed them on the colt, one on which no man had ever ridden. Matthew says "on them" (the ass and the colt). But Mark and Luke say that they were placed on the colt. There is no necessary contradiction here. They may have put garments on both animals as Matthew says. The other two writers single out only the colt upon which Jesus rode.

Evidently the multitude which had gathered caught the significance of the occasion. For they knew their prophecy. However, not all of them joined in the event. For Matthew 21:8 says literally, "The most part of the multitude...." Some of them did not believe in Jesus as the Messiah, and so would not join in such a royal entry. This would be true of some from Galilee and Perea, and especially some pilgrims from outside Palestine. Luke records that the Pharisees called on Jesus to rebuke His disciples (19:39). They saw the significance of the event, and sought to prevent it.

However, those who regarded Jesus as their King-Messiah joined heartily in the occasion. Since there were no carpets over which Jesus might ride, as was customary in such events, they spread their garments in the path over which the colt must walk. By a change of verb tenses Matthew describes vividly what happened. They "spread [aorist, one time] their garments in the way; others kept on cutting [imperfect] branches from the trees [John 12:13 says "palm trees"], and kept on strawing [imperfect] them in the way" (Matt. 21:8). A crowd from Jerusalem came out to meet the procession (John 12:18). Then converging into one great multitude they escorted Jesus into the city. In one great chorus their voices echoed back and forth from the Mount of Olives to Mount Moriah and Mount Zion. They "kept on crying [imperfect], saying repeatedly [present], Hosanna to the son of David: Blessed is he that cometh in the name of the Lord; Hosanna in the highest" (v. 9).

Each of these sayings is significant. "Hosanna" means "save now." "Son of David" and "he that cometh" *(ho erchomenos,* cf. Matt. 11:3) were definite Messianic terms. "Hosanna in the highest" is a call to God in the highest heaven to "save now." It is apparent that they expected an immediate deliverance from Jehovah, even though their concept of this deliverance doubtless carried military and political overtones. But despite this fact it is evident that they were ready to receive Jesus as their King-Messiah. Subsequent events would stun them for the moment, and probably cause some of them to turn from Jesus. He knew how fickle popular acclaim can be (cf. John 2:24-25; 6:66). It is possible that some who acclaimed Him as their King-Messiah on Sunday cried, "Crucify him," on Friday. But we can hope that the latter came largely from those who refused to join in this royal entry. Even the Twelve forsook Jesus for a time, but all save Judas returned to proclaim Him as the Christ of God. Nevertheless, Jesus presented Himself as the King. He courageously challenged His enemies in the center of their greatest power. Henceforth the response was their responsibility.

Presently the procession entered Jerusalem. The city was shaken as by an earthquake ("was moved," *eseisthē*, cf. *seismos*) by the tumultuous shouting. From everywhere the people ran together. "Who is this?" they asked. Who is the cause of such a demonstration? Perhaps many of the Jews of Jerusalem knew Jesus as a person. Many, especially those from outside Palestine, had never seen Him. But all of them would recognize the Messianic nature of the demonstration. So they asked as to the identity of Him who was its center.

It is at this point that a note of sadness enters into the picture. "Who is this?" the people asked. And there is no reason to doubt the sincerity of their inquiry. But note the answer which they received. "This is Jesus the prophet of Nazareth of Galilee" (v. 11). Not a word about a King or a Messiah! Outside the city He was the "son of David," "the Coming One" to "save now." But inside the city they said, "This is Jesus the prophet of Nazareth of Galilee." Intimidated by the hostile powers in the city, what a change in their testimony. And what an indictment against each of us as in moments of great crisis and opportunity we tone down our witness concerning Jesus.

Now everything which they said about Jesus was true. But there was so much which they could have said, and did not, which was so much more the truth. They said not a word about Jesus' person, teachings, or miracles. Let us analyze their answers from the standpoint of the inquirers. "This is Jesus." But there were many men named "Jesus" or "Joshua" in that day. "The prophet." There had been many prophets, even false ones. "Of Nazareth." Can anything good come out of Nazareth? (cf. John 2:46). "Of Galilee." This would be a matter of pride to the Galileans. But the Judeans would say, "Shall Christ come out of Galilee?" (John 7:41). Or "Search, and look: for out of Galilee ariseth no prophet" (John 7:52). And we may well imagine that "every man went unto his own house" (John 7:53).

What had begun as a great Messianic demonstration ended on a low note. Not because of Jesus, but because of those who professed to follow Him. They missed their opportunity then as multitudes of faint hearted disciples have done since. But Jesus had accomplished His purpose. He had presented Himself as the King-Messiah. However, this was but the first in a series of events designed to set forth His authority, purpose, and mission. It was to be a momentous week indeed!

The Assertion of Kingly Authority (21:12-22)

Matthew records that immediately following the incident in verses 10-11 Jesus entered the temple and cleansed it (vv. 12-13). But Mark, who usually follows a chronological sequence states that on that occasion Jesus only entered the temple, looked around, and departed for Bethany (11:11). He places the cleansing on the following day after the incident of cursing the barren fig tree. There need be no problem at this point. For here, as in other places, Matthew arranges his material topically in keeping with his purpose to reveal Jesus as the King. His purpose at this point is to show that following His royal entry the King asserted His regal authority. Broadus points out that when the King entered Jerusalem He did not go to the palace of Herod or to the city of David. His Kingdom was not of this world. Nor was it to be brought in by worldly means. It was a spiritual Kingdom which centered in spiritual instruction and worship.

It was fitting, therefore, that He should assert His authority in and over the temple. Indeed it had been prophesied that the Messiah would "suddenly come to his temple" (Mal. 3:1). Note that it was "his temple." The temple was the temple of God. So when Jesus asserted His authority over the temple He was identifying Himself with God. As He claimed authority to give a fresh interpretation to the Law and to be the Lord of the Sabbath, so He also claimed authority over the temple. In effect, when the King presented Himself to the capital city of Judaism, He also stormed the very citadel of Jewish power as He dared to cleanse the temple itself. So He added defiance to defiance as He challenged the power of the Jewish rulers.

It is well to note what is meant by the "temple." Two Greek words were used to designate the temple. One (*naos*) referred to the Holy of Holies, the small area behind the veil, where God was said to dwell in mercy. Only the high priest might enter this "temple," and that only on the Day of Atonement. The other word translated "temple" (*hieron*) referred to the temple area in general. It included several "courts." There was the Court of the Gentiles into which anyone might go. But Gentiles were forbidden to go further under the penalty of death. Next there was the Court of the Women into which any Israelite might enter. Archaeologists have discovered a sign, of which there were many, which was posted at each entrance to the Court of the Women and which prescribed death for any Gentile who entered this court (cf. Acts 21:28ff.). Beyond the Court of the Women was the Court of Israel where the people assembled for worship. Next there was the Court of the Priests in which only the priests might enter to minister in the sacrifices. Finally there was the *Naos*. There is no evidence that Jesus ever went beyond the Court of Israel. Since He was not a priest in the Jewish sense of the word, He would not be permitted to do so. His sacrifice was made in a greater tabernacle (cf. Heb. 9:11-12). And He bore the blood of His sacrifice into the heavenly Holy of Holies (cf. Heb. 9:24).

The scene of the cleansing occurred in the Court of the Gentiles.

John 2:13-16 records a similar cleansing at the beginning of Jesus' ministry. There is no reason to confuse the two. It is entirely proper and probable that the Messiah would do both, one at the beginning and the other at the close of His ministry.

Matthew says that Jesus "cast out all them that sold and bought in the temple, and overthrew the tables of the money-changers, and the seats of them that sold doves" (21:12). There are certain differences from the earlier cleansing. There Jesus drove out the sheep and oxen, and simply told the dove sellers to leave with their merchandise (John 2:15-16). In our present event no mention is made of sheep and oxen, and here Jesus overthrew the seats of the dove merchants. It could be that they had not gained enough courage to bring sheep and oxen back into the temple. However, they could be implied in the words "them that bought and sold." But it is evident that Jesus used harsher measures with the dove merchants because they had ignored His former order.

What was the occasion of this cleansing? In a way this merchandising had begun as a convenience to the worshippers. Certain sacrifices were required, and it was often inconvenient for the people to bring their own sacrificial victims. This was especially true of those from outside Palestine. Also each animal had to be approved by the priests as being without blemish. The doves were used as an offering by the poor. Furthermore, every Jew was required to pay the temple tax of a half-shekel, and payment should be made near Passover time. As a convenience to the people collection booths were set up in all of the towns and villages throughout the land. But after a certain date it could be paid only at the temple. And since the tax could be paid only in Jewish coin, moneychangers were established in the temple to exchange, for a fee, other currency for this coin. Such was especially convenient for Jews coming from other lands.

However, what began as a convenient service came to be a form of extortion. For exhorbitant prices were charged for the animals far beyond that charged for animals bought outside the temple. The same was true of the rates of exchange for currency. Since this enterprise was carried on by the former high priests, Annas and his sons, it came to be called the "Bazaars of Annas." And the name carried a stigma. For while certain of the profits were used for public service or placed in the temple treasury, much of this ill-gotten gain found its way into the pocket of those who dealt in this service.

It is easy to imagine the scene which greeted Jesus' eyes and ears as He entered the Court of the Gentiles. The noise of the animals, the disputes and oaths of those who bargained. It must have been much like the din and confusion seen today in the bazaars and market places of Palestine. But what was even worse the religious leaders were exploiting the very people who came to worship.

Some object to the authenticity of the two cleansings of the temple, saying that it is out of character for the gentle Jesus so to act. But when we recognize the abuses and the crass materialism which had invaded the temple of God, we could not understand had Jesus done otherwise. People coming to worship, and being robbed by those who were responsible for leading them in worship. Perhaps a Gentile longing for a knowledge of the true God. And yet when he came to pray he found an atmosphere conducive to everything but prayer. We must not mistake the "gentle Jesus" for an insipid Jesus. God is love. But He is also righteous love. His indignation and wrath (*orgē*) abide against every kind of evil. And on occasion His wrath (*thumos*) boils over in judgment. It was such an occasion when the King asserted His authority over His temple. His righteous wrath boiled over as He drove these perpetrators of evil from His "house of prayer."

In justification for His act Jesus quoted two passages from the prophets as one sentence (v. 13). "My house shall be called the house of prayer [Isa. 56:7]; but ye have made it a den of thieves" (Jer. 7:11). The latter statement is all the more meaningful when we recall that this very atmosphere in the temple had made it a rendezvous for criminals who met there to plan their crimes.

It is difficult to find an exact parallel to this scene in our present day. But one is certainly reminded of it in many parts of the world as one has to fight his way past the hucksters of relics and curios on the outside to find his way into a church or cathedral. In one case a man was selling pornographic literature. Perhaps an even closer likeness is any system of religion which *charges* for spiritual services beyond the stewardship of possessions as taught in the Bible. However, this action of the King condemns any religious practice which becomes a means of human exploitation, or which stifles spiritual worship by an overemphasis upon the material.

Following this tumultuous event in the temple Matthew alone mentions a scene of infinite beauty and tenderness. "And the blind and the lame came to him in the temple; and he healed them" (v. 14). Such unfortunates always swarmed about the temple. The outcasts in Israel! And Jesus always had time and compassion for them. From His condemnation of the mighty for their abuses of the physical temple of God, He turned in mercy to heal the lowly from the abuses of evil inflicted upon the human body, the true earthly temple in which God longs to dwell. But in both instances it was the assertion of the authority of the King.

The chief priests and scribes were not long in counter-attacking this onslaught against their domain (vv. 15-16). Maybe they had seen the actual cleansing of the temple, but, fearing the people, were helpless to prevent it. Now in a quieter moment they confront Jesus. It is more likely, however, that they did not witness the actual cleansing. But when it was reported to them they hastened to the scene, arriving in time to see the "wonderful things" or healings which Jesus did. Even as they approached Jesus little children, probably boys, were crying, "Hosanna to the son of David." The adults who had uttered this cry outside the city were cowed by the chief priests, and so were silent. But the children were less susceptible to such intimidation. So as A. T. Robertson was fond of saying, right under the nose of Rabbi Smellfungus they cried, "Hooray for Jesus!"

But the Jewish rulers "were sore displeased" with the whole thing. Despite the King's demonstration of Messianic authority they would have none of it. Their minds and hearts were closed against this Galilean peasant who had no approval of the Sanhedrin and to them was an imposter. Already they had determined to get rid of Him lest He foment a rebellion and bring the wrath of Rome down upon them (cf. John 11:47ff.). They were concerned about their "place and nation." But their "place" came before their "nation." And as for the healing of the blind and lame, they cared nothing for them.

But note that when they accosted Jesus they made no mention of the cleansing or the healings. They asked, "Hearest thou what these say?"—the children. They were saying, " 'Save now' to the 'son of David.' " They were proclaiming Him as the King-Messiah, and that right in the temple. But the chief priests wanted this to stop.

However, Jesus did not accede to their request. Instead He cited to them Psalm 8:2 (Septuagint version) and fitted it to the occasion. "Out of the mouth of babes and sucklings thou hast perfected praise" (v. 16). If the chief priests remained silent God would be praised out of the hearts of the young and innocent. To these children God had revealed truth unseen by the wise and prudent (cf. Matt. 11:25), a phenomenon which sadly is so often the case.

And with this reply Jesus left them to return to Bethany (v. 17).

We may imagine that He "lodged" in the home of Martha, Mary, and Lazarus. At any rate He was among friends where He found rest, peace, quiet, and understanding, the things which were denied Him in the hostile atmosphere of the city.

On Monday morning with the Twelve Jesus returned to the city (vv. 18-22). It was the Jewish custom to eat the first meal of the day about the middle of the morning. Thus Jesus had left Bethany without breakfast, and so "he hungered." Note the human element in the person of the King. And His walk in the morning air had sharpened His appetite. So seeing a fig tree He came to it expecting to find figs. (We must not press the foreknowledge of Jesus at this point. He was in the flesh which embodied certain human limitations, cf. Matt. 24:36.) In keeping with the custom of the time, as with grain (cf. Matt. 12:1) so it was permissible for a passerby to pluck some fruit. But when He came to it He "found nothing thereon, but leaves only." Mark notes that it was not "the season of figs" (11:13). But the fact that it had leaves prematurely would lead one to expect to find figs also. Nevertheless, finding it fruitless Jesus said, "Let no fruit grow on thee thenceforth for ever. And presently the fig tree withered away" (v. 19).

Several problems evolve from this incident. Some are troubled with what was a destructive miracle wrought by Jesus to teach the lesson contained therein. An even greater problem involves the time element. Mark records that the cursing of the fig tree occurred on Monday and that it was not discovered as having withered until Tuesday. But Matthew includes both the cursing and the withering in the events of Monday. Furthermore, it is held that in Mark the withering was gradual, whereas in Matthew it was "immediately." Let it be noted that Mark does not state how or when the tree withered. He only notes that on the next day the disciples "saw the fig tree withered away" (11:20). It could have happened immediately without the disciples' knowledge.

However, there is no such solution to the problem of days. We may assume that Mark is correct in the order of events. But this involves no real problem with Matthew. For here as in some other places Matthew arranged his material topically rather than chronologically, in keeping with his purpose. In this incident Matthew records that the King used the occasion of the fig tree to pronounce condemnation upon a nation which has rejected Him. For that reason it is destined to wither and die insofar as God's redemptive purpose is concerned.

Matthew is not so much interested in the tree itself as in what it represents. And this also explains the *destructive* nature of this miracle. For as it was with the fig tree, so it was with the Jewish nation. The Jews gave great promise in their "leaves" of outward piety and religiosity with no real religion. But when the Lord came to them for fruit He found none. The hunger of Jesus for physical food was as nothing when compared with His hunger for the souls of men. He had come repeatedly to Israel's "fig tree," but had found no fruit thereon. And the curse of perpetual fruitlessness pronounced upon the fig tree was but a figure of the fruitlessness which did exist and would continue to do so in Judaism. Presently the King will make this condition more emphatic (cf. vv. 43-45).

And this explains Jesus' words directed to His disciples immediately following this incident. "If ye have faith, and doubt not, ye shall not only do this which is done to the fig tree . . ." (v. 21). Then follows His promise of great accomplishments to be wrought through faith and prayer (vv. 21-22). If they are faithful to the mission upon which Jesus will soon send them, they will in truth see Israel's "fig tree withered away." And in its place they will go on to incredible victories in His name (cf. Matt. 28:18-20).

So instead of stumbling over some imaginary problems, we would do well to profit by the principle involved in the story. Profession without practice is always under the condemnation of the Lord. And any "tree" of religion which promises fruit but bears none is destined to wither away and die. But even the smallest faith exercised in the authority of the King shall be blessed of Him far beyond our expectation.

The Challenge to Kingly Authority (21:23-32)

It is quite clear from Mark's Gospel that the remainder of Matthew 21 and continuing through Matthew 23 occurred on Tuesday of what we call Passion Week. Nor does this time element in any sense conflict with Matthew's account. For he simply says, "And when he was come into the temple" (v. 23). This occurred probably early on Tuesday morning, the last day of Jesus' public ministry. It has appropriately been called a "day of controversy." The Jewish leaders were closing in for the *kill*. And they brought every power at their command to accomplish their evil purpose. While the Pharisees were involved, it is quite clear that at this time the Sadducees (chief priests) were in charge of the proceedings against Jesus. This was no sudden decision on their part. It was a premeditated plan born out of their deep hatred for Jesus who threatened their position of power and privilege. In Chapter 16 we saw where the Sadducees joined with the Pharisees in opposing Jesus in Galilee. From John's Gospel we know that the Lord had had repeated brushes with them. But it is of interest to note the two occasions which firmed their determination to destroy Jesus. The one is in John 11:53 following Jesus' raising of Lazarus from the dead. The other comes in Luke 19:47 after He had cleansed the temple. In these two events Jesus had acted counter to their denial of the resurrection and their claim to authority over the temple. In both instances the Sadducees saw a dire threat both to their teachings and their position of power. So realists as they were they set themselves to break Jesus' power with the people and subsequently to destroy Him.

The chief priests and elders began their present attack upon Jesus by challenging His authority. Mark and Luke add "the scribes." These were the constituent groups in the Sanhedrin. So this was an official inquiry, and one which probably had been arranged following Jesus' royal entry and assertion of authority over the temple. Broadus notes that they had the right to make this inquiry had they done so in the proper spirit. But their spirit was decidedly wrong.

In challenging Jesus' authority they asked a twofold question. "By what authority doest thou these things? and who gave thee this authority?" (v. 23). Thus they asked as to the nature and the source of His authority. Did He claim prophetic or Messianic authority? And if not, what kind of authority? Whence came this authority? The Jewish leaders were very zealous in this regard. If any Jew proposed to be a Rabbi he must have certain training and credentials, either from other Rabbis or from the Sanhedrin itself. Certainly they knew that Jesus did not have the latter. So, in effect, they were asking Him to name the Rabbi or group of such which had conferred this authority upon Him. But beyond this Jesus was acting as more than a Rabbi. By working miracles and cleansing the temple He was acting like a prophet or the Messiah. Furthermore, He had precipitated a situation in which He accepted without protest the acclamation as the Messiah. Hence the questions as to the nature and source of His authority.

Now Jesus might have answered that He claimed absolute authority as the Son of God (cf. Matt. 28:18). But to have done so would have precipitated His death before His hour. At the proper time He will make such a claim. But not yet. Instead He replied with one of His unanswerable questions which He employed throughout this day of controversy. "I also will ask you one thing [word], which if ye tell me, I in like wise will tell you by what authority I do these things" (v. 24). And then the question. "The baptism of John, whence was it? from heaven, or of men?" (v. 25).

One word and only one did they need to reply. They could have said either "heaven" or "men." It was as simple as that. But was it? So they called a conference. "They reasoned with themselves." The imperfect tense (*dielogizonto*) indicates a prolonged and thorough conference. If they said "heaven" He would ask why they did not believe John (v. 25). But if they said "men" they feared the reaction of the people who held that John was a prophet (v. 26). This would have alienated the people from them, the very thing which they were trying to do to Jesus (cf. Luke 19:48). So with one simple question Jesus turned the tables on them. Finally, they announced their learned decision. Literally they said, "We do not know" (*ouk oidamen*). This word "know" means a knowledge which comes by perceiving a truth until it becomes a conviction of the soul. They had never thought through the matter. And while they knew what they wanted to say (men), they were on the horns of a dilemma. How tragic it is when men are driven by prejudice rather than by soul knowledge!

As a result the Jewish leaders sought a refuge in agnosticism. "We do not know." Such an attitude is often regarded as one of a superior intellect. When actually the opposite is true. Agnosticism is the fruit of a lack of perception. It is experiential knowledge which lacks the courage to press on toward faith which bears fruit in soul knowledge or a conviction of the soul. And, alas, these Jewish rulers were not the first nor the last to come face to face with truth, and because of prejudice against it to answer with a weak "We do not know."

So Jesus replied, "Neither tell I you by what authority I do these things" (v. 27). If they had not even thought through John the Baptist, why should He cast His pearls before swine?

However, there is more to Jesus' question than meets the eye. They had asked Jesus about the nature and source of His authority. The only human ecclesiastical authority which Jesus could claim was that of John the Baptist who had baptized Him. If John's authority was from men, then that of Jesus was also. But if John's authority was from heaven, then Jesus' authority was likewise from heaven. The Sanhedrin was unwilling to admit the latter, and was afraid to claim the former. So how could they then be dogmatic about Jesus? Furthermore, since the people regarded John's authority as being from heaven, they would regard Jesus in the same way. So without saying it Jesus did claim heavenly authority for His ministry. And the Jewish rulers were left without a rejoinder.

Then Jesus disposed of them with a parable (vv. 28-32). A man had two sons. He told the one to go and work in His vineyard. He refused abruptly by saying, "I will not." But later he repented and went. The word here used for "repented" means to be sorry after an event (*metamelomai,* cf. Matt. 27:3). This is not the word used for true repentance (*metanoeō*). The disobedient son merely experienced remorse. Then the father said the same thing to his other son. And politely he replied, "I go, sir: and went not." To Jesus' question as to which really did his father's will there could be but one reply, "the first."

Now at first glance one might say that these sons represent the Gentiles and the Jews. But Jesus' conclusion shows that this is not the case. He was still thinking of these professed religious leaders. The contrast is between the grossly sinful people, as represented by publicans and harlots (v. 31), and these outwardly righteous Jewish leaders. And Jesus concluded that the former would go into the kingdom of God before the latter. It was easier for these grossly wicked people to suffer remorse which would bring them to true repentance (cf. II Cor. 7:9) than it was for these outwardly righteous ones to do so (v. 32). Furthermore, Jesus was saying that these lowly outcasts actually possessed a greater spiritual perception than these supposed teachers of religion. It was a terrible indictment against these Jewish leaders, as it is for all who like they profess to serve God but who do not. They felt the sting of Jesus' words and recognized their meaning (cf. v. 45). But before they could reply the King said an even more condemning thing to them.

The Exercise of Kingly Authority (21:33-46)

"Hear another parable," said Jesus. And with these words He introduced one of the most momentous things that He ever uttered. He exercised kingly authority indeed.

The parable pictured a man who possessed an excellent vineyard (v. 33). Having made every preparation for fruitfulness, he leased it to certain husbandmen, and departed to a far country. At harvest time he sent a series of servants to receive his share of the fruits. But the husbandmen refused to pay him his due. In turn they "beat one, and killed another, and stoned another" (vv. 34-36). Finally, thinking that they would respect his son, he sent him to collect his fruits (v. 37). But the husbandmen reasoned that if they killed "the heir" they could seize his inheritance. So they killed him (vv. 38-39).

It is quite evident from this parable that Jesus had in mind

Isaiah 5:1-7, a parable with which these Jewish rulers were familiar. Under similar circumstances God is the owner of the vineyard which He identifies as "the house of Israel, and . . . Judah" (Isa. 5:7). He planted it with "the choicest vine" or the *Sorek* grape. But when He came seeking grapes, "it brought forth wild grapes" (Isa. 5:4), literally "stinking grapes."

So in Jesus' parable again the owner of the vineyard is God. The vineyard here also is the house of Israel and Judah or the Jewish nation. The "husbandmen" in this case were the religious rulers of the Jews in that and former generations. So this parable actually views the entire scope of the Israelite nation from its beginning until the moment that Jesus was speaking.

Shortly after Israel's deliverance from Egypt God entered into a covenant with the new nation. This is recorded in Exodus 19:1-8. It was a covenant whereby Israel was to be a priest-nation to the rest of the world. Note the words of this covenant. "Now therefore, *if* ye will obey my voice indeed, and keep my covenant, *then* ye shall be a peculiar treasure unto me above all people: for all the earth is mine: and ye shall be unto me a kingdom of priests, and an holy nation" (Exod. 19:5-6, author's italics). Note the "if" and "then." It was a conditional covenant involving both privilege and responsibility. Only as Israel kept the responsibility could she claim the privilege.

But the nation rejected the responsibility and thought only of the privilege. The history of Israel from that time on was just a series of events in which God sent His "servants" to call the priest-nation back to its responsibility of bearing fruit in winning the other nations to the worship of Jehovah. It is not necessary to identify with exactness the servants who were beaten or killed. But certainly one is reminded of such prophets as Isaiah, Jeremiah, and Zechariah (cf. II Chron. 24:21f.). The point is that repeatedly Israel refused to render fruit unto God.

Now in these latter days God sent His Son. Surely they will reverence or respect Him, and, if not Him, then nobody. The Jewish rulers (husbandmen) refused Him. And at this very moment they were plotting His death, thinking thereby to secure their "place and nation" (John 11:48). The picture was so vivid and applicable that we cannot fail to catch its import. But apparently the Jewish rulers did not yet see the point.

However, when Jesus asked them a question regarding the parable there could be but one answer. "When the lord therefore of the vineyard cometh, what will he do unto those husbandmen?" (Matt. 21:40). They replied, "He will miserably destroy those *wicked men*, and will let out his vineyard unto other husbandmen, which will render him the fruits in their seasons" (v. 41, author's italics). Note the words "wicked men." Not one time did Jesus refer to the husbandmen as "wicked." These were the words of the rulers themselves. Mark and Luke record Jesus' words "he will come and destroy the husbandmen." Probably Jesus repeated the idea contained in their words. And when they heard them, they evidently got the point of the parable. For Luke reports them as saying, "God forbid" (20:16). But they themselves had pronounced their own sentence. The Revised Version translates their words, "He will miserably destroy those miserable men." And Weymouth renders it, "He will put the wretches to a wretched death." They were "wicked men," and their end will be in keeping with their character.

And then Jesus applied the lesson. "Did ye never read in the Scriptures, The stone which the builders rejected, the same is become the head of the corner: this is the Lord's doing, and it is marvellous in our eyes?" (v. 42). This passage is taken from Psalm 118:22f. And it is more meaningful when we note that it precedes immediately the words "Save now" (hosanna), the very words adopted by the shouting multitude during Jesus' royal entry. The multitude recognized and accepted Jesus as the Messiah, the chief cornerstone, but the "builders" (Jewish rulers) rejected Him. However, God's purpose will not be defeated by them. He will yet make Him "the head of the corner."

The story of Michelangelo's "David" draws a striking parallel to this fact. In a quarry a large piece of stone had been cast aside because it had a flaw in it. But when the master sculptor examined it he saw that this very *flaw* fitted into his purpose. So out of the rejected stone he carved a masterpiece. The Jewish rulers rejected Jesus because of what they considered to be a *flaw*, His role as the Suffering Servant. But it was around this very role that God proposed to build His redemptive purpose.

We may well imagine that the Sanhedrin remembered these words of Jesus when Peter said to them, "The God of our Fathers raised up Jesus, whom ye slew and hanged on a tree. Him hath God exalted . . . a Prince and a Saviour, for to give repentance to Israel, and forgiveness of sins" (Acts 5:30-31). But they rejected Jesus then as they did when He confronted them with God's rejection of them.

It was at this point that the King exercised His regal authority with words which are astounding within themselves, and which have altered the very course of history according to the eternal purpose and method of God. "Therefore [on the basis of the lesson in the parable, Israel's history, the rulers' own sentence and God's purpose] say I unto you, The kingdom of God shall be taken from you, and given to a nation bringing forth the fruits thereof" (v. 43). Mark well these words, for they are the words of the King. Only Matthew records them. And they are climactic in his purpose. He has presented Jesus as the King of the Jews. The Jews rejected Him. And when they rejected Him they rejected the Kingdom of God. The word "you" (*humōn*) is plural. So Jesus' words included not simply the rulers but the nation which they represented. This meaning is fortified in the words "given to a nation bringing forth the fruits thereof."

It is worthy to note the words "bring forth." They render a word meaning "to make" or to produce. The implication is that as a nation Israel had not only failed *to give* but *to produce* the fruits intended of God.

The new nation to which Jesus referred is called by Peter "a holy nation" (I Peter 2:9). At this point it would be well to read this passage in I Peter 2:4-10, and compare its wording with that of Exodus 19:5-6 and Matthew 21:42-44. Peter was writing to Christian people "which in time past were not a people, but are now the people of God . . ." (I Peter 2:10). Peter was familiar with the passage in Exodus 19:5-6. With his own ears he had heard Jesus' words in Matthew 21:42-44. So he combines their meaning to show that henceforth God's purpose will not run through a constituted nation as such. It will be "a holy nation," a "people of God," a spiritual Israel composed of all who receive the King as their Lord and Saviour.

Did this mark a change in God's purpose? No. For His is an "eternal purpose" (Eph. 3:11). Nor did it mark a change in His method. For we must not confuse national Israel as such with the spiritual Israel. "For they are not all Israel, which are of Israel" (Rom. 9:6). Even in the Old Testament we find a "remnant" or the true Israel within the nation of Israel. Only those Israelites who "will obey my voice indeed, and keep my covenant . . . shall be a peculiar treasure unto me . . . a kingdom of priests, and an holy nation" (Exod. 19:5-6), said Jehovah. Now Jehovah had revealed Himself through the King-Messiah. He was rejected by the Jewish rulers, and, as we shall soon see, by the nation as such. But within that nation there were some who did receive Him. It is they and others, not of Israel's fold but who receive the Messiah of God, who now comprise this "holy nation" "which in time past were not a people [a constituted nation], but are now the people of God" (I Peter 2:10). The selection is not on a racial or national basis, but upon a personal spiritual relationship (cf. Matt. 3:9).

Jesus goes further in His condemnation of the nation of Israel. "And whosoever shall fall on this stone shall be broken: but on whomsoever it shall fall, it will grind him to powder" (v. 44). Not only will one who falls on this foundation stone be shattered. The second clause says even more. It suggests that this stone is placed higher upon the corner. If it fall on one it will grind him to powder and he will be scattered as dust (cf. Dan. 2:35). The words "it will grind him to powder" render one Greek word *(likmēsei).* It means basically to winnow out chaff, and then to grind as powder. Both of these ideas are present in this passage. Not only had the Jews stumbled over this "stone." But God has made it the "head of the corner." The Jews will endeavor to pull it down by killing Him. Instead it will fall on them, grind them to powder and blow them away like chaff or dust. A. T. Robertson translates this as "will scatter as dust." This literally became a reality when in A.D. 70 Jerusalem was destroyed and the nation scattered as dust over the earth.

"The chief priests and Pharisees . . . perceived that he spake of them" (v. 45). From our vantage point it would seem that they would have cried out for mercy. However, so fixed were they in their rejection of Jesus that His words served only to drive them forward in their evil designs. But for their fear of the multitude they would have seized Him there. It is a pitiful picture indeed. For not only did they plunge on blindly to their ruin. They took their nation with them.

Jesus presented Himself to them as their King-Messiah. And they rejected Him. The King did not need them as being indispensable in His purpose. But they desperately needed Him. Let this be a lesson to us. Christ still presents Himself. He wants to use us in His purpose. But our refusal does not defeat Him or His cause. We may delay it, but we will not destroy it. For God is marching on. A very striking definition of successful living is to determine in which direction God is moving, and then to move with Him.

Matthew 22

The Rejection of the King

In order to understand this chapter we must refer back to the preceding one. The King had presented Himself to the Jewish nation as the Messiah. But through its official religious leaders it had refused Him as such. Even though outside Jerusalem some of the people dared to proclaim Jesus as the "son of David" and "the coming one," when they came under the influence of the hostile city even they were strangely silent. The Sanhedrin officially challenged Jesus' regal authority, and was in turn denounced by Him. But for their fear of the people they would have seized Him.

So actually Matthew 22 is a continuation of the controversy which began in Chapter 21. And it contains two distinct sections: Jesus' parabolic denunciation of the Jewish nation and its rejection; and the Jewish leaders' formal rejection of the King as seen in their efforts to discredit Jesus with the people. This was necessary in order that they might carry out their purpose to destroy Him.

So as we consider this chapter and the lessons that it teaches we may outline it as (1) the privileges in the kingdom; (2) the problems relating to the kingdom; (3) the person of the King.

The Privileges in the Kingdom (22:1-14)

Matthew says that Jesus "answered again" in parables. This was not necessarily an answer to spoken words but to the thoughts of the Jewish rulers relative to taking Jesus. In two previous parables the King had spoken with regard to rejected kingdom responsibility on the part of the Jews. Now He speaks of their lost privilege in the kingdom. The atmosphere of the former parable was that of labor in the King's vineyard. In this present one the atmosphere is that of a feast in the King's house. And this distinction is important in the lesson which Jesus taught. Rejected responsibility results in forfeited privilege.

The picture which Jesus drew was as always true to life. In Jewish life a marriage was the occasion of festivities which lasted for several days. So Jesus said that a certain king made "marriage festivities [*gamous,* plural] for his son" (v. 2). For such an occasion it was customary to send out invitations without naming a date.

Then when all was in readiness for the festivities servants were sent to bid the guests to come. So Jesus said, "And sent forth his servants to call them that were bidden ["the ones having been called," note the previous invitation] to the wedding festivities [*gamous*]." The perfect passive participle (*keklēmenous*) shows that the invitation had been given and still was in effect. But the guests "kept on not willing [imperfect tense] to come." Subsequently the king sent other invitations which were more insistent (v. 4). But the invited guests "made light of it" (v. 5). Literally, they did not care for it, neglected and disregarded it. Some of them were engrossed in other matters of material concern, good within themselves but evil in that their indifference kept them from enjoying the privileges of the marriage festivities. But others were not so gentle (v. 6). They were positively vicious, mistreating some servants and killing others. And all this in response to a gracious invitation. We can therefore understand why the king sent for bands of troops, not entire armies, which destroyed the murderers and burned their city (v. 7).

And then the emphasis of the parable shifts. Since the king's supposed friends refused to come to the festivities, he sent his servants to the "highways" or the crossroads to invite whosoever would come, "both bad and good." And so the "marriage dining hall" (*numphōn*) was filled with guests (v. 10).

In a sense this parable is a repetition of the truth taught in the parable of the husbandmen, only the emphasis is placed upon privilege rather than upon responsibility. The covenant which God made with Israel involved both. Jesus had shown how the nation was rejected because of a refused responsibility. Now He shows that consequently they also lose the privilege which they regarded so highly, but for which they were not willing to pay the price.

Note that in this parable we have the relationship of God the Father and Christ the Son. The Father is the King and the Son is the Prince. But this further shows the intimate relationship of Father to Son. For they are in reality one. To refuse the King is to refuse His Son.

The picture involves the marriage feast of the Son as He takes unto Himself His Bride, the Church, not the local church in this case, but all of the redeemed of all the ages. In one sense the Kingdom of God involves His sovereignty over the universe. But there is another sense in which the kingdom must be regarded in the spiritual sense. It is that which Jesus had in mind here.

As we seek the meaning of this parable we find a progression of thought. God proposes a marriage festival for His Son. When He made His covenant with Israel (Exod. 19) in a sense He invited privileged ones to the marriage festivities. Repeatedly He had sent His servants, the prophets, to call Israel to the happy occasion. But she would not come. Finally, God sent John the Baptist, and even the Son Himself, but Israel made light of the whole matter. Some were so engrossed in material pursuits that they disregarded God's call altogether (cf. I Sam. 8:4-20). In rebellion against God's covenant others mistreated the prophets, even killing some of them. They slew John the Baptist and now are plotting Jesus' death. The end result will be the carnage in the imminent fall of Jerusalem and the scattering of the Jewish nation (cf. v. 7).

The marriage festivities were ready, but those who had been offered the privilege of participation in it were not worthy (v. 8). They had refused the Prince of peace. In turn the King refused them. But He refused them only because they first refused Him. The privileges of the covenant were lost to them because they did not accept its responsibilities. God was under no obligation to grant the former until they fulfilled the latter. The "if" and "then" of Exodus 19:5 were the determining factors. *If* they accepted the responsibility, *then* they would enjoy the privilege. Conversely, *if* they refused the responsibility, *then* they would lose the privilege. And it is a timeless principle.

The emphasis of the parable suddenly shifts between verses 7-9. With the destruction of Jerusalem (v. 7). God writes off Israel as a total loss insofar as His redemptive purpose is concerned (v. 8). Then He says to His servants, "Go ye therefore into the highways, and as many as ye shall find, bid them to the marriage" (v. 9). Thus Jesus foresaw that day when the King would send His messengers into all the world. This actually happened prior to A.D. 70. But it was the destruction of Jerusalem and the temple which historically marked the end of Israel and the complete distinction of Christianity as the instrument in God's overture of grace through Christ to a lost world. Henceforth it would be through a people "which in time past were not a people, but are now the people of God" (I Peter 2:10).

In this new phase of God's eternal purpose these "servants" will go into the "highways." The "highways" were any place where two roads came together. Whoever passed by was to be invited to the marriage festival. This would include the "bad and good." Those who considered themselves as the morally and spiritually elite had refused to come. So the invitation is to be delivered without regard to moral character. This presages the preaching of the gospel to all men without discrimination of nationality, race, or spiritual achievement. It was an invitation of grace. Of course their acceptance of the invitation involved a change of nature and character (cf. v. 11). Nevertheless the import of Jesus' words is that of a universal proclamation of the gospel. The marriage dining hall will be furnished with guests!

The matter of a proper character is involved in verses 11-13. Some interpreters allude to a custom whereby the host furnished proper garments for his guests. And this is an intriguing approach. But Broadus questions any basis for this position. Whatever may be the background, it is clear that one man was not properly dressed (v. 11). It would appear that the man knew better and that the proper garments were available to him. For "he was speechless" (v. 12). He had no defense for his condition. Therefore, he was cast "into outer darkness," which is in direct contrast to the brilliantly lighted banquet hall.

When we look for the meaning behind these verses, it becomes clear that the man appeared at the marriage festivities without the proper preparation to be received as a guest by the host. Various suggestions have been made as to the meaning. Some see the "wedding garment" as baptism. But this puts upon it a strained, outward meaning which is unwarranted by Scripture and which does not satisfy the imagery of the parable. Nearer to the meaning is that the garments are the imputed righteousness of Christ which covers the sinner's "filthy rags" (Isa. 64:6) or the nakedness of the unrighteous. Still again this involves an inner condition which hardly coincides with outer garments. In all probability the wedding garment refers to one's outward and self-evident conduct which reveals an inward holiness of character or evidence of a changed nature.

In the widespread invitation of the Gospel there will be some who will show up at the marriage dining hall but without the required character and nature to qualify them as true "guests" or Christians. Judas himself was such a person. But only those who meet the conditions set forth by the King will be able to participate in the marriage festivities themselves. "For many are called, but few are chosen" (v. 14). There is a distinction between the ones called (*klētoi*) and the "called out ones" (*eklektoi*). The *call* goes out to all men. But only those are "called out" from among them to join in the marriage festivities who meet the conditions set forth by the King. This implies more than a token gesture of allegiance to Christ which falls short of the nature and character which are required for true kingdom citizenship. We should, therefore, beware of a mere surface allegiance to the King. We may fool the other "guests," but we cannot fool the King. When we come under His discerning eye, those who fall short of His demands in kingdom righteousness (cf. Matt. 5:20) shall be cast "into outer darkness; there shall be weeping and gnashing of teeth" (v. 13), an oft-repeated picture of hell (Gehenna) which fell from the merciful lips of Jesus.

The Problems Relating to the Kingdom (22:15-22)

If the enemies of the King caught the meaning of His words, it served only to spur them on in their evil purpose. The one thing which deterred them was not their spiritual sensitivity but their fear of the multitude (cf. 21:46). Regardless of what the Jewish rulers thought of Jesus, the people "took him for a prophet." Apparently even those who did not accept His Messianic claims regarded Him as a prophet. So for the rulers to seize Him would serve only to bring the wrath of the people down upon them. Therefore, they determined to break His hold upon the people. The best way to do this was to discredit Him as a teacher and as to His Messianic claims. Therefore, they came to Him, one group after another, with some of their pet problems, problems which they doubtless had debated among themselves. And since they in their learned disputes had failed to find suitable answers, they did not expect Jesus to find any. But as we shall see their evil intentions served to give to us some of the choicest teachings of Jesus on vital subjects.

The Pharisees were masters in debating. So they were chosen for the first attempt to discredit Jesus (v. 15). Their purpose was not to elicit information but to "set a trap" for Him in His talk. For this purpose they chose some of their disciples or pupils, probably their best. These joined with the Herodians to confront Jesus (cf. Mark 3:6).

What a strange coalition! For there were no two groups in Palestine which were farther apart politically. The Pharisees were a highly nationalistic group. They longed to return to a purely theocratic rule under the Messiah. Their slogan might well have been "Judea for the Jews." Thus they were highly antagonistic toward both the house of Herod and the Romans. They were violently opposed to paying taxes to any foreign pagan power. The Herodians, on the other hand, were those who longed to restore the rule of Palestine to the House of Herod. It is possible that they favored paying taxes to Rome in order to court them for their own purpose. Or in their desire for an independent nation they may have shared the Pharisees' aversion to Roman taxes, while differing with them on all other matters. At any rate, like the Pharisees and Sadducees (cf. Matt. 16:1) they resolved their personal differences in their common hatred for Jesus. Politics does make strange bedfellows!

Notice the hypocrisy in their approach. "Master [teacher, *didaskale*], we know that thou art true, and teachest the way of God in truth, neither carest thou for any man: for thou regardest not the person of man" (v. 16). There is not a word of truth in this statement insofar as their own attitude toward Jesus was concerned. They compounded their sin by their choice of the word for "know" (*oidamen,* cf. 21:27). They claimed to have studied the matter, to have perceived the truth, and to have a conviction in their souls, when all the while they were driven by ignorance, prejudice, and hatred. They called Him "true" when they regarded Him as false. His teachings they attributed to God despite the fact that they said that He was an instrument of Satan. They said that He did not care for man's opinion, when all the while they accused Him of trying to start a rebellion. A. B. Bruce comments that this suave flattery implied "that Jesus was a reckless simpleton." Truly the poison of asps was under their lips! But it was out of the abundance of their evil hearts that their mouths were speaking.

It is understandable that this coalition would confront Jesus with a political question. "Tell us therefeore, What thinkest thou? Is it lawful to give tribute unto Caesar, or not?" (v. 17). The Caesar reigning at the time was Tiberius Caesar who reigned A.D. 14-37. But the term was used here more in the sense of the office of Caesar or the Roman empire. The "tribute" was a "census" (*kēnson*). This was a head tax or *tributum capitis* paid with a silver coin called a *denarius.* Thus the question involved the idea of whether or not they should submit to a pagan foreign power.

Obviously this question was designed to place Jesus in a dilemma. They figured that either way He answered He would be in trouble. If He said, "Yes," they could accuse Him of being a traitor to His own people who themselves resented Roman rule and taxation. But if He said, "No," they could accuse Him of teaching rebellion against Rome. For Rome was very sensitive about refusal to pay taxes. And there was a further complication. For in their own judgment this involved Roman law versus Messianic law. According to their teachings the Messiah would not advocate paying taxes to other than His own kingdom. Therefore, if Jesus had given an affirmative answer to their question, to them it would have been an admission that He was not the Messiah. The question carried both political and religious overtones.

But Jesus was not taken in by either their feigned courtesy or their question. He called them the "hypocrites" which they were (v. 18). And then He said, "Shew me the tribute money" (v. 19). And they brought him a *denarius*. He did not answer with a coin of His own or of His disciples. He used one of their own. It was a Roman coin. Their very possession of it implied their subservience to and dependence upon Rome. In His action Jesus neither condemned nor condoned Roman rule. He simply recognized an evident fact to which they themselves were a party.

Jesus simply held up the coin for them to look at. On one side of it was Caesar's image, and on the other side the inscription "Tiberiou Kaisaros." The coin belonged to the Caesar who had minted it. Then Jesus asked a simple question. "Whose is this image and superscription?" (v. 20). To which they answered, "Caesar's" (v. 21). So Jesus said, "Render [give back] therefore unto Caesar the things which are Caesar's and unto God the things that are God's" (v. 21). There was nothing in this answer with which to accuse Jesus to either the people or Caesar. So they simply wondered, left Him, and departed. And the King was the victor.

But there was more than mere passing interest in this encounter. Because in it Jesus declared one of His greatest principles. In essence He said that the Christian is a citizen of two kingdoms, the Kingdom of God and a kingdom of the world. What is to be his relationship to each? Does loyalty to Christ precede obedience to human law? Furthermore, what is to be the relationship between the Church and the State?

These words of Jesus are basic in the religio-politico doctrine of the separation of Church and State. Is this separation to be absolute? Or are there grey lines where each is related to the other? These are questions which are still debated among men.

It is clear from Jesus' words that there is to be no union of the two. And yet He implies that each has its place in the economy of God. Both the Church and the State are ordained of God (cf. Matt. 16:18; Rom. 13:1). In an ideal society each bears responsibilities to the other. The State should provide an orderly society in which the Church can perform its mission. The Church, on the other hand, should produce the type of Christian character which is conducive to righteous government. But neither is to control the other or to invade the specific domain of the other. It is under such an ideal that both Church and State have realized their greatest potential.

As a citizen of two kingdoms the Christian owes a loyalty to each. He is not to live a monastic life, but is to be a part of the society in which he lives. Christianity lives under many and varied types of government. Christians are exhorted to be law abiding citizens (cf. I Peter 2:12-17). Where laws are wrong he is to use his influence to change them. But he is to abide by them, unless they involve a matter of Christian conscience (cf. Acts 4:19-20). Even when persecuted by the State for conscience's sake, the Christian is to suffer not as an evil-doer but as a Christian and as a testimony unto the Lord (cf. I Peter 3:14-15).

While the Pharisees and Herodians licked their wounds, some Sadducees took their turn against the King (v. 23). And as might be expected they came to Him with a question about the resurrection. As noted previously (Matt. 16:6) they did not believe in the resurrection from the dead. And, in the light of Jesus having raised Lazarus, this would be a particularly sensitive point with them. So they came to Him with an overly exaggerated case, one which they probably used to confuse and confound the Pharisees (cf. Acts 23:6-9). Note that they also addressed Jesus as "Teacher," a title they really denied to Him (v. 24).

In their problem they cited Deuteronomy 25:5-6. According to this Mosaic law if a man died childless, his brother should marry his widow and produce children in his name. Now the Sadducees posed a problem which they overstated for obvious reasons. They wanted to make Jesus seem ridiculous before the people. If He was such a great teacher of the Law, let him unravel this knotty problem.

There were seven brothers. One died childless. Then each of the other brothers in turn married the widow and died childless (vv. 25-27). And then the Sadducees posed their problem. "Therefore in the resurrection [if there be one] whose wife shall she be of the seven? for they all had her." (v. 28). What will this learned teacher say? They thought that they had asked the unanswerable. And so they settled back smugly to watch Jesus squirm.

But Jesus gave them a twofold answer which made them appear ridiculous in the eyes of the people (v. 29). In the first place, He said that they did not know the Scriptures. And they were supposed to be the teachers of Israel! In the second place, they did not know the power of God. And they claimed to be His representatives! Jesus could have made no greater charges against them. And then He enlarged upon these charges in reverse order. In the first, He cited no Scripture but declared a principle. In heaven there will be no marriage relationship such as exists on earth (v. 30). And in His second enlargement Jesus shattered the Sadducees' position on the resurrection. "But as touching the resurrection of the dead," the very doctrine which they denied (v. 31). They did so on the claim that the five books of Moses were the only genuine Scripture, and that these did not teach the resurrection. They claimed to know the Scriptures, a claim which Jesus had denied. And now He proved it. For He quoted from Exodus 3:6. "Have ye not read that which was spoken unto you by God, saying, I am the God of Abraham, and the God of Isaac, and the God of Jacob?" These men had been dead for many years when God spoke these words. Yet He did not say, "I *was* the God of Abraham. . . . He said, "I *am* the God of Abraham. . . ." (author's italics). And on this basis Jesus drove home His truth. "God is not the God of the dead, but of the living" (v. 32). So with their own Scriptures Jesus routed them. He was truly a "Teacher," and they were no teachers at all.

In His answers Jesus clearly declared that the physically dead are not truly dead. They live on after they have departed this earthly sphere. Of course, He did not go into the matter of the unrighteous dead at this point. Elsewhere He clearly taught that they also live on, but in a condition of punishment (cf. Luke 16: 19ff.). The righteous dead He pictured as being with God. Furthermore, He set forth the relationship of the righteous dead in heaven. Family ties as we know them on earth will give place to the greater relationship as the family of God. And that will be a richer experience by far than any present happiness of family and home.

The result of the encounter between Jesus and the Sadducees was disastrous for the latter. Instead of discrediting Jesus they had been the occasion of establishing Him more firmly than ever before in the eyes of the people. For "when the multitude heard this, they were astonished at his doctrine [teaching]" (v. 33). They were not so much astonished at the thing taught. For it was a common doctrine propounded by the Pharisees. Their astonishment was over Jesus' ability to teach, to handle the Scriptures. The masters of Israel were no match for the Master of men.

We may well imagine that the Pharisees were inwardly pleased when they heard that Jesus "had put the Sadducees to silence" (v. 34). Literally, Jesus had *muzzled* or *gagged* them. At least they had done no better than the Pharisees. But now it was their turn again. And for this effort they chose a "lawyer" or one of their number who was skilled in interpreting the Mosaic law (v. 35). Since Jesus had shown such ability in handling the law, they confronted Him with an *expert.*

"Master [teacher], which is the great commandment in the law?" (v. 36). Literally, "What kind of commandment is great in the law?" The scribes listed the commandments as heavy and light, with the former carrying the greater authority and punishment if broken. This would correspond to Roman Catholic mortal and venal sins. Vincent notes that they divided the law into 248 affirmative precepts, corresponding to the number of members in the human body; and 365 negative precepts, as many as there were days in the year; the total being 613 or the number of letters in the Decalogue. So apparently the lawyer wanted to know which of these two groups Jesus considered to be the more important.

However, Jesus brushed aside all such classification. Instead He quoted two commandments. "Thou shalt love the Lord thy God with ["in," *en,* in the sphere of] all thy heart, and with [*en*] all thy soul, and with [*en*] all thy mind" (v. 37; cf. Deut. 6:5). Mark adds "and with all thy strength" (12:30). This, said Jesus literally, "is the first and great commandment" (v. 38). And then He added, "And the second is like unto it, Thou shalt love thy neighbour as thyself" (v. 39; cf. Lev. 19:18).

It will be noted that these two commandments combine all of the laws in the Ten Comamndments. The first four deal with man's relation to God; the last six deal with man's relation to man. But Jesus went even further in saying that "On [*en,* in the sphere of] these two commandments hang all the law and the prophets" (v. 40). So to the Jewish mind this would mean that the entire Old Testament centers about these two commandments. They were the peg upon which all of the teachings of their Scriptures hung.

Therefore, with these brief words the King brushed aside all of the Pharisees' multitude of meticulous rules and sub-divisions of the Scriptures. So devoted had they become to a *system* that they had missed the main points of God's revelation. They loved neither God nor man in the sense that Jesus spoke. That was the very reason why they were right then hounding Him to His death. Alas, how many times the true spirit of religion has been nailed to a cross by those who major on the *letter* of the Bible but miss its *spirit* altogether.

Jesus spoke words about "love." But they blister and burn as they search the innermost spheres of our beings. We would do well to ponder them. For only as they become a reality in our hearts will the teachings of God's word become to us truth and light indeed.

The lawyer was impressed by Jesus' answer. Mark records that he spoke approvingly of His words (12:32-33). Thus a critic of Jesus became His admirer. In turn Jesus responded with words of kindness and hope. "Thou art not far from the kingdom of God" (Mark 12:34). He was not in it. But he was near. We may well hope that he later became a disciple of Jesus.

The Person of the King (22:41-46)

With His enemies in retreat the King now took the offensive. They had sought to discredit Him as a teacher. Without question He had proved to be a master of the art of pedagogy. However, to accept and admire Him as a teacher only is not enough. For Jesus claimed to be more than a teacher. He was the King-Messiah. And lest the Jewish rulers should succeed in sidetracking the principal issue, Jesus once again brought them and the multitude face to face with the matter. And He did so immediately while the Pharisees were still present (v. 41).

"What think ye of Christ? whose son is he? They say unto him, The son of David" (v. 42). Note that Jesus did not ask them what they thought of Him. That was quite evident. And while they rejected Him, they had firm convictions about the Messiah. Indeed, central in their theology was the Messiah and His coming kingdom. But as we have seen elsewhere their concept of both was erroneous. Nevertheless they were correct in calling the Messiah "the son of David." This was the most widely held belief as to the identity of the Messiah. But due to their own false interpretation of His person and work, the term "son of David" to them carried a highly nationalistic and revolutionary connotation.

Throughout this day (Tuesday) Jesus' critics had been bringing to Him their tricky questions. Now He gave them a dose of their own medicine. Admitted that the Christ is the son of David, "How then doth David in spirit [the Spirit] call him Lord, saying, The Lord [Jehovah] said unto my Lord [*Adonai*], Sit thou on my right hand, till I make thine enemies thy footstool? [Psalm 110:1]. If David then call him Lord, how is he his son?" (vv. 43-45).

Note the two words "Jehovah" or *Yahweh* and *Adonai*, Lord. "Jehovah" is the name used to distinguish the God of the Hebrews from all other gods. It is God's redeeming name (cf. Exod. 3:14-17), and is used 6,823 times in the Old Testament. "Adonai," appearing 340 times in the Old Testament, usually implies that God is a helper in time of need. It was used with reference to "Jehovah." In the Septuagint both names are translated by the Greek *kurios,* Lord. The Authorized or King James Version renders them "Lord." So both names refer to Jehovah.

Jesus quoted from one of the greatest of the Messianic psalms, a fact which the Pharisees recognized. Here then were two self-evident facts. The Messiah would come out of the tribe of Judah. Thus He would be a descendent of David, and in that sense his son. Furthermore, David writing of the Messiah called Him "my Lord." This was an evident ascription of deity to the Messiah. So here was one who was David's son by natural descent. Yet of Him David said "in spirit" that He is "my Lord." So by some means this one out of the tribe of Judah would also be "Lord" or God.

But Jesus was not dealing in theological analysis so much as in a practical problem. He Himself was of the tribe of Judah, and so David's son. Yet He had also by design been the center of a recent Messianic demonstration. In so doing He laid claim to the Messianic office. And since He did, in the light of Psalm 110:1, He was also David's Lord. Thus He laid claim to both humanity and deity. He is not only the "son of David" but the Son of God. And that which He soon would admit plainly under oath (cf. Matt. 26:63-64), He here stated in a veiled fashion. So the revelation rapidly moves toward a climax.

Matthew 27:46 says, "And no man was able to answer him a word...." Was this due to a lack of an answer? Or was their silence caused otherwise? It would appear that the latter was true. For the Pharisees were adept at Scripture analysis. In fact that very skill had become their downfall. They had so divided the meaning of the Scripture as to empty it of all true meaning. Therefore, they certainly could have analyzed the problem of giving an exegesis of Psalm 110:1 in the light of the genealogy of the "son of David." No, their problem was not one of analysis but of application. They saw the point of Jesus' question. But to have answered it would have meant to admit that He was not only the "son of David," the Messiah, but also the Son of God or the Lord. Furthermore, they would have been forced to admit to the humanity-deity of Jesus, a thought which they repudiated. Rather than to admit these things they suffered their intellects to be defeated. In the face of Scriptural proof as to His identity, the Pharisees hardened their hearts against it. It is in this light that we can understand Matthew 23.

"Neither durst any man from that day forth ask him any more questions" (v. 46). The Jewish rulers had engaged Jesus in their favorite battle of wit and words. And they had lost. But there were more things involved than either *wit* or *words,* their immortal souls and the life of their nation. And they lost on all counts. The King stands victor as He always is in the conflict between truth and error. Happy indeed are those who stand with Him!

Matthew 23

The Condemnation by the King

Matthew 23 contains some of the most excoriating words ever spoken by one man to another. If they were the words of one given to sudden outbursts of temper we might well ignore them. But when spoken by one such as Jesus who was ever gentle, mild, and merciful they call for the most serious consideration. The fact that they were spoken by the King Himself, who came to save men from their sins, adds immeasurably to their gravity.

This denunciation is the condemnation of the King upon the entire system of religion characterized by Pharisaical self-righteousness which evolved into hypocrisy and outward form but which was devoid of any inner spiritual reality. Repeatedly Jesus had sought to turn the mirror of God's truth upon the Pharisees. But they had refused to see. There was, therefore, no alternative for Jesus but to unveil their empty pretense before the multitude, and then to leave them to their fate.

As we approach this chapter we may outline it into three sections (1) the general condemnation; (2) the specific condemnation; (3) the final condemnation.

The General Condemnation (23:1-12)

The words in Matthew 23 were spoken not to the Pharisees directly but "to the multitude, and to his [Jesus'] disciples" or the Twelve (v. 1). But it is evident that the Pharisees were present and heard them.

The King began with an evident fact. "The scribes and the Pharisees sit in Moses' seat." The verb form is a timeless aorist meaning that they "sat" here and are accustomed to doing so. The word for "seat" (*kathedras*) corresponds to our thought of a professor's *chair*. So they sat in Moses' chair as the teachers of the Law. This word was borrowed by the Latin *cathedra*. Roman Catholics speak of the pope speaking *ex cathedra* or out of the chair. The Vatican Council of 1870 decreed that when the pope speaks *ex cathedra* in matters of faith and morals he is infallible. However, this thought is not involved here, since Jesus plainly went on to condemn any teaching which is not in keeping with the Scriptures themselves.

The point of Jesus' statement of a fact is that the scribes and Pharisees among the Jews were the accepted teachers of the Law. The Jews had a saying, "Moses received the Law and delivered it to Joshua; and Joshua to the elders; and the elders to the prophets; and the prophets to the men of the Great Synagogue." Therefore, the scribes and Pharisees laid claim to the right to sit in Moses' seat.

And Jesus did not dispute that claim. Rather He substantiated it as He said, "All therefore whatsoever they bid you . . . that observe and do" (v. 3). Literally, "keep on doing and keeping strictly." Insofar as they taught the Mosaic Law the people were to follow their teachings. This had no reference to their multitudinous rote laws, as Jesus presently pointed out. Nor should it be construed as in any sense replacing the gospel message. At the time Jesus spoke these words they were still living under the Mosaic system. The gospel message, while soon to be completed, was not yet known in its fulness. At that time the King will send forth His proclaimers of the *good news* of salvation. But even then the moral and spiritual laws of Moses will continue in effect, for they are timeless in their meaning. Only those ceremonial laws of ritual and sacrifice will pass away through their fulfilment in Christ. The Christian is still bound by the Ten Commandments and all of the moral and spiritual principles embodied therein (cf. Matt. 22:37-40).

"But do not ye after their works: for they say, and do not" (v. 3). "Works" involves both their system of outward deeds of righteousness and their evil practices which Jesus set forth subsequently.

Barclay is helpful at this point as he calls attention to the fact that the *Talmud* lists seven different kinds of Pharisees. There was the *Shoulder Pharisee*. He meticulously kept the Law, but he wore his good deeds on his shoulder in order to be seen of men. There was the *Wait-a-little Pharisee*. He accepted the Law, but could always find an excuse for delaying its practice. He said, but did not do. There was the *Bruised* or *Bleeding Pharisee*. Believing that a Rabbi should not speak to a woman in public, even his own wife, and fearing to look on a woman lest he be guilty of lust, he shut his eyes and was constantly running into buildings or other obstacles. Hence he was always bruised or bleeding. There was the *Mortar* and *Pestle Pharisee*. He was also called the *Hump-back* or *Tumbling Pharisee*. He displayed his humility by walking humped over so that he looked like a mortar and pestle. He dragged his feet along the ground, and so was constantly tumbling or falling. There was the *Ever-reckoning* or *Compounding Pharisee*. He was constantly keeping books on his good deeds, thinking that each one put God a little further in debt to him. There was the *Timid* or *Fearing Pharisee*. He lived in constant dread of divine punishment and fear of ceremonial pollution. Therefore, he was ever cleaning the outside of the cup and platter as an evidence of his goodness. Finally, there was the *God-fearing Pharisee*. He truly loved God, and kept the Law as a delight rather than a duty.

Barclay notes that among the Pharisees there were six bad types to one good one. So while there were some good Pharisees, some who even received Jesus as the Christ, it is clear from the above description that as a group they had degenerated into a system which was void of spiritual vitality; and in some instances was corrupted so as to divorce moral conduct from spiritual truth. It is in this light that we can understand Jesus' words of condemnation.

"For they say, and do not" (v. 3). For this Jesus condemns them negatively and positively. Negatively, "they bind heavy burdens . . . and lay them on men's shoulders; but they themselves will not move them with one of their fingers" (v. 4). "Bind" connotes the act of binding pieces of wood into one heavy bundle. The Pharisees had bound their many little precepts into one large burden, and had placed them upon the *shoulders* of the people, requiring them to keep them. Yet with one *finger* they did not will to move this burden. "Move" is an aorist infinitive meaning "to move" or "to set in motion." So not one time with one finger did they will to set these precepts in motion in their own lives or to help the people to bear them. This figure throws additional light upon Jesus' words in Matthew 11:28-30. The people were weighted down by the burden of the Pharisees. In its place He offered "His burden" which was "light." In one sentence (23:4) Jesus condemned the entire Pharisaical system in which they were only the task masters and the people were the burden-bearers.

Positively, Jesus condemned the scribes and Pharisees for what they did do (vv. 5-7). Even their righteous deeds were evil, for they were performed out of an evil motive. "All their works they do for to be seen [*theathēnai*] of men" (v. 5; cf. Matt. 6:1). They were theatrical performers, *hypocrites,* and loved to perform before an audience a role which was not truly themselves. So what Jesus warned against in Matthew 6 He now identified as being personified in the Pharisees.

In this general condemnation Jesus cited three things: a public show of personal piety; a personal love for public prominence; a personal love for public recognition. And as we consider them, it will be profitable if each of us searches his own heart rather than simply to point an accusing finger at the scribes and Pharisees.

Jesus condemned the Pharisees for a public show of personal piety. "They make broad their phylacteries, and enlarge the borders of their garments" (v. 5). The "phylactery" (from *phulassō,* to guard) was a small leather case from the skin of a clean animal, colored black, and worn on the forehead and the arm. This practice was based upon Exodus 16 and Deuteronomy 6:8; 11:18. What Jehovah had taught as a spiritual truth the Jews had made a material practice. They took literally the words "a sign unto thy hand," "a memorial between thine eyes," and "frontlets." Thus the practice of wearing "phylacteries."

In these little cases were placed four passages of Scripture: Exodus 13:1-10; 11-16; Deuteronomy 6:4-9; 11:13-21. In the case of the forehead phylactery these passages were written on four pieces of parchment and placed therein. A. T. Robertson notes that each piece was to be tied with a well-washed hair from a calf's tail. If thread or wool were used it might become polluted by a fungus growth. The arm phylactery contained only one parchment containing these passages of Scripture, written in four columns of seven lines each. The box was fastened high up on the left arm, nearest to the heart, and held in place by a black strap wound seven times around the arm and three times around the hand. Broadus notes that this was fastened with a mystically knotted string, and the phylactery covered with the sleeve. The purpose of these was to remind the Jews to keep God's law before their eyes and near their hearts.

These were worn by Jews generally, but usually at the time of prayer. Hence they were called *tephillin,* "prayers." Jewish men wore them during public worship, but the Pharisees apparently wore them constantly in public. Since the arm phylactery was covered by the sleeve, it seems that Jesus made primary reference to the forehead phylactery.

But even though these phylacteries involved a material expression of a spiritual truth, Jesus did not speak in condemnation of the practice. His condemnation was that they made their phylacteries larger than those worn by others. They said, "The bigger the phylactery the greater the piety, and the easier to be seen by men." For a Jew to wear one constantly and in public meant that he had taken a vow of perpetual devotion to the study of the Law. The Pharisees wanted to advertise this fact not in the classified ads of the newspaper, but in billboard signs along every street and highway. It was this attitude which Jesus condemned.

Furthermore, the Pharisees enlarged "the borders of their garments" (v. 5). This also reverts back to the Mosaic Law (cf. Num. 15:38). In the case of the phylacteries it is evident that Jehovah only spoke a spiritual principle. But in the matter of the "borders," a tassel or fringe of their garments, He gave specific instructions that such should be made and worn as a reminder of the Law. So even Jesus followed this practice (cf. Matt. 9:20), one which was commonly observed among the Jews. Jesus did not condemn the practice since it was ordered of God. What He condemned was the practice of the Pharisees of making theirs larger than others in order to demonstrate their superior piety.

Likewise, the Lord condemned them for a personal love for public prominence. When they went to a banquet they wanted to occupy the "uppermost" or chief reclining couches. In ancient times guests did not sit at the banquet table but reclined on couches about it. The couches nearest to the host were regarded as places of prominence and honor. The Pharisees wanted to sit at the speaker's table right next to the host. When they went to the synagogue they wanted the "chief seats" or "first seats." Some understand these to be the front seats nearest to the place where the Law was kept; and were given to those who were most conspicuous in their devotion to the Law. But Robertson cites Zuchermandel as holding that they were seats on the platform looking toward the audience and with the back to the ark in which the *Law* was kept. This would seem to fit Jesus' imagery better. At any rate they *loved* the places of prominence as another show of their piety.

One cannot refrain from noting that they would hardly have felt at home in a modern congregation where the back seats seem to be the choice ones. It is no greater sin to seek prominence by sitting on the front seats than by a show of mock humility to choose the back seats. Of course, one's choice of either may be due to other and legitimate reasons. Jesus was not speaking of such. His words were directed toward those who for ulterior motives *love* either.

Again, Jesus condemned the Pharisees for a personal love for public recognition. "And love . . . greetings in the markets [*agorais*, marketplaces], and to be called of men, Rabbi, Rabbi" (v. 7). The usual Hebrew greeting was *Shalom*, "peace." But this did not satisfy the Pharisees. They loved to be called "Rabbi." The word means "teacher." Basically it means "great one" or one who is superior. In a sense it corresponds to our word "doctor" in the sense of one who is a teacher. The office of teacher was a most respected one among the Jews, and so the title "Rabbi" was a most coveted one. And the Pharisees *loved* to be called such. It was a token of the highest public recognition. It was not the title but the *love* for it which Jesus condemned.

From verse 8 it might appear that Jesus meant otherwise. "But be not ye called Rabbi." However, Jesus on occasion was called "Rabbi" with no protest from Him. He did not court the title but He accepted it. Now the sense of this prohibition, and those which follow in verses 9-10, turns on the emphatic words "but ye." This refers back to the attitude of loving to be called "Rabbi." The disciples are not to love being called by this title. The word "be called" is an ingressive aorist passive subjunctive form. It may be translated, "Do not seek that you may be called by others." The prohibition is in the *seeking,* not in the *being called.* If others call you that it is their doing, not yours.

It is one thing to *receive* a doctor's degree. It is something else to *seek* one for the sake of being called "Doctor." It is one thing, having such a degree, to be called "Doctor." It is quite another thing, either with or without one, to love, to expect, or to demand to be called "Doctor."

"For but one is your Master ["Christ" not in the best manuscripts, but genuine in verse 10, and the meaning is implied here.] . . . and all ye are brethren." The word "master" here is "teacher" (*didaskalos*). Note the change from "Rabbi." So the sense of "Rabbi" here is more that of "my great one," involving a position of superiority. In the Christian fellowship there are to be no *great ones* (cf. v. 11). All are to be "brethren" or considered on an equality. Therefore, this verse is aimed not only at the preacher who seeks or demands to be called "doctor"; it also involves any "Diotrephes, who loveth to have the pre-eminence" (III John 9).

The second prohibition is quite different. For whereas in verse 8 Jesus used the *passive* subjunctive, in verse 9 He employed the aorist subjunctive *active.* Here, then, He specifically forbids us to "call" any man "father upon the earth." Of course, He was not speaking with reference to one's earthly parent or forebears (cf. Acts 7:2). His meaning goes far deeper than that. The word "father (*abba*) was also applied to religious teachers among the Jews. And the Pharisees loved this title also. In this sense "father" was related to the source of spiritual life, even as its natural usage is related to the one from whom we receive physical being. To call a man "father" in the spiritual sense is to infer that he possesses power to confer spiritual life. So Jesus said that we are not to regard any one "upon earth" in such a manner. The source of our spiritual life is not earthly but heavenly. "For one is your Father, which is in heaven" (v. 9).

G. Campbell Morgan sees this as our Lord's forbidding us to recognize any man's power to impart spiritual life to his fellowmen, either by rite or ceremony or by any other method. The "father" is the one who begets. It is from him that life comes. Any so-called *life* imparted by man is false. Such a religion is *on* but not *in* man. Spiritual life in the soul of a man must be begotten of God.

In the third prohibition Jesus returns to the aorist subjunctive *passive (klēthēte).* "Neither be ye called masters: for one is your Master, even Christ" (v. 10). The word for "master" in both instances is *kathēgētēs.* And this is its only occurrence in the New Testament. The word most frequently rendered "master" in the New Testament is *didaskalos* or teacher. This is especially true where the sense is that of instruction (cf. v. 8). Why did Jesus use this particular word at this time? Because it carries a higher connotation than *didaskalos. Didaskalos* corresponds to the Aramaic *Rab,* teacher. But *kathēgētēs* corresponds to the more honorable title *Rabban.* It means one who leads or guides, but in the sense of one who is authoritative. A *didaskalos* might teach, but a *kathēgētēs* is one who does so as an authority. So Jesus did not say that His followers should not be called *didaskaloi* or teachers. In fact He commissioned them to be teachers (cf. Matt. 28:20, *didaskontes,* teaching).

By one's learning and understanding one may be regarded as a competent and trustworthy interpreter of the Scriptures. But even so he is not *Authority.* The *Authority* is Christ by whose words and work all interpretations must be measured. One may be put into a place of responsibility in administering the affairs of kingdom work. But he is not *Authority.* He is still but an underservant of the King who is *Authority.*

What Jesus prohibited was the desire or *love* that we might be called *kathēgētai* or authorities. "For one is your *kathegetes* or Authority, Christ."

The matter of authority in religion is a most vital one. The Pharisees had set themselves up as such. The words of the rabbis were said to be more binding upon men than the words of the Scriptures themselves. It mattered not what the Law said. The Law was what they said that it said. So they assumed the place of supreme religious authority on earth. Jesus said that no man should assume such a position. Only Christ is Authority (cf. Matt. 28:18). Here, therefore, He taught the Lordship of Jesus Christ. Nothing or no one should stand between the soul and the Saviour. And any man or institution which claims such authority is doing so in violation of the King's express command.

So in these three verses Jesus set forth three tremendous, timeless, but timely truths. No Christian should seek excellence or position above his fellow-Christians. For "all ye are brethren." The Christian should regard no man on earth as the source or conveyer of spiritual life. "For one is your Father, which is in heaven." And "God was in Christ, reconciling the world unto himself" (II Cor. 5:19). No Christian should seek to become Authority in Christianity. "For one is your Master [Authority], Christ."

The paradoxical statements in verses 11-12 served to drive home these truths. Greatness in the kingdom of God comes through the rendering of the most menial service (*diakonos,* servant). If one seeks to exalt himself, God will bring him low. If one accepts a lowly place of service, God will exalt him according to His will and grace. What heartache and strife would have been (would be) spared if those who profess to follow the King took to heart these words from Him who is our *Kathēgētēs!*

The Specific Condemnation (23:13-32)

This section deals with what A. T. Robertson calls Jesus' "thunderbolt of wrath" against the scribes and Pharisees. It is found in *Matthew* alone. But it is to be expected that He would record this full and final break on the part of the King with this group which from the beginning had set themselves and their empty system of religion against Him. But He delivered it only after they had thoroughly repudiated His every overture of grace. However, we should not fail to see in this expression of divine wrath the sob of a refused love.

This condemnation is delivered in the form of seven *woes.* (Matthew 23:14 is not found in the best manuscripts, but is genuine in Mark 12:40 and Luke 20:47). The first six all revert back to the fact that the Pharisees "say, and do not" (v. 3). The seventh deals with their present design to destroy Jesus. However, we may further subdivide them. The first three reflect the Pharisees' relation to their role as teacher. The second three reflect their attitude toward personal righteousness. And the last one reflects their attitude toward Jesus. And in each instance, save one (v. 16), Jesus addresses them as "scribes and Pharisees, hypocrites!" We have encountered the word "hypocrite" before (cf. Matt. 6:2). So Jesus charges them with playing a role which is not their true selves.

Let us examine the first section (vv. 13, 15-22). "Woe unto you ... for ye shut up the kingdom of heaven against men; for ye neither go in yourselves, neither suffer ye them that are entering to go in" (v. 13). The words "shut up" render a verb which is related to the Greek word for "key" (*kleis*). Luke 11:52 uses this word where Jesus accuses the lawyers of taking away "the key of knowledge." Every scribe upon admission to his office was given the symbol of the key, suggesting that he was to open the door of understanding for others to enter. Jesus said that the only use that they had made of this key was to lock the door of the kingdom of heaven. Like the lawyers in Luke 11:52 they had locked the door and thrown the key away. The phrase "against men" is most picturesque. "Against" *(emprosthen)* means "before." The word *pros* is related to "face." So in effect Jesus said that in locking the door they had slammed it in the faces of those who were endeavoring to enter. They would not enter into the kingdom, nor would they permit others to do so.

This is a condemnation of the entire system of empty religion as taught by the scribes and Pharisees. The common people were eager to receive both the King and the kingdom. It is true that due to their false teachers they had a warped concept of both. But, even so, had the scribes and Pharisees recognized and admitted their error they could have led the people to accept both King and kingdom in their true meaning. However, so wedded were they to their system that they refused both. And they led the people to do the same.

It is tragic beyond words to express it when responsible religious leaders become a barrier to those who "keep on entering" or trying to enter the kingdom of heaven. And the "woe" which Jesus pronounced upon such ancient teachers is an abiding one in every age.

"Woe unto you...for ye compass sea and land to make one proselyte, and when he is made, ye make him twofold more the child of hell than yourselves" (v. 15).

Not only did the scribes and Pharisees refuse the gospel of the kingdom. They were a failure in their own efforts at proselytizing. The Jews were quite active in their efforts to win Gentiles to Judaism. In the first century many conscientious Gentiles, having failed to find spiritual satisfaction in paganism, were seeking to find it in other religions. Those who recognized Jehovah as the true God were by the Jews called *proselytes.* There were two kinds of proselytes: *proselytes of the gate,* not actual Jews but God-fearers or those who looked with favor on Judaism but who did not become Jews (cf. Acts 10:2); and *proselytes of righteousness,* those who received circumcision, became actual Jews, and endeavored to keep the Law. It was to this latter group that Jesus referred. Although A. T. Robertson holds that He spoke of proselytes to Pharisaism out of this group.

At any rate Jesus' condemnation stands in either case. A Gentile came to the Pharisees seeking eternal life. They put him through their ceremonies and taught him their precepts. But he found only emptiness (cf. Matt. 12:43-45). He sought something and found nothing. So he was worse off than before. Furthermore, he underwent no inner change. He only added to his fleshly pagan vices the insidious vice of spiritual formalism and emptiness. Thus he was twofold (pagan and Pharisaical) more a "son of hell" (*Gehenna*) than the Pharisees themselves. H. J. Holtzmann comments succinctly, "The more converted the more perverted."

You do not make a man a child of God simply by outward form or reformation. To enter the kingdom of heaven requires a new nature. If we merely make a man respectable or give him the false hope involved in *belonging* to the church, he is twice condemned. Trusting in a false hope, either self-righteousness or an institutional relationship void of a new nature, he thinks that he is saved from hell when he is not. But in his false sense of security he is less susceptible to the true gospel than one who is lost and knows it. It is a grave matter beyond compare to stand before men as one commissioned to lead them into the kingdom of heaven. And those who are wilfully "blind guides" shall not escape the judgment of God!

"Woe unto you, ye blind guides..." (v. 16). Note that Jesus omitted the word "hypocrites" here. There are possibly two explanations of this. That which follows unveils their deceitfulness or hypocrisy, and so the word was unnecessary. But since this is the only place where Jesus did not use the word, it is suggestive of another thought. Verses 16-22 are really a continuation of the thought expressed in verse 15. So this is a part of one larger lesson as to the Pharisees' failure in ministering to the needs of those who looked to them as teachers.

These verses (16-22) unmask the hypocrisy of the Pharisees with respect to the matter of taking and keeping oaths (cf. Matt. 5:33-37). An oath taken by naming the name of Jehovah was considered as absolutely binding, regardless of the cost in keeping it (cf. Exod. 20:7). However in order to get around this the scribes and Pharisees had devised a system of oaths which would be less binding. And yet in the course of time as men took these oaths and broke them a further system was drawn up to distinguish between oaths which were binding or which might be broken. It represented a system of religion which did not adhere to God's standard of truth, but which sought to adapt religious rules to the erratic conduct of men. It was based upon the age-old practice of saying that if men do not keep a given law the law must be bad, and should be changed or lowered in its demands. Thus instead of seeking to transform men according to truth one should make truth relative and, therefore, adapted so as to conform to the conduct of men.

Jesus called those who did so 'blind guides" (cf. Matt. 15:14). Note that in each case cited He refers to the scribes and Pharisees as "fools and blind" (vv. 17, 19). In Matthew 5:22 He warned against calling a man a "fool" (*mōros*) in a fit of anger. Here Jesus Himself calls this group "fools" (*mōroi*) or "blind fools." He does so in righteous anger bereft of temper. McNeile rightly suggests that the sin is not in the word itself but in the spirit in which it is uttered (cf. I Cor. 15:36).

To illustrate this deceitful practice concerning oaths Jesus selected two examples. The scribes and Pharisees said that if one swore an oath "by the temple [*naos,* Holy of Holies], it is nothing" (v. 16). The same thing was true of "the altar" (v. 18). Such an oath could be broken with impunity. But if one swore an oath "by the gold of the temple [*naos*]" or "by the [sacrificial] gift" on the altar, "he is a debtor" or is under obligation to keep it. Broadus sees the "gold" as referring both to the gold plates which adorned the building as well as the gold coins and/or bullion which were brought as offerings. This latter was the Corban or sacred treasure (cf. Mark 7:11). Josephus notes that when Crassus plundered the temple he took away eight thousand talents of gold, or about ten million dollars. However, in the light of the sacrificial gift mentioned in Matthew 23:18 it would appear that "gold" referred to that which was brought into the temple as an offering. Thus the Jewish teachers placed a greater value on the gifts and offerings than upon the temple itself. They were like so many leaders today who place greater importance upon the tithes and offerings than upon the program of evangelism!

But in each instance Jesus pointed out the hypocrisy of such an attitude. The greater value and importance should be placed upon the temple and altar which make holy the things that are offered.

So much gold and meat are just that apart from the purpose for which they are given. It is the spiritual value and not the material substance which is important in God's sight (vv. 17, 19).

Jesus brushed aside all of these hypocritical pretensions by saying that it is impossible to judge between oaths. For any oath, regardless of that by which it is taken, ultimately goes back to God (vv. 20-21). This is true even if the oath be taken "by heaven... the throne of God, and by Him that sitteth thereon" (v. 22), some of the most binding of oaths. Therefore, any oath taken by any sacred thing is an oath taken before God. Thus none is to be taken as "nothing." To break any one of them is to "take the name of the Lord thy God in vain" (Exod. 20:7).

The above teachings are remindful of the customs of taking an oath with one's hand on the Bible, by kissing the Bible, the medieval practice of taking an oath, or upon the relics of the saints. No one oath should be considered more or less binding than others. For they all rest ultimately upon our relationship to God Himself. Of course the ideal as set forth by Jesus in the Sermon on the Mount should be that one's "yea" means "yea" and one's "nay" means "nay." The Christian should be so honest that his *word* is his *bond.* If all men should so live there would be no need for "oaths." But life being what it is, when one takes an oath or gives his word (in the right sense, of course) he should regard it as binding even as a promise to God Himself.

The second section of "woes" has to do with the Pharisees' regard to personal righteousness (vv. 23-28). The one has to do with legalism as opposed to spiritual attitudes (vv. 23-24). The other two deal with outward ceremonial cleanliness as over against inward purity and righteousness (vv. 25-28).

"Woe unto you... for ye pay tithe of mint, anise, and cummin, and have omitted the weightier matters of the law, judgment [justice)], mercy, and faith" (v. 23). The law of the tithe was one of the most sacred to the Jews. We have noted how scrupulously the Pharisees observed it (cf. 15:1). Apart from the teachings of Jesus the New Testament makes few references to the tithe (cf. Heb. 7:6, 8-9). Jesus used the verb "to pay tithe" (*apodekatoō*) three times (Matt. 23:23; Luke 11:42; 18:12). Other than its use in the parable of the Pharisee and Publican (Luke 18:12), He used it in a similar statement on two different occasions in direct address to the Pharisees (Matt. 23:23; Luke 11:42).

Some regard this scarcity of treatment as evidence that the tithe is no longer binding upon the Christian. A more likely explanation would be that it was so universally accepted among the Jews that there was no need for further emphasis. We may well assume that Jesus tithed. Such would have been a part of His training as a faithful Jew. The Pharisees, who placed such great emphasis upon it, never criticized Jesus for not tithing. Had this been the case it is difficult to understand how they would have missed such an opportunity to do so. However, even these items do not get to the heart of the matter. The law of the tithe was basic in God's development of His people. It was not a part of the ceremonial law which was fulfilled in Jesus. In fact it antedated the Mosaic code (cf. Gen. 14:20). Even the Old Testament taught the giving of "tithes and *offerings*" (Mal. 3:8, author's italics), or giving beyond the tithe. In every instance where Jesus interpreted an Old Testament law He went beyond its letter to require more in its observance (cf. Matt. 5:20ff.). He did not criticize but rather commended the Pharisees for tithing. It is true that both Jesus and His interpreters taught the stewardship of all of one's life and possessions. But this is no excuse for ignoring the tithe as a basic minimum in giving. It should not be the *goal* but the starting point. No Christian can be obedient and give less than the tithe. The question is not how little *must* one give, but how much *may* one give. And since the Christian and all that he has belongs to God, the whole of his life should be used for man's good and God's glory.

Jesus did not condemn the scribes and Pharisees for tithing. Implied is His condemnation for the *bookkeeping system* by which they tithed. For they tithed every leaf of mint and every little seed (anise and cummin), no more but no less than one tenth. "Anise" or dill seeds were used for flavoring and medicine. "Cummin" seeds were used for flavoring only. But while the Pharisees were so scrupulous in keeping this law they ignored the "weightier" or more important laws of *justice, mercy and faith.* This latter statement would remind them of Micah 6:8. The prophet did not condemn Judah for her many sacrificial offerings. He condemned her for being so meticulous in observing the outward forms of religion, and at the same time neglecting the ethical and spiritual requirements of God, "to do justly, and to love mercy, and to walk humbly [humble thyself to walk] with thy God." The Pharisees were guilty on all counts. "These ought ye to have done, and not to leave the other undone" (Matt. 23:23). Jesus commended them for their righteous deeds of commission, but He condemned them for their sins of omission.

And then in a striking bit of hyperbole He draws a picture for them to see. Literally, "Blind guides, the ones straining out *the* gnat, but the ones swallowing down a camel" (v. 24, author's italics). Note the use of the definite article with "gnat" and its omission with "camel." This was not accidental on Jesus' part. They see "the gnat," *one little gnat,* floating on the surface of their drink. So they very carefully pour the drink through a strainer in order to remove the gnat. Then in their blindness they gulp down a *whole camel* that was also in the drink.

The scribes and Pharisees were so scrupulous in observing the minute letters of the Law. Yet with no compunction of conscience they ignored the spiritual aspects of its teachings. It was this very attitude which had robbed their religious system of any semblance of power. Thus it was not only ineffective in meeting the needs of the Jews; it was also powerless to make any vital impact upon a world that hungered for an experience with the living God.

But this condition did not confine itself to the first century. It plagues the people of Christ in the twentieth century also. With most Christians the greater problem is not sins of commission but sins of omission. Religious truth must express itself in life, or else it becomes rote ritual or meaningless teaching. It is much more serious for a man to swallow a camel than it is to swallow a gnat. He should avoid a diet of gnats, to be sure; but he should watch out for the camels as well.

The next two "woes" are related in meaning. They both speak of an overly cautious attitude with respect to ceremonial cleansing which neglects God's demand for inner spiritual holiness and purity. We have noted the care with which some Pharisees cleansed the outside of their dishes (the surface) lest they may have been polluted through the touch of a Gentile (cf. Matt. 15). But Jesus says that they themselves are "full of extortion and excess' (v. 25). "Extortion" suggests that the very food which filled the dishes was the fruit of their crooked dealings. "Excess" suggests their gluttony in eating and drinking. So the dishes are their bodies, and the contents are their lives or spirits (v. 30). The spirit of man indwells his body. No matter how ceremoniously clean the body may be, if the spirit be evil and gluttonous it pollutes the whole. On the other hand, if the spirit be clean it sanctifies the body. And such a body will through its conduct give evidence of the right spirit which indwells it.

Verses 27-28 are most picturesque. The Jews believed that to touch a dead body was to become ceremonially unclean for seven days. In such a condition they were unfit for worship. Therefore, before the Passover they whitewashed the tombs so that they would not inadverdently touch one and become ceremonially unclean. Even as Jesus spoke these words, just before the Passover, the tombs about Jerusalem must have been "whited sepulchres" (v. 27). But inside them were dead men's bones and decaying flesh. Jesus called the Pharisees "whited sepulchres." So clean outwardly, but so filthy and dead inwardly! To men they appeared to be so righteous. But God looked inside the graves and saw only "hypocrisy and iniquity" (v. 28). They had reversed the whole order. They cared what men thought of them, but were so careless as to how they appeared before God. Jesus could have said no more stinging a rebuke to them than this.

Again, we do not paint tombs with lime powder. But are we not just as guilty as they? We adorn the outside of our bodies and lives to be approved of men. But we are so careless about the inside. How carefully we groom our bodies before going out in public, even to church services, yet we carry along our spirits and attitudes which are as dead men's bones and rotting flesh. There is no sin in being careful about the outside so long as it does not belie our inner selves. But our first concern should be for the latter, not the former. If we be filled with an inner beauty it will make the outer self beautiful also.

The third section of "woes" reflects the attitude of the scribes and Pharisees, and the Jewish nation, toward Jesus Himself. "Woe unto you . . . because ye build the tombs of the prophets . . ." (vv. 29-30). Even today one may see the Tombs of the Prophets (Zechariah, Absalom, Jehoshaphat, James) at the foot of the Mount of Olives. Some of these may well have been under construction at this very time. Jesus' reference to Zechariah (v. 35) may have been chosen for this reason. At any rate Jesus points out an abiding principle. Their fathers slew the prophets, and they themselves built and adorned tombs or monuments in their names (v. 29). In so doing they piously said that had they lived in those days they would have acted differently from their fathers (v. 30). But by their very words they bore testimony that they were the children of those who were guilty of the "blood of the prophets" (v. 31). They were partners ("partakers," v. 30) with them in their evil deeds. For even then they were plotting to kill not a *prophet* but the *Son of God.*

"Fill ye up then the measure of your fathers" (v. 32). Crown their sins by killing the Prophet of God! Go ahead and do what you are planning to do! The hour is at hand! "Ye serpents, ye generation [offspring] of vipers, how shall ye escape the damnation [*krisis*] of hell [*Gehenna*]" (v. 33)? These climactic words blister and burn. "They cut to the bone like whip-cords" (Robertson). The word "damnation" renders a word which means *found guilty and sentenced.* The scribes and Pharisees had been convicted by their own testimony. They had been "witnesses unto [against] themselves" (v. 31). And on the basis of their own testimony the King, or Judge, pronounced them guilty and sentenced them to Gehenna or hell.

The scribes and Pharisees had deliberately and completely refused to enter into the kingdom of heaven. Therefore, they are fit only to be cast into God's *cosmic garbage dump* (*Gehenna* was the garbage dump of Jerusalem). Outwardly righteous but inwardly corrupt, they will spend eternity with all of the unrighteous. So concerned about ceremonial cleanliness, yet they are consigned to the place symbolized by one where filth, dead animals, and the unclaimed dead bodies of executed criminals were thrown.

These are terrible words indeed (v. 33). But they are not those of some sadist who delights in the torture of his victims. They come from Him who is infinite Love and Mercy. This very fact adds force to their meaning. We could not tone them down if we attempted to do so. Many would deny categorically the existence of a place of eternal punishment. But the word "Gehenna" (cf. Matt. 5:22) as a place of punishment for the lost is found in the New Testament only on the lips of Jesus. We cannot deny the reality of hell without denying the words of the King Himself. For like streaked lightning in a cosmic storm they strike forth against every unregenerate soul. What Jesus said to the scribes and Pharisees, as the Judge He will one day say to all who reject Him as Saviour and King. When his rejection becomes complete and final man leaves the King no other choice. But the decision ultimately is ours, not His. Infinite justice can only recognize the situation as it is.

The Final Condemnation (23:34-39)

The judgment of God is not only pronounced upon all of the lost at the end of the age. It is operative within the context of history against both men and nations. The religious system of the scribes and Pharisees will come to an end along with their capital city and nation. In verses 34-35 Jesus cited the sinful history of the Israelite nation. Not only had they persecuted and slain God's messengers in the past. They will continue to do so, as is seen in the words "scourge in your synagogues, and persecute them from city to city" (v. 34). Therefore, God will require at their hand "all the righteous blood shed upon the earth, from the blood of righteous Abel [the first man to be murdered] unto the blood of Zacharias . . ." (v. 35) .

Who was this Zacharias? Various attempts have been made to identify him. Broadus is probably correct in linking this name with Zechariah the son of Jehoiada (II Chron. 24:20-22) who was stoned "in the court of the house of the Lord." The problem of "son of Barachias" remains. He may have been called by both names. However, the words of Jesus become clear when we remember that Abel is mentioned in Genesis, the first book in the Hebrew canon. Zechariah is mentioned in II Chronicles which was placed last in the Hebrew canon. So the Lord said that all of the righteous blood shed and which was recorded in the Hebrew Scriptures will be required of the Jewish nation. And this judgment will come in that generation (v. 36) . This prophecy was literally fulfilled in A.D. 70 when Jerusalem fell to the Romans in a carnage seldom seen upon this earth.

That all of this condemnation broke the heart of the Saviour is seen in verse 37. "O Jerusalem, Jerusalem, thou that killest the prophets, and stonest them which are sent unto thee, how often would I have gathered thy children together, even as a hen gathereth her chickens under her wings, and ye would not!" (v. 37) . Plumptre notes that only here in *Matthew* do we find the Hebrew, *Jerousalēm,* rather than the Greek, *Jerosoluma,* as though these very syllables had impressed themselves upon the mind of Matthew. The figure is that of a hen seeing a storm coming. Frantically she tries to gather her brood under her wings to save them from it. But they ignore her calls. Jesus saw the storm coming. Rebellion was in the heart of the Jewish nation. Repeatedly He had called to her, but she would not heed.

"Behold, your house is left unto you" (v. 38) . The word "desolate" is absent from the best texts. Does "house" refer to the temple, city, and/or nation? In all probability it refers to all three. Furthermore, it involves the whole system of Judaism. God had sought repeatedly to use them, but to no avail. They had rejected the King, and now He fully and finally rejected them. "Your house is left unto *you*" (author's italics) . Since they chose their way rather than His the King departed, leaving them to their own will and desires. These will finally result in the destruction of their temple, city, and nation. They themselves will be scattered. And their system of religion as they had known it will be no more. Their teachings will continue, but without the temple and the sacrifices. A people which were not a people will be called the people of God.

One final word remained to be said. "Ye shall not see me henceforth, till ye shall say, Blessed is he that cometh in the name of the Lord" (v. 39). They did see Him when He appeared before them first for judgment and then as He was crucified. But He spoke of His second coming. They had rejected Him as the King-Messiah. But when He returns all, including them, will recognize Him as the Messiah, some gladly and others sadly. This does not in any sense refer to a "second chance." It simply means that while some may refuse Jesus as Lord and Saviour now, at His second advent all men, both saved and unsaved, will recognize Him as the King-Messiah. The former will do so joyfully even as they did in life. The latter by the force of His rule will be compelled to admit that the One whom they rejected was in truth the Christ of God. For every knee shall bow, and every tongue shall confess, either willingly or unwillingly, that "Jesus Christ is Lord, to the glory of God the Father" (Phil. 2:10-11).

With these final words Jesus left the temple. And there is grim realism in that fact. For when *Jesus* left the temple it was *God* leaving it, nevermore to dwell in its *naos* or Holy of Holies. Truly, their house was left unto *them!*

Matthew 24

The Predictions of the King

The disciples were stunned by the merciless words of Jesus to the scribes and Pharisees. The very atmosphere was filled with tension. Perhaps they felt that they should say something to break that tension. If so, then they said the wrong thing. Or else they thought that words of theirs might cause Jesus to recall His terrible predictions. For they knew that whatever their meaning they involved the destruction of their beautiful temple. Therefore, they began "to shew him the buildings of the temple" (*hieron*), the temple area (v. 1). This was a useless exercise for Jesus was quite familiar with it. It would seem, therefore, that we may read into these words, "Surely you do not mean to destroy all of this!"

Of course, the temple in question was Herod's temple. Herod the Great began its construction in 20-19 B.C. The *naos* was completed in about eighteen months, but the courts and cloisters required about eight years in building. However, certain constructions were still in progress during Jesus' public ministry (cf. John 2:20). It was not entirely completed until A.D. 64, just six years before it was destroyed by the Romans. It was one of the most beautiful buildings ever constructed. Josephus described its view from the Mount of Olives as like unto a mountain of snow. The Talmud says, "He that never saw the temple of Herod, never saw a fine building." Even Tacitus said that it was "a temple of immense wealth," and so constructed as to make "an excellent fortress." So glorious was it that the Roman general Titus wished to preserve it when he destroyed Jerusalem. But even while he was crying, "Save the temple!" a Roman soldier fired it and it went up in flames.

Evidently Jesus and the Twelve were outside the temple area when the disciples spoke of it to Jesus. Thus He probably pointed to some of the foundation stones of the temple. They were tremendous in size. Some of them were twenty to forty feet in length and weighed one hundred tons. It is still possible to see some of them which were gathered out of the debris, and used in building the present walls of Jerusalem. Their very size adds weight to Jesus' answer to the disciples. "There shall not be left one stone upon another [one stone upon a stone], that shall not be thrown down" (v. 2). Jesus predicted the absolute destruction of the city and the temple.

It was late in the afternoon on Tuesday. Presently Jesus and His little band had crossed the Kidron brook, and had ascended to a point on the Mount of Olives overlooking the city of Jerusalem to the west. It is still an awesome sight to this day. But it must have been even more so then, with the glistening white temple bathed in the rays of the rapidly setting sun. They had probably sat down to rest. While doing so the disciples asked Jesus about His words which had been spoken earlier in the temple area.

Note that they asked Him three questions. "When shall these things be?" "What shall be the sign of thy coming?" "And of the end of the world [age]?" (v. 3). Jesus had spoken of the destruction of Jerusalem and the temple (23:38; 24:2). He had referred to His second coming (23:39). And this implied the end of the age. It is important to keep these three distinct questions in mind. Failure to do so will involve the danger of reading Jesus' answer to one question as referring to another. And while He will at times refer back to previous thoughts, in essence He answered these questions in the order in which they were asked.

Therefore, we may divide this chapter into the following sections: (1) the warning against false signs; (2) the destruction of Jerusalem; (3) the sign of His coming; (4) the end of the age.

The Warning against False Signs (24:4-14)

"Take heed [beware] that no man deceive you [lead you astray]" (v. 4). Jesus knew that this would be the case. So He gave a general warning against false signs of His second coming. For there is no one facet of His teachings which has been subjected to more confusion. And it is amazing how successful have been the various schemes to do the very thing against which Jesus warned us. To exercise caution at this point does not mean that one does not believe in or share this "blessed hope, and the glorious appearing of the great God and our Saviour Jesus Christ" (Titus 2:13). It is always an imminent event. But as Jesus told His people to "watch," He also said, "Beware, lest anyone may lead you astray."

The first sign against which Jesus warned is that of false messiahs. "For many shall come in my name, saying, I am Christ; and shall deceive many" (v. 5)). Literally, "I am the Christ." Josephus tells us that these false Christs were one reason which brought on the Jewish War (A.D. 66-70). The minds of the Jewish people entertained the thought of a political military

Messiah. And this made them most susceptible to those who offered to lead them in rebellion against Rome. Even fifty years after the destruction of Jerusalem Bar-Cochba ("son of a star") arose, claiming to be the "star" of Balaam mentioned in Numbers 24:17. Throughout Christian history, even in our present time, false messiahs have offered themselves to the public. More than fifty years ago two men in Illinois claimed to be the Messiah. More recently Mrs. Annie Besant sought to foist upon us an Indian theosophical Messiah. Mrs. Mary Baker Eddy made claims for herself equal to those of Jesus.

These should not be confused with the Antichrist mentioned elsewhere in the New Testament. Jesus warned not against one who would be anti-Christ but against those who would make false claims to being the Christ Himself. He said that His people should not be led astray by such.

The second sign of which to beware is the cataclysmic disturbances in history and nature. "And we shall hear of wars and rumours of wars" (v. 6). "And there shall be famines, and pestilences, and earthquakes" (v. 7). Josephus and Tacitus tell of such conditions prior to the Jewish War in A.D. 66-70. It is surprising that such things are so often interpreted as signs of the Second Coming, when Jesus specifically said that such is not the case. Every time that some great upheaval, social or natural, comes, we break out in a rash of predictions that the return of the Lord is near. His return is always imminent, but no more so in a conflagration of war than in a time when life moves along more normal courses.

In World Wars I and II both the Kaiser and Hitler were called the Antichrist by some. During World War II a volume was issued which hailed Mussolini as the Antichrist. According to it he would be victorious in the war, re-establish the old Roman Empire, and lead his forces against Christ. Ironic was the fact that by the time the book was published, *Il Duce* was dead, having made one of the most ignominious exits ever accorded so pretentious a ruler.

Jesus warned His people not to be misled by such cataclysmic events. They will come as a part of history, but are not a sign of the end of the age. "See that ye be not troubled [disturbed or frightened, cf. II Thes. 2:2]: for all these things must come to pass, but the end is not yet" (v. 6).

Jesus said that these things are not signs of the end. Instead they are "the beginning of sorrows" (v. 8). The word for "sorrows" *(ōdinōn)* literally means "birth-pangs." The Jews used this word to express the sufferings of the Messiah which were to come prior to the coming of the Messiah. But which coming? Broadus in his *Commentary on Matthew* (*in loco*), observes, "But does not the expression mean that in the preparation for the complete reign of the Messiah, conflict is unavoidable, not simply individual and domestic variance, but conflict of the races and nations, as afterward depicted in the visions of John on Patmos?"

This "beginning of sorrows" Jesus blended with His description of the struggle which has characterized the experience of His people through the ages as they have endeavored to preach the gospel (vv. 9-13). Some see these as descriptive of conditions which existed just prior to the destruction of Jerusalem. And they are a fitting description. But Jesus' words "and ye shall be hated of all nations for my name's sake" seem to encompass all of the sufferings of His people through the ages until His return. They certainly describe the persecution of the Christians by the Romans. Pagans handed them over ("deliver") to be tortured and slain (v. 9). Many so-called Christians stumbled ("offended") because of persecution and betrayed their fellow-believers (v. 10). Even members of the same household did this to members of their own families. False prophets abounded (v. 11). And because of lawlessness "the love of many [for Christ] waxed cold," literally, "blew or breathed cold" (v. 12). This was true of many, but not of all. The chaff was separated from the wheat.

But it should be remembered that these conditions obtained in every age where persecution abounded. (i.e. the Middle Ages). It is under such conditions that the gospel is to be proclaimed through the ages. "But he that shall endure unto the end, the same shall be saved" (v. 13). The word "endure" is an aorist participle of a verb meaning to have an inner fortitude. It expresses the idea of one having the quality which enables him to withstand all that the enemy can throw against him, and still have the reserve power with which to counter-charge to victory. This does not teach a *future salvation*, whereby one is saved in the end if he holds out until death. It speaks of the genuine Christian as one who possesses the kind of character which will enable him to endure. Such an one will maintain a warm love for Christ. He will endure the trials and will thereby prove the genuineness of his faith and spiritual life which he already possesses.

Jesus closed this warning against false signs by stating the only sign which He gave with respect to His coming and the end of the age. "And this gospel of the kingdom shall be preached in all the world for a witness unto all nations; and then shall the end come" (v. 14). Plumptre sees this as meaning that the gospel will be preached throughout the Roman empire before the destruction of Jerusalem. And this was practically true. But this did not include all of the "world" or "inhabited world" (cf. John 3:16). Nor was it "a witness unto all nations" or ethnic groups (Greek, *ethnesin*). Furthermore, the destruction of Jerusalem was not "the end" of the age (cf. v. 3). It would appear, therefore, that Jesus was not looking merely to A.D. 70. He took a panoramic view of history from that moment until "the end of the age." The gospel is to be proclaimed as a witness to all people before the end comes. It is of interest to note that such a possibility exists today through means of mass media of communication that never existed before. But even so it is not our responsibility to try to plot the course of the end of time. We are to herald the gospel, and leave the time of "the end" in the mind and will of God.

The Destruction of Jerusalem (24:15-22)

Having warned against false signs Jesus proceeded to answer the questions of the disciples. The first was "When shall these things be?" So Jesus first dealt with the destruction of Jerusalem.

The Lord said that they would know "when [*hotan*] ye therefore shall see the abomination of desolation... stand in the holy place" (v. 15). The disciples had asked as to *time* (*pote*). But Jesus spoke of condition (*hotan*), for this word speaks primarily in that sense. So Jesus did not name a date, although He could have done so, but a condition. And the condition was "the abomination of desolation" standing in "the holy place" (*en topōi hagiōi*).

Jesus ascribed these words to the prophet Daniel, which is His own authentication of Daniel as the author of the prophecy which bears his name, despite some modern claims to the contrary. These latter hold to a date after the time of Antiochus Epiphanes (175-163 B.C.) which would rob the book of its prophetic element (cf. Dan. 7). But Jesus placed it in the time of the Babylonian captivity, the time which the book claims for itself. This writer prefers the words of Jesus to those of certain modern scholars.

But what did Jesus mean by "the abomination of desolation"? This is a definite allusion to Daniel 9:27; 11:31; 12:11. The word "abomination" means a nausea caused by a stench, and so something to be abhored and detested. This word is used oftenest in the Old Testament to denote idolatry. So we may assume that to be the meaning here. But to what incident does it refer?

In his persecution of the Jews Antiochus Epiphanes, the

Seleucid ruler of Syria, erected an altar to Zeus on the altar of Jehovah in the temple in Jerusalem. And the author of I Maccabees sees this as fulfilling the prophecies in Daniel. However, Jesus saw these prophecies as still referring to an event after His earthly ministry. So in all likelihood He referred to some incident connected with the destruction of Jerusalem in A.D. 70. In a parallel passage Luke says, "And when ye see Jerusalem compassed with armies, then know that the desolation thereof is nigh [has drawn near, perfect tense]" (21:20). Under Titus the Roman armies besieged Jerusalem. After its fall the Roman legions proclaimed Titus the emperor, offering heathen sacrifices to their ensigns placed by the eastern gate of the city. However, Jesus' reference to the Christians fleeing the city would seem to rule out this last event as being meant specifically as the "abomination." When that occurred it would have been too late to flee. The "holy place" does not necessarily mean the temple itself. A pagan ensign placed anywhere in the city would have been an "abomination" to the Jews. On a previous occasion Pilate had outraged the Jews by bringing such into the city. But when we compare Matthew's account with that in Luke, it appears that the pagan armies surrounding Jerusalem are the *abomination* referred to by Jesus. At any rate His reference could include the entire seige and fall of the city. Josephus notes that during the seige Titus permitted certain Jews to leave the city, and this could have included the Christians.

So Jesus answered the first question of the disciples by saying that they would know "when" as they saw the Roman armies surrounding the city, a fact that ultimately sealed its doom. And then He added parenthetically, "Who readeth, let him understand" (v. 15). So He referred them back to the prophecy of Daniel which told of the Messiah being cut off (crucifixion, Dan. 9:26) and the ceasing of "the sacrifice and the oblation" (destruction of the temple, Dan. 9:27). And although forty years separated the two events, Jesus in a sweeping glance saw them as one event related as *cause* and *effect*.

When the Christians see these events connected with the siege and destruction of Jerusalem transpiring, they are to flee to the mountains where they might hide (vv. 16-20). Those in Judea, outside the city, are to flee to the mountains (v. 16). Those inside the city, probably on the housetops watching the armies gather, are not to go down to get any of their possessions. They are to flee from roof to roof, called by the rabbis "the road of the roofs," and escape (v. 17). A man working in the field, and who had laid aside his outer garment, should not return to get it (v. 18). Haste was of the very essence. It will be bad for women with child or who have a nursing child, because they will not be able to run fast enough (v. 19). Furthermore, they should pray that this will not happen in the winter time because of rough, cold weather. Nor on a sabbath day because Jewish law would permit them to travel only about ten thousand and fifty yards (v. 20). Some held that this law might be violated when one's life was in danger. But many strict Jews would have died rather than to break it.

These words of Jesus take on vivid meaning as one reads Josephus' account of the fall of Jerusalem. And Eusebius tells how the Christians fled to Pella, a small town at the foot of the mountains about seventeen miles south of the Sea of Galilee. Evidently they recalled Jesus' warning and were saved thereby.

Jesus described the "great tribulation" connected with this event as exceeding anything that had ever before been seen or would be seen in all of history (v. 21). Some see this as referring both to the fall of Jerusalem and to events immediately preceding the return of the Lord. Without entering into this latter thought, it is sufficient to note that Jesus probably had in mind only the former. For He said, "No, nor ever shall be." He focused the disciples' attention on the one event as involved in their first question. Josephus tells us that when Jerusalem fell a million Jews perished in one day. Titus said that God was against the Jews on that day. And Jesus said that the carnage would have been greater, even to the wiping out of the Christians, had not God for their sake shortened the days of it (v. 22).

Thus Jesus answered the first question. Then He turned to the second.

The Sign of His Coming (24:23-35)

In verses 23-26 Jesus repeated His warning with respect to false messiahs. This was epecially appropriate in the period leading up to the destruction of Jerusalem. Even during the siege many came forward with wild schemes as to deliverance from it. But they served only to add to the misery of the beleaguered people. But this warning is of equal value throughout the ages. It must be remembered that in the remainder of this chapter, with the exception of verse 25, Jesus was using apocalyptic language, vivid imagery and speaking with the broad panoramic view of prophecy.

But during this broad sweep of history many false Christs and false prophets will appear. Some will even work "signs and wonders." This could mean "miracles" or it could refer to any phenomenon which *appears* to be accompanied by the power of God (e.g. occult powers so-called, v. 24). But the point is that even these are not to be considered as an authentic evidence of one's being the Christ or a true prophet. We must judge the work by the evidence of true results. John warns us to test the "spirits" to see if they be of God (I John 4:1). For there is also an evil spirit at work in the world.

Even so, such evidences and claims should not deceive the true Christians (v. 24). If anyone says, "Lo, here is Christ, or there; believe it not" (v. 23). Jesus reminded His disciples that He was telling them, and us, beforehand that they/we might not be led astray. "Wherefore, if they shall say unto you, Behold, he is in the secret chamber; believe it not" (v. 26). Both of these ideas point to claims of a secret appearing of the Christ. It is suggested that such would be the case of pretenders in order to avoid the possibility of their claims or those made about them being tested. But Jesus specifically negated any idea of a *secret* coming of Christ prior to the grand and climactic event of the age. Pastor Russell (Jehovah's Witnesses) claimed that the Lord appeared secretly to him in 1914 telling him to gather out the one hundred and forty-four thousand (cf. Rev. 14:1). Such a claim should be judged in the light of Jesus' words in Matthew 24:24-26.

From these negative warnings Jesus turned to the positive side (vv. 27-31). In contrast to the idea of secret comings, He said that when He comes His appearing (*parousia,* coming) will be seen by all. The *Parousia* was used in that day for the visit or appearance of a king among his people. The New Testament adopts this term for the second coming of Christ. So when the *Parousia* occurs it will be "as the lightning [which] cometh out of the east, and shineth [is seen] even unto the west" (v.27).

The thought has been expressed that significance should be placed on "as the lightning cometh out of the *east*" (author's italics). When lightning is seen in the west it heralds an approaching storm. But when we see it in the east it means that the storm has passed. Thus Jesus' choice of words suggests that the storm of tribulation has passed. And then Christ appears. This is an intriguing and suggestive thought. But whether it should be pressed is a matter of conjecture.

The primary point is that when Christ returns all will see Him simultaneously, even as all in a given locality see a flash of lightning across the sky. No one will have secret knowledge which has been withheld from others. This within itself should spare us from being misled by pretenders. For despite the seeming "signs and wonders," none of these false Christs will be able to duplicate the condition laid down by the King.

From this celestial figure Jesus turned to a most earthly one. "For wheresoever the carcase is, there will the eagles [vultures] be gathered together" (v. 28). Four interpretations have been offered concerning this verse. One sees the carcase as a dead Judaism with the Roman eagles gathered to destroy it. Another, that of some of the early Church Fathers, saw the carcase as Christ Himself, crucified and slain, and the eagles as His true saints and servants who will hasten to meet Him when He comes. Plumptre contends that the carcase is any decadent church or nation which in the end will be destroyed by God's ministers of vengeance, thus making way for new forms of life. But none of these seems to fit the context. The fourth, and most likely one, is that when conditions are right the Lord will return. In addition to this Broadus adds that when conditions are right Jerusalem itself will be destroyed. This is a possible inference. For throughout this section it is possible that Jesus was thinking of both the destruction of Jerusalem, which may be regarded as a *coming of the Lord* in an intervention in history and of the final event of the ages. The meaning would be true in either event. But on the whole the context seems to refer it entirely to the second coming of Christ. Anyone who has been in Asia and Africa, even today, will recognize that this was/is a common sight. Wherever a dead body is, there one will find vultures. The condition produces the phenomenon. So in vivid language Jesus simply said that when in God's judgment the condition is right the Son will return. Note that here also Jesus did not mention *time* but *condition.*

And then the mind of the Lord turned to apocalyptic language as He swept the scope of future history looking toward the Second Coming (vv. 29-31). "Immediately after the tribulation of those days..." (v. 29). What did Jesus mean by these words? The word "immediately" causes trouble if one presses the time element. Some regard "tribulation" as referring to the time of great suffering in connection with the fall of Jerusalem (cf. v. 21). However, Mark's words "But in those days, after that tribulation" (13:24), followed by his description of the second coming, seem to project this event into the future. In this light what are we to understand by Matthew 24:29? There are those who see the "tribulation" as referring to a period of great suffering on earth following the rapture of the saints, or the taking of the saints out of the world ahead of the lost people. And to those who follow this line of thought this would be a natural conclusion. However, verse 31 suggests that God's elect will still be on earth at this time. "From one end of heaven to the other" draws on the idea of the earth being bounded on all sides by the sky or "heaven," a view which is understandable in the popular language of one on earth.

In this light, therefore, the writer concludes that the "tribulation" refers to the suffering of the saints in preaching the gospel throughout the period from Jesus' ascension until His return (cf. Matt. 24:8-13). So in the mighty sweep of prophetic utterance our Lord looks toward the end of that suffering when the phenomena described in verse 28 shall appear.

"And then shall appear the sign of the Son of man in heaven [cf. Acts 1:11]" (v. 30). The "sign" then is not some secret appearing. As the "lightning" all shall see the Son of man coming in all of His glory! The trumpet will sound, the unsaved "tribes" will mourn because they have rejected the King (cf. Rev. 6:12-17). But the "elect," or those who have received Him, shall be gathered together to greet Him with rejoicing (v. 31). There are many details in connection with this event which do not call for treatment here. The Lord is dealing in grand pictures, and we shall leave it there.

Once again from these cosmic views Jesus turned His disciples to a common, earthly example. "Now learn the parable of the fig tree" (v. 32). "When" (*hotan,* condition, not time) you see a fig tree putting forth its leaves, you know that summer is near. Likewise, when you see the conditions described above, you shall know that "it is near, even at the doors" (v. 33). To what does "it" refer? The Revised Version translates it "he." Actually in the Greek text the verb "is" (*estin*) has no subject written out. So either translation may be considered correct from the standpoint of language. The decision rests in one's interpretation of the verb. If Jesus was referring to Himself in the second coming, then the subject is "he." Edersheim says that it is unlikely that Jesus would refer to Himself in the third person. However, in verse 31 "shall send" has no subject written out; "he" is inferred from the use of "the Son of man" in verse 30. But the case in verse 33 is quite different. The example of the fig tree refers to a condition or event, not a person. So in verse 33 the meaning is the same. Thus "it" seems to be the more likely subject of the verb *estin.* Therefore, it refers to an event, not to a person. Of course, the event could be the return of the Lord. But if that alone be regarded as the meaning, then we run into difficulty in verse 34. For obviously the second coming of Christ did not occur in that "generation." What event did occur during that generation? The destruction of Jerusalem. For it came in A.D. 70, exactly forty years after Jesus spoke these words. So evidently this event was in Jesus' mind.

However, we may well ask if this thought exhausts the meaning of the parable of the fig tree? If Jesus had stopped with the mention of "this generation" we might so agree. But He did not do so. To complete the thought we must also include verses 35-36. Verse 36 definitely refers to the second coming. Is it possible to relate both the destruction of Jerusalem and the second coming to this parable? Not only is it possible, it is only in that light that these words of Jesus make sense.

Up to this point He had been answering two questions: "When shall these things be? and what shall be the sign of thy coming?" Now before turning to the third question He summarized what He had said about the other two matters. In both cases He said that when they saw the conditions which He had set forth, then they would know that "it is near," on the one hand the destruction of Jerusalem, and on the other the second coming. And then in verse 35 He spoke of the former when He said, "This generation shall not pass, till all these things be fulfilled"— the destruction of Jerusalem. In this instance He practically named the date.

But then He turned to the second event, the second coming of Christ. "But of that day and hour knoweth no man, no, not the angels of heaven, but my Father only" (v. 36). The Nestle Greek text adds the words "not even the Son." Some question the genuineness of these words, but there is strong manuscript evidence that they are the true text. There is no question as to their authenticity in Mark 13:32, and so they may be regarded as genuine in Matthew also.

Does Jesus mean to say that even He did not know the time of the second coming? He said so in plain language. Some will see a problem at this point. For if in Him dwells "all the fulness of the Godhead bodily" (Col. 2:9), how could this be possible? The answer is found in Philippians 2:6-8. When the Son emptied Himself into the form of man He took upon Himself the "infirmities" (weaknesses, Heb. 4:15) of man, apart from sin. In a mystery which defies our understanding He took on a limitation of His omniscience. He possessed it, and yet He did not possess or express it in keeping with the condition of His incarnation. We cannot explain it; we can only accept it as the teachings of Scripture. E. Y. Mullins likens it to a master playing the piano while wearing gloves. Or to the mathematician setting aside his great knowledge to explain 2+2=4 to a child. The knowledge and skill were present, but in both cases the master adapted himself to a given situation. So the omniscient God as Jesus adapted Himself to the conditions required in a complete incarnation apart from sin. Only thus could He be our Saviour.

However, a more practical element is present in this statement of Jesus. If even He did not know the day or hour of His second coming, it is useless for man to try to speculate. All such efforts end in failure, to say nothing of bordering upon the ridiculous. Jesus spoke of condition, not time. It is our responsibility to be busy producing the *condition,* and to leave the *time* with God.

While we cannot know the time, we can know the certainty. For Jesus said, "Heaven and earth shall pass away, but my words shall not pass away" (v. 35). This statement He wisely placed between the two events under consideration. They refer to both the destruction of Jerusalem and the second coming of Christ. The King said that Jerusalem would "pass away," and it did. That event we can pinpoint in history. He also said that the present heaven and earth would give way to a new heaven and a new earth (cf. vv. 29-30; cf. II Peter 3:13; Rev. 21:1). We cannot pinpoint this event. But we can look forward to it as our "blessed hope, and the glorious appearing of the great God and our Saviour Jesus Christ (Titus 2:13). "Even so, come, Lord Jesus" (Rev. 22:20).

The End of the Age (24:37-51)

The thought of the second coming continues throughout this section. For it is impossible to separate it from "the end of the age" (24:3). It would seem, however, that Jesus was answering this third question as He turned to the use of parables. The thought which permeates this series of parables is the unexpected nature of the Lord's return heralding the end of the age.

The example of "the days of Noe" (Noah) may not strictly be called a parable, but it is certainly "an earthly story with a heavenly meaning." For "as the days of Noe were, so shall also the coming of the Son of man be" (v. 37). A recent volume stretches this statement to include various conditions spanning the first eleven chapters of Genesis to show that the same conditions exist today. The conclusion is the imminency of the second coming. The fact is true, but the examples go beyond the meaning of Jesus' words.

The meaning of the example of "the days of Noe" is not hidden under a maze of words. It is quite simple. Noah's contemporaries ignored his preaching. They went right on "eating and drinking, marrying and giving in marriage, until the day that Noe entered into the ark" (v. 38). That last day before the flood may have dawned bright and beautiful. Then suddenly the flood came, taking "them all away." Only Noah's family was saved. "So shall also the coming of the Son of man be" (v. 39). Men will ignore the warning. Life will proceed on its normal way, including sinful living. Until without warning the end will come. Only those who are "in Christ" will be saved. All others will be taken away or will be lost forever. This event will mark a great separation (vv. 40-41). Some see this as the rapture of the saints, leaving the lost on the earth. Many competent Bible students hold to this position. But the writer sees only one *second coming of Christ* with a separation of the saved from the lost. In many references in the New Testament mention is made only of the saved being caught up to be with the Lord. But in such passages the emphasis is upon the Christians with no reference to the unsaved. However, by putting all the passages together, the more likely picture seems to involve one coming and one judgment, with the separation of the saved and unsaved described therein. One cannot be dogmatic at this point, but can only interpret it as he sees it. For most Christians one's interpretation of the details of the end of the age is not a test of fellowship or orthodoxy. The fact is sure; the details call for one's own interpretation.

But whatever one's position may be, it is clear that Jesus does teach this separation. Two shall be in the field (father and son?). One will be taken, and the other left (v. 40). Two shall be grinding at the mill (mother and daughter?). The one shall be taken, and the other left (v. 41). We must not press the imagery at every point. For this is a parable. The one clear thought here is separation. For this reason Jesus cautioned us to be watchful or prepared, since we do not know the hour of the Lord's return (v. 42).

Verse 43 involves one of the "thief" passages. The point of this parable is not a *secret* coming but of the unexpectedness of the coming of Christ. Had the "goodman of the house" known, he would have been prepared. We should no more stress the point of the "thief" than that of the man preventing "his house to be broken up." The point is not to try to *prevent* the second coming, but to be ready when it happens.

This is clearly stated in verse 44. "Therefore [because the hour is not known] be ye also ready." "Ye" is written out, and so is emphatic. This is in contrast to the "goodman" who was not prepared. "For in such an hour as ye think not the Son of man cometh."

We agree with Broadus when he notes that this verse alone

should be sufficient to show that the Lord's return will not come at the end of a thousand years of peace and piety. If so, then men could date it. The sum-total of verses 37-42 teaches that the Lord's return will come unexpectedly with no possibility of the time being determined by man.

The closing thoughts in the parables of the "faithful and wise steward" and the "evil servant" are quite evident (vv. 45-51). Those who are prepared will be rewarded according to their faithfulness. Those who are not will be punished according to their unfaithfulness and evil deeds.

So as we conclude this chapter several lessons stand out. The time of the Lord's return and the end of the age is uncertain. The fact of both is certain. The need for readiness is imperative. Failure to be ready is fatal, and eternally so. God grant that we may be "faithful and wise" servants!

Matthew 25

The Valedictory of the King

The message of Chapter 25 is a continuation of the one in Chapter 24. Were it not for the chapter break we would make no division in our thoughts. For Jesus in reality is still speaking of preparedness looking toward the second coming of Christ and the end of the age. The word "then" in verse 1 serves to connect the two chapters. It points forward from the present moment, the first moment, the first or the twentieth centuries, to the consummation of the age.

It was still late on Tuesday afternoon. Jesus and the Twelve were still seated on the Mount of Olives. From John's Gospel we know that some of our Lord's richest teaching is yet to come (Chapters 14-16). But in keeping with his purpose to present Jesus as the King, Matthew closes His formal teaching with the three teachings listed in this chapter. There will be other brief words, but they will be more of an occasional instruction. So we may in a sense regard this chapter as "The Valedictory of the King."

As we follow His thoughts we may consider them as (1) the necessity for preparation; (2) the demand for faithfulness; (3) the principle of judgment.

The Necessity for Preparation (25:1-13)

This truth Jesus taught in the parable of the virgins. And since this is a parable we must be careful not to endeavor to press every detail for some hidden meaning. It is quite clear that Jesus' purpose was to teach the necessity of preparedness when the Lord returns.

The figure is that of a wedding feast, a figure that is used often in the Scriptures to depict the relation of Christ to His people (cf. Rev. 21:2). However, we must let each usage tell its own story. The relationship in this parable is not primarily that of the Bridegroom to the Church as a whole. It depicts the relationship of the individual to Christ.

In order to comprehend this parable we must recall something as to wedding customs among the ancient Jews. When a couple married they did not go on a honeymoon. Instead they remained at home, and for a week held open house with wedding festivities.

To the occasion they invited their chosen friends. If the groom came from another locality the festivities were held in the home of the bride's parents. But if the groom were a local person, his home was the scene of the joyful occasion. It would seem that the latter was the case here. Apparently the bridegroom had gone to the home of the bride's parents to claim his bride, and to take her to his own home for the festivities.

From the one house to the other a joyful procession accompanied the happy couple. But friends might join the procession along the way. Because of the darkness of ancient cities everyone was required to carry a light, either a torch or a lamp. Those without them would not be permitted to join the bridal procession, and so could not enter the bridegroom's house.

Now against this background Jesus said that ten virgins "took their lamps, and went forth to meet the bridegroom" (v. 1). The lamps in question probably were torches with a wooden staff and a dish on top in which was placed a piece of rope or cloth dipped in oil. It was customary for one to carry an extra supply of oil just in case the wick became dry.

Five of these virgins were foolish and five were wise or prudent (v. 2). All took their lamps, but the foolish ones failed to take with them their extra supply of oil (vv. 3-4). Evidently the virgins had not yet lighted their lamps, waiting until they heard the procession approaching. As was so often the case, the bridegroom "tarried" or delayed his coming. So while the virgins waited "they all slumbered and slept" (v. 5). Literally, "they all nodded and went on sleeping."

Suddenly at midnight they were awakened by a cry, "Behold, the bridegroom cometh; go ye out [come ye forth] to meet him" (v. 6). The virgins arose and prepared their lamps for lighting (v. 7). But when the foolish ones lit theirs they cried to the wise, "Give us of your oil; for our lamps are gone out [are going out]" (v. 8). The sputtering flame revealed that the oil in their lamps was exhausted. And they had brought no extra supply. But the wise virgins refused, since they had only oil for themselves. Instead they told the foolish ones to go and buy oil (v. 9). Where they would buy oil at midnight is not stated. This may imply the impossibility of doing so. While they were gone in search of oil, the wise virgins joined the procession and the bridal festivities (v. 10). Later the foolish ones came to the bridegroom's house and repeatedly sought admission, "saying, Lord, Lord, open to us" (v. 11). "Saying" is a feminine form of the present participle *(legousai)* expressing repeated action. But it was too late. The door was shut.

Because of their unpreparedness they had missed their opportunity. For the bridegroom "answered and said, I know you not" (v. 12). "Answered" is an aorist participle, "the one answering." The aorist means that he answered *one time*. It was terse and final.

What is the meaning of this parable? There is no particular significance in the fact that these young women were "virgins." Nor should the number "ten" be pressed. The important fact about them is that five were "foolish" *(mōrai)* and five were "wise" *(phronimoi)*. The former were dull or senseless in that they did not look or plan ahead. The latter were thoughtful or prudent in that they did look and plan ahead. It is significant that in the Greek text the "foolish" ones are mentioned before the "wise" ones. This would appear that the object of the parable is to place the greater emphasis upon the "foolish" virgins or those who were caught unprepared. The "bridegroom" corresponds to Christ Himself. And the wedding festivities are suggestive of His marriage to His bride the Church, an event which comes at the end of the age (cf. Rev. 21:2).

But where do the ten virgins fit into the picture? Plumptre notes that the bride as such is not mentioned in the story. Therefore, we are to think of the virgins and other guests as those who are invited to make up the bride. Barclay sees the immediate significance of the foolish virgins as referring to the Jews who, despite their invitation to become a part of the kingdom of heaven, had made insufficient preparation to do so. This may be true by implication. But the fact is that this was spoken not to the Jews but to the apostles. So evidently the parable has a broader meaning, a meaning for which Barclay allows.

May we not say, therefore, that the ten virgins along with other guests, represent all those who are invited to become a part of the bride of Christ. Certain conditions have been laid down for their doing so. The five wise virgins met these conditions, and the five foolish ones did not. The conditions, of course, are that one shall accept Jesus Christ as King (Lord) and Saviour. Both groups of virgins went out to meet the Bridegroom. So apparently both expected to join in the marriage feast. The fact that the Bridegroom tarried and the virgins "nodded, and kept on sleeping" signifies only the interval of time prior to the second coming of Christ. But when He does come some will be prepared to meet Him and others will not. The preparedness of the one will not suffice for the unpreparedness of the other. Nor can the unprepared in the crisis make preparation. There is no such thing as a gospel of a second chance.

There will come a time when opportunity will be past. The door will be shut. And all of the repeated pleading of the unprepared will be met with the one answer of the Bridegroom, "I know you not." This parable should be a ringing warning to everyone not to presume upon time, opportunity, or the tarrying of the Lord.

A doctor said that he did not know when the Lord would return in power and great glory. But according to the mortality tables He would come for him within the next few years. So for him it was vitally important that he be ready whenever Jesus came, either at the end of the age or at the end of his life.

Jesus closed this parable with His oft-repeated call for preparedness. "Watch [be constantly vigilant, present imperative] therefore, for ye know neither the day nor the hour" (v. 13). The best manuscripts omit "wherein the Son of man cometh." But this is the meaning nevertheless (cf. Matt. 24:44). This is the refrain which runs through all of these parables (cf. Matt. 24:37–25:12). Lack of readiness is inexcusable. Uncertainty as to the time of the end is no excuse for neglect. Rather it is every reason for one to be ready when it occurs.

The Demand for Faithfulness (25:14-30)

The parable of the talents draws upon another facet of ancient life. A man going into a far country handed over his goods or belongings to "his own servants" or slaves (v. 14). He gave them five, two, and one talents respectively, "to each according to his own ability" to use them (v. 15, literal translation). A "talent" was money (cf. 18:24). Immediately after the man's departure the first two began to trade with their talents, and in the course of time doubled them (vv. 16-17). But the third simply buried his one talent in the ground (v. 18). "After a long time" the owner "comes . . . and makes a reckoning" with the slaves (v. 19). Jesus used the historical present to portray vividly the action. The phrase "makes a reckoning" is found in the papyri as a business idiom. Literally it reads, "He takes up an account" with a view to settling it. In the case of the first two slaves they brought the successful results of their labors. And each received the same commendation, for each had been equally successful with that which had been entrusted to him (vv. 20-23). Each was termed a "good and faithful servant." "Enter thou into the joy of thy lord" could mean that they were invited to join in the feast given at the master's return. Or it could be that they shared with him the joy over a job well done.

"Then" (v. 24) sets the third slave over against the others. So in reality he is the main point of the story. Instead of reporting a successful venture he began to make excuses (vv. 24-25). Not once did he blame himself. The blame he sought to heap upon his master. Literally he said, "Lord, knowing you that you are a hard man, reaping where you did not sow, and gathering whence you did not winnow, and being afraid within myself, going forth I hid your talent in the earth: behold, you have your own." He accused his master of being ruthless and dishonest. The word "hard" *(sklēros)* is found on an inscription in the phrase "both inhuman and harsh." And while the servant did not use the word "inhuman" this phrase serves to color his accusation. The slave himself was not dishonest. He did not squander the talent. He simply did not use it. He returned it exactly as he had received it.

But note the master's reply (vv. 26-28). He called the slave a "wicked and slothful servant." The word "slothful" means to be slow or "pokey" (Robertson). We would say "lazy." So laziness is wickedness. The slave did not steal the talent, but he robbed his owner of any expected return from it. Note that the master did not challenge the slave's accusations. This does not mean that they were true. But the owner condemned the slave with his own words. Even if the things which he said were true, he should at least have put the money in the bank where it would have drawn interest. Instead, he had buried it in the ground where it had remained idle.

So the owner ordered the one talent taken from the wicked and lazy slave, and given to the one who had ten (vv. 28-29). The man who shoulders responsibility will receive more, and with it a greater opportunity. But the one who shirks responsibility loses the corresponding opportunity.

Instead of the "unprofitable" or *useless* servant being invited into the brightly lighted banquet hall, he is cast into outer darkness (v. 30). He does not share in his owner's joy of achievement. Instead he spends the rest of his life in the sorrow of a wasted opportunity.

So much for the "earthly story." What is its "heavenly meaning?" It is evident that the owner is the Lord Himself. His going away is the Lord's return to heaven, and the return is the Second Coming. "After a long time" is the interval in between these events. Which within itself negates the thought of some that Jesus expected His return to be in that generation. The *reckoning* suggests the judgment at the end of the age.

But what are we to understand by the "servants?" Again, in keeping with his position, Barclay sees the wicked servant as the Jews who missed their opportunity to enter into the kingdom of heaven. And likewise it can be said that this is true only by implication. For the Lord was looking beyond that moment across the sweep of time to the end of the age. So the lesson involves more than the Jews alone.

Note that all three slaves were "his own slaves," not children but slaves. All men belong to the Lord by right of His creation, providential care, and redemption. But only those are truly His in the spiritual sense who have willingly given themselves to Him in faith. So in essence Jesus said that each of these slaves proved his real relationhip by the character which he displayed in his works. Through the gospel the Lord extends equal opportunity to all men, to each according to his own ability. We should not become so involved in the several amounts and values of the talents as to lose the lesson contained in the story. The lesson is not money but character. The first two servants already loved their owner and were loyal to him. The talents only afforded them an opportunity to demonstrate them. The third slave despised and feared his owner. His talent served only to illustrate that fact. While the master claimed him as his slave, the slave in his heart did not claim or submit to him as his master. So the master's punishment was his recognition of that condition which the slave's actions had proved.

Thus Jesus said that through the ages men will prove their true relationship to Him by the attitudes shown in their works for Him. Those who show evidence of Christian character will enter into heaven, "into the joy of thy Lord." Those whose works prove the absence of Christian character will be cast into hell. This does not in any sense teach that some who are once saved will later be lost. The main point of the parable is that by his attitude and character the evil servant was never truly a servant of the Lord. He *belonged* to Him by the forced ownership of creation. But he was not His by a willing submission of love and loyalty to His will.

Those in heaven will enjoy heaven to the full extent of their ability to do so. And this ability is now being determined by their faithfulness to the Lord. But all will be supremely happy. And it will not be a happiness of idleness. Each one in heaven will continue to work with and for the Lord in whatever way He shall design. And each according to his ability as proved in this life. This very achievement speaks of the degrees of happiness or reward in heaven. But the wicked one will be no part of this. He will be in "outer darkness" where "there shall be weeping and gnashing of teeth." A preacher said that one of the worst sufferings in hell will be for one to know what God is doing and to know that he will never be a part of it.

One further word remains to be said about this parable. We must not press the point, but it is highly suggestive as to the number of words in the Greek text used by the servants in their reports. The two faithful ones used *ten* words each. The useless servant used *thirty*. (In English, KJV, the numbers are *sixteen* and *forty-three* respectively.) The two needed only ten words to report their success and faithfulness. The third needed thirty words to try to explain his failure and unfaithfulness. And it was to no avail. In the final judgment Christ will not be interested in excuses but results. Every man should ponder long and carefully this truth.

The Principle of Judgment (25:31-46)

It is most fitting that Jesus should conclude His formal teaching (in Matthew) with this sublime scene of the final judgment. And it forms a glorious climax to Matthew's Gospel up to this point. It was his purpose to present Jesus Christ as King. Now we see the King sitting "upon the throne of his glory" (v. 31). It is customary to call this passage the *parable* of the sheep and goats. But is it a parable in the truest sense of the word? The parable (vv. 32c-33) serves only to illustrate the divine scene which Jesus portrays. It was/is a common sight in Palestine at the close of day to see the shepherd separating the sheep from the goats. So Jesus said that this would be the case at the end of the age. The saved will be separated from the lost (cf. 24:40-41). These things stand out in this scene: (1) the fact of judgment; (2) the results of the judgment; (3) the principle of judgment. And the last one seems to be foremost in the mind of the King.

"When the Son of man shall come in his glory . . . then shall he sit upon the throne of his glory" (v. 31). Notice that Jesus uses *hotan* ("when") which expresses *condition,* not time. Whenever that condition obtains the Son of man will return. And it will be a glorious return. His first coming was an inglorious one according to worldly standards. For that reason many refused Him. They looked for the very kind of coming which will be true of His second coming. But then for them it will be too late. When He came the first time men, by their wills, could either receive Him or reject Him. But no choice will be given at His second coming. For all will be required to stand before Him in judgment.

"And before him shall be gathered all nations: and he shall separate them one from another" (v. 32). There are those who see this as one of several judgments, calling this the "Judgment of the Nations." Some even hold that the standard of judgment will be how these nations have treated the Jews (cf. v. 40, "my brethren").

But these positions seem to press the details out of a reasonable meaning. God judges nations as nations within the context of history, and not at the end of the age. And apart from the one reference to "all nations" the emphasis soon flows into a judgment of individuals. The meaning of this wording is simply that all people, Jews and Gentiles, who have ever lived upon the earth will be gathered together for one final judgment. And they will be separated to the right and left even as a shepherd divides the sheep from the goats.

"Then," after the separation, "shall the King say unto them on his right hand" (v. 34). Note that the "Son of man" is now "the King." "Come, ye blessed of my Father, inherit the kingdom prepared for you from the foundation of the world" (v. 34). Like the wise virgins and the faithful servants, the "blessed of my Father" enter into the glory and joy of heaven. It is into a kingdom prepared for all who will receive the King. And it was prepared or made ready "from the foundation of the world" (*kosmos*). How was it prepared? Through the redemptive work of God in Christ. While in history the cross loomed just before Jesus, in the cosmic sense He was "the Lamb slain from the foundation of the world" (Rev. 13:8). That which was accomplished in the heart of God in eternity was wrought out in history. Redemption was in the heart of God before sin was in the heart of man. But while the kingdom was "prepared for you," it is quite clear that it was prepared only for those who are *prepared* or fit for the kingdom.

On what basis did the King say, "Come, ye blessed of my Father?" "For I was an hungered, and ye gave me meat [gave me to eat]: I was thirsty, and ye gave me drink: I was a stranger, and ye took me in: naked, and ye clothed me: I was in prison, and ye came unto me" (vv. 35-36). Plumptre notes that this passage furnishes six out of the seven corporal works of mercy in Christian ethics, the seventh being the care of the fatherless (cf. James 1:27).

Two of these call for special mention. "I was a stranger [*xenos*], and ye took me in." Foreigners were quite often treated roughly in that time. The papyri gives evidence of this fact. A man wrote a letter home saying that he was despised by everyone "because I am a stranger" (*xenos*). Another wrote, "Do not be anxious about me because I am away from home, for I am personally acquainted with these places and am not a stranger here." So to treat a stranger kindly was evidence of one's benevolent character. In the case of the sick the word "visited" means more than a mere visit. It includes the thought of *looking after* the sick.

There will be surprises at the judgment. For the ones on the right hand, the righteous or justified ones, will ask when they had done all of these things (vv. 37-39). When had they so ministered to the King? For most of them would never have seen Him in the flesh. And then the King shall answer, "Inasmuch as ye have done it unto one of the least of these my brethren, ye have done it unto me" (v. 40). "My brethren" should not be construed to refer to the Jews, Jesus' kindred in the flesh. He Himself had said that relationship to Him was to be determined not on a genetical but on a spiritual basis (cf. Matt. 12:48-50). One might press these words to mean only Christians. But even this would seem to limit the thought of Jesus. In His own ministry of mercy Jesus did not limit Himself to either Jews or Christians. He ministered to the poor, sick, and needy whoever they were and wherever He found them. So it is more proper to understand Jesus to say that He identifies Himself with the needy and suffering altogether. And to minister unto them is to minister unto Him. This conduct was proof that the "righteous" loved Christ and followed Him. Had they been with Him in the flesh, and had He needed their ministry in person (of course He was never sick), they would have given it unto Him. But they had ministered to Him in their ministry to others. It is this spirit through the centuries which has ministered to the needy and suffering in Christ's name.

"Then shall he say also unto them on the left hand, Depart from me, ye cursed, into everlasting fire, prepared for the devil and his angels (v. 41). Note the contrast between "blessed" (v. 34) and "cursed" (v. 41). Furthermore, note that the former will receive "the kingdom prepared for *you*" (author's italics). But the latter are to depart "into everlasting fire, prepared for the *devil* and his *angels*" (author's italics). It was not *prepared* for the souls of men, but for the devil and his angels. This does not mean that some souls will not be there. It simply means that God did not prepare hell for that purpose. He prepared the kingdom for all of His children; He wants all men to become His children; all of His children will be there. But none of the devil's children will be in heaven. In his natural state man is a child of the devil (cf. John 8:44). Such can become a child of God only by receiving Christ as his Saviour (cf. John 1:12), whereby he is born again with a new nature as a child of God (cf. John 3:3). If a man goes to hell it is his choice, not God's. Someone put it picturesquely when he said that God will take all of His children to His house, and will send all of the devil's children to their father's house.

There is another way of looking at this matter. Jesus often used *Gehenna,* the garbage dump of Jerusalem, as a figure of hell. It would seem that He employed that imagery in "everlasting fire" in verse 41. If man has a garbage dump into which he casts all that is useless, may we not assume that God does the same? In Matthew 25:30 the words "unprofitable servant" actually mean "useless servant." So hell is God's cosmic garbage dump into which He casts all that is dead and useless.

And this thought blends into the basis upon which the King said, "Depart from me . . . into everlasting fire." For the King said this to them because they had *not* done the very things which the righteous *had* done (vv. 42-43). Nothing is said about vicious evil. It was what they had *not done.* A. T. Robertson notes that the repetition of the negative particles *ou* and *ouk* (five times) in verses 42-43 is like clods falling on a coffin. Like the "righteous" the unrighteous also will be surprised. They will ask as to when they failed to do these things (v. 44). Again the King will identify Himself with the needy and suffering (v. 45). And as the unrighteous failed to minister to them they failed to minister to Christ. Had they been with Him in the flesh they would have ignored Him personally.

So for these reasons Jesus said, "And these shall go away into everlasting punishment: but the righteous into life eternal" (v. 46). It is strange how some students of the Scripture try to tone down "everlasting punishment." Actually the word "punishment" (*kolasin*) comes from *kolazō,* to mutilate or prune. So they seize upon this thought to hold that that to which Jesus referred was a penal pruning or purgatory looking toward the time in eternity when even these shall enter into the kingdom. But they ignore altogether the fact that Jesus said "everlasting" punishment. It is the same word (*aiōnion*) as is used with "life" in the same verse. So if they are consistent they will limit "life" as they limit "punishment." The word *aiōnios* is as strong a word as the Greek language possesses to express that which is unending. We should remember that this is the King speaking. To discredit His words is to discredit Him. We would be wise to let the language say what it says, and to leave the matter with Him.

Looking back upon this climactic scene one question calls for consideration. What is to be the principle employed in the final judgment? Did Jesus mean to say that men will be saved by their good works and lost because of a lack of such? In the light of the overall teachings of the New Testament this cannot be the meaning of His words. What, then, do they mean?

We can best answer this question by examining two words: "blessed" (v. 34) and "cursed" (v. 41). Both are perfect passive participles: *eulogēmenoi,* the ones having been blessed; *katēramenoi,* the ones having been cursed. Both express an action performed by another in the past and which continues as a completed state. So the *being blessed* and *being cursed* are not things which will take place at the judgment. They will already have been accomplished prior to the judgment and will continue thereafter as a finished state. In their natural state of sin all men abide under the wrath of a holy and righteous God. But God set forth the condition by which every man may be saved or redeemed from his sinful nature: conviction of sin, repentance from sin, and faith in Jesus Christ as one's Saviour. Thereby one receives a new nature or character. The moment that this happens one is "blessed," a state which is a finished condition. But one who does not receive this new nature continues to abide under God's wrath, and at death there is no possibility of a change in condition (cf. John 3:18). So all men will come to the judgment with a nature or character determined not by good works or the lack of them, but by one's relation to Jesus Christ. The *works* or lack of them will reveal the kind of character which each one possesses. "Ye shall know them by their fruits" (Matt. 7:16).

So the final judgment will not determine character; it will reveal it. The King will not arbitrarily say to one, "Come," and to another, "Depart." The shepherd does not so act (vv. 32-33). He sets the sheep on the right because they are sheep. He sets the goats on the left because they are goats. Sheep with the sheep and goats with the goats, each according to its nature. And the King also separates men in the judgment according to character, a character which is already there but which will be revealed by their works.

A man does not have a good character because he does good works. He does good works because he has a good character. The same holds for the unrighteous. He is not unrighteous because he does not perform righteous works. He does not perform righteous works because he is unrighteous. The former performs the works of Christ because he has the nature of Christ. The latter does not perform the works of Christ because he does not have the nature of Christ.

Actually this truth runs throughout Matthew 25. The foolish virgins did not have the character of the Bridegroom. Therefore, they were unprepared. The useless servant did not possess the character of the Master. Therefore, he was unfaithful. The "cursed" did not have the character of the King. Therefore, they did not perform the work commensurate with the King's nature. And the opposite is true of the wise virgins, the faithful servants, and the "blessed of the Father."

So the preparation for which the Saviour calls is inward. But its presence or absence will be demonstrated by the outward evidence. This is a challenge not only for inner purity but for outward performance, not according to rote rules but according to Christian character. The only way to have such is through absolute commitment and loyalty to Christ.

The King has spoken, and we must answer. What will your answer be?

Matthew 26

The Tribulation of the King

The teaching was over, and now the King turned toward the cross. So we enter into what is called the Passion of the Lord. That this was of supreme importance in the minds of the Evangelists is seen in the fact that all four Gospels join in relating the remainder of the story, each in his own way and according to his particular purpose. Except for occasional references to the other Gospels, we shall confine ourselves to *Matthew*.

One thing to be noted throughout this account is that Jesus died as a King. He was not suddenly caught up in a maelstrom of fury and hate which He was helpless to contain. While those who were involved in Jesus' death are not free from guilt, the King was in control throughout. They will kill Him according to their evil designs. But while they will regard Him as a criminal, He will die as a King. A king represents his people. So the King will die in the place of all who dwell under the shadow of death.

Evidence that the King was in control is seen in the fact that on Tuesday afternoon He correctly predicted the date of His death on Friday (v. 2). For six months He had clearly pointed to the event. Now He named the date. He was the King all the way!

As we enter into the tribulation of the King let us note the following events: (1) the betrayal of the King; (2) the Supper of the King; (3) the agony of the King; (4) the arraignment of the King.

The Betrayal of the King (26:3-16)

The black storm clouds were gathering even as Jesus taught His disciples on the Mount of Olives. For the Sanhedrin had gathered to plot His death (vv. 3-5). The day of controversy had ended in the utter defeat of these enemies of Jesus. Since they could not defeat Him with words they had but two choices. Either they could acknowledge Him as the King-Messiah or else they could destroy Him. They chose the latter course. So they counselled together how they might seize Jesus quietly and kill him (v. 4). They would bide their opportunity and take Him without the knowledge of the people if possible. It was agreed that they would wait until after the Passover. The people were always restless at this time, as seen in the fact that the Roman governor during this week always came from Caesarea to Jerusalem personally with additional troops. One thing Rome would not condone and that was a mob scene or uproar. The chief priests did not want this to happen lest it endanger their own position. So they plotted and waited.

It may seem strange that Matthew would introduce so ominous an event as Jesus' betrayal with the joyful scene of a supper honoring Jesus in the home of a friend. But this supper was a vital link in the chain of events. For even on this happy occasion the forces which gathered about Jesus were evident. These were His friends who, while not yet comprehending all that was involved, were concerned, sympathetic, but bewildered. And then even in this intimate company itself the hand of hate reached forth to seize Him.

Jesus spent Tuesday night, all of Wednesday, and the greater part of Thursday in Bethany or its environs, probably as a guest in the house of Martha, Mary, and Lazarus. On Tuesday night He was a guest at supper in the home of Simon the leper (v. 6). This supper has been the source of great conjecture among the scholars. Some see it as the same supper which is related in Luke 7. But there are many differences between the two. There is no reason why we should identify them. John places this event on Saturday evening shortly after the close of the Sabbath (12:2-8). But this is probably due to the fact that that was his final mention of Bethany, and he thought that the supper was of sufficient importance to be recorded. In fact it is his account of the supper which makes its relationship to subsequent events understandable. In all probability Mark and Matthew are correct in their chronology which places it on Tuesday evening.

During the feast a nameless woman (in Mark and Matthew) came bearing an alabaster box (cruse) of "very precious ointment" (v. 7). Matthew does not name the kind of ointment. But Mark and John say that it was "spikenard" or *nard.* Matthew implies this since he says that it was very costly. *Nard* was considered as a gift fit for a king. Herodotus lists it as one of five gifts sent by Cambyses to the king of Ethiopia. Evidently it was one of the choice possessions of this woman. Therefore, hers was an act of great love as she broke the cruse and poured the ointment on the head of Jesus (v. 7). John notes that she poured it on His feet, and then wiped them with her hair. This adds to the picture of tender love. There is no reason why she could not have poured it on both Jesus' head and feet.

When the disciples saw this they were indignant, saying, "To what purpose is this waste?" (v. 8). The word for "waste" means ruin, destruction, or a "dead loss" (Robertson). Pliny wrote that the indulgence in costly perfume is more luxurious than in gems or garments, since it perishes with the using. It is understandable, therefore, why these pragmatic men would think that this act was a waste. It might have been sold and used for relieving the poor (v. 9), so they said. Thus we see something of their crusted natures. Apparently they still had not caught the significance of Jesus' words about His impending death. If they had, then their words are all the more inexcusable. For no cost should be considered in carrying out an act of love for a loved one who is about to die.

But Jesus rebuked them strongly. "Why trouble [beat with your words and attitude] ye the woman? for she hath wrought a good [*kalon*, beautiful] work upon me" (v. 10). She had expressed her personality in her own way, and the disciples, despite their misunderstanding, should leave her free to do so. It is so cruel for us to criticize the actions of others when we are incapable of judging them.

The poor? There are always the poor to be ministered to. "But me ye have not always," said Jesus (v. 11). Thus He related this act of love to the needs of the moment. Even if the Twelve did not understand, He did. She had anointed His body for burial before His death (v. 12). It is so comforting to realize that while men may not understand our acts of love for the Lord, and criticize us for them, there is One who does understand and who approves.

Then Jesus spoke some of the most beautiful words that He ever uttered. "Wheresoever this gospel shall be preached in the whole world, there shall also this, that this woman hath done, be told for a memorial of her" (v. 13). This shows how much this act of love meant to Jesus at a time when hatred toward Him was racing toward its most dastardly deed. A memorial unto her. Not a memorial in stone but in the terms of tenderest love. And whereas memorials in stone will perish under the ravages of time, time only serves to enlarge and make more beautiful this mysterious act of unbridled and unselfish devotion of one tender and delicate woman.

"Then one of the twelve, called Judas Iscariot, went unto the chief priests" (v. 14). Such a jarring note in a symphony of indescribable beauty! And yet it is the very point of Matthew's recording of this event. Because it was from the supper in Simon's house that Judas went on his evil errand. We can understand this only as we consider Matthew's account in the light of John's record of the same event.

In his account Matthew omits all personal names except those of the host and guest. Certainly Jesus and possibly Simon the leper had passed from the earthly scene at the time when Matthew wrote. If the other guests were still living, to have mentioned their names might have subjected them to the danger of persecution or intimidation by the Jews. This could possibly explain Matthew's omission of personal names. But John wrote late in the first century, sometime after A.D. 80. By that time all those involved in this event probably were dead. Therefore, he felt free to mention them by name. Furthermore, one of John's purposes in writing was to supplement the other Gospels by recording events omitted by the others and by filling in details not given in other events where he parallels the others. Therefore, in his account of this supper John mentions the presence of Martha and Lazarus (12:2). He identifies the woman who anointed Jesus as Mary (12:3). It is fitting that he should do so. For but for John the memorial to this wonderful deed would have been nameless. Furthermore, John points out that the complaint against Mary's deed was uttered by Judas Iscariot (12:4). Apparently he initiated the criticism and was joined by the other apostles. Furthermore, John helps us to understand Matthew 26:14. It was evidently the sting of Jesus' rebuke which prompted Judas to seek out the chief priests with a view to betraying Jesus.

The question naturally arises as to why Jesus chose Judas as one of the Twelve. For whatever it may be worth it is of interest to note that Judas was the only one of the Twelve who came from Judea. Outside of the Gospels we know nothing about him other than speculation. Some hold that he may have been an unsuccessful business man in Jerusalem since he seems to have known his way about the city. It is evident that he entertained ideas of grandeur and greatness. So when Jesus came preaching a kingdom he attached himself to this new Teacher, possibly thinking that he might achieve a place of prominence in this kingdom. At any rate when Jesus chose His twelve apostles Judas was among them. Did Jesus choose him for the purpose of betrayal? Some insist that He did. But if this be true then it violates all that we know about God's dealings with men. No man is a puppet on the strings of fate. Each man is a personality endowed with the right of choice.

And while Jesus knew one year before the deed that Judas would betray Him (John 6:70-71), this does not mean that Judas was not responsible for his deed (cf. Matt. 26:24). We must not malign the character of God in an effort to clear the character of Judas. There is absolutely no evidence in the Scriptures that Judas was ever a Christian. He was a follower of Jesus in name only. He never did give his heart and loyalty to Him. Of course, the whole affair of this man poses problems which are too deep for human minds to plumb. We can only judge by the fruits of his life. Why Jesus chose him will ever remain a mystery. But there are some things about which we can speculate in search for an answer.

When Jesus chose the Twelve it appears that each possessed certain qualities which if dedicated to Jesus would be of value in the Kingdom. The fact that Judas was intrusted with the meagre funds of the Twelve would seem to indicate that he possessed certain business ability (cf. John 13:29). However, he never did dedicate it to Jesus, but used it for his own selfish purposes (cf. John 12:6). There is good reason to believe that Judas was the moving force in precipitating the crisis of trying to force Jesus to become a political Messiah (cf. John 6:15). It could be that it was his inordinate ambition which produced wrangling among the Twelve as to which should be the greatest in the kingdom. At any rate we do know that sometime after Jesus' royal entry into Jerusalem Judas resolved to betray Him. The secrecy surrounding the arrangements for this event suggests that Jesus was aware of Judas' growing resentment over what seemed to him to be frustration as to Jesus' program of action. Evidently he thought that the King had missed His one grand opportunity of establishing His kingdom when He did not do so following the royal entry. The subsequent events probably led him to conclude that Jesus would be destroyed by His enemies. If so, then all of his dreams of grandeur and glory would come to nothing. This realization only served to deepen his resentment and hatred toward Jesus. It is even suggested by some that Judas had good but ill-advised intentions in betraying Jesus. Perhaps He needed a push. If he created a crisis maybe that would cause Jesus to declare His Kingship in accord with Judas' own ideas about it. However, this is only speculation with no basis of fact. The entire picture of this man points in another direction altogether.

The supper scene in Bethany seems to give us the best clue as to why Judas betrayed Jesus. It would appear that Mary and Judas, strangely enough, were the first two people about Jesus to realize fully that He was going to be crucified. Perhaps Mary had heard from some of the Twelve Jesus' words as recorded in Matthew 26:2. Judas certainly had heard them, and his conniving mind agreed that recent events pointed in that direction. Through connections in Jerusalem he may have known about the session of the Sanhedrin recorded in John 11:47-53. It is hardly possible that he knew of the meeting held that very day (Matt. 26:3-5). Jesus' words at the supper with respect to His "burial" (v. 12) would have confirmed any thoughts in Judas' mind.

When Mary and Judas realized that Jesus was soon to die, each asked a question in keeping with her/his nature. Mary, a delicate woman of boundless love for Jesus, probably mused thusly. "He is going to die. I cannot prevent it. The best that I can do is to try to express my love for Him and possibly to relieve His spiritual suffering through an act of understanding. *What can I do for Jesus?*" And so she anointed Him for burial, using the most precious thing which she possessed. Judas, a man of conniving selfishness, mused otherwise. "Jesus is going to die. I have left all to follow Him in hopes of using Him to satisfy my own ambition. Repeatedly I have tried to get Him to declare Himself, but to no avail. He is not a King, but only an idle dreamer. It seems that He is going to die, and there is nothing that I can do about it. But out of the debacle I may as well try to salvage something for myself. *What can Jesus do for me?*" And so he bargained to sell Him for whatever he could get.

This may be mere imagination on the part of the writer. But the end result in both cases is true nevertheless. For Mary did anoint Jesus for His burial. And Judas did betray Him into the hands of His enemies.

So Judas went to the chief priests with his proposal. Literally he said, "What are you willing to give to me, and I will hand him over to you?" (v. 15). The chief priests had not counted upon treachery within the ranks of Jesus' own little band. But they seized upon the opportunity. It was now unnecessary to wait until after the Passover. So they readily accepted Judas' offer. It is a sad sight to see religious leaders acting thusly. It was a dark hour indeed! But they showed their utter contempt for both Jesus and Judas in the amount of their offer. "Thirty pieces of silver." The price of a slave (cf. Exod. 21:32; Zech. 11:12). It was less than twenty-five dollars! Judas most likely could have gotten more had he held out for a higher price. But so greedy was he that the thought of money blotted out all reason from both his soul and mind. "And from that time he sought opportunity to betray him" (v. 16).

The Supper of the King (26:17-35)

Jesus probably spent Wednesday quietly resting, meditating, and praying. On Thursday morning, the first day of the feast of unleavened bread, the disciples inquired as to where Jesus wished to observe the feast (v. 17). He replied, "Go into the city to such a man, and say unto him, The Master saith, My time is at hand; I will keep the passover at thy house with my disciples" (v. 18). There is every evidence that, like the donkey incident (Matt. 21:2-3), Jesus had made previous arrangements privately. The betrayer must not know Jesus' movements in advance until He was ready to die. The words "such a man" (*ton deina*) are found in the papyri in our sense of "Mr. X." Modern Greek so uses them. Thus Jesus did not name the man. Furthermore, Mark and Luke note that Jesus told them (Luke says "Peter and John") to go into the city where they would see a man carrying a pitcher of water. They were to follow him to a house (cf. Mark 14:13ff.). It was there that they were to speak the words recorded in Matthew. Water carrying was a woman's task. So a man doing this could be readily identified. This evidently was a sign which Jesus had arranged with "Mister X." The home was probably that of Mary, the mother of John Mark.

Specific preparations were required for the Passover meal. Certain food was necessary: unleavened bread, bitter herbs, wine (cf. Matt. 26:29). At the time of Jesus certain sweet fruit preserves were also used. In addition to purchasing these it was necessary also to purchase a lamb. This would have to be approved by, the priests as being without blemish, and then slain by them in the courts of the Temple. This was done during the afternoon of the 14th of Nisan. The lamb was then roasted, and the food prepared on the table in the guest room (v. 19).

Shortly after sunset at the beginning of the 15th of Nisan Jesus and the remainder of the Twelve arrived at the appointed place (v. 20). Luke and John record certain events at this point which are omitted by Matthew (e.g. the disciples' struggle for the chief places and Jesus' washing the disciples' feet). The very atmosphere was charged with emotion for Jesus (cf. Luke 22:15). It was His last Passover meal with the Twelve. But even though He walked under the shadow of the cross, He had a consuming desire to eat it with them. Though Jesus had ignored the traditions of the Jews, He did not neglect the true religious duties of His people.

Furthermore, He planned to use this Passover meal as the occasion to inaugurate a greater *meal* which would commemorate an even greater deliverance.

Presently this little company was reclining on couches about the table as they ate the meal. Jesus had probably recounted the significance of Israel's deliverance from Egypt.

Now the disciples likely were engaged in the usual conversation which accompanies such festive occasions. When suddenly Jesus tossed a bombshell into their midst. "Verily I say unto you, that one of you shall betray me" (v. 21). It was a solemn and sobering utterance. It would seem that, apart from Judas, such a thought had not entered into their minds. And while Jesus had known that this would be true, even had alluded to it in a veiled fashion, He had not mentioned it before. But now this terrible truth was out. Evidently Jesus was aware of Judas' bargain. At least He knew that it was in his heart. Also knowing that the "hour" was near, there was no need to hide the fact any longer.

The disciples' exceeding sorrow was combined with their excitement. A buzz went about the table as they asked which of them would do such a thing (cf. Luke 22:23). Each began to look at the other with questioning glances (cf. John 13:22). Presently one after another they began to ask, "Lord, is it I?" (v. 22). Actually the question is preceded by the negative particle *mēti,* which invites a negative answer. Literally, "It is not I, is it, Lord?"

They had not thought of doing such a thing. Yet how little one really knows himself. Most of us can look back upon things that we have done, which at a previous time we thought that we would never do. Hopefully the disciples asked for a negative reply, but they were not sure. How we should search our own motives in the light of Jesus' declaration!

In response to their questions Jesus said, "He that dippeth his hand with me in the dish, the same shall betray me" (v. 23). A bowl of gravy was placed on the table into which all might dip their bread. So this did not point out any particular person. But it served to show the intimacy which would be betrayed. Then Jesus stated that the betrayal was necessary that God's purpose might be accomplished. But that did not absolve the one who did it. His choice would be his own, and he must bear the guilt (v. 25).

Up to this point Judas had been silent. But lest his very silence betray him, he asked, "Master, is it I?" (v. 25). He asked exactly the same question, even to the negative particle *mēti*—with one exception. He did not call Jesus "Lord" but "Rabbi." He acknowledged Him only as a *teacher,* but not as his *Lord.* Even then he invited a negative answer. Though he knew that he was the betrayer, he was hoping against hope that Jesus did not yet know it. But the Lord answered, "Thou hast said." Was this because Judas had used the word "Rabbi" instead of "Lord?" At least, even though the other disciples did not know, Judas knew that Jesus knew.

John records at this point that *the beloved disciple* was leaning on Jesus' bosom in the choicest place about the table (13:23-26). Peter caught his attention, asking him to ascertain the identity of the betrayer. Jesus' reply to this inquiry was "He it is, to whom I shall give a sop, when I have dipped." And He did so to Judas. For the host to do this for a guest was to show him a special honor. Was this one last generous gesture on Jesus' part to call Judas back from his evil purpose? At any rate it is evident that, apart from the beloved disciple (John), no one else knew except Judas. Had they known it is doubtful that he would have gotten out of the room alive. But even if Jesus did extend one last appeal to Judas, it was wasted effort. Now that Jesus knew, there was no reason for pretending further. So John records that at this point Judas left the room to hasten on his errand of treachery (13:30).

This is an important point to consider. For none of the other Gospels records this fact. It was for this reason that John added this note when he wrote his Gospel. He supplemented the other accounts to show clearly that Judas was not present when Jesus instituted the Last Supper. No unregenerated person is eligible to come to the Lord's table. Christian groups generally agree that only those who have been baptized should partake of the Lord's Supper (cf. Acts 2:41-42). But another note needs to be added. Only baptized *believers* should do so. Judas had been baptized so far as we know. But he was not a *believer.* We are indebted to John for clarity at this point.

Following the departure of Judas Jesus instituted the Memorial Supper or the Lord's Supper. "Jesus took bread, and blessed it, and brake it, and gave it to his disciples, and said, Take, eat, this is my body. And he took the cup [a cup], and gave thanks, and gave it to them, saying. Drink ye all of it; for this is my blood of the [new] testament, which is shed for many for the remission of sins" (vv. 26-28).

How simple! And yet how profound! As they were eating Jesus simply took one of the passover wafers, blessed it, broke it into small pieces, and gave one to each of the Eleven. There is no spiritual significance in the fact that He *broke* it. The word "broken" in I Corinthians 11:24 is not in the best texts. As a matter of fact John points out that the body of Jesus was not "broken" on the cross (19:33,36). In accord with prophecy it was "pierced" (19:37) but not broken. Then He took a cup and passed it among the disciples. His instructions were to eat the bread and drink from the cup (cf. v. 29).

"This is my body... this is my blood" (vv. 26, 28). It is amazing the ideas and practices which have been derived from these simple words. It is out of keeping with the character of Jesus for Him to have intended them to be magical formulae by which these simple elements were transubstantiated into His actual body and blood, or that they were present with those elements. It is contrary to the spiritual religion which He taught to see them as becoming some *fetish* or object of worship. These elements were no more the actual body and blood of our Lord than the lamb's flesh was the actual lambs which were slain in Egypt preceding the first *passover*. They were but symbols to remind the followers of Christ through the ages of that which Jesus did for their redemption. They are what Bruce calls "a beautifully simple, pathetic, and poetic symbol of his death."

Jesus specifically pointed out the cup as symbolic or a remembrance of "my blood of the covenant" (v. 28). The word "new" is not genuine in either Matthew or Mark 14:24. It is highly questionable in Luke 22:20. But it is unquestioned in I Corinthians 11:25. It is probable that the word was added by copyists to bring the Gospel accounts into line with Paul's account. But whether the word "new" appears or not, it is evident that it is implied. For here Jesus spoke of sealing the new covenant promised in Jeremiah 31:31ff., the fulfilment of which is discussed in Hebrews 8-9. However the significance of the absence of "new" in Matthew and Mark (probably Luke) is seen in that Jesus quoted from Exodus 24:8, "the blood of the covenant," the Mosaic Covenant. But in the Gospels Jesus said, "My blood of the covenant." "My blood" is in the emphatic position, which contrasts it with the blood of animals under the old covenant.

The words "for [*eis,* unto, with respect to] the remission of sins" are found only in Matthew. But they express a truth involved in all of the accounts. Jesus was not merely a teacher of ethical principles. In these words He clearly saw His death on the cross as necessary and the means for the removal of the sins of men.

This simple ordinance is one of two (baptism) which Jesus gave to His people to portray in symbolism that which He did for the salvation of men. In baptism (*baptisma,* the meaning of baptism, not the act; cf. Rom. 6:3-5) the believer symbolizes Jesus' death, burial, and resurrection; the death of the believer to sin, his burial, and resurrection to walk in a new life in Christ; and his faith in the final resurrection from the dead. In the Supper he symbolizes and remembers the body and blood of the Lord as a sacrifice for his sins; proclaims the Lord's death for sin; and portrays his faith in the second coming of Christ (cf. I Cor. 11:25-26).

From the New Testament it is evident that New Testament baptism is an initiatory ordinance, and should therefore be administered one time for each believer. (We do not go into the matter of what constitutes New Testament *baptism*.) But the Lord's Supper is an ordinance to be observed repeatedly and periodically. Jesus did not say how often this should be done. At first the early Christians probably observed it daily (cf. Acts 2:42) and then on the first day of the week (cf. Acts 20:7). But Jesus did say "as oft" as we do it it should be a "remembrance" (cf. I Cor. 11:25). So it is a memorial Supper. It is a communion, not between Christians, but between the believer and his Lord (cf. I Cor. 10:16-17, note v. 20 where "fellowship," *koinōnia*, is the same word as "communion"). It bestows no grace, but its observance should provide an occasion for self-examination and reconsecration of one's entire being to Christ.

Matthew 26:29 affords us some interesting thoughts. Jesus said, "I will not drink henceforth of this fruit of the vine, until that day when I drink it new with you in my Father's kingdom." While Jesus ate with His disciples after the resurrection, there is no record that after this night He ever drank "the fruit of the vine" with them. Thus He made it clear once again that His kingdom is not of this world. It is a spiritual kingdom, His "Father's kingdom." And while the Memorial Supper shall cease at His second coming ("till he come," I Cor. 11:26. There will be no further need for a *memorial* Supper), Jesus foresaw that it will give way in His "Father's kingdom" to festivities and joy embodied in the marriage feast of the Bridegroom.

But how may we understand "the fruit of the vine"? Did Jesus use actual wine in instituting this Supper? The word "wine" does not appear in the New Testament with reference to this event. It is implied from the contents of the "cup." Lightfoot notes that one of the prayers offered at the Passover was "Blessed art thou Jehovah our God, who hast created the fruit of the vine." But are we to understand this as the intoxicating beverage commonly called "wine"? The words for "wine" in both Hebrew and Greek were used to denote the beverage in various stages of fermentation. In fact the Hebrew word is sometimes used for the juice while it was still in the grape (cf. also Matt. 21:33). Strictly speaking "the fruit of the vine" is unfermented grape juice. Wine is the fruit of bacteria which has changed the grape juice into something else. Was Jesus speaking generally or specifically when He spoke of "the fruit of the vine?" It is this writer's opinion that He was speaking specifically.

But this leaves us the problem of the "cup." Did this contain intoxicating wine? We are not confined to such an opinion. The teachings of the Scriptures warned against the use of such. And Jesus obeyed the Scriptures. We should not be confused on this issue by the charges that Jesus was a "winebibber." For these were the words of His enemies. And whatever wine was used by the Jews for the Passover meal was diluted by two portions of water (Edersheim). However, even if one holds to this position with respect to the Passover meal, does this necessarily explain the "cup"? Both Matthew and Mark have no article with the word "cup." But Luke and Paul read "*the* cup" (author's italics). Was this a particular cup provided for the occasion? Its contents were to symbolize Jesus' blood. And it was pure blood not contaminated by sin. Would He have used "the fruit of the vine" contaminated by bacteria for this symbolism? Each person, of course, will decide the matter for himself. But from the evidence cited above it would seem that the contents of the "cup" was pure grape juice, "the fruit of the vine" only.

At the completion of the Passover supper the group sang a hymn (v. 30). It was customary at such a time to sing the *Hallel,* a part of Psalms 115-118. And then they departed unto the Mount of Olives, to Gethsemane. That which follows (vv. 31-35) is placed by John in the upper room. He also records an extended discourse and prayer by Jesus (14-17). But since Matthew omits this he places Jesus' warning to the disciples on the way to Gethsemane.

The end is drawing near. Soon the Shepherd will be taken from His sheep. Therefore, Jesus said that in that very night all of the disciples would "be offended" or stumble because of Him. This would be in keeping with prophecy (cf. Zech. 13:7). Judas had gone to betray Him. And all the rest will forsake Him in His hour of crisis. But Jesus foretold His resurrection, after which He would go before them into Galilee. Actually He appeared to them prior to this time. However, Matthew, in keeping with his purpose, lists only Jesus' appearance to the *Eleven* in Galilee where He gave the

Great Commission (cf. 28:7ff.). So he focuses on this one promise of the Lord.

Peter declared his loyalty to Jesus even to the point of dying (vv. 33-35). The others might stumble but not Peter (v. 33). Literally, "I will never [not one time] be made to stumble." The "I" (*egō*) is written out. So Peter sets himself apart from the others. But Jesus said, "That this very night, before a [no article] cock crows, three times you will deny me." (author's translation). Note the emphatic position of "three times." Not once, but thrice! Peter will do worse than all the rest. But he still persisted. "Even if it should be necessary me with you to die, not ever you I will deny" (v. 35, literal translation). The double negative *ou mē* shows how strongly Peter said this. The other disciples joined with him in this avowal of loyalty.

And they meant it. For later Peter will risk his life to defend Jesus (v. 51; John 18:10). But while he possessed the physical courage to die for Him, he and the others lacked the moral and spiritual courage to stand with Him in His hour of trial. How little they knew themselves! And how little do we understand ourselves! Such a sober reflection makes us all partners in cowardice. Only he who is without this sin should cast a stone at the Eleven.

Jeus knew them/us better than they knew themselves. Matthew lists no reply (but cf. Luke 22:35-36). He left events to prove the truth of Jesus' words.

The Agony of the King (26:36-56)

Jesus and the Eleven walked past the temple area, through the eastern gate (now called St. Stephen's Gate), down the hill across the Kidron brook, and came "unto a place called Gethsemane" (v. 36). The name "Gethsemane" means "oil press." It was an enclosed garden or olive orchard in which there must have been a press used to crush the oil out of the olives.

As one stands today at St. Stephen's Gate and looks eastward his eyes fall on one of the most sacred spots in all Christendom, the garden of Gethsemane. From this elevated viewpoint he sees a small garden enclosed by an iron fence. In season beautiful flowers bloom. Eight old olive trees stand in the enclosure. While not the same trees which were there in Jesus' day (the Romans under Titus cut down all the trees on the Mount of Olives during the siege of Jerusalem), some believe that they may grow from their roots. At any rate they are very old. Plumptre suggests that they may have been planted by pilgrims in the fourth century A.D. or soon thereafter. Alongside these trees stands the Church of all

Nations, which is built over the Rock of Agony said by tradition to be the very rock on which Jesus lay as He prayed. Even if this is not the exact garden, it is near the place where Jesus prayed in agony. It is no wonder then that modern pilgrims feel that there they are standing on holy ground amid the hushed atmosphere of prayer.

The garden of Gethsemane may have belonged to some friend of Jesus. In all probability our Lord often came here for prayer. If so, its location and His custom would be known to the Twelve, including Judas. So on this night, probably around midnight introducing Friday, Jesus came with the Eleven. Upon arrival He told the disciples, "Sit ye here, while I go and pray yonder" (v. 36). Literally He said, "There," probably pointing to a definite place. But He took Peter, James, and John a little farther (v. 38). Until He was through praying He did not wish to be disturbed. Hence the placing of the disciples.

Matthew notes that Jesus "began to be sorrowful and very heavy" (v. 37). Thus he calls attention to the burden of grief which overwhelmed the Lord. Mark is even more specific in his words "greatly amazed and sore troubled" (14:33). Robertson renders this a "feeling of terrified surprise." It is his effort to express the human reaction of the Lord to the ordeal which He knew awaited Him. He shared this feeling with the three disciples as He said, "My soul is exceeding sorrowful" (v. 38, *perilupos*). He was literally surrounded (*peri*) with sorrow (*lupos*). And it was "even unto death." It was as though death had already laid hold upon Him. Someone said that the agony of Gethsemane was greater than the agony of Calvary. So Jesus asked this trio to tarry and "watch," which means that they were to stay awake. The hour was late and the disciples were under a great strain. So this admonition was necessary. In His hour of deep sorrow it would be a source of strength to Jesus to know that this inner circle was sympathetically and watchfully near.

With these words Jesus faded into the shadows as "he went a little farther" (v. 39). Out of their sight He gave way to His grief. He did not stand or kneel to pray. He fell on His face. And as He prayed He said, "O my Father, if it be possible, let this cup pass from me" (v. 39). This prayer is even more moving in the Greek language. For He began "Father of mine" (*pater mou*). But Mark reveals even more the agony involved in it. "Abba, Father." He used both the Aramaic (*abba*) and Greek (*ho pater*). It is like a grief-stricken child dropping back into the language of His childhood. Some say that Jesus prayed in Aramaic, His native tongue. But that Jesus spoke Greek is most certain. At any rate Mark's use of "Abba" with the Greek is most suggestive.

Jesus made no demand of His Father. He did not ask to be relieved of the ordeal before Him at any price. He prefaced His petition with "if it be possible." If there is any other way to redeem man, then "let this cup pass from me" (cf. 20:22). If there is no other way He is ready to take the cup. But "if it be [morally and spiritually] possible."

What is the "cup" from which Jesus sought relief? There are those who see the "cup" as death in Gethsemane short of the cross. Thus Jesus who was sorrowful *unto death* prayed that He would live until He was nailed to the cross. This is a suggestive and intriguing thought. We cannot agree with those who see the "cup" as Jesus' death on the cross unless this *death* be enlarged to include more than physical suffering and dying. Physical death alone involved only His human nature. And if this was the "cup," then His oft-expressed knowledge of the resurrection on the third day would have removed much of death's sting. As the King He had repeatedly called upon His followers to be faithful to Him even to the point of dying. And multiplied thousands of such willingly and joyfully have done so. Jesus was no less courageous than they were. The cup to which He referred was not physical death but that which His death involved. This cup was His becoming *sin*. Jesus had come to bear away in Himself the sin of the world. Paul tells us that "he [God] hath made him [Jesus] to be sin for us, who knew no sin; that we might be made the righteousness of God in him" (II Cor. 5:21). Literally, "The one not knowing [by experience] sin, for us [on behalf of or instead of us] sin he made, in order that we might become a righteousness of God in him."

Jesus, virgin born, was without a sinful nature. In His experience He did not commit or know one single sin. And yet He was to be made not *sinful* but *sin* for us. All of the sin from Eve to the end of time was poured into one bitter potion, and He was to drink it. What a nauseous thing it was! And this divine Son of God, sinless and spiritually sensitive in nature, drew back in horror from such. It was not then His human nature alone which struggled with this problem. It involved His divine nature as well. The mystery of this union in Jesus defies our understanding. But here we see His human-divine nature in the throes of an experience into which finite man cannot enter. Like the disciples we can only tarry and watch.

But note that not for one moment was the will of the Son

in conflict with that of the Father. "Nevertheless not as I will, but as thou wilt" (v. 39). Nor should we regard this as another temptation from Satan. Repeatedly he had sought to lead Jesus aside from His redemptive purpose into some worldly program which would have left man in his lost condition. Without hesitation Jesus had brushed these efforts aside. He came to redeem man, and He would not deviate from that purpose. The struggle in Gethsemane was not whether or not He would redeem man, but how. So the Gethsemane experience was not a struggle between Jesus and Satan. It was one within the divine-human nature of Jesus Himself. Physical death held no terror for Jesus. He had faced its possibility many times with no evidence of fear. To die as sin or a sin offering was another matter. All of the abhorrence of God toward sin was bound up in this struggle. "If it be possible"; if there is some other moral and spiritual possibility—"nevertheless not as I will, but as thou wilt." Thus ended the first prayer.

Jesus then returned to the three disciples and found them asleep. Apparently Peter awoke at His approach. So He said to him, "What, could ye not watch [stay awake] with me one hour?" (v. 40). Then with a further exhortation to stay awake and pray, He faded into the shadows again (v. 41).

In His second prayer we note a progress from the first. From "If it be possible" Jesus prayed, "If this cup may not pass away from me, except I drink it, thy will be done" (v. 42). The possibility of not drinking the cup has faded away, and the probability of drinking it becomes certain. This is seen in the Greek form of conditional sentences employed in verse 42. "If this cup may not pass away from me" reads in the best manuscripts, "If it is not possible this to pass away." This is a first-class conditional sentence expressing a condition which is determined as fulfilled or is assured to be true. It cannot pass away. The cup must be drunk. And then Jesus added, "Except I drink it." This is a second-class condition stating something which is undetermined, but with the likelihood of being done. So Jesus said that since it could not pass away, He had not yet drunk it but would do so. And then He added, "Thy will be done."

A second time Jesus returned to find the disciples sleeping (v. 43). Again He seeks human sympathy but in their sleepy state these men were unable to give it. So Jesus did not awaken them, but turned again to pray a second time the same prayer (v. 44; cf. v. 42). This is suggestive of the fact that Jesus had now passed beyond that point where men cannot go. They may sympathize in their finite way, but it cannot begin to enter into the experience which now had become a reality to Jesus. For when He said, "Thy will be done," in effect He drank the last bitter dregs of the "cup." When did Jesus actually become sin? We can only surmise. But may we not say that this occurred when He received the cup. For the receiving involved the drinking. And this occurred when He said, "Thy will be done." The actual drinking may be said to be yet in the future (cf. John 18:11), on the cross, but the event was accomplished in Jesus' will when He accepted the cup. John 18:11 reads literally, "The cup which my Father has given [dedōken, perfect tense, He gave it and Jesus has it] to me, not [strong double negative, *ou mē*], may I drink [aorist subjunctive] it?" We must not split hairs between Gethsemane and Calvary. The time element is ours, not God's. We may even say that in a cosmic sense the Son accepted the cup in eternity before the foundation of the world (cf. Heb. 10:5-7). That which was effected in eternity must be wrought out in the arena of history.

Henceforth after Jesus accepted the cup, He was not merely the God-man. He was *Man* to be sure. And He was *God* no less. But He was the God-Man now become *sin,* that upon His person the wrath of God against sin might be wreaked without mercy. So all of the suffering from this moment on was Jesus' suffering for sin.

During the ordeal in Gethsemane Luke says that Jesus in His agony sweated great drops of blood (thick, clotted blood), which fell to the ground (22:44). In this we see the hand of Satan as he sought to kill Jesus in Gethsemane short of the cross. But an angel from heaven stayed his hand as it strengthened Jesus. Luke mentions only one prayer as embodying all three. We may, therefore, assume that this bloody sweat came during the first and second prayers. But God stayed Satan's hand that His redemptive purpose should be fulfilled according to His will.

However, when the victory had been won and in effect the cup had been drunk, the staying hand of God was removed. Now let evil do its worst to God. Let it storm the very citadel of God the Son Himself. It is only in the light of God's removal of restraint upon evil that we can understand the things which were about to take place.

"The hour is at hand, and the Son of man is betrayed into the hands of sinners" (v. 45). Heretofore Jesus had said that the *hour* had not yet come, that the Son of man *will* be betrayed. But now He used the perfect and present tenses. "The hour has drawn near and is here [perfect], and the Son of man is handed over [present] into the hands of sinners." With these words Jesus aroused the sleeping disciples, and moved toward the gate of the garden, saying, "Behold, the one handing me over [to His enemies] has drawn near and is here" (perfect, v. 46; cf. v. 45, literal translation).

At this very moment Judas arrived with a band of temple police (v. 47; cf. Luke 22:52) and a cohort of Roman soldiers (cf. John 18:3). This explains the "swords" (Roman soldiers) and "staves" or clubs (temple police). A cohort of Roman soldiers was the tenth part of a legion, or about six hundred men. The number sometimes varied. This could have been a full cohort (cf. "a great multitude," v. 47) or a part of a cohort stationed in the tower of Antonia. At this hour of the morning it is hardly likely that this "multitude" would have been ordinary citizens. Furthermore, the soldiers would hardly have permitted such to go along. The very object of their presence was to prevent a riot in an effort to rescue Jesus.

We may wonder why it had taken Judas so long to arrive. For since he left the upper room Jesus had instituted the Supper, probably involving only a matter of moments; had taught the Eleven and prayed both in the upper room and on the way to Gethsemane (John 14-17), which may have involved an hour; and had spent at least one hour in the garden. So it had taken Judas at least two, maybe three, hours to arrive. We may retrace his steps somewhat in this order. From the upper room he went some distance to the house of Caiaphas. It took time to gather the temple police and to secure a cohort of Roman soldiers from the tower of Antonia which was near the temple area. Then they probably had gone back to the upper room (cf. Mark 14:51-52; was this young man John Mark who had followed the group from his mother's home?). Failing to find Jesus there, Judas surmised that He had gone to Gethsemane where He often went for prayer. They arrived just after Jesus' third prayer.

Following a prearranged signal Judas came to Jesus and said, "Hail, master; and kissed him" (vv. 48-49). Note that Judas again called Jesus "Rabbi" ("master") not "Lord." This was all that Jesus meant to him. He was not "Lord" but simply a visionary rabbi. One cannot really grasp the depths of evil which Judas plumbed without examining this statement in the Greek text. He greeted Jesus with "hail" (*chaire*). It is the second person singular present imperative form of the verb *chairō,* rejoice. It has in it the idea of joy and gladness, to rejoice over something. In this sense the imperative form, as here, had come to be a greeting of good will. It corresponds to modern greetings such as "Welcome," "I am glad to see you," "How do you do?" or even "Hello." This last may be the actual meaning here, but even so it contained every element of friendliness and goodwill. Furthermore, Judas *kissed* Jesus. The Greek word means that he kissed Him much or fervently (*katephilēsen*). Since he called Jesus "Rabbi" he probably kissed Him on the hand, the usual way that a pupil kissed his *rabbi.*

Jesus brushed aside this seeming affection with the word "friend" (v. 50). It is not the usual word for "friend," but carries more the idea of "companion." Jesus reminded Judas of the close association which he now violated. "Wherefore art thou come?" The Revised Version reads, "Do that for which thou art come." This terse phrase (*eph' ho parei*) has caused much difficulty in translation. Both Moffatt and Goodspeed render it, "Do your errand." But Deissmann has shown that *eph' ho* is a question. On a Syrian tablet dated in the first century A.D. it reads, "Why here?" So the Authorized Version is correct when it reads, "Wherefore art thou come?" Jesus knew his purpose, but rebuked him with this question.

Seeing Judas' kiss the soldiers seized Jesus (v. 50). Peter was equal to his word (cf. John 18:10). He was willing to die for Jesus. So he pulled out his sword to defend his Lord (v. 51). The person nearest to him was a slave of the high priest, but as such he was of an official character on this occasion. John notes that his name was Malchus (18:10). It is interesting to note that only John mention Peter's name. By the time he wrote Peter was dead. So mentioning his name then would not endanger him with the Roman authorities.

Peter tried to cut off Malchus' head. Evidently the apostle was right-handed. Had the servant moved to the right Peter might have succeeded in his act of violence. But apparently Malchus expertly dodged to the left so that Peter's sword cut off his right ear (v. 51; cf. John 18:10). Jesus paused long enough to heal the ear (Luke 22:51). Except for this act and the fact that Jesus rebuked Peter and took him in hand, the apostle might well have died in the garden.

Jesus said to Peter, "Put up thy sword into his place: for all they that take the sword shall perish with the sword" (v. 52). How shall we understand these words? Some take them to be a prohibition of all armed conflict or violence. Certainly Jesus spoke a true principle when He said that "the ones taking a sword by [*en,* in the sphere of] a sword shall be destroyed" (literal reading).

If one takes a sword against another he must be prepared to die by the other's sword in the doing of it. But from this principle we are not warranted in denouncing a war of defense, be it against an army or a man. We must interpret this statement in the light of all of Jesus' teachings and actions.

That Jesus taught love for all men is true. But He opposed the evil designs of men and devils, not with a sword to be sure, but with the weapon of truth. He was opposed to war. But He did recognize it as a fact in history. So long as sin reigns among men and nations we must be prepared to endure "wars and rumours of war" (Matt. 24:6-7), whether we approve of them or not.

However, apart from these general truths, how shall we interpret Jesus' words in their larger and immediate context? Going back to Luke 22:38, just as Jesus and the Eleven were leaving the upper room He spoke also about the sword. He reminded the disciples that in the past when He had sent them forth they had been told to make no personal provision for their journey. And they had lacked nothing. "But now," He said, "he that hath a purse, let him take it, and likewise his scrip: and he that hath no sword, let him sell his garment, and buy one. For I say unto you, that this that is written must yet be accomplished in me, And he was reckoned among the transgressors: for the things concerning me have an end" (Luke 22:35-37). In the Authorized Version it seems that Jesus said, "The one not having a sword." But in the Greek text the meaning is different. For "the one not having" (*ho mē echōn*) refers back to *purse* and *scrip*. So what Jesus said was that those who had *purse* and *scrip* should take them, and the one having neither was to "sell" (*pōlēsatō,* imperative) his garment (it was that necessary), and "buy" (*agorasatō,* imperative) *"a sword"* (author's italics). And the fact that Jesus used the aorist imperative in both cases meant that they were to do it immediately.

Why did Jesus so command His disciples? Because they were about to leave the secrecy and safety of the upper room to go to Gethsemane. Already evil forces were prowling the night bent upon destroying Him. This must not happen prematurely. He must not die in the streets or anywhere else at the hands of violent men short of the cross. It had been written that He should be "reckoned," or put down in the books, "among the transgressors" (v. 37, cf. Isa. 53:12). This must be "accomplished [fulfilled] in me," in Jesus. He will die, but it will be through the constituted courts of the Jews and Romans, not by some other means. Satan will do everything that he can to kill Jesus short of the cross! The *cross* was God's way and purpose.

Furthermore, Jesus said, "For the things concerning me have an end" (v. 37), or a goal (*telos*). He was moving toward a *goal,* a purpose, according to the timetable of God. Nothing must prevent that from reaching its desired *end.* He must arrive safely at the garden of Gethsemane. He must not be disturbed or arrested before He had won the victory to be accomplished there through His agony or struggle in prayer.

When the disciples heard these words they understood Jesus to be talking about actual swords. They said, "Lord, behold, here are two swords" (v. 38). Jesus replied, "*It is enough. And he came out* [of the upper room], *and went...*" to Gethsemane (author's italics).

If these words sound strange to us it is because we are guided by sentimental feelings rather than by the truth of the Scriptures. Here it is in plain language. Jesus, the Lord Himself, told His innermost circle to sell their very clothes, if necessary, and to purchase a sword, and to do so at once. He did not tell them to go forth and use these swords to establish His kingdom. But He did tell them to be prepared to resist any effort by those who sought by violence to prevent His kingdom from being established in God's own way and time. They were to guard Him until His *hour* arrived. When He found that they already had two swords (they also knew of the danger that lurked on every hand or else they found them in the room of the host), He did not rebuke them for taking them. He simply said, "It is enough." They did not need enough armor to start a revolution, just enough to guard Him for the next few hours. The "two swords" may explain Jesus leaving two groups of disciples in Gethsemane, a sword with each group. Jesus, who had looked ahead so as not to betray His movements for His royal entry and the last supper, with grim realism also prepared for His safety until He was ready to go to the cross.

It is in this light that we can understand Peter's action in the garden and Jesus' reply to him. It is natural that Peter of the inner circle of three would carry the sword entrusted to that group. He had been asleep, and so did not know what had transpired within the shadows. When he awoke to find this armed band approaching Jesus he did the natural thing, that which Jesus had told him to do. He sought to guard or protect Jesus. But Jesus, having won His victory and being ready to be taken, told Peter to put up his sword lest he should get himself killed.

Then Jesus repaired the damage which Peter had done by healing Malchus' ear.

And He said to Peter, "Thinkest thou that I cannot now pray to my Father, and he shall give me more than twelve legions of angels?" (v. 53). Three things are worthy of note in this verse. In the Greek text Jesus introduced this statement with the little particle *ē*. It sets it over against or in contrast to what Peter had just done. The need for Peter's protection was past. Again, the word "now" (*arti,* even now or right now) appears not with "pray" but "send," "he shall send to me [shall stand alongside me] even now [*arti, p*resently, without a moment's delay] more than twelve legions of angels?" *Twelve,* for each apostle, including Judas! The need for the protection of the Eleven is over. At that very moment over 72,000 angels were poised in heaven just waiting for the Father's word to swoop down and rescue the Son from this little band of soldiers and police! All that was needed was for Jesus *to pray one prayer* (*parakalesai,* aorist infinitive). But He never prayed it. His hour had come (Matt. 26:52). Instead, with a rebuke to the arresting mob for taking Him under the cover of darkness when they might have seized Him any day in the temple area, He went with them. "Then all the disciples forsook him, and fled" (v. 56). They had courage enough to fight for Him with swords. But their moral courage failed in this crisis. Jesus was all alone!

The Arraignment of the King (26:57-75)

The trial of Jesus may be divided into two parts: the Jewish and the Roman. And these may be divided further into three parts each. The Jewish: preliminary hearing before Annas; informal trial before the Sanhedrin; formal trial before the Sanhedrin. The Roman: a first examination before Pilate; appearance before Herod Antipas; final sentence by Pilate. The Jewish trial shows every evidence of haste and disorganization, brought on probably by the unexpected turn of affairs through Judas' treachery, plus their hatred for Jesus and their determination to destroy Him by any means which was at their command.

According to John (18:12-14, 19-23) Jesus was taken first to Annas, the father-in-law of Caiaphas the high priest. Annas had been the high priest A.D. 7-14. Originally this office was held for life. But the Romans made and deposed high priests at will. When one displeased them they got another. We see something of Annas' corruption in His deposition. In turn he was succeeded for short terms each by his five sons. Finally his son-in-law came to office. The fact that Caiaphas held the office for eighteen years speaks for his ability as a politician. But despite what the Romans said, for many Jews Annas was considered to be the high priest. So he still was the power behind the office. Any charges brought against Jesus by both Annas and Caiaphas would more likely be accepted by both the Jews and the Romans.

This, plus the unexpected turn of affairs, probably explains why Jesus was first taken before Annas. At this hour (perhaps around 2:00 A.M.) it took time to assemble the Sanhedrin in the home of the high priest. Furthermore, they evidently had not agreed on what specific charge to bring against Jesus. So it could be that this was the purpose of bringing Him before Annas for a preliminary hearing. But when this failed in its purpose He was brought before the Sanhedrin for an informal trial. It is at this point that Matthew begins his account of Jesus' trial. The Sanhedrin was now assembled (v. 57).

In the truest sense of the word this was not the *trial.* It was illegal to hold a trial at night. But for all practical purposes this was *the* Jewish trial. That which followed was a mere formality to satisfy the demands of Jewish law. However, for purposes of distinction we choose to call these appearances before Annas and the Sanhedrin an *arraignment.*

Since Annas had been unable to bring any legitimate charge against Jesus, the Sanhedrin "sought [kept on seeking, imperfect tense] false witness [false evidence] against Jesus, to put him to death" (v. 59). Literally, "so that they might put him to death." They did not seek to ascertain whether or not He was guilty. That was inconsequential to them. Since there was no real evidence against Him they would manufacture some in order to accomplish their already determined purpose. They simply wanted to get the trial over so that they could *hang* Him.

The Authorized Verson reads, "But found none: yea, though many false witnesses came, yet found they none" (v. 60). Many scholars, including Bruce and Robertson, follow this reading. But the Greek text of Nestle (also Tischendorf, Westcott and Hort, and some of the best texts) reads, "And they did not find many false witnesses coming." Mark 14:56 in an undisputed reading says, "For many bare false witness against him, and their testimony was not alike" or "the same" (author's translation). Is this a contradiction in the record? Of course, if we follow the Authorized Version of Matthew 26:60 there is no problem, a fact which may have led many modern interpreters to do so. But by the same token what reason would some copyist have for changing *Matthew* so that it conflicts with *Mark?* The more natural procedure would have been to do the opposite. In the light of the strong manuscript support for Nestle's reading, this writer is inclined to agree with him.

Does this pose a conflict between the two Gospels? Not at all. They are simply reporting two aspects of the same thing. Matthew is saying that they had difficulty finding witnesses. At that hour of the night this would be understandable. And besides the treachery of Judas found them unprepared. They had been biding their time, and now they must act in haste. Furthermore, this may not have been the procedure they had planned to follow at all. After all, mob violence could be arranged under the proper conditions (cf. Acts 7:54-60). Little did they know that they were to do this according to God's purpose, not theirs. And since Annas had failed to elicit from Jesus anything with which to charge Him, Caiaphas had to *play it by ear.*

As the hearing proceeded, and word of it swept like wildfire through the city, either a crowd could have gathered from which came volunteers to bear testimony, or else previously enlisted witnesses could have been summoned from their homes. From wherever these witnesses came they were, as Mark says, "many." But no two told the same thing. The Mosaic law required at least two agreeing witnesses. Even the Romans might ask about this. So they must do this illegal thing legally.

Finally, two false witnesses came who claimed to have heard Jesus three years earlier say, "I am able to destroy the temple of God, and to build it in three days" (v. 61; cf. John 2:19). Even had this been a true report, it was no charge worthy of death. It would have been merely the boast of a madman. But they did not report Jesus correctly. He said to the Jews, "[You] destroy this temple, and in three days I will raise it up" (not build it). He spoke of His resurrection (John 2:21-22), but these men brought a garbled report of the way that the Jews had understood it (John 2:20). Caiaphas and other members of the Sanhedrin may have heard Jesus on that occasion. They may even have planted this perverted version in the minds of these false witnesses. If a witness has been coached and is not telling his own experience, he is more likely to get mixed up in his testimony. And Mark says that this very thing happened to these two. "But neither so did their witness agree together" (14:59).

This was poor evidence on which to try to build a case. But Caiaphas did the best that he could. When Jesus remained silent the high priest arose and said, "Are you answering nothing with respect to what these are testifying of you? But Jesus continued to be silent" (vv. 62-63, author's translation). So failing at this point Caiaphas took the most solemn step of all. He put Jesus on oath. "I adjure thee by the living God, that thou tell us whether [if, *ei*] thou art the Christ, the Son of God" (v. 63). From the Greek form of Caiaphas' question, "if thou art the Christ, the Son of God," he invited an affirmative answer. Had a more believing person asked it, it would have been equal to a confession that it was true. But the High priest had no such faith. He doubtless knew that Jesus had made such a claim (cf. John 5:18; 8:58; 9:37; 10:24-30). So he invited Him to repeat it.

All that Jesus needed to do was to say, "No," and He might well have walked out of there a free man. But to have done so would have been perjury. Of course, He would not do this. So under oath that which He had implied many times to His enemies, that which He had permitted His disciples to call Him, He now plainly declared (v. 64). "Thou hast said." This was the answer which Caiaphas had invited, but with a nefarious purpose. This was the answer which he received in a solemn declaration of truth. Mark reports it, "I am" (14:62). But Caiaphas got more than that which he asked. For Jesus continued, "Hereafter shall ye see the Son of man sitting on the right hand of power, and coming in the clouds of heaven" (v. 64; cf. Dan. 7:13; Ps. 110:1).

One would like to think that the arraignment could have ended in dignity at this point. They had their charge, and could have presented it in the formal trial within a matter of hours. But it was not to be so. For when Caiaphas heard Jesus' words he "rent his clothes." When the judges in a Jewish trial for blasphemy heard the accused speak the blasphemous words they were supposed to tear their garments, and never mend them again. Caiaphas cried, "He hath spoken blasphemy; what further need have we of witnesses? behold, now ye have heard his blasphemy." Probably at this point all of the members of the Sanhedrin followed the high priest in tearing their clothes.

They accused Jesus of blasphemy, a charge which of course was false. For He had spoken the truth. Nevertheless when Caiaphas asked for their verdict, they answered in unison, "He is guilty [held in the bonds] of death" (v. 66). The verdict was unanimous. For this reason we may be sure that Nicodemus and Joseph of Arimathea were absent. Their feelings toward Jesus probably were known, and so they were not called to the meeting of the court.

Then all pandemonium broke loose. While the Sanhedrin tore their clothes the men (temple police?) who held Jesus (cf. Luke

22:63ff.) began to spit in His face, to beat on His neck with their fists, and to slap His face with their open hands (Matt. 26:67f.). Luke 22:64 says that before slapping Jesus they blindfolded Him, and then taunted Him, "Prophesy unto us, thou Christ, Who is he that smote thee?" (Matt. 27:68). What had begun as an orderly arraignment ended in a shameful bedlam which is impossible to believe or describe. But God had removed His restraint from evil that it might do its worst. And it did.

This chapter closes with the sad spectacle of Peter's denial of His Lord (vv. 69-75). Jesus had prophesied it, and now Peter fulfilled it. But whereas within the palace of the high priest those who were completely in the bonds of evil did their worst – and were satisfied – outside the palace one held in the bonds of Jesus' love did his worst – and "wept bitterly" (v. 75). And all waited for the dawn – the dawn of the blackest day in the history of the world!

Matthew 27

The Crucifixion of the King

The arraignment of Jesus ended shortly before dawn. Not long after this meeting ended in diabolical confusion Peter heard a rooster crow heralding the approaching dawn of a new day. For those involved in the dreadful events of that day it would have been better had it not dawned. But those who follow the King look back upon it as the day when truly the hopes and fears of all the years met. For on that "Black Friday" the evil in men was at its worst, and the love of God appeared at its best.

There is no event in ancient history which is more authenticated than the crucifixion of Jesus. For it is recorded by both secular and sacred writings. But while the secular historian can relate the fact that Jesus was crucified by Pontius Pilate, only the sacred historian can declare that "God was in Christ, reconciling the world unto himself" (II Cor. 5:19). It is this latter thought which is the guiding principle in the four Gospels. And Matthew, true to his purpose, records that when Jesus died He died as the King.

As we consider this fact we may analyze Matthew 27 as (1) the King before the Sanhedrin; (2) the King before Pilate; (3) the King on the cross; (4) the King in the tomb.

The King before the Sanhedrin (27:1-10)

The arraignment of Jesus by the Jewish authorities actually became His trial before them. For what began as an effort to determine what charge to bring against Him had indeed ended in their pronouncement of the sentence of death. But since Jewish law forbade that a capital trial should be held at night, it was necessary that Jesus be brought before the Sanhedrin after dawn. It was a mere formality in order to confirm the illegal actions already taken. This session of the court was held not in the house of Caiaphas but in the regular council chambers of the court (cf. Luke 22:66).

In truth the entire Jewish trial was a mockery. For the Sanhedrin was forbidden by the Romans to sit in judgment on any other than religious questions or matters involving only civil judgment. They reserved capital cases for their own courts. And since the preconceived purpose of the chief priests was to put Jesus to death, they should not have judged Him at all. But judge Him they did, and declared Him to be guilty of death. However, this judicial murder must be done legally.

Hence Jesus after dawn was brought before the Sanhedrin in formal session. Luke records that there they asked if He were the Son of God, and received an affirmative answer (22: 67-70). Then they said, "What need we any further witness [evidence]? for we ourselves have heard of his own mouth" (v. 71). Therefore, they bound Jesus and "led Him away, and delivered [handed over] him to Pontius Pilate the governor" (Matt. 27:2). What they had already determined must now be made official by the Roman court.

That Jesus' trial by the Jews was something of a "kangaroo court" is seen in the many illegalities found in their procedure. The Sanhedrin had no jurisdiction in capital cases. The same officers who caused Jesus' arrest sat in judgment against Him. The trial was held at night in violation of their law. The prisoner was condemned before His arrest. They sought to convict Him on false testimony, none of which agreed. Failing in this they forced Him to *incriminate* Himself under oath. Jewish law required that such trials be conducted in mercy; this was filled with venomous hate. In cases involving the death penalty the verdict was not to be rendered on the same day as the trial. In order to prevent the older members of the court from influencing the younger ones, the latter were to vote first. In this case the high priest cast the first vote. The verdict was unanimous, whereas Jewish law said that to prevent mob injustice a unanimous vote was equal to an acquittal. Any legal review of this case would have reversed the verdict. But the chief priests were not interested in any such legal niceties. They wanted only one thing – the death of this hated Nazarene. So they handed Him over to Pilate.

Just as they were leaving for the Roman court they were interrupted in their proceedings. For when Judas saw that Jesus was found guilty and sentenced to death (by the Sanhedrin), he suffered a fit of remorse. Matthew says that he "repented himself" (v. 3). The word used is *metamelomai* (cf. 21:29). It was not a true repentance *(metanoeō)* involving a change of mind, heart, and nature. It was only regret after an act. Such regret might lead to true repentance (cf. II Cor. 7:8-9), but the context in Matthew shows that this was not true with Judas. He just wanted out of his bargain. Like some rapist who suffers remorse after he has satisfied his lust, but would repeat it if the occasion should arise, so Judas brought back the thirty pieces of silver. He cried, "I have sinned in that I have betrayed innocent blood" (v. 4). He was convicted of sin, but that was as far as it went. Peter confessed his sin, and it led him back to Christ. Judas admitted his and committed suicide.

One might think that this confession would have caused the chief priests to reconsider their actions. But not so. They were not interested in new evidence. They had what they wanted, and that ended the matter. In effect they said to Judas, "That is no concern of ours. It is your problem." They had used him, and since they had no further need for him they turned their backs on him. They were so much in the bonds of Satan that they acted as he does when his victim is trapped.

Judas then flung the money at their feet, went somewhere outside the city, and hanged himself. Tradition says that he did so in an area alongside the vale of Hinnom or Gehenna. Whether he did so or not, it would be most fitting had he chosen this place. For in truth he went "to his own place" (cf. Acts 1:16-25), the place which was described by Jesus as being akin to the nausea and horror of Gehenna.

But the chief priests who were so scornful of law when it stood between them and their evil purpose, now became very meticulous as to the disposal of this money. They had taken it from the temple treasury *(Corban)*. But now that it was *blood money,* made so by them, it could not be returned to the treasury (Matt. 27:6). So after taking counsel they used it for purchasing a "potter's field" in which to bury foreigners *(xenois,* vv. 7-10). It was not fit for a Jewish burial place. Tradition points this out as the same area in which it says that Judas committed suicide. But they did not even name it "Judas Memorial Cemetery." This man who reached for selfish grandeur and glory received only the nethermost place in infamy. Michelangelo in his "Last Judgment" painted Judas in the deepest part of hell. And he may not have been wrong at all.

The King before Pilate (27:11-31)

"And Jesus stood before the governor" (v. 11). Who was this governor? We know practically nothing about him prior to his appointment as governor of Judea, an office which he held A.D. 26-36. Apparently he was a man of certain ability and strength, or else he would not have been entrusted with the responsibility placed upon him.

The Roman empire was divided into provinces, such as the province of Achaia and the province of Syria. The more peaceable ones, e.g. Achaia, were ruled over by proconsuls under the authority of the Roman senate. Those requiring large number of troops to keep order, e.g. Syria, were ruled over by propraetors under the direct authority of the emperor (cf. Luke. 2:2). Lesser provinces of the latter class were placed under procurators. In A.D. 6, following the banishment of Archelaus, son of Herod the Great (Matt. 2:22), Judea and Samaria were made such a province, and placed under the authority of the propraetor of Syria. Pilate was the sixth such procurator over this province with his headquarters at Caesarea on the Mediterranean coast. Since he came to this post in A.D. 26 he had been ruling over Judea for four years when he was confronted with the trial of Jesus.

Pilate had experienced much trouble with the Jews. Josephus relates three specific instances. Shortly after coming to Judea he set his army up in winter quarters in Jerusalem. Since their standards contained images of Caesar, the Jews regarded them as graven images in the Holy City. A delegation of Jews went to Caesarea to implore Pilate to remove them. After six days he threatened to turn his soldiers loose to slaughter them. But they fell down and bared their throats, saying that they would rather die than to have these images in Jerusalem. So Pilate relented and removed them. Later he placed guilt shields bearing the names of pagan deities on the walls of Herod's palace in Jerusalem. Again the Jews protested. But Pilate was less pliable in this case, removing them only on direct orders from Tiberius Caesar. In an effort to provide more water for Jerusalem Pilate took money from the temple treasury (Corban) to build an aqueduct. In the tumult which followed, his soliders killed many of the rioters plus some innocent spectators. In addition to these, in Luke 13:1 mention is made of an occasion when Pilate's soldiers slew some Galileans in the temple even while they were worshipping, their own blood being mixed with that of the sacrifices slain on the altar. This was a most serious profanation of the temple and its altar, a matter which must have outraged the Jews. Philo also tells of Pilate's "murders without trial" stating that he feared any appeal to Tiberius by the Jews lest they tell also of his "acceptance of bribes, plunderings, outrages, and wanton insults, continual and most grievous cruelty." He also characterized Pilate as "unbending, self-willed, harsh, and malignant." So Pilate came to his supreme test with quite a sordid record, one which the Jews used to advantage with their implied threat to tell Caesar should Pilate not grant their wishes (cf. John 19:12). Pilate's chickens had come home to roost.

When "Jesus stood before the governor" we view the most dramatic moment in history. The King of the universe stood before the ruler of one small portion of earth. He thought that Jesus was on trial before him, when actually he was on trial before Jesus—and history.

The first thing which Pilate had to do was to ascertain the charges which the Jews brought against Jesus (cf. John 18:29). Luke 23:2 records their formal accusation (cf. Matt. 27:12). "We found this fellow perverting the nation, and forbidding to give tribute to Caesar, saying that he himself is Christ a King" (literally, "an anointed king"). Note that the charges which they brought were political in nature. Pilate would care nothing for their religious bickerings. The chief priests brought in the religious question only in desperation, when it appeared that the Roman governor might release Jesus (cf. John 19:7).

Obviously the first two charges made against Jesus were false, but may have been gathered from the false witnesses. Or they may have been their own perversions of truth. The last charge could have been concocted from their interpretation of the royal entry or from Jesus' words in Matthew 26:64 (cf. Luke 22:69-70). Even so, their implication that Jesus claimed to be an earthly rival of Caesar was a false one. But note that they did charge Jesus with claiming kingship. John records that Pilate tried to evade the issue by throwing the matter back on the Sanhedrin. But they countered by reminding him that they had no power to inflict the death penalty (18:31-32). Thus they demanded Jesus' death even before presenting any evidence to support their charges.

From John's Gospel we know at this point Pilate took Jesus inside the *Praetorium* (18:33) into which the Jewish rulers would not go. This was the dwelling place of a Gentile (probably Herod's palace where the Roman governor lived while in Jerusalem), and to enter would defile these Jews so that they could not participate in the remainder of the Passover feast. Therefore, in the privacy of this place Pilate questioned Jesus as to the charge. "Art thou the King of the Jews?" Literally, "You are the King of the Jews?" "You" is written out, and so is emphatic. In Jesus' present condition after the night's ordeal He looked like everything but a king.

To Pilate's question Jesus gave one answer. "Thou sayest" (v. 11). As in the trial before the Sanhedrin, so here Jesus gave but one answer. And in each instance He replied to statements which related to His identity and which invited affirmative answers. Caiaphas had said, "In order that you may say to us *if you are the Christ, the Son of God* (26:63, author's translation and italics). This italicized statement called for an affirmative answer. And Jesus replied, "You said it" *(su eipas,* aorist of *legō).* Pilate simply put a declarative statement in the form of a question. "You are the King of the Jews?" Note "You are the Christ, the Son of God" (26:64); "You are the King of the Jews" (27:11). In Greek as in English these are two exact statements except for the designated titles. And to Pilate's statement Jesus replied, "You are saying it" *(su legeis,* present of *legō).* And these are the only answers which Jesus gave at the two trials as to His identity. (John records that Jesus did explain to Pilate the spiritual nature of His Kingdom, 18:33-38, and that Pilate's only power came from God, 19:11.)

The point of all this is that Jesus did not endeavor to defend Himself against obviously false charges. There was no reason why He should. He willed to die. But He also willed to die not as a martyr or criminal. He would die as "the Christ, the Son of God" and as "the King of the Jews." He was the King directing the evil manuevers of men toward the accomplishment of God's eternal purpose. He did not do so simply by declaring Himself to be who He is. He evoked from Caiaphas and Pilate these declarations to which He simply gave assent. So if they crucified Him it would be their crucifying Him whom they had unwittingly declared to be "the Christ, the Son of God" and "the King of the Jews."

After this Jesus was silent. Even when Pilate urged Him to defend Himself (Matt. 27:13), He refused to answer. Literally, "And he did not reply to him up to even one word" (v. 14). So much so that the governor marvelled greatly. This suggests not only wonder at Jesus' silence but admiration or awe before His dignity.

Luke records that at this point Pilate sent Jesus to Herod Antipas in order to get Him off his hands (23:6-12). Here also Jesus remained silent. So much so that after making sport of Him Herod sent Him back to Pilate. The governor still had Jesus on his hands. In all of this it is of interest to note the quiet dignity of Jesus and the excited frustration of those who thought that they had Him on trial.

So clutching at straws to get out of his predicament Pilate suddenly remembered a custom of releasing one prisoner whom the people chose (v. 15). The origin of this custom is obscure. No parallel case to this has been found, but Josephus mentions it. It probably was a Roman custom designed to placate their captive peoples. And Pilate thought that he had just the man to use in gaining Jesus' release. For he was holding "a notable prisoner, called Barabbas." Apparently he was a notorious prisoner. Matthew does not describe him further. But Mark and Luke call him an insurrectionist and a murderer (15:7; 23:19). John adds that he was a "robber" (18:40). He was probably one who had sought to lead a rebellion against Rome (a political messiah, the very crime of which the Jews accused Jesus), and had finally ended up as a common robber and murderer preying on his own people. This was often the pattern of would-be political and military messiahs. He was probably scheduled to be crucified that very day. The governor thought that they surely would not want such a man turned loose upon them again. So he gave them their choice between Barabbas and Jesus.

"Whom [*tina,* which one of the two] will ye that I release unto you? Barabbas, or Jesus which is called Christ?" (v. 17). There is more to this question than meets the eye. Origen of Alexandria at the beginning of the third century mentions having seen some manuscripts of the Gospels which read "*Jesus* Barabbas." And there are a few manuscripts in existence today which read thusly, probably due to Origen's words. Whether this be a true reading or not, it is most suggestive. For it places Jesus opposite the very kind of messiah which He had refused to be.

The name *Barabbas* simply means "son of father" (Aramaic, *Bar,* son, *abbas,* father). So we see "Jesus, son of father" and "Jesus, the Son of the Father." The one offered himself as a military messiah; the Other offered Himself as a spiritual Messiah. The one would set up an earthly kingdom; the Other would establish the kingdom of heaven. The one brought revolution; the Other brought regeneration. The one represented political and military deliverance from the power of Rome; the Other represented spiritual deliverance from the power of sin. The one called upon the people to shed their blood to make him a king; the Other came to shed His blood as their King. So the Jews on that day were called upon to choose more than they knew. They were to choose not a man but a way of life and salvation. One is constantly amazed at the compounded elements which God had poured into this one decisive event of the ages!

Pilate knew that the only reason that had prompted the Jews' actions against Jesus was envy (v. 18). For he was convinced that He was innocent of their charges (Luke 23:15). He even suggested that he should release Him (John 18:30). And the people evidently favored the release of Jesus over that of Barabbas (Mark 15:11). So much so that the chief priests had to stir up the people in order to get them to call for the release of Barabbas.

Apparently their opportunity to do this came when Pilate was interrupted in the proceedings. For he had just sat down on the "judgment seat" *(bēma),* probably to render his judgment in favor of Jesus. But at that moment a messenger came from his wife telling him literally, "Nothing between you and that just one. For many things I suffered today in a dream because of him" (v. 19). The Romans put great importance upon dreams. And so this message upset the governor no end. But his problem was such that he could not get rid of Jesus so easily. For there was *much between him and that Just One*. Indeed, more than Pilate knew!

But the chief priests and elders had used this brief interlude to their advantage (v. 20). For when Pilate asked for their decision the multitude with one accord said, "Barabbas" (v. 21). Pilate was flabbergasted. He could hardly believe his ears. Evidently he hoped that in gay, holiday mood the people would choose Jesus also. Therefore, he asked, "What shall I do then with Jesus which is called Christ?" (v. 22). Never was there a greater question asked. It was asked by a pagan Roman governor. But he asked it for every man. For the multitudes then, and for the multitudes in every age. "What shall I do then with Jesus which is called the Christ?"

Note the word "then." They had chosen a political and military messiah. But they still were responsible for a decision concerning Jesus. You cannot be rid of Him simply by choosing another. For He quite evidently stands before you as He stood in Pilate's hall. Escape Him you cannot do. "What shall I do with Jesus . . . the Christ?"

And "they say *all,* Let him be crucified" Did we say "all"? There was one who did not say it. Not a chief priest. Not a Jew at all. But a pagan Roman. For he still cried, "Why, what evil hath he done?" (v. 23). Oh, the irony of it all! The Jews who claimed to be the people of God crying for the Son of God to be nailed to a cross! And a pagan pleading for His life! He was weak. Yes. He was evil. He was trying to save his own skin. Yes. But he recognized innocence when he saw it. And even now his sense of Roman justice cried out against this mob violence. But still he lacked the courage to stand by Jesus. With the power of the mighty Roman empire behind him he still lacked inner fortitude to do his duty. His sins of other years tied his hands. Indeed, the issue had resolved itself into whether or not Pilate would espouse Jesus' cause or by default try to *save* his own skin. He chose the latter. Alas, how many in Pilate's shoes still walk the way of Pilate! He pleaded for Him. He said nice things about Jesus. But he gave way to the pressure of the mob. For when they saw Pilate's hesitation "they kept on crying exceedingly [imperfect], Let him be crucified!" (v. 23). "Hosanna" on Sunday. "Crucify" on Friday. But how many of us, in the way we live, even wait until Friday to change our tunes?

Pilate was whipped. Instead of an orderly court of Roman law, through his vascillation the scene had turned into a mob. So in one weak and futile gesture of defiance toward the Jews, Pilate called for a bowl of water (v. 24). Then in symbolic fashion he "rinsed off" *(aponiptō)* the guilt from his hands, saying, "I am innocent of the blood of this just person: see ye to it" (v. 24). Why did Pilate do this? It may have been a universal symbol of feigned innocence (Plumptre). Maybe he did this to assuage the conscience of his wife.

But one thing is certain. The law of Moses (Deut. 21:6-8) required that if one were found slain in the field with no knowledge of the slayer, the city nearest to the slain man should go through a ceremony designed to remove the guilt from that city. After the sacrifice of a heifer the elders of the city were to wash their hands over the heifer, saying, "Our hands have not shed this blood, neither have our eyes seen it. Be merciful O Lord, unto thy people Israel, whom thou hast redeemed, and lay not innocent blood unto [in the midst of] thy people of Israel's charge. And the blood shall be forgiven them."

We would not say that Pilate knew of this law. But the chief priests and elders, probably the people, knew about it. And regardless of Pilate's motive, his symbolic deed would remind the Jews of the required occasion and meaning of this law. Pilate had just called Jesus innocent. Yet they "kept on crying exceedingly, saying, Let him be crucified." So in the face of this pagan's symbolic transfer of guilt to them, and the meaning which it suggested to them, their answer is all the more terrible. "His blood be on us, and on our children" (v. 25). Were there ever more terrible words uttered? "On us, and on our children." Children who were not even present, some not even yet born. Apparently they were proud of what they were doing. *Such is evil freed from God's restraint!*

But the guilt was not so easily removed from Pilate's hands or from his soul. To save his own skin, not his soul, he permitted Jesus to be crucified. But six years later he was recalled by Rome and banished to Gaul. Just outside Lucerne, Switzerland one may view Mount Pilatus. A legend says that Pilate's ghost dwells in that mountain. When storms rage about it his ghost comes out and still washes his hands in the storm-clouds. And all the while he cries, "It won't come off! It won't come off!"

No, there was guilt enough for Pilate, Judas, the Jewish leaders, and the people, yes, for us all. For not the Jews only crucified Jesus. Nor the Romans. He died for the sins of the whole world. And the guilt will not come off by the rinsing of hands in a bowl of water, in the storm clouds, or even over a heifer. There is but one cleansing power. Only "the blood of Jesus Christ his Son cleanseth us from all sin" (I John 1:7).

The verdict had been given. Not in the orderly and solemn tones of a judge. But in the howling madness of a mob. And Pilate, craven coward that he was, handed Jesus over to the soldiers who were to carry out the crucifixion (v. 26). He did so after he had caused Him to be scourged. This was done by stripping Jesus, binding Him, face downward, to a whipping post. Then He was whipped unmercifully with a whip composed of several thongs, the end of each loaded with bits of bone or metal, which tore pieces of flesh from His back and shoulders, leaving His quivering flesh one bloody mass.

Then the soldiers took Him to some place in Herod's palace (praetorium), probably into some open court (v. 27). Other soldiers gathered about to see the *sport*. It was customary to mock condemned criminals before their execution. Jesus had been condemned as a King. And so they would fit their mockery to the occasion. A king must have a robe. So they put about him a scarlet robe. This was the nearest thing to royal purple that they had. It was a military cape which probably belonged to one of the soldiers. A king must have a crown (v. 29). So they made one for Jesus out of a thorn branch, similar to a bush which grows today alongside the Tower of Antonia in Jerusalem. The thorns tore into the Lord's flesh as they cruelly crushed it down on His head. Also a king must have a sceptre. So some soldier added to the fiendish glee as he pulled up a reed growing nearby, and put it in Jesus' hand. And of course one must do obeisance to a king. So they kneeled before Jesus. Mark says that they "kept on kneeling" (imperfect, 15:19), suggesting that each of the soldiers did so in turn. And as they did so they mocked Him, saying, "Hail, King of the Jews!" (v. 29). This showed not only their contempt for Jesus, but for the Jews also. Then they began to spit on Him and to strike His head with the reed (v. 30). With the imperfect tenses Mark again shows that these acts were done repeatedly. It is impossible to add to the horrible nature of these acts. The words speak for themselves.

Finally, when the soldiers had so vented their scorn upon the Son of God that it no longer delighted them, they clothed Jesus and led Him away to Calvary to crucify Him (v. 31). It was before 9:00 A.M. on Friday.

The King on the Cross (27:32-54)

In keeping with custom Jesus was compelled to carry His own

cross to the place of crucifixion (v. 32). If any of the disciples were near enough to see this, they no doubt remembered with a shudder the words of Jesus spoken to them six months previously (Matt. 16:24). But the ordeal of Gethsemane, the sleepless night, and the terrible punishment inflicted upon Jesus that morning (plus the spiritual sorrow which weighed upon Him) took their toll. Seeing that He was weakening under the load, the soldiers "compelled" "a man of Cyrene, Simon by name," to bear Jesus' cross. He was from a town in Libya in North Africa. Some would like to suppose that he was a black man. But his name implies that he was a Jew. Cyrene was an ancient trade town, and so would probably have many Jews living there (cf. Acts 2:10). In all probability he had come to Jerusalem for the Passover. Mark points out that he was "the father of Alexander and Rufus" (15:21; cf. Acts 19:33; I Tim. 1:20; II Tim. 4:14). Whether these references all refer to the same *Alexander* is open to question. But apparently Alexander and Rufus were two Christians who were well-known to Mark's readers. This would indicate that Simon himself became a Christian, and was followed in the faith by his sons. What at the moment appeared to be a màrk of shame came to be his glory.

"And when they were come unto a place called Golgotha [Latin, Calvary], that is to say, a place of a skull" (Matt. 27:33). We cannot say with exactness where this place was located. It was outside the city walls (Heb. 13:12), but no definite wall has yet been identified with certainty as the outside wall of Jersualem at that time. The traditional site is located at the Church of the Holy Sepulchre. But archaeologists are not agreed as to whether this was within or without the wall in Jesus' day. Jack Finegan suggests the possibility that it was outside the "second wall" which may have been the wall in Jesus' time. But it is inside what is called Hadrian's wall, the present one, finished by the Jews in A.D. 66-70. A popularly held location of the crucifixion is "Gordon's Calvary." It is to the north and outside the present wall of the city. From a distance its rugged side has the appearance of a skull. Nearby is "Gordon's Tomb" located in a garden. In recent years archaeologists have unearthed the ruins of a small chapel located just before and to the right of this tomb. This suggests that this must have been a sacred site to early Christians. Of interest is the fact that a guide told the writer that originally the hill called "Gordon's Calvary" was used by the Jews as the place of execution by stoning; the Romans continued to use it as their place of crucifixion. But this, of course, is only surmise. The truth of the matter is that no one really knows the exact spot on which Jesus died. And this is probably as God intends that it should be. The important thing is that it did take place and for a definite purpose, the redemption of a lost race.

Man has never devised a method of execution which surpassed crucifixion in bodily suffering. Roman law forbade it being done to a Roman citizen. There were three types of crosses used. One was shaped like the letter "X", another was shaped like the letter "T", and a third was the "†" so familiar to Christians everywhere. It was most likely this last type on which Jesus died.

Following the usual method of crucifixion we may well visualize the experience of Jesus. When He arrived at Calvary the soldiers offered Him a drink of wine mingled with gall, a kind of narcotic, in order to deaden the suffering (v. 34). But Jesus refused to drink it. He would endure the full agony of crucifixion as He died for the sins of the world.

The cross piece was laid flat on the ground, and the upright part was stood up in a hole in the ground. Jesus was stripped naked.

The Roman custom was to strip the victim naked. However, since the Jews required that when one was about to be stoned his person should not be left exposed, some think that the Romans would respect that custom by allowing the victim to wear a loin cloth. We can certainly hope so in this case, but it is more likely that these crude and cruel Romans did not indulge the hated and despised Jews. In all likelihood Jesus' person was exposed to public view, thus adding to the shame and suffering.

He then was caused to lie down with His arms stretched along the cross piece. To render Him helpless His arms and legs were jerked out of joint. His hands were nailed to the cross piece. He then may have been stood up with His feet resting on a small shelf about two feet from the ground. Or he may have been suspended only by the nails. The latter was probably true in Jesus' case (cf. Ps. 22:17). The cross piece was fastened to the upright pole, and His feet were fastened to the cross with large spikes. There He was left suspended for hours. Sometimes it took even days for a victim to die. But Jesus remained there for six hours, 9:00 A.M. until 3:00 P.M., before He died.

As Jesus was hanging there His body was so stretched that every rib stood out (Ps. 22:17). The joints were wracked with agony. Every nerve throbbed with pain. The sun like leeches sucked the moisture from every pore in His skin. Fever mounted and parched His lips. His tongue grew dry and thick. Thirst caused His voice to become hoarse. The flow of His blood was hindered, the blood causing great distress as it gathered in His head and lungs. Gradually His body grew stiff and His strength ebbed away. And His physical suffering was enhanced beyond measure by His mental and spiritual agony. We cannot enter into His suffering; we can only try to describe and imagine it (Read Psalm 22).

It was while the soldiers were fastening Him to the cross that Jesus prayed, "Father, forgive them: for they know not what they do" (Luke 23:34). He prayed for the soldiers and for all who had brought Him to the cross. Did He not also pray for all sinners who actually made His crucifixion necessary?

The soldiers were permitted to keep the clothes of their crucified victims. There were four soldiers in such a detail. Barclay notes that every Jew wore five articles of clothing: shoes, turban, girdle, inner garment and outer cloak. So each of the soldiers took one item. John notes the unusual value of Jesus' seamless cloak (19:23-24). So the soldiers gambled for the cloak instead of tearing it into four pieces (Matt. 27:35). They did not know and cared less that they were fulfilling Scripture (cf. Ps. 22:18).

Matthew notes that the soldiers then sat down and "watched him there" (v. 36). The imperfect tense tells of the long hours while they guarded against anyone trying to rescue Jesus from the cross. But before they sat down, probably even before they gambled for Jesus' clothes, they nailed a sign to the cross just above His head. This was called a *titulus* (Latin, note *titlos,* Greek, John 19:19) on which were written the name of the victim and the crime for which he was crucified. In the case of Jesus it read, "THIS IS JESUS THE KING OF THE JEWS" (v. 37). The other Gospels have slightly different wording (cf. Mark 15:26; Luke 23:38; John 19:19). But all agree that the accusation read "THE KING OF THE JEWS." *So the official pronouncement of the Roman empire was that Jesus died as a King.* The chief priests objected to this wording, and requested that it read that "he said, I am King of the Jews" (John 19:21). But Pilate refused, saying, "What I have written I have written" (John 19:22). *Ho gegrapha, gegrapha.* He used two perfect tenses meaning, "What I have written and stands written, I have written and it stands written." It carries the double meaning of finality. And while Pilate had no particular conviction as to Jesus' identity, only being stubborn with the Jews, yet he has given final evidence that Jesus died as THE KING OF THE JEWS.

John further notes that this title was written in Hebrew, Latin, and Greek: Hebrew, (Aramaic), the local native tongue; Latin, the official Roman language; Greek, the universal language of the day. Pilate wanted it to be read and understood by both the Palestinian Jews and those from outside Palestine, Jews and Gentiles who might not understand Aramaic. Of course, he must use the official language of the Empire. But everyone could read the title and understand its meaning.

While Pilate had no concern beyond this there is a highly suggestive thought in the use of these three languages. Hebrew was the language of *religion*. Latin was the language of *government*. Greek was the language of *culture*. So when we ask as to who crucified Jesus, these three languages say, "Everybody crucified Him!" And more specifically, instituted religion condemned Him; official government and power killed Him; pagan culture rejected Him. These were the great streams of life in that ancient day. So the crucifixion of the Son of God actually stemmed from all of these great centers of man's existence. And this thought may well be timeless in its scope. Let no man point the finger of guilt toward the first century as he pulls his self-righteous robes about him. For the same streams of life which nailed Jesus to the cross then continue to ignore Him, and in so doing seek to defeat the purpose for which He died.

Isaiah had said that the Christ would be numbered with the transgressors (53:12). Our Lord was crucified between two robbers *(lēistai,* cf. John 18:40), not "thieves" *(kleptai)* as the Authorized Version reads (v. 38). In all probability they were members of the band of Barabbas. Assuming this to be true it is likely that they had been sentenced to the cross along with their leader. So here we see a further suggestion with respect to Jesus' relation to Barabbas. Barabbas had been chosen by the people instead of Jesus. Because of that Jesus is being crucified in the place of *(huper)* Barabbas. This is the very essence of the gospel. It is the substitutionary atonement. Jesus took the sins of Barabbas and of all men, and bore them in their place on Calvary's tree. Barabbas was sentenced to death. But because of Jesus he went free. We can only hope that he saw the day when through faith in Jesus he became free indeed. And in this picture we see ourselves. As we gaze upon the Son of God dying on a cross we should say, "Except for the grace of God, there hang I!"

As if the horror of the crucifixion itself were not enough Matthew says that Jesus was the object of the taunts and jeers of those who watched Him die (vv. 39-44). To us it is incredible that even Jesus' enemies would be guilty of such. But evil was having its day. And we see to what extremes it will go when once God removes His restraining hand.

Golgotha was probably located alongside a road leading into the city. Therefore, "they that passed by reviled" Jesus (v. 39). The word "reviled" renders the word for "blaspheme." So they spoke insultingly against Him. They shook their heads in mock sorrow as they repeated the false charges made against Jesus. "Thou that destroyest the temple, and buildest it in three days, save thyself. If thou be the Son of God, come down from the cross" (v. 40). Evidently word had spread as to the charges brought against Jesus. For here they repeated one false and one true charge. Jesus had admitted under oath that He was the Son of God. And the form of the conditional sentence used by the passersby implies that He is God's Son. In effect they said, "You say that you are the Son of God. Prove it, and come down from the cross." They hurled their insults at Jesus, and then went on their way.

If at any place one would expect to find dignity and respectful quiet it would be in the person of the leaders of religion. But, if possible, they were acting worse than the rest. "The chief priests ... with the scribes and elders" were the Sanhedrin. The night before they had acted like madmen. Now they were acting like silly children who love to taunt one another. For that is the meaning of the word translated "mocking." They said literally, "Others he saved, himself he is not able to save" (v. 42). The word "save" had a variety of meanings. It could mean to heal, to rescue from danger, or to save in a spiritual sense. The first two would apply here. He had healed others, but He could not rescue Himself from the cross. He had raised Lazarus from the dead (a tender point with the chief priests), but He could not deliver Himself from death.

They spoke more truth than they knew. For indeed Jesus had *saved* others. But He could not save Himself and be the Saviour. If He saved His life, He would have lost His life. Only by losing His physical life could He achieve the very purpose of His *living* or being (cf. Matt. 16:24-25).

Putting this taunt in the present time men may say, "He saved others; himself he *could* not save." And this is still true. He could not save Himself and be our Saviour. But if we change just one letter we get a fuller meaning. "He saved others; himself he *would* not save." He willed not to save Himself in order that He *could* save others.

The Authorized Version loses the strong irony which was in their next jeer. It reads, "If he be the King of Israel, let him *now* come down from the cross and we will believe [upon] him" (author's italics). But the Greek text has no "if" phrase. It reads,

"King of Israel he is." They looked at the sign over His head. THIS IS JESUS THE KING OF THE JEWS. They simply changed "Jews" to "Israel" as they read it aloud. "King of Israel he is!" But look at him *now* nailed to a cross! "Let him now [right now] come down from the cross, and we will believe [upon] him."

This was their condition upon which they would believe that He was "King of Israel." But was it? They soon will learn of a greater miracle (Matt. 28:11ff.). But they did not believe upon Him. Like so many in every age, they made what they thought were impossible demands upon which to condition their faith in Jesus. However, such is not a condition of faith. It is an excuse for a lack of it.

But the Sanhedrin was not through. "He trusted in God; let him deliver him now, if he will [s]: for he said, I am the Son of God" (v. 43). In effect, this was a double insult. They insulted the Son with respect to His claim to Sonship. And they insulted the Father with regard to His love and loyalty to His Son. Of course, they did not believe Jesus' claim, and implied that God would not will to save such a blasphemer. But the sum-total of it all was that they actually *dared* God to save Jesus from death. They dared Him to give them "a sign from heaven" (Matt. 16:1). Satan incarnate! But they knew nothing of the love and purpose of God the Father even as they did not with respect to God the Son. Compounded ignorance in those who thought that they were so enlightened. And their successors are ever with us.

We see the motley elements which met at the cross as we pass to verse 44. "The thieves [robbers] also [like the Sanhedrin], which were crucified with him, cast the same in his teeth [literally, began to reproach or revile him]." What a combination! The elite and the outcasts. The rulers and the robbers. Religious leaders and criminals. Truly Satan ran the scales in his diabolic symphony that day. But Luke 23:39-43 tells us that one of these robbers repented, confessed his sins, and trusted in Jesus as his Saviour and King. Fifty percent of the robbers at the cross were saved; none of the Sanhedrin that was there was saved (we assume that two did not join with the others at the cross). Yes, the publicans, harlots, and robbers went into the kingdom before them!

At this juncture it is well to pause a moment and examine these repeated demands that Jesus should come down from the cross. How may we understand them? Of course, we can regard them simply as impossible demands made by unbelieving hearts. And that is true. But is that all of the truth?

From the beginning Satan had endeavored to keep Jesus off

the cross. Repeatedly he tried to turn His efforts into another channel. And Jesus was determined to die on a cross. Because both Satan and Jesus knew that was how God purposed to save lost men. Now Satan wanted Jesus dead. But he did not want Him to die on a cross. He tried to kill Him when He was born (Matt. 2:16). He tried to get Him to jump from the pinnacle of the temple (Matt. 4:6). He sought to throw Him off a cliff in Nazareth (Luke 4:29). In a storm at sea he tried to drown Him (Matt. 8:24). He endeavored to bleed Him to death in Gethsemane (Luke 22:44), and to beat Him to death in Pilate's palace (Matt. 27:26). But in all of these he failed.

We often say that Satan nailed Jesus to the cross. But this is not the case. For that was the one way that he did not want Jesus to die. Well, if Satan did not nail Him to the cross, who did? We can hardly say that God did. For it was done at the hands of wicked men. And who would accuse a loving heavenly Father of such a vile deed? So the question remains. If neither Satan nor God nailed Jesus to the cross, who did? *Unbridled sin or evil nailed Jesus to the cross!*

Now we have three elements involved in the question of Jesus being nailed to the cross: God, Satan, and evil. The Bible assumes the eternal being of God. But whence came Satan and evil? Did Satan produce evil, or did evil produce the rebellious character of Satan? The origin of evil is one of the unsolved mysteries of the universe. It seems to be involved somehow in the element of *choice* which God has given to the highest of His creations. Such an element is necessary for the development of God's creatures. But before there can be a right choice, there must be the possibility of a wrong choice. And as the right choice is related to righteousness, so the wrong choice is related to unrighteousness or evil.

The origin of Satan is almost as obscure as the origin of evil. But we know that Satan is a created being, a creation of God, and so is not eternal. For only God is eternal. While the Bible does not clearly state it, it gives glimpses (cf. Isa. 14:12; II Peter 2:4; Jude 6) which lead us to understand that Satan was an archangel who rebelled against God and was cast out of heaven. Satan had the choice of obeying God or rebelling against Him. He rebelled and so sinned. Whatever we may say about the origin of evil, it would appear that the evil character of Satan is the result of evil. Therefore, Satan did not create evil.

But Satan is still in rebellion against God. And he uses the principle of evil as his weapon. Satan opposes God in nature. But his principal area of combat is in the heart of man. Since God made man for His own fellowship, Satan could best attack God through man and endeavor to alienate him from God's fellowship. And he does so by enticing man through evil as he endeavors to get man to follow him in making wrong choices with respect to the will of God.

While Satan possesses tremendous power his power is second to that of God. And the Bible clearly teaches that God holds both Satan and evil in restraint (cf. Job 1-2). Thus when man trusts in God He overrules Satan and his evil designs for man's good and God's glory (Rom. 8:28). The supreme example of God's overruling power is seen in the incarnation of the Son in Jesus Christ for man's redemption from the penalty and power of sin (by which Satan has separated man from the loving fellowship of God). And God proposed to do this through the death of His Son on the cross. The struggle between Jesus and Satan as related in the Gospels is simply the transfer of the cosmic struggle to the arena of this world.

Satan claims the sovereignty of the universe, including the souls of men. And when the King-Messiah came He was God contesting Satan's false claim. So in the Gospels we see the battle joined unto the death between the false sovereign and the true Sovereign. Satan sought to destroy God's sovereignty by killing God Himself in the person of His Son. But God purposed to break Satan's claim to sovereignty by His own death on the cross in the person of His Son. And since the Son was to become sin, in His death and resurrection God would break the power and remove the penalty of sin or evil. So the battle raged. Satan endeavoring to kill God short of the cross. And God determined to die on the cross.

Finally, in Gethsemane the Son said to the Father concerning His drinking of the cup of evil, "Thy will be done." In that moment He took the cup. And in that moment God removed His restraining power from Satan and from evil. They wanted to kill God. So let them do their worst. God will still triumph over them. Therefore, Satan was loosed, and evil was loosed. It is only in this light that we can understand the unbridled evil of the trial and crucifixion of Jesus. "God was in Christ, reconciling the world unto himself" (II Cor. 5:19). So what they did they did to God.

However, remember that while Satan wanted to kill God, he did not want Him to die on a cross. For if that happened he knew that God had won. Thereafter Satan would fight a guerrilla warfare, but his power would have been broken and his ultimate defeat assured. So he did everything that he could, even after

Gethsemane, to kill Jesus short of the cross. But unbridled evil got out of Satan's hand. It did its worst to God. It insulted Him. It spit in His face. It sought to kill God in the most terrible way possible. It nailed Him to a cross. Satan knew that if Jesus died on that cross he was defeated. So even as He was dying on the cross, Satan, in the person of those about the cross, cried, "Come down from the cross! Come down from the cross! Come down from the cross!"

But Jesus did not come down. He *could* have (physically) but He *would* not. Because He knew that it was in the eternal purpose of God. He was held to the cross not by spikes but by the bonds of God's love for a lost human race!

For some it may be difficult to relate the will of God to the cross and all that it involved. But we must recall the various facets of the will of God. God's *intentional will* intends only good for His creation. But due to the element of choice in man, there is God's *permissive will* wherein He permits that which He does not propose. Man is responsible for his choices, his wrong ones being his committed sins. Thus he acts in accord with his sinful nature. So there is God's *punitive will* whereby He punishes sin in keeping with His holy nature. When man sinned it produced the circumstance whereby his fellowship with God was broken. Thus we have God's *circumstantial will* or the will to act in that circumstance for man's redemption. And since the wages of sin is death, God willed that in the person of His Son He would die to redeem man back into His fellowship. The result is God's *ultimate will* or that His *intentional will* ultimately shall be done for all who believe in His redeeming work.

It was in God's permissive will that man lost his relation to God. This made necessary that God's *punitive* will be expressed toward man and his sin. But in that *circumstance* God willed to save man by the death of His Son, a will which the Son accepted. So God's *permissive* will allowed Satan and evil to do their worst to Jesus Christ. Thus God *permitted* the cross because of the *circumstance* of man's sin, in order that God's *intentional* will *ultimately* might be done.

And then the crucial moment came. For from the sixth hour (noon) until the ninth hour (3:00 P.M.) the land was shrouded in darkness (v. 45). It was the hour of dense darkness indeed. We shall never know the cosmic and personal struggle which raged within that darkness. We can only note the fact, and leave it in the mind of God.

"But at the ninth hour Jesus cried with a loud voice, saying,

Eli, Eli, lama sabachthani? that is to say, My God, my God, why hast thou forsaken me?" (v. 46). Thus Jesus in His darkest hour cried out in Hebrew (or Aramaic, Mark 15:34, *Eloi, Eloi,* and some manuscripts of Matthew) the words of Psalm 22:1, the psalm which clearly depicts the crucifixion of Christ. While this saying on the cross (the only one of seven recorded by Matthew and Mark) fulfilled this prophetic psalm, it was no formal act of Jesus. In a mystery beyond our comprehension it expresses the deepest agony of His soul. Whatever else it may mean it means that at that moment the Son felt the loneliness of being God-forsaken. We may well imagine that at that moment He drank the last bitter dregs of the "cup." And for that moment a holy God turned His face from Him who had become sin. G. Campbell Morgan notes that the beginning of sin is to forsake God. And the end of sin is to be God-forsaken. So in that mysterious moment Jesus plumbed the very depths of sin for us. He was God-forsaken—for us. He suffered all of the agonies of hell—for us. It was for only a moment as men reckon time. But it was the infinite suffering of the infinite God for the infinite guilt of men.

And then there was quiet. It was broken only by a murmur from Jesus, "I thirst" (John 19:28). The soldiers mistaking Jesus' words "Eli, Eli" thought that He had cried for "Elias" (v. 47). They wanted to wait to see if Elias would come to save Him (v. 49). But one kindly man put a sponge soaked in vinegar on a reed, and pressed it to Jesus' lips. And He drank (v. 48). At the beginning He had refused drugged vinegar. But now He accepted the sour, undrugged vinegar which the soldiers drank while on this cruel detail.

Why did He drink it? He did so with a purpose. He was about to give the cry of victory. His tongue was thick and His throat husky from thirst. But He wanted this cry to be clear and strong. For it was not the cry of defeat but of triumph. He had won the struggle. So John records that which Matthew implies when he says that "Jesus . . cried with a loud voice" (v. 50). "It is finished" (John 19:30). He did not die of slow exhaustion. He died the victor. *Tetelestai!* "It is finished!" This word has a number of meanings in the papyri (See my *The Crucial Words from Calvary,* Baker, 1958). One is that in which a father sent his son on a mission, saying that he should not return until it was accomplished. When the son returned he said to his father, "*Tetelestai.*" The mission was accomplished. It is the perfect tense of finality or of a finished work.

So the Father had sent the Son on a mission of redemption. He was not to return until it was finished. Now the Son reports to the Father, *"Tetelestai."* "It is finished. The mission is accomplished, and it stands accomplished."

"Jesus . . . yielded up the ghost" (v. 50). Literally, "Jesus . . . dismissed his spirit." He permitted it to return to the Father. He did not dismiss His spirit until the mission was accomplished. No man took His life from Him. He gave it of His own will. King all the way!

The picture is not complete without Luke's report. Just before Jesus dismissed His spirit He said, "Father, into thy hands I commend my spirit" (23:46). The word rendered "commend" means to place something on deposit. In the papyri it is used for placing something on deposit with another for safe keeping and to be used for its intended purpose. So the Son in His "spirit" placed His redemptive work on deposit with the Father to be safeguarded and used for its intended purpose—the redemption of all who should believe on Him.

The death of Jesus was accompanied by strange phenomena (vv. 51-53). "And, behold, the veil of the temple [*naos*] was rent in twain from the top to the bottom; and the earth did quake, and the rocks rent" (v. 51). A. T. Robertson notes that the Talmud speaks of a quaking in the temple forty years before its destruction. This would be in A.D. 30, the year of Jesus' death. Whether it refers to this earthquake is not clear. Apparently the earthquake mentioned in the Gospels did not do sufficient damage to warrant being mentioned by the historians of the period. But it was quite evident to those who were there that it was a significant thing (cf. v. 54). It was nature in revulsion against the dastardly deed done that day.

Two specific results of the earthquake are mentioned. First, the veil of the temple was torn in two—from the top to the bottom. This was the large veil, sixty feet long and thirty feet wide, which separated the Holy of Holies from the court of the priests. The fact that it was torn from top to bottom indicates that it was not an act of man. Later the author of Hebrews will interpret this event as meaning that this veil no longer shuts man off from access to God. In Christ our High Priest we can "come boldly to the throne of grace" (4:16). Man no longer needs an earthly mediator. "For there is one God, and one mediator of God and men [partaking of the nature of God and men], a man Christ Jesus, the one giving himself a ransom for [*huper,* on behalf of] all" (I Tim. 2:5-6, author's translation). Because Christ Jesus partakes of the nature of both God and man they meet in Him in reconciliation.

Second, "the graves [tombs] were opened; and many bodies of the saints which slept arose, and came out of the graves *after his resurrection* [rising up], and went into the holy city, and appeared unto many" (vv. 52-53, author's italics). Did these saints arise before or after Jesus' resurrection? Paul says that Christ is the "firstfruits" (I Cor. 15:20, 23). So we must conclude that this happened after Jesus' resurrection. The tombs were evidently opened by the earthquake which was itself an act of God. But the rising of the dead was most assuredly an act of God. Matthew alone reports this event. It would appear, therefore, that his purpose in relating it was to show that after Jesus' resurrection these "saints" who had received Jesus as King but died before His death, were raised after His resurrection; and appeared to other believing saints to show that they were living and would, therefore, also participate in the kingdom (cf. I Thess. 4:14-18).

Matthew closes his account of the crucifixion with the reaction of the centurion and his soldiers who had carried out the sentence of death upon Jesus (v. 54). They beheld the earthquake which followed the strange three hours of darkness. Perhaps by this time some priest had come running to report the rending of the veil. At any rate in wondering awe *they* said (*legontes,* plural participle), "Truly this was the Son of God" (v. 54). The Greek text reads "Son of God" or "a Son of God," since it has no definite article. Some would tone down this statement due to the absence of the definite article. They insist that a pagan Roman would have no concept of "the Son of God." Furthermore, they note that Luke reads, "Certainly this was a righteous man" (23:47). But Luke prefaces this statement with "he glorified God." It is entirely possible that the centurion made this statement in addition to the one made by him and the soldiers. And Plumptre notes that the terms "just man" and "son of God" are used interchangeably in the *Wisdom of Solomon.* These men had heard the people accuse Jesus of claiming to be "a Son of God" (literal reading in Matt. 27:40, 43). So they simply said, "Truly this one was who he claimed to be. He was a Son of God." (From Luke's account it appears that the multitude, apart from the Sanhedrin, also realized this, 23:48.) In the light of their knowledge they made this assertion. And in the light of our understanding we may say with them, "Truly this was *the* Son of God."

The King in the Tomb (27:55-66)

The King was not without friends on that awful day (vv. 55-56). For watching from afar was a small band of faithful women: Mary Magdalene, Mary the mother of James and Joses, and the mother of Zebedee's children (Salome, Mark 15:40). They had ministered to Jesus in His life. Now in His death they were an island of love in an ocean of hate.

After Jesus' death two other friends appeared, Joseph of Arimathea and Nicodemus (v. 57; John 19:38-39). Both were members of the Sanhedrin, but were secret disciples of Jesus and had not participated in the actions of that body (cf. Luke 23:50-51; John 19:38-39). In all likelihood they had witnessed the crucifixion, but had had no part in it. After Jesus' death Joseph, a righteous, wealthy, and influential man went to Pilate and requested that he be granted the privilege of burying Jesus' body. Pilate granted his request (v. 58). So he and Nicodemus wrapped the body in linen cloth, having placed myrrh and aloes about it, and buried Jesus in Joseph's new tomb (vv. 59-60). This was a tomb in a garden near Golgotha, which had been hewn out of rock. Joseph had prepared it for himself and most likely for his family. But he forsook his own wishes and used it instead for Jesus. And having "rolled a great stone to the door of the sepulchre" (v. 60), they departed.

No one knows the exact location of this tomb. In the Church of the Holy Sepulcre one is shown a tomb prepared for one body. But of interest is the fact that in Gordon's tomb, located in a garden adjacent to Gordon's Calvary, on one side to the right of the door there are places for two bodies (a man and his wife?). On the other side there are *unfinished* areas for two other bodies (for children?), as though it was a "new tomb" the completion of which was interrupted for some reason. Before the door is the groove in which a large stone might be rolled to close the entrance to the tomb. This is not to say with certainty that Gordon's tomb is the actual tomb of Jesus. But if not, then it must have been one like it. There is no wonder, therefore, that one stands today in this quiet garden and experiences an awe which defies description.

This *Black Friday* Matthew closes with a note of beauty and pathos. For as the sun was setting looking toward the beginning of the Sabbath, the departing light of day bathed the lingering and loving presence of "Mary Magdalene and the other Mary [mother of James and Joses], sitting over against the sepulchre"

(v. 61). Salome had gone to comfort and care for her sister, Jesus' mother. But these two women, so helpless to prevent the deed of that day, lingered long at the silent tomb. They did not even hope, but they loved.

But hate had not died. It pursued Jesus even into the tomb. For "the next day, that followed the day of the preparation, the chief priests and Pharisees came together unto Pilate" (v. 62). The "day of the preparation" (*meta tēn paraskeuēn*) was Friday. It was the day before the Sabbath, and was the day on which *preparation* (cooking, etc.) was made for the Sabbath (cf. Luke 23:54). In Modern Greek *paraskeuē* is the word for Friday. Therefore, the day "after the preparation" was the Sabbath day. Such a holy day to the Jewish rulers on which they did such an unholy thing!

For they came to Pilate with a request. "Sir, we remember that that deceiver said, while he was yet alive, After three days I will arise again" (v. 63). Literally, "we just remembered" (ingressive aorist, Robertson) as though it was a mere coincidence that they had recalled it. But we may well imagine that it had never been out of their minds. They had asked Jesus for a sign from heaven, and He had given it (cf. Matt. 16:4; cf. 12:40). To give them the credit of the doubt, it may be that the significance of Jesus' replies and His words about the "temple" being raised in three days (John 2:19) had just dawned on them. But in any case it made no difference. They would not wait to see if it were true. Instead they asked Pilate for a guard to be placed before the tomb "until the third day." They wanted to prevent Jesus' disciples from stealing the body, and then saying to the people, "He is risen from the dead" (v. 64). For to them "the last error [defraud] shall be worse than the first." The first "fraud" was belief in Jesus as the King-Messiah. The second "fraud" would be belief in His resurrection.

To the deceitful all people are deceitful. The chief priests had deceitfully conspired with one of the Twelve to get Jesus in their clutches. They knew what they would do were they in the disciples' place. So they attributed to them their own motives. We can understand why the Sadducees would want to be sure that there was no resurrection true or false. But one would think that the Pharisees would have waited. However, they had committed themselves, and their last *error* was greater than the first.

Pilate gave them a guard of Roman soldiers, saying, "Make it [the tomb] as sure as ye can" (v. 65). Actually, "Make it secure for yourselves [aorist middle] as ye know how" (*oidate*).

"So they went, and made the sepulchre sure, sealing the stone, and setting a watch" (v. 66). The sealing of the stone rolled across the door was done in the presence of the soldiers. The best texts read "with the guard" (*meta tēs koustōdias*).

The Jewish rulers went home satisfied that they had made the sepulchre "sure." But God causes even the wrath of man to praise Him. For only one thing had the chief priests and Pharisees made "sure." They had made "sure" one of the strongest proofs of our Lord's resurrection from the dead!

Matthew 28

The Vindication of the King

According to the Jewish method of reckoning time any part of a day was considered an entire day. Jesus' body was placed in the tomb late on Friday, and the tomb was found to be empty early on Sunday morning. So the Lord was in the tomb a part of Friday (first day), all of Saturday (second day), and a part of Sunday (third day). When Jesus spoke of "three days and three nights" (Matt. 12:40) He was speaking in general terms of three whole days. There is no conflict between this and the actual event. For to the Jewish mind each means three entire days. And thus in the words of an unknown poet we can say

> But Calvary and Easter Day,
> Earth's blackest day, and whitest day,
> Were but three days apart.

Matthew has been recording the revelation of the King. The King-Messiah presented Himself to His nation and was rejected and crucified. Its religious leaders had challenged Him to give them a sign which would prove His identity as such. He gave them only one sign—His resurrection from the dead. So in Matthew 28 the Evangelist records the fulfilment of that promise. The Jews rejected their King, but God vindicated Him as "the Son of God with power... by the resurrection from the dead" (Rom. 1:4).

As we examine this vindication of the King we may outline Matthew 28 as (1) the fact of the resurrection; (2) the denial of the resurrection; (3) the authority of the King.

The Fact of the Resurrection (28:1-10)

Mary Magdalene and the other Mary were the last to leave the tomb of Jesus on Friday. And they were the first ones to visit it on Sunday (v. 1). In Mark's introductory statement to his account of the resurrection he says that Salome was also with them (16:1). But he clearly says that these three "when the sabbath was past" went to buy spices. Matthew harmonizes with this when he begins, "In the end of the sabbath" or "late on the sabbath" (28:1). It was their purpose further to anoint Jesus' body with spices. Therefore, late on the sabbath they left their abode, and arrived at the place of their purchase after the sabbath had ended, a time when they could buy the spices. Then the next morning, before dawn (John 20.1), they left their abode to go to the sepulchre, arriving there "as it began to dawn toward the first day of the week" (Matt. 28:1; Luke 24:1).

It should be noted that they did not expect to find the tomb empty. Mark notes that they even wondered as to who would roll away the huge stone for them (16:3). So far as they were concerned Jesus' dead body still lay in the tomb. Their purpose in going there was to complete what they considered to be a hurried and inadequate preparation for His burial on Friday. So theirs was not an errand of faith, or even of hope. It was one of love.

We may wonder at the disciples' failure to remember Jesus' promise to rise on the third day. The Jewish rulers recalled it. Perhaps the dead body of Jesus had made death seem so final, and their faith had faltered. More likely the explanation lies in their deep grief. They were too stunned to remember. In any case their failure to expect the resurrection is an important point to remember as the story unfolds.

Matthew alone mentions an earthquake in connection with the resurrection. "And, behold, there was a great earthquake" (28:2). He does not tell when it occurred, simply that it happened. It occurred between sunset on Saturday and sunrise on Sunday. One writer notes that as the earth trembled in sorrow at the crucifixion, so it leaped with joy at the resurrection. If anyone is troubled by this supernatural element, he should remember that this is the greatest miracle of the ages. And we should be surprised were there no evidence of the supernatural in this greatest of all of God's interventions in history and in the natural order.

The cause of the earthquake is given as an angel of the Lord descending from heaven to roll away the stone from the tomb. When he had done so, he sat upon it. "His countenance [appearance, *eidea,* only here in the New Testament] was like lightning, and his raiment white as snow" (v. 3). This within itself suggests that the earthquake occurred while it was still dark. It is no wonder that the Roman soldiers were so frightened that they shook like an earthquake. For the word "shake" is the verb form akin to *seismos,* earthquake. The earth was not the only thing that quaked that night. So frightened were the soldiers that they "became as dead."

Matthew's account would allow for saying that the women saw this supernatural phenomenon. But from the other Gospels it is clear that this all happened before they arrived. Evidently the soldiers had recovered from their shock and had fled before they arrived. One would hardly expect these superstitious men to linger long before such a spectacle.

When the women arrived they found the soldiers gone and the tomb open. From Mark we learn that they did not yet see the angel, who now had moved inside the tomb (16:5). They did the natural thing by rushing into the tomb. When they saw the angel they also were frightened. But the angel said, "Fear not ye [stop being afraid]: for I know that ye seek Jesus, which was crucified" (v. 5). Literally, "Jesus the Crucified." It is the perfect tense expressing a state of completion. He was and will always be "the Crucified."

And then the women heard the most glorious words ever spoken. "He is not here: for he is risen, as he said" (v. 6). He told them that He would rise on the third day. And He did! Was ever anyone so thankful for a failure as were these women? They had come to find the dead body of Jesus. And they found it not. Failing to find the soldiers, and seeing the open tomb, they probably feared foul play, perhaps a grave robbery. But instead they found a messenger from heaven saying, "He is not here: for he is risen."

Then to verify his words the angel said, "Come, see the place where the Lord lay" (v. 6). The best manuscripts do not have the words "the Lord." But this is the sense nevertheless. For even though they are absent, the subject of the verb "lay" is "he" referring back to "Jesus" in verse 5. And note that the angel did not say "lies" but "lay." Actually he said, "was lying" (imperfect). But He is not lying there any longer. "He is risen" or raised up.

Now looking back over this account a question is in order. When did Jesus rise from the dead? Was it before or after the stone was rolled away? There is no mention in the account of Jesus coming out of the tomb. John suggests that the grave clothes were lying exactly where the body had lain (20:7). They had not been unwound from Jesus' body. The body had simply come out of them, leaving them as they were, but empty. We would conclude that Jesus came from both the grave clothes and the tomb by His own power or by the power of God through the Holy Spirit (cf. Rom. 1:4). Therefore, the stone was not rolled away to let Jesus out of the tomb. It was removed in order to let the women in, that they might see that the tomb was empty. Jesus had already left the tomb before the angel rolled away the stone.

The angel's mission was finished ("lo, I have told you") when he announced the resurrection, and told the women to tell it to the other disciples (v. 7). They were to do so "quickly." And with the promise that Jesus would meet the disciples in Galilee, his work was done. While it is not so stated, we may surmise that the angel then returned to heaven.

This verse is fraught with suggested meaning. As soon as an angel from heaven had proved the fact of the resurrection, the task of telling others about it was entrusted to those who believe in Jesus and are convinced that "He is risen." The privilege of preaching the gospel was not given to angels but to men and women. Only those who were lost and are now saved can comprehend the grace of God. So feeble, erratic, and sinful are we. Yet to us God has entrusted the gospel, the good news of salvation. Someone defined the gospel as "Something wonderful has happened!" And, indeed, it has. It is our responsibility and opportunity to "go quickly" and tell this good news, not only to "his disciples" but to the whole world.

And the women "departed quickly" (v. 8). So excited were they that they "ran" to bring the disciples word. Such good news could not wait. But even as they ran they were to see more than an empty tomb and an angel. They saw the living Lord Himself (v. 9). Literally, "Jesus suddenly met them" (aorist). And notice His greeting. "All hail!" This is but one word in the Greek text. *Chairete* (cf. Matt. 26:49). This was the common form of greeting. It could mean "hello" or even "good morning." The point is that Jesus greeted them in a natural way. The risen Lord did not appear to them with great dramatics or fanfare. This within itself speaks for the authenticity of the account. Left to himself to create such a story man would not have related it so simply. Jesus merely said, "Good morning!"

Never was there a greeting so sweet and wonderful! The women recognized Jesus, held Him by His feet, and worshipped Him. But they were still frightened. It was too much for them, too good to be true, and yet it was. So Jesus said, "Stop being afraid" (literal meaning). "Go tell *my brethren* that they go into Galilee, and there shall they see me" (v. 10, author's italics). "My brethren" refers to His disciples, not to His half-brothers by birth. Although Jesus Himself did appear later to James (I Cor. 15:7). Jesus' disciples are still His "brethren." They forsook Him and fled. But they were to Jesus still "my brethren." Nothing could separate them from the love of Christ (cf. Rom. 8:35-39)!

Jesus repeated the instructions of the angel about going to Galilee. That He appeared to them on that very night we know from the other Gospels. Jesus made ten post-resurrection appearances in all. But Matthew records only two of them, the one in

28:9-10 and the one in Galilee (28:16-20). We are not to suppose that Matthew was unaware of the others. For he was present at at least three of them (John 20:19-21:23). But he records only these two in keeping with his purpose. For he is concerned only with reporting the authority and commission of the King. He clearly and completely records the resurrection of the Lord. And that is enough.

The Denial of the Resurrection (28:11-15)

Even while these joyful events were transpiring the ominous voice of denial was heard with regard to the resurrection of Jesus. For there were other heralds of the event in addition to the women. "As they are going [present participle], behold, some of the guards having come [aorist participle] into the city, told to the chief priests all the things which were come to pass" (v. 11, author's translation). By his use of participles Matthew shows that the soldiers reported the resurrection to the chief priests even before the disciples heard about it. Pilate had placed the guard at the disposal of the chief priests, and so it is natural that it would report to them.

Notice the reaction of the chief priests. They did not go to ascertain the facts for themselves. The last thing that the Sadducees wanted was proof of a resurrection, and especially in the case of Jesus. So they called a council of the Sanhedrin, no doubt without notifying Joseph of Arimathea and Nicodemus. The decision was not to investigate the matter but to endeavor to squelch the report. So "they gave large money unto the soldiers" (v. 12). Literally, they gave them "considerable silver." As they had bribed Judas to betray Jesus so did they bribe the soldiers to deny His resurrection. And in both instances the money evidently came out of the Corban or *sacred* treasury.

They further compounded their sin of bribery with that of a lie. The bargain was that in return for the money the soldiers were to say, "His disciples came by night, and stole him away while we slept" (v. 13). If they were asleep how could they know? But those who would use perjury to secure Jesus' death had little concern for the smaller details of truth. Pilate himself would see through this story if it came to his ears. But there were ways of handling this crafty Roman. His record showed that he was not above taking bribes himself. Therefore, "if this should be heard by the governor, we will persuade him, and will make you free from anxiety" (v. 14, author's translation). The chief priests were old hands at *persuading* officials. And there is always the Corban with which to do it. So the soldiers took the silver, "and did as they were taught" (v.15). And they had competent teachers in the art of lying.

"And this very word is being spread abroad [timeless aorist] among the Jews until this day" (v. 15, author's translation). This explains why Matthew alone relates this incident. He was writing with the Jews in mind. And at the very time when he wrote, maybe twenty-five years later, this story of a grave robbery was being circulated among the Jews throughout the Roman empire. Justin Martyr (circa A.D. 100-165), in his *Dialogue* with Tryphon the Jew, mentions this report as being current among the Jews in his time, with the Jews having sent "chosen men" into all parts of the world (Roman empire) to propagate it. It was indeed "spread abroad."

This story suggests the entire matter of the efforts made to deny and/or discredit the story of the bodily resurrection of Jesus. And there have been/are many. In addition to the *grave robbery* theory, which is not accepted even in our skeptical age, let us examine briefly some of the others. It was suggested by Joseph Klausner, noted Hebrew scholar, that the tomb was empty because of a *legal removal.* According to him Joseph of Arimathea, the only one having legal authority to do so, removed the body to another place. But why would he change his mind so suddenly about his tomb? And if so, what about the guard? Their report made no mention of Joseph. Nowhere in almost two thousand years of careful scrutiny has one shred of evidence been uncovered, either in the New Testament or elsewhwre, to support such a theory. Two modern scholars, Kirsopp Lake and P. Gardiner-Smith, suggest that the tear-blinded women got lost and came to a *mistaken tomb.* Those who strain out gnats and expect us to swallow camels are still around. The women had been to the tomb before. Upon hearing of the resurrection Peter and John ran to the tomb (John 20:2-10). Did they also get lost? The women were not blinded by their *tears.* But it seems that some scholars are blinded by their *fears.*

Another attempt to deny the resurrection is the *fraudulent story* theory. This charges the disciples with deliberately inventing the story in order to perpetuate a fraud on the basis of Jesus' words about rising on the third day (cf. Matt. 27:64). Apparently those who set forth this theory chose to disregard altogether the *fraudulent story* of the chief priests. Such a theory runs counter to the evidence in the *stories* themselves. For the disciples did not expect Jesus to rise from the dead. All that the Sanhedrin needed to do to refute this story was to produce the dead body of Jesus (cf. Acts 3:14-16). They did not do so. But the greatest answer to this theory is the disciples themselves. To accept this theory is to say that these men endured untold suffering, even death, for what they knew to be a lie. This within itself would be a psychological impossibility.

And then there is the *swooning Saviour* theory. It says that Jesus did not die on the cross, but merely fainted. After the burial He revived, and came forth from the tomb under His own strength. But where is the evidence? The Roman soldiers were experts in the art of killing, and they judged Jesus to be dead (John 19:32-37). Had there been even the slightest evidence of breathing on His part those who buried Him would have detected it. Was Jesus some Houdini to get out of the carefully wound grave clothes? But let one of the most fanatical opponents of the resurrection of Jesus answer this theory. Strauss many years ago wrote, "It is impossible that one who had just come forth from the grave half dead, who crept about weak and ill . . . could ever have given to the disciple that impression that He was a conqueror over death and the grave . . . which lay at the bottom of their future ministry."

Of more modern ilk is the *hysteria* theory. It holds that the report of the resurrection was caused by the grief and hysteria of the early disciples. It bases its position on Luke's account that when the women first told the disciples this story that to them their word seemed as "idle talk" (24:11ASV). This phrase *hos lēros* was a medical term used of the wild talk of those in delirium or hysteria. The fact that the apostles so regarded this report adds to the truth of the resurrection. For when they came to the tomb they found it empty (Luke 24:12; John 20:3-8). Another form of this theory attributes the post-resurrection appearances of Jesus to hypnosis brought on by grief and shock. It insists that the disciples merely *saw* what they wanted to see. Would this explain the experience of Saul of Tarsus? Certainly he did not see what he *wanted* to see at that time. Some would explain his experience as a seizure of epilepsy in a thunderstorm. If that be true then, judging by his subsequent life, we should pray for an epidemic of epilepsy and thunderstorms. And what about the appearances to groups of people—above five hundred on one occasion? Was this mass hypnosis? If so, it was quite a feat on someone's part. Paul says that Jesus "was seen" by many (I Cor. 15:5ff.). He used the verb (*horaō*) which means to see with the natural eye and to retain the vision of what was seen. Furthermore, of the "five hundred" he says that they all saw Him at "once" (*ephapax,* the strongest word for this expression). And many of these were alive when he wrote, if anyone cared to check on it (I Cor. 15:6).

But the most widely held theory among modern skeptical scholars is the *spiritual resurrection* theory. It says that Jesus did not rise bodily, but that His spirit continues to live. If this be the case then why believe in Jesus? Why not Buddha, Moses, Ghandi, or some other great teacher? For their *spirits* live on. Furthermore, such a theory denies the very meaning of the word "resurrection." It means "a standing again." For something to be resurrected it must first be dead. And even these skeptics do not claim that Jesus' spirit died.

This interpretation of the resurrection is not New Testament theology. It is pagan Platonic philosophy. For Plato taught that *matter* is nothing and the *spirit* is everything. Therefore, said he, the body dies and that is all. But the spirit lives on. It was to refute this very philosophy that Paul wrote his great treatise on the bodily resurrection from the dead (I Cor. 15; see my *Messages on the Resurrection,* Baker, 1959).

So the fact remains that either we accept the bodily resurrection of Jesus or we do not. It is not enough to say with Matthew Arnold that we do not believe in the resurrection of Jesus because it involves a miracle, and "miracles do not happen." If we are to be intellectually honest we must consider the evidence. And there is much at hand. One of the greatest legal minds in British history once said that he knew evidence when he saw it, and that the evidence of the resurrection of our Lord has never broken down yet. Let us cite four such evidences.

First, there is the record of the Four Gospels. The resurrection is reported by all four Evangelists, three of which were eyewitnesses of the fact. The fourth, Luke, was a physician, a scientist, who has been declared to be a historian of the first rank. Even where his accounts contradict the official records of the Roman empire, archaeology has confirmed Luke's historical data. As a scientist he knew how to ferret out and interpret evidence. And after thorough investigation (Luke 1:1-4), despite what his medical training might say to the contrary, he wrote the most beautiful and complete account of the resurrection in existence. The Gospels and other New Testament writings have been submitted to the most careful, and sometimes hostile, criticism. And they stand today vindicated as credible historical evidence. Thus we know more about the death of Jesus than about that of any other personality of ancient times. And the data concerning His resurrection is just as firmly established.

Second, there is the evidence of the empty tomb. When the critics have done their worst they still must explain the empty tomb. The Gospels agree that Jesus' dead body was placed in the tomb of Joseph of Arimathea on Friday. The verdict of scholarship is that the Gospels report that the tomb was empty on Sunday morning. We have seen something of the futile attempts to explain this fact away. The truth of the matter is that there are some places into which *science* cannot go. When it has exhausted its power, then *faith* must lead. This is true in every realm of life, even in so scientific an endeavor as scientific research. The research scientist begins with the proposition that there are some things which he does not know. But he believes (faith) that by diligent application of all of his powers he can discover them. Thereafter, without prejudice, he must follow the evidence gained in research—wherever it may lead. If one applies this same technique in regard to the resurrection of Jesus it will lead him to exclaim, "My Lord and my God" (John 20:28).

Third, there is the evidence of the Christian movement through the ages. We have noted the transformation which was wrought in the early disciples. From a frightened, defeated, and disillusioned group they suddenly became bold as lions as they challenged the powers which crucified Jesus. And always their message centered in the resurrection of Jesus. There is no other adequate psychological or spiritual basis upon which to explain this transformation. The apostle Paul always went back to his having seen the risen Lord on the Damascus road to explain his ministry for Christ. From those early beginnings Christianity has swept throughout the world, empowered by the living Christ who indwells, moves, and works through His people.

Fourth, there is the evidence of personal experience. The court from which there is no appeal is the experience of the human heart. Those who have trusted Christ as Lord and Saviour know that He lives and reigns. Even where Christian apologetics may fail Christian experience can supply the answer. It is like the little woman who said, "I know that Jesus lives, because I was talking to Him this morning."

Yes, Jesus lives. It is of interest to note that insofar as the written record is concerned the enemies of Jesus never one time went to the tomb after His resurrection. After Peter, John, and Mary Magdalene left it no friend of Jesus went there. The chief priests did not go to the tomb because they were *afraid* that they would find it to be empty. The apostles never went back because they *knew* that it was empty. The enemies of Jesus posted a guard before the tomb to keep Jesus from coming out; the friends of Jesus must stand before the empty tomb, armed with faith supported by evidence, to see that none of His enemies ever put Him back in it again.

The Authority of the King (28:16-20)

Had Tiberius Caesar from his palace in Rome been able to see and hear the event which transpired on a mountain in Galilee, he probably would have laughed in derision. But that event heralded the day less than three centuries later when his successor would espouse the cause of the Christ who was the center of that mountain scene. For so numerous had become His followers that, even though history has proved it to be a blight for Christianity rather than a blessing, Constantine considered it politically expedient to proclaim the Christian religion as the state religion of the Roman empire. What was it that gave such an impetus to this movement so that from such a small beginning it became as the sands of the seashore? The answer is the *authority* of the living Christ.

The Eleven went into Galilee as they had been told (v. 16). Along the way from Judea others had probably joined them so that we may regard this as the appearance of Jesus to "above five hundred brethren" mentioned by the apostle Paul (I Cor. 15:6). Matthew says that they came to "the mountain," the definite article signifying a specific mountain where Jesus had designated beforehand as the place where He would meet them. The text reads "where Jesus had arranged with them" (*etaxato autois*). When they saw Jesus they all bent their knees before Him in worship. "But some doubted" (v. 17). These were probably those from Galilee who were seeing Him for the first time after the resurrection. It was too good to be true! But we may well suppose that they lost their doubts when they heard Him speak.

What an astounding claim Jesus made! "All authority hath been given [aorist] unto me in heaven and upon earth" (v. 18, author's translation). The word "authority" ("power" in KJV) means "out of being." It is the authority which resides in the nature of one's being. Jesus used it in the compound form *(katexousiazō)* of the verb referring to pagan rulers in the sense of tyranny (Matt. 20:25). Paul uses it in Colossians 1:13 when he speaks of the "power of darkness" where it means the "tyranny" of Satan. In both of the above senses it has a bad meaning, or authority which expresses itself in tyranny. But this word is also used in the good sense with reference to Jesus (cf. Matt. 7:29; 9:6). So whether or not the "authority" be good or bad depends upon the nature of the one out of whom it comes.

The "authority" of Jesus had been great prior to His death and resurrection. But now He lays claim to "all authority ... in heaven and upon earth." It is boundless in scope and nature. He said that this "hath been given" (aorist) or "was given." When was it given? For the aorist tense suggests a given point in time. Broadus suggests that it may have been done in the councils of eternity. But he leans toward the incarnation (cf. Matt. 11:27) with its consummation at Jesus' resurrection.

But was "all" authority given to Him at His incarnation? It was then that the Son of God took on man's weaknesses, apart from sin. In His incarnation Jesus did have "authority." But His claim to "all authority" suggests that this came at a time other than at His incarnation. It would seem that the point of its bestowal was at His resurrection. For this is the resurrected Lord speaking.

Help at this point may be found when we recall Jesus' contest with Satan. Satan made a false claim to "authority" or sovereignty in the world as seen in the third temptation (Matt. 4:8-9). This included not only the kingdoms of the earth but the souls of men. The very point of the incarnation was to challenge Satan's claim, to put him down, to break his assumed power over the souls of men and in the universe; and to make it possible that God's sovereignty might be received in the hearts of men. Satan even sought to establish his sovereignty over heaven itself, both by inducing the Son of God to worship him, and when He refused, by killing Him. But in His death Jesus broke the power of sin, and in His resurrection He triumphed over death itself. Thus the false claim of Satan to sovereignty was refuted. The absolute sovereignty of God was proved to be a reality.

It is to this fact that Revelation 11:15 alludes. For literally it reads, "The sovereignty [singular] of the cosmos [universe] became [*the sovereignty,* not in the Greek text, but understood] of our Lord [Jehovah] and of his Christ; and he shall reign unto the ages of the ages." Here again we find the aorist tense of a point action in time ("became," *egeneto*). So the event referred to is not in the future but in the past. The verb "became" (*egeneto*) does not express eternal, essential being, but that something came into being. So at a given point in time "the sovereignty of the cosmos" came to be that of Jehovah and His Christ.

How are we to understand this astounding statement? Since

God is eternal and omnipotent we cannot agree that there was ever a time when He was not sovereign in the universe. But there was a point in eternity when this sovereignty was disputed by Satan. And since this dispute involved the souls of men, is was necessary that the sovereignty of God should be proved in the arena of history. Hence the incarnation. And when we focus upon this period we come again to Jesus' death and resurrection. It was there that Satan's false claim was refuted absolutely. And when that was accomplished the uncontested sovereignty of God "became" or "came into being" in the arena of history. The "unto the ages of the ages" shows that it will extend beyond history into eternity.

Therefore, we return to Jesus' words "all authority was given unto me in heaven and upon earth." It is the "sovereignty of our Lord [Jehovah] and of His Christ." But although Satan's claim to sovereignty has been refuted, he still seeks to reign in men's hearts. There remains then the conquest of these remaining strongholds of Satan. And since the Christ had broken the power of Satan in His death and resurrection, "all authority in heaven and upon earth" was given to Him to accomplish this task.

Jesus Christ is reigning in heaven and upon earth. He is reigning in His mediatorial kingdom. And Paul says that "he must reign, till he hath put all enemies under his feet" (I Cor. 15:25). And this mediatorial reign will continue until His purpose is accomplished. Paul is careful to point out that "all things" does not include God the Father (I Cor. 15:27). It is the Father who gave "all authority" unto the Son. But he also notes that this gift of "all authority" is of a temporary nature. For "when [*hotan,* condition, not time] all things [*ta panta,* the universe both material and spiritual] shall be subdued unto him [Christ], then shall the Son also himself be subject [subdued, same word as above] unto him that put all things under him, that God may be all in all" (I Cor. 15:28).

This does not mean that God the Son and God the Holy Spirit will cease to be. God is one, who reveals Himself as Father, Son, and Holy Spirit. In an unsubdued universe we see God in His several revelations. But in a redeemed and subdued universe we shall see God as He is: God the Father, God the Son, and God the Holy Spirit—but God as He is. "That God may be all in all." Thus "He shall reign unto the ages of the ages."

When God the Son died on the cross and arose from the dead the redemptive work was finished. But the work of subduing the universe had just begun. In His own power and way Christ will exercise His "all authority" in subduing the material universe.

But also in His "all authority" He has chosen to subdue the spiritual universe, or men's hearts, through the efforts of those who believe in Him. And this thought adds sublimity to the words of the resurrected and reigning King on the mountain in Galilee.

"Going, therefore, disciple all the nations, baptizing them in the name of the Father, and of the Son, and of the Holy Spirit: teaching them to observe all things which I commanded you" (vv. 19-20, author's translation).

Note that this verse contains three participles, one imperative verb, and an infinitive. "Going... baptizing... teaching"; "disciple" or "make disciples" (Christians); and "to observe." But the one imperative colors all of the participles and the infinitive. They can *make disciples* only as they *go*. And once they have *made disciples* they are to *baptize* and *teach* them. They are to teach them "to observe ...." These words involve the whole of evangelism. They were not simply to win, but also to develop. Someone has wisely said that the process of evangelism is not completed until the evangelized becomes an evangelist. Dr. Gaines S. Dobbins was asked, "But is not conversion the end of salvation?" He replied, "Yes, but which end?"

In this regard the infinitive "to observe" *(tērein)* calls for added study. While this meaning is correct in the text, the verb carries a much larger one. It means basically "to keep watch over, guard"; "keep" in the sense of preserving, protecting, not losing, or to keep something unharmed. Those who are won to Christ are to do all of these things to that which Jesus has commanded. And in so doing they are to pass on His commandments, His gospel, to those who come after them. Each generation of Christians has its responsibility, beginning with the first and continuing "unto the end of the age."

So the living King sent His messengers out into the world. It was a hostile and wicked world. But they were to challenge it for Him. They were to establish His sovereignty in the hearts of men, and, through them, in the world. For this seemingly impossible task He gave them no army, government, or treasury. He gave them only Himself in the Holy Spirit. For "lo, I am with you all the days until the consummation of the age" (v. 20, author's translation). "I am" speaks of His constant, abiding presence. "All the days" suggests all kinds of days; days of joy and sorrow, accomplishment and disappointment, victory and defeat. "All the days." And He will be with us "until the consummation of the age." The "age" moves toward a goal *(sunteleias)*. That goal is the subduing of all things "unto himself." Then the Son will present a redeemed and subdued universe unto the Father – that God may be all in all. And as the King reigns in the Godhead supreme, He will in truth be KING OF KINGS, AND LORD OF LORDS.

In the meantime the subduing goes on. The labor is ours; the subduing is His. The King has not told us to be successful, but to be faithful. We can leave the results with Him.

A young minister asked the Duke of Wellington for advice as to how he might have a successful ministry. The Iron Duke asked, "What are your marching orders?" The young man replied by quoting the Great Commission. Then the great general replied, "Well, what are you waiting for?" Indeed, what *was* he waiting for?

And for that matter, what are *we* waiting for?

The Gospel of Mark

CONTENTS

IV. The Journey to Jerusalem

V. The Approaching Climax

VI. The Climax of the Gospel

INTRODUCTION

When we read the Gospel of Mark we are at the headwaters of the designed written accounts of the life of Jesus. Portions of that life were probably written by various ones. But in all likelihood Mark represents the first attempt by one to record an orderly account of the greatest life ever lived. Some have questioned the priority of Mark. And the studies continue. But the evidence is strongly in favor of its being the first of the four Gospels to be written. Barclay calls it *"the essential gospel."* It is basic in any study of the other Gospels, especially Matthew and Luke. It is exactly what it claims to be: "The beginning of the gospel of Jesus Christ, the Son of God" (Mark 1:1).

Mark, Matthew, and Luke are called Synoptic Gospels. "Synoptic" means *a seeing together*. While each has certain material not found in the others, they tell the story from the same point of view. John follows a different pattern although it parallels the others at given points. A glance through Robertson's *A Harmony of the Gospels,* reveals the synoptic quality of the first three Gospels.

Barclay gives a careful analysis of these works. He notes that Mark may be divided into 105 sections: 93 of these appear in Matthew and 81 in Luke. Mark contains 661 verses, 606 of which are reproduced in Matthew and 320 in Luke. Matthew uses 51 per cent of Mark's words; Luke does likewise for 53 per cent. Of 55 verses from Mark not found in Matthew, 31 are found in Luke. Thus only 24 verses in Mark are not found in either of the other two Synoptics. Furthermore, both Matthew and Luke largely follow Mark's order of events. Where one or the other varies the order, neither agrees with the other against Mark. One or the other always keeps Mark's order of events. This shows their dependence upon Mark. It appears that each wrote with this Gospel before him.

This Gospel does not name its author. But the weight of opinion holds him to be John Mark (Acts 12:12) in whose mother's home the early disciples gathered in Jerusalem (cf. Acts 12:25; 13:13; 15:37ff.; Col. 4:10; II Tim. 4:11). Colossians 4:10 shows that he was a relative of Barnabas. Although he had figured in the separation between Paul and Barnabas, before Paul's death Mark had proved to be a helpful ally of Paul in the ministry.

The Scriptures do not relate a joint ministry of Mark with

Peter. But the fact that in I Peter 5:13 Peter calls him "Mark, my son" who was with him in "Babylon" indicates that they did work together. It could also mean that Peter had won him to Christ. Robertson notes that "the early writers all agree that Mark was the interpreter for Simon Peter." This fact is borne out by Papias, bishop of Hierapolis in Asia Minor in the second century, who called Mark Peter's interpreter. Furthermore, Moule says that "a recently discovered copy of what seems to be a genuine letter of Clement of Alexandria (about A.D. 190), also speaks definitely of Peter's notes as forming part of Mark's material." Thus it is traditionally held that Mark's Gospel reflects the preaching of Peter. Indeed, Acts 10:37-43 forms a very good outline of this Gospel.

This would explain the eyewitness effect found throughout Mark. Furthermore, since Peter probably preached to the Jews in Aramaic, we are not surprised to see that Mark uses more Aramaic words than any of the other Gospels. And his Greek is colloquial, that which both he and Peter would speak.

Mark probably wrote his Gospel for Roman readers. Thus he always translates these Aramaic words. Also he uses more Latin words than any other Gospel. The Romans were people of action. They would be more interested in what Jesus did rather than in what He said. This is also a characteristic of this Gospel. It places emphasis upon Jesus' mighty works, and it is characterized by movement. One of Mark's favorite words is *euthus,* immediately or straightway. In this Gospel Jesus moves rapidly from one event to another.

The more conservative dates for Mark have ranged all the way from A.D. 50 to beyond A.D. 65, the probable date of Peter's death. One cannot be dogmatic at this point. But this writer sees it as being dated sometime between A.D. 50 and 55, probably nearer to A.D. 50. One problem with this date lies in the matter of Mark's association with Peter. We know that he was with Paul and Barnabas for a brief period prior to A.D. 49, the probable date of the Jerusalem Conference (Acts 15). Thereafter, he went with Barnabas to Cyprus (Acts 15:39). We are not told how long he remained with him. But he could have been with Peter prior to this time (cf. Acts 10:37ff.) and soon have returned to him.

The dates of Matthew and Luke hinge upon that of Mark. If Luke's date be fixed at the latter part of Paul's Caesarean imprisonment or the early part of the one in Rome it would fall sometime in the period A.D. 59-62. Assuming that Matthew precedes this date, time prior to that would be needed for Mark's Gospel to be available to them. Hence the suggested date sometime before A.D. 55. At any rate Mark's Gospel must have been written within a period reaching not more than twenty-five years after Jesus' death and resurrection.

In this exposition the basic English text is the King James Version. The author has sought to follow rather carefully Nestle's Greek version. At times he has made his own translations from the Greek text. The primary purpose of this study is not to deal with critical problems, although the author has sought to reflect them in a degree in the work. The basic purpose has been exposition of the text itself. This has been done within the framework of a busy pastorate and a heavy schedule elsewhere – which will account for any seeming deficiencies with respect to many current studies with regard to Mark. However, it is this author's conviction that none of these has greatly affected the basic meaning of this Gospel.

No effort has been made to compile an exhaustive bibliography. But certain standard works and others applicable to this study have been followed.

William Barclay, *The Gospel of Mark,* Westminster, Philadelphia, 1956.

A. B. Bruce, "Mark," *The Expositor's Greek Testament,* Eerdmans, Grand Rapids, 1951.

Charles R. Erdman, *The Gospel of Mark,* Westminster, Philadelphia, 1956.

Herschel H. Hobbs, *An Exposition of the Gospel of Matthew,* Baker, Grand Rapids, 1965.

The International Standard Bible Encyclopedia, James Orr, General Editor, Volume III, Eerdmans, Grand Rapids, 1949.

G. Campbell Morgan, *The Gospel According to Mark,* Revell, New York, 1927.

C. F. D. Moule, *The Gospel According to Mark,* University Press, Cambridge, 1965.

A. T. Robertson, *Word Pictures in the New Testament,* Volume I, Sunday School Board of Southern Baptist Convention, Nashville, 1930.

———, *A Harmony of the Gospels,* Broadman, Nashville, 1950.

J. W. Shepard, *The Christ of the Gospels,* Eerdmans, Grand Rapids, 1938.

Kenneth S. Wuest, *Mark in the Greek New Testament,* Eerdmans, Grand Rapids, 1950.

This completes the effort which began several years ago to write an exposition of the Gospels. Since the other Synoptic Gospels followed Mark but gave their own peculiar presentations, with design we treated these Gospels before Mark. Because John is unique in his Gospel, it was chosen as the third volume. And now Mark, the first of the Gospels, is presented as the fourth of the expositions.

This has been a labor of love — love for Him who is the *Good News* of salvation—and love for those who will read these works. The writer himself has been the greatest beneficiary of this effort. He prays that it may in a small way be beneficial to you—the readers.

Herschel H. Hobbs

First Baptist Church
Oklahoma City, Oklahoma

I

The Beginning of the Gospel

Mark 1:1-8

The Ministry of the Forerunner

The Introduction (1:1-3)

Without any preliminary warning Mark plunges immediately into his story. Each of the four Gospels has its own peculiar method of beginning according to the author's individual purpose. Matthew, writing to present Jesus as the King of the Jews, naturally begins with His legal genealogy. Luke, writing for Gentile readers to declare Jesus as the universal Saviour, sets forth his method of careful research and writing. John, whose purpose was to present Jesus as the eternal Son of God become flesh, introduces his Gospel with a philosophic treatment of the eternal Christ, or Word. But Mark, writing for Roman readers who were primarily activists, simply says, "The beginning of the gospel of Jesus Christ, the Son of God" (1:1). The Romans were not so much interested in a man's origin or even his teachings as they were in what he did. So Mark set forth in a terse statement the purpose of his writing, and then proceeded with his account.

Actually verse 1 is a title which encompasses the entire Gospel. This is evident in the absence of the definite article with "beginning" *(arché)*. Thus this is the beginning not of Mark's Gospel but of the facts of the gospel.

The "gospel" *(euaggelion)* is the word whence comes the English word "evangel." "Gospel" is from the Anglo-Saxon *God spel* which means "good news." The Greek word, meaning "a message of good news," was currently used for any kind of good news. For instance, it was used of the proclamation of the occasion of a new Roman emperor. But the Christians appropriated it to refer to the good news of salvation in Jesus Christ. A newspaper writer was asked to put the gospel in one headline. He wrote, "SOMETHING WONDERFUL HAS HAPPENED"' Mark says that this "SOMETHING WONDERFUL" concerns "Jesus Christ, the Son of God." This does not mean the gospel which Jesus preached but the gospel which He wrought and was.

Note how Mark in these names combined the larger meaning of the One about whom he writes. "Jesus" is the Greek equivalent of the Hebrew *Jehoshua,* which means, "Jehovah saves." It was the human, saving name. "Christ" means "the anointed One." He was the eternal one anointed of Jehovah to provide redemption.

It was the Greek equivalent of the Hebrew "Messiah," and thus was the official title. However, it came to be used as a proper name as here. So in these two names we see the eternal anointed One revealed as the human Jesus for the salvation of lost men. And He is "A Son of God." Note the absence in the Greek text of the definite article. This does not mean that He was one among many sons of God. Rather it speaks of Jesus Christ's relation to God as "a son." He *is* the Son of God revealed to enable men *to become* sons of God (cf. John 1:12).

But even though Mark is writing to Romans he does not forget that this "gospel" is grounded in Hebrew life and literature. Jesus was not simply a man who lived in a given period of history. He was One whose life and work were foretold in the Hebrew prophets. Thus the Evangelist quoted from the prophets. "As it is written in the prophets" (v. 2). The best manuscripts read, "In Isaiah the prophet." Actually Mark quotes from both Malachi (v. 2) and Isaiah (v. 3). A later copyist corrected this to read "in the prophets" to make it conform to the facts. However, this should not be construed as an error on Mark's part. He was following current literary practice in grouping prophecies under one name. And he named Isaiah since he was regarded as the chief of the prophets. Bruce notes that this is the only prophetic citation used by Mark on his own account.

In citing these two prophecies Mark has two purposes: (1) to show that a messenger would precede the Christ; (2) to set forth that that Christ would be the "Lord." "Lord" in this sense is used with the meaning of "Jehovah." So Jehovah revealed in His Christ became Jesus of Nazareth who bore to Jehovah the relationship of "a Son of God."

In Malachi 3:1 Jehovah had said, "Behold, I will send my messenger, and he shall prepare the way before me: and the Lord, whom ye seek, shall suddenly come to his temple, even the messenger of the covenant, whom ye delight in: behold he shall come, saith the Lord of hosts." In verse 2 Mark says that this One has come to fulfil the hopes of Israel and of all who delight in Him.

Furthermore, in Isaiah 40:3 Jehovah had said, "The voice of him that crieth in the wilderness, Prepare ye the way of the Lord, make straight in the desert a highway for our God." This reflected the ancient custom of preparing a smooth roadway through the rough country over which a king might ride in a visit to a portion of his realm. So in verse 3 Mark says that the Lord, the King, is coming, and one has been sent before to prepare the way for Him to be received into men's hearts.

Mark says, "It is written." He used the perfect tense of the verb which here expresses the idea of a past action with present results. So that which had been written hundreds of years previously was now yielding the results which had been promised. The King is at hand, and the messenger goes before Him to prepare the way.

The Messenger (1:4-6)

This "messenger" Mark identifies as John the Baptist (v. 4). Later Luke will give the account of his supranatural birth and the significance of his ministry. But in keeping with his style and purpose Mark simply presents him full-grown and active in his work. The Jews believed that before the Messiah came Elijah would appear (cf. Mal. 4:5). So one cannot fail to note the sudden appearance of Elijah out of nowhere and without warning to pronounce God's judgment upon Israel (I Kings 17:1). In like fashion Mark presents John the Baptist as he springs full-grown into the arena of history with his message of judgment and call to repentance.

"John did baptize in the wilderness, and preach the baptism of repentance for the remission of sins" (v. 4). The best manuscripts read, "John came [*egeneto*], the one baptizing in the wilderness." He came as a *herald* of the King. The word "preach" renders the verb *kērussō*. It was used of a king's herald who went throughout the realm proclaiming the message of the king. He was to be heard and obeyed as if the king himself were delivering the message. So John came in the authority of the King, declaring the message of the King, and was to be heeded and obeyed as though the King had come in person.

His message was "a baptism of repentance." The word rendered "baptism" is *baptisma* which denotes not the act of baptism but the meaning in the act. And the meaning was that it denoted or symbolized *repentance*. The word "repentance" *(metanoia)* connotes a change of heart, mind, and attitude. It means a complete change in the direction of one's life.

Note that this "baptism of repentance" is "for the remission of sins." Since this was not Christian baptism in the truest sense of the word, it should not be interpreted as teaching baptismal regeneration. However, from Acts 2:38 some do so interpret Christian baptism. The key word in both cases is "for" *(eis)*. This preposition may be translated variously: for, at, as the result of, with respect or reference to, or on the basis of. In Matthew 12:41 it is rendered as "at." The men of Nineveh repented *at* the preaching of Jonah. Their repentance did not result in Jonah's preaching. To the contrary Jonah's preaching preceded their repentance. Their repentance was the result of Jonah's preaching. So "for the remission of sins" may be better understood as "at," or "on the basis of," or "as the result of the remission of sins." A. T. Robertson translates it "with reference to." Even the English word "for" is used in this sense. "He was executed for murder." He was executed not that he might murder, but because he had already murdered. So John the Baptist preached that because their sins had been remitted, men should be baptized with a baptism which was characterized by or symbolic of their repentance from sin.

Such preaching attracted multitudes of people. "And there went out unto him all the land of Judaea, and they of Jerusalem, and were baptized of him in the river of Jordan, confessing their sins" (v. 5). The verb tenses in this verse make a moving picture. The people "kept coming out" as a steady stream (imperfect), and they "were from time to time being baptized" (imperfect), "keeping on confessing" (present) their sins. This was no idle mass movement of curiosity seekers. They did not merely come to look and nothing more. They went out for a "face to face" confrontation with this preacher. This is evident in "unto him." They did not merely come *unto* John. If so, this would have been expressed by the preposition *eis*. Instead Mark uses the preposition *pros, pros auton,* face to face with him. Those who believed his message were baptized "in [*en*] the river Jordan." The Greek preposition *en* means "in the sphere of." And this corresponds to the basic meaning of the verb "to baptize" *(baptizō)*. It means to immerse or to submerge. The total picture is of a steady stream of people coming from Jerusalem and from all parts of Judea. And out of this multitude there were those who repented, and *one by one* were being baptized in the waters of the Jordan river. In verse 7 Mark describes John. It is evident that he was a desert dweller. Some suggest that as a lad following his parents' death he had been reared by the Essenes, a Jewish ascetic sect which had a community in the Judean wilderness just west of the Dead Sea. The ruins of this community have been discovered in recent years. However, there is no evidence to support their relation to John other than asceticism. One strong argument against this position is that while John sought to reform society the Essenes withdrew from it. But wherever John had lived it is evident that his life had been a rather primitive and solitary one.

He was "clothed with camel's hair." This was a garment woven out of camel's hair, with a leather girdle about his loins. There are those who see in his dress a designed affectation as he assumed the role of the Elijah who was to come (cf. Mal. 4:5f.; II Kings 1:8). However, the perfect tense of the verb rendered "clothed" indicates that this was his customary form of dress. It is not surprising to see a desert-dweller so clothed.

Furthermore, John's usual fare corresponded to his environment. For "he customarily ate locusts and wild honey." Dried locusts were regarded as palatable. And "wild honey" would be plentiful in the wilderness. The limestone rocks provided the shelter necessary for wild bees to make honey. One writer notes that even today Bedouins make a living by hunting such bees and by selling jars of wild honey in the markets of Jerusalem.

The question naturally arises as to why such a man as John would draw such large crowds in this wild, desert area. To answer this question one must recall the Messianic hope among the Jews. In olden times their forefathers had been accustomed to hear men who came as messengers from God. But for four hundred years there had been a famine "of hearing the words of the Lord" (Amos 8:11). Now there came this desert prophet who had the ring of God in his voice. His message was about the immediate appearance of the Messiah. And he reminded them of Elijah. So with excitement and spiritual hunger the people flocked to him. He did not seek out a congregation. The congregation came to him. And they heard a message not about himself but about another.

The Message (1:7-8)

John heralded the baptism of repentance. But it was done against the background of an even greater message. Men were to repent because of Him who would come after John.

"There cometh one mightier than I after me" (v. 7). Here Mark used the definite article. It was not "a one" but "the One mightier than I." So John was not the center of the message. He but pointed to another, a definite Person, the Christ, the Anointed of Jehovah. The people had come out to see and hear John. But he pointed away from himself to Another. This is the picture of the Baptist found in all of the Gospels. The movement which he heralded did not culminate in him. It looked beyond him to One infinitely greater than himself. Henceforth John must decrease that the Christ may increase (John 3:30).

So much greater was He than John that "the latchet of whose shoes I am not worthy to stoop down and unloose" (v. 7). This referred to the custom wherein a menial slave stooped down and unloosed the shoes of an arriving guest that he might rinse the dust from the guest's feet (cf. John 13:4ff.). John could not have placed himself in a lower position with respect to Jesus. He was not even worthy to perform for Him so menial a service.

And then John compared his ministry to that of Jesus. "I indeed have baptized you with water: but he shall baptize you with the Holy Ghost [Spirit]" (v. 8). Thus he contrasted his baptism with that of Jesus. This contrast is clearly seen in the Greek text. In both cases the pronoun is written out in addition to being present in the verb form. So "I on my part baptized you with [in] water: but He on His part will baptize you with [in] the Holy Spirit." John's baptism was water-baptism; Jesus' baptism was Spirit-baptism.

It is clear as to the meaning of John's water-baptism. But what did he mean by Jesus' Spirit-baptism? Some see this latter as a reference to the coming of the Spirit at Pentecost. But this event occurred after Jesus' earthly ministry. John's words apply more naturally to what Jesus would accomplish within the context of His redemptive work. And that which Jesus would accomplish would be of a more vital nature than that which John did.

The contrast turns upon baptism. John baptized in water symbolizing outwardly an inward change. It is likely, therefore, that Jesus' baptism in the Holy Spirit refers to the vital, inner work which Jesus would perform in men's hearts. It is the Holy Spirit who effects this inner cleansing and transformation. To Nicodemus Jesus said that one must be born of the Spirit (3:5-6). So by the Holy Spirit Jesus will work inwardly what John's baptism signified outwardly. Charles R. Erdman comments on this. "John administered an external rite, Jesus would effect an inner change; the baptism of John symbolized moral cleansing, Jesus would secure purity of heart and life. John pledged the recipients of his baptism to break with sin, Jesus would deliver his followers from the guilt and power of sin; John brought men into contact with a material element, water, Jesus would bring them into spiritual fellowship with a divine Person; the act of John was momentary, the influence of Jesus would be abiding."[1]

So in a few terse verses Mark introduces "the gospel of Jesus Christ, the Son of God." He shows that while John's ministry was necessary, it was not final. It connected the Messianic prophecies of the Old Testament with their fulfilment in the New Testament. And having done so he passes from John to Jesus.

---

1 *The Gospel of Mark,* Westminster, Philadelphia, 1956, p. 27.

Mark 1:9-13

The Baptism and Temptation of Jesus

The Appearance of Jesus (1:9a)

"And it came to pass in those days, that Jesus came from Nazareth of Galilee."

With the same abruptness by which Mark introduced John he also introduces Jesus. True, he had mentioned Him in the caption of his Gospel. But here he presents Him in the story itself. While in the caption he declared Him to be the Christ bearing to God the relationship of "a Son of God," in bringing Jesus into the action he says nothing about His eternal existence or about the manner of His birth. Like John, in Mark's Gospel Jesus springs full-grown into the arena of history.

In Jewish life a rabbi began his public ministry at thirty years of age. Luke notes that this was Jesus' age when He began His ministry (3:23). John was six months His senior (Luke 1:36). So apparently John's ministry had been going on this long when Jesus appeared before him in the Jordan valley.

Since early childhood Jesus had lived in Nazareth of Galilee. His foster-father Joseph had been the village carpenter. But at his death, probably when Jesus was about sixteen years old, He had assumed this trade. From Luke's account it is evident that at twelve years of age Jesus had been aware of His Messianic role (2:42ff.). One cannot be dogmatic as to when He reached this awareness. But it is this writer's conviction that He had had such an understanding from the time that He could reason out anything.

At any rate there came the day when news of the Baptist's ministry reached Nazareth. There must have been a stirring in Jesus' spirit as he realized that the hour had come for His showing to Israel. So leaving His carpenter's shop He set forth upon the journey which led Him to the threshold of His eternally marked mission.

The Baptism of Jesus (1:9b-11)

In one terse phrase Mark says that Jesus "was baptized of John in Jordan." Literally, "into the Jordan." He makes no mention of John's hesitancy to baptize Jesus (cf. Matt. 3:14f.). He merely states the fact that he did.

However, one thing is worthy of notice. Mark says that Jesus was baptized "in [*eis,* into] Jordan." A. B. Bruce in *The Expositor's Greek Testament* "Mark" notes that *eis* carries the idea of John and Jesus descending into the river.[1] Couple this with the statement in verse 10 that Jesus came up "out of [*ek*] the water." These two prepositions correspond to the meaning in the verb "baptize," that of immersion. Gould in his *International Critical Commentary* volume on "Mark" comments on this. *"Eis ton Jordanēn—into the Jordan.* The preposition here coincides with the proper meaning of the verb, indicating that the form of the rite was immersion into the stream. The preposition *ek* in the next verse,—going up *out* of the water,—implies the same."[2]

But one cannot pass by this brief phrase in verse 9b without a question. Why did Jesus submit to baptism by John?

To say that for Jesus it was a baptism of repentance would be contrary to the entire New Testament teaching. He had no sin of which to repent. But there are definite reasons why Jesus came to John for baptism. Though without sin He identified Himself with sinners who received this baptism of repentance. But more to the point, it was Jesus' own authentication of the ministry of the Baptist. It linked His forthcoming ministry with that of John. John was the forerunner; Jesus the one who came after him. Thus His baptism was the occasion for the formal launching of Jesus' public ministry. John had come baptizing. But his baptism was not Christian baptism. His baptism symbolized repentance from sin and a willingness to participate in the coming Kingdom. Christian baptism, on the other hand, symbolizes a death, burial, and resurrection. So in truth Jesus in submitting to baptism at the hands of John symbolized that which He would do to redeem those who repent of their sins and thus to enable them to become citizens of the Kingdom of God. In this sense, therefore, John's baptism of Jesus marked a transition from the one to the other.

G. Campbell Morgan calls the baptism of Jesus one of the "Crises" in His ministry.[3] This he lists along with His birth, temptation, and ascension. He calls Jesus' baptism "the parting of the ways" between the thirty preparatory years and the more than three years of His public ministry. It was in His baptism, therefore, that Jesus dedicated Himself to His work.

The importance of this event is seen in that which happened immediately following Jesus' baptism. "And straightway [*euthus,*

---

1 P. 342.

2 P. 11.

3 *The Crises of the Christ,* Revell, New York, 1936..

immediately] coming up out of the water, he saw the heavens opened, and the Spirit like a dove descending upon [*eis*] him" (v. 10). The word "straightway," appearing here for the first time in the Gospel, is one of Mark's favorite words. It depicts the swift movement of events.

Simultaneously with His coming up out of the watery grave Jesus "saw" the heavens "opened," or "split asunder." It was no mere vision. The verb "saw" *(eiden)* means to see with the natural eye. The verb "opened" renders a participial form of the verb which means "to cleave asunder, to divide" *(schizō)*. This Jesus *saw*. Furthermore, He saw "the Spirit like a dove descending upon him." Luke says that it was in the form of a dove. And John *saw* it also (cf. John 1:32).

What was the significance of this phenomenon? Bruce calls attention to the fact that the Spirit descended not "upon" *(epi)* but "into" *(eis)* Jesus. He took up His abode in Jesus. This does not mean that the Holy Spirit was not with Jesus prior to this event. The Holy Spirit is the Spirit of God sent forth to do His work. He had been active in the world since creation. With respect to Jesus He was conceived in the power of the Holy Spirit. But at Jesus' baptism He came upon Jesus or into Him in a special manifestation. Of interest is the fact that in the New Testament the Holy Spirit is called both the Spirit of God and the Spirit of Christ. So He is intimately identified as doing the work of both God the Father and Christ the Son.

But what is the significance of the "dove." The dove is symbolic of purity, meekness, and gentleness. It is also a symbol of sacrifice. So in this descent into Jesus the Holy Spirit characterizes both the character, nature, and manner of Jesus' redemptive ministry.

The coming of the Holy Spirit at Jesus' baptism, therefore, was the anointing of Jesus for His work. Thus He was empowered for His task (cf. Luke 4:18). Of interest is the fact that Jesus never worked a miracle until after the Holy Spirit came into Him. This does not mean that He was merely a man who was at this time indwelt by divine power. The disciples were Christians prior to Pentecost. But there the Holy Spirit came upon them to work in and through them in their mission. Likewise, Jesus was the Son of God from the beginning. But henceforth He would work in the power of the Holy Spirit, the Spirit of God, the Spirit of Christ sent forth to do their work. He will teach and work in the power of the Spirit. He will go to the cross in the eternal Spirit (Heb. 9:14). And He will be raised from the dead in "the spirit of holiness" (Rom. 1:4).

Also there was another heavenly phenomenon at the baptism of Jesus. For "there came a voice from heaven, saying, Thou art my beloved Son, in whom I am well pleased" (v. 11). This was the voice of the Father acclaiming Jesus as His Son. He had been the Son of God all along. But here the Father placed His approval upon the Son's life thus far, an approval which will continue to the end. It is not definitely stated that John heard this voice, but it is likely that he did. Certainly Jesus heard it. There is no evidence that the multitudes heard it.

So here as Jesus stood on the threshold of His public ministry, we see the presence of the triune God. And in the full consciousness of His Person the Son went forth to do His work.

The Temptation of Jesus (1:12-13)

"And immediately the Spirit driveth him into the wilderness" (v. 12). Note again Mark's characteristic word "immediately" *(euthus)*. Without any further ado Mark takes note of Jesus' temptation experience. Whereas Matthew and Luke say that the Spirit "led" Jesus into the wild country, Mark uses the stronger statement that He "driveth" Jesus. This should not be construed as a reluctance on Jesus' part. Rather it expresses the strong conviction which the Spirit gave Him that this experience was necessary. It was to be a time of testing as Jesus faced the question as to the nature of His forthcoming ministry.

Whereas Matthew and Luke give the details of this experience, Mark disposes of it with two brief verses. He says that Jesus spent forty days in the wilderness, a wild region perhaps just west of Jericho (v. 13). His only companions were "the wild beasts." Robertson notes that it was the haunt at night of wolves, boars, hyenas, jackals, and leopards. So it was a lonely, dangerous place. But the Spirit who drove Jesus into this place watched over Him.

While here He was "tempted of Satan" (v. 13). Mark gives no details. But from Matthew and Luke it is clear that the temptations revolved about the nature of Jesus' Messiahship.[4] Jesus triumphed over Satan in each one. "And the angels ministered unto him" (v. 13). This was certainly true at the end of the temptation experience (Matt. 4:11). But we may also see God's protecting care over Him throughout the forty days.

After the two "crises" in the Jordan and in the wilderness Jesus

---

4 For a discussion of these temptations see my *Exposition of the Gospel of Matthew,* Baker, Grand Rapids, 1965; *Exposition of the Gospel of Luke,* Baker, Grand Rapids *(in loco).*

went forth to meet the challenge of a sinful world. And through it all He was well-pleasing to the Father and empowered by the Spirit.

II

The Ministry in Galilee

Mark 1:14-20

The Call of Four Fisherman

The Intervening Ministry (1:14a)

Were it not for John's Gospel it would appear that following His temptation experience Jesus entered immediately into His Galilean ministry. However, John shows that Jesus returned to Galilee, and after a brief ministry there made a journey to Jerusalem for a feast of the Passover and a brief ministry in Judea (1:43–3:36). This period consumed about a year, a year which Robertson calls "the year of obscurity." It was after this that Jesus returned to Galilee through Samaria (John 4). At this point Mark, followed by Matthew and Luke, relates Jesus' return to Galilee.

There is no conflict between Mark and John. John shows a continuing ministry of the Baptist after Jesus' baptism (3:22-36). And Mark notes that Jesus returned to Galilee "after that John was put in prison" (v. 14). Later he enlarges upon this matter (6:17ff.). His mention of it at this point is to show the stage of Jesus' ministry that is involved in his account.

The Beginning of the Galilean Ministry (1:14b-15)

"Jesus came into Galilee, preaching the gospel of the kingdom of God" (v. 14b). This had been the theme of John's preaching (Matt. 3:1-2). So once again we see the continuity between his ministry and that of Jesus. But there was a different emphasis. Whereas John's message centered in "repentance" as an evidence that one was willing to participate in the kingdom when it came, Jesus preached "the gospel of God," or the good news that the kingdom had come with the King. The words "the kingdom of" are not found in the best manuscripts. Note that Jesus did not use the word "Christ." This title had taken on a highly nationalistic sense, that of a military-political Messiah. For this reason Jesus never applied this term to Himself in direct, public discourse. But one cannot read His claims for Himself without seeing that He was the Christ in the true sense of the word as God's anointed for salvation.

However, Jesus did not omit the kingdom idea from His preaching. For He said, "The time is fulfilled, and the kingdom of God is at hand: repent ye, and believe the gospel" (v. 15). The word for "time" is *kairos* not *chronos* or time as such. *Kairos* referred to some particular time as an epochal event. This "fulness of time," as Paul called it (Gal. 4:4), was a time of God's own choosing, when He marked the end of the dispensation of law and the beginning of the dispensation of grace. This meant that the long-heralded "kingdom of God" was now here. And the clarion call of the King was "Repent ye, and believe the gospel." John had called for repentance. Jesus does the same, but adds that those repenting must also "believe the gospel." Not the baptism of John, but faith in the good news that the kingdom had come in the person of the King. So the call now was for allegiance to a Person. The "good news" at this point did not connote the saving work of Jesus. For that was yet to come. But it was "good news" that that which had been promised was now taking place. And it centered in "Jesus Christ, the Son of God" (1:1).

The Call to Service (1:16-20)

Other than the general statement in verses 14-15, this event sets the beginning of Mark's account of Jesus' "Great Galilean Ministry." The other Gospels note that prior to this occurrence Jesus had paid a second visit to Cana (cf. John 2:1-11; 4:46-54), had been rejected by Nazareth (Luke 4:16,31), and had set up headquarters in Capernaum a city on the northwest shore of the sea of Galilee (Matt. 4:13-16).

In addition to His own ministry it was in Jesus' purpose to select others to work with Him and to be trained by Him for future service. So one day He was walking along by the sea of Galilee near Capernaum. "He saw Simon and Andrew his brother casting a net into the sea: for they were fishers" (v. 16). About a year earlier in the Jordan valley they had become believers in Jesus as the Christ. Andrew had first believed in Jesus. Then he sought out his brother and brought him to Jesus (John 1:37-42). At that time Jesus had predicted that one day Simon would be called "Peter," a stone. According to John's Gospel they, along with others, had traveled with Jesus. But apparently upon their return to Galilee following Jesus' visit to Judea they had returned to their trade as fishermen. So Jesus saw them "casting" a net into the sea. This word means that they were casting the net first on one side of the boat and then on the other. With vivid imagination Mark tells a moving story. This reflects the clear memory of Simon Peter. Fish was one of the important items on the diet of the Galileans. And so these men evidently had a prosperous business.

But seing them Jesus said, "Come ye after me, and I will make you to become fishers of men" (v. 17). This was a challenge to leave their secure livelihood to cast their lot with Jesus. There was no promise of economic security. But there was the promise of a more satisfactory vocation. Now they fished for fish. But Jesus challenged them to fish for men. Rather than to cast their string nets for fish to satisfy the physical needs of men, they were to cast the net of the gospel to meet the spiritual needs of men.

Jesus' use of terms is most suggestive. Fishers for fish were to fish for men. They were to use their economic skills for spiritual ends. And what Jesus said to them He says to all who would follow Him. For there is no skill used in a legitimate business which cannot be used in the work of the Lord. If a man can sell soup he can *sell* salvation. A lawyer who can plead before the bars of justice can plead with men to receive the grace of God. Whether one be a teacher, farmer, executive, or clerk—he is challenged to devote his life and energy to the Lord—either apart from his present position or else within it. If any man will he can transform his vocation into a calling in God's service. Note that Jesus would make them "to become" fishers of men. They would do so crudely at first. But under His patient skill they would become fruitful evangels for Jesus.

"And straightway they forsook their nets, and followed him" (v. 18). In the Greek text "forsook" is an aorist participle. This plus the word "straightway" *(euthus)* doubly expresses the immediacy of their action. The aorist tense also expresses permanence. Without hesitation they broke completely with their former occupation to become followers of Jesus. The words rendered "followed him" mean literally to follow, or to walk side-by-side with Him. Kenneth Wuest comments: "It implies fellowship, joint-participation, a side-by-side walking with another. Thus it has come to mean, 'to join one as a disciple, to cleave steadfastly to one, conform wholly to his example, in living and, if need be, in dying.' "[1]

Going a little farther along the shore Jesus "saw James the son of Zebedee, and John his brother, who were also in the ship mending their nets" (v. 19). It is a common sight even today around the sea of Galilee to see fishermen doing this. James and John had finished their catch and were mending their broken nets for future use. Luke tells us that Simon, Andrew, James, and John were "partners" (5:7).

Seeing these two brothers who also had believed in Jesus previously, He issued to them the same challenge that He had given

[1] *Mark in the Greek New Testament,* Eerdmans, Grand Rapids, 1950, p. 29.

to Simon and Andrew. And they responded in similar fashion. "They left their father Zebedee in the ship [a large fishing vessel] with the hired servants [workers for wages], and went after him" (v. 20). The size of the boat plus the hired servants suggest that they together with Simon and Andrew had a large fishing business. But they left it to the care of Zebedee and the servants while they became companions of Jesus in service.

Nothing is said about the size of the catch these fishermen had made. But Jesus made a prize catch in these two sets of brothers. Simon will become Peter one of the early stalwarts of the faith. Andrew, while not so talented as his brother, became a great soul-winner. Other than in the list of the twelve apostles and this incident, each time that Andrew is seen he is bringing someone to Jesus. John and James were first cousins of Jesus. The former became the "beloved disciple" whose Gospel gives one of the greatest presentations of Jesus. James became one of the early martyrs, the first of the twelve apostles to pay for his faith with his life.

Yes, Jesus demonstrated His skill as a fisher of men. And that skill He will impart to these four fishers of fish.

Mark 1:21-45

The Pattern of Jesus' Ministry

Prior to Jesus' death on the cross His ministry followed the pattern of teaching, preaching, and healing. All three of these activities are found in this passage. He taught, and preached in the synagogues; He healed there and elsewhere. It is in this passage that Mark records the first teaching and miracles reported in his Gospel (but see John 2). It is significant that Mark's first recorded miracle of Jesus was the healing of a demoniac. This showed His power over the realm of evil.

The Healing of a Demoniac (1:21-28)

With His newly-made disciples Jesus returned to Capernaum. "And straightway on the sabbath day he entered into the synagogue, and taught" (v. 21). Jesus had taught previously (cf. John 3-4; Luke 4:16ff.). But Mark begins his record of Jesus' teaching here. However, it should be noted that he merely states the fact. His Roman readers were not particularly interested in this phase of Jesus' life.

The synagogue was a good place to begin teaching. For it was the local place of assembly for teaching and worship. The origin of the synagogue is shrouded in mystery. But it arose sometime during the Babylonian captivity when the Jews had no temple in which to worship. After their return to Palestine it became a permanent institution. Wherever there were ten heads of Jewish families there was a synagogue. So that by the time of Jesus synagogues were found throughout Palestine and the Roman empire. To both Jesus and Paul they were a focal point since it was there that they found a ready-made audience to hear the gospel. It was customary for the presiding officer to invite visiting dignitaries to read the Scripture and to address the people (cf Luke 4:16-21; Acts 13:14-43).

The synagogue in Capernaum was the scene of much of Jesus' teaching and works of wonder. It had been built by a Roman centurion as a gift to the Jews of that city (Luke 7:4-5). In modern Capernaum one may see the ruins of a later synagogue built upon the site of the one that stood there in Jesus' day.

As Jesus taught the people were amazed at His teaching (v. 22). The words "were astonished" render a verb which meant to be struck with astonishment or amazement throughout His lesson. For He "taught them as one that had authority, and not as the scribes" (v. 22). The scribes taught largely by quoting other important rabbis. So their teaching was a dry rote devoid of freshness or of authority. But Jesus taught out of Himself. The word rendered "authority" means "out of being." So out of His own being Jesus taught. He did not need to cite other rabbis, though at times He did undergird His teaching by quoting from the Hebrew Scriptures. But, even so, there was a freshness and a certainty to which the people were not accustomed. It is no wonder that they hung on His every word with growing interest and astonishment.

In the synagogue that day was "a man with an unclean spirit" (v. 23). Literally, "in an unclean spirit." This spirit was in the man and the man was in this spirit. The phrase "unclean spirit" is the equivalent of *demon*. He was possessed of a demon. This demon indwelt the man, and he was under its control.

Demon-possession is a mystery. Some moderns call it a superstition among a primitive people. But Luke, a physician, scientist, and a historian whose accuracy is without question, speaks of demons as a reality. And Jesus certainly accepted them as such. Those who deny their reality either accuse Jesus of ignorance along with His contemporaries, or else hold that He did not believe in them but accommodated His language and actions to their ignorance. In either case it maligns His Person and character, making Him nothing more than a man or else making Him guilty of hypocrisy.

Still others see in demon-possession certain psychological disorders, conditions to which modern science assigns its technical names. There are cases which could fit into this category. But it is not necessarily true of all. The truth of the matter is that some people today are demon-possessed. How else can one account for the diabolic deeds of certain people?

But there is one other thought which should be considered. Demon-possession was regarded as existing among all ancients. But in no time was this phenomenon more common than in the time of Jesus. With this in mind one thought emerges. The Bible teaches the continuing conflict between God and Satan in the spiritual realm (cf. Eph. 6:11-12). Paul says that in this conflict Satan uses evil men. Jesus was God in the flesh. Is it not possible, therefore, that to counter this revelation Satan in an especial way through his demons indwelt men during this time?

At any rate accepting the Gospel record we see this demon-possessed man. And in the presence of Jesus the demon "cried out." This means that through the throat of its victim it cried with a cry reflecting its fears of impending doom. In the presence of deity and holiness the demon saw its doom. And all who were present heard its words.

"Let us alone; what have we to do with thee, thou Jesus of Nazareth? art thou come to destroy us? I know thee who thou art, the Holy One of God" (v. 24). Note the interplay of singular and plural words. This demon cried out on behalf of all demons. Or else it spoke for itself and its victim.

What did demons have in common with Jesus? How could evil abide the presence of goodness? The coming of Jesus could mean but one thing. He had come to destroy demons and their evil works (I John 3:8). If men did not recognize the purpose of Jesus' ministry, demons did. Furthermore, he called Jesus "the Holy One of God." Men may deny Jesus' deity, but devils, wise in spiritual things, confessed Him as such. Beyond the pale of His mercy, still they knew Him for who He was.

But Jesus rebuked the demon, saying, "Hold thy peace, and come out of him" (v. 25). Jesus did not want the testimony of demons. All too soon there would be those who accused Him of being in league with Satan. So Jesus told the demon to "be quiet" (Moffatt). Literally, "be muzzled" like an ox. Gould translates it "Shut up." And this is a good colloquial rendering of it. Then Jesus commanded, "Come out of him." The aorist imperative of these two verbs shows that Jesus ordered the demon to do both immediately.

What did the demon do? It obeyed Jesus. But in doing so it showed its rage at being disembodied. It *tore* the man. This means that it threw him into a convulsive spasm. Medical writers used this word for the rotating of the stomach. Luke says that it threw the man to the ground (4:35). "And he cried out with a loud voice." This was a veritable screech. Then it came out of the man. What an exciting moment in the synagogue!

The people were even more amazed at this than at Jesus' teaching (v. 27). They asked literally, "What is this? A new teaching according to power! even the unclean spirits he lines up as a troop under command, and they obey him!" Jesus said, "Forward march out of the man!" And they marched forth at His command.

So before their eyes they had seen Jesus' power and authority over the evil spirits. No incantations or magic words as the exorcists used in pretending to cast out demons. A word of command, and it was done.

"And immediately his fame spread abroad throughout all the region round about Galilee" (v. 28). Like wildfire the news spread through the land. And well it might have done. For Capernaum had heard and seen wonderful things.

The Healing of Peter's Mother-in-law (1:29-34)

Apparently while in Capernaum Jesus lived in the home of Simon Peter. So after the service on this sabbath day He went with the four disciples to "the house of Simon and Andrew" (v. 29). Mark says that they did so "forthwith" *(euthus)*. "Simon's wife's mother lay sick of a fever" (v. 30). The word for "fever" comes from the Greek word for "fire." So she was burning up with a fever. The sense is that she had been sick for some time. This could have been malaria. "And anon [*euthus*] they tell him of her." So Jesus coming and taking her by the hand lifted her up. "And immediately the fever left her, and she ministered unto them" (v. 31). The word "immediately" is not in the best texts. But the idea is present in the aorist form of the verb. It is a miracle. The fever did not gradually subside. It left her immediately. The miraculous element is further seen in the words "and she ministered [imperfect, went on ministering] unto them." Had this been a natural cure she would have been left weak. But the fever left her immediately, and immediately she was strong enough to serve her son-in-law's guests. Perhaps she prepared the noon meal for them.

He who so recently had shown His power over evil spirits now demonstrated His power over disease. And it was done in the privacy of the home of friends. In no sense was this a public demonstration. It was an expression of Jesus' tender compassion.

Word spread throughout Capernaum about these miracles. But since it was the Sabbath Jesus evidently spent a quiet afternoon. Sabbath law forbade people to bear a burden on that day. "But at even, when the sun did set, they brought unto him all that were diseased and . . . possessed with devils" (v. 32). "Brought" means to bear a burden, the sick. At sunset the sabbath day ended. Thereafter a throng of people brought their loved ones to Jesus for healing. So much so that all the city was gathered together at the door (v. 33). One can imagine the excitement and anticipation throughout this crowd. And they were not disappointed. For Jesus "healed many that were sick of divers [various] diseases, and cast out many devils" (v. 34). "Many" does not mean that some were not healed. It simply means that many were diseased. Jesus healed all of them.

This was a beautiful sight. Just after sunset, perhaps in the twilight, Jesus with tender hands touching the sick so that they were healed. And with authoritative voice commanding demons to depart from their victims, and they obeyed. Mark alone mentions the size of the crowd (v. 33). Assuming that Peter was the source of his information, it reflects the prideful joy of Simon that his door should be the site of so great a scene. His eager mind retained every detail of it.

Jesus "suffered not the devils to speak, because they knew him" (v. 34). He "kept on not permitting" them to speak. This implies that they insisted upon speaking as the demon had done in the synagogue that morning. But Jesus refused them the privilege. He did not want the testimony of such.

The Healing of a Leper (1:35-45)

Jesus had spent a busy day. Healing was a drain upon His strength, both physically and spiritually. So that night He slept the sleep of the blessed.

"And in the morning, rising up a great while before day, he went out, and departed into a solitary place, and there prayed" (v. 35). Mark with exactness sets the time. It was *prōi,* or the last watch of the night, from three to six A.M. Furthermore, it was *ennucha lian,* or the early part of that watch while it was still dark. So arising from sleep He *went out* of the house and *went from* the city into a solitary place. "And there he kept on praying." He continued in prayer until after day had dawned.

If the scene at twilight had been a glorious one, this one was even more so. For alone with the Father Jesus poured out His soul in sweet communion. It is mere speculation as to that about which He prayed. But speculation is in order. Surely He was lonely and hungry for fellowship with His Father. Perhaps He prayed for renewed strength after the strenuous day. With His growing popularity He may have prayed that it might not become a snare to Him. Furthermore, He was planning a preaching tour through Galilee (v. 39). Maybe that was the burden of His prayer. But pray He did, both long and fervently.

If Jesus needed to pray, surely His people need to do so. It is said that before the beginning of each day Martin Luther spent an hour in prayer. But if he anticipated an unusually hard day, he prayed for two hours. So often Christians let a busy schedule interfere with their prayer time. Jesus did not, and neither should we.

Simon and the others awoke to find Jesus gone. So they went

in search for Him (v. 36). Moffatt says that they hunted Him out. Having found Him they said, "All men seek for thee" (v. 37). "All are seeking you." What preacher would not have been lured back by the call of the crowd! This was the thought in the minds of the disciples. Opportunity was knocking. And Jesus should open the door.

But Jesus had other plans. "Let us go [elsewhere, Nestle] into the next towns, that I may preach there also: for therefore came I forth" (v. 38). The "next towns" were country towns or villages without walls, out-of-the-way places. Most preachers would go from such places to the city where the crowds are greater. But Jesus proposed to go from the teeming city to the sparsely settled villages. A soul without Christ is as lost, and as precious to God, in a village as in a city. And they too must have opportunity to hear the gospel.

"For therefore [unto this] came I forth." One might see in these words the purpose of the incarnation. But it probably means that Jesus had come out of Capernaum with the intention of making this first tour of Galilee. So with the four fishermen He made this tour, preaching in the synagogues and casting out demons (v. 39).

It was while on this tour that "there came a leper to [*pros,* face to face] him" (v. 40). Leprosy was a common and terrible disease. Those afflicted with it were ostracized from society, usually living in caves or empty tombs. They were considered as the living dead. A leper was not permitted to enter a walled town or city. It was against Levitical law for one to touch them. One rabbi boasted that he had thrown rocks at a leper to drive him away. They were not permitted to come nearer than six feet to a clean person. If the wind were blowing from them toward the person the allowed distance was one hundred feet. And wherever a leper went he was supposed to wear a mask or else to keep his hand over his mouth. To warn any unsuspecting person who approached him he was required to cry, "Unclean! Unclean!"

It is against this background that Mark tells this moving story. Perhaps in the open country or else in an unwalled village the leper came face to face with Jesus. At once he was both "beseeching" and "kneeling" before Jesus. And he said or was saying repeatedly, "If thou wilt, thou canst make me clean." If Jesus were willing He had the power to do so. The leper did not doubt Jesus' power. But he was not sure about His attitude. He was not accustomed to being treated kindly. Would this *rabbi* also throw stones at him?

But he did not reckon with Jesus' heart. For "Jesus, moved with compassion, put forth his hand, and touched him, and saith unto him, I will [I am willing]; be thou clean" (v. 41). Jesus was moved with compassion. Only Mark mentions this. The pitiful plight of the man aroused Jesus' pity and love. The fact that Jesus touched him shows that the man had dared to come nearer than six feet.

Did Jesus touch the leper before or after he was healed? Wuest concludes from a grammatical analysis that it was afterward. However, the natural sequence suggests that He touched him prior to his healing. This seems to be the case from verse 42. The King James Version says, "And as soon as he had spoken, immediately [*euthus*] the leprosy departed from him, and he was cleansed." Literally, "And immediately left him the leprosy." The word "immediately" plus the aorist tense both emphasize the miraculous cleansing. At any rate, the touch of Jesus was significant. For as Wuest says, "The first kind touch of a human hand that leper ever experienced, was the gentle touch of the Son of God."[1]

Having performed this deed of mercy Jesus "straitly charged him, and forthwith sent him away" (v. 43). The words "straitly charged" render the verb *embrimaomai* which means to snort as a horse or to be moved with anger. In Greek classics it meant to be moved with anger or indignation. However, in the New Testament it carries the idea of an earnest admonition. Did Jesus sternly charge the leper not to tell of the healing since to do so would excite the people prematurely? This could be the meaning. But this was done in public. So there must be another possible meaning. In the light of verse 44 it would appear that Jesus sternly charged him to go to the priest, in accord with the Mosaic law, that the priest might officially pronounce him clean. Thereafter, he was to make the required offering in connection with his being pronounced cured of leprosy (cf. Lev. 14). Even though Jesus healed by a miracle, He did not ignore the laws prescribed for those who had been healed.

But the man went out and told everyone he saw about his cleansing. So much so that Jesus was forced to avoid populated areas (v. 45). However, even so, the crowds flocked to Him "from every quarter." And why not? For Jesus had healed what to the Jews was the most terrible of diseases.

---

[1] *Op. cit.*, p. 41.

Mark 2:1-12

The Claim of Jesus to Deity

Did Jesus ever make a claim to deity? Some deny that He did. To be sure, He never in so many words said, "I am God." But it is impossible to read the Gospels without seeing that in one way or another He claimed a relationship with God which can be explained in no way short of deity. Some see John's Gospel as written for the express purpose of proving His deity. And this truth is more pronounced there than it is in the other Gospels. But do they ignore this element altogether? The answer must be in the negative. The birth narratives in Matthew and Luke certainly teach it. The death and resurrection of Jesus likewise do so. This truth is seen as the background of the Synoptic narratives.

Certainly the passage under consideration teaches it. And it is paralleled by both Matthew and Luke.

The Return to Capernaum (2:1)

"And again he entered into Capernaum after some days; and it was noised that he was in the house." This would be at the close of Jesus' first tour of Galilee. Does this mean that "after some days" He returned to Capernaum? This could be. Yet this expression hardly allows for the time evidently spent in this tour. However, Robertson suggests that this phrase involves the time from Jesus' departure from Capernaum to His return.

But Bruce makes a more likely comment. He suggests that "after some days" may be related to "it was noised." Jesus returned quietly to Capernaum, to Simon's home. And then "after some days . . . it was noised [or heard] that he was in the house."

The Paralytic Man (2:2-4)

The news that Jesus was back in Capernaum produced a phenomenal result. The people crowded in to see Him, "insomuch that there was no room to receive them, no, not so much as about the door" (v. 2). Not only was the house filled, but a crowd stood outside so that no one could enter at the door. "And he preached [kept on saying] the words unto them."

"And they came unto him, bringing one sick of the palsy [a

paralytic, Greek, *paralutikon*], which was borne [being borne] of four" (v. 3). This is a good example of Mark's use of the historical present tense, one of his favorite forms. Though the event was in the past, he tells it as though it were just happening. Mark also gives the detail that the man was borne by four friends, a detail omitted by both Matthew and Luke. Each man carried a corner of his bed or pallet. He evidently was seeing through the eyes of Peter.

But due to "the press," or the crowd about the door, they were unable to bring the man into the house where Jesus was (v. 4). But they were not to be denied. So they took him up on the top of the house. The roof of an oriental house was flat, and reached by stairs outside the house. Often, and especially in hot weather, dwellers would go up to this roof at night. Then the men "uncovered the roof." Literally, "they unroofed the roof." Then through the hole they lowered the man on his pallet down into the house before Jesus.

Their persistence was admirable. They did not falter before an obstacle in their effort to bring their friend to Jesus. One can only wish that all men were as persistent in bringing lost men to Jesus.

The Act of God (2:5-12)

"When Jesus saw their faith, he said unto the sick of the palsy, Son, thy sins be forgiven thee" (v. 5).

When He saw "their faith." Whose faith? The faith of the four men. They had a faith which would not be denied. Even though Mark mentions only their faith, it is implied that the paralytic also had faith. Though he was physically helpless, he was a part of this persistent effort. So "their" could include him also. Faith is the basis of the work of Jesus. In Nazareth He could not do mighty works because of the townspeople's unbelief (Matt. 13:58). But here in Capernaum there was abundant faith upon which Jesus could act. The five men all believed in Jesus' power and willingness to heal.

But to their surprise Jesus said nothing about paralysis. Instead He said, "Son, thy sins be forgiven thee" (v. 5). The word "son" renders *teknon,* child, rather than *huios,* son or an adult son. *Teknon* was used to address a boy or a small child. But in the papyri this word is found as a form of kindly address, even to adults. Jesus used it as a tender address to this sick man. He did not upbraid him as a sinner, but spoke kindly to him as a sinner in need of His ministry. Jesus hated sin but loved sinners. Why did Jesus speak of sins, a spiritual ailment, rather than the man's physical condition? It is possible that his sins had caused his paralysis. So Jesus began at the proper place. He went to the heart of the matter. Though men might not think so, his greater need was spiritual healing.

Jesus' words astonished others besides the five men. For some scribes were present. Up to this point no mention has been made of the Jewish priesthood. But here they were. Up to this point, according to Mark, Jesus had encountered no opposition. But John notes that He had had a run-in with the chief priests in Jerusalem (2:13-22). And the Pharisees were watching Him (4: 1-3). These scribes may have been present in Capernaum for that purpose.

At any rate, Jesus' word about forgiving sins would arouse their animosity (v. 6). In their hearts they resented His words as blasphemy. For, asked they, "Who can forgive sins but God only?" (v. 7). It is evident, therefore, that they regarded Jesus as assuming a position which belonged only to God. Did Jesus, knowing their hearts, deliberately challenge them by first forgiving the man's sins? Perhaps so.

Nevertheless, knowing what they were thinking, Jesus asked, "Why reason ye these things in your hearts?" (v. 8). Then He challenged them to make a decision. "Whether it is easier to say to the sick of the palsy, Thy sins be forgiven thee; or to say, Arise, and take up thy bed, and walk?" (v. 9). "Whether" renders the Greek word *ti.* In this context it means "which of two?" So Jesus asked which of these two things was easier, to say that the man's sins were forgiven or to perform this physical miracle? The latter of these may be translated exactly as "Be arising [present], and immediately take up and carry [aorist] thy pallet, and go on walking about [present]."

Now if Jesus were an imposter He could still say, "Thy sins be forgiven thee," and no one could prove on the spot whether or not the man's sins had been forgiven. But obviously one could tell immediately whether or not Jesus had performed the physical miracle. And if Jesus did do the latter it would prove that He was more than a mere man. And if so, then it would be evident that He possessed supernatural, divine power. It would naturally follow, therefore, that He also had the power and right to forgive sins.

And then Jesus applied the clincher. "But that ye may know that the Son of man hath power on earth to forgive sins, (he saith to the sick of the palsy,) I say unto thee, Arise, and take up thy bed, and go thy way into thine house" (vv. 10-11).

These verses are rich in meaning. "Know" renders *eidēte* from *oida*. This means a deep down perception, or absolute knowledge. So Jesus' purpose is that they shall have a knowledge which cannot be denied. The word "power" basically means "out of being." This is a power resident in Jesus by virtue of His being; no tricks; no *hocus pocus;* but divine power.

Note also that for the first time Mark records Jesus as calling Himself "Son of man." This was His favorite term of self-designation. This was one title for the Messiah (cf. Dan. 7:13). The more popular titles were "Christ" and "Son of David." But to the Jewish mind in the first century they carried a highly nationalistic sense. Therefore, to avoid exciting the people unduly Jesus never used these titles of Himself in direct public address. He accepted the titles, when applied to Him by others. In private to the Samaritan woman at Jacob's well He admitted that He was the Christ. And under oath at His trial He admitted that He was the Christ. For this the Sanhedrin said that He was guilty of blasphemy, and, therefore, was liable to the death penalty. Throughout His public ministry they had sought to trick Jesus into an open claim to being the Christ. Had He made such a claim to them they would have used it to accuse Him of treason before Pilate. He admitted to being the Christ only when placed under oath. To have denied it then would have been perjury.

It is clear, therefore, why Jesus chose the title "Son of man." It both revealed and concealed His Messiahship. It related Him to both God and man.

So as the "Son of man" He commanded the paralytic to get up, take up his pallet, and go to his home. What did the man do? Literally, "And he arose, and immediately bearing his pallet he went out before all of them" (v. 12). The people were amazed, and they kept on glorifying God, saying, "We never saw it on this fashion." The scribes could not deny what they and the crowd had seen. They, too, were amazed. But they did not glorify God. Jesus had set the terms of the test. He had proved His point. If He could miraculously heal the man's body, He could also forgive his sins.

By their own admission the scribes had said that only God could forgive sins. Thus with their own words Jesus had proved His right to His claim to deity.

Mark 2:13-22

The Old and the New Revelation

A modern tourist in Palestine often wonders at different localities if he is where Jesus once was. For the most part one has to say of a given event that if it did not happen at a given spot it surely took place somewhere nearby. Jacob's well in Samaria is said to be the one certain spot where one may be sure that Jesus once was there.

But there is also another place. For when today one walks along the shores of the sea of Galilee near Capernaum he may be certain that he is walking where Jesus walked. For Mark says that "he went forth again by the sea side" (v. 14). Bruce says that the incident at hand did not necessarily follow immediately after the preceding narrative. However, one likes to follow Robertson who says that Jesus probably went directly from Simon's house and from the crowd. For Him it would be a joy to get a breath of fresh air by the seaside. But even there the crowd followed, and Jesus "kept on teaching" (imperfect) them.

The Call of Levi (Matthew) (2:14)

Mark is indefinite as to the time when this call was given. It could have been while Jesus continued His walk by the seaside after teaching the people. Or it could have come later. The time element is unimportant here.

But as Jesus was passing along He saw "Levi the son of Alphaeus sitting at the receipt of custom." This was a tollgate on the Great West Road which ran from Damascus to the Mediterranean. It also served as the customs office at Capernaum, the landing place for the ships which plied their trade on the sea of Galilee. Levi was a toll collector for Herod Antipas, the tetrarch of Galilee. Mark, followed by Luke, calls him Levi. But Matthew uses the name Matthew, the name by which he was known among the apostles. It was a common custom for a man to have two given names, then as now.

Levi was a publican. In the Roman tax system the collection of taxes was not done by the government directly. Tax collection in a given area was sold to the highest bidder. The one thus chosen had others who worked for him. Under this system a man had to get back his investment plus a profit. So the system lent itself to corruption and oppression. For this reason publicans were a hated lot. This, plus the fact that in Palestine the publicans were Jews, led them to be classed as traitors to their nation. It is not surprising to see that they were classed along with the lowest of sinners.

Seeing Levi Jesus simply said, "Follow me." But since He used the present imperative it was a command. No previous mention has been made of Levi. However, in all likelihood he was familiar with Jesus. It is unlikely that anyone living in Capernaum had not heard of Jesus. More than likely he had heard Him teach. Furthermore, such a command from Jesus shows that He knew Levi, or at least knew about him. Working in a public place as he did, it is likely that Jesus had observed him carefully over a period of time.

The word "follow" *(akolutheō)* means to walk the same road, to join one as an attendant or disciple, to side with one's cause, and to follow after one who precedes him in the way. All of these thoughts were involved in Jesus' command to Levi. And the present tense means that he was to begin and to keep on doing these things. They were to become the habit of Levi's life. However, Jesus added an additional touch when He said literally, "Follow with me." So Jesus did not simply say for Levi to come after Him but to walk with Him. He was to associate himself with Jesus in His spiritual enterprise. This could suggest that as a tax collector Levi was not merely an employee but one who shared in the profits of his business. It appears that he may have been a man of means (v. 15). If this be a proper surmise then Jesus commanded him to change partners, to become His partner. Previously He had challenged the four fishermen to become fishers of men. So now He called Levi to form a spiritual partnership with Him. He spoke to men in terms of their present position and understanding.

Levi immediately "arose" (aorist participle) and "followed [aorist] him." Literally, "with him." So at a financial cost to himself Levi without hesitation entered into a new partnership. Wuest comments, "This meant for Levi, that henceforth he would walk the same road that Jesus walked, a road of self-sacrifice, a road of separation, a road of altruism, a road of suffering, a road of holiness."[1] This decided change in life for Levi indicates the transformation which his commitment to Jesus made. And He demands this of all who would follow *with* Him.

---

1 *Op. cit.*, p. 52.

The Dinner in Levi's Home (2:15-20)

Levi's new *partnership* was quite an event in his life. So to celebrate it he made a great feast in his house (cf. Luke 5:29). The number of guests present suggests that it may have been a garden or a court party. Levi's purpose for this dinner may have been to announce to his friends his decision to leave his customs seat and to become a follower with Jesus.

At any rate Mark is careful to point out the large number and type of people present. "Many publicans and sinners sat also together with Jesus and his disciples: for they were many, and they followed him" (v. 15). Who other than publicans and sinners would accept such an invitation? The fact that "they were following" (imperfect) Jesus shows that by this time He had a considerable following among this class.

But there were also some uninvited people at the dinner, "the scribes and Pharisees." They were not guests. Indeed, they would have refused to come had they been invited. They were there to spy on Jesus. It was customary for outsiders to stand about and watch as the guests reclined about the table. So seeing Jesus eating with such despised people they asked His disciples, "How is it that he eateth . . . with publicans and sinners" (v. 16)? "And drinketh" is not found in the best manuscripts. To these self-righteous ones such an act was considered immoral.

Jesus, overhearing their critical question, replied, "They that are whole have no need for a physician, but they that are sick: I came not to call the righteous, but sinners to repentance" (v. 17).

The scribes and Pharisees were a self-righteous group. This is Mark's first mention of the Pharisees. They were the orthodox among the Jews. They accepted all of the Old Testament as Scripture, believed in miracles, angels, and the resurrection from the dead, and held to a strong Messianic hope. The Pharisees were the *separatists*. As a group they had arisen during the period following the Babylonian captivity. They had been strongly opposed to the efforts to force Greek culture and religion upon the Jews. In this regard they rendered a useful service. But they had degenerated into a group of rote ritualists. In emphasizing the letter of the law they had lost its spirit. And in addition to the law of Moses they had devised a multitude of rules designed to regulate the least details of conduct. Highly nationalistic they were the champions of Jewish rule. Thus they were opposed to the house of Herod and to the Romans. This meant that they were strongly antagonistic to the publicans. Since the "sinners" ignored their rules of conduct they were also against them. It is no wonder then that they were indignant at seeing Jesus eating with them.

Jesus took them at their own appraisal. They would be the last to acknowledge that they were in need of Jesus' ministry. Thus they were the "whole" or the "well." A physician would not be expected to be found among such a *healthy* group. On the other hand, the scribes and Pharisees certainly regarded the publicans and sinners as "sick," even fatally so. Therefore, the Physician of souls would naturally be found among them striving to heal them of their illness.

Bruce points out that "Jesus would not meet such people in the synagogue, as they seem to have been excluded from it." So since they could/would not come to the synagogue, Jesus went where they were. Too often today in the churches one finds largely the "whole." Present-day followers of Jesus would do well to follow the example of their Lord, going where the "sick" are when they do not come to the stated meeting places of the churches.

Present also were disciples of John the Baptist and of the Pharisees. They "used to fast" (v. 18). Literally, they "were accustomed to fasting." And so seeing Jesus and His disciples eating they asked Him, "Why do the disciples of John and of the Pharisees fast, but thy disciples fast not?" (v. 18).

This was a strange coalition. The Pharisees had no love for John who had called them a brood of vipers (Matt. 3:7). He had even dared to call them to repentance. And yet we find this mixed group of their learners allied against Jesus. Their only common cause was their criticism of Him.

Why this coalition? It is possible that this occurred during a fast period. Certainly John's disciples would resent Jesus going to a banquet when their leader was in prison. So ascetic was John that he would not have attended such an occasion had he been free. On the other hand, Jesus was a social being. And His conduct made Him the target of criticism from these disciples.

Jesus replied by reminding them that His disciples had no reason to fast. Fasting was a sign of mourning. So why should "the children of the bride-chamber" mourn while the "bridegroom" was still with them (v. 19)? Doubtless Jesus chose His figures of speech deliberately. For John's disciples had heard him call Jesus the "bridegroom" (John 3:29). But the time will come when He will be taken from His disciples. Then they will fast (v. 20). Of course, Jesus here spoke of His death. But their fasting would be of short duration. With His resurrection fasting will give place to unspeakable joy.

Jesus' words should not be construed as being against fasting as such. On occasion He Himself fasted (Matt. 4:2; cf. 5:16-18). Fasting should not be according to dates on the calendar or for a public display of piety. It should be the result of one's preoccupation with the things of God so that one loses any thought or desire for food. *Fasting* as such is not necessarily a sign of piety: *eating* is not necessarily a sign of worldliness. In both cases the important thing is how and for what reason one does them.

The New and the Old (2:21-22)

Jesus concluded this scene with a lesson of tremendous import. In it He contrasted the new revelation of God with the old.

"No man . . . seweth a piece of new cloth on an old garment: else the new piece that filled it up taketh away from the old, and the rent is made worse" (v. 21). The figure is that of patching an old garment with new unfulled cloth. To begin with the two do not match. Even if they had the same design the new patch would not be the same in color as that which had faded with time. Furthermore, in time the new cloth would shrink. In so doing it would tear the old cloth, making a hole larger than that which it was designed to cover.

"And no man putteth new wine into old bottles [wineskins]: else the new wine doth burst the bottles, and the wine is spilled, and the bottles will be marred [destroyed]: But new wine must be put into new bottles" (v. 22). Old wineskins were brittle, having lost their elasticity. New wine was still in a state of fermentation. If it were put in old wineskins the fermentation would produce gases. And since the old skins would not stretch, they would burst. Thus the skins would be destroyed and the new wine would be lost.

In these two parables Jesus was contrasting God's new revelation in Him with the old revelation which with age had degenerated into ritualism and institutionalism. The critics were proposing that Jesus should conform to their rules and regulations. He likened it to trying to patch up their old worn-out system. But the two had little or nothing in common. To be sure, the new revelation was the flower of the old. But the Pharisees had torn too many holes in the old so that it no longer expressed the original intent of God. And since the old, or that which they had made it, was no longer usable, God had brought forth new cloth altogether.

Again, the Pharisees wished to confine Jesus' work to their old forms. But Jesus said that such was impossible. Theirs was a system of legalism; His was a way of grace. Theirs was one of bondage;

His was one of freedom. Theirs was the brittle form of ritual; His was the expanding expression of the spirit. The new revelation in Christ could not be contained in the rigid ways of Judaism. New wine must have new wineskins. To try to combine them would be to lose both. One has but to examine those systems of Christianity which have sought to combine the two in order to see the tremendous truth which Jesus set forth.

Mark 2:23 – 3:6

The Rise of Opposition to Jesus

There is no break in Mark's account between verses 22 and 23, other than the words "and it came to pass." But this suggests a complete change in the situation. By comparing the various Gospels one learns that some time had elapsed between the two verses.

John 5 records that during His Galilean ministry Jesus made a trip to Jerusalem. The occasion was "a feast of the Jews" (v. 1). This probably was a Passover Feast. While there Jesus healed a lame man at the pool of Bethesda. And He did so on the sabbath day. Prior to this time the Pharisees had been critical of Jesus. But they had no specific case upon which to base their opposition. In Capernaum Jesus had cast a demon out of a man on the sabbath day. Doubtless the Pharisees knew about it. But it took place in Galilee. In Jerusalem it was easy to explain it away as the wild tale of the country bumpkins of Galilee. So they chose to ignore it for the time. But when Jesus healed on the Sabbath in Jerusalem, the seat of Pharisaic power, they could no longer deny or ignore it. They had to face it. Furthermore, they had a case against Jesus. And they played it to the hilt.

The Sabbath Day (2:23)

The sabbath day was the most sensitive nerve in Pharisaism. There were certain key points in Judaism: the temple, the Scriptures, the traditions, and the Sabbath. However, other religions had their temples, scriptures, and traditions. But only Judaism had the Sabbath. So more than any other, the Sabbath was the distinctive element in the Jewish faith.

However, it would be difficult to identify the simple commandment concerning the sabbath day (Exod. 20:8-12) with the elaborate system of sabbath observance in Judaism. The fourth commandment simply forbade work on the Sabbath. But Jewish interpreters had defined work. In so doing they laid down thirty-nine basic actions, and then subdivided these into hundreds of prohibitions.

For instance, no burden could be borne on the Sabbath, a burden being defined as anything which weighed as much as two dried figs. Lengthy debates were held as to what was permitted and what was forbidden. A man gets off his donkey just at sunset on Friday. Should he take the saddle off the donkey? If so, he was working. If not, the donkey was working. Should one eat an egg laid on the Sabbath? For in laying it the hen worked. Many simple things were denied and forbidden as labor. Drawing a stick along the ground was plowing; pulling a hair out of one's head was shearing. Healing was forbidden on the Sabbath. A man had a sore throat. Could he treat it on the Sabbath? It was finally decided that he could not. He might drink oil for food. If in doing so it helped his throat, that was purely incidental.

One can see, therefore, why the Jews were so sensitive about the Sabbath. It is also understandable why Jesus ignored these silly regulations. He never broke the fourth commandment. But He refused to be bound by the man-made laws of the Jews. Nevertheless, it was on this issue more than upon any other that the Pharisees constantly hounded His steps.

The Incident in the Grain Fields (2:23-28)

This incident took place while Jesus and His disciples were returning from Jerusalem to Galilee. Mark does not locate the place where it occurred. But it probably was somewhere in southern Galilee. "And it came to pass, that he went through the corn fields on the sabbath day" (v. 23). Actually the Greek text says that He *went alongside* through the grain fields (not maize, but either wheat, rye, or barley). Farmers left footpaths through their fields for the convenience of travels. So the picture is that Jesus went through the grain field on a footpath with grain growing on either side.

Assuming that the feast of John 5:1 was a Passover, this return journey to Galilee would come while the grain was ripening but not yet ready for the harvest. "And his disciples began, as they went, to pluck the ears of "corn" or "grain." The words "as they went" render two words meaning "to make a way." This suggests that they left the path, went among the grain, and were plucking some ripened heads of grain.

This was permitted by the Mosaic law (Deut. 23:25). A hungry traveler might pluck a few heads for food, but could not use a scythe to gather grain. So they were following an accepted, legal custom. They were rubbing the heads in their hands, blowing away the chaff, and eating the grain.

But as Jesus and His little group traveled they were not alone. Apparently, following the sabbath incident in Jerusalem, some Pharisees had gone along to spy on Jesus. So they said, "Behold why do they on the sabbath day that which is not lawful?" (v. 24). "Behold" carries the element of surprise. "Look!" They did not question what they were doing, but that they were doing so on the Sabbath. The disciples were not breaking one of God's laws, but one of the meticulous rules of the rabbis. But they reckoned that they broke at least two, perhaps three, such rules. To the Pharisees plucking the ears was reaping, rubbing them in their hands was threshing, and blowing away the chaff was winnowing. The entire process was preparing food on the sabbath day.

The Pharisees were supposed to be experts on the Scriptures. But Jesus gave them a Bible lesson in answering their question (vv. 25-26). He reminded them that when David and his men were hungry they ate the shewbread which was reserved for the priests (I Sam. 21:1-6). Matthew records that He further reminded them that the priests ministered (worked) in the temple on the sabbath day (12:5; cf. Num. 28:9-10). And then He added, "The sabbath was made for man, and not man for the sabbath" (v. 27). God made the Sabbath to bless man. The Pharisees had made it a burden to be borne. The implication of Jesus' words is that a man's needs, both food and worship, are more important than an institution. The Pharisees had no compassion for men. Their only concern was to safeguard their rules about sabbath observance.

In this light it is well to note Jesus' own teaching and practice regarding the Sabbath. He countenanced deeds of mercy, necessity, and worship. This does not justify a wide-open Lord's Day. But it does throw light upon a proper regard for that day.

From all this Jesus drew a conclusion. "Therefore the Son of man is Lord also of the sabbath" (v. 28). Note again the use of "Son of man." While at times this title emphasized Jesus' humanity, here it is related to His deity. He is "Lord" in the sense of Jehovah. To be "Lord . . . of the sabbath" could mean no less. Jehovah gave the Sabbath. Jesus claimed the right to control it. Recall again the four principal elements of Judaism: temple, Scriptures, traditions, and Sabbath. In cleaning the temple Jesus had acted as Lord of the temple (John 2: Mark 11:15ff.) Later he will show His Lordship over the Scriptures (Matt. 5), and with authority He will brush aside Jewish traditions (Mark 7:1ff). And here He claimed to be "Lord of the sabbath." It is easy to see, therefore, why the enmity of the Pharisees would become a consuming fire. Mark makes no mention of their answer to Jesus in the grain fields. But His claim as Lord did not phase them. They continued to watch His every move.

The Healing of a Withered Hand (3:1-6)

Jesus continued on to Capernaum. Perhaps on the next sabbath day He went into the synagogue (v. 1). Present was a man with a withered hand. With a physician's eye Luke notes that it was his right hand, his working hand (6:6). The word rendered "withered" is a perfect passive participle. This means that the hand was completely withered. But the man was not born with it. It was the result of either an accident or a disease. "And they watched him" (v. 2). The "they" refers to the Pharisees (v. 6). The verb "watched" is an imperfect tense of a Greek verb meaning to watch alongside or on the sly. They kept on watching Jesus on the sly to see if He would heal on the sabbath day – "that they might accuse him" (v. 2). So including the incident in John 5 this was the third sabbath controversy with the Pharisees.

Jesus, knowing their thoughts, did not dodge the issue. Instead He met it head-on. For He said to the afflicted man, "Stand forth" (v. 3). Literally, "Arise in the midst." Apparently the man was sitting among the people. Jesus told him to stand up in the middle of the room in order that all might see him. The Pharisees covertly watched from the side. But Jesus proposed to act openly before the eyes of all.

With the man standing in the middle of the synagogue, Jesus then posed a question to the Pharisees. "Is it lawful to do good on the sabbath days, or to do evil? to save life, or to kill?" (v. 4).

Jesus deliberately placed the Pharisees in a bind. Certainly they could not say that it was lawful to do evil or to kill on the Sabbath, or at any other time, for that matter. But the question tied them to the sabbath issue. On the other hand could they admit that it was lawful to do good, to save a life, on the Sabbath? Their position with regard to that day was morally neutral or indifferent. It was a *do nothing* position. And that was one purpose of Jesus' question, to show that indifference to human need in order to preserve their sabbath laws.

Of course, in a general sense they might have answered that it was lawful to do good or to save a life. But how would they apply that prinicple in a concrete situation? Here before them was a man in need of help. Was it lawful to do him good on that day? They held that it was unlawful to heal on the Sabbath. But obviously if one had the power to heal him, but did not because of the sabbath law, the result was to do him evil. If one could save a life on the Sabbath, but did not, that was tantamount to killing him.

So the Pharisees were caught on the horns of a sabbath dilemma. To answer either way would be to incriminate themselves. So "they kept on holding their peace" (v. 4, imperfect tense). The silence weighed heavily upon the congregation as Jesus let them stew in their own juice.

During this time Jesus "looked round about on them in anger" (v. 5). The aorist participle shows that it was one long unbroken look. The word for "anger" (*orgē*) was used for God's abiding opposition to evil. It was not simply a sudden burst of emotional anger (*thumos*). At the same time Jesus' anger was tempered with grief "for the hardness of their hearts." The present tense of "being grieved" means that this was an abiding state of Jesus' heart. The word for "hardness" means a state of moral ossification (*pōrōsis*) like hardened hands or feet (Robertson). This word *pōros* was used of a kind of marble, and came to refer to the *callus* on broken bones. Gould notes that the Pharisees "were hardened by previous conceptions against the new truth."

Then Jesus told the man to "stretch forth" his hand. The man obeyed, and his hand "was restored." The aorist tense means that it happened immediately, a miracle. This verb means to restore to its former state. The words "whole as the other" do not appear in the best texts. But the sense is there nevertheless. His withered hand was immediately restored to its former state of health. And there it was stretched forth for all eyes to see. The Pharisees could not deny that Jesus had worked a miracle of healing. But they condemned Him for doing it on the sabbath day.

"And the Pharisees went forth, and straightway took counsel with the Herodians against him, how they might destroy him" (v. 6). This is Mark's first mention of the Herodians. They were a political party which championed the return of a Herod to the rule of Judea. Herod the Great, a half-Jew, half-Idumean, had ruled 36-4 B.C. Since he was not a pure Jew he had no rightful claim to the throne. He ruled as a puppet ruler under the Romans. At his death his son Archelaus succeeded him in Judea, but was soon deposed by the Romans in favor of a Roman procurator. The Herodians favored the return of a Herod to rule. Naturally they were on the opposite side of the fence from the Pharisees who wanted to return to Jewish rule. But the Pharisees forgot their political differences in order to form a coalition against Jesus. This healing took place in Galilee, the domain of Herod Antipas. Doubtless the Herodians had his ear in political matters. Bruce takes note of this as the reason why the Pharisees sought the help of this group. In their efforts to destroy Jesus "they would naturally regard the assistance of people having influence at court as valuable."

And the Herodians were ready and willing tools. It was quite clear by this time that Jesus made claims for Himself which could belong only to the Messiah. Furthermore, the people so regarded Him. And the political-military interpretation which they placed upon that office posed a threat to Herod Antipas. He had already imprisoned John the Baptist. It is even possible that by this time John was dead by his hand. Probably he had already begun to take note of Jesus and His relation to John (Mark 6:14ff.). So the Herodians entered into a collusion with the Pharisees "how they might destroy him."

One cannot help but note the similarity between the Pharisees' actions and the question posed earlier by Jesus. On the Sabbath Jesus did only good; He saved life. But the Pharisees who withheld any answer to Jesus' question on the Sabbath were doing evil. They were plotting to take Jesus' life.

Thus the lines were drawn. Jesus versus the Pharisees. And they will hound Him to His death.

Mark 3:7-12

The Growing Popularity of Jesus

Due to the venomous purpose of the Pharisees and Herodians Jesus withdrew from them. He left the synagogue to walk along the shore of the sea of Galilee. In this open place He would be safer than in a crowded building. Vincent points out that on eleven occasions Jesus retired from His work in order to escape His enemies, to pray in solitude, to rest, and/or to teach His disciples (1:12; 3:7; 6:31, 46; 7:24, 31; 9:2; 10:1; 14:34). Bruce calls attention to the phrase "with his disciples" (v. 7). Coming before the verb this places emphasis upon them. Perhaps this prominence is given to them as a prelude to the account of Jesus' selection of the Twelve (cf. vv. 13ff).

But though Jesus left the synagogue He did not get away from the crowd. Because "a great multitude followed him." The word "great" is in the emphatic position in the Greek text. It shows how large the crowd was. Thus with design Mark points to the growing popularity of Jesus. Such a marvelous ministry could not be hidden. Like wildfire the news of it spread throughout Palestine.

Mark shows how the news had spread by listing areas whence came the multitude. Of course, they came from Galilee. But there were also present those from Judea and from the city of Jerusalem (v. 8). Furthermore they came from Idumaea to the south of Judea. This is the only mention of Idumaea in the New Testament. This region had been conquered by John Hyrcanus. George Adam Smith notes that at this time it was practically a part of Judea with a large circumcised population. Likewise, there were those from "beyond Jordan" or from Perea and the Decapolis, a Gentile area made up of ten Greek cities. In addition people had come from Phoenicia or from the region of Tyre and Sidon northwest of Galilee. This was an old Canaanite territory. From south, east, and northwest they came, or from everywhere. Both Jews and Gentiles flocked to hear Jesus and to receive His ministry.

Some came out of curiosity. Others came to be healed. But many, no doubt, came with hungry and expectant hearts. They came "when they heard [hearing constantly, present participle] what great things he did" (v. 8). "Did" in some Greek texts is an imperfect tense. But the best texts have it in the present tense.

But both speak of a continuing work of Jesus either in the past or the present, probably the latter.

So great was the crowd that Jesus was in danger of being thronged by them (v. 9). The word rendered "throng" (*thlibō*) means to press hard upon or to squeeze into a tight place. It was used of pressing grapes in order to extract their juice. Since He was by the sea He probably was standing at the water's edge. So as a caution He told the disciples to have a small boat, perhaps a rowboat, handy. If necessary, He would stand in the boat away from them to teach.

The enthusiasm of the crowd is understandable. "For he had healed many" (v. 10). Perhaps others were pressing upon Him hoping to be healed. "They pressed upon him to touch him, as many as had plagues." "Plagues" (*mastigas*) might mean a paralytic stroke or some other widespread disease such as influenza (Robertson). The word for "pressed upon" is *epipiptō,* "to fall upon." Evidently this eager crowd had become a pushing, shoving mob. This merely emphasizes the need for the boat.

This passage is typical of Mark. It presents a moving spectacle of an eager, pushing, shoving, and shouting throng intent upon coming into bodily contact with Jesus. If only they could touch Him, or even be shoved against Him, they hoped to be healed.

Among this group were those who were demon possessed (v. 11). Mark describes them as "the spirits, the unclean ones." The double use of the definite article serves to point them out as a particular kind of sickness. The demons indwelt the bodies of their victims, speaking and acting through them.

"When they saw him, [they] fell down before him, and cried, saying, Thou art the Son of God" (v. 11). The verb "saw" (*theōreō*) means that they carefully watched Jesus. It was a critical, understanding investigation, not that of mere spectators. Though they were demons they understood better than men the spiritual realm. They recognized Jesus as the embodiment of holiness. And so they declared Him to be the Son of God.

This verse and verse 12 contain four imperfect tenses which present a moving picture of repeated action in the past. The unclean spirits "kept on beholding" Jesus. They "kept on falling down before" him. And they "kept on crying," "Thou art the Son of God," Or intensive as the pronoun is, "Thou and no other art the Son of God." And Jesus "kept on rebuking them that they should not make him known" (v. 12).

Once again Jesus rejected the testimony of demons as to His deity. Though they spoke the truth, Jesus did not want such testimony from the realm of evil. The crowds were flocking to Jesus. He never courted popularity. But when they came He wanted them to learn of Him from His lips, not from the lips of those under the control of the servants of the archenemy Satan.

Mark 3:13-19a

The Choice of Twelve Apostles

Although one would not surmise it from Mark's account, at this point we are approximately at the mid-point of Jesus' public ministry. From the beginning, in all likelihood, Jesus had planned to select a small group of disciples who would bear a special relationship to Him and His work. Among other things they were to assist Jesus in His work while on earth and after He was gone. The rising opposition of the enemy made it evident that He would be killed. So Jesus prepared for the inevitable. His rising popularity, plus the time element in His ministry, made such a choice a wise one at this time.

The Place of the Choice (3:13)

So "he goeth up into a mountain, and calleth unto him whom he would: and they came unto him" (v. 13). Both Bruce and Robertson see this as a group larger than the twelve. How the call was made we do not know. It may have been verbal. Or it may have been done by certain chosen ones who went throughout the crowd. But however it was done, Jesus called those whom He wished. The basis of choice probably was those who gave evidence of being true believers in Him, not merely the curiosity seekers or those who came merely for healing.

Mark does not mention it, but Luke says that in the mountain Jesus spent the night in prayer (6:12). He often slipped away from the crowds to commune with His Father. It appears, however, that this prayer session had a peculiar purpose. For He was about to make the choice of twelve apostles.

The Reason for the Choice (3:14-15)

The next morning (Luke 6:13) Jesus called the disciples to Him. Apparently they had waited at a respectful distance from Him while He prayed. Out of this group He "ordained twelve" (Mark 3:14). Literally, He "made" twelve. Certain manuscripts add "whom he also named apostles." These words are footnoted by both Nestle and Bruce. But Robertson holds to their genuineness. This phrase is genuine without question in Luke 6:13. The word "apostle" (*apostolos*) comes from *apostellō,* to send off from one's self, as one furnished with certain credentials and sent on a mission. Literally, it means "the sent one."

Mark gives two distinct reasons why Jesus chose the Twelve. First, "that they should be with him" (v. 14). The verb "should be" is a present subjunctive form. They were to be continuously with Him in order to receive His teachings, observe His methods, and to share in His spirit. Second, "that he might send them forth." "Send forth" is the verb *apostellō.* They were to be His ambassadors.

Note the sequence. They were *to be with* Him; they were *to be sent forth* by Him. This is the divine order. They were not ready to be sent forth until they had been with Him. Jesus ever says, "Come" and then, "Go."

Sending them forth involved two purposes. These are seen in the two infinitives of purpose. "To preach" (v. 14). This word is *kērussein* from *kērussō,* to preach or to herald. They were to go forth declaring officially the message of their King. And those who heard were to receive and obey them as though Jesus came and spoke in person. "To have power ... to cast out devils" or "demons." The words "to heal sicknesses" are not found in the best texts. Robertson comments, "This double ministry of preaching and healing was to mark their work. The two things are, however, different, and one does not necessarily involve the other."

The Group Chosen (16-19a)

Then Mark proceeded to name the twelve apostles. "And Simon he surnamed Peter" (v. 16). This, of course, is Simon, son of John or *Barjona.* Actually, "he placed upon Simon a name Peter." This relates to Jesus' promise to Simon in John 1:42, and anticipates its fulfilment in Matthew 16:18. "Peter" is *petros* (masculine). In Matthew 16:15 Jesus also used *petra* (feminine). A *petra* was a large ledge or foundation rock. A *petros* was a smaller rock broken off of the *petra* and one which betook of its nature. In Matthew's words the *petra* is Christ in His divine nature, and the *petros* is one who partakes of this nature.[1]

James and John were surnamed *"Boanerges,"* the sons of thunder (v. 17). No explanation is given of this *nickname.* It means that they were of a tumultuous nature as seen in Luke 9:34. Of interest is the change which Jesus effected in Simon and John. Simon became a "rock" and John became the apostle of love.

The other apostles were Andrew, Philip, Bartholomew (Nathan-

[1] See Hobbs, *An Exposition of the Gospel of Matthew, in loco.*

ael, John 1:45), Matthew, Thomas (Twin, Didymus, John 11:16), James the son of Alphaeus, Thaddaeus, Simon the Canaanite (Zealot, Luke 6:16), and Judas Iscariot.

This was quite a diverse group. One thing which they had in common is that there was not a priest or theologian among them. They were ordinary *laymen* in the popular sense of that word. Among them were fishermen and a tax-collector. Otherwise their vocations are not given. It is interesting to note two especially. Matthew had been a publican, one who had been in the service of the Romans and who was regarded as a traitor to his country. Simon Zelotes evidently had been a member of the party called Zealots. They were fanatically patriotic and sought to free their land of Roman rule by revolutionary methods. Yet these two men were drawn together by their mutual faith in Jesus. In fact, in all this group one sees the suggestion as to how the Christian faith can bring together in harmony of purpose men with such varied personalities and backgrounds.

But the greatest mystery of all is Judas Iscariot. He was the only Judean in the group. And in each of the Gospel lists of the Twelve he is described as a traitor. Because of his suicide his name does not appear in the list in Acts 1:13f. It is evident from the Scriptures that Judas was not a Christian. His purpose in following Jesus was purely selfish. Thinking of Jesus as a political-military Messiah, he evidently followed Him hoping for a prominent place in the Kingdom. The question as to why Jesus chose him as one of the Twelve defies a complete answer. Apparently Judas, along with the others, possessed some quality which if dedicated to Jesus would make him of peculiar value in the Kingdom. In Judas' case it may have been a business ability. But he never gave himself or his ability to Jesus. He will ever remain a warning to anyone who proposes to attach himself to Jesus to any degree short of a self-denying faith in and a full commitment to Him.

Was there ever a group of men that could be labeled more as the least likely to succeed? Yet Jesus took this raw material and forged it into a mighty force in the Kingdom of God, so that the march of these eleven men, and those who have come after them, has blazed a path of faith down the centuries and around the world.

Mark 3:19b-30

The Unpardonable Sin

From Matthew and Luke it is evident that some time elapsed between Jesus' choice of the Twelve and the incident which Mark begins in 3:19b. Following the Sermon on the Mount (Matt. 5-7; Luke 6:17-49) Jesus returned to Capernaum, paid a visit to the village of Nain, and spent some time ministering in Galilee. Then He came once again to Capernaum.

This gives added meaning to Mark's words "and they went into an house" (v. 19b). The tense of the verb "went" is a singular historical present. "House" is without the definite article. It might well read, "And he comes home." Home to Jesus would be Peter's house in Capernaum.

The Popular Error Concerning Jesus (3:19b-21)

When the word spread as to His return the crowds came together again (v. 20). So great was the crowd and their needs for ministry that "they [Jesus, His apostles, and the crowd] could not so much as eat bread." They had no time for rest or food. "And when his friends heard about it, they went out to lay hold on him: for they said, He is beside himself" (v. 21). Who were these friends? The word "friends" is not in the Greek text. Literally, "the ones from the side of him." Robertson, following the usage of this phrase in the Septuagint, says that most likely this refers to Jesus' family (cf. v. 31). But he allows for the possibility that these were some of His disciples. There seems to be no necessity of relating "the ones from the side of him" with the family group mentioned in verse 31. Indeed, the verb "went out" suggests another possibility and probability. It would seem that Jesus was outside Simon's house ministering to the people. He was oblivious to time, food, or the need for rest. Such dedication was strange to the Twelve. They thought that Jesus was "beside himself." This renders the word *exestē* from *existēmi,* to throw out of position, to displace, to amaze, to throw into wonderment. Classical Greek used this word for the act of driving one out of his senses. So they said that Jesus was out of His mind.

Bruce holds that this means that they thought that He was in a state of unhealthy excitement which bordered on insanity. His friends thought that He was absorbed in His work to the extent that He was endangering His health and mind. So benevolently they "went out" of the house to bring Jesus in away from the crowds.

The Criticism of the Scribes (3:22)

In the meantime, the Pharisees and Herodians who were bent on destroying Jesus probably had sent to Jerusalem for help. It was at this time that "the scribes which came down from Jerusalem" began to criticize Jesus (v. 22). Note that they "came down" from Jerusalem even though they had traveled northward. They came down out of the mountains about Jerusalem to the rolling hills of Galilee.

These scribes who were regarded as experts in the Law proposed to give an opinion as to the nature of Jesus' miraculous works. They said, "He hath Beelzebub, and by the prince of devils [demons] casteth he out devils [demons]" (v. 22). From Mark's account alone one might infer that the scribes were joining with those who said that Jesus was bordering on insanity. Only they went one step further to say that He was an ally of Satan.

However, from Matthew's parallel account (12:22-37) it is clear that their charge was in response to Jesus having cast a demon out of one who was both blind and dumb. So they passed off this miracle as one which was performed by the power of Satan.

"Beelzebub" is a name related to the pagan Canaanite god Baal. The best Greek text of Mark reads "Beelzebul." It was an adaptation of the words Baal-Zebub, the fly god of Ekron (II Kings 1:2-3, 6, 16). The combination of *Baal* (lord) with flies was probably due to the fact that when this god of nature was said to be in the ascendency, namely, in the growing season, Palestine was overrun with flies. So in contempt for Him He was called Baal-Zebub, the god of flies. Further to show their contempt for Him the Jews attributed the name Beelzebub to Satan. Hence the scribes called him "the prince of demons." Thus they said that Jesus worked in partnership with Satan.

The Answer of Jesus (3:23-30)

Jesus answered this charge in a series of brief parables. How can Satan cast out Satan? (v. 23). If a kingdom or a house be divided against itself, it cannot stand (vv. 24-25). "And if Satan rise up against himself, and be divided, he cannot stand, but hath an end" (v. 26).

The entire position of the scribes was preposterous. It maligned the intelligence of Satan, to say nothing about the character of

Jesus. Why would Satan work in league with Jesus to destroy his kingdom or house? On the other hand, granted that Jesus had cast out a demon. Before a man could enter a strong man's house and plunder his goods, he must first overcome or bind the strong man (v. 27). Even so, before Jesus could tear up Satan's playhouse, He must show His power to be superior to that of the evil one. Jesus recognized the great power of Satan. But His very work showed that He possessed the greater power. The "goods" (*skeuē*) were the utensils of one's house. Demons, therefore, are recognized as the instruments of Satan to do his evil work. And Jesus was in the process of destroying them. Jesus was manifested that He might destroy the works of the devil (I John 3:8).

At this point Jesus spoke some of the most awesome words which ever fell from His lips. And since He is the very essence of love and mercy, they take on a more ominous meaning.

Note that He began with the words "verily I say unto you" (v. 28). Thus He called attention to the serious nature of that which followed. "All sins shall be forgiven unto the sons of men, and blasphemies wherewith soever they shall blaspheme: But he that shall blaspheme against the Holy Ghost [Spirit] hath never forgiveness, but is in danger of eternal damnation: because they said [kept on saying, imperfect tense], He hath an unclean spirit" (vv. 28-30). Actually the best Greek text of verse 29 reads, "But whosoever may blaspheme against the Holy Spirit does not have forgiveness unto the ages, but he is guilty of an eternal sin." This translation better suits the context.

What is meant by "blaspheme?" It means to speak slanderously against. And this specific sin is to speak thus regarding the Holy Spirit. Jesus said that to do so is to commit a sin which is eternal as to its guilt. So that this sin is called the unpardonable sin.

What is the nature of this sin? It is not a sin committed in a fit of anger. It is a deliberate sin. Neither is it a sin of ignorance but one of full knowledge. According to Matthew's account it was a sin of deliberation, coming as the result of repeated refusals to believe in Jesus. And it was a sin committed with full understanding. The people saw Jesus cast out the demon, and thus called Jesus the Son of David, a Messianic title (Matt. 12:23). The scribes or Pharisees saw it, and said that Jesus was an ally of the devil (v. 24). In so doing they spoke slanderously against the Holy Spirit.

The issue here was as to whether Jesus worked by an evil spirit (Mark 3:30) or by the Holy Spirit. And the words of the scribes kept on calling the Spirit evil. What had happened was that they had so resolutely rejected Jesus that they had lost the power to discern between good and evil. Jesus had performed an obviously good work which could have been done only by the Holy Spirit. But the scribes said that this Spirit was evil. Like John Milton's Satan in *Paradise Lost* they said, "Evil be thou my good." Unable to recognize the good work of the Holy Spirit they were thus hardened against His work. And since it is He who convicts of sin, they rejected His work altogether. No conviction, no repentance; no repentance, no faith; no faith, no salvation. Thus, an unpardonable sin.

It is impossible for a Christian to commit this sin. For he is already saved and sealed by the Holy Spirit (Eph. 1:13). The person who thinks that he has committed it has not done so. His consciousness of sin is evidence that he is still sensitive to the work of the Spirit. He is capable of discerning between good and evil. The person who insists that he has no sin of which to be forgiven should beware.

Is it possible to commit this sin today? Some say not, insisting that the condition for committing it demands the bodily presence of Jesus at work in the world. However, this is a sin, not against Jesus, but against the Holy Spirit. And the Holy Spirit continues to convict of sin and to reveal Jesus as the Saviour from it.

This writer believes that it is possible for men to commit this sin today, indeed, that some people do so. Obviously to save from sin is a good work of Jesus through the Holy Spirit. To reject it is to say that it is an evil work or that Jesus works through an evil spirit. To be sure, if one continues to reject Jesus until death, there is no forgiveness after death. But even this is not the unpardonable sin spoken of by Jesus. The scribes were still alive. Yet they had committed this sin. By a continued rejection of Jesus one can become so hardened that he loses any sense of sin or a need for salvation. And somewhere, sometime he can well reach that state where he loses any sense of sin and any ability to respond to the Holy Spirit. In such a state, and beyond our sense of comprehension, the Holy Spirit ceases to strive with such a person. Thus he is in a state of living death. Alive to the world, but dead to God.

How may one be certain never to commit this sin? By surrendering to the Holy Spirit's wooing and by receiving Christ as his Saviour. For "there is therefore now no condemnation to them which are in Christ Jesus . . . for the law of the Spirit of life in Christ Jesus hath made me free from the law of sin and death" (Rom. 8:1-2).

Mark 3:31-35

The New Relationship

The atmosphere within Peter's house was charged with the lightning of divine condemnation. But outside a tender scene was transpiring. For "there came then his brethren and his mother, and standing without, sent unto him, calling him" (v. 31). The word "then" is not in the best text.

But why were they come? Many interpreters relate this with verse 21. Thus they hold that Jesus' mother and brothers came to take Him home, thinking that He was out of His mind. For instance, Bruce says, "The evanglist resumes the story about Christ's friends, interrupted by the encounter with the scribes." But is this necessarily the case?

It seems more natural to see in the visit of Mary and her sons a simple desire to see Jesus. He had long been absent from Nazareth. To be sure, Jesus' half-brothers were not in sympathy with His cause. They may well have come at Mary's insistence, perhaps caused even by her desire to effect a family reconciliation. At any rate, if the Scripture be allowed to say what it says, the simple fact is that they appeared outside Peter's house calling for Jesus. This fact shows how great was the crowd which was present, perhaps even jamming the door of the house.

Inside the house Jesus sat in the midst of a circle of people surrounding Him (v. 32). Some of them said to Jesus, "Behold, they mother and thy brethren without seek for thee" (v. 32). Nestle's text adds "and thy sisters." But this is omitted from the text of Expositor's (Bruce). This may have been added by a later copyist to correspond to Jesus' words in verse 35.

In any event, Jesus made a strange reply. "Who is my mother and my brethren?" (v. 33). And then after sweeping the crowd with His eyes, He said, "Behold my mother and my brethren! For whosoever shall do the will of God, the same is my brother, and my sister, and mother" (vv. 34-35).

Thus Jesus spoke of a new relationship. The fact that His earthly family called for Him to interrupt His work for even a visit implied that they may have felt a prior claim upon Him. This may have been the case through the years in Nazareth. But it is no longer true. His primary relationship is no longer genetical but spiritual. His *family* was now those who did the Father's will by believing in the Son.

Already at Cana Jesus had gently suggested this fact to Mary (John 2:4). Now He announced it formally. The relationship between Mary and Jesus was no longer that of mother and son. It was that of a sinner saved by grace and her Saviour. With respect to His brothers, there was a much more intimate bond between Jesus and His followers than there was between Him and His unbelieving earthly kin. The day will come after His resurrection when they too will believe in Him. Even then the relationship will not be that of half-brother to half-brothers and half-sisters. It will be that of Saviour and sinners saved by grace. Of interest is the fact that neither James nor Jude in their epistles makes mention of a family relationship to Jesus. James is "a servant of God and of the Lord Jesus Christ" (1:1). Jude is "the servant of Jesus Christ, and brother of James" (v. 1).

So in truth Jesus' *family* is spiritual, not genetical. There is no prior privilege of family, race, or class in the household of our Lord.

Mark 4:1-34

The Earthly Stories with Heavenly Meanings

For some time Jesus had been majoring on teaching His disciples. Now He "began again" to teach to a wider group (v. 1). He had left the synagogue to teach by the sea side where a larger audience was available. But the crowd became so great that He entered into a small boat (*ploion*), pushed it shortly away from the shore, and from there continued His teaching. This served a dual purpose. He escaped the press of the crowd, and in the boat He could be seen and heard by more people.

"And he taught them many things by parables" (v. 2). Heretofore, Jesus had used many short parables. But on this particular day He taught in parables only, using for the most part longer ones. Matthew records more parables than Mark on this occasion. But the heart of this teaching is preserved in Mark.

A parable has been called an earthly story with a heavenly meaning. Again, someone said that a parable was a handle by which one might take home a spiritual truth. The word rendered "parable" (*parabolē*) comes from the verb *paraballō,* to cast alongside. So the use of parables was a form of teaching by which an earthly story was cast alongside a spiritual truth in order to give understanding to the latter. It should be noted that a parable teaches one primary truth. While many secondary meanings may be involved, they all contribute to the central truth.

Why did Jesus use parables? A parable both concealed and revealed. It concealed the truth from those who used Jesus' teachings only as a means of criticizing Him. But it also revealed truth to those who were prepared to receive it (vv. 11-12). It caused those who were sympathetic toward Him to think through the story in order to catch its true meaning. Furthermore, parables enabled His hearers to retain the truth which was taught. Many of Jesus' most precious truths are thus retained even today by these pictures painted with words.

A parable is different from a fable. A fable is not necessarily true to life. But a parable draws spiritual truth from life as it was lived by the hearers. This element is evident in the parables in Mark 4.

The Parable of the Soils (4:3-9)

This parable is often called that of the sower. When in truth the point of this story is that similar seed sown in different soils bear differing results. So this may more exactly be called the *parable of the soils.*

Jesus began with the word "hearken." It renders the present imperative form of the verb "to hear" (*akouō*). It is the equivalent of "listen" or "be listening." "Behold, there went out a sower to sow" (v. 3). "Behold" suggests the element of surprise. "Look!" It is even possible that a farmer was sowing seed nearby. If so, this makes the parable all the more vivid. Even so, the scene described by Jesus was a familiar one.

There were two methods of sowing seed in Jesus' day. One was to balance a bag of seed on a donkey's back, cut holes in either side, and let the seed run out as the donkey walked over the ground. The other method was to broadcast the seed by hand. This apparently was the method described in the parable.

As the farmer broadcast the seed it fell on various types of soil. "Some fell by the wayside, and the fowls of the air came and devoured it up" (v. 4). "Wayside" renders *hodos,* the word for "way" or "road." Literally, "alongside the road." Farmers left paths for travelers through their fields. This ground naturally would be hard. So birds would quickly eat the seed which fell there.

"And some fell on stony ground, where it had not much earth" (v. 5). The word "some" renders *allo,* meaning other seed of the same kind as that which fell on the foot path. Galilee is underlaid with limestone rock. In some places this rock is covered only by a thin layer of soil. This created a condition in which the early spring sun would warm the rock, which in turn kept the soil warm. Seed which fell on this soil would germinate quickly. So that "immediately it sprang up, because it had no depth of earth." However, this warm soil would also have less moisture. Furthermore, the little plants would be rooted only in shallow soil with no subsoil supply of moisture. So "when the sun was up [arose], it was scorched; and because it had no root, it withered away" or "dried up" (v. 6).

"And some [*allo* again) fell among thorns, and the thorns grew up, and choked it, and it yielded no fruit" (v. 7). Barclay notes that Palestinian farmers were lazy. They did not endeavor to rid the soil of foreign growths. Perhaps the meaning here is that the seed fell on ground which also contained the seed or roots of thorns or other wild plants. This is suggested by the words "and the thorns grew up." The thorns grew with the planted seed. A given amount of soil can nourish only so many plants. So the wild growth "choked" or "strangled" the good plants. The result was a stunted plant which bore no harvest.

"And other [*alla,* plural form of allo] fell on good ground, and did yield fruit that sprang up and increased; and brought forth, some thirty, and some sixty, and some an hundred" (v. 8). The plural *alla* in contrast to *allo* in the preceding verses suggests that more of the same kind of seed fell on the good soil. The imperfect forms of "did yield" and "brought forth" indicate continuing processes. The harvest varied with these seed, some thirty, some sixty, and some an hundredfold. This last may seem like a bumper crop. But ancient records show that in some cases such was possible.

The point of the story is that the same kind of seed was sown in all of the soils. So the difference in results was due to the soil not to the seed. Hence *the parable of the soils.* Jesus cautioned His hearers to hear with understanding the lesson of the parable (v. 9).

The Question of the Disciples (4:11-12)

As soon as the disciples were alone with Jesus in the house away from the crowd, they asked Him to explain the parable (v. 11). Robertson suggests that they did not want to show their own lack of understanding to the crowd.

So Jesus said, "Unto you it is given to know the mystery of the kingdom of God" (v. 12). The words "to know" do not appear in Mark, though they are genuine in Matthew (13:11) and Luke (8:19). So Mark records, "Unto you the mystery of the kingdom of God is given."

The word "mystery" (*mustērion*) means a knowledge known only to the initiated. In pagan cults this referred to secrets known only to their members, such as a secret society. But in the New Testament it refers to the secret counsels of God which are revealed by Him to those who are spiritually able to receive them. So to those within the circle of believers this mystery was given in order to reveal truth, even though Jesus had to explain it to them.

However, this mystery had a different purpose or result regarding those whose hearts were hardened against Jesus and His truth. So that "seeing they may see, and not perceive; and hearing they may hear, and not understand; lest at any time they should be converted, and their sins should be forgiven them" (v. 12). Literally, "it should be forgiven them."

This verse presents a difficulty to interpreters. Does it express a purpose or a result? Were parables used by Jesus deliberately to prevent the unbelievers, particularly the Pharisees, from seeing and hearing with understanding, turning from their unbelief and being forgiven? Or did their hardness of heart simply prevent them from doing so?

It should be noted that this is a quotation from Isaiah 6:9-10. And this passage troubled even the Jewish interpreters. Barclay in his *The Gospel of Mark* cites two rendering of this passage given by W. O. E. Oesterley. He translates Isaiah 6:9-10 from the Hebrew.

"And he said, Go, and say to this people, 'Go on hearkening, but understand not; go on looking, but perceive not.' Make fat the heart of this people, and its ears make heavy, and its eyes besmear; lest it see with its eyes, and with its ears hear, and its heart understand, so that it should be healed again."

However, when in the third century B.C. the Old Testament was translated into Greek (Septuagint) the translation read

"And He said, Go and say to this people, 'Ye shall hear indeed, but ye shall not understand; and seeing, ye shall see, and not perceive.' For the heart of this people has become gross, and with their ears they hear heavily, and their eyes they have closed; lest at any time they should see with their eyes and hear with their ears, and understand with their heart, and should be converted, and I should heal them."

A comparison of these two renderings shows that they differ in tone. The former says that Isaiah is to speak in such fashion that his sinful hearers would not understand. The latter says that their failure to understand is due to their self-hardening of heart. But does the passage in Isaiah speak of a deliberate design on God's part? Or does the meaning lie in the fact that people who constantly reject truth lose the ability to comprehend truth when they hear it? There is a spiritual law involved here. To reject the Spirit repeatedly means that one will lose his spiritual sensitivity. God's messenger must speak God's truth. If in doing so his message is concealed from those who reject truth, then in a sense he does make their hearts fat, their ears heavy, and their eyes besmeared. It is not God's will that it shall be so. But there comes a time when even He must accept the negative decision of man's sinful will.

This seems to be the meaning which Jesus attached to Isaiah's statement. He had taught the truth. But His enemies rejected it and even used it as a weapon against Him. One can hear the tone of frustrated love and disappointment in His words. Yet as His Father had done in Isaiah's day, so He must do in His. He must continue to speak the truth. But circumstances dictated that He should do so in a fashion that would reveal it to those who would hear with understanding, and conceal it from those who would reject its content and abuse its purpose. Thus Jesus spoke in parables.

The Parable of the Soils Explained (4:13-20)

Jesus expressed surprise that the disciples did not discern the truth taught in this parable (v. 13). If they did not understand it how would it be possible to comprehend others? So He proceeded to explain it to them.

"The sower soweth the word" (v. 14). Jesus did not identify the sower. In this case it was He. However, anyone who scatters the "word" or the Word of God is the sower. But he does so with different results, governed not by the seed but by the soil into which it is sown. And Jesus identifies the difficult soils as seen in men's hearts.

"These are they by the wayside" (v. 15). They are those whose hearts are hardened by the traffic of the world. God's word falls upon them like seed falling on a path. And Satan quickly takes it away before it can have a chance to do its work. Every sower of the gospel seed knows this type of hardened *soil.*

"These are they likewise which are sown on stony ground" (v. 16). Such receive the word with gladness. They may be likened to superficial hearers. The seed quickly germinates. But shallow lives provide it no root. And they "endure but for a time" (v. 17). This does not mean that they are saved and then lost again. They have no genuine experience of grace. They readily agree to follow Christ, but fail to count the cost. So that when affliction or persecution comes because of their surface profession, just as quickly as they received the word they renounce it for personal safety. They are willing to give their allegiance to any group which happens to be popular at the moment. Fairweather friends are they. But when the rain begins to fall they run for cover.

"These are they which are sown among thorns" (v. 18). They "hear the word." They truly receive it into their hearts. But they never progress beyond that point. They remain wedded to the "cares" or distractions of the "age" (v. 19). They want to be in step with the worldly drummer. They are ensnared by "the deceitfulness of riches, and the lusts of other things" which enter into their lives. These things "choke the word, and it becometh unfruitful." Their Christian life endures. But they are dried up. And the result is that they bear no fruit unto Christ.

"These are they which are sown on good ground" (v. 20). They are the fruitful Christians, each bearing a harvest in keeping with his ability.

In each case the *soil* had its opportunity. So it is not the "seed" but the "soil" which tells the story in the final analysis. Every man should examine himself carefully to determine which type of soil he is.

The Parable of the Lamp (4:21-25)

"Is a candle [lamp, *luchnos*] brought to be put under a bushel, or under a bed? and not to be set on a candlestick [lampstand, *luchnia*]?" (v. 21).

In vivid fashion Jesus pointed out the absurd. Why did a man light a lamp? To put it under a grain measure *(modios,* a dry measure holding about a peck)? Or to place it under a bed *(klinē,* a bed or reclining couch at the table)? Obviously the answer is "no." And Jesus invited such an answer by using the negative *mēti*. If one puts a lamp under a peck measure, not only will it give no light but will soon be extinguished from lack of oxygen. To put it under a couch will diminish the light and will set the couch on fire. It is inconceivable to think that a lamp would be placed anywhere except upon a lampstand. That is where it belongs in order that it may light the entire room.

The purpose of this parable was to teach the disciples the importance of revealing truth. In fact, this was the purpose of all of Jesus' parables. This He states in verse 22. Vincent points out that the King James Version has Jesus saying that everything which is hidden shall be revealed. But a literal translation says otherwise. "For there is not anything hidden [*krupton*] except in order that it may be manifested; neither become an absolute secret [*apokruphon*], but that it may come into full view." Jesus had not spoken in parables for the ultimate purpose of hiding truth. He had concealed it temporarily from His enemies in order that ultimately His disciples might bring it out into the open in a fashion that it could be grasped. Robertson quotes Swete to the end that this temporary concealing is for final manifestation and a means to an end. Thus He charged His disciples to declare it fully after His ascension back to the Father. Like a lamp on a lampstand they are to cause truth to shine abroad. And He cautioned them to hear and heed this admonition (v. 23).

With added emphasis Jesus said, "Take heed what ye hear" (v. 24). Luke 8:18 reads, "Take heed therefore how ye hear." Both *how* and *what* are important. They are to hear attentively and with understanding. And they are to be watchful over what they hear, not only to remember it but to share it (v. 24). With the same measure with which they share they shall receive — and more. For, as Wuest says, there shall be some on top of that which one receives in proportion to what he gives. By sharing truth one shows his ability to receive and use more truth. "For he that hath, to him shall be given: and he that hath not, from him shall be taken even that which he hath" (v. 25). This is the law of return. A proper stewardship of anything, for instance, knowledge or skill, will add to it. Failure in this regard causes one to lose what he has. A pianist must practice and perform or else he loses his skill and touch.

Many missionaries on furlough from their stations illustrate this truth. After several years of speaking a foreign language with little use of their native tongue, they have difficulty for a time with vocabulary as they endeavor to use the latter. So truth unused or unshared slips away.

Had the apostles not shared Jesus' truth with others they would in time have lost their own understanding of it. But because they declared it, the Holy Spirit guided them into even greater understanding of God's revealed truth concerning His Son. So that to His disciples in all ages Jesus says, "If any man has ears to hear, let him hear" (v. 23).

The Parable of Mysterious Growth (4:26-29)

The purpose of this parable is to show that seed sown ultimately will bear a harvest. Evidently Jesus was thinking of the seed sown in good soil (v. 20).

"And he said, So is the kingdom of God" (v. 26). How is the kingdom of God? It is as a man sowing seed in the ground. He sows it. And then leaves it alone. In some farming cultivation of the plant enters into the picture. But Jesus was thinking of seed such as wheat or barley. The farmer does not plow the rows as he does, say, with corn. He merely prepares the soil, sows the seed, and then waits for the harvest. And the emphasis is upon *wait*.

Having sown the seed the farmer "should sleep, and rise night and day" (v. 27). These verbs are present subjunctives: "should be sleeping and rising night and day." And the seed "should be sprouting and growing" or "lengthening." While the farmer is sleeping and rising the grain is germinating and growing. Night and day the process goes on. To the farmer it is a mystery. For "he knoweth not how." Actually, "how he does not really know."

With all of his knowledge man does not understand this mystery of growth. But he waits. And the growth takes place.

Note the gradual process (v. 28). First, the blade or the herbage *(chortos)*. Then the ear or head forms. And then the grain *(sitos)* appears and fills out. Now the farmer does not force this to happen. "For the earth bringeth forth fruit of herself" (v. 28). The words "of herself" translate a word *(automatē)* whence comes the word "automatic." So the earth produces fruit automatically. Really the seed in the earth does this. It does so because it is within its nature to do so. Without the living seed the soil, sun, rain, and cultivation would be futile. These are but cooperative factors. The life principle is in the seed. And at the end of the process the farmer reaps a harvest (v. 29).

Now this parable is related to the seed as the Word of God. It is necessary for the gospel sower to sow this seed in good soil. But he does not reap an immediate harvest. He must wait patiently while the gospel does its work. But God's spiritual laws are as definite as His natural laws. The harvest will come.

So often God's people are impatient. They want immediate results. But Jesus was content to wait. And so should His disciples. To endeavor to force results is to destroy the plant and to negate the harvest. Someone has noted that Jesus was revolutionary but He was no revolutionist. His gospel is dynamitic but not dynamite. The sower should keep on sowing the seed in men's hearts. But he should be patient to leave the results with God.

The Parable of Comparison (4:30-34)

"Comparison" is the thought in the word "liken." Jesus asked, "Whereunto shall we liken the kingdom of God?" (v. 30). "Liken" renders the verb *homoioō*, to compare. Already Jesus had spoken of the kingdom of God in terms of sowing and reaping. He sought for a figure to depict the kingdom.

"It is like a grain of mustard seed" (v. 31). In what way? When it is sown it is the least of seeds. But it grows into the largest of herbs (v. 32). Matthew says that it becomes a tree (13: 32). Actually it is still an herb, but one as large as a tree. Some interpreters have questioned this. However, one Talmudist describes the mustard plant as a tree, producing enough wood to cover a potter's shed. Vincent quotes Professor Hockett as saying that on the plain of Akka he found mustard plants from six to nine feet high. He also cites Thompson as having seen near the Jordan one that was over twelve feet high. Barclay notes a traveler in Palestine who saw such a plant higher than a horse and rider.

Jesus said that in the branches of such an herb birds find shelter among or underneath its shaded limbs. Actually birds did just this, finding food from the little black mustard seeds.

What was Jesus saying? He was saying that even though the kingdom had a small beginning it would become a great thing in the earth. At this juncture the kingdom was numerically small indeed. But again Jesus said, "Wait." It was destined to fill the earth, growing out of all proportion to its beginning. And men would find both shelter and food in its great growth.

The disciples needed this assurance then as they do now. At times the kingdom may seem to move on leaden feet. But it is moving. And patient perseverance will win the day.

So it was that Jesus taught in parables (v. 33). On this occasion He did so altogether. And those who heard with understanding received great truth indeed. How fortunate were these early disciples to hear and to have interpreted these fresh revelations concerning the kingdom of God (v. 34). And their pungent truths abide as a benediction upon all who hear and heed them today.

Mark 4:35-41

The Lord over Nature

The day when Jesus spoke the foregoing parables A. T. Robertson calls the "Busy Day," noting that it was likely just one of many such days in His life. It spans events recorded in Mark 3:19–5:20. Beginning in Galilee (Capernaum) it also carried Jesus across the sea of Galilee to the region of Gerasa.

"And the same day, when the even was come, he saith unto them, Let us pass over unto the other side" (v. 35). Mark usually does not relate temporal connections. But here he points out that the following events occurred on this *busy day*. "Even" could be either before or after sundown. In this context it probably means late in the afternoon but before sunset. After so trying a day it would be refreshing to get away from the crowds for a cooling trip across the lake.

The Side Journey (4:35-36)

So after dismissing the people the Twelve took Jesus into a large fishing boat "even as he was." That is, without previous preparation. They were not prepared with food or other apparatus, being unaware in advance of Jesus' plan to cross the lake. Mark alone notes that people in other boats went along. It was not so easy to get away from the crowds. But since no other mention is made of them, it is likely that they soon turned back probably because of the approaching storm (v. 37).

The Crisis at Sea (4:37-38)

While Jesus' boat was crossing the lake "there arose a great storm of wind." Mark calls this storm a *lailaps* (cf. Luke 8:23). But Matthew calls it a *seismos* (8:24). It was like a violent earthquake as the sea rolled and tossed. It was a furious hurricane. Evidently it arose suddenly. The hot air of this area 682 feet below sea level suddenly drew this storm system down from the lofty area of Mt. Hermon. Such sudden storms on the sea of Galilee are common even today.

Mark vividly describes the action. The waves "beat into the ship, so that it was now full." "Beat into" renders the verb *epiballō,* to throw upon. It is an imperfect tense showing repeated action. The wind took up the waves and repeatedly threw them upon the ship. Insomuch that "the boat was now filling." One can see them desperately rowing and bailing water. But to no avail.

All the while Jesus "was in the hinder part of the ship, asleep on a pillow" (v. 38). He was in the stern of the boat asleep, either on the bench where the steersman sat or else with His head resting on the leather cushion provided for the steersman. It is reasonable to assume that He lay on the bench with His head on the cushion. This "pillow" was a *proskephalaion,* that towards which one puts the head. Both Matthew and Luke note that Jesus was asleep. But only Mark mentions the pillow. This reflects the accurate eye-witness report of Peter, a seaman who would be familiar with this detail.

Two things may be noted about Jesus sleeping at such a time. The evident one is His humanity. He was exhausted after this busy day. But back of this idea is His deity. As the Son of God He had no need to fear the waves.

But the Twelve had no such assurance. So having done all that they could, they now awoke Jesus. They said, "Master [Teacher] carest thou not that we perish?" (v. 38). They rebuked Jesus for sleeping while "we are being destroyed." Mark alone records this rebuke. Luke reads, "Master, Master, we are perishing" (8:24). Matthew simply says that they cried, "Lord, save [rescue from danger]; we are perishing" (8:25). It is of interest that Luke in his exact language uses the word *epistata* (Master), the technical name for the captain of a ship.

Even though they rebuked Jesus, it is evident that they recognized His power to come to their aid. He was a tired man sleeping; but He was the Lord of the sea and wind.

The Sufficient Lord (4:39-41)

Now awake, Jesus arose and "rebuked the wind, and said unto the sea, Peace, be still" (v. 39). He spoke with authority to the wind and sea even as He did to men. "Peace" renders a word which means to be silent, still, or calm. "Be still" means literally, "Be muzzled." The present imperative of the former verb means to keep on being calm. The perfect imperative of the latter verb means to be muzzled and to remain so.

Note the results. "And the wind ceased [immediately, aorist], and there was [immediately, aorist] a great calm." The aorist tenses show that this was a miracle. Naturally, the wind would have abated gradually and likewise the sea would have become still. But when Jesus ordered them they obeyed instantly.

Bruce comments on this. "Observe the poetic parallelism in this verse: wind and sea separately addressed, and the corresponding effects separately specified: lulled wind, calmed sea. The evangelist realizes the dramatic character of the situation—*siōpa, pephimōso,* silence! hush! laconic, majestic, probably the very words."

Having attended to nature Jesus then turned to His disciples. "Why are ye so fearful? how is it that ye have no faith? (v. 40). Wuest translates this, "Why are you such timid, fearful ones? How is it possible that you do not have faith?" But Robertson renders the latter question, "Have ye not yet faith?" Did they not know that the Lord, the Creator and Sustainer of the universe, was in the boat? God would not let His Son drown at sea, for He had a different goal. The Twelve had accepted Jesus as the Messiah. But it is clear that they have much to learn about Him and His mission.

"And they feared exceedingly" (v. 41). Literally, "they feared a great fear." If they had been frightened at the power of the wind and waves, they were more frightened in the presence of One who commanded and they obeyed. So they asked among themselves, "What manner of man is this, that even the wind and sea obey him?" (v. 41). The word "man" is not in the Greek text. Actually it reads, "Who then is this?" They had seen His power over demons and disease. But this miracle, to them, was the greatest yet. They failed to recognize the terrible power of evil in men's lives. To them the natural force of nature on the prowl was even greater. But they saw that even this was subject to the power of Jesus.

The Twelve learned a great lesson that day. It is a pity that modern man with his great wisdom has not yet fully accepted the power of God in nature as also in men.

Mark 5:1-20

The Lord over Demons

Following the stilling of the storm Jesus and the disciples arrived on the eastern shore of the sea of Galilee (v. 1). They disembarked at a place described by Mark as "the country of the Gadarenes" (KJV). This place name once created a problem. Matthew calls it "the country of the Gadarenes" (8:28). But the best texts of Mark read "Gerasenes." And this reading is followed by Luke 8:26. Was this necessarily a conflict between the Evangelists? What might seem to be the case has been cleared up. The ruins of a village called Khersa or Gerasa have been discoverd which lie near the coast. The city of Gadara is located about thirty miles to the east. But Khersa could be described as being in the country or territory of Gadara. Thus it may be called "the country of the Gerasenes" or "the Gadarenes."

Since it was late evening when they began their journey across the lake, they probably arrived on the eastern shore after dark. The distance across the lake at this point is about five miles. The boat had been slowed up by the storm. So the time involved would make their arrival sometime after dark. This fact, as Barclay notes, added to the eerie nature of the scene which transpired there.

The Demonized Man (5:2-7)

For when He came out of the boat, Jesus was met by a man coming out of the tomb (v. 2). There are many caves in the area which were probably used as places for burial. The man had an unclean spirit, and dwelt among the tombs (v. 3). The word rendered "dwelling" means that he made his home in this place. A demon-possessed man would be driven from among other men. So it was customary for such to dwell in solitary places as among the tombs. And most likely he would be prowling about at night.

Matthew mentions two such men (8:28), but Mark and Luke mention only one. This does not necessarily mean a conflict. While there were two men, Mark and Luke concentrate upon the one, probably the more prominent of the two on this occasion.

So crazed was he that "no man could bind him, no, not with chains" (v. 3). Evidently he was a maniac. Because of this many times he had been bound with fetters (ropes?) and chains (v.

4). The word for "bound" is a perfect tense, showing that he had been thoroughly bound. Nevertheless he broke the chains and fetters. So that no one could tame or restrain him.

Naturally he terrorized the entire area. Night and day the residents could hear his screaming as he wandered in the mountains and among the tombs (v. 5). In his times of wild frenzy he kept cutting himself with jagged stones. So evidently his body was covered with scars. He was an ominous sight indeed.

"But when he saw Jesus afar off, he ran and worshipped him" (v. 6). Assuming that it was night, he evidently simply saw a gathering of people. So he ran toward them, probably screaming and raging. This may well have filled the Twelve with fear. But to their surprise when he came near Jesus, he knelt or prostrated himself before Him. This fact, plus the miracle at sea, must have caused the disciples to wonder even more.

There is no reason to suppose that the man as such recognized Jesus. But the demons residing in him did. So, in fact, it was they who fell before Jesus. They did recognize Him for who He was. Wuest comments that "the spiritual power and grace that always pervaded the Son of God, quieted his spirit and caused him to fall on his knees in reverence."

Then the demoniac cried with a loud voice, "What have I to do with thee, Jesus, thou Son of the most high God? I adjure thee by God, that thou torment me not" (v. 7). Literally, "What to me and to thee?" What did they have in common? So the demon put Jesus on oath that He would not begin to torture him. The verb is an ingressive aorist subjunctive and the negative *mē*. It meant to test metals and then to test one by torture.

The Response of Jesus (5:8-13)

Why did the demon make this cry? Because Jesus "had repeatedly been saying [imperfect], Come out of the man, thou unclean spirit" (v. 8). Demons did not want to be disembodied.

With the man's cry Jesus asked him his name. And he replied, "My name is Legion: for we are many" (v. 9). A "Legion" was a Roman troop containing 6,826 men. Such was a common sight in Palestine. The name had come to mean a well-organized group possessing great power. Therefore, we are not necessarily to suppose that this exact number of demons indwelt this man. But it is true that "many" had, probably a very large number. The man's conduct would indicate this to be true.

"And he besought him much that he would not send them away out of the country" (v. 10). The imperfect tense of the verb plus the word "much" indicates how earnestly one demon, speaking for the group, kept on pleading with Jesus. Though they were powerful they still recognized the greater power of Jesus. Why not "out of the country"? This was in the Gentile area called the Decapolis, so-called because of ten Greek cities that were in the region. Bruce quotes Grotius as saying that the Decapolis was a favorite haunt of demons since one found there so many apostate Hellenistic Jews. But for whatever reason they did not want to leave that region.

Mark notes that a great herd of swine was feeding nearby (v. 11). This was Gentile country. Such a sight would not be seen in Jewish territory. "And all the devils besought him, saying, Send us into the swine, that we may enter into them" (v. 12). "All the devils" does not appear in the best texts. But the sense of this phrase is present in the plural verb form. The verb "send" is an aorist imperative, suggesting the frantic state of the demons. Demons were said to have no rest unless thy inhabited a physical body. Knowing that Jesus would cast them out of the man, they wanted to enter the swine rather than to be made homeless altogether.

And Jesus gave them permission to do so (v. 13). He did not command but permitted. Some raise the question as to why Jesus permitted this rather than to send the demons back into the abyss. It is an idle question which promises no answer. But certainly one thing is clear. Jesus valued a man more than many hogs. As to the subsequent destruction of property, one can only say that it was by our Lord's permissive will, not His perpetrative will. This is akin to the destruction of life and property by natural phenomena such as earthquakes and tornadoes. Job 1 shows that such are the work of Satan. God permits such in that He does not work a miracle to prevent it. It would appear that all destructive works of nature are caused by Satan. Nature, as well as man, is out of joint because of evil. And in His redemptive work Jesus ultimately will redeem nature back into the perfect will of God (cf. Rom. 8:21ff.).

The Response to Jesus' Act (5:14-20)

When the demons entered into the swine, the herd ran violently down a cliff into the sea. "And were choked in the sea" (v. 13). The verb "were choked" (drowned) renders an imperfect tense. It expresses the successive action. Robertson sees it as describing graphically "the disappearance of pig after pig into the sea." Mark alone notes that there were "about two thousand" hogs. This reflects the eyewitness account of Peter.

Such a spectacle stirred the swine feeders into action. They fled, doubtless filled with fear. "And told it in the city, and in the country" (v. 14). The verb "told" *(apaggellō)* means to bring tidings or word. They were responsible for the swine, and now they lay dead in the sea. Doubtless they told the owners of the swine. But they also related the event to everyone they met.

"And they went out to see what it was that was done" (v. 14). This evidently included both the owners and others.

"And they came to Jesus" (v. 15). Bruce notes that their journey brought them face to face with Jesus. But what they did with Him was another matter.

The people saw the man who had been possessed of demons "sitting, and clothed, and in his right mind" (v. 15). The verb "see" *(theōreō)* means to look at carefully. They thoroughly surveyed the situation. "And they were afraid" (v. 15). Heretofore, they had been afraid of the insane man. But now they were more afraid of what they saw, the man now sane.

Those who were present when the incident occurred confirmed the story of the swineherds. They told what had happened to both the man and the swine. "And they began to pray him to depart out of their coasts" (v. 17). The aorist tense of the infinitive rendered "depart" shows that they wanted Jesus to leave without delay.

Why did they wish this? Many interpreters see the reason to be the loss of their property. They cared more for swine than for souls. This is possible. And it makes for good preaching. But "they" seems to involve more than the owners of the swine. A more probable reason seems to be their fear in the presence of the supernatural. This was an area inhabited largely by Gentiles or pagans. Pagans lived in fear of their gods. And Jesus' display of supernatural power struck terror in their hearts. So they asked Him to leave the area. They rejected Him who in love would have saved them. Alas, how often this is true!

But the healed man had quite a different reaction. Rather than to be out of Jesus' presence, he wanted to go with Him (v. 18). The Greek text is most vivid. As Jesus was entering the boat, the man began to beg or was begging Him to let him accompany Jesus. This, of course, was a natural reaction. He who had been so signally blessed did not want to be out of Jesus' presence. Did he fear that the demons might return to him?

At any rate Jesus denied his request. He readily granted the request of the people of the area. But in denying the man's plea He provided him with a greater privilege. "Go home to thy friends, and tell them how great things the Lord hath done for thee, and hath had compassion on thee" (v. 19). Literally, Jesus told him to return to his home to his own family. The man had been forced to dwell away from them. Now there would be a happy reunion. And he was to tell them what *the Lord* had done for him. Note that Jesus called Himself "Lord." And the perfect tense of the verb "hath done" shows how thoroughly the man was freed from demons.

"And he departed [immediately, aorist], and began [immediately, aorist] to publish in Decapolis how great things Jesus had done for him: and all men did marvel" (v. 20). "To publish" renders a present infinitive of the verb to herald or to preach. Immediately he began and continued to do this. Not only to his own family but to the entire region of the Decapolis. Probably he was widely known as a madman. It is no wonder that everyone who heard him marvelled at his message.

Jesus left the region of Gerasa never to return insofar as the record shows. But He left a powerful witness behind.

Mark 5:21-43

The Lord over Death

No sooner had Jesus returned to Galilee than He was again thronged by the multitudes (v. 21). And there He was confronted by another crisis. "There cometh one of the rulers of the synagogue, Jairus by name: and when he saw him, he fell at his feet" (v. 22). Note that he was one of several rulers (cf. Acts 13:14-15). The rulers of the synagogue were charged with seeing that the services were conducted in orderly fashion. Among other things they selected those who read and taught the Scriptures, taking care to see that the discourses were rendered in order and in keeping with the Jewish faith. The name "Jairus" means one whom Jehovah enlightens.

The Sick Daughter (5:22-24)

Now Jairus' little daughter lay at the point of death (v. 23). So he implored much that Jesus would come to his house, lay His hands upon her, and that she might be healed. Evidently Jairus was from the synagogue in Capernaum. He had seen Jesus heal others. So he had faith that He could heal his daughter.

Jesus started immediately to go to Jairus' home (v. 24). The immediacy of His response is seen in the use of the aorist tense. And as He went the people "kept following him and thronging him" (both verbs are imperfects). The word rendered "thronged" means to press in on all sides. Wuest translates this "they kept on pressing upon Him almost to the point of suffocation."

The Afflicted Woman (5:25-34)

In this throng was a sick woman "which had an issue of blood twelve years" (v. 25). Mark notes that she "had suffered many things of many physicians, and had spent all that she had, and was nothing bettered, but rather grew worse" (v. 26). This is typical layman's language. But Luke 8:43 in the neat language of a physician says that she had an incurable disease. Nevertheless, she had exhausted her resources with doctors, to no avail. But she had faith to believe that Jesus could heal her (v. 27). She felt that if only she could touch His clothes she would be healed (v. 28). Hers was a superstitious faith. But she did have faith.

So she touched the hem of His garment (cf. Luke 8:44). "And immediately the fountain of her blood was dried up; and she felt in her body that she was healed of that plague" (v. 29). It was a miracle. What many doctors had not been able to do, the great Physician had done.

Though apparently Jesus did not see the woman, He knew that something had happened. For "immediately knowing in himself that virtue had gone out of him, turned him about in the press, and said, Who touched my clothes?" (v. 30). The word rendered "knowing" is a verb which means a full knowledge gained by experience. Thus it was personal and clear knowledge gained by experience. "Virtue" may better be translated "power" *(duamin)*. In this case it was Jesus' supernatural power. Literally, "Jesus, knowing fully in himself the out of him power going out."

The disciples were surprised at Jesus' question, since He was pressed in on all sides (v. 31). People were pushing and shoving so that many were touching Him. But this touch of the woman was more than this. It was a deliberate, purposeful touch of faith.

Therefore, Jesus "looked round about to see her that had done this thing" (v. 32). The imperfect form of the verb shows that He kept on looking around as His eyes searched the crowd near Him. And He was looking for a woman. This is evident in the feminine gender of the definitive article and the participle "doing." Did Jesus know this by divine knowledge? Did Mark use these feminine forms in retrospect of the event? Or is there another possible explanation? It could be that Jesus knew by the nature of the touch that it was a woman. A man probably would have grasped His garment. According to the Mosaic law a woman in this diseased condition was forbidden to touch Him at all. But so desperate was her condition that she dared to ignore it. Yet in her timidity she just barely touched Jesus' garment. But it was enough.

However, as Jesus swept the crowd with His eyes, the woman felt that she was discovered. So "fearing and trembling, knowing what was done to her, [she] came and fell down before him, and told him all the truth" (v. 33). The verb "done" is a perfect tense, denoting a complete cure. But why did she fear and tremble? A woman's position in society could explain it. But probably Bruce is right in his explanation. The woman was forbidden by law to touch Jesus. In a sense she had violated His rights, if He should choose to see it thus. Would He resent her action, and, perhaps, recall His healing power? These things could well have been in her mind as she fell at Jesus' feet. Nevertheless, she made a clean breast of her actions. She told the Lord of her long period of suffering and of her desperate faith. And Jesus responded with mercy. This poor woman had heard of Jesus' power. Now she learned of His sympathy and love.

"Daughter" (v. 34). Note that He did not say, "Woman." This word *(Thugatēr)* was used when speaking tenderly to a mature woman. And as Bruce notes, Jesus spoke not as a man to a woman but as a father to a child. "Thy faith hath made thee whole." This verb form may mean to heal from disease or to save from sin. Its perfect form expresses completeness. Actually both meanings may apply here. Through her faith she had been both healed of disease and saved from sin. It is no wonder, then, that she could go away in peace! Or more exactly, "Go away into peace." A new door of life had opened for her.

The Dead Child (5:35-43)

This beautiful and merciful interruption was ended as one came from Jairus' house with the sad news, "Thy daughter is dead: why troublest thou the Master further?" (v. 35). The aorist tense should read, "Your daughter died." All hope was gone, so there was no further need to bother Jesus with the matter. There was nothing left but a funeral and grief.

Jesus overheard the bad news. But He did not merely shake His head and turn away in resignation. Rather, He spoke reassuring words to the already grieving father. "Stop fearing, only keep on believing" (v. 36). This was a tremendous challenge to Jairus. Fear already gripped his heart with icy fingers threatening to snuff out his candle of faith. But Jesus told him to put aside his fear and to hold on to his faith even in the presence of death.

Having spoken thus Jesus told the crowd to cease following Him (v. 37). Peter, James, and John were the exception. The definitive article before "Peter" shows that these were selected as a group. This is the first of three instances when they were permitted to be an inner circle of the Twelve on an auspicious occasion (cf. Transfiguration and Gethsemane). Perhaps the home of Jairus was too small to include more. But, further, these three disciples were chosen to witness a great miracle.

Arriving at the house Jesus was greeted with a pitiful scene. The place was literally in an *uproar (thorubos)*. There was much weeping and wailing. No doubt the grief of the family was genuine. But much of this turmoil was caused by paid mourners who had crowded into the home. The word for "wailed" is an onomatopoetic word, a word whose very sound is related to its meaning. It is *alalazō,* to repeat over and over the cry *alala*. It was used by soldiers entering battle. This word is also found in I Corinthians 13:1 of a "tinkling [or clanging] cymbal."

Entering the house Jesus asked, "Why make ye this ado, and weep?" (v. 39). Or, "Why do you make this uproar, and weep?" And then He made an astounding statement. "The damsel [little girl] is not dead, but sleepeth." Some would suppose that "sleepeth" means that the girl had not died but was in a coma. But the entire scene speaks of death itself. *Sleep* was used in the sense of rest. This does not mean that souls exist in an unconscious state until the resurrection (cf. Luke 16:19ff.). In this particular case Jesus meant that the child was not dead to remain so.

"And they laughed him to scorn" (v. 40). "Laughed" renders the verb "to laugh at" with the prefix "down" *(katagelaō);* thus "to ridicule." The form of the verb is what is called an inceptive imperfect. They began to laugh at Jesus and kept on doing so. Robertson notes that "the loud laughter was ill suited to the solemn occasion."

But Jesus took charge of the situation. He cleared the house of all save the parents and the three disciples. Then they entered the room where the dead girl lay. What a prophetic picture. The Lord of life entered into the chamber where death reigned for the moment. But it was only for a moment. For Jesus took the little girl by the hand and spoke to her. Here was the touch of life and the voice of authority over death. Though she was dead Jesus knew that she would hear His voice and live.

"Talitha cumi" (v. 41). Though Jesus doubtless spoke Greek, He employed the native language of Himself and the damsel. Such would be natural in so tender a scene. Peter heard these words and never forgot them. Years later he passed them on to Mark. But for his Roman readers Mark translated them. "Little girl, I say unto thee, arise." And she responded immediately. She "arose, and walked" (v. 42). Weak in death, and yet she immediately "arose" (aorist) and "kept on walking about" (imperfect). Mark alone notes that she was twelve years old and thus able to walk. Another touch of Peter's vivid imagery. Wuest adds a tender note. She "kept on walking about, first, possibly to her mother, then to her father, and, then, finding out what had happened, to the Lord Jesus who had restored her to life."

Naturally those who witnessed this were greatly amazed. "They were astonished with great astonishment" (v. 42). Nestle employs the word *euthus* (immediately) twice. "Immediately" the little girl arose . . . "immediately they were amazed with a great amazement." The verb and noun for *amaze* mean to put out of one's self. They were out of their senses, in an ecstasy. They could not believe what they saw. But it was true.

Then Jesus strongly ordered those who had seen this that they should not relate it to others (v. 43). It could not be hidden that the damsel was alive. But Jesus did not want the people outside to know what He had done, lest the people's excitement should get out of hand. But apparently from Matthew 9:26 it was told nevertheless. Did the three disciples ignore Jesus' orders? Or the parents? Or both?

The story closes with a very realistic note. For Jesus "commanded that something should be given her to eat" (v. 43; cf. Luke 8:55). She had strength to walk. But a living body needs food to maintain that strength. So the Great Physician employed divine powers to raise the dead. But He also relied upon natural means to sustain the living.

Bruce notes that "she could walk and eat; not only alive, but well."

Mark 6:1-6

The Prophet Not without Honor

A City of Unbelief (6:1-3)

Following the raising of Jairus' daughter Jesus and the Twelve paid a visit to Nazareth. This is the natural meaning of "his own country" (v. 1). It means "his native place." Jesus had been born in Bethlehem. But His home had been in Nazareth. Some would equate this visit with the one recorded in Luke 4:16ff. But there is no reason why Jesus would not return there a second time. Though His native town had rejected Him earlier, He may have proposed to give it another chance. Since this rejection He had made Capernaum His headquarters.

But why did Jesus choose to revisit Nazareth at this time? It could have been a natural desire to visit His mother. Or it may have been prompted by the excitement as news spread about the raising of the little girl. He had spent some time in a busy ministry. And this would afford a period of comparative quiet and rest.

However, even while on a *vacation* Jesus did not neglect the privilege of worship. So on the sabbath day He went to the synagogue (v. 2). There He was invited to teach. Evidently the fame of Jesus led the ruler of the synagogue to extend this invitation despite the unhappy ending to His former visit. Perhaps things would be different this time.

But as the people heard Jesus' words they were amazed. "From whence hath this man these things? and what wisdom is this which is given unto him, that even such mighty works are wrought by his hands?" (v. 2). They could not deny His "wisdom" *(sophia)*. And they had heard about His miracles. But were they genuine or just so much *hocus-pocus?*

For, you see, they knew Jesus from former days. "Is not this the carpenter, the son of Mary, the brother of James, and Joses, and of Juda, and Simon? and are not his sisters here with us" (v. 3)? The word rendered "with" is *pros*. It means before or face to face. This could mean that Jesus' family was present in the service. It would be the natural thing to expect. They had all gone to the synagogue together. It may well be that on this occasion Jesus' unbelieving brothers looked with askance upon the place given to him in the service. But doubtless Mary felt a mother's pride in her illustrious Son.

But the people sat in stunned disbelief. Jesus had grown up among them, had done their carpenter work, and they knew His family. So, they concluded, that He could not be much. "And they were offended [caused to stumble] at him." It was a typical case of a hometown *boy* who had made good and now was back among His provincial neighbors.

No mention is made of Joseph who probably died while Jesus was in His "teen" years. But what about His brothers and sisters? Those who hold to Mary's perpetual virginity see them either as cousins of Jesus or else children of Joseph by a former marriage. But this is to argue around a difficulty. The term "brother" *(adelphos)* means just that. The New Testament clearly shows that after Jesus' birth as Mary's "firstborn son" (Luke 2:7) she entered into normal marriage relations with her husband Joseph (Matt. 1:25). So in truth these were Jesus' half-brothers and half-sisters.

Seeing the reaction of His former neighbors, Jesus said, "A prophet is not without honor, but in his own country, and among his own kin, and in his own house" (v. 4). This within itself suggests that Jesus' family, except Mary, shared the feeling of the townspeople. Some hold that Jesus quoted a proverb. At least it has become proverbial in meaning. The people of Nazareth thought that they knew Jesus. But, alas, they did not know Him at all!

A City of Lost Opportunity (5:5-6)

If this was a sad occasion for Jesus, it was even more so for Nazareth. For Jesus "could there do no [*oudemian,* not even one] mighty work, save that he laid his hands upon a few sick folk, and healed them" (v. 5). Evidently these few did believe, and they received His healing power. But note that it was only a "few," probably those in the synagogue. Bruce notes that the Nazarenes were so unbelieving that, contrary to other places, they did not even bring their sick to Jesus for healing.

Charles R. Erdman makes a telling comment. "The real pathos of the story is expressed in the words which follow the proverb: 'He could there do no mighty work.' This is the pity of it all. Where appreciation and love are lacking there our friends cannot be, and there we cannot do what otherwise would be possible; where faith is lacking, there Christ, however near, however powerful, cannot, will not, do any mighty work."

"And he marvelled because of their unbelief" (v. 6). On one

occasion Jesus marvelled at the great faith of a Roman centurion. Now He marvelled at the great unbelief of the people of Nazareth. In this one sees the humanity of Jesus. As God He would not marvel at anything. But as Man He wondered that people who had been so favored as those in Nazareth should not believe.

One still wonders at such unbelief. Several years ago a group of preachers were visiting Jerusalem. One of them asked an Arab boy, "Son, do you know Jesus?" He replied, "No, I don't believe he ever lived around here." A prophet without honor in His own country indeed!

Jesus had expected so much out of Nazareth. But He suffered bitter disappointment. So He left His own city. And insofar as the Gospel record is concerned, He never returned. Instead He "went round about the villages, teaching" (v. 6). If Nazareth would not hear, other villages would. And they were given their chance.

Mark 6:7-13, 30

The Noble Experiment

The Disciples' Mission (6:7-11)

Jesus had been teaching the Twelve to prepare them for a greater role in the ministry of the kingdom. Now the time had arrived when they should be sent on a preaching tour about Galilee. It was a noble experiment in learning by doing. So one day He "called" the Twelve to Him (v. 7). The verb is *proskaleō*. *Kaleō* means "to call." And the prefix *pros* means "to" or "face to face." He "began to send them forth by two and two." (v. 7). The Greek reads *"duo duo"* or "two two." There would be strength and courage in companionship. "Began" suggests that He prepared them before sending them out on their mission. To equip them "he gave [kept on giving, imperfect] them power over unclean spirits." "Power" *(exousian)* here means delegated power. He kept on giving them His delegated power throughout this mission.

Then before their departure He instructed them. The journey was to be one of haste. So He commanded them that they should take no excess baggage along (v. 8). They were to take a "staff" or walking stick. They were to carry "no scrip, no bread, no money in their purse." What was a "scrip?" It was generally thought to be a satchel or a bread bag. But since they were to travel lightly a satchel would be unnecessary. And they would need no bread bag since they were not to carry bread. Adolph Deissmann in *Light from the Ancient East* cites the meaning of "scrip" as a beggar's bag. Pagan priests carried such in which to put that which they received as they begged money for their gods. It would seem, therefore, that Jesus told the Twelve that they were not to go as beggars. They had an entirely different purpose in going.

And they were to carry no money or brass coins in their "purse." A *purse* was a belt used to hold in place their long, flowing robes. Since purses were hollow they were also used to hold money. They were to wear sandals but not carry an extra pair (v. 9). And they were to wear only one under garment. Truly they were to *travel light*. Erdman notes that "they were such as an Oriental peasant might observe today if sent on a short and important mission."

What were they to do for food and lodging? They were to stay with friendly people along the way (v. 10). If any home refused to welcome them or to hear their message, they were to leave it. And leaving it they were to shake off the dust under their feet "for a testimony against them" (v. 11). This was an act of extreme contempt. When a faithful Jew entered Judea from a pagan land, he shook the pagan dust from off his feet. So the Twelve were to regard those refusing them as though they were pagans. The remainder of verse 11 about Sodom and Gomorrah is footnoted in Nestle's as lacking sufficient manuscript evidence to be regarded as genuine Scripture.

The Disciples' Ministry (6:12-13)

Having received their instructions, the Twelve went forth and preached that men should repent (v. 12). This was the message delivered by both John the Baptist and Jesus. The word "preached" renders the verb for one who went as a herald of the king. He went with the king's authority. Those who heard him were to regard him and his message as though the king delivered it in person. So the Twelve went out as heralds of the King. They went in His authority (cf. v. 7b). And they were to be heeded as though Jesus were doing this in person. It is a great responsibility so to represent the King. It is equally as great a responsibility to hear His heralds.

The Twelve had a successful mission (v. 13). They cast out many demons, and anointed with oil many sick and healed them. The Gospels make no other mention of anointing with oil. However, oil was widely used as a means of healing. The word for healing used here is the one generally used for healing by treating one. This could be the meaning of anointing with oil. But this word *(therapeuō)* is sometimes used interchangeably with *iaomai* which denotes healing by miracle. So the *treatment* idea should not be pressed to the exclusion of miraculous healing. It is possible that the Twelve did both.

The Disciples' Report (6:30)

Finally, "the apostles gathered themselves together unto Jesus" (v. 30). This is the first time that "apostles" is used concerning the Twelve. They doubtless returned tired but happy. For they reported all the things which they had done and taught.

The "noble experiment" was noble indeed. The Twelve had

learned; now they had put into practice what they had learned. It was a foretaste of the greater work which they would do in the future.

Mark 6:14-29

The Death of John the Baptist

The Fear of Herod Antipas (6:14-16)

Meanwhile during the absence of the Twelve an event occurred which showed that Jesus' life was in danger, not only from the religious rulers, but from Herod Antipas, the tetrarch of Galilee and Perea. A tetrarch was one who ruled over a fourth of a kingdom. Herod Antipas was the son of Herod the Great. Upon his father's death in 4 B.C. he received his appointment from Augustus Caesar. And he reigned until A.D. 39. At that time he was sent into exile to Lyons in Gaul.

This was the same Herod who had arrested John the Baptist (Mark 1:14). Later he had beheaded him. But his guilty conscience continued to trouble him.

Word of Jesus' ministry had reached his ears. And in his superstitious nature he said, "John the Baptist was risen from the dead, and therefore mighty works do show forth themselves in him" (vv. 14, 16). Other people regarded Jesus as Elias or as some other prophet (v. 15). But Herod saw in Him a risen John the Baptist. "Mighty works" may better be rendered "the powers." This means supernatural powers which were a dread to Herod. He thought that John had come back from the dead to torment him.

The Fate of John the Baptist (6:17-29)

At this point Mark inserts a historical note as to the fate of John the Baptist. He gives only the bare details. But from Josephus may be learned the background of Mark's account.

Herod Antipas had two brothers named Philip. One reigned over Iturea and Trachonitis. Caesarea Philippi bears his name. But the other brother lived in Rome as a private citizen. He was married to a woman named Herodias. She was a conniving, ambitious woman. On a visit to Rome Herod Antipas seduced her and persuaded her to divorce her husband to marry him. It took little persuading to convince her to exchange her place as the wife of a private citizen for that of the wife of a tetrarch. Herod also was married to the daughter of Aretas IV, the king of Arabia. But he divorced her in order to marry Herodias.

When John the Baptist heard of this iniquitous affair he boldly condemned it (v. 17). Apparently he had gone to Herod's palace or fortress at Machaerus and said to him, "It is not lawful for thee to have thy brother's wife" (v. 18). Note that he did not call her Herod Antipas' wife. This event shows the corruption in Herod's court. But John condemned this part-Jew for violating the law of God.

For this reason Herod had John arrested and placed in prison at Machaerus, a fortress built by Herod the Great and located near the Dead Sea. Josephus tells of this arrest. But he says that it was done lest John should cause a political revolution. This evidently was Herod's publicly-stated reason for the arrest. But Mark gives the real reason for it.

"Therefore Herodias had a quarrel against him" (v. 19). Literally, she "had it in for him." The imperfect tense shows her abiding wrath. She wished to kill him, but she was not able to do it. The reason being, that even though he was steeped in evil Herod still feared (kept on fearing, imperfect) John, knowing that he was both just and holy (v. 20). Therefore, Herod kept him safe in custody. Also from time to time he heard (imperfect, heard from time to time) John preach to him. But it always left him greatly perplexed (imperfect tense, kept on leaving). The imperfect tenses make this story live. Herodias kept on after Antipas to slay John. But his occasional visits with John steeled his resistance to her. As Swete says, his visits braced "his jaded mind as with a whiff of fresh air." But Herodias bided her time waiting for the opportune moment.

Finally that "convenient day was come" (v. 21). It was on Herod's birthday. He gave a banquet attended by his lords, chief captains, and the chief men of Galilee. It was a notable gathering. At the right moment when the wine had flowed freely Herodias sent her daughter (Salome) to dance before the men. Gould points out that "such dancing was an almost unprecedented thing for women of rank, or even respectability. It was mimetic and licentious, and performed by professionals." Herodias degraded her daughter in order to accomplish her vicious purpose against the Baptist. For Salome's dance pleased Herod and his guests.

The drunken ruler took the bait dangled before him by his scheming wife. "Ask of me whatsoever thou wilt, and I will give it thee" (v. 22). He took a public oath that he would do this even "unto the half of my kingdom" (v. 23). Bruce calls this "maudlin [drunken, silly] amorous generosity." Within itself this was an empty promise. He ruled by the favor of Rome. And the emperor would certainly have had something to say about this. Doubtless Herod himself would have felt otherwise once he was sober.

Quite obviously the daughter was not in on the plot of her mother. Not knowing what to ask she went to her mother. "What shall I ask?" (v. 24). And Herodias was prepared with a ready answer. "The head of John the Baptist" (v. 24). Salome must have been shocked at so ghastly a request. However, Bruce notes that she was ready enough to comply. She came immediately to Herod with her request. "I will that thou give me by and by [immediately] in a charger the head of John the Baptist" (v. 25). A "charger" *(pinoki)* was a platter such as was used to serve food. She asked for a gruesome dish indeed!

Herod must have been sobered by this request (v. 26). His conscience said, "No." But his pride said, "Yes." He had taken a foolish oath. But rather than back down before his drunken guests, he acquiesced. He ordered a soldier to carry out the execution (v. 27). Soon he returned with the bloody head on a platter (v. 28). He gave it to the daughter who, in turn, presented it to her gloating mother.

John the Baptist had delivered his soul. But he lost his head in the process. There was nothing left to do but for John's disciples to take his headless body and place it in a tomb (v. 29). Matthew 14:12 says that they then went and told Jesus about the death of His faithful cousin, friend, and forerunner. And in the dire news Jesus saw the foretaste of that which awaited Him.

Herod was left with his conscience. It was a conscience tormented with fears; fears which were compounded by the subsequent reports of the miraculous works of Jesus.

Herodias is a perfect picture of a woman scorned. Her one redeeming feature is seen in the fact that when her husband finally was banished to Gaul, she chose to share his fate.

III

The Period of Withdrawals

Mark 6:31-46

The Feeding of the Five Thousand

For eighteen months Jesus had carried on a busy ministry in Galilee. During this time He had made a trip to Jerusalem (John 5). At this point His ministry took a different turn. He began a period of withdrawals from Galilee marked by occasional returns to that area. It was one year prior to the crucifixion. These withdrawals involved about six months from Passover to Tabernacles A.D. 29.

The First Withdrawal (6:31-34)

When the Twelve returned from their preaching tour of Galilee Jesus said, "Come ye yourselves apart into a desert place, and rest a while" (v. 31). The demands of the ministry to the throngs were such that "they had no leisure so much as to eat." Actually one may discern five reasons for these withdrawals: the jealousy of Herod Antipas, the hostility of the Jewish rulers, the fanaticism of the people, the need for rest, and the necessity for Jesus to spend time in teaching the Twelve. Thus we see Jesus leading His little band away from the crowded area of Galilee, the region ruled over by Antipas. In so doing they were out of the hot summer climate of the area about the sea of Galilee. They were largely away from the Jewish rulers. And Jesus was afforded opportunity to prepare the Twelve for the storm which would descend upon them. However, He was not so successful in avoiding the crowds.

The first withdrawal was to a region on the eastern shore of the sea of Galilee. "And they departed into a desert place by ship privately" (v. 32). This was a sparsely-settled area on the northeastern shore of the lake. The people did not attempt to follow in boats as on a previous occasion. But they noted His direction and surmised His destination. So they ran ahead on foot around the northern edge of the lake (v. 33). When Jesus disembarked He found them waiting for Him. Seeing them He was moved with compassion for they seemed "as sheep not having a shepherd" (v. 34). They had their "hirelings," but these left them tired, hungry, and scattered. Therefore, He began to teach them. No mention is made of healing. This is understandable since the sick and lame could not have accompanied this crowd on their race after Jesus.

The Miracle of the Loaves and Fishes (6:35-44)

It was now late in the day, sometime after 3:00 p.m. on the first evening. In their haste the people had brought no food. Not having eaten since morning they were hungry. And the disciples took note of this fact (v. 35).

"Send them away, that they may go into the country round about, and into the villages, and buy themselves bread" (v. 36). John 6:5 says that Jesus asked Philip where they might buy bread for the people. This evidently came in response to the disciples' words. Mark's account blends into this idea. For Jesus said, "Give ye them to eat" (v. 37). The Twelve said, "Send them away." Jesus said, "Give ye them to eat." They suggested that the people should shift for themselves. But Jesus placed the responsibility squarely upon His disciples.

Quite naturally the Twelve faced the problem of finances. "Two hundred pennyworth" (*dēnariōn*) would be about thirty-five dollars. But even that sum was lacking in their meager treasury. As they were soon to learn, however, they reckoned in their own power rather than in the power of God.

For Jesus asked, "How many loaves have ye? go and see" (v. 38). Looking about they found a lad who had "five, and two fishes" (v. 38; cf. John 6:9). It was probably the lunch which his mother had fixed him. It consisted of five little cakes and two dried fish, the food of the poor. But even this was but a morsel for one, not food for a multitude (cf. John 6:9). However, with Jesus it was sufficient.

"And he commanded them to make all sit down by companies upon the green grass" (v. 39). John notes that it was the time for the passover (6:4). In the springtime the hills would be covered with green grass. So "they sat down in ranks, by hundreds, and by fifties" (v. 40). Note Jesus' use of organization. In a mob some would not be able to get any food. But in this orderly arrangement each person could be fed efficiently and systematically. To Jesus organization was not an end but a means. But it was necessary for successful results.

It is interesting to note the verbs used in verses 39-40. In verse 39 Jesus said to cause the people *to recline* on the grass. Verse 40 says that they *fell down*. Like exhausted cattle they *fell down* and *reclined* on the green grass. And they did so "in ranks." This phrase renders two Greek words *praisai praisai*. Literally, "garden beds garden beds." These groups dressed in their multi-colored garments looked like "garden beds" of beautiful flowers nestling among the green grass. This was what this scene looked like to Peter. And he passed this vivid imagery on to Mark.

With these arrangements made, Jesus proceeded to act. He took the loaves and fishes, gave thanks, "and brake the loaves, and gave them to his disciples to set before them; and the two fishes divided he among them all" (v. 41). The verb forms are most expressive. He "brake" (aorist) the loaves, and "gave" (imperfect) to His disciples, in order that they "might set before" (present subjunctive) them. In the aorist tense of instant action one can almost hear the snap of the little cakes as Jesus broke them. And both the imperfect and present tenses speak of continuous action. He "kept on giving" to the disciples that "they might keep on setting before" the people. This same action may be implied with respect to the fishes. The meager supply was not exhausted. The more Jesus broke the more there was.

Various attempts have been made to explain away this miracle. Some say that Jesus and the Twelve shared their lunches and this set off a chain reaction of generosity among the people. This, of course, is contrary to the record. Others suggest that the disciples found a military cache of food and with it fed the people. It takes more credulity to accept this than to believe the miracle of Jesus.

Once one accepts Jesus for who He was the problem vanishes. If the Lord of nature could by natural laws produce the grain and fish, could He not by laws unknown to men multiply them? A miracle may be defined as an act of God contrary to natural laws understood by men, but in keeping with laws of God's understanding, which God does to accomplish His benevolent purposes. In the light of the marvels performed by man who can say what God can or cannot do?

"And they did all eat, and were filled" (v. 42). The word rendered "were filled" is a verb meaning to fill full or to gorge (cf. John 6:26). It was used of feeding cattle. So all the people ate to their fill. Furthermore, the Twelve took up "twelve baskets full of the fragments, and of the fishes" (v. 43). A basket was a *kophinos* or a food basket. When a Jew traveled he usually carried one. It was customary for those who served a meal to get the leftovers. And each diner was supposed to leave some food for that purpose. Twelve disciples served. There were twelve baskets full of fragments. This was not garbage, but broken pieces of food just as the guests had received it. So they evidently followed the custom of saving some food for the servers. Of interest is the fact that Jesus provided food, but He did not allow it to be wasted.

Mark notes that "five thousand men" were fed (v. 44). Matthew adds the note that there were also women and children (14:21). No one knows. But it does show that the crowd was decidedly more than five thousand.

The Reaction to the Miracle (6:45-46)

Mark says that "straightway he constrained his disciples to get into the ship, and to go to the other side before unto Bethsaida, while he sent away the people" (v. 45). He does not report the revolutionary attempt of the people to declare Jesus their military Messiah (cf. John 6:14ff.). But he implies it. The fact that Jesus "constrained" the Twelve indicates that they did not want to go. Some suggest that He wanted to get them out of this revolutionary atmosphere. But there is another possibility. Did the Twelve arouse the people? If so, it was necessary to send them away before He could quiet and dismiss the people. In either event this shows the fanatical atmosphere which Jesus wished to avoid at this time. To precipitate a revolution would bring the wrath of Rome down upon Him. Thus His mission would have ended in failure as had those of so many pretenders. Jesus had another role and a divinely-given end. And He pursued it despite the alternatives presented to Him by Satan and those under his control.

Having dispersed this abortive attempt, Jesus went away to pray (v. 46). When men misunderstood, He could always find fellowship and strength with His Father.

According to John's Gospel this event marked the high-water mark in Jesus' popularity with the Galilean people. When he refused to be a bread Messiah they left Him. But He continued to walk the path designed for Him by His heavenly Father.

Mark 6:47-56

The Return to Galilee

The Solitary Jesus (6:47)

The feeding of the multitude and subsequent events had absorbed about three hours (cf. vv. 35, 47). For it was now "even" (*opsias*). This was called the second evening from sunset on. At this season of the year this would be about 6:00 P.M. By this time the disciples were "in the midst of the sea." Jesus had finished His prayer period, and now stood alone on the shore. This is a vivid scene as the Saviour stood alone in the twilight. Robertson suggests that evidently Jesus remained here for some time. Because John 6:17 notes that it was long after dark before Jesus came to the disciples in their boat.

The Miracle of the Wind and Waves (6:48-52)

"And seeing them being distressed in the rowing, for the wind was contrary unto them, about the fourth watch of the night he comes to them walking upon the sea, and would have passed by them" (v. 48). A strong wind had made large waves, so that rowing was difficult. The fourth watch was between three and six A.M. John says that they had rowed about three miles or about half way across the sea at this point. This plus the time element shows how slow was their progress. All three Synoptic Gospels mention Jesus as walking on the water. But only Mark notes that He willed to pass by them. No explanation is given for this wish. It is possible that since they had presumed to take matters into their own hands in the attempted revolution, He proposed to let them learn in the rough sea how little power they really possessed.

At any rate when they saw Jesus walking upon the sea, they thought that they were seeing a spirit or an apparition (v. 49). Quite naturally they were terrified. The word rendered "cried" means a shriek or scream of terror. But Jesus put them at ease by saying, "Be of good cheer: it is I; be not afraid" (v. 50). "It is I" were the words of cheer. Literally, "I am," with emphasis upon "I." "I AM" was the title assumed by Jehovah with Moses at the burning bush. So the miracle of walking on the water, plus this claim "I am," showed Jesus to be more than a military Messiah. He was God in the flesh. In this light He said, "Stop being afraid."

At this point in his Gospel Matthew tells of Peter's request that he also be permitted to walk on the water (14:28ff). Evidently Peter avoided any mention of this incident. Hence its absence from Mark's record.

Mark simply notes that Jesus entered the boat, and "the wind ceased" (v. 51). The aorist tense shows that it ceased immediately. Thus here is another miracle. A natural phenomenon would have been a gradual subsiding of the wind and waves. So once again the disciples "were sore amazed . . . beyond measure."

One would think that by this time the Twelve would have grown accustomed to such events (cf. 4:39ff.). But they seemed to have short memories and hard hearts (v. 52). In their terror they even forgot the miracle of feeding the multitude. At least they did not regard it as a miracle to be compared with Jesus walking on the sea and His power over the angry elements. Barclay quotes Augustine to this effect. "He came treading the waves; and so He puts all the swelling tumults of life under His feet. Christians – why afraid?"

The Arrival in Galilee (6:53-56)

With a calm sea they arrived shortly in the area of the plain of Gennesaret (v. 53). This was several miles south of their intended goal of Bethsaida (v. 45). The wind had driven them off course. So they moored to the shore there.

Immediately upon leaving the boat Jesus was recognized by the people there (v. 54). So the word went like wildfire that He was back. And people began to bring their sick to Him (v. 55). From this point of landing Jesus returned to Capernaum (cf. John 6:24). Along the way the sick were brought to Him. For they said that if they could just touch the tassel of His garment they would be healed. Evidently they had heard of the healing of the woman with the issue of blood. "And as many as touched him were made whole" (v. 56). In these two verses one may see something of the scope of Jesus' healing ministry. A few instances here and there are related in detail. But these were but a few among many.

But with all of this popularity John tells how the people turned away from Jesus that very day (6:22ff.). They had come to think of Him largely as a healing and feeding Messiah. When He presented His greater spiritual claims they rejected both them and Him. Later in Judea great crowds will follow Jesus. But the Galilean throngs left Him to seek succor elsewhere. It is tragic. But sadly it is ever thus. Man is so earth-bound that he too often loses the true blessings which Jesus would give.

Mark 7:1-23

The Rejection of Tradition

One of Jesus' reasons for withdrawing from Galilee was the growing opposition to Him on the part of the Jewish religious leaders. There is evidence of friendship between Jesus and the religious leaders who resided in Galilee. This is shown by their repeated invitations for Him to speak in the synagogues. Jairus was a ruler of the synagogue who turned to Jesus in his hour of need. But the Jewish rulers from Judea or Jerusalem were quite another matter. The scribes and Pharisees opposed Him at every turn even to the point of plotting His death. John's Gospel relates how this opposition began in Jerusalem (2:13ff.; 4:1; 5:1ff.).

Already it has been noted that their enmity against Jesus centered about His attitude toward their position on the temple, the law, the Sabbath, and their traditions. Conflict over this last matter comes out in the open in Mark 7.

The Criticism of the Pharisees (7:1-2)

Sometime after Jesus fed the multitude a delegation of Pharisees and scribes arrived in Galilee from Jerusalem (v. 1). Or they may have been the same ones who had been in Galilee since shortly after the beginning of Jesus' Galilean ministry. At any rate they were from Jerusalem. The Pharisees were zealous for their rules. And the scribes were experts in the law. Of course, there was the written law of Moses. But the *traditions* were the oral law which had been devised by various Jewish teachers down through the years. These traditions or things handed down were efforts to interpret the written law. But as with the Sabbath so with other matters this resulted in a multitude of rules for the regulation of conduct. The Mosaic law dealt with things that were clean and unclean. But the traditions sought to apply these in a manner never intended by God. One group of traditional laws dealt with both things and people regarded by the Jewish teachers as being unclean.

Jesus ran head on into these when the Jewish leaders criticized His disciples for eating bread without first washing their hands (v. 2). They were said to be eating with "defiled" and "unwashen" hands. The word "defiled" renders the word meaning "common" (*koinais*). Originally *koinos* meant that which was common to everyone (cf. *Koinē* Greek, or the common language of the people). Later it came to mean vulgar or profane. And finally it took on the meaning of being ceremonially unclean. That is the meaning in this passage. Furthermore, the word "unwashen" renders *aniptois* or unrinsed.

The Problem of Tradition (7:3-5)

Now this charge by the Jewish rulers stemmed from a custom which they followed. "For the Pharisees, and all the Jews, except they wash [rinse] their hands oft [diligently], eat not, holding the tradition of the elders" (v. 3). This custom was related not to physical but to ceremonial cleanliness. This related to both things and people.

For instance, they had a superstition that the demon Shibta got on their hands so as to enter their bodies. Therefore, they *rinsed* their hands to remove this evil spirit. This was done before and at intervals during a meal. Large stone jars filled with pure water were kept conveniently nearby for this purpose. In this ceremony the hands were held so that the finger tips pointed upwards. Water was poured over them so as to run down the arms as far as the elbow. Then while still wet the arm and hand were scrubbed with the fist of the other hand. This practice is seen in the word "diligently" (*pugmei*) from the word meaning "fist."

Furthermore, when they came from the marketplace they *sprinkled* water over themselves to remove any ceremonial uncleanness received by inadvertently touching a Gentile (v. 4). The word "wash" renders the verb "to sprinkle" (*rhantizō*). And lest eating utensils had been touched by a Gentile they dipped them in water. The word "washing" renders *baptizō,* meaning to dip, submerge, or immerse. This is the verb often rendered "baptize."

Having described the traditions of ceremonial cleansing Mark proceeded with the narrative. The Pharisees and scribes asked Jesus, "Why walk not thy disciples according to the tradition of the elders, but eat bread with unwashen hands?" (v. 5). In the best Greek texts the word "unwashen" reads "defiled" or "common." To the Jewish rulers this was not simply bad hygiene. It was an evil. For to them the disciples were unclean in God's sight. Barclay notes that to them bread eaten with defiled hands was no better than excrement. The story is told of a Rabbi who was imprisoned by the Romans. He used his drinking water for ceremonial cleansing and almost died of thirst. He preferred death to defilement.

The Answer of Jesus (7:6-16)

To the Pharisees this was the very essence of religion. One can understand Jesus' scorn of such as He said, "Well hath Esaias prophesied of you hypocrites, as it is written, This people honoreth me with their lips, but their heart is far from me" (v. 6). Note the term "you hypocrites." They were play actors pretending to be religious when they were not. They emphasized the outward form of cleanliness. But their hearts were defiled. Their worship was empty as they taught men's commandments but ignored God's commandments (vv. 7-9).

Then Jesus showed how hypocritical they were. God through Moses had said, "Honor thy father and thy mother" (Exod. 20:12). And "Whosoever curseth father and mother, let him die the death" (Exod. 21:17) (v. 10). But what did they do? They devised a rule by which a man might be free from any responsibility for his parents.

"If a man shall say to his father or mother, It is Corban, that is to say, a gift, by whatsoever thou mightest be profited by me; *he shall be free*" (v. 11). The italicized words are not in the Greek text. But the sense is there nevertheless. "Corban" means a gift, and particularly a gift to God. A man's parents were in need. But the son could escape any responsibility to them by merely speaking this word. This meant that his money was dedicated to God. He might keep it until he died. He might even reject his dedication at a later time. But still he was freed from any obligation for his parents (v. 12). Thus by this tradition they made God's clear commandment void or without authority (v. 13). With this one example Jesus clearly showed the hypocrisy of the scribes and Pharisees.

With this He called the multitude to Him (v. 14). Most likely they had heard the exchange of words. But now Jesus proposed to apply His lesson. Therefore, He cautioned the people to hear His words with understanding. He wanted them to see the utter hypocrisy of their religious leaders.

"There is nothing from without a man, that entering into him can defile him: but the things which come out of him, those are they that defile the man" (v. 15). Now in the Mosaic code certain foods were considered as unclean and unfit for human consumption. But here Jesus exercised authority over the law itself in saying that no food, even that which was eaten with unwashed hands, defiles a man. Certainly in some cases the Mosaic code dealt with certain foods which were subject to spoiling in Israel's migratory life. But here Jesus anticipates the words spoken to Peter in Acts 10:11-15. At any rate He was striking at the Jewish tradition showing that the thing which truly defiled one was the evil which came out of him. Verse 16 does not appear in Nestle's text.

When Jesus' words are considered in the light of the cited passage in Acts one sees a deeper thought. The beneficial dietary laws of Moses had been extended to include the Gentiles among the unclean things. It is possible, therefore, to see a veiled condemnation of the Jewish rulers for their attitude toward the Gentiles. So not only food but people as such are neither clean nor unclean. And the Jews were being defiled by their attitude toward the Gentiles.

The Explanation of the Lesson (7:17-23)

Jesus left the crowd and entered into a house, probably that of Simon Peter (v. 17). There in privacy the disciples asked Him to interpret the "parable" about the clean and the unclean (v. 15). Jesus was provoked at their lack of understanding (v. 18). They were as dull as the Pharisees. In fact, they had not yet escaped from their narrow ways and practices. Gould notes that they had been brought up in Judaism, and were unable to accept their Lord's words in which He abrogated the distinction between the clean and unclean.

Nevertheless Jesus proceeded to explain the parable. Food entering into a man could not defile him (v. 18) because it did not enter the heart. Rather it entered the stomach and passed through the body (v. 19). The phrase "purging [making clean] all meats" does not seem to be a part of Jesus' statement. Evidently this is a comment by Mark himself. He means that by His words Jesus made clean all meats. This reflects Peter's own comments with respect to his vision on the housetop in Joppa. "What God hath cleansed, that call not thou common" or "defiled" (Acts 10:15). Peter did not really understand the meaning until that time. But Mark, benefited by Peter's later lesson, adds this note here.

However, Jesus continued His lesson (vv. 20-23). It is not that which enters into a man's stomach which defiles him, but that which comes out of his heart. What a lesson for modern man! Pure food and drug laws protect his stomach. But he is so careless about his heart. And one needs but to look about today to see how defiled modern man is.

Mark 7:24-37

The Dramatized Truth

The Second Withdrawal (7:24)

Following the incident with the Jewish rulers Jesus again left Galilee on His second withdrawal. He left Jewish territory altogether and went into the pagan region of Tyre (v. 24). "And Sidon" does not appear in the best text of Mark. But it is genuine in Matthew 15:21. Some interpreters question whether Jesus ever left the land of Israel. But these references (cf. Mark 7:31) show that He did.

The Plea of a Pagan (7:25-26)

In that pagan area He entered into a house (v. 24). He was in search for privacy, but such was impossible. "For a certain woman, whose young daughter had an unclean spirit, heard of him, and came and fell at his feet" (v. 25). Nestle has the word "immediately" (*euthus*). She did not hear about Jesus immediately upon His arrival. But when she did hear she went immediately to Him.

Mark is careful to identify this woman by religion, language, and race. She was a "Greek." This means that she was a Greek by religion, and so a pagan. And she was a "Syrophenician by nation" or "by race." This word is a combination of *Sura,* Syrian, and *Phoinikissa,* Phoenician. This shows that her language was Syrian, and her race was Phoenician. She was a Phoenician of Syria in contrast to a Phoenician from North Africa. Matthew 15:22 calls her "a woman of Canaan" or a "Canaanitish woman." The Phoenicians were descended from the Canaanites, the original inhabitants of Palestine. They were descendants of Canaan the son of Ham (Gen. 10:6, 15-19).

It would hardly be possible for one to be more non-Jewish than was this woman. She was a descendant of the hated Canaanites, a pagan people to the core. She spoke not Hebrew or Aramaic but Syrian, which within itself would not endear her to the Jews. And her present religion was that of the pagan Greeks. The Pharisees were mortal enemies of Greek customs and religion. So to the Jews she was a Gentile of the worst sort.

Nevertheless, she was a woman, a human being in need who

came to Jesus, a Jew. "And she kept on begging [imperfect tense] him that he would cast forth the devil [demon] out of her little daughter" (v. 26).

The Attitude of Jesus (7:27-30)

In response Jesus showed a strange attitude. "Let the children first be filled: for it is not meet [*kalon,* well or fitting] to take the children's bread, and cast it to the dogs" (v. 27). To the Jews Gentiles were dogs. But Jesus did not use the ordinary Greek term for "dogs" (*kuōn*). Rather He softened the term as He used *kunarion,* a little dog. Instead of wild dogs He spoke of the family pets. Wuest points out that Jesus evidently spoke Greek to the woman, since she would not understand Aramaic.

But the woman was equal to the occasion. For she said, "Yea, Lord: yet the [little] dogs [*kunaria*] under the table eat of the children's crumbs" (v. 28). Robertson notes the combination of "little dogs, little scraps of bread . . . little children." Gould speaks of the woman's "unique combination of faith and wit." Barclay says, "Here was a sunny faith that would not take no for an answer." Instead of being resentful of Jesus' seeming rebuff she answered with a smile. She took His own words and turned them to her advantage. She admitted that the little children must first be fed. But the little dogs must eat also. Her desire was not to recline at the table and eat to her fill. She accepted the term of *little dog,* and asked only for the crumbs which Jesus had to give.

Jesus did not resist further. Instead He said that because of her saying, a saying supported by a persistent faith, her daughter was made whole. And returning to her home she found it to be true (vv. 29-30).

But the question remains as to why Jesus spoke thus to her. He certainly did not share the Jewish prejudice against Gentiles. Some interpreters hold that Jesus was saying that the Jews had the first claim in hearing the gospel. To be sure, it was preached to the Jew first and then to the Greek (Rom. 1:16). But this incident did not involve preaching the gospel as such. It dealt with the merciful healing ministry of Jesus. And there was the prior case of the Roman centurion in which Jesus did not withhold it from a Gentile (cf. Matt. 8:5ff.). Still others see Jesus as testing the woman's faith. This is a possible reason.

But in the light of the larger context there seems to be a more appropriate reason. Just prior to His visit to this region Jesus had been confronted with the Jewish traditions which involved Gentile prejudice. And the Twelve showed that they were not immune to it. It is one thing to hold prejudice against a group. But it is another matter when it involves just one individual. It would seem, therefore, that Jesus deliberately portrayed this typical Jewish attitude toward this Gentile woman that He might teach the Twelve a lesson. In Himself He held up a mirror in order that they might see how utterly vicious this attitude was. Thus His hesitancy was not His own attitude. It was not for the woman's benefit but for that of the Twelve. The most unlikely prospect imaginable could ask for and receive the merciful ministry of Jesus. The Gentiles were not outside the mercy of God. But in faith they could receive His benevolent ministry.

Jesus proposed to use these withdrawals to teach the Twelve. And in this incident He dramatized before them a lesson which they sorely needed to learn. It is a lesson not for them only but for all who propose to follow Him. Of interest is the fact that Barclay calls this section of Mark (7:24-30) "The Forecast of a World for Christ." Here then was a lesson not only in healing but in world evangelism. Jesus has sheep other than Jews. And the day will come when the Twelve (and others) will be told to disciple all nations (Matt. 28:19-20).

The Third Withdrawal (7:31-37)

This lesson in the region of Tyre was compounded in Jesus' third retirement. For "departing from the coasts of Tyre and Sidon, he came unto the sea of Galilee, through the midst of the coasts of Decapolis" (v. 31). Note that He went north toward Sidon and then east and south into the Decapolis. Someone has noted that this may have been the only time that Jesus saw the Mediterranean sea. But the point of present interest is that He went from Phoenicia into the Gentile area of the Decapolis. Note how carefully He avoided the area ruled over by Herod Antipas. In the area east of the sea of Galilee He was in the territory of Herod Philip. Philip was a better man than his brother Antipas. Furthermore, he had no reason to be concerned about Jesus.

In the Decapolis Jesus was confronted by "one that was deaf, and had an impediment in his speech" (v. 32). He was deaf but not entirely dumb. Rather the Greek word *mogilalon* means that he spoke with difficulty. Since this was Gentile territory it is entirely possible that this man was a Gentile. If so, it adds meaning to the story.

Jesus took him aside, "put his fingers into his ears, and he spit, and touched his tongue" (v. 33). These things were not necessary for Jesus' healing power, but probably were done as an aid to the man's faith. Among the ancients saliva was regarded as having healing properties. This does not mean that Jesus held to this idea. But He accomodated His actions to the man's own understanding (cf. John 9:6).

Having done these things Jesus looked up to heaven and "sighed" (v. 33). This could mean either a sigh or a groan. It shows Jesus' sympathy for the man. Furthermore, it indicates the mental and spiritual strain upon Him to perform an act of healing. With this Jesus spoke. "Ephphatha, that is, Be opened" (v. 33). Here is another of Mark's uses of Aramaic which he translates for the benefit of his Roman readers. Immediately the man's ears "were opened, and the string of his tongue was loosed, and he spoke plain" (v. 35). The aorist forms of the verbs for *opened* and *loosed* show that this was a miracle. The words "string of his tongue" render words meaning "that which bound his tongue." "Spake" is what is called an inchoative imperfect tense. The man "began to speak correctly [*orthōs*]."

To prevent undue excitement Jesus charged that this miracle should not be told (v. 36). But the report of it was spread abroad anyway. Those who heard it were constantly amazed beyond measure. They said, "He hath done all things well: he maketh both the deaf to hear, and the dumb to speak" (v. 37).

This was a new phenomenon in this pagan area. Not only the miracle, but the fact that it had been performed upon a Gentile by a Jew. Matthew adds a most interesting note. "And they glorified the God of Israel" (15:31). Why "the God of Israel?" Because these people were Gentile pagans. Thus they learned that Israel's God had compassion for them also.

In two healing incidents, therefore, Jesus had dramatized the truth that even though the Jews might regard the Gentiles as unclean, Jesus did not so regard them. They were souls in need of a Saviour, the Saviour which He proposed to be.

Mark 8:1-9

The Feeding of Four Thousand

The Hungry Multitude (8:1-5)

As the news of Jesus' healing of the deaf man spread, naturally the people of the Decapolis flocked to Him. This is quite a different reaction from that in another part of the Decapolis when Jesus had healed the demoniac (cf. Mark 5:17ff.). Could it be that the preaching of the healed demoniac had made possible this new attitude?

At any rate the people came in great numbers (v. 1). And as in the area of Bethsaida Julias, these people also had no food. So Jesus pointed out to His disciples the situation. "I have compassion on the multitude, because they have now been with me three days, and have nothing to eat" (v. 2). Had they been without food so long? Or was their meager supply now exhausted? In any case, Jesus' heart went out to them in their need. He could not simply send them home (v. 3). For many had come quite a distance. So He asked the Twelve how much food they had (vv. 4-5). They reported that they had seven loaves of bread and a few small fishes (vv. 5-7).

The Compassionate Christ (8:6-9)

So as before Jesus had the people sit down in orderly fashion, and He fed them miraculously. The people ate their fill. "And they took up of the broken meat that was left seven baskets" (v. 8). The word for "baskets" here is different from the one in Mark 6:43. There the word is *kophinos,* a Jewish bread basket. Here the word is *sphuris,* a basket or hamper used by Gentiles.

Mark notes that here the people who were fed were "about four thousand" (v. 9). But here there was no effort to make Jesus a political, military Messiah, Such would have been contrary to the Gentiles. Rather, after Jesus had fed them He "sent them away" (v. 9).

Now some commentators question the genuineness of this miracle of feeding, insisting that it is just a repetition of the former one. However, this question is without a factual basis. For one thing, both Mark and Matthew record both feedings. Both preserve the distinctions in the two accounts, including that of the kind of baskets used. And both record a later reference by Jesus to both feedings (Matt. 16:9f.; Mark 8:19f.).

There is no valid reason as to why Jesus did not feed both a Jewish and a Gentile multitude. Indeed, there is ample reason as to why He did. The latter feeding certainly demonstrated that He cared for Gentiles as well as Jews. And by suggestion He was saying that God's Bread from heaven was to be given to all men, both Jew and Gentile, who would receive it.

Mark 8:10-13

The Continuing Opposition

At this point Jesus made a brief visit back to Galilee. Bruce holds that He was still in the Decapolis. But the fact that He took a boat suggests Galilee. He "came into the parts of Dalmanutha" (v. 10). Matthew says, "Magadan" (15:39). The truth is that the location of neither is known. But Robertson holds that it was "apparently the same region of Galilee on the western side of the lake not far from Tiberias." Mark 8:13 also suggests that on His next move after this Jesus also recrossed the lake on His fourth withdrawal.

The Strange Alliance (8:11)

That Dalmanutha was in Galilee is further suggested by the presence of the Pharisees (v. 11). So long as Jesus remained in Gentile territory He was not bothered by them. But the minute that He returned to Jewish territory there they were. Matthew 16:1 notes that they had been joined by some Sadducees. This is a new development. Apparently they thought that it was time that they joined in the fray. It had been more than a year since Jesus had been to Jerusalem. So they had left that center of Sadducean power to oppose Jesus in Galilee.

No stranger alliance could be imagined than that between these two groups. Theologically and politically they were at opposite ends of the poles. The Pharisees were arch-conservatives theologically and highly nationalistic politically. The Sadducees, on the other hand, were very liberal in theology and were aligned with the Romans politically. They hated the Romans, but since they enjoyed power and affluence under them they favored the *status quo*. But these two groups found a common cause in their opposition to Jesus.

They challenged Jesus to give them "a sign from heaven" (v. 11). They did so, tempting or testing Him. He claimed to be the Messiah. So they asked for a sign to prove it. Previously the Pharisees had asked Jesus for a sign (Matt. 12:38). They ignored Jesus' many signs or miracles. But here they asked for a sign from heaven. Brushing aside His miracles as *earthly* signs, they asked for some great display of divine power – perhaps some cosmic display.

This "from heaven" reflects the touch of the Sadducees. They did not believe in the supernatural. So they expected Jesus to fail in this demand. The Pharisees did believe in the supernatural. But in their doubts concerning Jesus, they also expected Him not to deliver.

The Refusal of Jesus (8:12-13)

Again Jesus "sighed" (cf. 7:34). But this time He "sighed deeply in his spirit." "Sighed deeply" renders a compound verb which gives the perfective force to "sigh." Robertson quotes Swete: "The sigh seemed to come, as we say, from the bottom of his heart, the Lord's human spirit was stirred to its depths." This was, of course, a physical sigh. But it expressed the deep agony in Jesus' soul. For here were not ordinary unbelievers. They were the religious leaders who in spite of abundant evidence as to His person and work, were repeatedly rejecting Him and finally will drive Him to the cross.

Nevertheless He did not grant their demand. Asked He, "Why doth this generation seek [keep on seeking] after a sign . . . there shall no sign be given . . ." (v. 12). It distressed Jesus that His contemporaries saw Him as a miracle worker and nothing more. Matthew 16:4 adds "but the sign of Jonah" (cf. Matt. 12:39-40). In this Jesus spoke of His resurrection. This would truly be a "sign from heaven," but the Sanhedrin will deny even that.

Charles Kingsley once said that one should not be afraid of doubt so long as he has a disposition to believe. The Pharisees and Sadducees had no such disposition. So they were left in their doubts to their own destruction. There is poetic meaning in the words "And he left them, and entering into a ship again departed to the other side" (v. 13).

Mark 8:14-21

A Timely Warning

The Fourth Withdrawal (8:14)

Jesus' departure across the lake was the beginning of His fourth retirement. This time He went north to the region of Caesarea Philippi. Mark notes that the disciples forgot to take along bread for their journey. So that they had with them not more than one loaf (v. 14).

As they were plying their way across the lake Jesus "kept on charging" (imperfect tense) them, "Take heed, beware of the leaven of the Pharisees, and of the leaven of Herod" (v. 15). His repetition of this warning showed that it was needed. Matthew does not mention Herod, but he adds the Sadducees (16:6). Robertson likens Herod to *bad politics* and the Pharisees and Sadducees to *bad politics* and *bad theology.*

The Twelve reasoned that Jesus was chiding them because they had no bread (v. 16). When Jesus knew of this misunderstanding He charged them with being spiritually blind and hard of heart (vv. 17-18). How short were their memories. Did they not recall His two feeding miracles? Why then should He or they worry about physical bread (vv. 19-20)?

Mark ends his account with Jesus' question, "How is it that ye do not understand?" (v. 21). But Matthew adds that they then realized that He was talking about the teachings of the Pharisees and Sadducees (16:12).

They need to beware of this teaching indeed. They were steeped in such, and Jesus was having a difficult time in getting them to look beyond it to see Him in the true light. It is a sad picture to see religious leaders, then and now, who blind men's eyes to the truth. One cannot help but feel that had they been left to themselves the common people of that day (and now) would have received Jesus. But their teachers misled them so that they, for the most part, turned away from Him. And this *leaven* which silently worked in their minds and hearts finally led to the death of Him who came to give life.

Mark 8:22-26

The Healing of the Blind

The Case of Need (8:22)

The boat touched land at "Bethsaida" (v. 22). This was Bethsaida Julias near to the place where Jesus had fed the five thousand. When Jesus arrived, there was brought to Him a blind man. Those who brought him begged Jesus to touch him.

The Case Resolved (8:23-26)

But Jesus "took the blind man by the hand, and led him out of town" (v. 23). This is a neat detail—Jesus Himself leading the blind man. Though Herod Philip had enlarged Bethsaida into quite a city, it was still called a village. Jesus' purpose in leading the man out of the village evidently was in order that His healing would not attract attention. He would not turn His back upon this needy case. But He was desperately seeking privacy. Were this miracle known He would have been swamped with additional cases.

Note that once again Jesus spit on the man's diseased members. This He did as an aid to his faith. Then putting His hands upon the man He asked, "If you see somewhat?" Bruce renders this "Do you possibly see anything?" "And he *looked up,* and said, I see men as trees walking" (v. 24). Literally, "I see men, because I behold them as trees walking about." He saw, but he did so indistinctly. Then Jesus again touched his eyes "and made him *look up* [through]: and he was restored, and *saw* every man clearly" (v. 25). Bruce calls attention to these italicized words (author's italics). Respectively they render compound verbs (*blepō* with *ana, dia,* and *en*). First, the man *looked up,* as is common with a blind person. Second, he *looked through* as through a mist so as to see clearly. Third, he *looked in* or seeing distinctly. The word rendered "clearly" is *tēlaugōs* composed of *tēle,* afar, and *augē,* radiance or far-shining. This means that he saw "all things" (*apanta*) clearly and at a distance.

This is the only example where Jesus effected a gradual cure. No reason is given for this. But, even so, it was a miracle. Mark alone relates this incident.

Jesus sent the man away to his home (v. 26). But He forbade him to return to the village. The words "nor tell it to any in the town" are absent from the best texts. Jesus did not wish to cause undue excitement there before He left for Caesarea Philippi. But there certainly was joy in the healed man's home upon his return.

However, one may regard this gradual healing, there is symbolic truth in it. Bruce explains it as showing how slowly and gradually the disciples were comprehending the truth concerning Jesus. But it also suggests the gradual nature of any Christian's growth in Christ. Immediately the man saw whereas he had been totally blind. But he saw indistinctly. However, with further experience with Jesus he saw all things clearly and even at a distance. So one may be saved in a moment. He then comes out of darkness into light. But as a babe in Christ his spiritual vision is not yet clear. As he goes on growing in grace and knowledge of Christ, he comes to see clearly and even afar.

No Christian should be content merely to see. He should let Christ develop him until he sees all things with a distinct vision. Thus he shall see through the eyes of the Lord.

Mark 8:27 – 9:1

The Confession and the Conflict

Leaving Bethsaida Jesus led His little group northward into the region of Caesarea Philippi (v. 27). Since Mark notes that He entered "villages" of the area, evidently He avoided the city itself. This area was ruled by Herod Philip. It was here that Jesus put the Twelve to the test as to His person and work.

The Locale of the Test (8:27a)

No more fitting place could have been chosen for this test. Caesarea Philippi was located about twenty-five miles northeast of the sea of Galilee, in the northern extremity of Jewish territory. This region is the headwaters of the Jordan River which plays so great a part in Jewish history. The city itself was built upon a rock cliff several hundred feet high. The cliff rested upon a huge strata of rock (cf. Greek, *petra,* Matt. 16-18). It was an ancient city which had been rebuilt by Herod the Great and had been beautified by Herod Philip. The latter named it Caesarea Philippi in honor of the Roman Caesar. "Caesarea" means "Caesar's town." Philip added his own name to distinguish it from Caesarea located on the Mediterranean coast.

However, there is even more significance to this location. George Adam Smith identifies it as the site of Dan which had long been associated with Hebrew worship. It also became under Jeroboam I a center of Baal worship as is seen in the name *Balinas* which it bore at one time. However, in later times it was the center of the worship of the Greek god Pan. Thus it had also been called *Panias.* The Greeks said that Pan had been born in a nearby cave. During the reign of Herod the Great he built there a white marble temple to Caesar Augustus, thus making it a center of Roman emperor worship. As noted above Herod Philip had improved it and named the city after Caesar. At a later time Herod Agrippa called the city Neroneas in honor of Nero.

The Test Presented (8:27b-30)

One can see, therefore, the mingled religious and political influences found in this area: Hebrew and pagan worship; Roman emperor worship. It represented the forces which were so contrary to what Jesus was in His person and work.

It was in such an atmosphere that Jesus asked, "Whom do men say that I am?" (v. 27). This area was filled with relics and monuments of ancient kings and conquerors. It may be that in a holiday spirit the disciples were seeking to identify them. If so, Jesus' question illustrates His method of seizing upon events of the moment as means of teaching. As the disciples were guessing as to whose this or that monument was, Jesus interrupted them with His question.

"Whom do men say that I am?" (v. 27). It is even possible that the Twelve kept looking at the monuments as they replied, "John the Baptist: but same say, Elias; and others, one of the prophets" (v. 28). These were some of the popular ideas as to Jesus' identity. Certainly Herod Antipas thought that He was John the Baptist come to life again.

But whether or not they had continued to look at the monuments, Jesus stung them into alertness with His next question. "But whom say ye that I am?" (v. 29). He put the emphasis upon "ye." In the Greek text it is included in the verb form and also written out at the beginning of the sentence. So "ye" has a triple emphasis: in the verb, written out, and first in the sentence. Literally, "Ye, but whom me are you saying to be?" It was one thing to recite popular ideas about Jesus. It was quite a different matter as to their own concept of Him. He had taught them repeatedly. But had they learned their lesson? One may well imagine that Jesus waited with bated breath to hear their answer.

And then it came. Peter was ever quick to speak. So he replied for the group, "Thou art the Christ" (v. 29). Luke says, "The Christ of God" (9:20). Matthew combines the two thoughts, "Thou art the Christ, the Son of the living God" (16:16). The Greek text of Mark followed by Matthew, uses the pronoun "you" with the same triple emphasis: present in the verb, also written out, and at the beginning of the sentence. Actually Peter said, "You and no other are the Christ of God. [None of the gods represented by the atmosphere of Caesarea Philippi or any other god or person]." "You only are the Christ of God."

So the disciples had learned their lesson. But as is presently seen they still had much to learn. For Jesus strongly "charged them that they should tell no man of him" (v. 30). Later Jesus will tell them to declare this truth to the whole world. But they were not yet ready to do so. For even though they had grasped this truth it must be refined in their hearts before it is ready to be presented to the world. To the Jews "Christ" meant a political-military figure. The disciples also still held to this concept. And had they gone forth immediately to proclaim Jesus as the Christ, it would have been that kind of Christ. Such a message could well have fanned the fires of revolution against Rome. As with so many false messiahs it would have brought the wrath of Rome down upon the movement. Thus Jesus' mission would have ended in failure.

In passing it is well to note that Mark does not record Jesus' subsequent words about the church (cf. Matt. 16:17-19).[1] Apparently Peter did not dwell upon this event in his preaching. This is difficult to understand had Peter thought of himself as occupying a place in Jesus' program above the other apostles; but as is presently seen he evidently did not spare himself as to his mistakes.

The Confused Disciple (8:31-33)

Therefore, Mark does record the stinging rebuke given to Peter by Jesus. For on the heels of Peter's great confession there came a conflict between him and Jesus. This conflict arose as Jesus sought to lead the apostles to understand the nature of His Messiahship. "He began to teach them, that the Son of man must suffer many things, and be rejected of the elders, and of the chief priests ,and scribes, and be killed, and after three days rise again" (v. 31). The word "must" expresses a moral and spiritual necessity. And it should be read with each item in this verse. Jesus "must suffer... be rejected... be killed... rise again."

Thus Jesus presented to them the concept of a suffering Christ, the Suffering Servant of Jehovah (cf. Isa. 52:13—53:12). Some interpreters see in this the idea that Jesus *at this point* became convinced that He would be brought to death by His enemies. However, there is ample evidence that He had known this from the beginning (cf. John 2:19.). Heretofore He had taught this by veiled reference. But now, just six months before the crucifixion, He began plainly to teach it to the Twelve. They had grasped the idea that He was the Christ. But it was vitally important that they should know what kind of Christ He was. He must experience the things enumerated in verse 31 if He was to fulfil His role as the Redeemer.

He must suffer many things or much. Among other things He must be "rejected." This renders the verb *apodokimazō*. *Dokimazō* means to put to the test to prove that one is genuine. *Apo* means

1 See Hobbs, *An Exposition of the Gospel of Matthew*, pp. 215ff.

off or away from. The thought is that the Jewish leaders put Jesus to the test to determine if He were the Messiah. But since He did not meet their specifications as a political-military messiah they judged away from Him or rejected Him. He was not the kind of messiah that they wanted. They were not interested in a Saviour from sin. Their desire was a Saviour from political and military bondage. So, having found Jesus to be other than the Christ they wanted, they killed Him.

Bruce comments on this rejection as "fitly indicating the precise share of the religious authorities in the coming tragedy. Their part was solemnly to disapprove of the claimant to Messiahship. All else was the natural sequel of their act of rejection." The fact that Jesus used the definite article before each group (elders, chief priests, and scribes) shows that they all shared equally in the guilt concerning the death of Jesus.

Unknown to them was the fact that by His death Jesus atoned for man's sin. And by His resurrection He conquered both death and sin.

These things Jesus "spake . . . openly" (v. 32). The imperfect tense shows that He kept on speaking them. The word rendered "openly" *(parrēsia)* is a word which means that He held back nothing. He fully and without reserve explained what was involved in His coming death and resurrection.

But "Peter took him, and began to rebuke him" (v. 32). The word rendered "took" is an aorist participle of the verb *proslambanō*. The verb *lambanō* means "to take." The prefix *pros* carries the force of "face to face." The compound verb means to take hold of someone so as to be face to face with him. Thayer gives this the sense of leading Jesus aside or away from the other disciples. This may have been the case. But the verb itself in the aorist participial form suggests that Peter suddenly grabbed Jesus by His clothing and stood facing Him as he began to rebuke Him for what He had said. Peter had spoken so nobly about Jesus' Messiahship. But his concept had no place for a suffering and dying Christ. It would appear that Peter's mind froze on the words "and be killed," so that he did not hear "and after three days rise again." Certainly he was not opposed to Jesus rising from the dead. His rebuke was with respect to His death. The fact that Jesus "began" to teach and Peter "began" to rebuke suggests that these things may have happened more than once.

How did Jesus react to Peter's rash act? "But he turning about and seeing his disciples rebuked Peter" (v. 33). The word rendered "turning about" is an aorist participle of *epistrephō* It is the verb "to turn" with the prefix *epi* which makes the verb intensive in force. This, plus the aorist participle, means that Jesus suddenly and vigorously turned about or away from Peter toward the other disciples. He was indignant at Peter's words. So He said, "Get thee behind me Satan, for thou savorest not the things that be of God, but the things that be of men" (v. 33). Here was Satan's temptation all over again to avoid the cross and to receive the kingdom in some other way. And this time Satan spoke through one of Jesus' own inner circle! Satan would rather work through a saint than through a notorious sinner any time.

One might say that Peter often suffered from hoof-in-mouth disease. So recently he had spoken under the inspiration of God (Matt. 16:17); now he was the mouth-piece of Satan speaking the things of men, the popularly held worldly concept of the Christ. How are the mighty fallen! And what a warning to all of the children of God!

The Larger Lesson (8:34 – 9:1)

Mark alone notes the presence of a crowd with Jesus at this time (v. 34). Indeed, some scholars would reject this statement as not being genuine Scripture. However, there is no reason why people other than the Twelve were present. To be sure, Jesus was seeking privacy, but He did not always succeed as has been noted on previous withdrawals. Matthew is noncommittal as to whether or not others were present (16:13). Luke notes that just prior to asking His question of the Twelve He was alone praying (9:18). But this does not mean that there were not other people present nearby with the Twelve. Mark simply says that as Jesus journeyed, "in [*en*] the way he asked his disciples" (8:27). There is no conflict in these three reports. And there is every possibility that other "people" were present.

So Jesus called the people with the disciples, and taught them all as to the necessity of the cross. He was counteracting any adverse effect Peter's words may have had on them.

Peter rejected the thought of a cross for Jesus. And he doubtless spoke for the other disciples. But Jesus said that not only He must bear a cross. All who propose to follow Him must be prepared to do the same. "Whosoever will come after me, let him deny himself, and take up his cross, and follow me" (v. 34). The verb tenses in this verse make it live. "Deny" and "takeup" are aorist imperative tenses, expressing once-for-all acts. "Follow" is a present imperative, meaning a repeated, continuous, or habitual act. So assuming that one wishes to follow Jesus as His disciple, he must once-for-all deny self and take up his own cross. Then he must go on following Christ. Actually he must follow "with me." Wuest explains this thus: "The idea is not that of following behind another, but that of accompanying the other person, taking the same road that he takes and fellowshipping with him along that road." Denying oneself may mean renouncing any dependence upon self for salvation and/or self denial in serving Jesus. Both ideas are consistent here. But the aorist tense seems to weigh it in favor of the former. At any rate denial of self and taking up one's cross express a determined way of life. And going on following "with me" suggests the continuing process of traveling in that way.

But what did Jesus mean by taking up a cross? It was customary for one sentenced to crucifixion to bear his own cross to the place of execution. This, Jesus was compelled to do. And one following "with me" must be willing to do the same, if necessary, in order to be true to Jesus. Thus the "cross" is not merely some hardship which one must endure. It is total commitment of one's life to Jesus.

Now Peter had suggested that Jesus save His life by avoiding the cross. Little did he know that by doing so Jesus would have forfeited His very life or the purpose of His being. And this principle applies to everyone. "For whosoever will save [may will to save] his life shall lose it; but whosoever shall lose his life for my sake and the gospel's, the same shall save it" (v. 35). The words "life" render *psuchē*. *Bios* (cf. biology) refers to the physical life. But *psuchē* (cf. psychology), while it may refer to the animal principle of life, also connotes the soul, the willing, thinking, reasoning person. In a sense it refers to what is called the personality or the real person as opposed to the physical body. It is that which abides about a person.

Actually as Jesus used this word He employed a play on words. He spoke of saving and losing one's *psuchē*. If one wills to save his animal principle of life, he shall lose the true meaning of life. But if he submerges his true self in the work of Christ he shall in the process realize the true meaning of life in the highest form. Jesus was not telling how one may be saved from sin through self-denial. He was relating His philosophy of life. It was by losing Himself in the will of God that He found His purpose for living. Likewise shall it be for all who propose to follow with Him.

And then Jesus struck a balance of life. "For what shall it profit a man, if he shall gain the whole world, and lose his own soul? Or what shall a man give in exchange for his soul?" (vv.

36-37). Here again "soul" may be regarded as the true spiritual self or as the true purpose of being. Either or both make sense. If one gains the whole world to the loss of his soul, he has made a bad bargain. Likewise if he gains wealth, power, and worldly glory, but in the process misses the highest purpose of living.

But suppose that having made this bad bargain, he desires to regain his soul. What shall he give in exchange for it? The "whole world" would not be legal tender in heaven for such a transaction. The only way that one may be saved in any sense is by God's grace as he loses himself in the good and perfect will of God in Christ.

One's relationship to Jesus is of infinite importance as is seen in verse 38. The way men treat Jesus now will determine how He treats them when He returns to earth in great power and glory. If one is *ashamed* of Him now, He will be *ashamed* of him then. And *ashamed* in both instances involves rejection.

The chapter division is unfortunate at this point. For 9:1 is a part of Jesus' present discourse. Men may debate about Jesus and the nature of His person and work, but the time will come when they shall see the kingdom of God coming in great power.

But Jesus said, "That there be some of them that stand here, which shall not taste death, till they have seen the kingdom of God come with power" (9:1).

Now in 8:38 Jesus obviously spoke of His second coming. But to what event did He refer in 9:1? Certainly this was no reference to the second advent. For none of those present lived to see that. Note that He said "some" not *all* would live until this event which He had in mind. He could not then have been speaking of the transfiguration. For all of the Twelve lived beyond that point. It is possible that He had reference to Pentecost. For all save Judas lived to see that. However, "some" suggests that more than one would die prior to the event in mind. It would appear, therefore, that Jesus was speaking of the destruction of Jerusalem in A.D. 70. How many lived to see this, one cannot say. Certainly John lived beyond that time. And perhaps others.

But in what sense could this event be "the kingdom of God come with power?" Any signal event was considered as God's intervention in history. Certainly the destruction of Jerusalem and the temple would qualify for such an event. Keep in mind that during this fourth withdrawal the burden of Jesus' teaching had to do with the "leaven" of the Pharisees and Sadducees contrasted with the person and work of Christ. It is evident that Jesus' followers were contaminated with the former. Jerusalem and the temple were the centers of the power of Judaism. So long as they stood they would be a problem and hindrance to the spread of the kingdom of God.

History records that the destruction of Jerusalem marked the end of the Jewish nation as such and largely the end of Judaism as a power in religion in the Roman empire. Up until that time Christianity was regarded by the Empire as a branch of Judaism. But thereafter it was delivered from such a concept. Thus in a very real sense the fall of Jerusalem saw the movement of Christ loosed upon the world in a new relationship. It was in this sense that the kingdom of God came with power.

Jesus, therefore, was saying that while men might be shackled to the narrow concepts of Judaism, the day would come when this system of religion would no longer be a hindering power to the spread of the gospel of Christ. God was moving in that direction. And those who would save their lives *(psuchē)* would do well to move along with Him.

Mark 9:2-13

The Transfiguration of Jesus

The Time and Place (9:2a)

The transfiguration is one of the most mysterious yet beautiful and meaningful events in the life of Jesus. Tradition places it on Mt. Tabor in southern Galilee. But there are several reasons why this is improbable. The Synoptic Gospels indicate that it took place during Jesus' fourth withdrawal. This found Him in the region of Caesarea Philippi. This city was located near Mt. Hermon. Jesus was seeking isolation. This would hardly have been possible on Tabor, since at this time it had a fortress on its summit. Furthermore, both Matthew and Mark say that the location was "a high mountain apart." Tabor is only about one thousand feet high, while Hermon is ninety-two hundred feet high. It is highly probable, therefore, that Jesus was transfigured on Mt. Hermon not far from Caesarea Philippi.

Mark and Matthew say that this event occurred "six days" after the incident near Caesarea Philippi. Luke says "about an eight days." There is no conflict, since the point is that it took place about a week after the previous event.

At this time Jesus took Peter, James, and John and led them up into this high mountain. The other disciples were left behind at the mountain's base. Three times during His ministry Jesus took this inner circle into a significant event: the healing of Jairus' daughter, here, and in Gethsemane. No reason is given for this. But Peter was very close to Jesus as were His blood relatives James and John. (It seems that their mothers were sisters.) At any rate they were alone with Him.

The Transfiguration (9:2b-3)

Luke, who places great emphasis upon Jesus' prayer life, says that He went into the mountain to pray. "And as he prayed" (Luke 9:29) "he was transfigured before them" (Mark 9:2).

The verb rendered "was transfigured" renders *metamorphoomai* (note our "metamorphosis"). This verb expresses the act of giving outward expression of one's inner character. The meaning is especially significant in this incident. For in His transfiguration the three disciples saw an outward expression of the Lord's inner nature.

Mark says that "his raiment became shining, exceeding white as snow; so as no fuller on earth can white them" (v. 3). Assuming that the scene is Mt. Hermon "white as snow" takes on added meaning. For the peaks of this mountain are always covered with snow. Bruce renders the Greek word *stilbonta* as "glittering." Since it is a participle it indicates an active shining. Jesus' body was glittering as snow in the sunshine. According to Matthew "his face did shine as the sun, and his raiment was white as the light" (17:2). Luke describes it as "white . . . glistering" or "dazzling" (9:29).

It is difficult for mere men to explain this phenomenon. But since it was an outward expression of Jesus' inner character, we may suppose that this brilliant light did not shine upon Him from without. Evidently it was His deity shining forth from within. What He essentially was in His inner nature was manifested in outward expression.

Such an experience testifies to Jesus' sinless nature. Some will recall the old coal-oil lamp chimneys or globes. If one had a flaw a sudden rushing of heat into it would break it. Likewise, had there been a flaw in Jesus' character this sudden outrushing of deity would have killed Him. But because of His holy nature, the deity shone forth in a brilliance which defies human description. Like a lamp wick turned low and suddenly turned up to full brightness, so was His deity turned up for the disciples to see.

Note that He was transfigured "before them." This suggests that Jesus may have had this experience at other times when at night He prayed alone in perfect communion with His Father. But there were no human eyes to see. Apparently the transfiguration took place at night, since the disciples were heavy with sleep (Luke 9:32). Thus the brightness was all the more emphasized as bright as the sun. And the disciples saw it.

The Heavenly Visitors (9:4)

"And there appeared unto them Elias with Moses: and they were talking with Jesus" (v. 4). The verb "appeared" renders the aorist form of a verb which means to see with the natural eye. So this was no hypnotic vision. And the aorist means that it happened suddenly. The verb for "were talking" is what is called a periphrastic construction. It is formed out of the imperfect verb "to be" and the present participle of talking with someone. Mark used this form to show that their conversation with Jesus was a protracted one. He does not say of what the conversation consisted. But Luke says that they were talking about Jesus' "decease which he should accomplish in Jerusalem" (9:31). "Decease" renders the word for *exodus*. So they talked about Jesus' *exodus* out of this world which should be effected in Jerusalem. This would include His death, resurrection, and ascension.

Now what is the significance of Moses and Elijah? In Jewish thought Moses was symbolic of *law*, and Elijah symbolized *prophecy*. Robertson notes that both were prophets and dealt with the law. "The law and the prophets" was a term used to refer to the Hebrew Scriptures or the Old Testament.

The Significance of the Transfiguration

With this scene before us the question emerges as to the purpose and meaning of the transfiguration. To understand these things it is necessary to review the scene following Peter's confession of Jesus' Messiahship (8:29). There He "began" to teach about His death and resurrection six months hence in Jerusalem. Peter "began" to rebuke Jesus. These words "began" suggest that this dialogue continued perhaps all the following week. Peter was actually arguing with the Lord. Despite Jesus' teaching the Twelve still did not comprehend the meaning of His mission.

This brings us to Luke's note about Jesus praying. It may well be that He was praying that the Father would give such a revelation that the disciples would believe and understand. If this be a true surmise then Jesus' transfiguration came in answer to His prayer. The three disciples saw not only Jesus the Man. They saw that this Man was truly God. And when they saw and heard Moses and Elijah talking with Jesus about His exodus, they were made aware in dramatic fashion that the law and prophets taught the same thing that they had heard from Jesus. The Son of Man *must* suffer, *must* be rejected, *must* be killed, and after three days *must* rise again (8:31). And even though these disciples would still stumble on this truth, they never forgot it. For years later Peter made reference to the experience (II Peter 1:16-18).

The Mistake and Rebuke of Peter (9:5-8)

However, at the moment in spite of this glorious experience Peter fumbled the ball. Luke notes that he spoke without knowing what he said (9:33). To Jesus he said, "Master [Rabbi], it is good for us to be here: and let us make three tabernacles; one for thee, and one for Moses, and one for Elias" (v. 5). It was near the time for the feast of tabernacles. So he proposed that they make three booths under which they might sit during this feast.

In keeping with Luke's account Mark notes that Peter knew "not what to say; for they were sore afraid" (v. 6). Actually, he did not know what to *answer*—to the phenomenon which they had seen. Robertson asks, "But why did Peter say anything?" Why indeed? But true to his nature he thought that someone should say something. He should have been listening rather than talking. For when he spoke he said the wrong thing.

Suddenly a cloud overshadowed the disciples (v. 7). Clouds form quickly at this high altitude on Hermon. But this was no ordinary cloud. It was the Shekinah Glory or the presence of God. For out of this cloud came a voice, "This is my beloved Son: hear him" (v. 7). As at His baptism so here, the Son was still pleasing to the Father. Peter might dispute His word, but it was well-pleasing to the Father.

These words not only spoke approval of the Son, but also rebuke to the disciples. And especially to Peter. For he not only erred in disputing with Jesus, he was wrong in his suggestion about the three tabernacles. For one thing he thought that these heavenly visitors were going to remain on earth. But more to the point, he placed them on an equality with Jesus. One tabernacle for each, with no distinction between Jesus and Moses and Elijah.

How often do we err in the same way. Jesus is not one man among men, even such giants of faith as Moses and Elijah. He is unique and apart from all men in glory and majesty.

So the disciples are to "hear him." Not Moses and Elijah, but Jesus. God's supreme revelation is not in the law and the prophets, but in Jesus (Heb. 1:1f.). The former revelation spoke dimly of that which Jesus taught with authority. In this admonition to hear Jesus only is the truth that the followers of Jesus are to break with the old revelation to follow the new. Not that we are going to reject the former. But we are to see its fulfilment in Jesus. Old cloth cannot be patched with new. New wine must be put into new wineskins.

Then the cloud was gone. And Moses and Elijah with it. For suddenly looking round about, the disciples "saw no man any more, save Jesus only with themselves" (v. 8). The transfiguration had come and gone. Had the three disciples learned its lesson? They could not take it all in at once. But they were subdued by it. And they never really forgot it.

The Charge and the Question (9:9-13)

As they were coming down out of the mountain Jesus strongly charged them that they should not tell anyone what they had seen "till the Son of man were risen from the dead" (v. 9). To do so would cause premature excitement. Furthermore, these men would not be able fully to comprehend its meaning until after the resurrection. Only then would all the pieces of this divine puzzle (to them) fall into place.

That they still did not comprehend is seen in their questions among themselves about the resurrection (v. 10). And they will not fully understand until after the event. Indeed, the nature of Jesus' kingdom will not be clear to them until after the Holy Spirit comes at Pentecost (cf. Acts 1:6).

The appearance of Elijah on the mountain posed another problem for them. The scribes taught that he would come before the Messiah (v. 11; cf. Mal. 4:5f.). The disciples recognized Jesus as the Messiah. And now they had seen Elijah. So to them it seemed that Elijah had come after the Messiah, not before.

In effect, Jesus replied that it is true that Elijah comes first, and restores all things (v. 12). But the question still remains as to why the Son of Man must suffer and be held in contempt by sinful men. And then He said that Elijah had already come (v. 13). He spoke of John the Baptist (cf. Matt. 11:14; 17:13). Already John had suffered martyrdom. As Jezebel had persecuted Elijah, so Herodias had effected the death of the Baptist.

Thus Jesus enlightened the disciples on the true meaning of Malachi 4:5. But they were still confused by the scribal teachings concerning the Messiah. However, the transfiguration had dramatized truth to them. And in time they will understand.

Mark 9:14-29

The Impotent Disciples and the Powerful Jesus

Following the scene of glory at the summit of Mt. Hermon, Jesus found one of shame at its base. Assuming that the transfiguration happened at night, it was probably the next morning when Jesus and the three disciples returned to the other nine. And it was to discover a scene of frustration.

The Failure of the Disciples (9:14-18)

Mark begins this account with the participle "coming." This suggests that Jesus was approaching the nine and those who had gathered about them. "And coming to the disciples, he saw a great crowd around them" (v. 14). In their midst were scribes questioning with them. The word "questioning" renders a compound verb showing that they were continually doing so with zest. Bruce notes that they were *wrangling* with the nine. The nine had failed to heal a young man. And the scribes were delighted. If they could not get Jesus in a corner, at least they could make capital of this. They may even have implied that their failure was His also.

When Jesus arrived on the scene unexpectedly the crowd was greatly surprised. But when they recovered from their amazement, "running they began to greet [welcome] him" (v. 15). This is the literal rendering of the text. The crowd forgot the embarrassed nine and the carping critics, and rushed to meet Jesus. Perhaps they wondered what He would do in the situation.

Taking in the scene He asked the scribes why they were wrangling with the nine disciples (v. 16). Perhaps the scribes refused to answer. But one of the crowd did so. And who was he? The father of the young man.

His was a pathetic story (vv. 17-18). He had brought his son *to Jesus*. Evidently he thought that He was with the nine. But, of course, he failed to find Him. There is no evidence that he had ever seen Jesus. But likely he had heard of His healing miracles in Galilee.

His son had "a dumb spirit." Jesus called it a "dumb and deaf spirit" (v. 25). The boy was unable to speak, and he attributed it to such a spirit. The father said that the spirit "taketh him."

The word for "taketh" is *katalabēi*. In English this word is *catalepsy*. It is used by Galen and Hippocrates for *fits*. So he had such seizures periodically. The effects are graphically described: "teareth," spasms or convulsions; "foameth"; "gnasheth with his teeth," a grinding of his teeth; "pineth away," withering as grass, suggesting the stupor in which the seizure left him. A pitiful picture indeed! And it was compounded by the words "I spake to thy disciples that they should cast him out; and they could not" (v. 18). The father's hopes had also been dashed to the ground.

The Response of Jesus (9:19-27)

We are not surprised at Jesus' reaction. "O faithless generation, how long shall I be with you? how long shall I suffer you? bring him unto me" (v. 19). "Faithless" means "no faith." While He applied this to the entire generation, He also included these impotent disciples. Of course, they had believed in Him, but they had no faith to cope with this situation. So in exasperation Jesus wondered how long He could put up with or endure such. With this He told them to bring or bear the son to Him. Apparently the son was some distance away from Jesus. The word rendered "bring" could be either a present indicative or imperative form. In this context it is the latter. Basically the word means to carry something. It is possible that in the son's present state this was necessary.

So "they brought him" to Jesus (v. 20). "And seeing him the spirit immediately tare him" (v. 20). When the dumb spirit saw Jesus it knew that its power over the boy was soon to be ended. The impotent disciples were one thing, but the powerful Jesus was another. So the spirit "completely convulsed" the boy. He threw him into a complete convulsion. Mark vividly describes the scene. Literally, "And falling upon the ground he [the boy] *kept on rolling* and *foaming*" (author's translation). The imperfect tenses show that this continued for some time.

So like any physician Jesus asked the father how long the boy had been so afflicted. The father said, "Of a child" or childhood (v. 21). This could mean from infancy. Then the father gave details of his son's malady. Many times "it hath cast him into the fire, and into the waters, to destroy him" (v. 22). Matthew says that he *fell* into fire and water. But Mark uses the word "cast." In his seizures the boy had done these things. But the father interpreted this to mean that the *spirit* was trying to destroy the boy.

And then the father made his appeal. "If thou canst do any thing, have compassion on us, and help us" (v. 22). Note the "us." The father identified himself with his son in this. He did not question Jesus' willingness as did the leper in Mark 1:40. The leper said, "You can if you will." The father said, "You will if you can." The failure of the disciples, plus the chronic condition of his son, dampened but did not extinguish his faith. His question implies doubt as to whether anyone, including Jesus, could heal his son. Note the words "have compassion on us, and help us." Literally, "having had compassion on us, help us." The participle and verb both are aorists. He knows that Jesus has compassion. So he asks for immediate help if such is possible.

In response Jesus shifted the emphasis from His power to the man's faith. The man said, "If thou canst do any thing." Jesus said, "If thou canst believe" (v. 23). Actually the Greek text uses what Robertson calls a "neat idiom." The definite article *to* precedes "if you can" *(ei dunēi; to ei dunēi)*. It reads, "With respect to the 'if thou canst,' all things can [are able or possible] to the one believing." So the issue turned not upon Jesus' power but on the man's faith. How often we accuse God of inability when the trouble is our lack of faith! As one has said, we need "a sense of the possible."

Jesus' words shocked the father. For immediately he cried out with a loud cry, "I believe; help thou mine unbelief" (v. 24). It is no wonder that he cried out ("with tears" not in best manuscripts), when he heard that his son's healing depended not upon Jesus' power but upon his faith. "I believe," "I do believe," or "I am believing ("Lord" not in the best manuscripts). That is why he came to Jesus in the first place. And despite the failure of the disciples, he still kept on believing. However, his faith was weak after what had happened and considering his son's chronic condition. So he prayed, "Help [keep on helping] my unbelief." The word "unbelief" *(apistiai)* means "no faith." Thayer says that here *apistia* in this context means "weakness of faith."

Barclay comments that the man's original faith had been shaken. But in Jesus' presence it "blazed up again." So he translates this, "I believe . . . if there is still some discouragement in me, still some doubts, take them away and fill me with an unquestioning faith." The present tense of "help" expresses continuous action. In verse 22 this same verb is an aorist, "Help immediately." He felt the need of help at once with his son. But he sensed a continuous need for help with his faith. And do not we all?

The crowd came running together about Jesus (v. 25). So apparently the conversation with the father had been private. It is possible that others, having heard, also came running. The crowd wanted to see what Jesus would do about the boy whose condition evidently was widely known.

So Jesus "rebuked the foul spirit." The Holy Spirit led Mark to choose exactly the word for "rebuke" *(epitimaō)*. This refers to an ineffectual rebuke. The word used for rebuke which brings conviction and confession is *elegchō*. Demons do not so respond. Rather, as Wuest says, they are "incorrigible. They will never repent."

Nevertheless, Jesus commanded the spirit to come out of the boy and never again to enter into him (v. 25). Note that He spoke to the demon as a real being, not merely a popular superstition. The word "charge" renders a verb used in military commands. Jesus would accept no less than obedience from the spirit. "Enter no more" reads literally, "No more may you enter." This reflects the intermittent seizures of the boy. The demon could not enter to seize him again.

And while evil spirits do not repent, they must obey the expressed command of God. So "crying with a loud voice and convulsing much it came out." All three verb forms are aorists, testifying to the miracle involved. The spirit had to obey Jesus. But it did its worst to the boy before doing so. So much so that the boy "became as dead." The violent convulsion left him in this state. It was such that many said, "He is dead" or "he died" (v. 26). To them the case was hopeless.

"But Jesus." Ah, there is the difference! What men consider to be hopeless is not so with Jesus. For He "took him by the hand, and lifted him up, and he arose" (v. 27). Again the verbs are all aorists. "Lifted up" may be called an ingressive aorist. Literally, "But Jesus, gripping firmly his hand, began to raise him up, and he stood up immediately."

Mark makes no comment as to the crowd's reaction. But Luke notes that "they were all amazed at the mighty power of God" (9:43). "Mighty power" should read "majesty, magnificence, glory." So that which the three disciples had seen on top of the mountain, the crowd saw demonstrated at its base. The nine disciples had failed, but Jesus had prevailed.

The Reason for Failure (9:28-29)

Since the excitement which His miracle had created did not provide an atmosphere for teaching, Jesus and the Twelve withdrew to some private abode. There the nine asked, "Why could not we cast him out?" (v. 28). In the Greek text "we" is written out for emphasis. "We" in contrast to Jesus. And Jesus replied, "This kind can come forth by nothing, but by [in] prayer" (v. 29, "and fasting" not in best manuscripts).

These disciples were a subdued group. On their tour of Galilee they had cast out demons (6:13). But here they had failed. Swete says that they failed because they felt that they possessed a "quasi-magical power," since Jesus had given them this power previously. Thus they had not prepared themselves spirtually for this challenge. He adds further, "Spirits of such malignity ["this kind"] were quick to discern the lack of moral power and would yield to no other." Bruce points out the need for prayer and faith. And then he notes that neither the nine nor the father were hopeful of a cure.

Another thought is suggested by this particular instance. Jesus had taken three disciples into the mountain, leaving the nine behind. Knowing the jealousy for position within the group, one wonders if the nine had not spent their time in grumbling rather than in praying. Such would drain them of spiritual power. Outwardly they were the same men who had gone on a successful mission for Jesus. But inwardly they were hollow shells when confronted with this spiritual challenge.

This event teaches many lessons. But none is more to the point than that while the Lord's people squabble among themselves, struggling for position and power, they are imperceptibly drained of spiritual power; so that the devil laughs in their faces as they speak words which once achieved for God but which have become but "quasi-magical" phrases to which the evil forces do not respond.

Still the Lord's people ask, "Why could not we cast him out?" And the Lord ever replies, "This kind can come forth by nothing, but by prayer." Lord, we believe; help Thou our unbelief!

Mark 9:30-50

The Teaching Concerning Kingdom Greatness

The period of withdrawals was now over. It was probably late in September A.D. 29, just about six or seven months before Jesus' death. He returned to Galilee preparatory to going south into Judea. The Galilean people had largely rejected Him (cf. John 6:66). Before the end He will have a ministry to the people of Judea and Perea. During this period He will spend some time in Jerusalem (John 7:11–10:39). But most of it will be spent outside that city. However, this juncture in Jesus' ministry marks the beginning of the end.

The Return to Galilee (9:30-32)

Leaving the region of Mt. Hermon Jesus and the Twelve went south through Galilee (v. 30). "Passed through Galilee" involves the events prior to His departure for Judea. On the journey back to Capernaum the Lord did not wish that His whereabouts be known. After all, the Galileans had forsaken Him. And His primary concern was to teach His disciples. It was evident to Jesus that they were far from being ready for His departure from them.

The substance of His teaching was still His coming death and resurrection. But a new note was added. He had taught the basic truth near Caesarea Philippi (8:31). But now He prefixed this with *"The Son of man is delivered into the hands of men,* and they shall kill him . . ." (9:31, author's italics). Why this new note?

The verb rendered "is delivered" means to give alongside. It may also read to hand one over to another for execution. It is so used of the Sanhedrin delivering Jesus to Pilate (15:1) and of Pilate handing Him over to the soldiers for crucifixion (v. 15). Had Jesus had these events in mind in 9:31a He probably would have used the future tense, although the historical present (as here) could mean that. However, there seems to be another meaning in Jesus' words at this point.

For in Mark 14:41 this word is rendered "betrayed." Wuest gives as its modern equivalent "to sell down the river." The fact that the verb form used in 9:31 is a present passive suggests that at that time He "is being betrayed into the hands of men." Back in the early spring Jesus had intimated that one of the Twelve is a devil (John 6:70). John notes that He referred to Judas, "for he was about to betray [*paradidonai,* the verb used in Mark 9:31] him" (v. 6:71). Jesus had seen evidences of that purpose forming in Judas' heart. Evidently it had been growing. So for the first time Jesus clearly said that His death would be brought about by His being betrayed into the hands of men.

"But they understood not that saying, and were afraid to ask him" (v. 32). What was it that they did not understand? And why were they afraid to ask Him about it? To be sure, they did not understand about the necessity for Jesus' death. And the resurrection was a mystery to them. However, they had heard these things before. Robertson suggests that they feared to ask questions because they remembered Jesus' rebuke of Peter as "Satan." Bruce comments that they did not ask because "they did not wish to understand, they would live on in hope that their Master was under a hallucination." But do either of these fully explain their fear?

Was not their fear related primarily to the words "the Son of man is delivered into the hands of men?" They understood this to mean betrayed. And who could *betray* Jesus but someone close to Him? Later at the last passover meal when Jesus plainly said that one of them would do it, the Eleven asked, "Is it I, Lord?" This question invited a negative answer. One by one they were not sure. But each hoped that it was not he. But he was not sure.

This same fear lurked in their hearts when they first heard of a betrayal. Certainly the Eleven had no thought of doing this. But, like all men, they were not sure but that some unknown seed of evil might even then be working within them. So each, hoping against hope, was afraid to ask the identity of such a person. Only Judas probably knew it. But even then the seed was just sprouting in his heart. It would bear its hellish harvest later. Certainly he feared to ask Jesus to identify the betrayer, lest he hear his own name. And the others feared, not only for that reason, but lest they should hear the name of any one of this intimate group. So no one dared to press the matter.

The Question as to Kingdom Greatness (9:33-37)

Back in Capernaum, probably in Peter's house, Jesus raised a question. "What was it that ye disputed among yourselves by the way?" (v. 33). This referred to a "reasoning" as they had returned to Capernaum. The imperfect tense of the verb shows that this had gone on for some time. At times Jesus walked ahead of His disciples. And while He had heard their words probably punctuated by heated arguments, He had not stopped them. Hence His question at this time.

"But they held their peace" (v. 34). Literally, "They kept on being quiet." His question put them to shame. For they had been disputing as to who should be greatest in the kingdom. This had probably been brought about by the seeming favoritism shown to the three disciples taken up into the mountain.

What a pitiful picture! As Jesus talked about His death, they argued about position. As Bruce says, "He went before, thinking His deep thoughts, they followed thinking their vain thoughts."

Since they would not answer Jesus, He proceeded to tell them (v. 35). "If any man desire to be first, the same shall be last of all, and servant of all." Instead of insisting on standing at the head of the line, he will be content to stand at the foot. And instead of insisting that others serve him, he will be the "servant" of all. He did not say slave *(doulos)* but *the lowest kind of slave (diakonos,* note "deacon"). This same word is found in Mark 10:43 as "minister." And the verb form is so rendered twice in 10:45. A *diakonos* was a slave who rinsed the feet of guests upon arrival. Since Jesus had no such slave, He performed this menial task Himself for His *guests* at the last passover meal (John 13:4ff.). It is obvious, therefore, that in Mark 9:35 Jesus taught a lesson in humility.

Then He proceeded to demonstrate the lesson. For He took a child, maybe Peter's, set him in the midst of them, and then took him in His arms (v. 36). With this He spoke. "Whosoever shall receive one of such children in my name, receiveth me: and whosoever shall receive me, receiveth not me, but him that sent me" (v. 37).

What did Jesus mean by this act and these words? Why did He use a child? Was it because of a child's simple, trusting nature? We can hardly say that a child is unselfish. What is there about a child that illustrated Jesus' lesson? Is it not a child's helplessness and being largely without influence in worldly affairs? So a child can give nothing. Rather we must give to him. Naturally one would not serve a child in order to gain worldly prestige. What influence can a child exert to advance your selfish ambitions?

The disciples were interested in getting ahead, in achieving power, prestige, and wealth. Jesus said to achieve kingdom greatness one must be willing to forego such aspirations and to lose himself in the most menial service. Such could not possibly advance one in worldly ambition. So in the figure of a child, Jesus said that those who aspire to kingdom greatness must *receive kindly* a little child. He must show loving concern for these helpless ones who need, but who cannot possibly reward him in a worldly, material way. He does it purely for the joy of serving with no thought of reward.

Those who do this for a little child, do it for Jesus, and for the Heavenly Father. It is He who will determine who is great in His kingdom. What a great lesson in humility! And what joyful words to those who serve little children in the home, school, and church. Such will not lose their reward from Him who sees, knows, and approves.

The Lesson in Christian Understanding (9:38-41)

Evidently this lesson was getting through to the disciples. At least that was true of John. For he sought to change the subject. Incidently this is the only remark attributed to the apostle John by the Synoptic gospels.

"Master, we saw one casting out devils [demons] in thy name, and he followeth us not: and we forbad him, because he followeth us not" (v. 38). Apparently he expected a compliment for his zeal for Jesus and His work.

Evidently this man was a disciple of Jesus. But He was not one of the twelve apostles. This would seem to be the sense of the twice stated fact that he "followeth not *with us*" (author's italics). The former of these is a present tense; the latter is an imperfect tense, "he was not following with us." Jesus had given to the Twelve the power to cast out demons. But this man was doing it *in Jesus' name* also. But what John thought was zeal actually was jealousy. This is more the attitude *of the son of thunder* than that of *the apostle of love* as seen in John's Gospel and Epistles. It reflects the later development in this apostle's spiritual life.

Jesus' response was quite different from that expected by John. "Stop forbidding him" (v. 39). For, said Jesus, no man doing such in His name could speak "lightly" or in an evil manner concerning Him. "For he that is not against us is on our behalf," or is on our side.

Thus Jesus taught a lesson in Christian understanding or tolerance. Simply because one is not a member of the Twelve is no reason to forbid him to work for Jesus. Every follower of Jesus is to witness to and work for Him. One Christian may not speak the exact words of another Christian. His methods may be different. But if he is doing the work of Christ he should have one's blessing.

Paul expressed this truth in Philippians 1:18. "What then? notwithstanding, every way, whether in pretence, or in truth, Christ is preached; and I therein do rejoice, yea, and will rejoice."

Any service rendered for Christ is rewarded by Him. "For whosoever shall give you a cup of water to drink in my name, because ye belong to Christ, verily I say unto you, he shall not lose his reward" (v. 41). In this closing phrase Jesus used a strong double negative. This emphasizes the certainty that such will be rewarded. Robertson calls this "the bond of universal brotherhood of the redeemed." Any service for Christ, however small, has upon it the Lord's blessing.

The Lesson of Humility Continued (9:42-50)

Having dealt with John's interruption Jesus returned to His lesson drawn from the little child. However, His thought turns from an actual child to that of a child in Christ. This seems to have been prompted by John's word about this non-apostle. For he was "one of these little ones that believe in me" (v. 42). The intent of John's forbidding was to "offend" him or to cause him to stumble, to cease casting out demons. This is the meaning of the word "offend." It would be better for one to have a millstone hanged about his neck and to be cast into the sea, than to keep one of Christ's followers from serving Him. This was a form of execution.

Furthermore, a man may be his own cause of stumbling (vv. 43, 47-58; verses 44-46 not in best manuscripts). These verses seem to refer to one who does not become a child of God because of the wrong use of his natural powers. It would be better to go through life maimed of limb or eye as a Christian, than to be whole of body yet lose one's soul. The words "hell" in verses 43, 47 are *Gehenna*. This was the Vale of Hinnom which ran around the southwest to the Kidron valley on the east of Jerusalem. It was the scene of the worship of the fire god Moloch where children had been sacrificed during the time of Ahaz. Josiah had put an end to it. But in revulsion against this practice this valley had become the garbage dump of the city. Fires burned constantly to consume the filth. And worms worked in the putrefaction. *Gehenna* had become the symbol of hell or eternal punishment.

Of interest is the fact that only Jesus uses this term in the Gospels. And its symbolism is all the more terrible because it fell from the lips of Him who is perfect love and mercy. Men may deny the reality of hell. But Jesus did not. He ever warned men to escape it, and He died to enable men to do so.

Jesus concluded His lesson on humility by reminding the Twelve that "every one shall be salted with fire" (v. 49, the remainder of this verse is not found in the best manuscripts). In this context this verse is related to Jesus' reference to fire in verse 48, and to the idea of self-discipline found in verse 50. Either one will exercise the self-discipline of committal (faith) to Christ or else he will suffer eternal punishment in hell. But behind this figure there is also a lesson for the Christian. Without self-discipline in serving Christ he will suffer the loss of a *life* of Christian ministry.

"Salt is good: but if the salt have lost his saltness, wherewith will ye season it" (v. 50)? Jesus called His followers the salt of the earth (Matt. 5:13). Salt is good as a preservative, a curative power, and as a flavor. Christians are to be all of these, preserving from corruption, curing the disease of sin, and giving flavor or zest to life. Salt can do these things only by being applied to that in which it is to serve. And salt loses itself in doing these things.

But if salt loses its quality as salt it is useless. It is here that Jesus comes back to the original question. Shall the Twelve lose themselves in service to God through men? Or will they lose their "saltness" in striving after selfish ambition? If the latter, then they will lose the very purpose of their being. This has no reference to loss of redemption but to loss of opportunity as Christians.

Thus Jesus closed by exhorting these men to "have salt in yourselves, and have peace one with another" (v. 50). Rather than to wrangle among themselves in striving for greatness, they are to be at peace on with another. They should lose selfish ambition in the greater cause of losing themselves in the purpose of God for His people. This is a much-needed lesson for Christian people in all ages—even today.

IV

The Journey to Jerusalem

Mark 10:1-12

The Lesson Concerning Divorce

A comparison of the Gospel accounts reveals that Mark passed over a considerable ministry of Jesus in Jerusalem, Judea, and Perea. This is reported by John (7:2–10:42) and Luke (9:51–17:10). After this extended ministry Jesus returned to Galilee (Luke 17:11), and then went back through Perea on His last journey to Jerusalem. It is during this journey that Mark, followed by Matthew, takes up the story again.

The Final Journey to Jerusalem (10:1)

If we had only the Synoptic Gospels, we would suppose that during His public ministry Jesus made only one appearance in Jerusalem, the one at the close of His ministry. Luke places Him at Bethany near Jerusalem (10:38-42) but not in the city itself. Only John reports four visits to Jerusalem prior to this time (2:13ff.; 5:1ff.; 7:10ff.; 10:22ff.). Without these accounts we would hardly be prepared to understand the final rejection of Jesus by the Jewish leaders.

Mark 10:1 takes up this final journey to Jerusalem. It was only a matter of weeks, perhaps less, before the final Passover. "And he arose from thence [Galilee], and cometh into the coasts of Judaea by the farther side of Jordan" (v. 1). Going from Galilee to Jerusalem Jews customarily followed this route. They crossed to the eastern side of the Jordan river, went southward through Perea, back across the Jordan near Jericho, and then up to Jerusalem. This is the route taken by Jesus. He went from Galilee to Judea by way of Perea.

This was done to avoid passing southward through Samaria. A Jew going northward through Samaria was accepted by the Samaritans, since he was going away from Jerusalem and the temple. But they resented one going southward *toward* Jerusalem and its temple. Early in His ministry Jesus had gone northward through Samaria (John 4). On this occasion He was welcomed by the people of Sychar. But just a few months prior to this final journey, because He was going toward Jerusalem a Samaritan village refused to let Him enter (Luke 9:51ff.).

So on this final trip to Jerusalem He went by way of Perea.

Evidently He traveled with a caravan of pilgrims bound for the feast. Such an arrangement provided both fellowship and protection from marauders. Mark says that "the multitudes again go together" with Jesus (v. 1). Caravan after caravan was making this journey. And apparently the largest of them all was the one about Jesus. For the most part this multitude was composed of Galileans who were friendly toward Jesus, and who perhaps were excited over the prospect that He might declare His kingdom at this feast. And as was customary Jesus was teaching them along the way.

The Problem of the Pharisees (10:2-4)

Somewhere in Perea Jesus was accosted by some Pharisees. They brought to Him the problem concerning divorce. While nothing is said specifically about re-marriage, it was certainly the crux of the problem. "Is it lawful for a man to put away his wife?" (v. 2). Their purpose in asking this question was to tempt Him. "Tempting" may mean just that. Or it may mean simply to test. Perhaps they had heard of a previous word of Jesus on this subject (Matt. 5:31f.). Knowing the Pharisees, however, their purpose probably was ulterior.

This was one of the burning questions of the hour. Moses had permitted a man to put away his wife. But he required that the husband write her "a bill of divorcement" (vv. 3-4; cf. Deut. 24:1-4). This was actually an improvement over the practice in which the man might send his wife away. Barclay notes that a woman was regarded as mere chattel at the mercy of the head of the family. A woman could be divorced either with or without her will. But a man could be divorced only by his consent. A woman could divorce her husband only if he were a leper, were engaged in a disgusting trade such as a tanner, if he ravished a virgin, or if he falsely accused his wife of a pre-marriage sin. At least under Moses' law she had a record that she was divorced and was free to marry someone else.

Now in Jesus' day there were two schools of thought on this matter. Hillel taught the more liberal view. He interpreted "that she find not favor in his eyes, because he hath found some uncleanness in her" (Deut. 24:1) to mean that a man might divorce his wife for any cause. It could be, according to one rabbi, because she had lost her beauty. Or because she had spoiled the food or was a loud talking, brawling woman. Other liberal causes of divorce were if the wife talked to a strange man, or if she spun in the streets. It is clear that under this view a woman had no rights whatsoever. She could be divorced for any cause or even without a cause. On the other hand there was the stricter view. Shammai taught that "uncleanness" meant adultery and nothing else.

One can see, however, that human nature being what it is, the more liberal view prevailed among men. The condition was such that women hesitated to marry at all. It is a compliment to Jesus to say that the Pharisees hardly expected Him to champion the liberal view. And if He sided with Shammai this would certainly lessen His popularity with the men of that day. In effect, the Pharisees proposed to put Jesus on the horns of a dilemma.

The Answer of Jesus (10:5-9)

What could Jesus say to such a question? Of course, He referred the Pharisees to the law of Moses (vv. 3-4). But the Jews did not agree as to its meaning. So with one terse statement Jesus disposed of this matter. Moses did not command divorce. He only permitted it because of the hardness of men's hearts (v. 5). And he sought to regulate the practice in order to protect the wife.

With this Jesus turned back to the original divine purpose of marriage. "From the beginning of the creation God made them male and female" (v. 6; cf. Gen. 1:27). And "for this cause shall a man leave his father and mother, and cleave to his wife; and the twain shall be one flesh" (vv. 7-8; cf. Gen. 2:24).

For what cause? Because God made them male and female. Neither is complete without the other. In this statement Jesus set forth three elements of true marriage: the divine intent, the social need, and the physical aspect. Marriage is ordained of God. Marriage involves social rules and relationships. And it is based upon the difference between sexes.

God has deposited love in the human heart. He has made it possible that one man and one woman might love one another. So the divine ideal in marriage is monogamous. Social well-being requires marriage regulations. In marriage a couple brings into being a new unit in society. And marriage is consummated in sexual union.

"What therefore God hath joined together [yoked together], let not man put asunder" (v. 9). The divine purpose in marriage should not be destroyed by man. Clearly Jesus taught that God's intent in marriage was that one man and one woman should be married until parted by death. Any deviation from that is due to the hardness of men's hearts.

The Lesson to the Disciples (10:10-12)

Later "in the house" (v. 10) the disciples asked for further explanation. So Jesus said, "Whosoever shall put away his wife, and marry another, committeth adultery against her. And if a woman shall put away her husband, and be married to another, she committeth adultery" (vv. 11-12). Bruce holds that in verse 11 Mark reported Jesus' words, but that in verse 12 he added these words to balance the teaching. However, there seems to be insufficient grounds for this position. Since Moses' law gave *rights* to the wife, Jesus simply reminded the disciples that she also had *responsibilities.* The point in these verses is not merely that of divorce but of remarriage.

It is here that we encounter a problem. According to Mark, Jesus' teaching was absolute. Whereas in Matthew's account He made one exception, fornication (19:9; cf. 5:32). Thus according to Matthew Jesus taught that fornication (adultery) was the only ground for divorce and remarriage. Some interpreters claim that the *exception* is not genuine Scripture. But Robertson holds to the contrary in both passages in Matthew. The objection is based upon two claims. The exception reflects a later practice; and it makes Jesus side with Shammai against Hillel. The former objection does not hold up in the light of history. And, as Robertson says, why should not Jesus agree with Shammai if he is right?

However, are we forced to see a conflict between Matthew and Mark? From Matthew's record it is clear that Jesus gave the exception in His discourse with the Pharisees. Mark's account was spoken to the disciples "in the house." In these words Jesus was dealing with divorce for any cause short of adultery. In Matthew He was answering the question regarding divorce "for every cause" (19:3). He said that there is but one cause, adultery. To the disciples He said that divorce and *remarriage* "for every cause" other than sexual infidelity is adultery. So the two Gospels agree.

Why did Jesus make one exception? It goes back to the very nature of marriage. It is divinely based upon "male and female." They are to be *one flesh.* Adultery breaks that *oneness.* Keep in mind the threefold nature of marriage: divine, social, physical. And in that order. The divine involves true love and also God joining together. The social meets the demands of a well-ordered society. The physical consummates the union. And it can be severed only in reverse order. Society may declare a legal end to a marriage. But so long as the physical oneness abides, God does not recognize a mere legal accommodation. But when the oneness is broken by sexual infidelity, if the innocent party so chooses the marriage is broken. Of course, that one may forgive and re-establish the physical oneness (cf. Hosea). But otherwise not. Having then dissolved the social aspect, God recognizes the marriage at an end.

It should be remembered, however, that this is not God's intentional but circumstantial will. But in such a circumstance the innocent party is free to remarry. The guilty party is not.

Jesus' teaching was not an accommodation to hard hearts. It was to protect the rights of the innocent. And it places a wall of protection about both the home and marriage.

Mark 10:13-16

The Lord and Children

The Children and Jesus (10:13a)

It is fitting that this incident should follow Jesus' teaching designed to safeguard marriage and the home. For it pictures mothers bringing their little children to Jesus to be blessed by Him. It was customary for them to be blessed by the ruler of the synagogue. But here was one who was greater than these rulers.

Mark says that "they were bringing [imperfect] young children to him." This pictures a procession as one after another the mothers did this. Matthew notes that the purpose was that Jesus might lay His hands on them and pray (19:13). This had nothing to do with salvation. And it is no Scriptural basis for infant baptism. It was a natural thing that these mothers would bring their little ones to this noted Rabbi. It was customary for children to receive such a blessing on their first birthday. Luke uses the word for "babes." However, since there were so many, this need not be limited to those only one year old. But it was a beautiful scene indeed.

The Disciples and Children (10:13b)

But even into so tender a scene a discordant note was injected. For as the mother's "were bringing" their children to Jesus, the disciples "rebuked" (aorist) them for it. But even though the aorist tense speaks only of the act of rebuking, it is colored by the preceding imperfect tense. The mothers *were bringing* and the disciples *were rebuking*. The word rendered "rebuked" means both to check unjustly and ineffectually. So while the disciples unjustly sought to prevent the mothers, they were having no success at it. What mother on such an occasion would have been deterred in her purpose by mere rebuking men?

Why did the disciples do this? To protect Jesus from being disturbed while He rested "in the house?" This could be the case. Or was it because they wanted to hear more on the subject of divorce and remarriage? Whatever the reason, it showed that the disciples tended to discount the importance of the children and the purpose for which their mothers were bringing them to Jesus.

It is a serious thing to look lightly upon children and their place in God's plan. For in them are bound up infinite possibilities. Each of them is the object of God's love. Rightly regarded they are the joy of today and the hope of tomorrow. It is a tragedy beyond measure to fail to lead little children to be rightly related to Jesus. What a fearful thing is the responsibility of adults in the care of little children, and especially with regard to their spiritual nurture. In effect to every parent God says, "Take this little one and rear him for me." Woe betide those parents and others responsible for children who do otherwise.

The Lord and Children (10:14-16)

Quite naturally when Jesus saw the disciples rebuking these mothers, He was "much displeased" (v. 14). This verb renders a Greek verb which means basically "to feel pain." It expresses deep emotion which is best expressed as indignation. So Jesus was indignant over the action of the Twelve.

Said He, "Suffer [permit] the little children to come unto me, and forbid them not: for of such is the kingdom of God" (v. 14). Literally, "stop hindering." Hindering was exactly what the disciples were doing. And it was the opposite of what Jesus wished. For both verbs, "suffer" and "forbid," are imperative modes. They are commands. The disciples were to stop forbidding. Rather they were to keep on permitting the children to keep on coming (present infinitive) to Jesus.

As a side thought this scene not only shows what Jesus thinks of children. It also shows what they think of Him. *The only hindrance to their coming to Jesus was the disciples!* By their coming to Jesus we know that He was one who attracted children. They were at ease in His presence. This was because they sensed His love. He was not one of stern countenance. We may well imagine that He greeted them with a winsome smile. You may fool adults, but not children. A child either likes you or he does not. And they respond to the spirit shown in an adult. They knew that in Jesus they had a friend.

Our Lord said that "of such [as little children] is the kingdom of God" (v. 14). Citizens of the kingdom of God must be as a little child. This opens up a vast area as to kingdom qualities: trust, humility, obedience, a forgiving spirit. But as in the case of the child in Mark 9:36, a child is helpless and dependent. So must one be who would enter into the kingdom of God. Helpless to save himself, he must depend entirely upon the Lord. He is saved by grace through faith in Jesus Christ.

And "whosoever shall not receive [receive warmly, cf. 9:37] the kingdom of God as [in the same manner as] a little child, he shall not enter therein" (v. 15). In this statement one can see how joyfully and eagerly the children came to Jesus. In the same manner must one come to Jesus for salvation. We must come to Him in trust, making no demands, obeying His word, receiving that which He gives, and in turn giving ourselves.

This scene closes on a beautiful note. Verse 16 reads, "And taking them in his arms he kept on blessing them fervently, placing his hands upon them." As each child came to Jesus, one by one He placed His hands upon them and blessed each one individually. Bruce comments "The process would last a while, but Jesus would not soon weary in such work."

The mothers never forgot this moment. And we may well imagine that as their children grew they were told repeatedly how they had been blessed by the Lord as He made His way to Jerusalem and the cross. The hands which had held them had been broken by the nails. The bosom to which He had pressed them had been pierced by the spear. And all that He might bless all who came to Him in faith as a little child.

Mark 10:17-31

The Lesson about Wealth and Reward

Jesus had left the house, and had resumed His journey toward Jerusalem. Somewhere along the way a man stopped Him with an earnest request. In the course of this experience Jesus opened up vistas of truth with respect to earthly possessions and heavenly reward.

The Request of Idealism (10:17)

How eagerly this young man came to Jesus: running and falling on his knees before Him. Earnestly he asked, "Good Master, what shall I do that I may inherit eternal life?" (v. 17). As the story develops we learn that he was a young ruler (Luke 18:18) of wealth. Matthew calls him a "young man" (19:20). The word so rendered *(neaniskos)* may refer to one from youth to middle age. Likely he was a young man. Luke uses the word *archōn,* a first one. He may have been a ruler of a synagogue or a town. How he achieved wealth is not stated. Did he inherit it? If so, then his question to Jesus is most suggestive. He had enough of this world's goods for a good life here. But what could he do to inherit life of the ages or age-abiding life?

Whatever else we know about him we know that he had high ideals. This within itself suggests his youth. He had a good life, but he was not satisfied with it. He was reaching out for something better. He wanted a life that would abide forever. Eternal life is often regarded in terms of time, or that which extends beyond death. But actually it also includes quality, that quality of life which is received now and which abides beyond one's earthly sojourn. This young man seems to have thought in this latter sense. He wanted to know how he could realize his highest ideals both now and forever. He was a "first one" among men, and wanted to be a "first one" with God.

The Answer of Truth (10:18-22)

Jesus did not immediately answer his question. Instead, He sought to lead him to a proper understanding of the moral and spiritual quality involved in "good."

"Why callest thou me good? there is none good but one, that is, God" (v. 18). The young man had called Jesus "Good Teacher."

Matthew relates "good" to that which he should do. But in any event it is essentially related to God.

Did Jesus reject for Himself the quality of "good?" That can hardly be the case. Was His question intended as a mild rebuke for a rather thoughtless use of the term? This could be true. But note that He related the quality of absolute goodness to God alone. And yet the young man had used it of Jesus as a Teacher.

May we not, therefore, see Jesus' play upon this word in relation to "Teacher" and "God?" The youth called Jesus "good," yet he also called Him "Teacher." Yet the term "good" should be used only of God. So was not Jesus saying that the young man should first of all get a proper understanding of Him? If Jesus was only a *Teacher* then He was undeserving of the term *good*. On the other hand, if He were truly *good* then He was *God*. Instead of refusing the term *good* He actually was claiming *deity*. And if the young man was to inherit eternal life, he must recognize that truth and accept it.

Then Jesus proceeded to answer the question. "What shall I do that I may inherit eternal life?" Jesus told him to keep the Ten Commandments. Then Jesus reminded him of the last six commandments (v. 19). These are the commandments which have to do with one's relationship with other men and women. But He made no mention of the first four commandments with regard to one's relationship to God. The Jews summarized the whole law in the words "Thou shalt love the Lord Thy God with all thy heart, and with all thy soul, and with all thy strength, and with all thy mind; and thy neighbour as thyself" (Luke 10:27; cf. Deut. 6:5; Lev. 19:18). In Jesus' reply to the young man He mentioned the latter but omitted the former. As we shall see presently this was not without purpose.

However, at this point a question calls for consideration. Could the young man have inherited eternal life by keeping the Ten Commandments? That is what Jesus said (cf. Luke 10:25-28). By this we may assume that He meant that one should keep every commandment perfectly. James says that if you break one commandment you are as guilty as if you had broken all of them (2:10-11). It is at this point that man fails. Because of his sinful nature he does not keep the commandments perfectly. For this reason he cannot be saved by law, but must be saved by grace. It was this very point that Jesus was endeavoring to get this young man to see. He wanted to know what he should do to inherit eternal life. And Jesus was leading him to see how impossible it was for him to have eternal life through any effort of his own. He must look to Someone outside himself.

The young man claimed that he had observed "all of them" from his youth (v. 20). This was quite a claim. But was it a true statement? Doubtless he thought so. Perhaps he was free from the overt acts of sinful living. But was he innocent of sins of the spirit? (cf. Matt. 5:20ff.). His very selfish clinging to his wealth when surrounded by so much need was within itself a sin. He was a perfect specimen of a self-righteous person, that is, righteous in his own eyes and by the accepted mores of his society. But such a person is far from the kingdom of God.

Nevertheless, Jesus "began to love" one with such high ideals (v. 21). Of course, He loves all men. But He was especially drawn to this rich young ruler. If He could win him he had so much to give the kingdom of God, not merely his wealth but himself. You can understand in part how Jesus felt. A person with such high ideals may himself form a barrier to becoming a Christian. But if you could only lead him to Christ, to harness those ideals to the cause of Christ. What a power for God he would be!

So Jesus, like a skilled physician, began to probe into this man's trouble. "One thing thou lackest" (v. 21). Matthew notes that the man asked, "What lack I yet?" (19:20). There need be no conflict here. Evidently the young man made this admission and Jesus agreed with him. His coming to Jesus showed his sense of need. And Jesus proceeded to meet it. And what did he lack?

"Go thy way, sell whatsoever thou hast, and give to the poor, and thou shalt have treasure in heaven: and come, follow me" (v. 21). "Take up thy cross" is not found in the best manuscripts. This was quite an order. We usually think of Jesus saying, "Come . . . go." But here He said, "Go . . . come." This young man had to "go" do something before he could "come" to Jesus in faith. What must he do? He must change his attitude from *doing nothing* to *doing something*. He claimed that he had never broken the Ten Commandments. Of course, this was an overstatement. But granting that this was true, his approach to life was in not doing the wrong thing. He must do the right thing. This is a much needed lesson for all of us. The popular concept of a good Christian is one who refrains from doing the wrong: not being immoral; not killing, stealing, lying, defrauding, or disobeying. But a clothing store dummy could qualify by this norm. One must avoid sins of omission as well as those of commission.

But more specifically Jesus told this man to do two things. First, he must *sell* and *give* if he would *have*. He must break with earthly treasures if he would inherit heavenly treasures. Second, he must "come, keep on following me." He must change allegiances from earthly things to Jesus. He would not be saved simply by disposing of his wealth through charitable deeds. But he must renounce his present allegiance; then by grace through faith in Jesus he would be saved. It was not what he did (v. 17) but what Christ soon would do which would enable him to inherit eternal life.

This brings us back to the matter of the first four commandments. These deal with man's relation to God. Essentially the man wanted to be rightly related to God. He had made a *fair* score in his human relationships; fair, not perfect, in that it was largely negative in nature. But what about his relationship to God? One cannot be rightly related to God unless that relationship leads him to a *positively* right relationship to man. He must, first, love God, and then, his neighbor. Both of these are involved in Jesus' words in verse 21.

As for the latter, Jesus touched upon it as He cited the last six commandments. But what about the first four? In effect Jesus cited these in His words to "go . . . sell . . . give." For in truth his possessions were his god, his graven image. So he must forsake that which stood between him and God. He must renounce allegiance to and trust in Mammon for a new allegiance to and trust in God. Evidence of this change would be seen in what he did with his wealth.

Did Jesus mean that he should take a pauper's oath? Not necessarily. In strong oriental expression He said that he must forsake trust in material things. His wealth must not be a barrier to God, but a means of serving God through serving men. So, in effect, Jesus, rather than calling for a pauper's oath, was calling for a dedication of self and substance. But even this alone would not give him eternal life. This would come through his trust in and committal to Christ. There must be the outward evidence of renunciation which is made possible only through inward dedication to Christ and His way.

For "follow" means to follow another in the way or to take the same road which another has taken. In His complete dedication to God's will Jesus had forsaken the pomp, glory, and wealth of the world to give Himself completely in serving men—even in His redemptive death. This man was called upon to do the same. He could not die for man's sin, but he could die to self in serving God through his service to man. Only through the power of a redeeming experience in Christ could this be possible for him.

But through this experience he could live according to the whole law: loving God with all his heart, soul, strength, and mind, and his neighbor as himself.

The interview which began with such high hopes ended on a sad note. "For he was sad at that saying, and went away being sorrowful." The word rendered "was sad" means to be gloomy as a lowering cloud. He brooded over these unwelcome words. His smile of anticipation gave way to a puzzled frown and then to utter disappointment. Jesus' words had punctured his balloon of easy optimism. The price was more than he was willing to pay. He was unwilling to give undivided allegiance and love to God or to lose himself on behalf of men. So instead of keeping the Ten Commandments, he became guilty of all. He went away sad, but he went away. Alas, how often this is the case!

The Peril of Wealth (10:23-27)

We may be certain that the young man was not alone in his disappointment and sorrow. Without question Jesus shared them also. Nevertheless, His immediate concern was the Twelve. What effect had this event had upon them? For "he looked round about." This renders an aorist participle which describes a quick glance about—at theTwelve. And then Jesus spoke.

"How hardly shall they that have riches enter into the kingdom of God" (v. 23) ! "Hardly" renders a word meaning "with difficulty." It is not impossible but "with great difficulty" for such to be saved. The young man had just demonstrated this. The popular attitude then as now was that wealth was a sign of God's blessing and good pleasure. If rightly regarded it may be. But riches have their problems and sorrows. Money may be a great servant, but it is a terrible master. Jesus said that one cannot give absolute allegiance to both God and Mammon or the money god (Matt. 6:24) . And the latter will deprive one of the former.

Proverbs 18:11 says, "The rich man's wealth is his strong city, and as an high wall *in his own conceit*" (author's italics) . He feels secure in his wealth when it may be his greatest peril. For "how with difficulty" shall a rich man enter into God's kingdom!

So revolutionary were these words of Jesus that the disciples were astounded (v. 24) . And seeing this, Jesus repeated His statement, fortifying it with the words, "It is easier for a camel to go through the eye of a needle, than for a rich man to enter into the kingdom of God" (v. 25) . Efforts have been made by some to relate this to a gate in the wall about Jerusalem. But this is without basis. In all likelihood Jesus was citing a current proverb which expressed the impossible. The Jewish Talmud speaks of the impossibility of an elephant passing through the eye of a needle. So it is impossible for one to enter God's kingdom who makes wealth his god.

These words of Jesus plunged the disciples into despair. Among themselves they said, "Who then can be saved?" (v. 26). Hearing their words Jesus looked upon them again. "With [*para,* alongside] men it is impossible, but not with [*para*] God: for with [*para*] God all things are possible" (v. 27). If a rich man will let Him, God can enable him to get a proper relation to both God and wealth.

Wuest makes a very helpful comment on the uses of *para*. "That is, take your stand beside man on the question of riches, and it is impossible to be saved. But, take your stand beside God on the matter, and the formerly impossible becomes possible."

The Question of Reward (10:28-31)

The failure of the rich young ruler turned on his refusal to forsake his wealth in order to commit himself to Jesus. This fact is reflected in Peter's statement to Jesus (v. 28).

Robertson says that Peter had had a difficult time keeping quiet up to this point. But finally he spoke. "Lo, we have left all, and have followed thee" (v. 28). "Have left" renders an aorist form of the verb meaning to send away or to give up. It means a once-for-all act. But "have followed" is a perfect tense of completeness. It means a past act which continues in the present and will continue in the future. So literally Peter said, "Lo, we gave up all things once and for all, and we have fully followed thee, we do so now, and will continue to do so."

What had they given up to follow Jesus? The four fishermen had given up their boats and nets. Matthew had forsaken his tax collector's position. Perhaps others had given up similar things. And while these were a far cry from the wealth and position of the rich ruler, still they also were all that they had. God does not count dollars; He weighs loyalty and love.

Now Peter did not mention reward. But it was implied in his statement. However, we may be sure that he was thinking of material not spiritual reward. In effect, he asked, "What reward will we receive?"

Jesus saw the implied reference to reward. This is evident from His answer given in verses 29-30. The best manuscripts omit "or wife" in verse 29. "Or father" is the only item in verse 29 which is not repeated in verse 30. Jesus said that for everything forsaken for His sake and the gospel's sake, they would receive an hundred-fold "now in this time." This most likely referred to the time then in existence.

Should we take Jesus literally in this? Hardly so. Certainly one would not receive a hundred *mothers.* This seems to be another strong oriental expression referring to spiritual blessings. As a Christian one enjoys a broader relationship to his fellow-Christians. And the spiritual rewards far exceed any material blessings enjoyed without Christ.

But note that Jesus added "with persecutions." "Now in this time," along with the blessings, they would endure persecution for Jesus' sake and that of the gospel. This was literally true. But like Paul they counted all things as loss that they might gain Christ.

Beyond this time "in the coming age" they would receive eternal life. This looks beyond the present to the *age* following the Lord's return. Of course, the Christian receives this quality of life here and now. But it is a life which endures in the age to come. It is a sad balance sheet which values earthly goods over the riches of Christ. Such a balance sheet was that of the rich young ruler. But those who follow Christ can leave the reward to Him. And he who does so shall not be disappointed.

However, Jesus added one final note. "But many that are first shall be last; and the last first" (v. 31). Literally, "But many shall be first last and the last first." This rather curious statement lends itself to several possible meanings, all of which may be true. The disciples wanted to be *first* in the kingdom of God. So this could mean that if one wishes to be first he must be willing to be last. He must be a menial slave to both God and men if he would be first in the kingdom. Furthermore, these words suggest that there will be many surprises in heaven. Many who think that they will be first will be last. And many who are content to be last will be first. Many whom the world judges to be first will be last in heaven. Contrariwise, many whom the world regards of no importance will be the most highly rewarded in heaven.

In the overall, Jesus was saying that such judgments belong to God. This does not mean that He will arbitrarily reward some more than others. He has set the standard of judgment. And eternity will reveal how each one has measured up to that standard. We are to serve God out of love and the joy of serving with no thought of reward. Our responsibility is to trust and serve. It is God's prerogative alone to reward. And the eternal God will do right.

Mark 10:32-45

The Contrast in Concern

Mark 10:32 clearly introduces the final phase of Jesus' ministry. Because for the first time the author mentions Him as going to Jerusalem. Previously he has mentioned people coming to Jesus from Jerusalem. With one exception (3:8) they have been those who opposed Him (3:22, 7:1).

As noted previously John's Gospel explains why Jerusalem was the center of their opposition. This city was the seat of the power of Judaism. The conflict between Jesus and the Jewish religious leaders began there and spread into Galilee. However, the battle had raged most fiercely in Jerusalem (cf. John 2:13ff.; 5:1ff.; 7—10). For the most part the struggle had been between Jesus and the Pharisees. But several weeks prior to this time He had brought down upon Himself the wrath of the Sadducees when He raised Lazarus from the dead (John 11). Since the Sadducees denied the resurrection, this was a direct challenge to them. And they promptly accepted the challenge (John 11:47ff.). So without question the matter would be brought to a head when Jesus again visited the city. In full awareness of the situation Jesus moved resolutely toward it.

The Rendezvous with Destiny (10:32-34)

"And they were in the way [road] going up to Jerusalem" (v. 32). The city was located near the highest point in the ridge which runs north and south between the Mediterranean Sea and the Jordan Valley. To approach it from any direction except the south one must go *up*. This is especially true when approaching it from the west. In a distance of less than twenty miles one goes from the Dead Sea (1,286 feet below sea level) to Jerusalem (about 2,500 feet above sea level).

As they journeyed Jesus was *going before (proagōn)* the Twelve. He was leading them. In all likelihood He customarily walked before them except when He was teaching them in the way. On this particular occasion one may see Jesus' eagerness to get to Jerusalem. As they followed Him the disciples "were amazed... were afraid" (v. 32). Both of these verbs are imperfect forms. They were constantly amazed and afraid. They were aware of danger in Judea (cf. John 11:7-16). And Jerusalem would be even worse. Jesus' eagerness, and perhaps His very countenance, amazed them; and knowing that He was walking into the very jaws of death (and taking them with Him) they were afraid.

At some point Jesus gathered the Twelve about Him to tell them clearly what awaited Him in Jerusalem. "Behold, we go up to Jerusalem; and the Son of man shall be delivered [betrayed] unto the chief priests [Sadducees], and unto the scribes [Pharisees]; and they shall condemn him to death, and shall deliver [hand over for execution] him to the Gentiles [Romans]: and they shall mock him, and shall scourge him, and shall spit upon him, and shall kill him; and the third day he shall rise again" (vv. 33-34). He had told them repeatedly that this was coming. Here He told it in the greatest of detail. Now it is at hand. They had not understood before, and they did not understand now (cf. Luke 18:34). They knew the danger, but they did not know the purpose of all this.

Jesus was in the throes of concern for lost men. But so captivated were the disciples by current Messianic expectations that they did not perceive. They were still concerned about personal position in the kingdom which they believed was soon to be established.

We are prone to judge these men for their spiritual density. But are we any better than they? And that after almost two thousand years of knowledge. If they sinned before the fact, we sin after the facts.

The Request of Selfish Ambition (10:35-41)

The complete failure of the Twelve to comprehend Jesus' words is clearly illustrated in this request. Because hard upon Jesus' expression of concern came theirs.

James and John came to Jesus asking Him to do for them whatever they wished (v. 35). They wanted His promise before they told Him of their desire. But Jesus asked them to be more specific (v. 36). So they said, "Grant unto us that we may sit, one on thy right hand, and the other on thy left hand, in thy glory" (v. 37). These were the positions of first and second power. Since James evidently was the elder, he apparently wanted the right side Matthew says that this request came from their mother. It seems that the two brothers made this request along with their mother. Since they did not understand Jesus' words about His death and resurrection, it is obvious that they were thinking about an earthly regal glory. At best, they thought of such a kingdom set up through His death and resurrection (cf. Acts 1:6).

Why should such a request come from this particular group? One interpreter suggests that they may have interpreted Jesus' rebuke of Peter at Caesarea Philippi (Mark 8:32-33) as meaning that he had lost favor with Jesus. And assuming that they regarded Peter somewhat as a leader among the Twelve, and one of the trio Peter, James, and John, they thought to replace him. But as interesting as this theory is, it does not fully explain their request.

May we not look for the answer in the persons involved? By comparing certain references (Matt. 27:56; Mark 15:40; John 19:25) it appears that the mother of Zebedee's children (James and John) was Salome, a sister of Mary, Jesus' mother. Assuming this to be true, then James and John were cousins of Jesus and Salome was His aunt. This could explain their boldness in assuming that they were entitled to special privilege. If Jesus was going to establish a kingdom, why not keep the reins of power within the family? Let the other disciples have lesser positions of power and glory, but reserve the chief places under Jesus for *Cousin James* and *Cousin John.*

To this request Jesus replied, "You do not know what you are asking for yourselves" (v. 38). The verb rendered "know" means a deep, perceptive knowledge. And "ask" translates a verb in the indirect middle (reflexive) voice. Their request was for themselves alone. But they were asking for more than they knew. So Jesus told them.

"Can ye drink of the cup that I drink of? and be baptized with the baptism that I am baptized with?" (v. 38). In the Greek text "I" with respect to both drink and being baptized is written out and so is emphatic. These refer to a particular cup and baptism. Both references deal with the suffering which awaited Jesus on the cross. "The cup" was the particular cup to which Jesus referred in Gethsemane, not death itself but that which His death involved. He was to become sin on behalf of men (cf. II Cor. 5:21). For this reason He was to be forsaken by both God and men.

The *baptism* was His being overwhelmed with calamity. This usage is common in the papyri. The word for "baptism" *(baptisma)* refers not to the act but to the meaning in baptism—death, burial, and resurrection.

Were James and John ready to do these things? They thought of power, privilege, and glory. Jesus spoke of suffering, rejection, and shame. Truly they asked for more than they knew. How little they knew is seen in their glib reply, "We are able" (v. 39). Are we not kin to them as we sing lightly, "Lord, we are able"?

Listen to Jesus' reply. "The cup which I am drinking ye shall drink, and with the baptism with which I am being baptized ye shall be baptized" (v. 39). How true, how true! James was the first of the Twelve to be martyred; he was beheaded by Herod Agrippa (Acts 12:2). John was exiled on Patmos. Tradition says that he died there from hard labor. But these were far more than they meant when they said, "We are able." At best this was an expression of moral courage, not of spiritual power and understanding.

But as for the positions of prestige and power that was another matter. Jesus said, "It is not mine to give, but to whom it has been prepared" (v. 40). This last verb is a perfect passive form. It is a preparation made by another than Jesus, made in the past, still stands, and will continue to stand. It has been prepared by the Father but will be distributed by the Son (Matt. 25:14ff.; II Tim. 4:8; Rev. 22:12). However, the bestowal will be in accord with terms set by the Father. These terms have no reference to selfish seeking or to greatness as the world judges greatness (cf. Mark 10:31). They will be on the basis of Christian character as evidenced in self-forgetful service.

Did the other ten disciples hear this exchange of the two with Jesus? Apparently it took place in a private interview (v. 35). But somehow the others heard about it. And doing so they were indignant (v. 41). This is the sense of the verb rendered "much displeased." Peter was a member of the inner circle along with the two brothers. He may well have been the most indignant of all. Knowing the rivalry which existed within the Twelve, this indignation can hardly be explained as resentment that such a request should be made in so delicate a spiritual moment. It was because such a request should be made at all. They were jealous because James and John had beaten them to the punch. For each of them desired these positions. We may be certain that Judas resented the request made by the two disciples. The fact that they began "to be indignant" (present infinitive) shows that this attitude was an abiding one. As Swete says, "It threatened the harmony and spiritual life of the Apostolate, and called for immediate correction."

The False and True Standards of Greatness (10:42-45)

Jesus proceeded to make this correction by pointing out conflicting standards of greatness.

He began by setting forth the pagan standard of the world. The

Gentiles, or pagans, exercise "lordship" (absolute rule) and "authority" (tyranny) over their subjects (v. 42). Their greatness is determined by the number of people who serve them.

But emphatically Jesus denied such a standard for Christian people. "But not so is it among you: but whosoever may will to be great among you shall be your menial slave [*diakonos,* cf. 9:35]; and whosoever may will to be first among you shall be a bondslave of all" (vv. 43-44). Christian greatness is determined by the number whom one serves.

This standard of greatness is perfectly revealed in Jesus. "For even the Son of man came not to be ministered unto [served menially], but to minister [to serve menially], and to give his life a ransom for many" (v. 45). He had so served throughout His public ministry. And soon He will give His life a ransom for all who will receive Him as Saviour.

So with sharp contrast this verse sets Jesus over against the Twelve. While He was preparing to die for men, they were contending for position. The one was concerned with saving men by giving Himself; the others were concerned with pomp and power which they hoped to receive for themselves. Nothing has hindered the fruit of Jesus' concern through the ages, even now, more than this false concern on the part of His people!

Mark 10:46-52

The Healing of Bartimaeus

It was probably at this point that Jesus and His company crossed the Jordan river into Judea. Because Mark mentions that "they came to Jericho" (v. 46). He was now in the area where He was under the power of the Roman governor Pontius Pilate and the Sanhedrin.

The Problem of Jericho (10:46a)

Jericho is located about five miles west of the Jordan River and about fifteen miles east of Jerusalem. It is one of the oldest inhabited sites in the world.

Mark 10:46, followed by Matthew, says that the event under consideration took place as Jesus went out of Jericho. Luke relates this incident and then has Jesus arriving in Jericho (18:35–19:1). Is there a conflict between the accounts? The truth is that both are correct. For there were two Jerichos, the old and the new. The older site of ancient Jericho is nearer to the Jordan River. Later Herod the Great had built the new, or Roman Jericho, some distance to the west. So this event occurred as Jesus was leaving old Jericho on His way to the Roman Jericho.

Because of its semi-tropical climate, due to its being so far below sea level, this was a favorite resort area. Its fertile surroundings made it the center of rich agriculture. This, together with its location on the main highway, made it a lucrative tax collection center (cf. Luke 19:1ff.). Barclay notes that many priests lived here when they were not taking their turn serving in the temple.

The Blind Beggar (10:46b-48)

As Jesus was leaving old Jericho accompanied by the Twelve and a large caravan of people, they came to a blind beggar sitting by the roadside (v. 46b). Mark and Luke mention only one beggar, but Matthew says that there were two. Evidently Mark, followed by Luke, concentrated on the one as being the more noticeable. Blindness was and is one of the great health problems of Palestine. It is a common sight even today to see blind people, both children and adults, begging for a subsistence. This beggar's name was Bartimaeus, the "son of Timaeus."

Though he was blind, he could hear. He heard the footsteps of the passing caravan. Doubtless there had been many such at this time. And from each Bartimaeus had asked for alms. But among the words of this particular caravan he caught the name "Jesus of Nazareth." Evidently he was aware of the healing miracles of Jesus. Therefore, "He began to cry out, and say, Jesus, thou son of David, have mercy on me" (v. 47).

The Greek text shows that he kept on crying out in a loud voice. The word rendered "have mercy" (aorist) asks that Jesus do it at once. Note the title "son of David." This was in Judea, David's land.

But as Bartimaeus kept on crying, those about Jesus "kept on rebuking" him that he should "become silent at once" (v. 48). It may be that Jesus was teaching, and they could not hear for the insistent crying of the beggar. A sad picture of selfish indulgence! But he only cried the more and louder. "Son of David, have mercy on me at once." This was his one chance, and he proposed to make the most of it.

The Compassionate Jesus (10:49-52)

The crowd might be indifferent to the man's need, but Jesus was not. For standing still He told those about Him to call the beggar. They did so, saying, "Be of good comfort [courage], rise; he calleth thee" (v. 49). The indifferent crowd responded to Jesus' compassion.

"And he, casting away his garment, rose, and came to Jesus" (v. 50). The aorist forms in the Greek text paint a vivid picture. "And the one quickly casting off his outer garment, leaping up immediately, came at once face to face with Jesus." In his eager haste he did not want to be hindered by this long outer cloak. And, though blind, he needed no guide. He followed the sound of Jesus' voice!

Jesus asked what he wanted Him to do. He knew, but He wanted the man to state his wish. Thus when it was granted, he would know of a certainty that it was Jesus' doing. Bartimaeus had forgotten all about alms. He had a greater need. So he said, "Lord, that I might receive my sight" (v. 51). "Lord" translates *Rabbouni,* "my master," a term of reverent respect. The verb rendered "receive sight" is *anablepō,* to see again. So he had at one time been able to see. What a pathetic plea! "That I might see again!" If so, he would no longer need to beg for alms.

In reply Jesus said, "Go thy way; thy faith hath made thee whole" (v. 52). "Hath made whole" is a perfect tense of the verb meaning to save, heal, or to rescue from danger. In this case the first two meanings certainly apply. And the perfect tense means that he was fully healed and saved.

Immediately he *saw again*. And the first sight to greet his eyes was that of the glory of God in the face of Jesus Christ. It is no wonder that "he kept on following [imperfect] him in the way" (v. 52).

V

The Approaching Climax

Mark 11:1-11

The Royal Entry

The arrival of Jesus in Bethany marked the beginning of the final phase of His public ministry. According to John's Gospel He came to Bethany perhaps on Friday afternoon prior to Palm Sunday (12:1). This was just before the Passover in A.D. 30. As previously noted this preceded the first visit to Jerusalem recorded by the Synoptic Gospels, although Luke tells of a previous visit to Bethany itself (10:38ff.). But John shows that Jesus had made previous visits to Jerusalem. Thus we may understand the strong opposition to Him in the city. However, in the previous visits recorded by John Jesus had come to Jerusalem without undue publicity. But on this occasion He made a public and formal challenge to the city and its people.

The Preparation for the Entry (11:1-6)

This entry shows evidence of careful preparation on the part of Jesus. Sometime during the period between Friday afternoon and Sunday morning He probably had arranged for a donkey to be left at a pre-arranged place. It seems that the owner himself did not know the exact purpose of the donkey.

Why this secrecy? Was it not due to Jesus' knowledge that Judas was even now near the brink of betrayal? Thus He guarded His movements to prevent Judas from knowing in advance His exact whereabouts at a given time. And besides the Jewish rulers had ordered that anyone seeing Jesus should report it to them in order that they might arrest Him (John 11:57).

Mark does not record Jesus' previous arrival in the area. He simply notes that He came to Bethphage and Bethany, two adjacent villages on the crest of the Mount of Olives near Jerusalem (v. 1). Since Bethphage (House of Figs) is mentioned first, it was probably the starting point for the entry.

From here Jesus sent two disciples to fetch the donkey. "Go your way into the village over against you," probably Bethany (House of Dates, v. 2) There they would find a colt "tied." Since donkeys usually ran loose, this would imply previous preparation. It was a donkey which had never before been ridden. If when they untied the donkey someone challenged them, they were to say, "The Lord hath need of him" (v. 3). At this word he would let them have the donkey. Was this a previously arranged sign?

At any rate they found the donkey "tied by the door without a place where two ways met" (v. 4). The italicized words render *epi tou amphodou,* "upon both ways." It probably means a winding street. As they loosed the donkey they were accosted. "What do ye, loosing the colt" (v. 5)? When the disciples gave the right reply they were permitted to take him (v. 6).

The Purpose of the Entry (11:7-10)

Seated on the donkey Jesus rode into Jerusalem (v. 7). As He went from Bethphage down the western slopes of the Mount of Olives. the Passover pilgrims caught the significance of the event. According to Jewish belief they expected the Messiah to present Himself at a Passover, effecting a deliverance of Israel comparable to her deliverance out of Egyptian bondage. And while their concept of deliverance was different from that of Jesus, it is evident that He used this occasion to present Himself officially to the Jewish nation.

But His purpose went beyond current expectations. Apparently He chose this season because it found Jerusalem and its environs overrun with Jews from both Palestine and beyond. Every Jewish male who was a Son of the Law, and living within twenty miles of Jerusalem, was required to attend this feast. Also Jews from everywhere were present. No matter where he lived every Jew hoped at least one time to attend the Passover feast in Jerusalem. So that many Jews of the Dispersion would be present.

About thirty years after this time a Roman governor took a census of the number of lambs slain at a Passover. The number was 250,000. And since one lamb was required for every ten people, this meant that approximately 2,500,000 Jews were present. So, in effect, Jesus presented Himself as the Messiah to world Jewry.

At the moment they saw Him as their King riding into the city. Therefore, in recognition of the event they began to spread their garments on the road before the donkey (v. 8). Others cut branches from trees for this purpose. They were making a royal path over which the King should ride.

The joyous shouts of these pilgrims attracted others from the city (v. 9). So Jesus found Himself preceded and followed by a shouting throng. They "kept on shouting" (imperfect), "Hosanna; Blessed is he that cometh in the name of the Lord" (v. 9). "Hosanna" means "O save!" "He that cometh" renders the words *ho erchomenos,* the Coming One, a technical title for *Messiah.*

It is evident, therefore, that they acclaimed Jesus as the Messiah. And as a King. For literally they cried, "Blessed the one coming a king of our father David!" (v. 10). Thus whatever may have happened in subsequent days, at the moment the populace hailed Jesus as their Messiah King.

It is customary to call this Jesus' Triumphal Entry. But was it? Such was the return to his capital city of a conquering king or general. He did so riding upon a white horse, symbolic of victory. Behind him walked captives in chains, perhaps a defeated king or general, to denote how thorough was his victory. As he did so the people shouted their praise, and the conquering hero threw coins to the people. Jesus' Triumphal Entry into His capital city, heaven, may more likely be seen in Ephesians 4:8ff.

However, Jesus' entry into Jerusalem was quite different. It happened *before* not after the battle (cf. crucifixion and resurrection). He rode upon a donkey as one coming in peace. This was customary for a king who in peace visited one of his subject cities. So this event may more aptly be called Jesus' Royal Entry. He came as a King of peace to present Himself to His subjects.

It is in this light that we may better understand Jesus' act on this Sunday. He challenged both Jerusalem, the Jews, and their religious leaders to receive Him as their Messiah King bringing peace. But, of course, the record shows that under the influence of their leaders both the city and people (world Jewry) rejected Him as such. It was a dramatic moment in history!

The Portrayal of Purpose (11:11)

Had Jesus been the kind of Messiah that the people expected, upon His arrival in Jerusalem He probably would have led a march against the Tower of Antonia. This was the garrison of Roman soldiers in the city. Instead He went directly into the temple (v. 11). This within itself indicated that His mission was spiritual, not military and political. His primary concern was not military bondage but spiritual bondage. It was from the latter that He came to redeem.

The term for "temple" is *hieron* which refers to the entire temple area with its complex of courts. The *naos* was the Holy of Holies into which only the high priest entered once annually. The various courts were those of the Gentiles, the women, of Israel, and of the priests. Since Jesus was not of the line of Levi, He never entered the Court of the Priests. In all likelihood the court entered this day was that of the Gentiles. And as He looked around His eyes fell upon the Bazaars of Annas (cf. v. 15).

At eventide Jesus, accompanied by the Twelve, left Jerusalem to return to Bethany. Knowing the evil designs of the Jewish leaders He avoided the city at night until He was ready to be arrested. Insofar as the record shows, the first night that He remained in or about Jerusalem He was taken by His enemies. He was not fearful of death. But he did not tempt God by taking unnecessary chances.

In all likelihood He spent His remaining nights in the home of Martha, Mary, and Lazarus. Swete holds that Sunday, Monday, and Tuesday nights before His passion were spent out under the open sky on the Mount of Olives. What about Wednesday night? But on what evidently was Tuesday night He definitely was in Bethany (14:3ff.). It is more natural to see all of these nights spent in Bethany. As Jesus moved within the shadow of the cross He would long for friendly companionship and understanding. Where better would He find these than in the home of His friends in Bethany?

Mark 11:12-26

The Judgments of Jesus

It was Monday morning of Passion week (v. 12). Jesus and the Twelve were returning from Bethany to Jerusalem. And "he was hungry." Note this element of our Lord's humanity. Matthew says that it was *prōi* (21:18). This would be in the fourth watch of the night before 6:00 A.M. This early hour would explain Jesus' hunger. He had left Bethany before breakfast.

The Fig Tree Cursed (11:13-14)

As Jesus walked along He saw a fig tree in the distance, "having leaves" (v. 13). The presence of leaves suggested that the tree was already bearing fruit. The later crop comes in August. Since this was the time of the Passover it was too early to expect figs to be ripe. However, this foliage gave promise of an early bearing. Perhaps the tree was in a protected place which enabled it to be ahead of the normal season.

But when Jesus came to the tree He found leaves but no figs. The tree gave promise but did not perform. So Jesus said, "No man eat fruit of thee hereafter for ever" (v. 14). Cynical minds see this as the angry reaction of one who had been disappointed at finding no breakfast. And the disciples evidently wondered at this. For they "were hearing" or "listening." Jesus offered no explanation at this time of His curse upon the tree. But His reason may be discerned by words spoken the next day (cf. vv. 20ff.).

The Cleansing of the Temple (11:15-19)

Jesus proceeded on to Jerusalem, and entered the temple (v. 15). Here He definitely was in the Court of Gentiles. For it was there that the "Bazaars of Annas" were located.

This term was given to the practice of selling sacrificial animals and birds and of exchanging foreign coins for Jewish money with which to pay the temple tax. It had begun as a service to the worshippers, but had degenerated into a system of profiteering. People coming from a distance, and especially from outside Palestine, found it difficult to bring their victims to sacrifice with them. Furthermore, the animal or bird had to be approved by a priest as being suitable for the purpose. One might bring such from afar and then find it unfit. So as a service, animals and birds were sold in the Court of the Gentiles.

Furthermore, every Son of the Law must pay the annual temple tax of a Jewish half-shekel (cf. Matt. 17:24ff.). Since Greek and Roman coins were not acceptable, money changing was also provided as a service. But an exchange fee was charged. This temple tax was collected in the villages and cities throughout Palestine prior to the Passover. But one might pay it at the temple instead. So this money changing was designed as a convenience for those who did so, and especially for Jews from outside Palestine.

The profits from these services were supposed to go into the temple treasury. But in time some of it found its way into the pockets of those who rendered the services. By the time of Jesus what had begun as a service to the worshippers had degenerated into a system of profiteering and misuse of funds. At the beginning of His ministry Jesus had cleansed the temple of such (John 2:14). But the money gougers had once again set up business. Some interpreters question the validity of John's account. But there is no valid reason why Jesus would not cleanse the temple twice.

So seeing the temple of God turned into an emporium Jesus "began to cast out them that sold and bought in the temple [note the two groups], and overthrew the tables of the moneychangers, and the seats of them that sold doves" (v. 15). John 2:15-16 notes that on that occasion He also drove out the animals and told the dove sellers to take out the cages of doves. Though the Synoptics do not mention these details, we may assume that this happened at the second cleansing also.

Furthermore, Jesus would not permit "that any man should carry any vessel through the temple" (v. 16). Only Mark has this item. The word rendered "vessel" could mean any implement, household utensil, or domestic gear. The people had made the temple area a short-cut between the city and the mount of Olives. Even though the temple authorities had prohibited it, the people ignored the order. Such a practice showed disrespect for the temple. Therefore, Jesus forbade it. This was a sacred place, not a footpath of convenience.

Having cleansed the temple Jesus then gave His Scriptural reason for doing so. Doubtless His action had attracted a crowd of people. And one may imagine that the victims of this so-called sacred extortion were pleased with it. So Jesus cited Isaiah 56:7 and Jeremiah 7:11. "My house shall be called of all nations the house of prayer. But ye have made it a den of thieves" (v. 17). A house of prayer for all nations, including Gentiles.

But a Gentile was permitted to enter only the Court of the Gentiles. For stone slabs were posted at each door leading from this court into that of the women. These slabs forbade Gentiles under the penalty of death to enter this inner court. One of these slabs was found in Jerusalem in 1871 by M. Clermont-Ganneau, and is now in the Museum of the Ancient Orient at Istanbul. A portion of a second slab has been discovered recently. The former slab is a limestone block about twenty-three inches high, thirty-four inches long, and fifteen inches thick. The inscribed letters are over one and one-half inches in height. And they read, "No foreigner may enter within the balustrade and enclosure around the Sanctuary. Whoever is caught will render himself liable to the death penalty which will inevitably follow" (cf. Acts 21:28f.).

In this light Jesus' words take on added meaning. Suppose that a Gentile seeking after Jehovah came to pray in His temple. Since he was permitted to enter only the Court of the Gentiles, what impression would he receive of Jehovah and His worship? He would be greeted by sounds which belonged in an oriental marketplace. Instead of voices rising in prayer he would hear the noise of animals, of bickering over prices, and of the clanking of coins. Rather than smelling the incense of prayer he would be stifled by the stench of animal filth. Instead of being drawn to Jehovah he would be driven from Him.

Furthermore, the sacred temple had been degraded into a den of robbers. This included the dishonest practices of the *Sons of Annas*. And tradition says that thieves and robbers were actually meeting in the temple area to plot their crimes! It is no wonder that Jesus revolted at such desecration of the temple of His Father.

But the Jewish leaders did not take this act of Jesus lightly. When the scribes (Pharisees) and chief priests (Sadducees) heard about it they set about to destroy Him (v. 18). Mark noted early in the Galilean ministry how the Pharisees and Herodians combined in their purpose to destroy Jesus (3:6). Matthew tells of the Sadducees joining forces with their arch-rivals, the Pharisees, in opposing Him (16:1). John tells of a firm resolve on the part of the Sanhedrin (Pharisees and Sadducees) to put Him to death (11:53, 57). But in 11:18 Mark for the first time records their combined venomous purpose.

The imperfect tenses make this verse live. "And the scribes and chief priests . . . kept on seeking how they might destroy him: for they kept on fearing him, because all the people kept on being astonished at his doctrine," or "teaching." His teaching was fresh and alive in contrast to the stale and powerless teaching of the Jewish rabbis. Jesus was the hero of the hour as shown by the demonstration on the previous day. The only answer to such was their nefarious plot. Even so, they would do their evil work furtively since they feared the people (cf. Luke 19:48).

In full knowledge of the rulers' purpose, Jesus again left Jerusalem to spend the night elsewhere, perhaps in Bethany (v. 19). He did not fear His enemies. But He knew the timetable and redemptive will of God. These could not be upset or defeated by the designs of wicked men.

The Cursing of the Fig Tree Explained (11:20-26)

It was now Tuesday morning. Here Mark also uses the word *prōi*. So before 6:00 A.M. Jesus and the Twelve were once again on their way back into the city. Coming to the place where Jesus had cursed the fig tree, they found that it was completely dried up—"from the roots" (v. 20). Matthew says that the tree withered immediately upon its being cursed (21:19). He then proceeded to relate the lesson concerning it. Is this a conflict between the two writers? Hardly so. Matthew writes topically and arranges his material thus. He completed the story before moving on to other matters. In fact we may render Matthew 21:19, "And immediately the fig tree began to wither away." Mark tells the story in its true sequence. The next day the tree which had begun to wither was now withered "from the roots."

Peter called attention to this fact (v. 21). Since the disciples had been wondering about the whole affair Jesus explained its meaning. "Keep on having faith in God," said He. This was the lesson which He desired to teach from the fate of the fruitless tree. But what is the meaning of this lesson?

The cursing of the fig tree was in effect an acted parable on Jesus' part. Interpreters generally agree that back of the event is a symbolic meaning. In Jesus' mind the tree was symbolic of the Jewish nation. It had promised so much, but had produced nothing in the redemptive purpose of God. Even then it had a great outward show of religion but no fruit of true godliness. For this reason it was withered away, dead "from the roots." This was due to its lack of faith in God and His redemptive purposes. Thus Jesus taught His disciples that if they were to escape a like fate they must keep on having faith in God to achieve His purpose through them and others like them. It is a message for Christ's people in every age, even for today.

Jesus proceeded to apply the lesson (v. 23). If they keep on having faith they shall see "this mountain" removed and "cast into the sea" or go into oblivion. Following Jesus' symbolic meaning "this mountain" probably refers to Mount Moriah on which stood the temple, or even the entire mountain upon which the city of Jerusalem was built. In either event the meaning is the same. "This mountain" stood for the power of Judaism with all of its implications. It was to be destroyed with the fall of the city in A.D. 70. Like the fruitless fig tree it will pass away. And as the disciples labored and prayed in faith they would see Christianity go forth to present God's redemptive purpose and work to a lost world.

Thus Jesus used the occasion to teach the Twelve a lesson in effectual prayer. Since faith is so vital in the achievement of spiritual ends, it follows that it is necessary in effective praying (v. 24). "What things soever ye desire, when ye pray, believe that ye receive them, and ye shall have them." Does this mean that you can get *anything* you want through prayer? Hardly so. The word rendered "desire" means "to ask" as in prayer. This is more than a selfish request. The asking must be in Jesus' name and in keeping with God's spiritual purpose. And one must ask believing that God will grant such. Such faith sees the fulfilment even before the asking.

That this promise is made apart from purely selfish desire is evident in verse 25. The disciples were constantly at odds with one another over selfish aims in God's kingdom. These things must be removed before they can claim the promise of answered prayer. God can forgive only those who are forgiving. And He promises to answer prayer which is devoid of all selfish ambition with respect to God's kingdom and work. Verse 26 does not appear in the best texts.

These things happened early in the morning of a day which promised to be unusually hard on Jesus. It was His last day of public ministry prior to Calvary.

Mark 11:27-33

The Challenge to Jesus' Authority

Following the discussion about the withered fig tree Jesus and the disciples went on to Jerusalem. And as was His custom He was walking in the temple area. There He found waiting for Him a deputation from the Sanhedrin: chief priests, scribes, and elders (v. 27). Their firm resolve to destroy Him was now taking place. In order to accomplish their purpose they must first break His hold on the people. So this was the opening volley of what Robertson calls "A Day of Controversy."

The Question of the Jewish Rulers (11:28)

"By what authority doest thou these things? and who gave thee this authority to do these things?" This was a double barreled question. What is the nature of Jesus' authority? And who gave it to Him?

They were within their rights in asking them. For they were the custodians of the temple. It was their authority to administer it. But on the previous day by cleansing the temple Jesus had presumed to exercise a greater authority. Hence their question as to its nature and source.

By their standards only God Himself, the Messiah, or a prophet possessed authority over the temple greater than theirs. They most certainly did not believe that He was God. Neither did they accept Him as the Messiah or as a prophet. So to them He had no authority to do what He did. Assuming that He had usurped this authority they demanded to know who had authorized Him to do so.

The Answer of Jesus (11:29-30)

Jesus was a master in debate. And as He often did, He answered His adversaries by asking them a question (v. 29). Thus He immediately put them on the defensive. If they would first answer His question then He would answer theirs. And then His question.

"The baptism of John, was it from heaven, or of men? answer me" (v. 30). Now Jesus did not mean that He received His authority from John the Baptist. Neither did He bother to answer directly their questions. Had He claimed deity or Messiahship, or even to being a prophet, they would not have believed Him. So rather than to enter into useless debate He simply posed this question to them.

It is obvious that in their unbelief they were thinking of some earthly source of His claimed authority. The nearest thing to such would be that He had been baptized by John. So assuming their own position for the sake of argument, He presented them with a problem.

The Dilemma of the Adversaries (11:31-33)

Jesus' question set them to reasoning among themselves. The imperfect form of the verb "reasoned" means that they kept on doing so. They must have had quite a conference on the side. And what did they reason? "If we shall say, From heaven; he will say, Why then did ye not believe him? But if we shall say, Of men; they feared the people: for all men counted John, that he was a prophet indeed" (vv. 31-32).

They were really caught on the sharp horns of a dilemma. Were it not so tragic it would be comical. It was like answering the question, "Tell me yes or no, have you stopped beating your wife?" They were trapped either way they answered.

So they gave the only answer which they could give and still escape the dilemma. "We cannot tell" (v. 33). They could have told what they really thought. But to do so would have strengthened Jesus' hold upon the people. It would have widened the gap between them and the populace. And it may well have brought bodily harm, even death, to them from mob violence.

Actually they said, "We do not really know" *(ouk oidamen)*. *Oidamen* is the first person plural of the verb *oida*. The verb to know by experience such as seeing or hearing was *ginōskō*. *Oida* means perceived experiential knowledge until it becomes a firm conviction of the soul. This soul-knowledge was expressed by *oida*.

So, in effect, they said that they had not really given the matter much thought. They presumed to sit in judgment upon Jesus when they had reached no conclusion about His forerunner. They had no conviction one way or another about John's baptism. In truth they sought refuge in agnosticism. When unbelieving men are confronted with the undeniable truth of the gospel, yet are unwilling to face the facts, they can always slink back into this cave of intellectual and spiritual darkness. But doing so does not change the facts. Even though they dwell in darkness the light still shines. It is lost only to them.

This is seen in Jesus' answer to His adversaries. "Neither do I tell you by what authority I do these things" (v. 33). Had He done so it would have been to no avail. For had He declared to them His true nature the bright light of divine revelation would only have blinded their eyes, which were adjusted only to the darkness of their unbelief.

The first skirmish of this day ended. And Jesus stood victor in the field.

Mark 12:1-12

The Parable of Condemnation

Having driven back this initial probing action of His enemies, Jesus launched a frontal attack against them. This He did in the form of a parable. Mark gives one, although he uses the plural "parables." Matthew precedes this parable with one about two sons (21:28ff.). It was designed to show that even publicans and harlots go into the kingdom before these religious leaders. All three Synoptic Gospels relate the parable of the wicked husbandmen.

The Target of the Parable (12:1a)

"And he began to speak unto them by parables." "Them" refers to this deputation from the Sanhedrin (cf. v. 27). So it was related to the Sanhedrin as a whole. But even more, since they were representatives of the Jewish people and the entire system of Judaism, the lesson was designed as a condemnation of the whole. Of course, this does not include those Jews who believed in Him.

In this light this parable marks the watershed of God's redemptive purpose as it relates to the human instrument of His will. For it pointed away from the old dispensation toward the new.

The Contents of the Parable (12:1b-11)

As one reads this parable he is reminded of Isaiah 5:1-7. In all likelihood the similarity was drawn with a purpose. One cannot fail to see its background as the rebellious nation of Israel (cf. Isa. 5:7).

A man planted a vineyard and provided every condition necessary for productive results (v. 12b). For protection he built a hedge-high fence about it and placed a watchtower in it. He provided a winevat for extracting the juice from the grapes. He left nothing to be desired. Then he rented it to husbandmen, "and went into a far country." This last clause is suggestive of the passing of time. He left the vineyard in their care, but naturally expected a return on his investment made possible by the faithful performance of the renters. It is hardly necessary to point out this parallel to God's providential care of Israel and His purposeful expectation from her.

In due course harvest time arrived (v. 2). So the owner sent a servant to claim his "fruit of the vineyard." But instead of giving the servant fruit, they beat or scourged him and sent him away empty-handed (v. 3). So the owner sent a similar *(allon)* servant (v. 4). They wounded him in the head, treated him shamefully, and also sent him away with no fruit ("casting stones" not in best manuscripts). Patiently the owner sent another *(allon)* whom they killed (v. 5). And then "many others." They beat some and slew others. Note the progression of violent rebellion. In a few brief words Jesus vividly portrayed Israel's attitude toward the prophets of God as they sought to bring her to honor her covenant relation with God in His redemptive purpose.

Despite this continued and progressively violent rebellion the owner persevered patiently in his efforts to get the husbandmen to honor their contract with him. He had one beloved son. So finally he sent him for the rent, saying, "They will reverence my son" (v. 6). The word rendered "reverence" means that they would regard him worthy to receive the rent. However, they recognized the son as heir to the vineyard (v. 7). By some crude reasoning they figured that by killing the heir they would inherit the vineyard. They failed to reckon with the father who was the present owner. Nevertheless, they killed the son (v. 8).

The meaning of the parable is clear. The owner of the vineyard is Jehovah. The vineyard corresponds to Israel as the covenant people in God's redemptive purpose in history. In Isaiah 5:7 the vineyard was identified as Israel and Judah, both of which composed the Israelite people. However, in the deepest sense it was not regarded as a political entity but as a covenant people. It would, therefore, refer specifically to the true or spiritual Israel within the corporate people. The husbandmen suggest the composite leaders of Israel through the succeeding generations. The fruit would be the spiritual harvest which God expected from His covenant people. The servants would represent the long line of prophets sent by Jehovah to call Israel to fulfil her covenant with Jehovah. And the beloved son corresponds to Jesus Himself.

Now the picture unfolds. Following her redemption from Egyptian bondage Israel entered into a covenant of service with Jehovah (Exod. 19:4-8). She was to be a priest-nation to bring other nations to Jehovah. It was a covenant which imposed conditions upon Israel. Note the "if" and "then" in Exodus 19:5. Until Israel fulfilled the conditions Jehovah was not bound by the covenant. The history of Israel was one of repeated failure on the part of that people with respect to the covenant. Prophet after prophet was sent to call her to honor this covenant. In turn, some were mistreated and others killed. Finally, Jehovah promised a new covenant with the true Israel, the faithful remnant within the national Israel (Jer. 31:31ff.; Heb. 8). As a last resort God sent His beloved and only Son. But now the nation as a whole led by their leaders were about to reject and kill Him.

It was in this light that Jesus asked, "What shall therefore the Lord [owner] of the vineyard do?" (v. 9). Matthew puts the answer in the mouths of the Jewish leaders (21:41). Mark reports Jesus as answering His own question. "He will come and destroy the husbandmen, and will give the vineyard unto others" (v. 9). Probably the Jewish rulers gave the answer as reported by Matthew, and then Jesus avowed it in His own words. At any rate the meaning is clear. As Jesus said in Matthew 21:43, "The kingdom of God shall be taken from you, and given to a nation bringing forth the fruits thereof."

This marked a promised end to the place of the Jewish nation as such in God's redemptive purpose. Jesus cited Psalm 118:22-23 as the Scriptural basis of this. "The stone which the builders rejected is become the head of the corner: this was the Lord's doing, and it is marvellous in our eyes" (vv. 10-11).

In order to get the full picture one should read Exodus 19:4-8; Mark 12:1-11; Matthew 21:33-45; I Peter 2:1-10. Note how Peter combines the language of the first three passages to show that the Christian people are the true Israel of God in proclaiming His redemptive purpose and work to a lost world. God's purpose will not fail. But a given segment of those who profess to follow Him may lose its opportunity to be used in that purpose.

The Reaction to the Parable (12:12)

It was clear to the Jewish leaders that Jesus had spoken this parable against them. However, that knowledge only drove them deeper into their purpose to kill Him. "They kept on seeking to seize him, but feared the people." They feared the crowd more than they feared God.

For the moment they had failed in their purpose to discount Jesus before the populace. So "they left him, and went their way" —still the way of rebellion against God and of venomous purpose toward His beloved Son.

Mark 12:13-40

The Battle of Wits

Evidently the deputation reported back to the Sanhedrin. For soon various groups were sent one by one to try their own hand against Jesus. Still trying to destroy the people's faith in Him they entered into a battle of wits. But before the day's end they were to learn that they marched into the fray half-armed.

The Question of Taxes (12:13-17)

The first group to challenge Jesus was composed of Pharisees and Herodians (v. 13). Already Mark has shown this coalition against Jesus (3:6).

On the matter of taxes no two groups could have been farther apart. The Pharisees were opposed to any kind of rule other than a theocracy through the Messiah. Thus they were against any kind of political taxes paid to a pagan foreigner, including the Herods. They were a highly nationalistic group. On the other hand, the Herodians were opposed to Roman rule. Herod the Great had, under the Romans, ruled all of Palestine. But at his death his kingdom had been divided among some of his sons. Archelaus ruled over Judea. But he had been deposed in favor of a Roman procurator. The Herodians longed for the restoration of the House of Herod. It is possible that they favored paying taxes to Rome as a means to courting favor which might enable them to achieve their purpose. Or they may have shared the Pharisees' aversion to all foreign taxes. At any rate these two groups buried their differences in their common cause against Jesus.

Note the hypocrisy in their approach. They despised Jesus, yet they began by complimenting Him (v. 14). "Teacher, we are convinced that thou art true, and carest for no man [He would tell the truth regardless of what others thought]: for thou regardest not the person of men, but teachest the way of God in truth" (v. 14). The word rendered "know" (convinced) is *oidamen* (cf. 11:33). They claimed to have studied all the evidence about Jesus and were convinced that He was genuine, that He would not lie. This statement is filled with truth, yet truth which they denied. It was designed to throw Jesus off guard. Their whole purpose was to trap Him in His reply. So having complimented Jesus they put their question.

"Is it lawful to give tribute to Caesar, or not? Shall we give, or shall we not give?" (vv. 14-15). The word "tribute" renders the word *kēnson*. It might refer to any tax, but especially to a poll-tax. Barclay points out that a poll-tax was levied on all men from fourteen to sixty-five and on all women from twelve to sixty-five. This tax was one *denarius*. This was a tax paid to the Emperor simply for the privilege of living. It may well be that this was the tax in mind, since it would have been resented more than any other.

This looked like a sure trap for Jesus. "Shall we give or not give?" Either way He answered He was in trouble; so they thought. If He said, "Give," the Jewish people would regard Him as a traitor. If He said, "Not give," they could charge Him with sedition. Two things more than any others the Romans demanded: to keep the peace and to pay taxes.

But underneath all of this there was an even more subtle trap. Jesus claimed to be the Messiah with a kingdom of His own. And according to Jewish belief the Messiah would not pay taxes to any other ruler. So to countenance taxes to Caesar would be tantamount to a denial of His Messiahship. How could He possibly avoid this booby trap? But avoid it He did.

Knowing their real purpose He said, "Bring me a penny, that I may see it" (v. 15). "Penny" renders *dēnarion* the very coin used in paying this tax. It was the coin of the pagan empire. Whether Jesus had such a coin on His person we cannot say. Probably not. But His purpose in asking them for one went beyond that question. The fact that they used such a coin was evidence that they were subjects of Rome.

Holding the coin which one had given Him He asked, "Whose is this image and superscription? And they said unto him, Caesar's" (v. 16). The image was that of Tiberius Caesar. On one side of this coin was his image. Around the coin were the words "Of Tiberius Caesar, the divine Augustus, son of Augustus." On the reverse side were the words "Pontifex Maximus" or "the high priest" of the Roman empire. So the questioners could not deny that this was Caesar's, a symbol of his power and ownership.

Then Jesus gave His answer. "Render to Caesar the things that are Caesar's, and to God the things that are God's" (v. 17).

Never did anyone declare a greater principle with respect to man's duty. As a citizen of an earthly nation one owes it certain political obligations. But the Christian also is a citizen of God's kingdom. And he owes spiritual obligations to Him. Where there is a conflict between the two obligations his prior duty is to God.

But in the ordinary course of affairs a good Christian must also be a good citizen. The Christian's prior loyalty to God does not mean that he should defy laws with which he does not agree, except where unjust laws seek to deny him his direct relation to God. Otherwise one should be willing to endure injustice rather than to bring shame upon the name of Christ. Unjust laws may be changed through legal processes. But so long as they are laws, where they do not affect one's relation to God, they should be obeyed. Government is ordained of God (Rom. 13:1ff.). Only in utterly extreme cases is revolution justified. And that by a composite people, not merely by small defiant groups within a society. We may be reasonably certain that Jesus did not agree with every law imposed by the Roman empire. But there is no record that He ever disobeyed one of them. He suffered injustice as He rendered to Caesar the things which belonged to Caesar. It was not Caesar's right to come between Him and His heavenly Father. He suffered death rather than to deny the will of God.

This maxim by Jesus is the foundation stone of the separation between Church and State. And while men still debate the various facets of this grand principle, one thing is quite clear. While Church and State do have certain relationships neither organically should seek to control or invade the realm of the other. In their distinctive spheres they are to respect one another. When each does this, the result is most wholesome indeed.

The Pharisees and Herodians had no answer to Jesus' words. They simply marvelled and went away.

The Question about the Resurrection (12:18-27)

The Sadducees were the next to try their hand against Jesus (v. 18). They held that only the Pentateuch, the five books of Moses, was genuine Scripture. Since, according to them, this body of Scripture did not teach the resurrection of the dead they denied the possibility of such. Perhaps the question which they put to Jesus was one with which they delighted to baffle the Pharisees who did believe in the resurrection.

"Master [teacher], Moses wrote unto us, If a man's brother die, and leave his wife behind him, and leave no children, that his brother should take his wife, and raise up children unto his brother" (v. 19; cf. Gen. 38:8). This law is found in Deuteronomy 25:5-6. Then they posed a situation in which a man had six brothers (vv. 20-22). In succession each brother married her; each died without having an heir. Finally, the woman died. And then the puzzling question. "In the resurrection therefore, when she shall rise [at this point they must have had a smirking smile], whose wife shall she be to them? for the seven had her to wife" (v. 23). No one had been able to answer their question, so they assumed that Jesus would fail also.

But hear His reply. "Do ye not therefore err, because ye know not [*ou*] the scriptures, neither the power of God?" (v. 24). In Greek the negative *ou* in a question invites an affirmative answer. This was a one-two punch. They were supposed to be experts in the Pentateuch. Yet they did not really understand it. The word for "know" is a form of *oida* (cf. 11:33; 12:14). They had read it but had not perceived its meaning. And they who posed as God's representatives did not really know *(oida)* His power. Then Jesus expounded these in reverse order.

First, the Sadducees did not reckon with God's power to produce a heavenly order different from the earthly one (v. 25). This was also a weakness of the Pharisees, which explains their inability to answer the riddle of their theological foes. Both thought of heavenly relations as corresponding to those of earth. (Do we not also do the same?) They thought of the marriage relationship of earth as continuing in heaven. But Jesus said that in heaven "they neither marry, nor are given in marriage" (v. 25).

Many years ago I conducted a funeral. The following Sunday she asked me if she would be her husband's wife in heaven. Before I could answer she added, "If not, then I don't want to go to heaven." Not wanting to dim her desire for heaven I simply replied, "Well, we will know one another in heaven." That seemed to satisfy her. Six months later she re-married. And she never raised the question again! Happily for her, in heaven they neither marry nor are given in marriage.

No, in heaven the relationship will be much sweeter. We shall all be children of God and sons and daughters with our elder Brother.

"But are as the angels which are in heaven" (v. 25). This does not mean that we shall be angels. We shall be more than angels. Angels are the servants of God and of His children which children we are. Wuest points out that angels are created beings. There are no more or no less angels than were originally created. Angels do not procreate themselves. It is in this latter sense that we shall be as angels. No marriage and no procreation.

Second, the Sadducees did not understand the teachings of their Scriptures. They denied the resurrection on the basis of their understanding that the Pentateuch did not teach it. But Jesus reminded them that at the burning bush God said, "I am the God of Abraham, and the God of Isaac, and the God of Jacob" (v. 26; Exod. 3:15-16). God spoke of the three patriarchs as living, even though in earthly terms they had been dead for hundreds of years. So the Pentateuch did teach life after death; God "is not the God of the dead, but of the living" (v. 27). The Sadducees got a lesson in exegesis from the master Exegete!

Luke reports that one of the scribes, a Pharisee, complimented Jesus for His reply (20:39). We may be certain that all the Pharisees were glad to see the sophisticated Sadducees put in their place, even by Jesus.

The Question as to the Greatest Commandment (12:28-34)

It was now the Pharisees' turn again. A scribe who was an expert in the Law stepped forward. He was evidently the one mentioned by Luke. His question was, "Which is the first commandment of all?" (v. 28). That is, first in rank and importance. He did not ask as to the first commandment in the Decalogue. He wanted to know "of what sort" *(poia)* or what class is the commandment of priority. Vincent points out that the scribes had devised a rather elaborate system of grading the commandments. They held that "there were 248 affirmative precepts, as many as the members of the human body; and 365 negative precepts, as many as the days in the year, the total being 613, the number of letters in the Decalogue." Lightfoot, on the other hand, points out the Jewish distinction between ritual and ethical, or positive and moral. Greater value by some was given to the positive such as circumcision, Sabbath-keeping, and the rules regarding phylacteries. Others placed the greater value on the ethical, such as loving one's neighbor. This scribe evidently belonged to this latter group.

But Jesus cut across all of this to come to the heart of the matter. He began by quoting the *Shema* (Hebrew "hear"). "Hear, O Israel; The Lord [Jehovah] our God is one Lord; and thou shalt love the Lord thy God with all thy heart, and with all thy soul, and with all thy mind, and with all thy strength: this is the first commandment" (v. 30; cf. Deut. 6:4f.). And then He added, "And the second is like namely this, Thou shalt love thy neighbour as thyself" (v. 31; cf. Lev. 19:18). "There is none other commandment greater than these" (v. 31). Matthew records Jesus as saying, "On these two commandments hang all the law and the prophets" (27:40).

This was an accepted Jewish teaching. In the Decalogue the first four commandments deal with man's relation to God; the last six deal with man's relation to other men. So the Jews used the above verses to summarize them. Hillel was asked by a proselyte to teach him all of the law while he stood on one leg. He replied, "What thou hatest for thyself, do not to thy neighbour. This is the whole law, the rest is commentary. Go and learn."

The scribe complimented Jesus for His answer, adding his own comments regarding two laws (vv. 32-33). In response Jesus replied, "Thou art not far from the kingdom of God" (v. 34). Not far from it, but not yet in it.

Jesus came through this battle of wits unscathed. He had defeated His opponents at every turn. And they were aware of the fact. For "no man after that durst ask him any question" (v. 34). They pulled back to lick their wounds. But they were not through with Jesus. The only answer to an unanswerable argument is violence. And even then they were plotting to use it.

The Question about the Son of David (12:35-37)

This battle of wits took place in the temple courts, most likely in the Court of the Gentiles. Now that the adversaries of Jesus had called off their attack, He took the offensive. "How say the scribes that Christ is the son of David?" (v. 35). This was not an idle question. It was true that the Christ was a descendant of David. This battle of wits had begun with the Sanhedrin's challenge to Jesus' authority. Essentially this was related to His person as the Messiah. So Jesus brought that issue back into the picture.

Though the Christ is the son of David, David himself, writing under the inspiration of the Holy Spirit, had said, "The Lord said unto my Lord, Sit thou on my right hand, till I make thine enemies thy footstool" (v. 36; cf. Ps. 110:1). The word rendered "Lord" is *kurios,* which was used in the Septuagint to translate the Hebrew word for *Jehovah.* This was the unique name for the true God. So, in effect, David had said that the Messiah was his Lord or Jehovah. How then could He be both Jehovah and also David's son (v. 37)?

David was human, and so his son would be human. Still as the Messiah He was also deity. And David had declared Him as such under the guidance of the Holy Spirit. Of interest is the fact that in His statement Jesus referred to the Trinity: Father, Son, Holy Spirit. So the Old Testament teaches this doctrine.

But His primary thought was the dual nature of the Messiah as both deity and humanity. The Jewish rulers had missed this teaching of David. So they were unprepared to accept Jesus as the divine-human Christ (cf. John 5:18; 10:33). Thus Jesus brought into focus the conflict which had raged on His previous visits to Jerusalem. Though the rulers refused to believe this, Jesus showed them that the Old Testament Scriptures taught it. Thus He faced His foes with the fact of His incarnation.

By His perceptive interpretation of the Scriptures Jesus had shown how shallow was the understanding on the part of these professed experts in them. "And the common people [the much multitude] heard him gladly" (v. 37). They delighted in His fresh understanding of the Scriptures. And they were overjoyed in His demonstrated mastery over the Jewish rulers. These had utterly failed to destroy His influence with the multitudes. His hold on them was greater than ever.

The Attack upon the Scribes (Pharisees) (12:38-40)

Therefore Jesus turned on these hypocrites. Matthew 23 gives an extended account of this.[1] But Mark tells enough to see how Jesus utterly condemned them. As one reads the Gospel accounts he senses a growing breach between Him and the Pharisees. It is now evident that they will never accept Jesus as the Christ. And their opposition was the chief obstacle which kept the people as a whole from accepting Him. Therefore, He utterly condemns them and exposes them for what they are. His words are all the more terrible since they come from one who is the very essence of love, mercy, and grace.

"Beware of the scribes, which love to go in long robes, and love salutations in the marketplaces" (v. 38). Long robes were symbols of regal and scholarly splendor. It enhanced their ego to be saluted as "rabbi" in the marketplaces. They loved the "chief seats" in the synagogues (v. 39). These were front seats or even seats on the platform. They also craved the chief places or reclining couches at banquets. They loved to sit at the speaker's table, and especially next to the principal speaker. Yet all the while they devoured widows' houses (v. 40). Under the pretense of leading widows to give their houses to the temple, they gained control of them for their own profit. All the while they made long prayers as a pretense at piety. These prayers were often given in the homes of their victims to convince them of their good faith, and as a possible blessing upon those who so contributed their estates to the temple.

For this reason they shall receive the greater condemnation.

---

[1] See Hobbs, *An Exposition of the Gospel of Matthew*, pp. 314ff.

Greater than that of openly dishonest men. For they do it in the name of religion.

The Jewish rulers had planned to show Jesus to be a sham. But He had revealed their avarice and emptiness instead.

Mark 12:41-44

The Calm after the Storm

The day of controversy was over. The enemies of Jesus had run for cover in the face of His condemnation of them. Evidently the crowds had departed in the calm after the excitement. The Twelve apparently had wandered away though remaining nearby. Jesus was alone in the Court of the Women. This court would provide greater privacy as Jesus rested from the ordeal.

The Lord of the Treasury (12:41a)

"And Jesus sat over against the treasury, and beheld how the people cast money into the treasury."

In the court of the women there were thirteen receptacles called the "treasury." They were also called "Trumpets" because of their shape. This word "treasury" translates a compound word meaning a safe place in which gifts may be deposited. Each "trumpet" was designated to receive gifts for specific purposes.

Jesus was watching the people as they cast in their gifts. This is a poetic picture. The Lord of the treasury is concerned about the *treasure,* not so much the amount as the spirit in which it is given. This is evident as the story unveils.

The Givers and the Gifts (12:41b-42)

As Jesus watched He saw "many that were rich cast in much" (v. 41b). The word "cast" renders an imperfect verb form. They "were casting." This pictures a procession of rich people giving large gifts. In the Greek text there is a play on words. *Kai polloi plousioi eballon polla.* Many wealthy ones were casting in much money. The implication is that they had much left after they gave.

"And there came a certain poor widow, and she threw in two mites, which make a farthing" (v. 42). The word "and" at the beginning of this verse may well be rendered "but." It expresses contrast between the rich givers and this poor widow.

The word for "poor" is *ptōchos.* It means a pauper. In describing her Luke uses this word, but also the word meaning one who works for a living (21:1-4). Despite what she earned it was insufficient for her needs. So she was in abject poverty.

Her material poverty is seen in her gift. It was two *lepta.* A *leptos* was the smallest of thin brass coins valued at about one-eighth of a cent. She gave one-fourth of a cent. A Rabbinic rule prohibited a smaller gift. However, Bruce points out that she had two coins. She might have given only one of them. So her gift was a generous one.

The Value of the Gift (12:43-44)

Jesus made no mention of the larger gifts of the rich. But calling His disciples to Him, He said, "This poor widow hath cast more in, than all they which have cast into the treasury" (v. 43). It was not more in monetary value. But it was more in love and sacrifice. Jesus measures our gifts only on this basis. He does not count the coins but weighs the spiritual power behind the gift. He measures our gifts not by what we give, but by what we have left over after we give.

"For all they did cast in of their abundance; but she of her want [poverty] did cast in all that she had, even all her living," or "the whole of her life" (v. 44). She probably went hungry that night because of her gift. But the rich made no sacrifice in giving. One should not claim to have given the *widow's mite* until he has given all that he has.

This was a beautiful ending to a day of storm. It showed that despite the hypocrisy of the Jewish leaders, there were some souls who loved the Lord completely, and their neighbors as themselves. This is the last recorded visit of Jesus to the temple area except His being brought there to appear on trial before the Sanhedrin. This poor widow's gift was quite a contrast to the emptiness of spirit which the Jewish temple had come to represent.

Her act was as the setting of a blazing sun in a clear sky after a day of storm. And we may hope that such a sun sent its westering rays across the slopes of Olivet as Jesus wended His way from the city of antagonism toward Bethany, the village of His friends.

Mark 13:1-37

The Olivet Discourse

Matthew, save one verse, closes his account of the controversy in Jerusalem with the words, "Behold, your house is left unto you." "Desolate" not in the best texts. They had rejected Jesus, and so He rejected them (23:38). It is this statement which perhaps promoted the conversation between Jesus and one of His disciples as they were leaving the temple. Since Mark alone reports the exact words of this disciple, it may well be that Peter was the one. It certainly fits his nature.

Not only the Jewish leaders but the disciples had been shocked by Jesus' words about the "house" being left unto them. There may have been a stunned silence within the group as they walked along. Perhaps Peter thought that someone should say something. So he said, "Master, see what manner of stones and what buildings are here!" (v. 1). The temple area was composed of many buildings, colonnades, and enclosures. And it was built out of massive stones. At present this area is the site of a Mohammedan mosque. But since Israel's victory in the brief war of June 1967, there is some talk about possible archaeological excavations there. If so, some of these ancient ruins may be brought to light. But even now one may see some of the massive stones in the ancient walls. They measure from twenty to forty feet long and weigh approximately one hundred tons.

One can learn something of the splendor of this temple from Josephus. He speaks of the sun shining on the eastern side of the temple which was covered with plates of gold. And its marble structure as appearing "like a mountain covered with snow." This temple was the pride of every Jewish heart. Herod the Great began building it in 20-19 B.C. In Jesus' day it was still under construction (John 2:20), and was not finished until A.D. 64, just six years before its destruction by the Romans in A.D. 70. One can understand the disciples' concern over Jesus' words.

In reply Jesus admitted that it was a great structure indeed. But He added, "There shall not be left one stone upon another, that shall not be thrown down" (v. 2). This prophecy was fulfilled literally within forty years.

From the temple area Jesus and His little band left Jerusalem, crossed the Brook Kidron, and began their ascent up the western slopes of the Mount of Olives. Somewhere on its sides overlooking the city and its temple area, they probably stopped to rest. It was then that Peter, James, John and Andrew came privately to Jesus with a question (v. 3). In response Jesus spoke to the disciples what is called His "Olivet Discourse."[1]

The Question of the Disciples (13:4)

Actually the question is two-fold. Matthew reports it as threefold (24:3). But the substance is present in Mark. "Tell us, when shall these things be? and what shall be the sign when all these things shall be fulfilled?"

Quite obviously the former part of the question relates to the destruction of Jerusalem. The latter part seems to look beyond that event to the consummation of the age, involving Jesus' second coming. Matthew closes his account of the controversies in the temple with the words "Ye shall not see me henceforth, till ye shall say, Blessed is he that cometh in the name of the Lord" (23:39). This statement pointed to a time in the future, even beyond the destruction of Jerusalem. So the disciples asked literally, "And what the sign when these things, all of them, are about to be consummated?" As we proceed through this chapter we shall see that Jesus deals with first one and then the other of these questions. At times He seems to have both in mind, with each being distinguished perhaps with some inflection or gesture. But it is possible to separate them through careful analysis.

The Warning against False Signs (13:5-8)

Before answering the distinct questions Jesus dealt with some preliminary matters. One of these was that the Christians should not be misled by false signs of His second coming. "Take heed [beware] lest any man deceive you" or "lead you astray" (v. 5). The word rendered "deceive" is *planaō*. Our word "planet" comes from this verb. The ancients thought of the planets as wandering aimlessly in space. Hence the idea of leading astray. Such a warning is needed today even as it was timely then. It is amazing how easily one may gather a following simply by claiming to have *inside information* with respect to the second coming of Christ.

The former warning had to do with false Christs (v. 6). Many would appear in the name of Jesus (falsely, of course) claiming to be the Christ. Palestine was plagued with such in the years just

---

1 See Hobbs, *An Exposition of the Gospel of Matthew*, pp. 332ff.; *An Exposition of the Gospel of Luke*, pp. 292ff.

prior to the Jewish War of A.D. 66-70. Indeed, they were one of the prinicipal factors which caused it. Through the centuries such pretenders have appeared, even in our time; and they have led many astray.

These are not to be confused with the Antichrist or one against Christ. They are pseudo-Christs or individuals who falsely claim to be the Christ. For instance, someone simply announces that he is the Christ. Such is not the Christ. The next time that men shall see the Christ it will be in a manner far different from this (vv. 26f.).

The latter warning had to do with disturbances in society and in nature. "Wars and rumors of wars" (v. 7). Hearing of these things should not trouble the Christian as a sign of the end of the age. "Be not ye troubled" should read, "Stop being troubled." They were already in a state of unrest about these. Vincent notes that three Roman emperors threatened war against the Jews: Caligula, Claudius, and Nero. None of these ever really materialized. These are a part of sinful history (v. 8a). So long as there are unregenerated men so long will we have wars and rumors of wars. We talk about a just and *lasting* peace. The Bible never promises such in this age. It is interesting to note that when wars rage, there are those who see this as a sign of the second coming of Christ. But Jesus said that in such conditions "not yet is the end" or the consummation of the age.

"Earthquakes . . . famines. "And troubles" is not in the best texts. Again Vincent points out that between this time (A.D. 30) and the fall of Jerusalem (A.D. 70) there were earthquakes in Crete (A.D. 46 or 47), Rome (A.D. 51), Apamaia in Phrygia (A.D. 60), and Campania (A.D. 63). Four famines came during the reign of Claudius (A.D. 41-54). One of these was in Judea (A.D. 44; cf. Acts 11:28). Such events are often mistakenly seen as signs of the end of time. But Jesus' warning against being led astray applies here also.

These things, says Jesus, are a beginning of anguish, or "travail." This word "travail" means "birthpangs." The Jews used this term to express the sufferings which were to come prior to the coming of the Messiah. Broadus in his *Commentary on Matthew* discusses this statement (24:8). "But does not the expression mean that in the preparation for the complete reign of the Messiah, conflict is unavoidable, not simply individual and domestic variance, but conflict of the races and nations as afterward depicted in the visions of John on Patmos?"

However, in view of Jesus' purpose at this point another idea presents itself. He doubtless foresaw the events mentioned by Vincent. These came prior to the destruction of Jerusalem. In this section Jesus was warning that His disciples should not interpret these events as signs of His return. Rather they are the beginning of the anguish which would be culminated in the fall of Jerusalem, one of the matters involved in the twofold question which Jesus was answering. And what applied in that period is of timeless import. Cataclysmic events in society and nature are not to be interpreted in terms of the Lord's return.

The Warning about Persecution (13:9-13)

That events of that period of history were primary in Jesus' thinking at this point may be seen in these verses. This beginning of anguish would also relate to the Christians personally as they strived to be true to Christ and His cause.

"But take heed to yourselves" (v. 9). "But" is adversative, focusing attention upon themselves rather than upon world events. "Yourselves" is emphatic. The Jewish nation will have trouble in the throes of war and rumors of war. The world generally will be afflicted by earthquakes and famines. But the Christians will also be in anguish. So Jesus said, "Look out to yourselves!" The persecutions described seem to relate to the period prior to the fall of Jerusalem.

They will be persecuted by the Jews (v. 9a). This is seen in their being delivered up to "councils" (Sanhedrin) and "synagogues." Furthermore, they will be persecuted by pagans (rulers and kings). All of this will be endured for Jesus' sake and as a witness to those who persecute the Christians.

"And the gospel must first be published among all nations" (v. 10). Matthew reports Jesus as saying that then, and only then, shall the end come (24:-4). So the only certain sign which Jesus gave as to His second coming was that prior to it the gospel must be preached to all nations as a testimony to them. Jesus' primary reference to His return had to do with *condition.* The *time* is when the *condition* obtains. Our task is to help create the condition and to leave the time in the mind of God.

When these Christians are led before the various constituted authorities, they are not to premeditate as to what to say in their defense (v. 11). That defense will be given to them by the Holy Spirit. This promise applied primarily to this particular period in Christian history. The forms of Christian doctrine had not yet been perfected. So the Holy Spirit would give them the words to speak. This truth may be seen in various events of persecution.

Note Peter and John (Acts 4:7ff.), Stephen (Acts 7), and Paul (Acts 24:10–26:36). This most certainly is not a promise given to lazy preachers who enter the pulpit unprepared. It has been my experience that when I do this my mouth is *filled with noise and hot air!*

During this time of persecution there will be treachery even within the family circle (v. 12). Brother will betray brother, fathers their sons, and children their parents. These conditions actually existed. And the Christians will endure the widespread hatred of men (v. 13). During Roman persecutions they were branded as enemies of the empire, even of the human race.

"But he that shall endure unto the end, the same shall be saved" (v. 13). The word "endure" renders the verb *hupomenō*. It was a military term meaning to take all that the enemy can throw against you yet still possess reserve strength to countercharge to victory. The verb rendered "saved" may mean spiritual salvation. But it also means to rescue from danger, to heal, or to solve a problem. The context must decide. Initial spiritual salvation is a finished fact for the Christian, by grace, not by one's works. So that does not appear to be the sense here. In the light of the persecution theme this could mean that those who exercised patient endurance would experience the full purpose of their being as Christian witnesses.

Indeed, *salvation* is used in the New Testament to refer to three spiritual experiences: regeneration, sanctification, and glorification. The very second that one is regenerated he is sanctified, set apart for the service of God. He will be glorified in heaven: resurrection of the body and the sum total of rewards and glory for faithful service rendered. Thus the Christian who is faithful to Christ in the state of sanctification will be fully rewarded in heaven. Even physical death in persecution cannot prevent but rather will enhance this.

The Destruction of Jerusulem (13:14-23)

Having dealt with preliminary matters Jesus now answered the question "When shall these things be?"–the destruction of Jerusalem and the temple.

"But when ye shall see the abomination of desolation, spoken of by Daniel the prophet, standing where it ought not, (let him that readeth understand,)" (v. 14a).

The disciples had asked as to *time* (*pōte*). But Jesus spoke of *condition*. For "when" in this verse renders *hotan*, which refers primarily to *condition*. Time is secondary; the time is governed by the condition. Jesus might have named the date for this event. But instead He spoke of the condition which would herald the time.

What did He mean by "the abomination of desolation?" He cited Daniel (9:27; 11:31; 12:11). The word for "abomination" means a nausea caused by a stench, or something to be detested. In the Old Testament it is used most often with reference to idolatry. So we may expect that meaning here. But to what particular incident does it refer? In I Maccabees 1:54 it is used with reference to the altar to Zeus erected by Antiochus Epiphanes, the Seleucid ruler of Syria, on the altar of Jehovah in the Jerusalem temple. That author saw this as fulfilling Daniel's prophecy. But that writing is not Scripture. Jesus saw its true fulfilment in the future. And since the matter under question was the fall of Jerusalem in A.D. 70, apparently it is related to that event.

In Luke's account he speaks thus. "And when ye see Jerusalem compassed with armies, then know that the desolation thereof is nigh ["has drawn near" (perfect tense), "it is all over"]" (21:20). Titus' armies besieged Jerusalem. After its fall his legions proclaimed him emperor, and offered pagan sacrifices to their ensigns placed by the eastern gate of the city. However, Jesus' reference to Christians fleeing the city (vv. 14b-18) seems to rule out this last event as being specifically "the abomination of desolation." When that event took place it would have been too late to flee. "Where it ought not" may refer not only to the Holy of Holies, it may include all of the city which was holy to the Jews and not to be desecrated by Gentiles. So in the light of Luke's account, along with that of Mark (and Matthew), it seems that Jesus was speaking of Jerusalem being surrounded by pagan armies, which eventually brought about the destruction of the city and temple. "When" they see this take place they will know that the prophecy is ready to be fulfilled. Jesus cautioned His followers to read the prophecy in that light (v. 14).

Seeing this, Jesus warns the Christians to flee the city. Josephus says that during the siege Titus allowed certain Jews to leave the city. What Jews? It is natural to see them as Christian Jews. For Eusebius reports that the Christians fled from Jerusalem to Pella, a small town at the foot of the mountains about seventeen miles south of the Sea of Galilee.

Evidently they remembered Jesus' warning to "flee to the mountains" (v. 14b). Haste would be of the essence. So those on the housetop, probably watching the approaching armies, were not to go into the house to take any belongings (v. 15). These probably fled by way of the "Road of the Roofs" from housetop to housetop. One working in the fields should not wait to get his outer garment which he had laid aside while working (v. 16). It would be hard on pregnant women and those who were carrying nursing children (v. 17). Such would make it difficult to run. Also they were to pray that this would not occur in winter because of the rigorous weather (v. 18). The affliction of those days would exceed that of any period in past or future history (v. 19). The word "affliction" renders *thlipsis,* tribulation. Some interpreters see this as referring to tribulation (Great Tribulation) of the unbelieving Jews and Gentiles near the end of the age. But the reference to the future (neither shall be) makes this appear to be in the midst of history. It is more likely the suffering accompanying the fall of Jerusalem. Josephus describes this as a horror which defies words to express it. Had these days not been of short duration no one could have escaped. But because of God's elect, Christians, the days were shortened (v. 20). After a long siege Jerusalem fell in a terrible carnage. But it was then soon over except for certain diehard resistance elsewhere.

One of the contributing factors to the Jewish war and the suffering which attended it was the many false Christs who appeared. Many such caused the Jews to rebel, and their false promises of deliverance led to fanatical resistance on the part of the Jews during the war. Jesus warned of these, telling His followers not to be misled by them (vv. 21-22). "But you beware" (v. 23). "You" in contrast to the Jews. He had warned them beforehand of such false pretenders. It is amazing that despite this warning so many are deluded by those who claim to be a messiah. This has been a favorite role assumed by dictators (cf. Lenin, Hitler, Mussolini), and the gullibility of people has repeatedly bathed the world in blood.

The Second Coming of Christ (13:24-37)

Jesus now proceeded to answer the latter question of His disciples. It is important to note that in keeping with current usage Jesus employed apocalyptic language to speak of this final consummation of the age. Such was never intended to be taken literally. It was symbolic language expressing great sweeping truths.

"But in those days, after that tribulation" (v. 24). "But" (*alla*) sets the second coming of the true Christ over against the appearing of false Christs. "In those days" gathers up the long sweep of history to point to the end of the age. "Tribulation" (*thlipsin*) is related by some to a period of great suffering near the end of time. The word means to be in a tight place, like grapes being pressed for their juice. It may refer to any anguish or suffering. This writer sees the "tribulation" as the suffering of the followers of Christ through the centuries as they seek to witness for Him. If this be a true surmise we are in that *tribulation* which extends from our Lord's ascension unto His return.

The various references to nature are apocalyptic, symbolizing natural disturbances connected with the Lord's return (vv. 24-25; cf. II Peter 3:7-10).

"And then shall they see the Son of man coming in the clouds with great power and glory" (v. 26). This will herald the end of the age. Note that this will not be a secret coming of the Lord (cf. Matt. 24:26ff.). References to Jesus coming as a thief in the night refer not to a secret coming but to its unexpected nature. He will come when men least expect Him. This within itself should warn against efforts to map out events connected with this event.

"And then shall he send his angels, and shall gather together his elect from the four winds, from the uttermost part of the earth to the uttermost part of heaven" (v. 27). Literally, "from the tip of earth to the tip of heaven" (Robertson).

Again some interpreters see this as one coming of Jesus for His saints to be followed by another at the end of the age. Jesus' thoughts at this time were of His own with no reference to non-Christians. In fact most Scriptural references to the resurrection are related to Christians only (cf. I Cor. 15; I Thess. 4:13ff.). But other references include both the saved and unsaved (cf. Matt. 25:31ff.; John 5:28f.). The matters related to the end of the age are too complicated to be discussed at length in this work. But by way of summary this author sees the overall teaching of the Scriptures as dealing with one second coming, one resurrection, and one final judgment. The Bible does not tell us all that we want to know but all that we need to know about these events. Jesus Himself here is dealing not in details but in the broad sweep of events. And we are content to leave it there.

Jesus' emphasis was upon condition not upon time. This is seen in His dual use of *hotan* in verses 28-29. A certain condition of the fig tree is a harbinger of summer. Likewise, certain conditions relate to the return of Christ.

At this point Jesus reverted back to the fall of Jerusalem (v. 30). "This generation shall not pass, till all these things be done." Did Jesus expect His return to take place in that generation? Some critical scholars so insist. Thus they make Jesus to be in error. But this does not hold up in the light of verse 32. He was speaking of a definite event at a definite time, something which He never did with respect to His return. What did happen in that generation? The fall of Jerusalem. Jesus was completing His answer to the former question before winding up the latter. Jerusalem and the temple would fall within that generation. And so it did forty years later.

We can gauge the certainty (not the time) of the second coming by the fulfilment of our Lord's prophecy concerning Jerusalem. "Heaven and earth shall pass away" (v. 31). As His word about the fall of Jerusalem will be fulfilled, so will His prophecy concerning His return be fulfilled. The event is certain. The time Jesus left in the mind of His Father.

For verse 32 reads literally, "But concerning that day and hour no one really knows [*oida*], not even the angels in heaven, not even the Son, but the Father." "Day" and "hour" are both preceded by the definite article, showing that Jesus was speaking of a definite event. This statement should be a blazing red light to all who seek to chart the end of the age. No stronger warning against such could have been uttered. "No one really knows, not even the angels, *not even the Son*" (author's italics). Only the Father really knows.

How may we understand this expression of Jesus about His own lack of knowledge concerning the day and hour of His return? While insisting upon His deity we must not ignore His humanity. It was in this latter light that He spoke these words. In His incarnation He assumed certain limitations which are a part of complete humanity, apart from sin. Indeed, sin is not a part of humanity as God intended it. And in His perfect humanity Jesus said, "My doctrine [teaching] is not mine, but his that sent me" (John 7:16). Again, "The Son can do nothing of himself, but what he seeth the Father do: for what things soever he doeth, these also doeth the Son likewise" (John 5:19). The heart of our answer is found in John 8:26, 28. "I speak to the world those things which I have heard of him.... I do nothing of myself; but as the Father hath taught me, I speak these things." The incarnation was a fact, but it is ever a mystery to finite minds.

So in the Father's good pleasure He had not "taught" the day and hour of Jesus' return. It is governed by condition. When the condition is right that will be the time. And while the triune God knows when the condition will obtain, the Father during the incarnation did not reveal it. It is that which is set in the mind of the Father (Acts 1:7).

Because of the uncertainty as to the day and hour, humanly

speaking, Jesus warned His followers to "watch" (v. 33, "and pray" not in best texts). "Watch" (*agreuō*) means to be alert, wakeful. It speaks of a sleeping man arousing himself. He illustrated this truth by means of a parable (vv. 34-36). His ascension is "as a man taking a far journey." Actually the word is *apodēmos,* away on a journey. He "left his house, and gave authority to his servants [bondslaves], and to each man his work, and commanded the porter [doorkeeper] to watch." The word here rendered "watch" is *grēgoreō,* meaning to stay awake. The "porter" is the Apostles, and the "servants" are the great body of Christians.

Vincent is helpful at this point. In the temple at night the captain of the temple made his rounds at uncertain times. As he did so the guards had to rise and salute him. Any guard found asleep on duty was beaten, or his garments set on fire (cf. Rev. 16:15). So every guard should stay awake at all times. The disciples were doubtless familiar with this custom.

Therefore, they also should "watch" or be constantly awake and alert. For the "master" (*kurios,* lord) of the house might come at any moment but at no certain time: at even, midnight, shortly before daylight, or in the morning. They should not be found asleep at their post. And what Jesus said to the Twelve He says to all Christians, "Stay awake!" (v. 37). Staying awake means to be busy about the task committed to them by the Lord.

In this light it is well to glance at Acts 1:6-11. The apostles were concerned about the future in the Lord's plans. But He told them that these were in the Father's hands alone. Their job was to witness to all nations, creating the condition for the Lord's return. After He had ascended into heaven the apostles stood gazing heavenward. Two angels appeared, and, in effect, told them that they were not to stand with their eyes fixed in the clouds. The Lord will return. But that is the Father's business. They are to get on with the work left for them to do.

We should leave in God's hands that which only He can do. We should be busy at the task which by His commission only we can do. The *future* belongs only to God. The *present* is our responsibility!

Mark 14:1-9

The Anointing of Jesus

The Olivet Discourse was delivered on Tuesday afternoon of Passion Week. Having finished it Jesus and the Twelve continued on to Bethany. By the time of their arrival at this village probably the sun had set. This meant that it was the beginning of the Jewish Wednesday.

The Plot Thickens (14:1-2)

"After two days was the feast of the passover, and of unleavened bread" (v. 1). Both of these terms were used of the feast. They might refer to the one day which began at sunset on Thursday or to the entire eight-day period of the feast. Either usage makes sense here. Matthew notes that at this time Jesus predicted exactly the day of His death (26:2).

All the while members of the Sanhedrin "kept on seeking" how to take Jesus by craftiness in order that they might put Him to death. They had been doing this for some time and they pressed their evil purpose. However, they decided to wait until after the Passover season. For they still feared an uprising among the people (v. 2). Their efforts to break Jesus' hold on them had failed. After the Passover the multitude of pilgrims would depart. They feared this group, especially those from Galilee. But apparently they felt that they could control the Jews of Jerusalem.

The Deed of Love and Understanding (14:3)

That evening in Bethany Jesus was the honored guest at a dinner in the home of Simon the leper. This man is not identified further. Most likely he had been healed by Jesus.

As they were reclining at the meal a woman came with "an alabaster box [cruse] of ointment of spikenard very precious; and she brake the box, and poured it on his head" (v. 3). John says that she poured it on His feet (12:3). Evidently she did both. Some interpreters see this as the same event recorded in Luke 7:36-50. However, there are sufficient differences between the two accounts to merit considering them as separate events.

This alabaster cruse contained a perfumed ointment which came from India. It was well known to the Greeks and Romans, and was regarded as a gift fit for a king. Herodotus lists it as one of five gifts sent by Cambyses to the king of Ethiopia. Mark describes it as genuine or unadulterated (*pistikos*) and very costly (*polutelēs*).

When a guest arrived it was customary to pour on him a few drops of perfume and to rinse the dust off his feet (cf. Luke 7:44ff.). Whether Simon did this for Jesus is not stated. But this custom adds significance to this woman's deed.

She broke the cruse, and poured the ointment on Jesus' head (and feet, John 12:3). This suggests that she broke off the narrow neck of the cruse and emptied its contents upon Jesus. Not just a few drops, but the whole of it. Hers was an act of loving abandon. She gave to Jesus that which was very precious to her.

The Criticism of Her Deed (14:4-5)

Some of those present (disciples, Matt. 26:8; John 12:4) were indignant at what they considered a waste of this costly substance (v. 4). They thought only in terms of monetary value and forgot the emotional value which it represented.

It might have been sold for more than "three hundred pence," or about fifty-one dollars, and given to the poor (v. 5, but see John 12:6). So "they murmured against her" (v. 5). The word rendered "murmured" expresses strong criticism. The imperfect tense shows that they kept on doing this.

This is ever the attitude of materialism. It becomes as hard as the coin it worships, so that any money spent for spiritual purposes is "waste."

The Reply of Jesus (14:6-9)

"Let her alone," said Jesus (v. 6). "Let alone" renders *aphete* which is sometimes translated "permit." He silenced the disciples' criticism, and approved of the woman's deed. To the poor they could always minister (v. 7), for they would still be around. But Jesus' days were numbered (cf. Matt. 26:2). What one would do for Him must be done now.

"She hath done what she could" (v. 8). Literally, "what she had she did." She did the best that she could with what she had. She had anointed Him for burial before He was crucified. Whether she understood fully the significance of her deed is not certain. She expressed her love, and Jesus interpreted its meaning.

The disciples might criticize her deed. But "wheresoever this gospel [the good news of redemption] shall be preached throughout the whole world, this also that she hath done shall be spoken of for a memorial of her" (v. 9). Her deed of love not only sweetened the atmosphere of Simon's home. It lightened the burden of the Lord. And the winds of time have wafted its sweet perfume throughout the earth and down the corridors of time.

Were it not for John's Gospel (12:2ff.) much of the significance of this event would be lost. For it is to him that we are indebted for the names of some of the principal characters involved. Lazarus was one of the guests, and his sister Martha helped with the serving. It has been suggested that she may have been Simon's wife. But this is pure conjecture. True to her nature she was a friendly neighbor lending a hand. Her sister Mary was the one who anointed Jesus. Were it not for John this memorial would have remained anonymous. Judas was the principal complainer but was joined by the other apostles.

In this light an interesting contrast arises. Both Mary and Judas were close associates of Jesus. Yet in the crisis they reacted so differently. Apparently each realized that Jesus was going to die. And in that realization each asked a question. Mary asked, "What can I do for Jesus?" Judas asked, "What can Jesus do for me?" Mary showed sympathetic understanding as she anointed Jesus for burial. Judas showed his avaricious hatred by betraying Jesus for gain.

In a sense these two are types of people. In which group do you belong?

Mark 14:10-11

The Bargain of Betrayal

The value of John's supplementary account appears further at this point. For he shows the immediate reason why Judas bargained to sell Jesus to His enemies.

The Act of Betrayal (14:10)

"And Judas Iscariot, one of the twelve, went unto the chief priests, to betray him unto them."

This evidently took place on Tuesday night. Judas went directly from Simon's house to see the chief priests. Note the plural, Caiaphas and Annas. He had been stung by Jesus' rebuke. And it triggered him to perform his nefarious act. This evil purpose had been working in his heart for at least a year (John 6:70f.). Which raises the question as to why Jesus chose Judas as one of the apostles. Of course, the simplest explanation, on the surface, is to say that Judas was chosen of God to perform this deed. But this runs into serious difficulty in that it runs contrary to the very nature of God. A more natural reason is that Judas possessed qualities which, if dedicated to Jesus, would have made him a valuable servant in the kingdom. But unlike the other apostles he never gave himself to Jesus. Instead he followed Jesus purely for selfish reasons. Some see Judas as a former unsuccessful business man. If so, this could explain why he was trusted with the small purse which probably was given by friends to Jesus and the disciples. But he was derelict to his stewardship (cf. John 12:6). Of course, this basis for Jesus' choice is only a surmise. Since the Scriptures do not explain the matter we must be content for this ever to remain a mystery. The fact is that Judas, "one of the twelve," betrayed Him. It was a betrayal of intimacy, and it was an act of selfish greed.

Efforts have been made to exonerate him (but see 14:21). In addition to the suggestion that he was divinely chosen for this act, it is held by some that he acted under the complete control of Satan. In either event he would be without personal guilt. Did he, as some suggest, act as an agent of the Sanhedrin who joined himself to Jesus for the purpose of betraying Him? This hardly fits the facts. Because he began to follow Jesus long before the issue was so tightly drawn. Some would make him a *super-patriot* who betrayed Jesus lest His movement provoke a revolution against Rome which would lead to his nation's destruction. But the opposite is more likely true. He may well have been the instigator of the abortive effort to make Jesus a political and military messiah (cf. John 6:14-15). At the opposite extreme is the position that Judas was a *super-Christian* who betrayed Jesus into the hands of His enemies in order to force His hand to declare His kingdom. These all are but futile attempts to whitewash the arch-fiend of history.

As one studies the record it becomes clear that Judas was the victim of his own greed. Satan worked on him ever so slowly but with great cunning to bring him to his evil end. Jesus said, "One of you is a devil" [*diabolos*] (John 6:70). He was not one when Jesus chose him. But one year before the end he *is* a devil. Judas never was a Christian. This is evidenced by the fact that while the other apostles called Jesus "Lord," Judas never did. Note Matthew 26:22, "Lord, is it I?" and Matthew 26:25, "Master [Rabbi], is it I?" Then note Matthew 26:49, "Hail, master [*rabbi*]." To Judas Jesus was not "Lord" but a "Rabbi." He was to him only a speaker of pious words, not the Christ of God.

He knew of the plot to kill Jesus. When He failed to declare His kingdom on Palm Sunday Judas knew that by his standards Jesus had failed. It was only a matter of time until His foes would slay Him. The rebuke in Simon's house was the straw that broke the camel's back. He might as well get what he could out of the *debacle.* So he sought out the chief priests to try to make a bargain.

The Happy Conspirators (14:11)

The chief priests had not counted upon such a stroke of luck. So when they heard Judas' words "they were glad." This changed the picture. No longer needed they to wait until after the Passover. This inside job made it possible to proceed without delay.

So they readily "promised to give him money." Mark does not mention the amount. But Matthew 26:15 gives the figure at "thirty pieces of silver" (cf. Zech. 11:12). This was about twenty-five dollars, the price of a slave. When Judas failed to get his hands on the fifty-one dollars (John 12:5), he settled for twenty-five. Whence came this money? Probably from the temple treasury. Yet the hypocrisy of the chief priests is seen in that they refused to put it back into the treasury because it was blood money (Matt. 27:6)! They used Judas for a purpose, and then forgot him. This is ever the way of Satan.

Judas reached for the stars and wound up with a handful of dirt, dirt stained by the blood of the Son of God. His ill-gotten gain was used to purchase a cemetery for non-Jews (Matt. 27:7ff.). And they did not even name it "Judas Memorial Cemetery!" Someone said that men name their boys after Paul and their dogs after Nero. But they use the name of Judas only for the goat which leads sheep to the slaughter.

Having made his bargain Judas "kept on seeking how he might betray [hand over for execution] him at a good time" (v. 11b). He sought a time when this could be done without exciting the multitude.

Mark 14:12-21

The Passover Meal

Nothing is said about Jesus' actions on Wednesday. Probably He remained in Bethany resting and teaching His disciples.

The Preparation for the Meal (14:12-16)

On Thursday afternoon the disciples inquired as to where Jesus would eat the passover meal. Mark uses the words "the first day of unleavened bread" (v. 12). This causes some confusion. For this would mean the Jewish Friday. The Passover began at sunset on Thursday which marked the beginning of Friday. This would mean that the preparations were made after the time for the meal. But note that Mark says that this was the time when the Passover lamb was slain. The Passover began at 6:00 P.M. on Thursday, the beginning of the fifteenth day of the month (Exod. 12:6). It is evident, therefore, that the disciples asked their question on the fourteenth day of the month or on Thursday.

So Jesus sent two of His disciples (Peter and John, Luke 22:8) into the city to prepare for the meal. He did not tell them where the meal was to be eaten. Already He knew of Judas' purpose to betray Him. So He kept secret the place. But He told the two disciples how to find it. In the city they would meet a man carrying a pitcher of water, and they were to follow him (v. 13). Since this was usually done by women, such a man would be conspicuous. Perhaps the man himself did not know why he was carrying the pitcher. It evidently was a prearranged sign made between Jesus and the owner of the house where the meal was to be eaten.

Wherever the man led them they were to say to the man of the house, "The Master saith, Where is the guestchamber, where I shall eat the passover with my disciples" (v. 14)? The man, in turn, would show them the room where the meal was to be eaten (v. 15). There they were to prepare for the meal.

Peter and John did as they were told (v. 16). The room itself was "furnished," or in a state of readiness (v. 15). The perfect tense of the verb shows how thoroughly this had been done. Among other things reclining couches were arranged about the table. But the disciples prepared the food for the meal.

Barclay gives this preparation in detail. First, they made a ceremonial search for leaven. Since the first Passover had been eaten with unleavened bread, every bit of leaven must be removed from the house. Second, at 6:00 P.M. the lamb was slain in the temple. After it was approved by the priests it was slain by the disciples. The blood was placed on the altar by the priests. After the carcass had been rendered, the edible portion was given to the disciples. In turn they took the lamb to the home and roasted it over an open fire. Third, certain other ingredients in addition to the lamb were secured. These included a bowl of salt water to remind them of the tears shed by Israel in Egypt and of the waters of the Red Sea crossed in the deliverance. Bitter herbs such as horse radish, chicory, endive, lettuce, and horehound were to remind them of the bitterness of the bondage of Egypt. A paste called Charosheth, a mixture of apples, dates, pomegranates, and nuts was a reminder of the bricks made in the land of bondage. Finally, four cups of wine, three parts wine and two parts water, were prepared. These were drunk at stages throughout the meal to recall the four promises found in Exodus 6:6-7.

"I will bring you out from under the burdens of the Egyptians."

"I will rid you out of their bondage."

"I will redeem you with a stretched out arm."

"I will take you to me for a people, and I will be to you a God."

The Eating of the Meal (14:17-18a)

"And in the evening [after 6:00 P.M.] he cometh with the twelve. And . . . they sat [reclined] and did eat."

Evidently Jesus and the *ten* came and joined Peter and John at the house. And they ate the meal. But with one difference from the way the Israelities ate the first such meal in Egypt. There they ate standing, or ready for a journey. Jesus and His group ate while reclining on couches. To the Jews this signified that they were free men, living in their own home and country. While this was the custom in eating in Jesus' day, it was most significant at the Passover meal. For this feast commemorated Israel's deliverance from bondage.

The Word about the Betrayer (14:18b-21)

As they were eating Jesus threw a bombshell into their midst. "Verily I say unto you, One of you which eateth with me shall betray me (v. 18b). Jesus had alluded to His betrayal before. But now He plainly said that the betrayer was one of the Twelve. This one was one of His most intimate associates, even one who at that time was eating with Him. This within itself did not point out the person. But it narrowed it down to those present about the table. To the oriental mind this made the deed all the more terrible. For one who ate at another's table was entitled to his protection. Arabs to this day will not violate hospitality by mistreating a table guest.

One may well imagine that the disciples looked at each other in shocked amazement, perhaps with suspicion. And then one by one they began to ask, "Is it I?" (v. 19). In Greek this form of a question invited a negative answer. In effect they asked, "It isn't I, is it?" Mark does not go into detail at this point. But Matthew reports that eleven of the apostles addressed Jesus as "Lord." "Lord, is it I?" To their knowledge they had not entertained such a thought. But they asked out of fear that some unknown sin of treachery lurked within them. They asked hoping that Jesus would say, "No." Had Judas remained silent that would have given him away. So finally he asked, "Rabbi, is it I?" (cf. Matt. 26:25). His question also invited a negative answer. He asked it hoping that Jesus did not know that he was the one.

John notes that at this point Peter asked the beloved disciple to inquire of Jesus as to the betrayer's identity (13:23-26). Mark agrees with John as seen in Jesus' reply to the question as to identity. "It is one of the twelve, that dippeth with me in the dish" (v. 20). This not only points up the intimacy betrayed, but it anticipates John's words. "He it is, to whom I shall give the sop" (13:26). And He gave it to Judas Iscariot.

The "sop" was a sauce composed of dates, raisins, and vinegar. All those about the table were dipping in it with unleavened bread. It was customary for the host to show special honor to a guest by placing the bread dipped in this sauce in the mouth of some chosen guest. Seeing Jesus do this to Judas may have provoked jealousy on the part of the others. But it did not reveal Jesus' true purpose in doing it. The beloved disciple (John) knew. But Peter did not know the meaning of this gesture on the part of the Lord. Had he known, it is questionable as to whether or not Judas would have gotten out of the room alive.

One wonders if Jesus did not have another purpose in this gesture. Was it to make one last effort to snatch Judas back from his evil purpose? If so, it failed to produce the desired result.

Previous notice has been given to efforts to absolve Judas from guilt. However, Jesus entertained no such sentimental thoughts. True, it was necessary that He should be betrayed. "But woe to that man by whom the Son of man is betrayed! good were it for that man if he had never been born" (v. 21). Judas' deed was his own. And he must ever bear the guilt.

Mark 14:22-26

The Institution of the Lord's Supper

By comparing the various Gospel accounts it seems that at this point Judas left the room to carry out his purpose to betray Jesus. There is an important doctrinal matter at this point. For Jesus was about to institute the Lord's Supper. This Supper is for baptized believers only. Most likely Judas had been baptized. But he was not a believer.

The Significance of the Bread (14:22)

At the end of the passover meal Jesus took a cake of unleavened bread. After offering a blessing He broke the bread and gave a piece to each of the Eleven. As He did so He said, "Take, eat: this is my body."

The natural way to understand "this is my body" is to see the bread as a symbol of Jesus' body. When understood naturally it is difficult to see it to mean that the bread actually became the flesh of Jesus. It symbolized that which Jesus did in His body to provide redemption for the sins of men. When He said, "I am the door" (John 10:7), we do not understand this literally but symbolically. It is natural to see the same meaning with respect to the bread.

The Significance of the Cup (14:23-25)

"Then Jesus took the cup" (v. 23). After giving thanks He gave the cup to each disciple, and they all drank from it.

Then Jesus explained its meaning. "This is my blood of the new testament, which is shed for many" (v. 24). The same principle applies here as with the bread. It is to be understood symbolically. The contents of the cup symbolized Jesus' blood which was shed for man's sin.

What cup did Jesus take? We have noted that there were four cups of diluted wine on the table. Wuest sees this as the third cup. But was it? In Luke's account of the Supper he uses the word "cup" preceded by the definite article. It points to one specific cup. Does this point out the third cup? Or was this a special cup provided for the occasion?

It is of interest to note that the word "wine" is never used for the contents of this cup. The term is "fruit of the vine." This suggests unfermented grape juice. Wine is the fruit of bacteria in the juice. Both the bread and the cup symbolize the pure body and blood of Jesus respectively. The bread was unleavened. It contained no foreign substance. May we not also apply the same principle to the cup? It would appear, therefore, that the cup contained pure grape juice unchanged by bacteria.

So the bread and the cup symbolize what Jesus did for man's redemption. He gave His body and He shed His blood for man's sin.

And Jesus said that He would "drink no more of the fruit of the vine, until that day when I drink it new in the kingdom of God" (v. 25). The Jews thought of heaven as a great banquet. So Jesus was saying that the next time that He drank of the fruit of the vine it would be in the heavenly marriage feast of the Lamb following His return. Thus the Lord's Supper not only *remembers* what Jesus did to save men, it points forward in faith to His return, which involves complete salvation including the resurrection of the body and the glory and reward in heaven (I Cor. 11:26).

There are two ordinances in the New Testament church: baptism and the Lord's Supper. Baptism symbolizes that which Jesus did for our salvation, that which He does in the believer, and one's faith in the final resurrection at the Lord's return (Rom. 6:3-5). The Lord's Supper symbolizes that which Jesus did for salvation and looks toward the end of the age. So both ordinances look back to what Jesus did in His death and resurrection. And they look forward in faith to the full-salvation [regeneration, sanctification, glorification] which shall be for every believer in heaven.

The Singing of a Psalm (14:26)

"And when they had sung an hymn, they went out into the mount of Olives" (cf. John 14:31b).

Only John reports that prior to His departure from the upper room Jesus spoke comfort to His disciples (14:1ff.). It had finally dawned upon them that He was going to die. Mark and Matthew tell of the singing of a hymn before leaving the room. This was the Hallel, composed of sections of Psalms 115, 118, which were sung at the close of a Passover meal.

And then they left Jerusalem for the Mount of Olives. On the way Jesus taught the Eleven about duty (John 15-16), and then prayed what is sometimes called His High Priestly prayer (John 17).

This nightly departure toward the Mount of Olives was customary on Jesus' part. So it would not have surprised the disciples. But this time they did not proceed to Bethany. For Jesus had a different destination, the garden of Gethsemane. His hour was rapidly approaching. But before it arrived there remained for Him yet one more soul-searching experience.

Mark 14:27-31

The Audacity of Peter

This event is reported by Matthew and Mark as occurring after Jesus and His band left the upper room. Luke and John place it in the upper room. In all likelihood the latter are correct as to sequence. But all four Gospels attest to its being a genuine event.

The Warning of Jesus (14:27-28)

Knowing the ordeal which awaited Him Jesus warned His disciples as to their conduct in it. "All ye shall be offended because of me this night: for it is written, I will smite the shepherd, and the sheep shall be scattered" (v. 27). They will act according to the prophecy found in the Old Testament (Zech. 13:7). The word rendered "offended" is *skandalizō,* to stumble or to find an occasion for stumbling. When Jesus was arrested the disciples forsook Him and fled. In Jesus' hour of trial they forgot Him in favor of their own safety. Are we any better?

"But after that I am risen, I will go before you into Galilee" (v. 28). Jesus' purpose in mentioning the behavior of the disciples was not to condemn them, but to warn them and to give them hope. This is seen in the adversative particle *alla,* "but." It sets the hope of an early reunion with Jesus over against their forsaking Him. He will die, but there is an even greater fellowship beyond His resurrection. No matter what dangers we face or how shamefully we fail, there is always the assurance of renewed fellowship which awaits us.

The Reply of Peter (14:29)

Jesus spoke His warning to all of the Eleven. But Peter put himself in a class apart from them. "Although all shall be offended [see in you a cause of stumbling], yet will not I."

We are not surprised to hear Peter say this. He probably meant it at the time. The form of his statement shows that the others most likely will do as Jesus had said. "But not I." He did not want to be put in the class of the chicken-hearted. Yet how little he knew himself! In fact a *chicken* will remind him of his chicken-heartedness.

The Dialogue between Jesus and Peter (14:30-31)

Jesus did not rebuke Peter. But patiently He reiterated His statement with emphasis. The others will forsake Jesus. But Peter will do so with emphasis. Peter never did anything halfway, even when he was wrong.

"This day, even in this night, before the cock crow twice [before daylight], thou shalt deny me thrice" (v. 30). Not stumble but deny. Not once but thrice. To Peter's emphatic assertion Jesus gave a more emphatic reply. "Certainly not I," said Peter. "Surely you," said Jesus. He would deny Jesus again, again, and yet again.

But as before (8:31ff.) Peter argued with Jesus. "He spoke the more vehemently" (v. 31). "Vehemently" means in both manner and in repetition. Only Mark reports this word, probably from Peter himself: "He kept on speaking" (imperfect). Not once, but many times.

"If I should die with thee, I will not deny thee in any wise" (v. 31). "I positively will not deny thee." Death rather than denial. And all the rest said, "Me too!"

The record shows that only Peter later tried to defend Jesus with a sword. But Jesus told him to cease. It was then that Peter fled. He had physical courage but lacked moral courage. He followed afar off. But he did follow.

Mark 14:32-42

The Rendezvous in Gethsemane

Through the eastern gate Jesus led the disciples out of Jerusalem, across the Brook Kidron, to the garden of Gethsemane. "Gethsemane" means "oil press." It was evidently a private garden, perhaps owned by a friend of Jesus. It was a place where He often went to pray while in this area. Just outside St. Stephen's gate and across the way one may still visit a lovely spot. It contains many old olive trees and beautiful flowers. In it stands the Church of all Nations, built over a huge rock called "the rock of agony." Tradition says that Jesus kneeled at this rock to pray. Whether this is the spot or not, it must have been some similar spot nearby.

The Distribution of the Disciples (14:32-34)

Perhaps near the entrance to the garden Jesus left eight of His disciples. He told them to sit there while He prayed (v. 32). Then He took Peter, James and John a little farther into the garden (v. 33). As He did so He "began to be sore amazed, and to be very heavy" (v. 33). "Sore amazed" expresses "terrified surprise" (Swete). "Heavy" means "uncomfortable" as one who does not feel at home. Though Jesus had known that the cross awaited Him, now as it loomed up before Him He was in a state of great agitation. Indeed, He said, "My soul is exceeding sorrowful unto death" (v. 34). "Exceeding sorrowful" renders *perilupos, peri,* around, *lupos,* grief. He was surrounded by or enveloped by sorrow. So great was His sorrow that He was almost dead from it.

In such a state He said to the three, "Tarry ye here, and watch" (v. 34). Wuest says that they were left there to witness Jesus' agony. But is this the purpose for their being nearby? The word "watch" renders *grēgoreō* to be awake, vigilant. They were not simply to *watch* Jesus suffer. They were to *watch while* He suffered. They were to *guard* Him from being arrested prematurely until He was ready to be taken.

This suggests Jesus' purpose in His distribution of the disciples at this time. He set an outer and an inner guard. In the upper room He had told them to get swords (Luke 22:35-38). Two were enough. Why these swords? As one reads the entire account it appears that they were for the purpose of guarding Him until He had finished His prayer vigil in Gethsemane.

Now we know that Peter (the inner guard) had one of these swords (cf. v. 37; John 18:10). Where was the other sword? Was it with the outer guard?[1]

At any rate Jesus told the inner group to be on its guard. They did not do a very good job at it. But they had their guard post nevertheless.

The Prayer of Jesus (14:35-42)

Having posted His watches Jesus "went forward a little, and fell on the ground, and prayed" (v. 35). His falling to the ground shows the utter grief of Jesus. There He prayed. This verb is an imperfect form. It means that He began to pray and kept on praying. And what did He pray? He prayed that if it were possible, the "hour" might pass from Him. Matthew 26:39 uses the "cup" as does Mark in verse 36. They refer to the same thing.

"Abba, Father, all things are possible unto thee; take away this cup from me: nevertheless not what I will but what thou wilt" (v. 36). Note the Aramaic and Greek words for "Father." This within itself indicates the extreme burden on His heart. Jesus recognized the omnipotence of God. This does not mean that God can do all things arbitrarily. He must act in accord with His nature and purpose. Jesus agreed with this when He prayed for God's will to be done regardless of what He asked.

Now to what do the "hour" and the "cup" refer? Was Jesus praying that He might not die in Gethsemane? Or was He praying that He would be saved through the cross in the resurrection? Neither of these positions satisfies the situation. Jesus had known all along that He was going to die on a cross. So this would rule out the former idea. And He also knew that He would be raised on the third day. This would rule out the latter idea. Was He praying to be spared from physical death? Did He, after knowing all along that He was to die on a cross, suddenly pray to escape death? This cannot satisfy the situation either. He did not fear death. And He knew that it was only for three days. So it seems that we must look further for an answer.

It would appear, therefore, that the "cup" symbolizes that which Jesus' death involved. In it He was made sin for us (cf. II Cor. 5:21). It was thus that He endured the wrath of God against sin. Though He did not fear death as such, His sensitive, sinless soul drew back in horror from the prospect of becoming, not sinful, but the very essence of sin. If there were any other way to save men, but, if not, or "nevertheless not what I will,

[1] See Hobbs, *An Exposition of the Gospel of Luke*, pp. 370ff.

but what thou wilt." The emphasis in the Greek text is upon "I" and "thou." He was willing to do what was necessary to redeem men.

What is the significance of the struggle in Gethsemane? Was it a struggle between Christ and Satan? Satan does not enter into the picture except by inference. Was it a conflict of wills, a conflict between the will of the Father and of the Son? There is no evidence of such. Jesus was willing to do the Father's will, whatever that might be. It seems that the struggle was within the will of Jesus Himself. Was He willing to be made or regarded as sin? And He ultimately won the victory to do so.

After the first prayer Jesus came back to the three disciples and found them asleep (v. 37). He spoke only to Simon. Note that He called him "Simon," not "Peter" (a rock). Mark has not used the name "Simon" since Peter's selection as an apostle. Evidently Peter recalled this incident with shame and sorrow. Apparently He singled out Simon because of his avowed loyalty above that of the other disciples. Already he was proving Jesus' words to be true. "Simon, are you sleeping? Do you not have strength to be vigilant one hour? Be constantly vigilant and praying in order that you not enter into trial" (v. 38). Jesus knew that Simon's spirit was eager, ready, and willing, but the flesh lacked strength to perform. Luke 22:45 notes that the disciples were exhausted from sorrow. And the hour was very late.

A second time Jesus went into the shadows and prayed the same prayer (v. 39). Returning He found the three in a sleepy stupor, so much so that they were unable to answer Jesus when He exhorted them again to alertness (v. 40). After a third prayer Jesus returned to find the disciples asleep. This time He said, "Keep on sleeping and resting" (v. 41). There was no longer need for their watching. "It is enough," said Jesus (v. 41). This renders the verb *apechō* which is used in the papyri as "paid in full." As used here it means that the prayer vigil is completed. Jesus had won the victory within Himself and is ready to be taken.

"Behold, the Son of man is betrayed into the hands of sinners. Rise up, let us go; lo, he that betrayeth me is at hand," or "drawn near" (vv. 41-42). Even as Jesus spoke He could hear the noise of the approaching band of temple police and Roman soldiers. And Judas walked before them.

Mark 14:43-52

The Betrayal and Arrest of Jesus

It was probably sometime after midnight but long before dawn on Friday. After Judas left the upper room he evidently went to the chief priests to tell them that he was ready to deliver Jesus into their hands. To make the arrest they assigned some temple police to go with Judas. Roman soldiers went along just in case there should be trouble with any people who might be present at that time of night.

It is likely that Judas first led them to the upper room. Failing to find Jesus there he surmised that he would find Him at Gethsemane where he knew that Jesus was accustomed to go for prayer and meditation (John 18:2). These movements would account for the lapse of time before Judas arrived at the garden.

The Kiss of Betrayal (14:43-45)

Mark describes the group which came with Judas. He points out that the betrayer was "one of the twelve" (v. 43). With him was a crowd bearing "swords and staves." These were sent by representatives of the Sanhedrin. The "swords" were used by the Roman soldiers; the "staves" were stout sticks used by the temple police. Also accompanying them was Malchus, the bondservant (slave of the high priest: cf. Luke 22:52; John 18:10).

Judas had told them that he would point out Jesus by kissing Him (v. 44). He said that when he had identified Him they were to "take him, and lead him away safely" (v. 44). "Safely" means "without a slip." They were to see that Jesus did not escape. When Judas sinned he did so with a vengeance. Without delay Judas went to Jesus and said, "Rabbi [only one in the best texts]; and kissed him" (v. 45). The verb rendered "kissed" is an aorist form of a compound verb *kataphileō* The prefix *kata* intensifies the basic verb. So it means that he kissed Jesus one time, and he did so fervently. He probably kissed Him on the hand, since this was the customary way for a pupil to greet his *rabbi.* Note that Judas called Jesus *Rabbi,* not *Lord.* To him Jesus was never *Lord,* just a Jewish *rabbi.*

The Arrest of Jesus (14:46-50)

As soon as Judas kissed Jesus the arresting detail "laid their hands on him, and took him" (v. 46). The word "laid" renders the aorist form of the verb *epiballō*. It means to cast upon. A derived meaning is violently to lay one's hands on someone. The aorist tense of instant action serves to emphasize the violence. So they roughly seized Jesus.

At this point things began to happen. Someone asked, "Lord, shall we smite with the sword" (Luke 22:49)? This probably came from one of the eight disciples which had been left at the gate. But one disciple did not wait for an answer. John identifies him as Peter (18:10). True to his impulsive nature he snatched out his sword and started swinging. He "smote a servant of the high priest [Malchus, John 18:10] and cut off his ear" (v. 47). Luke notes that it was his right ear (22:50). Peter was aiming at his head, but he dodged expertly. Only Luke, the physician, notes that Jesus healed the severed ear (22:51).

Matthew and John record that Jesus told Peter to put up his sword (26:52; 18:11). "For all that take the sword shall perish with the sword" (Matt. 26:52). This statement has been used to make Jesus an extreme pacifist. But from the context, including Luke 22:35-38, this does not seem to be a true position. It suggests that Jesus approved of defensive warfare but not offensive warfare. If one follows the extreme pacifist position to the letter, he would abolish police departments and all military forces, both of which should be law enforcement agencies to deter the evil designs of wicked men. There are some things worth fighting and dying for. Neither Jesus nor Paul belonged to the "better Red than dead" crowd.

Peter was doing exactly what he understood that Jesus had told him to do. In his sleepy state it had not dawned upon him that Jesus was ready to be taken. Jesus told him that He no longer needed guarding. He should put up his sword lest he be killed for no good reason. In telling him to do this He most likely saved His faithful but impulsive disciple's life.

Jesus then rebuked this group for coming after Him with an armed band (v. 48). They could have taken Him anytime as He taught daily in the temple (v. 49). However, Judas' betrayal and the manner of Jesus' arrest were fulfilments of the Scriptures.

"And they all forsook him, and fled" (v. 50). As Jesus had prophesied, the disciples fled for their lives, leaving Jesus alone.

The Strange Young Man (14:51-52)

Among those who fled was a young man whose name is not given. Since Mark alone records this, it is entirely possible that he was this lad. There is really no point to the story other than a personal reference.

He had a "linen cloth cast about his naked body" (v. 51). This cloth was such as was used in wrapping the dead. It may also have been used to make a boy's cloak or even a bed sheet. This last usage is most suggestive. It is usually thought that the passover meal had been eaten in the home of Mark's mother (Acts 12:12). If so, Mark may have been in bed when the armed band came to his home. With a boy's curiosity he may have wrapped a bed sheet about his naked body and have followed them to Gethsemane.

As the apostles fled some effort must have been made to apprehend them (cf. John 18:8). In the confusion Mark also fled. But somebody grabbed at him and got only the sheet. He fled naked.

This adds a personal note to the story. In keeping with custom the author of this Gospel would not mention his own name. But perhaps in this little story he has inserted himself into the record nevertheless.

VI

The Climax of the Gospel

Mark 14:53-65; 15:1

The Trial before the Sanhedrin

The trial of Jesus may be divided into two sections: Jewish and Roman. Each of these consisted of three phases. The Jewish section was before Annas (John 18:12-14, 19-23), before the Sanhedrin prior to dawn (Matt. 26:57, 59-68; Mark 14:53, 55-65; Luke 22: 54, 63-65; John 18:24), and before the Sanhedrin after dawn (Matt. 27:1; Mark 15:1; Luke 22:66-71). The Roman section was before Pilate (Matt. 27:2, 11-14; Mark 15:1-5; Luke 23:1-5; John 18:28-38), before Herod Antipas (Luke 23:6-12), and before Pilate a second time (Matt. 27:15-26; Mark 6:15; Luke 23:13-15; John 18:39—19:10). As is evident the appearances before Annas and Antipas are related only by John and Luke respectively.

The appearance before Annas was actually a preliminary hearing in preparation for the trial before the Sanhedrin. It was designed to obtain a specific charge to make against Jesus. Annas was a former high priest who had been succeeded in office by his sons and finally by his son-in-law Caiaphas. But he had remained the real power behind the high priesthood. He had great influence over the people and with the Roman authorities. Hence a charge brought by him would have borne great weight.

The Jewish Trial before Dawn (14:53-65)

From Gethsemane Jesus was led to appear before Annas. During this interval the Sanhedrin was hastily assembled (v. 53). Things were moving more rapidly than had been anticipated. While Mark speaks generally of "all" the various elements of the Sanhedrin being present, from Luke 23:50-51 we may understand that Joseph of Arimathea was not there. He had not consented to Jesus' death. Since the verdict of the Sanhedrin was unanimous this means that he was not present. By inference we may also assume that Nicodemus was absent (John 7:50ff.; 19:39). Perhaps, knowing their relation to Jesus, the authorities did not call them to the meeting.

Mark points out that Peter followed Jesus at a distance (v. 54). He had recovered from his panic, and was in the courtyard outside Caiaphas' dwelling in which the Sanhedrin was meeting. John 18:15 notes that another disciple, perhaps John himself, had entered the hall with Jesus. Evidently he had not run very far in the garden. He was acquainted with Caiaphas; and he had used his influence to get Peter admitted into the courtyard.

The hurry of events also had caught the Sanhedrin without witnesses against Jesus. Since Annas' efforts had been fruitless, a charge had to come from some other source. So they "were seeking" (imperfect, v. 55) those who might give testimony against Jesus worthy of death. Note that they were not searching for the truth, but for a basis upon which to condemn Him. The verb tense suggests that they sought for some time, but they "found none" or "did not find" any. What they finally found were false witnesses whose testimony did not agree (v. 56). Finally some false witnesses testified that they had heard Jesus say, "I will destroy this temple that is made with hands, and within three days I will build another made without hands" (v. 58; cf. Matt. 26:61). But Mark notes that even here their witness did not agree (v. 59).

This obviously was a reference to Jesus' words in John 2:19. Which incidently is a Synoptic testimony to the fact of the cleansing of the temple reported by John. These witnesses reported on what they had heard. The fact that their witness did not agree suggests that they were false witnesses who had been told to say what they said. They may have been *coached* by the chief priests. But they were not very good *players*. Furthermore Jesus had made such a statement. But His meaning was far different from the one which they attached to it. He spoke of the temple of His body, but they thought of the temple in Jerusalem. It is of interest to note that Jesus used *naos* for the temple, not *hieron,* the temple area as a whole. The *naos* might be used in the latter sense. But strictly speaking it was the Holy of Holies in which God was said to dwell with His people. Jesus' body was such a *naos*.

All the while Jesus had remained silent. And since other efforts had failed to produce damaging evidence, Caiaphas questioned Jesus Himself. "Answerest thou nothing? what . . . these witness against thee?" (v. 60). Though the false witnesses had really said nothing, the high priest implied that they had really stated a case against Him. It was pure bluff.

"But he held his peace, and answered nothing" (v. 61). The imperfect verb for "held his peace" means "he kept on being silent." This suggests how little Jesus spoke throughout His trial. His silence showed His contempt for them and His knowledge that answers were useless. They had already made up their minds to kill Him. An analysis of Jesus' replies shows that He spoke only at strategic points to prove His innocence of their charges and to assert that He was truly Christ the King. He would die, but only as Christ the King.

In the face of Jesus' continued silence Caiaphas resorted to the only recourse left to him. He put Him on oath (cf. Matt. 26:63). Then he asked, "Art thou the Christ, the Son of the Blessed [God]?" (v. 61). Literally, "You are the Christ, the Son of the Blessed?" In this form it asked for a positive reply.

So Jesus simply said, "I am" (v. 62). This was the first public admission by Jesus that He was the Christ—at least in so many words. To have answered otherwise under oath would have been perjury. Matthew 26:64 reads, "Thou hast said." Since the high priest's question invited a positive answer Jesus said. "You yourself said it." Thus Jesus turned the tables on him by reminding him that, even though he put it in the form of a question, he himself had admitted that He was the Christ, the Son of God.

But Jesus gave him more than that for which he bargained. He added, speaking to the entire body, "Ye shall see the Son of man sitting on the right hand of power, and coming in the clouds of heaven" (v. 62). Such would be obnoxious to the Sadducees, for it implied the supernatural which they denied. But more, it emphasized His claim to being the Son of God and the Christ coming in judgment. The Sanhedrin thought that they had Jesus on trial, when all the while they were on trial before Him. And though they shall kill Him He will be exalted to the right hand of God and will sit in final judgment upon them.

This was too much for Caiaphas. He had obtained the confession that he sought. And though it was the truth, he regarded it as blasphemy. Therefore, he tore his clothes, or his undergarments *(chitōnas)*. This was a sign of deep mourning (cf. Gen. 37:29). The law forbad the high priest to do this in case of personal troubles (cf. Lev. 10:6; 21:10). But when acting as a judge he was supposed to do this as a sign of horror and mourning when he heard blasphemy against God.

"What need we any further witnesses?" asked Caiaphas (v. 63). He accused Jesus of blasphemy without bothering to test His claims. He obviously was relieved from embarrassment by Jesus' own words. "What think ye?" he asked. Or "What does it appear to you?" Did they agree with his charge of blasphemy? They did. For "they all condemned him to be guilty of death" (v. 64). The verb *katakrinō* means to judge one, find him guilty, and pronounce sentence upon him. In this case the penalty for blasphemy was death.

With this pandemonium broke loose. What was supposed to be

a court of justice became a scene of mob violence. For "some" began to abuse Jesus unmercifully. Luke 22:63 identifies these as the temple police. They began to spit on Jesus. Some covered His face, slapped His face, and then challenged Him to tell who did it (v. 65). No greater insults could have been hurled at Him. The Sanhedrin accused Jesus of speaking insultingly about God. The officers insulted the Son of God. This ended the trial before dawn.

It was illegal in every sense. It was held at night which was contrary to Jewish law. Those who arrested Jesus sat as His judges. False witnesses were used. Under oath Jesus was required to incriminate Himself. They never examined His testimony. To avoid undue influence the younger men were supposed to vote first. In this case the high priest voted first. The verdict was unanimous. Under Jewish law there must be an element of mercy. So a unanimous verdict was equal to acquittal. In capital cases sentence was not supposed to be passed on the same day of the trial. And the one on trial was not supposed to be mistreated. Truly this was evil men's hour and the tyranny of darkness (Luke 22:53).

The Jewish Trial after Dawn (15:1)

To give a legal semblance to the proceedings the Sanhedrin assembled after dawn. There they officially condemned Jesus to death.

The Romans permitted the Sanhedrin to sit in judgment in civil and religious matters. But they reserved to themselves those cases involving capital punishment. Even if the Sanhedrin found one guilty of death, it had to turn the case over to the Roman procurator. So having arrived at this point with Jesus, they took Him to appear before Pilate. The word "delivered" renders the Greek verb used of Judas' betrayal. In this case it means to hand over to another for execution. In the minds of the Jewish rulers this was but a legal requirement. They were anxious to get the trial over so they could *hang* Jesus on a tree.

So shortly after dawn Jesus was on His way to Pilate's hall. It was the dawn of the blackest day in the history of the world.

Mark 14:66-72

The Denials of Peter

It was during the trial of Jesus before the Sanhedrin that Peter lingered in the open court of Caiaphas' palace. At this season of the year the nights were cold; so Peter was sitting with the servants *(hupēretōn,* under-rowers) by the fire (v. 54). The prophecy of Jesus as to Peter's conduct was about to be fulfilled.

The First Denial (14:66-68)

"Peter was beneath in the palace" (v. 66). This implies that the Sanhedrin was meeting in an upper story of the building. Peter was in the court which opened off the first floor. One of the maidservants of the high priest came to the fire. And seeing Peter she "looked upon him" (v. 67). Actually, she "gazed intently upon him." Then she said, "And thou also wast with Jesus of Nazareth" (v. 67). Perhaps she was aware of John's presence inside the palace. And here was another disciple of Jesus. Literally she said, "Also you [emphatic, in contrast to another] were with the Nazarene, that Jesus." There must have been contempt in her voice. Such an identification could endanger Peter, especially because of his use of the sword in Gethsemane.

So "he denied, saying, I neither know [*oida,* I do not really know] nor understand what you are saying" (v. 68). The aorist tense (denied) suggests a curt answer. It was an emphatic denial of any knowledge of Jesus or the matter about which she spoke.

So he left the fire where he was recognized, and "went out into the porch" (v. 68). This was the vestibule of the court. He went into the darkness, and possibly near the entrance through which he might flee if necessary. The words "and the cock crew" are not found in the best manuscripts. They were probably inserted by some copyist in order to agree with verse 72.

The Second Denial (14:69-70a)

But Peter could not hide in the dark. For the maid was persistent. The King James Version says, "And a maid saw him again" (v. 69). This could mean another maid. But the Greek text says, "The maid." It was the same maidservant who had asked the first question. In fact the original text reads, "And the maid, seeing him, began again to say to the ones standing about that this fellow is one of them." She did not speak directly to Peter but to those standing around the fire.

This was even more serious. So long as the maid thought so, that was one thing. But to arouse the others was quite another thing. In view of the situation everyone was doubtless on edge. So "he denied it again" (v. 70a). The imperfect form shows that he did this repeatedly. The verb may also mean to disown. So Peter disowned his Lord.

The Third Denial (14:70b-71)

Peter may have returned to the fire. For "a little after" suggests a short interval of time. Perhaps they would accept his repeated denial. But that was not to be. Because again those standing about the fire began to say and kept on saying (imperfect) to Peter, "Surely thou art one of them: for thou art a Galilean" (v. 70). "And thy speech agreeth thereto" is not in the best texts. It was probably added by some copyist to agree with Matthew 26:73. However, the sense of that statement is present. The Galileans had a peculiar brogue.

"But he began to curse and to swear, saying, I know not this man of whom ye speak" (v. 71). The word rendered "curse" is *anathematizein*. From it comes the word *anathema,* a thing cursed. The verb form means to call down a curse upon someone. Matthew 26:74 uses *katathematizein*. This is probably a contraction of the word used by Mark. "Swear" means to take an oath. "Know" is *oida,* to know by perception. This could mean that he knew Jesus as a man by seeing or hearing about Him. But he did not really know Him intimately. This was the strongest of all the denials. He took an oath and called down upon himself a curse if he did not tell the truth in avowing that he did not really know Jesus.

The Repentance of Peter (14:72)

"And the second time the cock crew." Jesus had said that "before the cock crow twice, thou shall deny me thrice" (14:30). And it had happened.

Peter heard the rooster crow. And evidently Jesus heard it. For Luke 22:61 says that at that point Jesus turned and looked upon Peter. At the sound of the rooster he also evidently looked at Jesus. And he saw Jesus looking at him. The Lord's words came flooding back into Peter's mind. This, plus Jesus' look, broke his heart. Therefore, he "began to weep" and "kept on weeping" (imperfect). Matthew 26:75 uses the same verb in the aorist tense, "he burst into tears."

This is an evidence of a godly sorrow leading to true repentance. It points up an interesting contrast between Peter and Judas. The word "repent" does not appear in this account of Peter's denials. Yet there is every evidence that he did so. He was a true disciple of Jesus who sinned, then repented and received forgiveness.

On the other hand the English word "repent" is used of Judas after he had betrayed Jesus. Peter *repented* and went on to a life of useful service. Judas *repented* and committed suicide. The difference is in the words for *repent*. The word describing Peter's action is *metanoeō*. It means to have a change of mind, heart, attitude. It means true repentance. But the word used of Judas is *metamelomai*. This word means "regret." But it involves no thought of a change in one's spiritual condition. Judas merely regretted his deed. Peter truly repented and reconsecrated himself to his Lord.

As we think of Peter's denials of Jesus, who can throw the first stone of criticism at him? We are so much like him in denying Jesus. God grant that we shall also be like him as we repent in bitter tears and go on serving Jesus the more.

Mark 15:2-20

The Trial before Pilate

There is no more dramatic moment in history than that in which Jesus stood before Pilate. This was a confrontation between the Lord of the universe, the King of the kingdom of God, and the legal representative of the empire which symbolized the essence of worldly pomp, power, and splendor. Pilate thought that Jesus stood on trial before him. Actually he stood on trial before Jesus—and before history.

Pilate came to this hour ill-prepared. He was the procurator of Judea A.D. 26-36. So he had been in this office about four years. During this time he had created a sordid record of bribery, violence, and many clashes with the Jews. He was hated by them, and, in turn, he despised the Jews. His official residence was in Caesarea on the Mediterranean coast. Many of the ruins of this city have been excavated in recent years. Pilate came to Jerusalem only when his official duties required it. Such a time was the Passover, when the normal Roman garrison was reinforced to prevent trouble. Jewish nationalism ran highest at this season of the year.

In Jerusalem Pilate stayed in the palace built by Herod the Great. When Jerusalem was destroyed in A.D. 70 this palace was preserved as quarters for troops left to guard the site. One may still see some of the ruins of it.

In all probability it was here that Jesus stood before Pilate. Some would place the scene at the Tower of Antonia, the place where Roman soldiers were garrisoned. They hold that at such a time Pilate would live near the troops. But knowing his proud nature this is difficult to believe. He would much prefer the luxury of the palace. And besides, he had officers over the troops with whom he could maintain communications. Since it was early in the morning it seems more likely that he would be at the palace. There is no valid reason to doubt this. There is much reason to believe it. But wherever it was the Sanhedrin brought Jesus to Pilate.

The Preliminary Examination (15:2-5)

The Sanhedrin refused to enter the building where Pilate resided. To enter the home of a Gentile would make them unclean, thus rendering them unfit to participate in the events of Passover week (John 18:28). So Pilate went outside to them. Assuming that this was just another case of Jewish law, he suggested that they try Jesus. But they revealed their previously appointed purpose to see Jesus put to death (John 18:29-32). When Pilate insisted upon specific charges which would merit such, they accused Jesus of forbidding the payment of taxes and claiming to be "Christ a king" (Luke 23:2). If true, these were serious charges to make before the Roman court. It is at this point that Mark takes up the narrative.

"Art thou the King of the Jews?" asked Pilate (v. 2). Literally, "You, you are the King of the Jews?" It was incredulous to him that such could be true. But for the sake of the proceedings he asked the question as though it might be true. For his form of question invited an affirmative answer. That is why Jesus replied, "Thou sayest it." Or "You, you are saying it." In both statements "thou" is in the emphatic position. Jesus' answer could read, "You yourself are saying it." This was Jesus' way of admitting that He was the King of the Jews. But note that He let Pilate say it; He only agreed with him.

In all the trial this is the only specific accusation with which the procurator dealt. And it was the only thing to which Jesus agreed. So in both the Jewish and Roman trials the issue was Jesus' Kingship. By fine points of language both Caiaphas and Pilate had said that Jesus was the King of the Jews. Jesus would die. But He would die as the King!

The chief priests "kept on accusing" (imperfect) Him of many things. The words "but he answered nothing" are not in the best texts. However, the idea is genuine in verse 5. It is evident, however, that Jesus did not reply to their charges. So as the Jewish rulers "kept on accusing" Jesus, Pilate "kept on asking" (imperfect), "Answerest thou nothing? behold how many things they witness [accuse] against thee" (v. 4).

"But Jesus yet answered nothing; so that Pilate marvelled" (v. 5). Literally, "But Jesus still answered not even one thing, so that Pilate was amazed," or "wondered." He had never before had a prisoner like this. Even he saw through the flimsy charges. Yet with a composure which amazed Pilate, He remained absolutely silent. The one charge to which Jesus would admit had been dealt with, so He said no more in the presence of His accusers. Later in private conversation He explained to Pilate the nature of His kingdom (John 18:37f.). But for His accusers He had only silent contempt.

It was at this point that the rulers mentioned that Jesus was a Galilean (Luke 23:6ff.). Seeing an escape from his problem Pilate sent Jesus to Herod Antipas who was in the city at that time. But He was soon back before Pilate. He still had Jesus on his hands.

The Choice of Barabbas (15:6-14)

To placate the Jews the Romans at the Passover were accustomed to release some prisoner of their choice (v. 6). It just happened that Pilate was holding a notable prisoner Barabbas. He may have been a false messiah. At any rate he had attempted to lead an insurrection, during which time he had committed murder (v. 7). Often these false messiahs would be forced to flee to the mountains where they became bandits. The Gospel descriptions highly suggest that this had been Barabbas' experience. It is possible that he was scheduled to be crucified on that day. At any rate the mob began to demand that some prisoner be released (v. 8).

Luke records that at this point Pilate reminded them that neither he nor Antipas had found Jesus guilty of any capital crime (23:13-16). So he offered to whip Him and then release Him. Whip an innocent man? Anything for Pilate to get out of his dilemma!

In response to the cry of the mob Pilate offered to release Jesus (v. 9). Matthew says that he gave them their choice between Jesus and Barabbas (27:17). He knew that the chief priests out of envy had brought Jesus to him (v. 10). Evidently he was aware of His popularity with the people. So he assumed that they would choose Jesus over this violent man. However, at this point a strange thing happened. Pilate's wife came and told him of a dream which she had had about Jesus (Matt. 27:19). The Romans placed much importance upon dreams. Apparently it was during this brief interval that the chief priests had opportunity to *coach* the people to ask for the release of Barabbas (v. 11). And the mob did as they suggested.

Hearing their request for the release of Barabbas, Pilate asked, "What will ye then that I shall do unto him whom ye call the King of the Jews?" (v. 12). Perhaps he hoped that they would ask for His release also. But they cried, "Crucify him!" (v. 13). The aorist imperative is a command for Pilate to crucify Jesus *at once*.

The entire trial had gotten beyond Pilate's control. He was at the mercy of the mob. So he asked, "Why, what evil hath he done?" (v. 14). It was no longer a matter of right and wrong. Mob violence had the upper hand. So the people "cried out the more exceedingly, Crucify him!" (v. 14). This was a sad day indeed for the vaunted Roman justice!

And the Jewish rulers and people made a choice greater than they realized. Origen tells of having seen a manuscript of Matthew's Gospel in which Barabbas is called "Jesus Barabbas." If this be a true combination of names, it is most suggestive. "Barabbas" means "son of father." "Jesus," of course, means "Jehovah is salvation." Thus we have Jesus Christ, the Son of His Father, and Jesus Barabbas the son of his father. One came as a spiritual Messiah, the other as a military-political messiah. The former offered salvation from the bondage of sin, the latter offered salvation from the bondage of Rome. The One offered to save by the shedding of His blood, the other offered to save by the shedding of their blood. Jesus Christ refused to be the very kind of messiah which the other proposed to be.

But whether or not this be a true reading, it is evident that the Jews rejected the Christ of God for a messiah of the kind that they sought. Their rejection of Christ sealed their doom. And it was the spirit expressed by their fateful choice which brought about their destruction as a nation.

The Infamy of Pilate (15:15-20)

This mob was now of such a nature that they might attempt anything, even to doing harm to the Roman procurator. So he was ready to do anything to placate them (v. 15). Therefore, he released Barabbas, and, having scourged Jesus, handed Him over for execution. If Barabbas was on the list of criminals to be executed, they probably erased his name and wrote Jesus' name instead. The Scriptures had said that He would be numbered with the transgressors (cf. Luke 22:37; Isa. 53:12). This means that His name would be put on the list of criminals to be executed.

Scourging was a merciless thing. Jesus' back was laid bare, and He was fastened to a post. The whip was made of leather thongs to the ends of which were fastened bits of bone or metal. As the lashes were laid on these bits beat out chunks of flesh. Since one could be beaten to death the number of lashes was limited to forty. To give a man more made the whipper liable for a similar punishment. To safeguard himself from a wrong count he would usually stop with thirty-nine (cf. II Cor. 11:24). One can easily imagine the horrible punishment which Jesus endured (cf. Isa. 53:5).

But this was not all. For the soldiers led Jesus back into the palace or the Praetorium (Matt. 27:27). Calling together the entire cohort of soldiers they proceeded to mock Jesus, pretending that He was an oriental potentate (vv. 16-19). A king needed a royal robe. So they put about Jesus a faded and probably cast-aside scarlet cloak of a Roman soldier. In its condition it may have looked like purple. A king must have a crown. So they plaited a crown out of twigs from a thorn bush. As they crushed this down on His head the thorns dug jagged gashes in His head. Then they began to salute Him saying "Hail, King of the Jews!" (v. 18). They kept on beating His head with a rod made of a reed. They kept spitting on Him, and bowed their knees before Him in mock obeisance. Having tired of their horse play they took off the robe and dressed Jesus in His own clothes. Then they led Him away to Calvary.

Jesus went out of the city with a lacerated body. But those responsible for His death were lacerated in their souls.

Mark 15:21-41

The Crucifixion of Jesus

On the way to the place of crucifixion the victim was required to carry his own cross. He walked in the midst of four soldiers. Before him marched a soldier carrying a sign stating the victim's crime. This board was later placed above his head on the cross. It was designed to serve as a warning to others.

While it is not stated that Jesus fell under the weight of His cross, this is implied in the record. The ordeal through which He had passed had taken its toll. So the soldiers compelled another to bear the cross for Him. The word "compel" renders the verb *aggareuō*. It was of Persian origin. To transmit messages rapidly the Persian rulers stationed men at given places along the route. They were called *aggaroi*. These had the authority to impress into service horses, ships, or men needed in transmitting the message. So the verb means "impressed into service." This could be done simply by tapping a man on the shoulder with a spear. Thus was Simon of Cyrene impressed into service.

Cyrene was on the coast of North Africa in Lydia. It contained a large colony of Jews. Apparently Simon had come to Jerusalem for the Passover. It may have been a once-in-a-lifetime experience for him. Since Jerusalem was so crowded at this season, he evidently was staying outside the city at night. As he came into the city that morning his own plans for the day were suddenly interrupted. And doubtless he resented it. But it was to prove to be the greatest event of his life.

Mark identifies him as "the father of Alexander and Rufus" (v. 21). Apparently these were two notable Christians by which to identify Simon. Mark wrote for the Romans. It is of interest, therefore, to note Paul's word in Romans 16:13. "Salute Rufus chosen in the Lord." This may have been the son of Simon. Several references are made to "Alexander" (Acts 19:33; I Tim. 1:20; II Tim. 4:14). Whether any one of these was the son of Simon is not certain. Nevertheless, the reference to Simon's sons would suggest that he became a Christian, and his sons after him.

The Arrival at Golgotha (15:22-23)

"And they bring him unto the place Golgotha, which is, being interpreted; The place of a skull" (v. 22). Mark uses the Aramaic word but translates it for his Roman readers. Its Latin name is Calvary.

The exact location of this place is unknown. It was outside the city wall (Heb. 13:12f.). Archaeologists are not agreed as to the location of this wall in Jesus' time. Tradition places Golgotha on the site of the Church of the Holy Sepulchre. However, this location presents the problem as to the place of the wall. Gordon's Calvary is definitely outside that wall. It is a hill whose very appearance is that of a skull. Some see "skull" as meaning that the place was littered with the skulls of previous victims. This is an unlikely position, however. More likely the name was derived from its appearance. No one can be dogmatic as to the location. But if this writer were required to choose between the two, Gordon's Calvary seems to be the more likely one. Perhaps God does not intend that we should know with certainty the exact spot.

Before the crucifixion began Jesus, according to custom, was offered a drink of drugged wine (v. 23). The imperfect tense of "gave" means either that they began to offer or did it repeatedly. Both meanings make sense here. But since the verb for "received" is an aorist, the former meaning is the more likely. They began to offer this drugged wine, and He rejected it emphatically. This wine was designed to numb the pain of crucifixion. Jesus was determined to endure it in His full senses.

The Former Three Hours on the Cross (15:24-32)

It was the "third hour," or 9:00 A.M., when Jesus was nailed to the cross (v. 25). In crucifixion the victim was stark naked. The four soldiers, under command of a centurion (v. 38), were permitted to keep the victim's personal belongings (v. 24). All that Jesus had was His clothing. Every Jew wore five articles of clothing: shoes, turban, girdle, inner garment, and outer cloak. John notes the value of Jesus' seamless cloak (19:23f.). So rather than to tear it the soldiers gambled for it (cf. Ps. 22:18).

Crucifixion was the most horrible method of execution ever contrived by man. The upright pole of the cross was placed in a hole in the ground, and the cross piece was laid flat on the ground. The victim was thrown to the ground; to render him helpless his arms and legs were jerked out of joint. His arms were stretched out along the cross piece, and his hands were nailed to the wood. He was lifted in place with the beam fastened to the pole. The victim's feet were then crossed and nailed with a spike to the upright pole. His feet rested on a little shelf about two feet above the ground.

There he was left until he died, death often taking days. During this time his naked body was exposed to the sun. Every pore of his skin became a flowing fountain as sunbeams like leeches sucked the vital fluid from his body. Blood dripped from his wounds. All this brought on a high fever. His mouth became dry and his throat raspy. His tongue became swollen. Every nerve in his body telegraphed pain to his brain. The flow of blood through his body was hindered, resulting in added aches and pains. As his body slumped under its weight the nails would tear his hands. And in this position it became almost impossible to breathe. As the victim struggled for breath the nails tore all the more. It was such a death that Jesus died for the sins of the world.

After Jesus was in place on the cross, the board stating His *crime* was nailed above His head. It read, "THE KING OF THE JEWS" (v. 26). This was the Roman empire's official sign. It crucified Jesus as "THE KING OF THE JEWS." Yes, Jesus died, but He died not as a criminal but as a KING! John 19:20 notes that this sign was in Hebrew, Greek, and Latin: the language of constituted religion, culture, and of the State. These were used for a reason. They were the language of the land, the universal language, and the official language of government. But they are suggestive of an even greater truth. These were the languages of the great streams of life in that day: Hebrew religion, Greek culture, Roman government. Institutional religion rejected Jesus; pagan culture ignored Him; constituted government crucified Him. So all men were there when they crucified the Lord.

Alongside Jesus on either side two thieves (robbers) were crucified (v. 27). Verse 28 is not found in the best texts, although the sense is true (cf. Luke 22:37). It is possible that these robbers were companions of Barabbas. He may have been destined for the central cross. But because of the choice of the people, Jesus was in fact Barabbas' *Substitute.*

Apparently Golgotha was located beside a road leading into the city. For the passers-by blasphemed Jesus as they wagged their heads in derision. They mocked Him, saying, "Ah, thou that destroyest the temple, and buildest it in three days, save thyself, and come down from the cross" (vv. 29-30). They were aware of the false charge brought against Jesus before the Sanhedrin.

But they were not alone. For also the chief priests and the scribes did likewise. They who were supposed to be a dignified court had become a mob taunting their victim. They had achieved their goal, and intended to enjoy every bit of this tragic scene.

"He saved others; himself he cannot save," they cried in fiendish glee (v. 31). Literally, "Others he saved; himself he is not able to save." Unknowingly they spoke a dual truth. He had saved and does save others. But in order to do so He could not save Himself. In effect they said, "He *could* not save Himself." The truth is that "He *would* not save Himself." He *could* not save Himself, and still be the Saviour of others. So He *willed* not to save Himself in order that He might be the Saviour of all who believe in Him.

Furthermore, they challenged Jesus, "The Christ the King of Israel: let him descend now from the cross, in order that we may see and believe" (v. 32). Note how they hurled His admitted claim into His teeth. Through them Satan made one last effort to prevent Jesus from dying on a cross, the manner of death by which God proposed to redeem men. He had tried many times to slay Jesus. But He did not want Him to die on a cross. Had Jesus done what they demanded He still would have been the Son of God, the Creator and Sustainer of the universe. But He would not have been the Saviour. He could have avoided the cross, even in this dire moment, but He would not have been in truth "Jehovah is salvation." He would have denied His very name, Jesus, and would have missed His greatest glory (Phil. 2:9-11). But, of course, Jesus remained on the cross to complete the work which the Father had given Him to do.

On the other hand, had Jesus come down from the cross before their very eyes would they have believed? Most probably not. He came from the tomb, and they sought to lie away the fact.

Mark with one simple statement takes note of the fact that the two robbers joined with them in reviling Jesus (v. 32). But Luke enlarges on the story to show that one of them later repented and was saved (23:39-43).

The Latter Three Hours on the Cross (15:33-39)

"And when the sixth hour [noon] was come, there was darkness over the whole land until the ninth hour [3:00 P.M.]" (v. 33). Nature itself rebelled at what men were doing to nature's God. This phenomenon created great fear among the people; so that a profound silence settled over the scene. Out of the gloom came the groans of the victims on the two crosses. We may assume that Jesus suffered in silence (cf. Isa. 53:7).

But at the ninth hour the silence was broken by a piercing cry. For Jesus cried, *"Eloi, Eloi, lama sabachthani?"* (v. 34). Again Mark translates the Aramaic for his readers. "My God, my God, why hast thou forsaken me?" The word "forsaken" renders a verb meaning to forsake or desert one in a set of untoward circumstances.

It may be read "to leave in the lurch." This is the only one of Jesus' seven sayings on the cross which Mark gives.

It is impossible for us to plumb the depths of meaning in this cry. Obviously Jesus quoted Psalm 22:1. This psalm is a vivid prophetic description of the crucifixion of Jesus. His cry was not simply a recitation of Scripture; it was a cry of dereliction. In this moment in some mysterious manner the Saviour entered into the greatest depths of His suffering. Here He was made to be sin for us (II Cor. 5:21). Throughout the incarnation the Son had ever been under the benevolent eyes of the Father. A holy and righteous God can not look with favor upon sin. So for this moment the Father turned His eyes from the Son. He was left in the lurch as He endured the wrath of God against sin. Someone has said that the beginning of sin is to forsake God; the end of sin is to be God-forsaken. So as One regarded by the Father as sin, Jesus endured the agonies of the doomed and damned for lost sinners. It was the agony of hell itself. It was for only a moment. But in that moment He endured the infinite suffering of the infinite God for the infinite guilt of finite man.

An English preacher was reading Isaiah 53:4-5. He read, "We did esteem him stricken, smitten of God, and afflicted." Then he paused. Suddenly, he said, "We were wrong! For 'he was wounded for our transgressions, he was bruised for our iniquities: the chastisement of our peace was upon him; and with his stripes we are healed.' "

Those standing by thought that He was calling for Elias or Elijah (v. 35). They misunderstood the word "Eloi" for Elijah. This probably was due to Jesus' physical condition. The Jews thought of Elijah as a deliverer in time of trouble. Mark notes that someone "ran and filled a sponge full of vinegar, and put it on a reed, and gave him to drink" (v. 36). The word rendered "vinegar" is *oxos,* a mixture with water which the soldiers were accustomed to drink. This was probably issued to the crucifixion detail. Mark also makes it appear that the one doing this said, "Let alone [wait]; let us see whether Elias will come and take him down" (v. 36). "Let alone" is a second person plural, as though this one man said this to others. But Matthew 27:49 probably has the correct reading. For this reads, "But the rest said, Let be [second person singular], let us see if Elias comes to save him." John 19:28-30 shows that Jesus' words "I thirst" came just before this incident. Immediately thereafter Jesus cried, "It is finished" (John 19:30).

Mark agrees with John when he says, "And Jesus cried with a

loud voice, and gave up the ghost [spirit]" (v. 37). Literally, he "breathed out." It was Jesus' dying breath. Matthew says, "And yielded up his spirit" (27:50, RV). He permitted His spirit to leave. In effect He said, "You can go now." No man took His life from Him; He laid it down of Himself. King all the way!

At this point a strange thing took place in the temple. "The veil of the temple [*naos*] was rent in twain from the top to the bottom" (v. 38). Not from the bottom to the top as if done by man. It was an act of God. This was the veil which separated the Holy of Holies from the Holy Place. Through this veil only the high priest might enter annually on the Day of Atonement. This rending of the veil indicated that hereafter through Christ every man had access to God for himself (cf. Heb. 4:16). Matthew notes that this phenomenon was accompanied by an earthquake (27:51). Robertson points out that the Talmud mentions such a quaking of the temple forty years before its destruction. This would be A.D. 30, the year of Jesus' death.

The centurion in charge of the crucifixion, noting how Jesus died, said, "Truly this man was the Son of God" (v. 39). The Greek text reads "Son of God," or "a Son of God." Some scholars insist that a pagan Roman would not call Jesus "the Son of God." To him "a son of God" would simply mean an extraordinary man. They point out that Luke reads, "Certainly this was a righteous man" (23:47). However, Luke prefaces this with "he glorified God." He likely had heard the people accusing Jesus of claiming to be "a Son of God" (literal meaning in Matthew 27:40, 43). So we may understand the centurion as saying that Jesus was who He claimed to be. Luke notes the reaction of grief on the part of the multitude (23:48). In the light of all of this and of our understanding we can say, "Truly this man was *the* Son of God."

The Island of Love (15:40-41)

Some days prior to Jesus' arrival in Jerusalem He had asked James and John if they could drink of His "cup" and be baptized with His "baptism" (10:38). So now He had drunk the last dregs of that bitter cup. He had been submerged in an ocean of hate. But in that ocean of hate there was an island of love. Because standing afar off "there were also women looking on" (v. 40). "Looking" is a feminine present participle of *theōreō*. This means that they were not mere spectators. They looked upon the terrible scene with interest, giving attention to every detail.

Who were these women? Mark mentions some by name: Mary

Magdalene, Mary the mother of James the less and of Joses, and Salome. Mary Magdalene had been healed of seven devils by Jesus (Luke 8:2). From this some see her as formerly a wicked woman. But there is no evidence to substantiate such a position. She may have been the victim of some terrible malady. Salome was the mother of James and John, Jesus' aunt (cf. Matt. 27:56). John had already taken Jesus' mother away (John 19:27).

These women were from Galilee. Mark notes that they had followed Jesus and had ministered to Him out of their possessions (cf. Luke 8:2f.). Besides these there were "many other women which came up with him unto Jerusalem" (v. 41). Though the Galilean crowds forsook Jesus one year before, not all Galileans did so. These women had reason to love Him, as indeed all women should. For because of Him womanhood has been raised from the position of chattel to that of queen in the home.

These women had followed Jesus in His ministry, lending to Him whatever aid they could. And they continued to follow Him to the end. Though they stood afar off to escape the ribald mob, their eyes intently followed Him to His death. And their hearts went out to Him in love. He died the victim of men's hate. But these women, and many others, loved Him to the end.

Mark 15:42-47

The Burial of Jesus

Jesus was dead. Insofar as men could see the end had come. He who had been the center of hope for so many was hanging lifeless on a cross. To them there remained nothing but the burial. Even then the sun was racing toward the horizon. But for the faithful the sun of hope had already disappeared in the darkness of a gloomy night of despair.

The Day Christ Died (15:42)

It was late afternoon on the day called "the preparation" (*paraskeuē*). Mark further identifies it as "the day before the sabbath."

There are those who debate as to the day of the week on which Jesus died. But it is clear from the record that the day was Friday. The term *paraskeuē* (preparation) had come to be used for this day of the week. In fact, this word is used in modern Greek for Friday. Being the day before the Sabbath it was used in preparation for that day when no work was to be done. All necessary work was done on that day in *preparation* for observing the Sabbath (cf. Luke 23:54; John 19:31).

One reason for debating the day is the time of Jesus' death. Those who argue against Friday insist that Jesus died at the hour when the paschal lamb was slain. And while certain items by themselves might be made to support such a position, the weight of evidence favors Friday. Another basis of argument is the time which Jesus was in the tomb. Jesus spoke of being in the heart of the earth "three days and three nights" (Matt. 12:40). In order to account for three twenty-four hour days the burial would need to have been on Thursday. However, Jesus spoke generally of three days. The Jews regarded any part of a day as one day. So figuring from Friday afternoon one has Friday before sunset (one day), Saturday (one day), and Sunday before sunrise (one day). Therefore in the light of the evidence it is concluded that Jesus died on Friday about 3:00 P.M.

The Friend Indeed (15:43-45)

The Jewish rulers wishing to get the bodies off the crosses

before the Sabbath, had requested that Pilate hasten their death by having their legs broken (John 19:31). However, it was found that Jesus was already dead. Had no one claimed His body it would have been buried in a common grave, or might even have been thrown into the Vale of Hinnom (*Gehenna*), the garbage dump of Jerusalem.

But "Joseph of Arimathaea, an honorable counsellor, which also waited for the kingdom of God, came and went in boldly unto Pilate, and craved the body of Jesus" (v. 43). This took courage since no one could predict what the procurator might do to any friend of Jesus, even to a member of the Sanhedrin.

The Gospel writers variously describe Joseph. He was a rich man and a secret disciple of Jesus (Matt. 27:57; John 19:38). And he was a good, righteous man who had not agreed to Jesus' being put to death (Luke 23:50f.). As previously noted, he evidently was not called to the meeting of the Sanhedrin. John notes that his companion in this merciful act of burial was Nicodemus (19:39).

Pilate consulted with the centurion, and was amazed to learn that Jesus was already dead without the breaking of His legs. Such a death usually took two or three days. But upon learning of it Pilate gave His body to Joseph (vv. 44-45).

The Manner and Place of Burial (15:46)

Having obtained the procurator's permission Joseph proceeded about his mission. First, he "bought fine linen." This was to be used in wrapping the body. Second, probably with the aid of Nicodemus, he took the body down from the cross. Third, in all likelihood they bathed the body, after which they wound it in the linen. Nicodemus had provided spices to use in preparing the body (John 19:39f.). As the linen was wound about the body the spices were placed within the folds. Fourth, the wound body was placed in the tomb. It was Joseph's own tomb which had never been used (Matt. 27:53; John 19:41). John says that it was a new tomb. The Synoptics all agree that it was hewn out of rock.

Where was this tomb located? It was in a garden adjacent to Golgotha (John 19:41). Therefore, the place of the tomb is linked with that of Golgotha. It was somewhere outside the wall of Jerusalem. In the Church of the Holy Sepulchre is a suggested tomb. It has room for only one body. If this is the location of Golgotha, it could also be the site of the tomb.

On the other hand, Gordon's Tomb is located in a garden alongside Gordon's Calvary. As previously noted this was definitely outside the north wall of that time. There is a place at the front into which a large stone was once rolled to seal the tomb (v. 46). Of interest is the interior of the tomb. To one's right as he looks in are places for two bodies, with a bone receptacle in between. This portion shows evidence of having been finished. But to the left a similar area is unfinished, suggesting a hurried use before this portion was ready. It is evident from the record that Joseph's decision to use his tomb as Jesus' burial place had not been planned in advance.

Now Joseph was a member of the Sanhedrin, and so was married. He would certainly have prepared a tomb for both himself and his wife. Probably he had children who would be included in his plans. This within itself would argue in favor of Gordon's Tomb.

Furthermore, just in front and to one side of Gordon's Tomb archaeologists have unearthed ruins dating to the Byzantine period, from the fourth century A.D. on. Among these ruins are the remains of a small chapel. This would indicate that possibly in the fourth century Christians regarded this as a sacred spot. Was it because they understood this to be the tomb in which Jesus was buried and from which He arose?

No one can speak dogmatically at this point. But as with Golgotha, so here. If the writer had to choose between the two suggested sites, his decision would be in favor of Gordon's Tomb.

The Watch of Love (15:47)

"And Mary Magdalene and Mary the mother of Joses beheld where he was laid." These were two of the women mentioned in verse 40. Possibly Salome had gone to comfort her bereaved sister.

But these two women had lingered near the cross. And they had followed Joseph and Nicodemus to ascertain the place of burial (Luke 23:55). Matthew 27:61 pictures them as sitting over against the tomb.

Doubtless long after the men had gone they maintained a silent vigil, held to the spot by bonds of love.

Mark 16:1-8

The Resurrection of Jesus

The next day was the Sabbath. Jews were supposed to rest on this day. But the Sanhedrin was busy (Matt. 27:62ff.). Even though Jesus' followers did not remember His promise to rise on the third day, His enemies did. They were determined to destroy completely any influence of Jesus which might extend beyond His death. So they asked Pilate to seal the tomb and to place a guard before it until after the third day. They feared that the disciples would steal Jesus' body from the tomb and then claim that He had risen from the dead. Strangely enough when He did rise they circulated the false rumor that this had happened, the very thing which they took such pains to prevent (Matt. 28:11-15). In their careful preparation unwittingly they provided one of the greatest proofs of the bodily resurrection of Jesus.

So the tomb was sealed with the Roman seal. And a guard detail was posted before it. Never did a guard detail have so hopeless a task.

The First Ones at the Tomb (16:1-3)

"And when the sabbath was past" (v. 1). This would be after sunset on Saturday. No purchases might be made on the Sabbath. But as soon as it was over "Mary Magdalene, and Mary the mother of James, and Salome, had bought sweet spices, that they might come and anoint him" (v. 1). These were the women who had watched Jesus' death from afar (15:40). The first two had followed Him to His tomb. In the meantime Salome had done what she could for her sister Mary. Now the three proposed to do what they could for the body of Jesus.

They certainly did not expect Him to rise from the dead. In their shock and grief they had forgotten His promise. Supposing, therefore, that the hurried burial on Friday had been insufficient, they proposed to do what was necessary for a permanent burial.

Therefore, before dawn on Sunday morning (John 20:1) they left Bethany on their errand of love and mercy (v. 2a). By the time that they reached the garden the sun had risen (v. 2b). As they walked along "they were saying" (imperfect) among themselves, "Who shall roll us away the stone from the door of the sepulchre?" (v. 3). This was a real problem because of the size of the stone. Certainly these women could not remove it.

The Message of the Empty Tomb (16:4-7)

With this problem still in their minds they came to the tomb. Evidently they had been walking with heavy hearts and downcast eyes. For before the tomb "looking up they see" (v. 4). They saw that the stone already was rolled away! Such a sight must have struck terror in their hearts. Who had done it? What did it mean? Had someone already removed the body? Could it be a grave robbery indeed? Apparently the women did not expect to find the body in the tomb. But their reason for not doing so was far different from the truth.

For "entering," or "rushing into" (aorist participle) the tomb, "they saw a young man sitting on the right side, clothed in a long white garment" (v. 5). Note that he was sitting "on the right side," the side where Jesus' body had been placed (cf. Gordon's Tomb). And he was clothed in "a long white garment," a *stolē*. This was a long stately robe which reached to the ground. Bruce notes that "no such robe [was] worn by men on earth." This implies that he was an angel.

The Gospel accounts vary as to details. Luke agrees with Mark, only he says that there were two young men (24:4). Matthew 28:2 speaks of an angel who sat upon the stone outside the tomb. He could have been inside when the women arrived. But these variations actually speak of the authenticity of the event (Robertson). Swete says, "The very diversity of the accounts strengthens the probability that the story rests upon the basis of truth; the impressions of the witnesses differed, but they agree upon the main facts."

Naturally they "were utterly amazed" (v. 5). Not only at the absence of the body but at the presence of the angel. But he put them at ease. "Stop being amazed: Jesus you are seeking, the Nazarene, the crucified one: he is risen; he is not here: behold the place where they placed him" (v. 6). And the place was empty! Not stolen, but risen! They did not find that which they sought. But they found much more. The evidence of a risen Lord!

Many efforts have been made by skeptics to explain away the bodily resurrection of Jesus.[1] None of them stands up under careful examination. And one of the greatest proofs of the event is the empty tomb. All four Gospels agree that the body of Jesus

---

[1] See Hobbs, *An Exposition of the Gospel of Matthew*, pp. 413ff.

was placed in the tomb on Friday and that it was empty on Sunday morning. No satisfactory explanation of this has been given except the one in the Gospels themselves. It was a miracle of God. Sometime between sunset on Saturday and sunrise on Sunday Jesus came forth from the tomb alive! He came forth without the stone being removed (cf. John 20:19). The stone was rolled away not to let Jesus out but to let the women in. Thus they saw with their own eyes the evidence of what had taken place. And of interest is the fact that, according to the record, after the resurrection no enemy of Jesus ever went to see the tomb. From the record, after Mary Magdalene, Peter, and John left it, no believer ever returned to it. The enemies of Jesus did not go because they *feared* that they would find the tomb empty. No friend of Jesus returned because they *knew* that it was empty. As someone has said, the enemies of Jesus placed a guard before the tomb to see that none of His friends took Him from it. The friends of Jesus must ever stand before the empty tomb, armed with an informed and intelligent faith, to see that no enemy of Jesus ever again places Him back into it.

The women were told not to stand gazing at the empty tomb. They were to "be going: tell his disciples and Peter that he is going before you into Galilee: There shall you see him, even as he said to you" (v. 7, cf. Mark 14:28). Note the special mention of Peter. Only Mark has this. He most likely received it from Peter himself. What joy this must have brought to Jesus' problem disciple. He never forgot it, and must have referred to it often.

Jesus would appear to various individuals and groups before the meeting in Galilee. But there to His followers He would speak some of the most majestic words which ever fell from His lips (cf. Matt. 28:18-20).

The Strange Reaction (16:8)

"And they went out quickly" (aorist participle, "going out quickly"). They fled from the tomb in trembling amazement. This was to be expected.

The strange thing is that "they said not even one thing to anyone." And why? Because "they were afraid." Afraid because of what they had seen? Or because they feared that no one would believe them? After all, it was too good to be true. But true it was.

Now from other accounts we know that they did tell "all these things unto the eleven, and to all the rest" (Luke 24:9). Even so, their words seemed to their hearers as "idle tales," or the tales of hysterical women (Luke 24:11). But their unbelief was to give way to a confirmed faith as in the next forty days they saw the living Lord on ten different occasions.

We may, therefore, understand the reaction of the women otherwise. It was not that they did not tell the glad news to believers. They simply did not stop to tell it to others along the way. Robertson makes a telling comment. "Hushed to silence their feet had wings as they flew on."

And well they might do. For they were the first heralds of the greatest news that the world ever heard.

THE LORD LIVETH INDEED!

Mark 16:9-20

The Disputed Ending

While many Greek manuscripts contain this passage, it is by no means generally accepted as genuine Scripture. Some manuscripts have a shorter ending, and others have both the shorter and the longer one. However, in textual criticism one does not merely count manuscripts. He evaluates them. Of interest is the fact that the oldest and best manuscripts end with Mark 16:8. But is this within itself the way that Mark ended his Gospel? Probably not. It is hardly likely that he would end so glorious a message with the words "and they were affrighted" or "afraid." Various efforts have been made to explain this: such as that Mark was either interrupted or that he died before finishing his work. However, neither of these thoughts appears to be satisfactory.

It is more likely that Mark's true ending has been lost. And because of this various later writers sought to compose an ending. This is supported by the fact of the different endings found in different manuscripts, plus the fact that this passage differs from the body of the Gospel in both style of writing and in vocabulary.

The thought of a lost ending to Mark is supported by two things among many others. Mark 16:7 reports the word about Jesus meeting His disciples in Galilee. Yet Mark as we now have it makes no further mention of this. Already we have noted the strange words that the women said not even one thing to anyone about the empty tomb. Yet they had been told to bear the message to Peter and the other disciples. Now Mark 16:9f. does relate this. But verse 9 reads like a separate account which takes no note of the preceding verses.

It is possible, therefore, that the true ending of Mark did tell how the women related the message, and how that later Jesus appeared to His followers in Galilee something like we find in the closing verses of Matthew.

However, even if one rejects this ending, one does not lose the basic teachings of Scripture contained in it. For these are found in unquestioned passages in other writings, especially Matthew 28; Luke 24:50-53; and Acts 1:8ff. And its rejection does serve to clear up certain problems (cf. 16:16-18). This writer does not see this passage as true Scripture. But since it appears in many translations, we shall seek to examine it.

The Appearances of Jesus (16:9-15)

The teachings of this passage may be found in genuine parts of the other Gospels. It is unnecessary to treat each verse specifically. However, it should be noted that they deal with various appearances of Jesus after His resurrection. For instance, verses 9-11 are suggestive of John 20:1-10 and Luke 24:9-12. Verse 12 suggests John 20:11-18 and Luke 24:13-32. Note the words "in another form." This means in forms of a different kind: Mary Magdalene thought that Jesus was a gardener, and the two disciples on the road to Emmaus regarded Him as just another traveller. Verses 13-14 remind us of Jesus' two appearances to the disciples on succeeding Sunday nights (Luke 24:33-43; John 20:19-29). And, of course, verse 15 is similar to Jesus' words in Matthew 28:19-20.

The Problem Passage (16:16-18)

Verse 16 is cited as supporting baptismal regeneration. "He that believeth and is baptized shall be saved; but he that believeth not shall be damned" (v. 16). Jesus is nowhere else recorded as placing such a value on baptism. The abundance of New Testament teaching does not support such an idea. Even those isolated passages cited elsewhere to support baptismal regeneration lend themselves more naturally to another interpretation.

For instance, in Acts 2:38 the word "for" (*eis*) may better read "on the basis of, because of, as the result of, or with respect to." In Matthew 12:41 *eis* is translated "at" where it definitely means something which happened as the result of Jonah's preaching. The Ninevites repented *after* Jonah had preached, not in order that he might preach. In Romans 6:3-4 "into" *(eis)* may better be rendered "with respect to." Even the English "for" (Acts 2:38) may be understood in the following manner. "He was executed *for* murder." Not that he might murder but because he had already done so.

In I Peter 3:20-21 the idea is that Noah and his family were saved *through* the flood by being in the ark. They were not saved by being in the water. The word "figure" refers to the *ark* or being in Christ. "Baptism" (*baptisma*) refers to the meaning of baptism, not to the act. So baptism is not a sacrament but a symbol of what Jesus did for one's salvation, and what He does in the believer (death, burial, resurrection).

Furthermore, in Mark 16:16 there is an inconsistency. For the latter part says nothing about being *condemned* (damned) if one is not baptized. "He that believeth not shall be damned," or "condemned." Certainly one should not build a system of doctrine upon this questionable verse.

In verse 17 the former part may be supported by teachings of Jesus elsewhere. But nowhere else is He reported as speaking of "tongues." "Tongues," or the ability to speak languages other than one's own without having studied them, sounds more post-Pentecost than like a statement of Jesus. There is no recorded instance where Jesus ever spoke in "tongues."

"They shall take up serpents" (v. 18). This might reflect Jesus' words in Luke 10:19. But more likely this latter reference was a symbolic promise of God's protection as the disciples proclaimed the gospel. It could also reflect Acts 28:3-5. The words about drinking poison sound strange from the lips of Jesus who said, "Thou shalt not tempt the Lord thy God" (Matt. 4:7). Jesus never crowded God into a corner in challenging Him to protect Him. There is no unquestioned saying of Jesus which teaches the drinking of poison or the handling of snakes.

Bruce has a very striking comment on verses 17-18. "Here also we find a great lapse from the high level of Matthew's version of the farewell words of Jesus: signs, physical charisma, and thaumaturgic powers, taking the place of the spiritual presence of the exalted Lord. Casting out devils represents the evangelic miracles; speaking with tongues those of the apostolic age: taking up venomous serpents and drinking poison seem to introduce us into the twilight of apocryphal story. Healing of the sick, by laying on of hands, brings us back to apostolic times."

In conclusion it may be stated that if on the basis of 16:16a one insists upon baptismal regeneration, he should also on the basis of verse 18 handle snakes and drink poison as a proof of his faith. However, one should beware of all of these, since they rest upon so insecure a Scriptural basis.

The Ascension of Jesus (16:19-20)

There is no reason to question the truths taught in these verses, since they are presented elsewhere in passages which are not open to suspicion. But as one reads them they reflect (v. 19) Luke 24:50-53; Acts 1:9; and His followers did go forth to preach the gospel every where. And in many instances their word was confirmed by supernatural evidences of God's presence.

There is nothing good that is lost from Jesus' teachings by rejecting Mark 16:9-20. And in so doing the Christian gospel is rescued from many erroneous ideas.

So without what was the true ending of Mark's Gospel, we may well end this treatment with words of assurance and certainty.

THE LORD LIVETH INDEED!